THE YALE EDITION

OF

HORACE WALPOLE'S

CORRESPONDENCE

EDITED BY W. S. LEWIS

VOLUME FORTY-ONE

HORACE WALPOLE'S MISCELLANEOUS CORRESPONDENCE

II

EDITED BY W. S. LEWIS

AND

JOHN RIELY

WITH THE ASSISTANCE OF

EDWINE M. MARTZ

AND

RUTH K. McCLURE

NEW HAVEN

YALE UNIVERSITY PRESS

OXFORD · OXFORD UNIVERSITY PRESS

TABLE OF CONTENTS

VOLUME II

LIST OF ILLUSTRATIONS

VOLUME II

HORACE WALPOLE'S CORRESPONDENCE

To Unknown, ?1766

Printed for the first time from the MS copy now WSL, acquired from Gabriel Wells in 1932.

The present text is an extract from a missing letter copied in an unidentified hand on paper watermarked 'Hayes & Wise 1801' and introduced as follows: 'Mr Horace Walpole (the Earl of Orford lately deceased) being a[t] Paris after the Peace in 1763 wrote to England the following.' The letter is dated conjecturally by this endorsement and by HW's visit to Paris in 1765–6.

I have observed amidst this agreeable society and dissipation a sect called *Les Philosophes*[1] and I have endeavoured to find out their object; if I mistake not their object is, to destroy their God and their King,[2] and as far as I can judge I think they will succeed in both.

To James Boswell,[1] ca Monday 20 January 1766

Printed from the MS in the Yale University Library (Boswell papers C3058). First printed in *Private Papers of James Boswell from Malahide Castle*, ed. Geoffrey Scott and F. A. Pottle, Mt Vernon, New York, privately printed, 1928–34, vii. 61, n. 1. Reprinted in *Boswell on the Grand Tour: Italy, Corsica, and France 1765–1766*, ed. Frank Brady and F. A. Pottle, 1955, p. 270, n. 9. The MS was among the Boswell papers from Malahide Castle purchased by Lt-Col. Ralph H. Isham and acquired from him by Yale University in 1949.

Dated approximately by Boswell's visit to HW 21 Jan. 1766 (see n. 4 below).
Address: À Monsieur Monsieur Boswell à l'Hôtel Dauphin, rue Taranne.

MR Walpole is extremely thankful to Mr Boswell for his obliging note[2] and shall be very glad of the honour of his acquaintance, and will endeavour to find him at home or hopes to meet him: is very sorry it has not happened, but as Mr Walpole, from conforming to the French hours while he is here,[3] and living much with the people, rises very late, and is seldom at home afterwards till very late too, he has been so unlucky as not to see Mr Boswell, but

1. 'The *savants*, I beg their pardons, the *philosophes*, are insupportable. Superficial, overbearing, and fanatic; they preach incessantly, and their avowed doctrine is atheism' (HW to Gray 19 Nov. 1765, GRAY ii. 144).

2. HW wrote Conway 28 Oct. 1765 that the French philosophers 'aim, many of them, at a subversion of all religion, and still many more, at the destruction of regal power' (CONWAY iii. 22).

———

1. (1740–95), the biographer of Samuel Johnson.

2. Missing.

3. See *ante* 19 Oct. 1765, n. 14.

flatters himself he shall soon have an opportunity of being acquainted with him.[4]

From the COMTESSE DE BOUFFLERS,[1]
Thursday 6 February 1766

Printed from the MS now WSL. First printed, Toynbee *Supp.* iii. 194. Damer-Waller; the MS was sold Sotheby's 5 Dec. 1921 (first Waller Sale), lot 95, bought in; resold Christie's 15 Dec. 1947 (second Waller Sale), lot 55 (with other lots), to Maggs for WSL.

The year of the letter is established by HW's entry in his 'Paris Journals' *sub* 12 Feb. 1766 (see n. 2 below).

Jeudi, 6 fevrier.

QUOIQUE Madame la Comtesse de Boufflers sache bien que Monsieur Walpole est engagé pour le mercredi des Cendres, cependant, elle le prie de se dégager si cela est possible, et de lui faire l'honneur de souper chez elle ce jour-là parce qu'elle aura quelques amis avec qui, il fera plaisir à Monsieur Walpole de se trouver.[2]

4. HW wrote in 'Paris Journals' 21 Jan. 1766: 'Mr Boswell came' (DU DEFFAND v. 296). The visit is described in Boswell's journal notes for 22 Jan., covering the events of the previous day: 'Went and found Horace Walpole, whom you [Boswell] had treated with by cards, lean, genteel man. Talked to him of Corsica. He said you should give something about them, as there are no authentic accounts. You said you intended to do so. He had seen [King] Theodore, but, whether from pride or stupidity, he hardly spoke any. Horace has the original writing for getting him out of prison' (*Boswell on the Grand Tour,* ed. Brady and Pottle, 1955, pp. 270–1). See F. A. Pottle, *James Boswell: The Earlier Years*

1740–1769, New York, 1966, pp. 275–6, and *post* 23 Feb. 1768.

———

1. Marie-Charlotte-Hippolyte de Campet de Saujon (1725–1800), m. (1746) Édouard, Comte (Marquis, 1751) de Boufflers-Rouverel. HW had become acquainted with her during her visit to England in the spring of 1763 (MANN vi. 135).

2. Ash Wednesday 1766 occurred on 12 Feb., when HW 'supped at Mme de Bouffler's with Duchesse d'Aiguillon, Duchesse de Boufflers, Maréchale de Luxembourg, Comte and Comtesse de Biron, Marquis de Villeroy, Mme du Deffand, Pont-de-Veyle, and M. Sorba and Mr Bentinck' ('Paris Journals,' DU DEFFAND v. 301).

To John Craufurd,[1] Thursday 6 March 1766

Printed from the MS now wsl. First printed (as 'To James Crawford'), Cunningham iv. 483–7. Reprinted, Toynbee vi. 431–6. The MS was sold Sotheby's 26 March 1898 (Johnson Sale), lot 1555 (with HW to Craufurd 26 Sept. 1774 and 2 Jan. 1775), to Potter; *penes* John W. Ford, of Enfield Old Park, Enfield, Middlesex, in 1900; resold Sotheby's 5 May 1904 (Ford Sale), lot 206 (as above), to Maggs; resold Sotheby's 19 July 1937 (Sir Herbert Leon Sale), lot 77 (as above), to Maggs for wsl.

The letter is listed in 'Paris Journals' as sent to England 8 March 'by Mr Nesbitt' (du Deffand v. 380).

Paris, March 6, 1766.

YOU cannot conceive, my dear Sir, how happy I was to receive your letters,[2] not so much even for my own sake, as for Madame du Deffand's. I do not mean merely from the pleasure your letter gave her,[3] but because it wipes off the reproaches she has undergone on your account. They have at once twitted her with her partiality for you and your indifference: even that silly Madame de la Valière[4] has been quite rude to her on your subject. You will not be surprised; you saw a good deal of their falsehood and spite, and I have seen much more. They have not only the faults common to the human heart, but that additional meanness and malice which is produced by an arbitrary government, under which the subjects dare not look up to anything great. The King has just thunderstruck the Parliament,[5] and they are all charmed with the thought that they are to continue to grovel at the foot of the throne—but let us talk of something more meritorious. Your good old woman wept like a child with her poor no eyes, as I read your letter to her. I did not wonder; it is kind, friendly, delicate and just—so just, that it vexes me to be forced to continually combat the goodness of her heart, and

1. (1742–1814), of Drumsoy and Auchenames, Scotland; called 'Fish' Craufurd; M.P.; friend of George Selwyn and Mme du Deffand (du Deffand i. 6 n. 21; Mann vi. 40 n. 4). He had recently been with HW in Paris, leaving for England 27 Jan. 1766 (Selwyn 207; 'Paris Journals,' du Deffand v. 379).

2. Missing.

3. Mme du Deffand's reply to Craufurd's letter, dated 8 March 1766, is printed in *Correspondance complète de Mme du Deffand*, ed. the Marquis de Sainte-Aulaire, 1866, i. 23–7.

4. Anne-Julie-Françoise de Crussol (1713–93), m. (1732) Louis-César de la Baume le Blanc, Duc de la Vallière.

5. 'He had lately [3 March] held a *lit de justice* in which he had asserted his authority in very strong terms, and forbidden the Parliament to dispute his acts' (HW's note on his letter to Mann 20 April 1766, Mann vi. 415 n. 13).

destroy her fond visions of friendship—Ah! but, said she at last, he does not talk of returning! I told her, if anything could bring you back, or me either, it would be desire of seeing her. I think so of you, and I am sure so of myself. If I had stayed here still, I have learnt nothing but to know them more thoroughly. Their barbarity and injustice to our good old friend is undescribable: one of the worst is just dead, Madame de Lambert[6]—I am sure you will not regret her. Madame de Forcalquier,[7] I agree with you, is the most sincere of her acquaintance, and incapable of doing as the rest do, eat her suppers, when they cannot go to a more fashionable house, laugh at her, abuse her, nay try to raise her enemies among her nominal friends. They have succeeded so far as to make that unworthy old dotard the President[8] treat her like a dog. Her nephew the Archbishop of Toulouse,[9] I see, is not a jot more attached to her than the rest, but I hope she does not perceive it as clearly as I do. Madame de Choiseul[10] I really think wishes her well; but perhaps I am partial. The Princess de Beauvau[11] seems very cordial too, but I doubt the Prince a little. You will forgive these details about a person you love and have so much reason to love; nor am I ashamed of interesting myself exceedingly about her. To say nothing of her extraordinary parts, she is certainly the most generous friendly being upon earth— but neither these qualities, nor her unfortunate situation touch her unworthy acquaintance. Do you know that she was quite angry about the money you left for her servants? Viar[12] would by no means touch it, and when I tried all I could to obtain her permission for their taking it, I prevailed so little, that she gave Viar five louis's for refusing it; so I shall bring you back your draught, and you will only owe

6. Louise-Thérèse de Menou (1714–66), m. (1740) Henri-François de Lambert.

7. Marie-Françoise-Renée de Carbonnel de Canisy (1725 – ca 1796), m. 1 (1737) Antoine-François de Pardaillan de Gondrin, Marquis d'Antin; m. 2 (1742) Louis-Bufile de Brancas, Comte de Forcalquier; 'la Bellissima'; HW's correspondent.

8. Charles-Jean-François Hénault (1685–1770), président de la première chambre des enquêtes; Mme du Deffand's *cavalier servant* since 1730; HW's correspondent (DU DEFFAND i. 3 n. 3).

9. Étienne-Charles de Loménie de Brienne (1727–94), Archbishop of Toulouse, 1763; Archbishop of Sens, 1788; cardinal, 1789; Mme du Deffand's cousin.

10. Louise-Honorine Crozat du Châtel (1735–1801), m. (1750) Étienne-François de Choiseul-Stainville, Duc de Choiseul; HW's correspondent.

11. Marie-Sylvie de Rohan-Chabot (1729–1807), m. 1 (1749) Jean-Baptiste-Louis de Clermont d'Amboise, Marquis de Renel; m. 2 (1764) Charles-Just de Beauvau, Prince de Beauvau.

12. Jean-François Wiart, 'Madame du Deffand's valet de chambre, who was her secretary, and read and wrote all her letters for her. He came into her service before the year 1758, remained with her till her death in 1780' (Mary Berry's note, DU DEFFAND i. 6 n. 25).

me five louis's, which I added to what you gave me, to pay for the two
pieces of china at Dulac's,[13] which will be sent to England with mine.

Well! I have talked too long on Madame du Deffand, and neglected too long to thank you for my own letter.[14] I do thank you,
for it, my dear Sir, most heartily and sincerely. I feel all your worth
and all the gratitude I ought, but I must preach to you, as I do to
your friend. Consider how little time you have known me,[15] and
what small opportunities you have had of knowing my faults. I know
them thoroughly; but to keep your friendship within bounds, consider my heart is not like yours, young, good, warm, sincere, and impatient to bestow itself. Mine is worn with the baseness, treachery,
and mercenariness I have met with. It is suspicious, doubtful and
cooled.[15a] I consider everything round me but in the light of amusement, because if I looked at it seriously I should detest it. I laugh,
that I may not weep. I play with monkeys, dogs or cats, that I may
not be devoured by the beast of the Gévaudan.[16] I converse with
Mesdames de Mirepoix,[17] Boufflers and Luxembourg,[18] that I may
not love Madame du Deffand too much—and yet they do but make
me love her the more. But don't love me, pray don't love me. Old
folks are but old women, who love their last lover as much as they
did their first. I should still be liable to believe you, and I am not
at all of Madame du Deffand's opinion that one might as well be
dead as not love somebody—I think one had better be dead than
love anybody. Let us compromise this matter; you shall love her,
since she likes to be loved, and I will be the confidant. We will do
anything we can to please her—I can go no farther—I have taken
the veil, and would not break my vow for the world. If you will
converse with me through the grate at Strawberry Hill, I desire no

13. Du Lac's, *marchand-mercier* in the
rue St Honoré (du Deffand ii. 302 n. 27a;
William Cole, *A Journal of my Journey to
Paris in the Year 1765*, ed. F. G. Stokes,
1931, pp. 233–4; F. J. B. Watson, 'Walpole
and the Taste for French Porcelain in
Eighteenth-Century England,' in *Horace
Walpole: Writer, Politician, and Connoisseur*, ed. W. H. Smith, New Haven, 1967,
pp. 189–91).

14. Missing.

15. Probably only since HW's arrival in
Paris in Sept. 1765.

15a. For HW's reaction to Henry Conway's 'neglect' of him in the formation of
the first Rockingham administration see
Appendix 7, Conway iii. 529–32.

16. 'Prodigious was the noise made
about that beast, which was believed to
be really some famished or mad wolves'
(HW's note on his letter to Mann 26
March 1765, Mann vi. 289 n. 12; see HW
to Conway 2 Oct. 1765, Conway iii. 14).

17. *Ante* 19 Oct. 1765, n. 26.

18. Madeleine-Angélique de Neufville
(1707–87), m. 1 (1721) Joseph-Marie, Duc
de Boufflers; m. 2 (1750) Charles-François-
Frédéric de Montmorency-Luxembourg,
Duc de Luxembourg, Maréchal de France.

better; but not a word of friendship; I feel no more than if I professed it. It is paper credit, and like other bank bills, sure to be
turned into money at last. I think you would not realize me, but
how do you, or how do I know, that I should be equally scrupulous?
The Temple of Friendship,[19] like the ruins in the Campo Vaccino,[20]
is reduced to a single column at Stowe. Those dear friends have
hated one another, till some of them are forced to love one another
again—and as the cracks are soldered by hatred, perhaps that cement
may hold them together. You see my opinion of friendship; it would
be making you a fine present to offer you mine!

Your ministers may not know it, but the war has been on the
point of breaking out here between France and England, and upon
a cause very English, a horse-race. Lord Forbes[21] and Lauragais[22]
were the champions; they rode, but the second lost, his horse being
ill.[23] It died that night, and the surgeons on opening it, swore it was
poisoned. The English suspect that a groom, who I suppose had been
reading Livy or Demosthenes, poisoned it on patriot principles, to
ensure victory to his country. The French, on the contrary, think
poison as common as oats or beans, in the stables at Newmarket. In
short, there is no impertinence they have not uttered; and it has gone
so far, that two nights ago it was said that the King had forbidden
another race, which is appointed for Monday between the Prince de
Nassau[24] and a Mr Forth,[25] to prevent national animosities. On my

---

19. The Temple of Friendship at Stowe
was furnished with busts of Frederick,
Prince of Wales, of Lords Chesterfield,
Westmorland,   Cobham,   Marchmont,
Gower, Bathurst, Lyttelton, and Temple,
and of William Pitt, men who had differed in politics at one time or another.
'The edifices and inscriptions at Stowe
should be a lesson not to erect monuments to the living' (HW to Montagu
26 May 1765, MONTAGU ii. 154; B. Seeley,
Stowe, 1769, p. 32).

20. The Roman Forum, so called since
the Middle Ages, when cattle were pas-
tured in the Forum itself.

21. George Forbes (1740–80), styled Vct
Forbes; 5th E. of Granard, 1769; M.P.
(Ireland).

22. Louis-Léon-Félicité   de   Brancas
(1733–1824), Comte de Lauraguais; afterwards Duc de Brancas.

23. HW noted in 'Paris Journals' 25
Feb. 1766: 'Went with Lady George [Len-

nox] and Mrs Trapaud to the Plaine de
Sablon to see the race between Count
Lauraguais and Lord Forbes, which was
won by the latter' (DU DEFFAND v. 304).
For further accounts of the race see Daily
Adv. 12 March 1766, MORE 106–7 and
CONWAY iii. 57.

24. Karl Heinrich Nicolaus Otto (1745–
1808), Prince of Nassau-Siegen, who insisted 'like a good patriot, on riding in
jack-boots' (HW to Anne Pitt 7 March
1766, MORE 112; Journal inédit du duc
de Croÿ, iii. 259–60).

25. Nathaniel Parker Forth (b. 1744),
grandson of Col. T. Forth, aide-de-camp
to the Maréchal de Schomberg, and son
of Samuel Forth, Irish M.P.; envoyé particulier to the French Court, 1777; agent
and correspondent of the Duc de Chartres
(Amédée Britsch, Lettres de L.-P.-J. d'Orléans duc de Chartres à Nathaniel Parker
Forth (1778–1785), 1926, pp. x-xv, 44–7).

side, I have tried to stifle these heats, by threatening them that Mr
Pitt is coming into the ministry again, and it has had some effect.
This event has confirmed what I discovered early after my arrival,
that the *Anglomanie* was worn out; if it remains, it is *manie* against
the English. All this however is for your private ear; for I have found
that some of my letters home, in which I had spoken a little freely,
have been reported to do me disservice. As we are *not* friends, I may
trust to your discretion—may not I? I did not use to applaud it
much.

Perhaps it is necessary to use still more caution in mentioning me
to Lord Ossory.[26] Do it gently, for though I have great regard for
him, I don't design to make it troublesome to him.

You don't say a word of our Duchess,[27] so superior to earthly
duchesses! How dignified she will appear to me after all the little
tracasseries of Paris! I trust I shall see her soon. Packing up is in all
my quarters: but though I quit tittle tattle, I don't design to head
a squadron of mob on any side. I hate politics as much as friendship, and design to converse at home, as I have done here, with
dévots, philosophers, Choiseul, Maurepas, the Court and the *Temple.*[27a]

What a volume I have writ! but don't be frightened; you need not
answer it, if you have not a mind, for I shall be in England almost
as soon as I could receive your reply. La Geoffriniska[28] has received
three sumptuous robes of ermines, martins, and Astracan lambs, the
last of which I suppose the Czarina had the pleasure of flaying alive
herself. *Oh! pour cela, oui,* says old Brantôme,[29] who always assents.
I think there is nothing else very new: Mr Young[30] puns, and Dr
Gem[31] does not: Lorenzi[32] blunders faster than one can repeat, Vol-

26. *Ante* 19 Oct. 1765, n. 18. It was
possibly in this letter to Thomas Brand
that HW spoke 'a little freely.'

27. Of Grafton, who after her divorce
married Lord Ossory in 1769.

27a. The building of the Templars, in
the rue du Temple, where the Prince de
Conti lived (DU DEFFAND v. 288).

28. Madame Geoffrin, so called because
of her maternal fondness for King Stan-
islas II of Poland (DU DEFFAND ii. 214
n. 5).

29. Pierre de Bourdeille (ca 1540–1614),
Abbé and seigneur de Brantôme; soldier
and chronicler of court scandal. HW

owned a copy of his *Mémoires,* Leyden,
1699 (Hazen, *Cat. of HW's Lib.,* No.
1211).

30. Not identified; for HW's encounters
with him at Paris see DU DEFFAND v.
293, 300, 309–10, 316.

31. Richard Gem (ca 1717–1800), English physician; HW's occasional correspondent.

32. Jacques Roland (d. 1784), Chevalier
de Lorenzi. Grimm collected a number of
his blunders in *Correspondance littéraire*
under the heading *Lorenziana* (v. 411–14,
433–5).

taire[33] writes volumes faster than they can print, and I buy china[34] faster than I can pay for it.

I am glad to hear you have been two or three times at my Lady Hervey's. By what she says of you, you may be comforted, though you miss the approbation of Madame de Valentinois.[35] Her golden apple, though indeed after all Paris has gnawed it, is reserved for Lord Holderness! Adieu!

Yours ever

H. Walpole

From the Duchesse d'Aiguillon,[1] ca Sunday 9 March 1766

Printed for the first time from the MS now WSL. Damer-Waller; the MS was sold Sotheby's 5 Dec. 1921 (first Waller Sale), lot 85, bought in; resold Christie's 15 Dec. 1947 (second Waller Sale), lot 55 (with other lots), to Maggs for WSL. Dated approximately by the reference to HW's 'mal des yeux' (see n. 2 below). *Address:* À Monsieur Monsieur de Walpol à l'Hôtel du Parc Royal à Paris.

MADAME la Duchesse d'Aiguillon est bien fâchée que l'incommodité de M. de Walpole l'ait privée du plaisir de l'avoir hier à souper chez elle. Elle envoie savoir de ses nouvelles et comment il se vienne de son mal des yeux.[2]

33. Who had been visited by Craufurd at Ferney.
34. For HW's purchases see Appendix I in Smith, op. cit. 327–36.
35. Marie-Christine-Chrétienne de Rouvroy de Saint-Simon (1728–74), m. (1749) Charles-Maurice Goyon-de-Matignon de Grimaldi, Comte de Valentinois. According to HW, 'Mme de Valentinois haïssait les Anglais' (DU DEFFAND i. 4 n. 10).

1. Anne-Charlotte de Crussol de Florensac (1700–72), m. (1718) Armand-Louis Vignerot du Plessis-Richelieu, Duc d'Aiguillon.
2. After suffering from a 'cold in my eyes' 7–10 March 1766, HW went out on the 11th 'to take the air' and paid a visit to Mme d'Aiguillon ('Paris Journals,' DU DEFFAND v. 306–7). The supper party that HW could not attend probably took place on Saturday, 8 March.

From the DUKE OF RICHMOND,[1]
Tuesday 11 March 1766

Printed from Toynbee *Supp.* ii. 135–6, where the letter was first printed. Damer-Waller; the MS was sold Sotheby's 5 Dec. 1921 (first Waller Sale), lot 177, to Maggs; offered by them, Cat. No. 492 (summer 1927), lot 1092; resold American Art Association-Anderson Galleries, Inc. 30 Oct. 1929 (John M. Geddes Sale), lot 134, to unknown; not further traced.

Whitehall, March 11th 1766,

Tuesday morning.

Dear Sir,

I DID not know of a messenger's going a few days ago or should have wrote to you, and now that I write by the post I cannot say all I would wish to communicate to you.

The Repeal is passed the H[ouse] of Commons,[2] as you must know; we are to read it a second time today and shall certainly have a long debate.[3] If Lord Bute goes against us, as most people think he will, we shall have a near division, but I take it we shall carry it by five or six. If he absents himself or votes with us, which I think just possible, we shall have a majority of 25 or more.

The first bill asserting the right[4] occasioned some talk and opposition from Lord Shelburne[5] and Lord Campden, but we had no divi-

1. Charles Lennox (1735–1806), 3d D. of Richmond, 1750; ambassador to France 1765–6. He arrived at Paris 6 Nov. 1765 and left on leave 17 Feb. 1766, but did not return to his post. He was appointed secretary of state for the southern department in the first Rockingham administration and kissed hands 23 May 1766 (D. B. Horn, *British Diplomatic Representatives 1689–1789*, 1932, p. 22; William Cole, *A Journal of my Journey to Paris in the Year 1765*, ed. F. G. Stokes 1931, p. 167; *The Letters of David Hume*, ed. J. Y. T. Greig, Oxford, 1932, ii. 46 n. 3; 'Paris Journals,' DU DEFFAND v. 270, 379). HW's admiration for him as a person and statesman was strengthened by a family tie: his wife was Lady Ailesbury's daughter by her first husband. Only three letters are extant in what must have been one of HW's major correspondences. HW's letters written before 21 Dec. 1791 were probably lost when Richmond House,

Whitehall, was destroyed by fire on that date.

2. The repeal of the Stamp Act, moved by Henry Seymour Conway (Lady Ailesbury's second husband), passed the House of Commons 4 March (*Journals of the House of Commons* xxx. 627; MANN vi. 404).

3. See *Journals of the House of Lords* xxxi. 303. It was carried by a majority of 34 votes (MANN vi. 409–10).

4. The Declaratory Bill, asserting the absolute right of Parliament to legislate for the colonies without limitation.

5. William Petty (1737–1805), styled Vct Fitzmaurice; 2d E. of Shelburne, n.c., 1761; cr. (1784) M. of Lansdowne; first lord of the Treasury 1782–3; HW's occasional correspondent. He succeeded Richmond as secretary of state for the southern department 23 July 1766 (SEL-WYN 228).

sion; it passed the Committee yesterday. Lord Mansfield[6] and Lord Campden have had two good battles; and though the first is certainly the finest speaker and ablest man, he has not come off so well as might be expected, having unluckily made a little trip, in quoting to the House a statute, which upon examination never existed.[7] In some other quotations also he has been detected of *mistakes* by Lord Marchmont.[8]

Lord Pomfret[9] yesterday proposed an amendment or additional clause, a test oath to be taken by all governors, judges, justices of the peace, *etc.,* allowing supremacy of England and right to bind by laws in all cases whatever.[10] The *etc.* alone was sufficient to throw it out. He tried to divide but could get but four with him.

The repeal or rather alteration of the Cider Act[11] has hitherto met with only verbal opposition; in the H[ouse] of Commons they have not divided upon it. Mr Dowdeswell[12] says, his method will produce as much money and without excise. G. Grenville and the Bedfords etc., in the H[ouse] of Commons, seem wearied out; in the H[ouse] of Lords, where they have not met with a Conway, they are very pert.

Very soon business of another sort will begin;[13] I will only say I wish you was here, though you would go mad if you was, to see some things.

As I think you know Madame de Monconseil,[14] may I beg of you

6. William Murray (1705–93), cr. (1756) Bn and (1776) E. of Mansfield; lord chief justice 1756–88.

7. 'Lord Camden took the same part as Mr Pitt, and declared against the right of taxing. He also detected Lord Mansfield, who had quoted two laws that had never existed. As I am possessed of no notes relative to the debates in that House, I do not pretend to extend the detail of them' (*Mem. Geo. III* ii. 218). Mansfield's speech is reported in Cobbett, *Parl. Hist.* xvi. 172–7.

8. Hugh Hume Campbell (1708–94), 3d E. of Marchmont, 1740.

9. George Fermor (1722–85), styled Lord Lempster 1722–53; 2d E. of Pomfret, 1753.

10. Pomfret's proposal appears in 'Debates on . . . the Repeal of the Stamp Act, 1766' in *American Historical Review,* 1911–12, xvii. 579, quoted from the Hardwicke papers in the BM (Add. MS 35,912).

11. 'The tax on cider had given great uneasiness to the western counties, particularly from its being collected by the mode of excise. . . . To alter that mode of collection was the next step taken by the ministers; and they found it no difficult task to obtain the assent of so time-serving a Parliament, who by turns enacted and repealed whatever was proposed to them . . . and the repeal of the excise passed easily' (*Mem. Geo. III* ii. 218–19; see also *Journals of the House of Commons* xxx. 637, 670, 707, 717; Cobbett, *Parl. Hist.* xvi. 206–7).

12. William Dowdeswell (1721–75), chancellor of the Exchequer 1765–6.

13. HW wrote Mann 22 May 1766 giving him a summary of political changes in England and news of the appointment of Richmond as secretary of state (MANN vi. 419–22).

14. Claire-Cécile-Thérèse-Pauline Rioult de Douilly (1706–87), m. (1725) Étienne-

to ask her if she can let me Sir Harry Jansen's[15] country house at *Ennery*,[16] which he had bought for his life of her nephew, Mons[ieur] d'Ennery,[17] who is now at Martinico. I would take it for one year, I mean the Manor, the *Chasse,* and house, and give two or three thousand livres for it, besides paying the *gardes-chasses*. I think this might accommodate them to let it for so short a time till the master can determine upon what he would have done with it; and it would suit me very well in *all* cases to have this autumn's shooting there.[18]

> Adieu, my dear Sir,
> I am ever yours most sincerely,
>
> RICHMOND

Louis-Antoine Guignot, Marquis de Monconseil. Her sister Madeleine-Angélique Rioult de Douilly married the Seigneur d'Ennery in 1730 (MASON i. 290 nn. 15, 16; Chesterfield's *Letters,* ed. Bonamy Dobrée, 1932, vi. 2968).

15. Sir Henry Janssen (d. 21 Feb. 1766), 3d Bt, 1765.

16. In the Baillage de Pontoise, north of Pontoise, Seine-et-Oise (E. Coüard, *Les Baillages Royaux en 1789,* Versailles, 1901, pp. 13–14).

17. Victor-Thérèse Charpentier (1732–76), Marquis d'Ennery, 1763; Comte du Saint-Empire, 1765; governor of Martinique, 1765 (*Dict. de biographie française* xii. 1313–14; La Chenaye-Desbois and Badier, *Dictionnaire de la noblesse,* 3d edn, 1863–76, v. 211).

18. Richmond's dogs had been sent to Paris in advance of his arrival there on 6 Nov. 1765. William Cole wrote in his Paris journal *sub* 26 Oct.: 'As the Duke of Richmond's pack of dogs were come over this day from England to Paris, it was not to be reasonably expected that his Grace would be long behind' (Cole's *Journal,* p. 80).

From the PRINCESSE DE TALMOND,[1]
Tuesday 18 March 1766

Printed for the first time from the MS now WSL. The MS was acquired in 1934 from Frank R. Brown, of Cambridge, England, who previously purchased it at auction; its earlier history is not known.

The year of the letter is established by HW's reference to it in his letter to Montagu 21 March 1766 (see n. 5 below).

Endorsed by HW: From the Princesse de Talmond.

Address: À Monsieur Monsieur de Walpol à Paris.

Mardi, 18 mars.

LA Princesse de Talmond vient d'apprendre que Monsieur de Walpol était sur son départ.[2] Elle est bien fâchée d'avoir si peu joui de sa bonne compagnie; elle en accuse en partie ses fréquentes absences de Paris. Elle se flatte d'avoir le plaisir de le voir avant son départ.[3] Cependant si le hasard voulait qu'elle ne se trouvât pas chez elle, elle le prie de vouloir bien se souvenir de la commission dont il a eu la bonté de se charger, d'une petite levrette, de la plus petite espèce, noire doublée de blanc.[4] Elle lui envoie son portrait, non pas pour [le] lui laisser, car elle ne peut pas s'en détacher; mais pour lui faire voir la beauté sans pareille de feue la petite Diane si chère à son souvenir.[5] Elle lui en sera sensiblement obligée.

1. Marie-Louise Jablonowska (1701–73), m. (1730), Antoine-Charles-Frédéric de la Trémoïlle, Prince de Talmond. Born in Poland, she came to France with her cousin Marie Leszczyńska, Louis XV's consort; she became the Young Pretender's mistress and was a well-known figure at the French Court. See HW's description of her in Appendix 3f, DU DEFFAND vi. 57–8.

2. HW left Paris 17 April 1766 ('Paris Journals,' DU DEFFAND v. 314).

3. HW paid a 'visit of leave' to the Princesse 1 April 1766 (ibid. v. 310).

4. When HW visited the Princesse 15 Jan. 1766 (DU DEFFAND v. 295), 'she desired me to get her a black and white greyhound marked exactly like the one she had lost, and which I had never seen. I promised, and took my leave, and

thought no more of her and her dog and my promise' (ibid. vi. 58).

5. HW wrote Montagu 21 March 1766: 'The Princess of Talmond sent me this morning a picture of two pug dogs and a black and white greyhound, wretchedly painted. . . . in her note she warned me not to hope to keep it—it was only to imprint on my memory the size and features and spots of Diana, her departed greyhound, in order that I might get her exactly such another' (MONTAGU ii. 208). In his reply (missing) HW indicated that he could not 'execute so impossible a commission. Two years after I met the Princess at the Duchesse d'Aiguillon's, and she told me with great good humour that she found I had never thought any more of her commission' (DU DEFFAND vi. 59).

To Pierre-Jean Mariette, ?Wednesday 16 April 1766

Printed for the first time from a photostat of the MS in the Bibliothèque Nationale (MS français 12765, ff. 246–7). The MS is in a four-volume collection of autograph letters acquired by the Bibliothèque Nationale from an unidentified owner during the 19th century.

Dated conjecturally by the references to Lord Nuneham and to HW's imminent departure for England (see nn. 1 and 3 below).

Address: À Monsieur Monsieur Mariette (not sent through the post).

COMME que je ne compte de partir que vendredi,[1] je m'étais destiné le plaisir de prendre congé de vous, mon cher Monsieur, cet après-dîner ou demain. C'est avec regret que je vous quitte sans avoir cette satisfaction, et avec encore plus de regret que je vous quitte pour quelque temps. Je n'ose pas me flatter de vous voir en Angleterre, mais l'estime, l'amitié et tous les agréments de la société, ne peuvent pas manquer de me ramener en France. Entre mille et mille marques de bonté et d'amitié je n'en ai reçu de plus fortes, Monsieur, que de votre part,[2] et je vous supplie de croire que j'en suis bien reconnaissant.

Je ne manquerai pas de faire vos compliments à Milord Nuneham,[3] et j'aurai grand soin de vous chercher les nouvelles estampes que vous m'indiquez. Si vous vous ressouvenez encore de quelque chose dont vous avez envie, soyez sûr que vous ne pourriez me faire de plaisir plus sensible qu'en me nommant votre commissionnaire.

J'ai l'honneur d'être

Monsieur
Votre très humble et très obéissant serviteur

HORACE WALPOLE

1. HW set out for England at four o'clock on Thursday 17 April 1766 ('Paris Journals,' DU DEFFAND v. 314).

2. See *ante* 21 Nov. 1765, n. 1.

3. George Simon Harcourt (1736–1809), styled Vct Nuneham 1749–77; 2d E. Harcourt, 1777; HW's friend and correspondent. He had left for France probably in June 1765 (see Lord Villiers to Nuneham 4 July 1765, in *The Harcourt Papers,* ed. E. W. Harcourt, Oxford, 1880–1905, viii. 56). As an amateur engraver and collector of engravings, he had doubtless met Mariette in Paris and gone to see his collection of prints and drawings.

From the Comtesse de Boufflers, Sunday 4 May 1766

Printed from Toynbee *Supp.* iii. 196–8, where the letter was first printed. Damer-Waller; the MS was sold Sotheby's 5 Dec. 1921 (first Waller Sale), lot 96 (with Madame de Boufflers to HW 6 Sept. 1766), to Maggs; not further traced.

Le 4 mai 1766.

JE serais fort confuse, Monsieur, d'avoir différé si longtemps de répondre à la lettre[1] que vous m'avez fait l'honneur de m'écrire, si ma paresse (car je n'ai pas d'autre excuse à donner), n'était un vice invétéré, connu de tous mes amis, qui ne prend rien sur la solidité de mes sentiments, et pour lequel je suis accoutumée à trouver de l'indulgence. Voilà ce que j'ai à dire en ma faveur. J'espère que cela est suffisant pour que vous m'excusiez, et qu'après m'avoir témoigné une prévention si favorable, vous ne me ferez pas l'injustice de me croire capable de vouloir manquer à ce que je vous dois.

Puisque vous voulez bien, Monsieur, vous ressouvenir de la recommendation que vous m'avez promise, je vous serai très redevable de me l'envoyer vers la fin de juillet. Mon fils[2] part dans ce temps-là pour Florence, et la remettrait lui-même; cependant, je serais bien aise aussi que vous écrivissiez d'avance et que la lettre que vous m'enverrez fût simplement une lettre de créance.[3] J'avais beaucoup vanté à Lady Hervey[4] le bon effet de l'air de France sur votre santé; elle n'en veut pas convenir; elle prétend qu'elle vous a trouvé maigri. Je vois qu'elle n'a pas tant de bonne volonté pour moi que je l'imaginais; elle craint d'être persuadé en notre faveur, mais j'espère, Monsieur, qu'elle ne vous detournera pas de tenir ce que vous avez promis;[5] vous savez à combien de gens cette promesse est agréable, et je vous prie de me mettre à la tête de la liste. Mr Hume[6] me mande que vous aviez encore écrit contre J. J.[7] en réponse à une lettre qu'il a

1. Missing.

2. Louis-Édouard (1746–94), Comte de Boufflers (DU DEFFAND i. 172 n. 7).

3. HW wrote Mann 11 July 1766: 'You will soon see at Florence the son of Madame de Boufflers, to whom I have been desired to give a letter' (MANN vi. 434). The same day he enclosed the 'lettre de créance' to Mann (printed ibid. vi. 435) in his reply (missing) to Mme de Boufflers. See *post* 6 Sept. 1766.

4. With whom Mme de Boufflers had doubtless become acquainted during Lady Hervey's occasional visits to L'Isle Adam, the seat of the Prince de Conti north of Paris (*Letters of Mary Lepel, Lady Hervey*, ed. J. W. Croker, 1821, pp. 187, 199). Mme de Boufflers was Conti's mistress.

5. That is, to make a return visit to France.

6. David Hume, 'the second idol of Madame de Boufflers' (HW to Mann 11 July 1766, MANN vi. 434).

7. Jean-Jacques Rousseau (1712–78). Mme de Boufflers and the Prince de Conti were Rousseau's patrons.

fait mettre dans les papiers, mais que vous avez fait le sacrifice de cette nouvelle production,[8] quoique très propre à faire honneur à votre esprit. Cela est fort digne de votre bon cœur, et doit vous coûter moins qu'à un autre. Votre réputation est établie et méritée. On m'avait assuré que l'allégorie d'un charlatan qui vend des pillules etc.[9] était de vous, je ne l'ai pas cru, cela m'aurait fait de la peine, et après la conversation que nous avons eu ensemble à l'Hôtel de Luxembourg,[10] je pense que cela n'aurait pas été bien fait à vous. Vous voyez, Monsieur, ma franchise et mon estime; je vous prie d'être convaincu que mon amitié pour vous n'est pas moindre. J'ai l'honneur d'être, Monsieur, votre très humble et très obéissante servante,

H. DE SAUJON DE BOUFFLERS

M. le Prince de Conty[11] vous fait ses compliments.

---

8. HW's first letter to Rousseau, signed 'Frederic,' King of Prussia, led to the famous quarrel between Hume and Rousseau; Rousseau's reply appeared in the *St James's Chronicle* 8–10 April 1766, causing HW to write a second letter, signed 'Émile,' which he then suppressed 'parce que l'auteur ne voulait pas pousser la querelle plus loin' (HW's note, quoted in DU DEFFAND i. 4 n. 5; see also ibid. vi, Appendix 6). For full accounts of HW's rôle in the affair see Hazen, *Bibl. of HW* 160–2; 'A Narrative of What Passed relative to the Quarrel of Mr David Hume and Jean Jacques Rousseau, as far as Mr Horace Walpole was Concerned in it,' *Works* iv. 249–56; and F. A. Pottle, 'The Part Played by Horace Walpole and James Boswell in the Quarrel between Rousseau and Hume: A Reconsideration,' in *Horace Walpole: Writer, Politician, and Connoisseur*, ed. W. H. Smith, New Haven, 1967, pp. 255–91. HW's correspondence with Hume concerning the hoax begins *post* 26 July 1766.

9. 'A Tale' in French, describing a quack who left Athens because his pills were no longer popular there and went to Sparta, where he was at first well received and later ignored, appeared in the *St James's Chronicle* 24–6 April 1766. The author of this piece was Georges Deyverdun (ca 1735–89), Swiss writer and friend of Edward Gibbon, later a clerk in the secretary of state's office in London.

10. Presumably 14 Jan. 1766, when HW had a 'long conversation with Prince [de Conti] and Mme de Boufflers on the letter' to Rousseau ('Paris Journals,' DU DEFFAND v. 295). Mme de Boufflers and Conti were highly offended by the letter when it was circulated in Paris during the winter of 1765–6; see CONWAY iii. 48 n. 8.

11. Louis-François de Bourbon (1717–76), Prince de Conti.

To the Duchesse de Choiseul,[1] Tuesday 6 May 1766

Printed from the MS copy in Jean-François Wiart's hand, now WSL. First printed, Toynbee vi. 457–8. The MS copy was among the papers bequeathed by Mme du Deffand to HW on her death in 1780; sold SH vi. 107 to Dyce-Sombre, whose widow (later Lady Forester) left them to her nephew, W. R. Parker-Jervis in 1893; resold Sotheby's 12 March 1920 (Parker-Jervis Sale), lot 394 (with other Du Deffand MSS), to Maggs; acquired from them by WSL, 1933. The original letter is missing; it is listed in HW's record of letters sent to Paris in 1766 (DU DEFFAND v. 381).

Dated by the endorsement.

Endorsed by Wiart: Copie d'une lettre de Monsieur Walpole à Mme la D. de Choiseul 6 mai 1766.

JE fus bien tenté, Madame, à mon retour dans mon pays, de vous marquer ma reconnaissance de toutes les bontés que vous avez daigné me prodiguer; mais votre politesse naturelle, Madame la Duchesse, m'en empêchait, et je n'osais mettre sur mon compte les grâces que vous répandez sur tout le monde, il ne résultait pas de ce que vous m'aviez été favorable que je l'eusse mérité; l'excellence de votre caractère aurait pu mettre vos lumières en défaut; je vous estimais trop, Madame, pour m'en estimer davantage. Madame du Deffand veut me persuader, car elle est très sujette à s'engouer, que vous m'aviez un peu distingué du commun, et pour preuve m'envoie votre billet;[2] je vous en remercie très humblement, Madame la Duchesse, et quoique mon peu de mérite me rend encore très défiant sur mon propre chapitre, je n'y suis pas moins sensible. Je suis persuadé que vous vouliez faire plaisir à ma bonne amie, et j'ai trop de raisons pour l'aimer pour ne pas goûter des attentions pour elle, pour le moins autant que si elles m'eussent été adressées. Voyez, Madame, jusqu'à quel point j'honore votre caractère quand j'ose vous faire un pareil aveu! Le fils d'un premier ministre ose être sincère avec la femme d'un premier ministre.[3] Ce n'est pas aux

1. Louise-Honorine Crozat du Châtel (1735–1801), m. (1750) Étienne-François de Choiseul-Stainville, Duc de Choiseul. HW met the Duc and Duchesse during his visit to Paris in 1765–6.

2. 'Je vous envoie l'original de la lettre de Mme de Choiseul; je n'en ai gardé que la copie. Vous pouvez montrer cette lettre si vous en avez envie à qui vous jugerez à propos; on verra le cas que Mme de Choiseul fait de votre nation et de vous en particulier' (Mme du Deffand to HW 23 April 1766, DU DEFFAND i. 15).

3. The Duc de Choiseul had held the office of minister of foreign affairs in alternation with his cousin, the Duc de Praslin, since 1758 (ibid. i. 1 n. 1).

disgrâces des cours, mais c'est vous, Madame, qui en retirez tout l'honneur, car vous jouissez; votre philosophie ne s'est pas attendu à se former aux leçons d'une chute; vous avez fait davantage, Madame, vous rapprochez les gens de partis opposés. J'ai eu l'honneur de causer une demie heure avec Monsieur le Duc de Bedford[4] sur votre chapitre; j'ai presque envie de vous raconter tout ce qu'il m'a dit sur ce sujet, cela serait vous exposer mes pensées sans vous offenser; mais quoiqu'on devient babillard en parlant de vous, Madame la Duchesse, je n'ose pousser trop loin la liberté que j'ai pris de vous écrire, je veux être sage pour que vous me continuiez vos bontés à mon retour.[5] Moi qui suis un peu glorieux vis à vis de mes compatriotes, ne rougirais pas d'être un des courtisans de votre antichambre; il n'y a point d'Anglais qui tiendrait contre un pareil charme. J'ai l'honneur d'être, Madame la Duchesse, votre très humble, très respectueux et très obéissant serviteur

Horace Walpole

To the Rev. John Hutchins, Saturday 10 May 1766

Printed from the MS now WSL. First printed in John Hutchins, *The History and Antiquities of the County of Dorset,* 3d edn, ed. William Shipp and J. W. Hodson, 1861–73, ii. 462. The MS apparently passed from Hutchins to John Nichols and remained in the Nichols family; sold Sotheby's 18 Nov. 1929 (J. G. Nichols Sale), lot 231, to Francis Edwards; resold by W. T. Spencer to WSL, 1932.

Endorsed in an unidentified hand: Walpole.

Arlington Street, May 10th 1766.

Sir,

I AM very sorry that I cannot furnish you with the materials you want for the life of Sir James Thornhill.[1] I went to Strawberry Hill on Thursday to search for them, but could find nothing to your purpose. There are 40 MSS. volumes of Vertue's collections,[2] all en-

---

4. John Russell (1710–71), 4th D. of Bedford, 1732; statesman and diplomatist. HW was at this time politically opposed to the Bedford faction in Parliament. See ibid. ii. 49.

5. HW returned to Paris in 1767, arriving 23 Aug.; he saw the Duchesse on

28 Aug. and supped at her house on 6 Sept. ('Paris Journals,' ibid. v. 316, 318).

1. See *ante* 22 Sept. 1765 and *post* 17 Feb. 1767.

2. Actually, thirty-eight volumes are known to have survived.

tered without method, and without any direction for finding anything.[3] I twice made an index to them,[4] when I was compiling my
Anecdotes; which I cannot find, nor am sure whether I did not burn
them with my blotted papers. I turned over the volumes in which
I thought it most likely to find accounts of Sir James, but there is
no such thing; and indeed in such a farrago, it would be impossible
without much more time than I have at present, to pick out a life
of him thence, if the materials are there.[5]

I beg, Sir, you will not think this an excuse to decline assisting
you, or that I am unwilling to anticipate any part of my own work.
God knows whether I shall ever finish it; and if I should, it would
not at all prevent my obliging you. I have told you the exact truth;
am sorry it is so, and more sorry for the account you give me of your
own misfortunes,[6] which I dare to say were not at all from your own
fault.

I am Sir
Your obedient humble servant

Hor. Walpole

From the Duc de Nivernais,[1] Sunday 11 May 1766

Printed from the MS now wsl. First printed, Toynbee *Supp.* iii. 198–200.
Damer-Waller; the MS was sold Sotheby's 5 Dec. 1921 (first Waller Sale), lot 165
(with Nivernais to HW 22 Aug. 1771, 30 April 1785, and 29 Feb. 1792), to
Wells; given by him to Thomas Conolly, of Chicago, from whom wsl acquired
it in 1937.

Le 11 mai 1766.

J E trouve en arrivant de Chantilly,[2] Monsieur, la charmante lettre[3]
dont vous m'avez honoré le 6 de ce mois. Ne croyez pas que je la

3. A description of the volumes is given
in 'The History of the Vertue Manuscripts,' *Walpole Society,* 1929–30, xviii.
xv–xxv.

4. HW's detailed listing of the contents
of the volumes, headed 'Abstracts from
Vertue's MSS,' is at Nostell Priory, Wakefield, Yorks.

5. Since Vertue set down his notes
without method or system, HW's state-
ment is not exaggerated. However, HW
did later include an account of Thornhill
in the fourth volume of *Anecdotes of
Painting,* SH, 1771.

6. Hutchins's letter to HW is missing.

———

1. Louis-Jules-Barbon Mancini-Mazarini
(1716–98), Duc de Nivernais; French ambassador to England 1762–3; translator of
HW's *Essay on Modern Gardening.*

2. The country seat of the Prince de
Condé.

3. Missing; the letter is listed in HW's
record of letters sent to Paris in 1766 (du
Deffand v. 381).

trouve charmante à cause de tous les compliments et remercîments infiniment flatteurs que vous m'y prodiguez. Je m'en offenserais plus volontiers car je sais bien que c'est à moi à vous remercier, et depuis le premier jour que vous m'avez accordé si généreusement vos bontés à Londres[4] sans que je les eusse en rien méritées, je me regarde et me dois regarder comme votre obligé et votre débiteur pour toute ma vie. Ce qui me charme dans votre lettre, Monsieur, c'est la promesse d'une seconde visite.[5] Je ne vous la laisserai pas oublier et je vous supplie de trouver bon que je vous la rappelle quelquefois.

Je ne puis vous dire combien je suis touché des bontés de Milady Hervey et de Mlle Pitt, et je vous supplie de vouloir bien chercher dans votre langue ou dans la mienne que vous savez mieux que moi, des expressions qui puissent leur faire connaître l'étendu de mon respect, de mon attachment et de ma reconnaissance. Pour moi, je n'y réussirais pas; c'est un besogne au-dessus de mes forces et c'est pour cela que je m'adresse à vous.

Je viens de passer trois jours dans le plus beau lieu et avec la meilleure compagnie de France que M. le Prince de Condé[6] y avait rassemblée pour faire honneur à Monsieur le Prince héréditaire.[7] J'espère qu'il ne s'y sera pas plus ennuyé qu'à la guerre, car on ne s'ennuie guère de ses succès et il est impossible d'en avoir plus qu'il n'en a ici. On ne fait pourtant que lui rendre justice. Mais nous la lui rendons avec une sensibilité et une abondance de cœur dont il doit être content. Il me comble de bontés et il doit me faire l'honneur de dîner chez moi le 22 de ce mois. En vérité vous auriez tout le temps d'y venir et ce serait une galanterie à lui faire, mais sans préjudice de la visite promise car nous ne prendrions pas celle-là pour nous.

Je m'en vais demain à une campagne où Mme de Rochefort[8] est

4. For HW's severe description of Nivernais when he was in London in 1762 to negotiate the peace see *Mem. Geo. III.* i. 151–2.

5. HW returned to Paris in 1767, arriving 23 Aug.; he supped at Mme de Rochefort's with Nivernais and others 4 Oct. ('Paris Journals,' DU DEFFAND v. 323).

6. Louis-Joseph de Bourbon (1736–1818), Prince de Condé.

7. Karl Wilhelm Ferdinand, the Hereditary Prince of Brunswick-Wolfenbüttel.

Mme du Deffand reported to HW 18 May 1766 that his 'voyage à Chantilly a été des plus brillants' (ibid. i. 42; see also i. 41 n. 7).

8. Later (1782) Nivernais's wife (*ante* 19 Oct. 1765, n. 25). She was doubtless at Saint-Maur, the country estate of the Comtesse de Pontchartrain, where she was in the habit of spending the warmer months; Nivernais frequently visited her there (Louis de Loménie, *La Comtesse de Rochefort et ses amis*, 1870, p. 141). See following letter.

depuis une dizaine de jours. Vous pouvez croire qu'il y sera parlé
de vous et de votre imprimerie car j'y porte votre volume de *Pièces
fugitives*[9] que j'estropie en français à Madame de Rochefort et qui,
tout estropiées que je les lui montre, lui paraissent faites à peindre,
parce qu'elle a le goût assez fin pour deviner l'original dans ma
grossière traduction. Quant aux fables,[10] nous en parlerons à la
visite que vous savez; on me tourmente beaucoup ici pour les rendre
plaisance et peut-être la vanité me font balancer. Je vous demande
quera de moi, et il me semble que je suis bien vieux pour cela. Je
n'ai pas encore pris de parti. *Video meliora proboque,*[11] mais la complaisance et peut-être la vanité me font balancer. Je vous demande
pardon de vous piller encore une pensée car il me semble qu'elle est
dans une de ces charmantes épîtres que vous écriviez il y a tantôt
deux mille ans.[12] J'ai le cœur, la mémoire, et l'esprit si plein de vous
que vous devez me pardonner de vous voler si souvent.

Adieu, Monsieur, je vous renouvelle avec bien de la sincérité le
tendre attachement avec lequel j'ai l'honneur d'être, votre très
humble et très obéissant serviteur,

LE DUC DE NIVERNOIS

M. Horace Walpole—Londres.

9. *Fugitive Pieces in Verse and Prose,*
SH, 1758.

10. HW had become acquainted with
Nivernais's fables, composed in the manner of La Fontaine, during his visit to
Paris in 1765–6. He wrote Anne Pitt 25
Dec. 1765: 'Monsieur de Nivernois has
been reading us a dozen new fables, all
prettier than one another' (MORE 90).

The fables formed the first two volumes
of Nivernais's *Œuvres,* 1796; an English
translation was published in 1799. See
post 6 Jan. 1785.

11. 'I see the better and approve it'
(Ovid, *Metamorphoses* vii. 20).

12. Nivernais apparently alludes to the
poet Horace, but mistakes the correct
source of his quotation.

From Madame de Rochefort,[1] Tuesday 24 June 1766

Printed from Toynbee *Supp.* iii. 200–2, where the letter was first printed. Damer-Waller; the MS was sold Sotheby's 5 Dec. 1921 (first Waller Sale), lot 180 (with the Marquis de Saint-Simon to HW 19 July 1755), to Wells; not further traced.

HW recorded in his list of letters sent to Paris in 1766 that he wrote to Mme de Rochefort 17 June; this letter, to which the present letter is doubtless her reply, is missing (DU DEFFAND v. 382).

À St-Maur,[2] ce 24 juin.

SI quelque chose, Monsieur, peut adoucir les peines de sentiment, c'est l'intérêt des personnes à qui on est véritablement attachée. Combien donc ne vous dois-je pas de remercîments de la lettre[3] que vous avez fait l'honneur de m'écrire? J'en suis sensiblement touchée pour moi et pour mon frère[4] et ma belle-sœur.[5] Je me hâte de les instruire des marques de votre amitié comme ce que je puis leur mander de plus doux dans leur affliction. Mon frère est parti immédiatement avant l'arrivée de votre lettre pour aller en Anjou trouver sa femme qui était chez Monsieur son père.[6] Il est parti en bonne santé, et je l'ai vu partir et s'éloigner de moi sans regret pour lui dans l'espérance que la dissipation des voyages lui ferait du bien. Son absence ne sera pas longue et à son retour nous nous entretiendrons ensemble du bonheur que nous avons et que nous sentons très bien d'avoir acquis, Monsieur, un ami tel que vous.

J'attends notre ambassadeur[7] avec la plus grande impatience, puisqu'il arrive les mains pleines de vos bienfaits pour moi. Ils seront d'une valeur inestimable puisque votre goût et ma reconnaissance y auront mis le prix dans ce petit coin du Luxembourg[8] que vous

1. Marie-Thérèse de Brancas (1716–82), m. 1 (1736) Jean-Anne-Vincent de Larlan de Kercadio, Comte de Rochefort; m. 2 (1782) Louis-Jules-Barbon Mancini-Mazarini, Duc de Nivernais. HW wrote of her to Gray 25 Jan. 1766: 'Madame de Rochefort is different from all the rest. Her understanding is just and delicate; with a finesse of wit that is the result of reflection. Her manner is soft and feminine, and though a *savante,* without any declared pretensions' (GRAY ii. 153–4). For the 'portrait' of her by Président Hénault see DU DEFFAND vi. 100–2.

2. See previous letter, n. 8.

3. Missing; see headnote.

4. Louis-Paul (1718–1802), Marquis de Brancas, later Duc de Céreste.

5. Marie-Anne-Renée-Jacqueline Grandhomme de Giseux (b. 1718), m. (1747) Louis-Paul, Marquis de Brancas.

6. René-Simon Grandhomme, Seigneur de Giseux in Anjou.

7. *Ante* 19 Oct. 1765, n. 13.

8. In 1759 Mme de Rochefort had moved into an apartment in the Luxembourg Palace given to her by the King; HW visited her there when in Paris (Louis de Loménie, *La Comtesse de Rochefort et ses amis,* 1870, p. 100; MORE 54, 90).

[avez] daigné ⟨   ⟩ votre place, qui ne saurait jamais être remplie non du moins ⟨   ⟩ pendant votre absence. Je vois, Monsieur, que vous n'êtes pas fort content de Mlle Pitt,[9] et en vérité je
ne suis pas propre à vous apaiser. L'air de sa campagne est apparemment un air très froid, car elle est devenue de glace pour moi; je n'en
reçois pas la plus petite marque de souvenir. Je suis aussi à la campagne, et cette campagne est à deux lieux de Paris aussi. Suivant
votre observation, il me serait bien permis d'être ⟨   ⟩ cam-
pagnarde, cependant je n'oublie point la ville et les amis que j'y
ai laissés. Il y en a un auquel vous n'aurez pas de peine à croire que
je pense souvent, c'est l'ami Newton.[10] Je lui ai écrit tout exprès
pour lui mander tout ce que vous me dites flatteur pour lui. Il en
sera aussi glorieux que moi tandis que le Duc de Nivernois sera
accablé de vos reproches. Il doit venir incessamment dans le lieu que
j'habite, et je lui garde votre lettre qui justifiera le désir que je lui
ai souvent témoigné d'immortaliser par ses ouvrages notre ami
Newton. Il a donné toujours pour excuse la crainte d'être au-dessous
de son sujet, et voilà comme il m'a fait prendre patience. J'espère
que vous l'encouragerez et je vous en remercie d'avance. Recevez,
Monsieur, une nouvelle assurance de l'attachement sincère avec lequel j'ai l'honneur d'être votre très humble et très obéissante servante,

BRANCAS DE ROCHEFORT

TO LORD ILCHESTER, Saturday 19 July 1766

Printed (for the first time as a letter to Ilchester) from a photostat of the MS
among the Holland House papers in the British Museum (Add. MS 51,350, f. 30).
For the history of the MS see *ante* 29 July 1762. For previous printings see head-
note, SELWYN 225, where this letter was mistakenly printed from a copy sent by
Ilchester to Lord Holland (Holland House papers, BM Add. MS 51,404, f. 212).
Endorsed by Ilchester: Mr Walpole July 19, rec[eive]d 21, 1766.

Arlington Street, July 19, 1766.

I SUPPOSE, my dear Lord, you will have twenty letters by this
post to tell you that Lord Temple has refused the Treasury and
is gone.[1] His creatures say Mr Pitt used him like a dog. 1 should not

---

9. Who frequently visited Mme de
Rochefort during her trips to France.
For an account of their friendship see
Loménie, op. cit. 221–3.

10. Possibly Sir Isaac Newton.

---

1. The only other letter to Ilchester
on this subject found among the Holland

think that either was very gentle to the other before they parted. Lord Temple insisted on bringing his brother George too, which Pitt flatly refused. Then poor Lord Lyttelton; no. When all was rejected, the Earl recollected Almon and Humphrey Cotes; not for lords of the Treasury; but as responsible to them. He asked what Mr Pitt intended to do for Mr Mckensie and Lord Northumberland? Considerably. This was the sum of the conference and quarrel, which in Ciceronian Billingsgate you know might be rolled out into a spirited dialogue of some hours. The next day his Lordship saw the King, was, I believe as well as I guess, very impertinent, was answered properly, called at Lord Gower's, who was not in town, left his commands for the people of England with Mrs Maccartney, and set out. I am so well satisfied that I am setting out too.

Mr Pitt has still much fever; the Duke of Grafton goes to him today, but he himself will not, they say, be able to see the King before Wednesday. I do not guess who will have the Treasury, nor care since I know who will not. Adieu! my dear Lord; I hope this charming weather will be of great service to you.

Yours ever

H. W.

House papers is from the Duke of Richmond 17 July, in which Richmond reports: 'Lord Temple is gone out of town tonight for Stowe, very angry at Mr Pitt, who he says may settle the administration as he pleases. He was with Pitt for seven hours yesterday after having seen the King the day before. 'Tis reported, and I believe truly, that Lord Temple wanted Grenville, which Pitt objected to; and afterwards Lord Lyttleton was proposed, but likewise in vain. He then picked a quarrel about what is to be done for Lord Northumberland and Mackenzie, and went to the Queen's House today at 3 o'clock, where he says he found H[is] M[ajesty] very much determined for Lord Bute's friends, and *therefore* he would have nothing to do with it' (BM Add. MS 51,350, f. 29). For further annotation of the present letter see SELWYN 225–6.

From DAVID HUME, Saturday 26 July 1766

Printed from *Works* iv. 257, where the letter was first printed. Reprinted in T. E. Ritchie, *An Account of the Life and Writings of David Hume, Esq.*, 1807, pp. 244–5; J. H. Burton, *Life and Correspondence of David Hume*, Edinburgh, 1846, ii. 355 (closing and signature omitted in Ritchie and Burton); *The Letters of David Hume*, ed. J. Y. T. Greig, Oxford, 1932, ii. 71. The history of the MS and its present whereabouts are not known.

Dated by HW's reply *post* 26 July 1766.

Saturday forenoon.

Dear Sir,

WHEN I came home[1] last night, I found on my table a very long letter from d'Alembert,[2] who tells me, that, on receiving from me an account of my affair with Rousseau,[3] he summoned a meeting of all my literary friends at Paris, and found them all unanimously of the same opinion with himself, and of a contrary opinion to me, with regard to my conduct. They all think I ought to give to the public a narrative of the whole. However, I persist still more closely in my first opinion, especially after receiving the last mad letter.[4] D'Alembert tells me, that it is of great importance for me to justify myself from having any hand in the letter from the King of Prussia: I am told by Crawford,[5] that you had wrote it a fortnight before I left Paris, but did not show it to a mortal, for fear of hurting me;[6] a delicacy of which I am very sensible. Pray recollect, if it was so. Though I do not intend to publish, I am collecting all the original pieces, and shall connect them by a concise narrative. It is necessary

1. Hume lived in Lisle Street, Leicester Fields.

2. Jean le Rond d'Alembert (1717–83), 'philosophe' and mathematician. His letter to Hume from Paris 21 July 1766 is printed in Appendix K, 'Letters to Hume about his Quarrel with Rousseau,' in Hume's *Letters*, ed. Greig, ii. 412–15.

3. See *ante* 4 May 1766, n. 8. Hume's letter to d'Alembert is missing.

4. Rousseau's long, accusing letter written from Wootton, Staffordshire, 10 July 1766, printed ibid. ii. 385–401. 'I received a letter from him, which is perfect frenzy . . . . He there tells me, that d'Alembert, Horace Walpole and I had from the first entered into a combination to ruin him;

and had ruined him . . . That the English nation were very fond of him on his first arrival; but that Horace Walpole and I had totally alienated them from him' (Hume to the Rev. Hugh Blair 15 July 1766, ibid. ii. 63–4).

5. John ('Fish') Craufurd (*ante* 6 March 1766, n. 1).

6. See following letter.

7. HW's letter in the name of the King of Prussia appeared in the *St James's Chronicle* 1–3 April 1766; Rousseau's answer, dated 7 April 1766, was printed in that *Chronicle* 8–10 April. For Mme du Deffand's comments to HW 21 April 1766 concerning Rousseau's reply see DU DEFFAND i. 9.

for me to have that letter and Rousseau's answer. Pray assist me in this work. About what time, do you think, were they printed?[7]

I am, dear sir,
Your most obedient humble servant,

DAVID HUME

To DAVID HUME, Saturday 26 July 1766

Printed from a photostat of the MS in the possession of the Royal Society of Edinburgh, kindly furnished by Dr James Watt through the good offices of Mr James Kendall. First printed in *A Concise and Genuine Account of the Dispute between Mr Hume and Mr Rousseau*, 1766, pp. 88–9 (salutation and first paragraph omitted). Reprinted, *Works* iv. 258; T. E. Ritchie, *An Account of the Life and Writings of David Hume, Esq.*, 1807, pp. 245–6 (closing and signature omitted); Wright v. 157–8 (closing and signature omitted); Cunningham v. 7 (signature omitted); Toynbee vii. 31–2; *The Letters of David Hume*, ed. J. Y. T. Greig, Oxford, 1932, ii. 423–4 (closing and signature omitted); extracts printed in *European Magazine*, 1797, xxxi. 300; J. H. Burton, *Life and Correspondence of David Hume*, Edinburgh, 1846, ii. 361–2; *Letters of David Hume to William Strahan*, ed. G. B. Hill, Oxford, 1888, p. 88; *Horace Walpole: Writer, Politician, and Connoisseur*, ed. W. H. Smith, New Haven, 1967, p. 271, n. 39. For the history of the MS see *ante* 15 July 1758.

Arlington Street, July 26, 1766.

Dear Sir,

YOUR set of literary friends[1] are what a set of literary men are apt to be, exceedingly absurd. They hold a consistory to consult how to argue with a madman; and they think it very necessary for your character to give them the pleasure of seeing Rousseau exposed, not because he has provoked you, but them. If Rousseau prints, you must; but I certainly would not, till he does.

I cannot be precise as to the time of my writing the King of Prussia's letter,[2] but I do assure you with the utmost truth that it was

1. Hume mentions by name the members of this group in his letter from Paris to the Rev. Hugh Blair ?Dec. 1763: 'The men of letters here are really very agreeable; all of them men of the world, living in entire or almost entire harmony among themselves, and quite irreproachable in their morals. . . . Those whose persons and conversation I like best are d'Alembert, Buffon, Marmontel, Diderot, Duclos, Helvétius, and old President Hénaut' (Hume's *Letters*, ed. Greig, i. 419).

2. HW wrote the pretended letter 23 Dec. 1765; it had been circulating in Paris since 28 Dec., or about a week be-

several days before you left Paris, and before Rousseau's arrival there, of which I can give you a strong proof; for I not only suppressed the letter while you stayed there, out of delicacy to you; but it was the reason why, out of delicacy to myself, I did not go to see him, as you often proposed to me; thinking it wrong to go and make a cordial visit to a man, with a letter in my pocket to laugh at him. You are at full liberty, dear Sir, to make use of what I say in your justification, either to Rousseau or anybody else.[3] I should be very sorry to have you blamed on my account; I have a hearty contempt of Rousseau, and am perfectly indifferent what *the litterati of Paris* think of the matter.[4] If there is any fault, which I am far from thinking, let it lie on me. No parts can hinder my laughing at their possessor if he is a mountebank. If he has a bad and most ungrateful heart, as Rousseau has shown in your case, into the bargain, he will have my scorn likewise, as he will of all good and sensible men. You[5] may trust your sentence to such, who are as respectable judges, as any that have pored over ten thousand more volumes.

Yours most sincerely

Hor. Walpole

PS. I will look out the letter and the dates as soon as I go to Strawberry Hill.[6]

fore Hume and Rousseau left Paris for London 4 Jan. 1766. Rousseau had arrived in Paris 16 Dec. 1765 (More 99–100; Gray i. 41 n. 277; L.-J. Courtois, 'Chronologie critique de la vie et des œuvres de Jean-Jacques Rousseau,' *Annales de la Société Jean-Jacques Rousseau,* 1923, xv. 180–2).

3. See *post* 30 Oct. 1766.

4. When using this letter to compile a documentary account of his quarrel with Rousseau, Hume wrote in the MS 'anybody' above 'the litterati' and changed 'think' to 'thinks.' He sent a transcript of the account to his 'literary friends' at Paris, who employed Jean-Baptiste-Antoine Suard to translate and edit his narrative. *Exposé succinct de la contestation qui s'est élevée entre M. Hume et M. Rousseau, avec les pièces justicatives* was published at Paris (with the fictitious imprint 'À Londres') in Oct. 1766. The passage above reads in translation: 'J'ai un mépris profond pour Rousseau et une parfaite indifférence sur ce qu'on pensera de cette affaire' (*Exposé,* p. 118). A London edition of the pamphlet (for the most part a retranslation from the French), supervised but not publicly endorsed by Hume, was published by Thomas Becket 20 Nov. 1766 as *A Concise and Genuine Account of the Dispute between Mr Hume and Mr Rousseau;* in it the passage reads, p. 88: 'I have a hearty contempt of Rousseau, and am perfectly indifferent what anybody thinks of the matter.'

5. This final sentence, as well as the entire first paragraph of the letter, was omitted from the French text printed in the *Exposé,* pp. 117–18.

6. HW had sent Mme du Deffand 16 July 1766 an up-to-date summary of the Hume-Rousseau quarrel (du Deffand i. 94–8). She called the present letter to Hume 'noble, franche, délibérée, comme vous' (Mme du Deffand to HW 4 Sept. 1766, ibid. i. 128).

From CHARLES JAMES FOX,[1] Wednesday 6 August 1766

Printed from the MS now WSL. First printed, Toynbee *Supp.* iii. 204. Damer-Waller; the MS was sold Sotheby's 5 Dec. 1921 (first Waller Sale), lot 125, bought in; resold Christie's 15 Dec. 1947 (second Waller Sale), lot 14 (with Fox to HW 10 Sept. 1783), to Maggs for WSL.

The year of the letter is established by the reference to HW's unsuccessful 'endeavours' to obtain an earldom for Lord Holland (see n. 5 below).

Winterslow,[2] August 6.

Dear Sir,

I RECEIVED the enclosed[3] yesterday, and though I understand that it came to London by express, I do not imagine there is any impropriety in sending it by the post.[4] I make no doubt from the last conversation I had with the Duke of Richmond, but all your kind endeavours proved ineffectual.[5] My father and all of us are more sorry on his account[6] than on our own. I am, dear Sir, your most obedient and most humble servant,

CHARLES JAMES FOX

1. (1749–1806), statesman.

2. Winterslow House, near Salisbury, Wilts, the country house belonging to Fox's brother, the Hon. Stephen Fox.

3. Missing; doubtless a letter from Fox's father, Lord Holland (see following note).

4. Lord Holland suggested to HW 31 July 1766 that letters between them be sent to his son Charles, who would send an express with them rather than 'trust by the post' (SELWYN 231).

5. HW and the Duke of Richmond, Lord Holland's brother-in-law, had been asked by Holland to solicit an earldom for himself. After speaking to the Duchess of Richmond 1 Aug., HW informed Holland that 'it would be impossible to persuade him [Richmond] to ask any favour now' (ibid. 232). Holland never received the long-coveted earldom; see *post* late Nov. 1766.

6. Richmond had been 'hurt' by the appointment of Lord Shelburne replacing him as secretary of state for the southern department in July 1766 (HW to Holland 29 July 1766, ibid. 228), and was doubtless unwilling to ask favours of the King on this account.

To Président Hénault,[1] Sunday 17 August 1766

Printed from the MS copy in Jean-François Wiart's hand, now WSL. First printed, Toynbee vii. 34–6. For the history of the MS copy see *ante* 6 May 1766. The original letter is missing; it is listed in HW's record of letters sent to Paris in 1766 (DU DEFFAND v. 382).

De Strawberry Hill ce 17 août 1766.

UNE lettre[2] de votre part, Monsieur, ne me paye que trop du petit présent que j'ai osé vous offrir, et Lucain doit être plus glorieux de votre éloge que de voir sortir sa *Pharsale* de la presse d'un simple particulier, comme moi. Vous, Monsieur, mettez le sceau à l'histoire, et quiconque ose parler avec impartialité de son propre pays, est plus en état que personne d'apprécier les auteurs étrangers. Pour nous autres presque républicains, Lucain doit être un auteur précieux, et il est vrai qu'il y a des hémistiches dans son poème qui me font oublier des centaines de vers ampoulés et gigantesques.[3]

À mon âge on est bien revenu du clinquant; il nous faut du bon sens même dans la poésie, et je vous avoue que j'aimerais mieux Virgile si j'en retenais autre chose que des vers harmonieux. On oublie de bonne heure les poètes qui ne parlent qu'aux passions naissantes. Votre Despréaux[4] plaira toujours, parce qu'on est plus longtemps sur le retour qu'on est jeune. Mais c'est La Fontaine[5] qui charme tous les ages. Il a l'air d'écrire pour les enfants, et plus on avance en âge, plus on lui découvre de beautés. Tous les autres auteurs, qui ont le plus approfondi le cœur humain, ne font que faire parler la nature; mais c'est la nature qui fait parler La Fontaine. Dans les tragédies, dans les satires, ce sont des vices, ce sont des crimes, qu'on voudrait n'attribuer qu'à des particuliers; dans La Fontaine tout émane de nos dispositions; c'est la marche de nos penchants naturels; et d'abord

1. Charles-Jean-François Hénault (1685–1770), président de la première chambre des enquêtes; cavalier servant to Mme du Deffand; author (DU DEFFAND i. 3 n. 3). HW, who met him often during his visit to Paris in 1765–6, described him as 'very old deaf and almost gone' ('Paris Journals,' ibid. v. 261). For Mme du Deffand's 'portrait' of Hénault see Appendix 5b, ibid. vi. 75–7.

2. Missing; doubtless a letter of thanks for a copy of Lucan's *Pharsalia*, SH, 1760, sent to him by HW.

3. 'Lucan, who often says more in half a line than Virgil in a whole book, was lost in bombast if he talked for thirty lines together' (HW to Mason 25 June 1782, MASON ii. 256).

4. Nicolas Boileau-Despréaux (1636–1711).

5. Jean de la Fontaine (1621–95), renowned for his fables.

qu'il a établi les passions, tout le reste semble devenir le résultat nécessaire. Est-on loup? on dévore; est-on renard? on est rusé; est-on singe? on est petit-maître. Ce n'est pas comme dans les pièces de théâtre où tout se fait de dessein prémédité, et où l'on souffle ses passions, plutôt qu'on ne les obéit. Pardonnez, Monsieur, cette petite critique; vous m'y avez entraîné, et votre exemple est bien séduisant. Mais je sais à qui je parle et je m'arrête; mais plaignez un étranger, Monsieur, qui se sentant du goût pour vos auteurs admirables, n'est que trop convaincu combien des beautés doivent lui échapper: car je ne suis pas de ces génies heureux, qui saisissent les meilleurs endroits des auteurs étrangers, et savent en enrichir leur propre pays. Tout le monde, après avoir lu notre Shakespear, ne produit pas un *François second*.[6]

Je ne dois pas quitter la plume, sans vous féliciter, Monsieur, du rétablissement de la santé de la Reine.[7] Je sais combien vous vous intéressez à cette vie précieuse, mais permettez-moi de vous dire que ce n'est pas uniquement sur votre compte que je m'y intéresse aussi. La vertu de la Reine la fait adorer de tout le monde; et rendez-nous la justice de croire, Monsieur, que si chez nous on ménage moins qu'ailleurs les défauts des princes, nous savons aussi respecter à proportion ceux qui méritent notre estime. Eh! que nous serions barbares si nous ne rendissions volontiers l'hommage dû au caractère incomparable de la Reine de France. Sa haute piété dans un siècle illuminé est toute autre chose que celles des princesses qui font la principal et peut-être le seul ornement de la première partie de votre inimitable *Abrégé chronologique*.[8]

Oserais-je vous supplier, Monsieur, de présenter mes très respectueux compliments à Mesdames vos nièces,[9] et de me conserver un

6. *François II, roi de France*, 1747. HW's copy of this 'livre très rare, écrit par le Président Hénault,' was kept in the Glass Closet at SH (Hazen, *Cat. of HW's Lib.*, No. 2394).

7. Marie-Catherine-Sophie-Félicité (Leszczyńska) (1703–68), m. (1725) Louis XV, K. of France. Mme du Deffand had reported to HW 10 May 1766: 'La reine est guérie, mais elle est encore faible' (DU DEFFAND i. 35). Hénault was superintendent of the Queen's household.

8. *Nouvel abrégé chronologique de l'histoire de France*, 1744. HW's copy of the 3d edn, 2 vols, 1749, is Hazen, op.

cit., No. 964; for HW's opinion of the work see MANN iv. 107.

9. Marie-Françoise Bouchard d'Esparbez de Lussan (1720–72), dau. of Marie-Françoise Hénault, Président Hénault's sister; m. (1738) Henri-Joseph Bouchard d'Esparbez de Lussan, Vicomte and Marquis d'Aubeterre. Élizabeth-Pauline-Gabrielle Colbert (d. 1786), m. (1736) François-Pierre-Charles Bouchard d'Esparbez de Lussan, Marquis de Jonzac, son of Hénault's sister (DU DEFFAND i. 3 n. 4, i. 11 n. 6). Both women attended Hénault during his last years.

petit coin de votre amitié. Vos bontés passées m'ont enhardi, et je sais que vous n'êtes pas homme à manquer à ceux qui ont autant d'attachement et de respect pour vous que n'a, Monsieur,

Votre très humble et très obéissant serviteur,

Horace Walpole

To Henry Sampson Woodfall,[1] ?September 1766

Printed from a photostat of the MS in the Pierpont Morgan Library. HW may have sent the MS to his deputy Grosvenor Bedford to copy and forward, but no printing of the letter in the *Public Advertiser* has been found and it seems probable that Woodfall never received the letter. The history of the MS is not known.

Dated conjecturally by HW's memoranda on the letter.

Endorsed in an unidentified hand: By the Honourable H. Walpole.

Address: To Mr H. S. Woodfall near the corner of Ivy Lane, Paternoster Row.

Memoranda (by HW, on the verso):

Mr Bower[2]

Mrs Trumbull[3]

farmer 2-2-0

Lady George Sept. 8th[4]

Mr Conway 9th

Memorandum (in a different hand): 14-18-11½

Sir,

STROLLING by chance lately into a public house, the landlord showed me the following lines, with which he was much transported and wished to get them set to music. They were written by an apprentice who frequents his house, and whom mine host extolled above Churchill[5] and Falstaff, the latter of whom he takes for a poet. As there is something very original in this little piece, at

---

1. (1739–1805), printer; publisher of the *Public Advertiser* 1760–93; Master of the Stationers Company, 1797.

2. Probably Archibald Bower (1686–1766), historian, who died 2 Sept. 1766 (Mann iv. 157 n. 22; GM 1766, xxxvi. 439).

3. Not identified.

4. The only extant letter written by HW to Lady George Lennox on 8 Sept. is in 1766 (More 124).

5. Charles Churchill (1731–64), poet.

least genuine strokes of nature, I thought it might not be unacceptable to many of your readers.

Yours
I. G.

The Joys of Spring.
A new song.

Returned is the spring,
And the nightingales sing:
My Phillis and I
To the country will hie,
Where we'll revel and love,
Like the blackbird and dove.
Nature calls us abroad,
And on one side the road,
At the Saracen's head,
In a snug little arbour a napkin is spread.
    Charming scenes!
    Peas and Beans!
    Union of hearts,
    And gooseberry tarts!
On cool tankard and cider and cream we regale,
And mix kisses and squeezes with cakes and ale:
Till with Bacchus and Cupid at length overcome,
We trudge home and all night sleep as sound as a drum.
    In joys like these O! let me live,
    Which rural life alone can give.
Nor ambition nor riches intrigue us:
    The golden age
    Contents the sage:
    His highest view
    But reaches to
His Phillis, a haycock, and negus.

From the COMTESSE DE BOUFFLERS,
Saturday 6 September 1766

Printed from Toynbee *Supp.* iii. 204–5, where the letter was first printed. For the history of the MS see *ante* 4 May 1766.

Ce 6 septembre 1766.

J'AI reçu, Monsieur, il y a bien longtemps, je l'avoue avec confusion, deux lettres de vous: l'une pour moi, l'autre pour Monsieur le Chevalier Mann.[1] J'aurais dû vous en remercier plutôt, et je n'y eusse pas manqué, si l'arrivée et le départ de mon fils ne m'en eussent empêché. Après une separation assez longue, et à la veille d'une autre qui ne le sera guère moins, vous concevez, Monsieur, qu'on n'est pas sans beaucoup d'occupations de toute espèce. C'est mon excuse pour avoir différé de vous écrire, et je ne doute pas que vous ne l'approuviez. Le Colonel Keene[2] m'a apporté depuis peu de votre part deux charmants éventails, qui m'ont fait beaucoup de plaisir[3] et dont je vous prie de recevoir mes remercîments. C'est un souvenir fort obligéant de votre part, surtout dans le moment ou j'avais l'apparence d'un tort avec vous.[4] Je ne vous parlerai guère de Rousseau, puisque ses étranges soupçons et ses emportements m'ont ôté tout moyen de le justifier, et qu'après l'avoir beaucoup admiré je suis reduite à le plaindre. Mais je vous dirai franchement selon la manière de procéder qui convient entre nous, que la satire que vous avez écrite contre ce malheureux homme a eu des conséquences que votre bon naturel doit vous faire regretter. J'ai l'honneur d'être, Monsieur, votre très humble et très obéissante servante,

H. DE SAUJON DE BOUFFLERS

1. See *ante* 4 May 1766, n. 3.

2. Whitshed Keene (ca 1731–1822), Maj. 5th Foot, Ireland, 1762, to serve as Lt-Col. (later as Col.) in Portuguese army; M.P. (BERRY i. 148 n. 10; Namier and Brooke). HW had met him three times at Paris ('Paris Journals,' DU DEFFAND v. 261–2).

3. 'Elle a reçu vos éventails avec toute la dignité d'une déesse qui reçoit des offrandes' (Mme du Deffand to HW 27 Aug. 1766, ibid. i. 120).

4. Mme de Boufflers strongly disap-

proved of HW's satirical letter to Rousseau. 'She was extremely angry . . . at the letter I wrote to him in the name of the King of Prussia. It was made up, but I believe not at all forgiven' (HW to Mann 11 July 1766, MANN vi. 434). She later broke with Rousseau as a result of his quarrel with David Hume; her letters to Hume 22 July and 6 Aug. 1766 concerning the quarrel are in the possession of the Royal Society of Edinburgh.

5. That is, Hertford.

Voulez-vous bien vous charger, Monsieur, de mes compliments pour Lord et Lady Hereford,[5] le Général Conway, Lady Allsbury,[6] et Lady Hervey. Vos amis ici se portent bien, et espèrent vous revoir bientôt.

To Madame de Forcalquier,[1]
Monday 8 September 1766

Printed from the MS, presumably a translation of HW's letter in English, in Jean-François Wiart's hand, now wsl. First printed, Toynbee vii. 43–5. For the history of the MS see *ante* 6 May 1766. The original letter is missing; it is listed in HW's record of letters sent to Paris in 1766 (du Deffand v. 382).

Dated by HW's entry in 'Paris Journals.'

Madame,

RIEN ne pouvait être aussi heureux pour moi que de trouver une personne à qui toujours j'ai désiré témoigner les marques les plus vraies de mon respect et de ma reconnaissance entendre l'anglais.[1a] Je suis, Madame, troublé à l'excès, et je ne sais si jamais je serai assez osé pour écrire ou pour parler un mot de français dorénavant. M. le Président Hénault a un tel zèle et attachement pour la Reine,[2] une telle partialité pour moi, qu'il a envoyé à Sa Majesté une lettre de moi[3] dans laquelle était un compliment pour lui à l'occasion de la bonne santé dont elle jouit maintenant; cela, Madame, m'a causé la dernière confusion, et si ce n'eût été de la plus grande méchanceté j'aurais désiré que la Reine n'eût pas possédé le quart de toutes ses vertus, parce qu'alors je n'aurais pas été tenté de m'étendre sur ses perfections. De grâce, Madame, ayez pitié de moi, songez que je suis un inconnu, un obscur étranger, dont la misérable lettre se trouve produite dans un français barbare; et où? à Versailles. Eh quoi, Madame, vous me blâmez de ne pas retourner à Paris! Dieu me par-

---

6. That is, Ailesbury; Conway's wife.

———

1. Marie-Françoise-Renée Carbonnel de Canisy (1725 – ca 1796), m. 1 (1737) Antoine-François de Pardaillan de Gondrin, Marquis d'Antin; m. 2 (1742) Louis-Bufile de Brancas, Comte de Forcalquier.

1a. *Sic;* presumably an error in Wiart's translation (see headnote).

2. See *ante* 17 Aug. 1766 and n. 7.

3. Ibid. Mme du Deffand wrote HW 4 Sept. 1766: 'Le Président ne va point trop mal. Il voulait me charger de vous envoyer l'extrait d'une lettre [missing] de la Reine qui ne devait vous rien faire du tout, et puis il me dit qu'il vous l'avait envoyé lui-même' (du Deffand i. 130). See Hénault to HW *post* 17 Sept. 1766.

donne, je n'aurais jamais la hardiesse d'y remontrer mon visage. Pourriez-vous même vous en étonner lorsque vos compatriotes me traitent ainsi? Vous pourrez me dire que tout cela vient de la grande bonté du Président; pour moi je sais que les extrêmes sont proches et je vous assure que j'ai souffert autant que s'il avait eu intention de me blesser; et ce qui me met au désespoir, c'est qu'au lieu d'être en colère je ne sens qu'un sentiment de reconnaissance, étant bien convaincu du motif obligeant qui l'a fait agir. Dans le vrai, Madame, je ne sais comment me venger de votre nation. Si votre lettre[4] n'était pas la plus aimable qui ait été jamais écrite je l'aurais déjà montrée à ma souveraine, mais la conséquence m'a arrêté; elle m'aurait dit, 'Pourquoi donc ne retournez-vous pas dans un pays où vous êtes invité par une femme charmante, qui écrit aussi agréablement qu'elle regarde?' Voulez-vous, Madame, accepter une condition? Celle de me dispenser de prononcer un mot de français—alors, tout aussitôt je m'embarque du premier instant que ma santé sera un peu rétablie, ou que les eaux de Bath me l'auront rendue.[5] J'ai été extrêmement incommodé depuis un mois,[6] sans quoi je n'aurais pas tant différé de vous rendre mille grâces de la lettre que vous m'avez fait l'honneur de m'écrire. Je suis mieux depuis un jour ou deux, mais il me semble qu'un invalide ne mérite pas l'avantage de vous faire sa cour, d'ailleurs je ne suis pas sûr d'être moins malade. Peut-être n'est-ce même que l'aventure de ma lettre à Versailles, qui m'a causé une agitation que je prends pour une existence plus vivante. Cela peut s'appeler une erreur de santé. Quant à Madame du Deffand, je déclare que si elle n'apprend pas immédiatement l'anglais, je ne veux plus retourner dans le cher petit cabinet bleu.[7] Je vous supplierais, Madame, de le lui apprendre, si je ne savais que vous êtes fort occupée par des soins tendres et affligeants auprès de Madame la Comtesse de Toulouse.[8] Madame du Deffand, comme si elle pensait

---

4. Missing.

5. HW made his only visit to Bath 1–22 Oct. 1766 to recover his health (CONWAY iii. 76; *The Letters and Journals of Lady Mary Coke*, ed. J. A. Home, Edinburgh, 1889–96, i. 82). See following note.

6. 'For these five or six weeks I have been extremely out of order, with pains in my stomach and limbs, and a lassitude that wore me out' (HW to Mann 9 Sept. 1766, MANN vi. 450).

7. Probably the 'petit cabinet pratiqué à côté dudit passage et tirant son jour sur l'antichambre,' described in the in-

ventory of Mme du Deffand's apartment in the convent of Saint-Joseph (DU DEFFAND vi. 17). In 'Paris Journals' HW records going to visit Mmes du Deffand and Forcalquier 'in the blue cabinet' (ibid. v. 314).

8. Marie-Victoire-Sophie de Noailles (1688–1766), m. 1 (1707) Louis de Pardaillan d'Antin, Marquis de Gondrin; m. 2 (1723) Louis-Alexandre de Bourbon, Comte de Toulouse. Mme de Forcalquier's first husband was the Comtesse de Toulouse's son by her first marriage.

que je n'admirais pas assez vos perfections, m'a donné un récit de ce que l'amitié vous faisait exercer dans cette triste circonstance,[9] et je ne doute pas qu'une conduite comme la vôtre ne soit récompensée par un cœur qui en sent le prix. Je n'en suis pas moins obligé à Madame du Deffand; elle a jugé par sa propre admiration de vous si je serais charmé de la partager.

Je ne me connais point en politique, Madame, et comme Milord Chatham[10] se propose d'aller aux eaux de Bath ainsi que moi, vous ne manquerez pas d'apprendre si lui et moi méditons quelque révolution considérable. Il doit être ami de la France ou nous ne nous conviendrons pas, car puis-je, Madame, vous connaître, et ne pas faire des vœux pour un pays que vous habitez?

J'ai l'honneur d'être, etc.

From the DUKE OF NEWCASTLE, Wednesday 10 September 1766

Printed for the first time from a photostat of the MS copy in Thomas Hurdis's hand in the British Museum (Add. MS 33,070, f. 273). An extract from the letter was printed in *Horace Walpole: Writer, Politician, and Connoisseur*, ed. W. H. Smith, New Haven, 1967, pp. 82–3. The whereabouts of the letter actually sent to HW is not known.

Endorsed by Thomas Hurdis: Copy to Honourable Hora[tio] Walpole September 10th 1766.

Claremont, September 10th 1766.

Dear Sir,

OUR friend General Conway[1] has been so good as to appoint this day se'nnight, Wednesday the 17th instant, to come to Claremont. You would make us both very happy, if you would honour us with your company that day; and, as I propose to have only some few friends, I hope it will not be disagreeable to you.

I am sorry to hear that you have been indisposed,[2] which I had not heard, or I should have sent sooner to inquire after you. I hope

9. In her letters of 16, 19, and 24 July 1766, Mme du Deffand reported Mme de Forcalquier's frequent attentions to her mother-in-law during her last illness (ibid. i. 92, 99, 102). The Comtesse died 29 Sept.

10. William Pitt, cr. (4 Aug. 1766) E. of Chatham. HW wrote Montagu from Bath 5 Oct. 1766 that 'Lord Chatham . . . and sundry more are here' (MONTAGU ii. 229).

1. Henry Seymour Conway, HW's first cousin and correspondent; at this time secretary of state for the northern department.

2. See previous letter, n. 6.

you are at present perfectly recovered, and that a little airing to Claremont will do you no hurt.

The Duchess of Newcastle sends her compliments to you, and hopes she shall have the pleasure of seeing you here on Wednesday next.[3]

I am, with great respect, dear Sir,

Your most affectionate humble servant,

HOLLES NEWCASTLE

Honourable Hora. Walpole, at Strawberry Hill.

From the DUKE OF NEWCASTLE, Friday 12 September 1766

Printed for the first time from a photostat of the MS copy in Thomas Hurdis's hand in the British Museum (Add. MS 33,070, f. 286). An extract from the letter was printed in *Horace Walpole: Writer, Politician, and Connoisseur*, ed. W. H. Smith, New Haven, 1967, p. 83. The whereabouts of the letter actually sent to HW is not known.

Endorsed by Thomas Hurdis: Copy to Honourable Hora[tio] Walpole September 12th 1766.

Claremont, September 12, 1766.

Dear Sir,

I AM extremely sorry to hear from General Conway that you are so much out of order, and that we are prevented from having the honour and pleasure of your good company here on Wednesday next with Mr Conway; a party which I am sure, at least I flatter myself, would have been as agreeable to you as it is to myself. I hope the gout will soon go off, and that your health will be the better for it; and that you will return from Bath perfectly re-established in your health.[1]

3. Conway wrote Newcastle from London 11 Sept.: 'I am now with Mr Walpole, who has this moment received your Grace's note; and am very sorry to be obliged to make his excuse on so disagreeable an account as that of his illness, which I doubt leaves no hope of his being able to wait upon you, which he much regrets' (BM Add. MS 33,070, f. 283). In the same letter Conway confirms his intention to visit Newcastle at Claremont on 17 Sept.

1. After returning to London from Bath, HW reported to Mann 26 Oct. 1766: 'My recovery has gone on fast: the Bath waters were serviceable to me, though they have not removed the pain in my stomach' (MANN vi. 461).

The Duchess of Newcastle begs you would accept her best compliments, and most sincerely joins with me in our best wishes, that you may receive all the benefit from the Bath that can be proposed. We also flatter ourselves with the hopes of seeing you at Claremont upon your return. I am, with great truth and respect,

Dear Sir,

Your most affectionate humble servant,

Holles Newcastle

Honourable Hora. Walpole, Arlington Street.

From Président Hénault, Wednesday 17 September 1766

Printed from Toynbee *Supp*. ii. 137, where the letter was first printed. Damer-Waller; the MS was sold Sotheby's 5 Dec. 1921 (first Waller Sale), lot 142, to Maggs; not further traced.

The year of the letter is determined by the reference to HW's letter of 17 Aug. 1766 to Hénault.

Paris 17 septembre.

NE pensez pas, Monsieur, que j'aie craint de vous commettre, en faisant lire votre lettre[1] à la Reine.[2] S'il y avait un tribunal encore plus redoutable, je vous y aurais cité; mais regardez plutôt cette indiscrétion comme une affaire de vanité; on aime à se parer de tous ses avantages, et la gloire de nos amis tourne à notre profit. Pouvez-vous croire que j'eusse manqué une si belle occasion de lui faire connaître, qu'un homme digne de la louer, avait quelque estime pour moi! Ah, mon cher Monsieur, que ne pouvez-vous la voir, l'entendre, juger d'une si belle âme, qui seule ignore tout son prix, à qui rien n'échappe, à qui les choses les plus fines sont familières, sans rien perdre dans sa simplicité . . . Je vais vous conter une hardiesse bien grande où je me laissai aller il y a quelques années (j'en meurs encore de peur). La Reine avait écrit de sa main quelques lignes à la fin d'une lettre que m'écrivait Madame la Duchesse de Luines,[3]

1. *Ante* 17 Aug. 1766.
2. See HW to Mme de Forcalquier *ante* 8 Sept. 1766 and n. 3. The same day HW wrote a letter (missing) to Hénault, presumably protesting the liberty Hénault had taken with his letter of 17 Aug. (DU DEFFAND v. 382).

3. Marie Brulart (ca 1685–1763), m. 1 (1704) Louis-Joseph de Béthune, Marquis de Charost; m. 2 (1732) Charles-Philippe d'Albert, Duc de Luynes. She was Mme du Deffand's aunt and, according to HW, 'the Queen's favourite' (ibid. vi. 55).

sa dame d'honneur et mon amie, sans signer.⁴ J'osai lui envoyer ces quatre vers en réponse:

> Ces mots tracés par une main divine
> Ne m'ont causé que trouble et qu'embarras:
> C'est trop oser si mon cœur le devine;
> C'est être ingrat de ne deviner pas.

HÉNAULT

To the DUKE and DUCHESS of NEWCASTLE, Thursday 25 September 1766

Printed for the first time from a photostat of the MS in the Albemarle Collection, Ipswich and East Suffolk Record Office, County Hall, Ipswich, Suffolk, kindly furnished by the late Sir Lewis Namier. An extract was printed in *Horace Walpole: Writer, Politician, and Connoisseur*, ed. W. H. Smith, New Haven, 1967, p. 83. The MS was deposited in the Ipswich and East Suffolk Record Office by the 9th Earl of Albemarle before 1954; its earlier history is not known.

Arlington Street, Sept. 25, 1766.

MR Walpole begs leave to return his most grateful thanks to their Graces the Duke and Duchess of Newcastle for their great goodness to him. He was not able to write himself when he had the honour of his Grace's letter;[1] but being much recovered, takes the first opportunity of assuring his Grace how sensible he is of that mark of his favour. Mr Walpole is going immediately to the Bath, and at his return[2] shall take the liberty of troubling their Graces with his thanks in person.

---

4. 'Un jour, la reine entra chez une duchesse, au moment où celle-ci écrivait au président; elle mit au bas du billet: "Devinez la main qui vous souhaite ce petit bonjour"' (*Biographie universelle*, ed. Michaud, 1811–62, xx. 49).

1. *Ante* 10 Sept. 1766.
2. HW left 27 Sept. and returned to London 25 Oct. (COLE i. 119 n. 2; MANN vi. 461).

ROBERT ADAM'S DESIGNS FOR THE
ROUND DRAWING-ROOM AT STRAWBERRY HILL

To Robert Adam,[1] ca Friday 26 September 1766

Printed from *The Builder* 6 Jan. 1866, xxiv. 6, where the letter was first printed from 'a copy . . . exhibited with other MSS at the Industrial Exhibition, Glasgow, by Mr J. Wyllie Guild.' Reprinted, *Times Literary Supplement* 25 Aug. 1921, xx. 548; Toynbee *Supp.* iii. 11–12. The history of the MS and its present whereabouts are not known.

Dated approximately by HW's only visit to Bath (see previous letter, n. 2).

MR Walpole has sent Mr Adam the two books,[2] and hopes at his leisure he will think of the ceiling and chimney-piece. The ceiling is to be taken from the plate 165 of St Paul's, the circular window.[3]

The chimney from the shrine of Edward the Confessor, at Westminster.[4]

The diameter of the room[5] is 22 feet. The enclosed little end is for the bed,[6] which Mr Walpole begs to have drawn out too. He is just going to Bath, and will call on Mr Adam as soon as he returns.[7]

1. (1728–92), architect.

2. Sir William Dugdale's *History of St Paul's Cathedral in London,* 1658, with plates by Wenceslaus Hollar, and John Dart's *Westmonasterium,* 2 vols [?1742]. HW's copies are Hazen, *Cat. of HW's Lib.,* Nos 591 and 566.

3. The Rose Window at the east end of old St Paul's.

4. Dart, op. cit. ii. 23.

5. The Round Drawing-room in the Round Tower, at the western end of the house at SH. Work was started on it in 1760 and continued intermittently until 1771; the progress may be traced in HW's *Strawberry Hill Accounts,* ed. Paget Toynbee, Oxford, 1927, pp. 106–7. 'The de-sign of the chimney-piece is taken from the tomb of Edward the Confessor, improved by Mr Adam. . . . The ceiling is taken from a round window in old St Paul's; the frieze was designed by Mr Adam' ('Des. of SH,' *Works* ii. 468–9). Adam's drawings for the ceiling and chimney-piece, dated 1766 and 1767, are in Sir John Soane's Museum; HW refers to Adam's chimney-piece design in his letter to Sir William Hamilton 22 Sept. 1768 (CHUTE 407). See illustrations.

6. The small recess is shown in the plan of the principal floor at SH, *Works* ii. following p. 512. The room was never used as a bedroom.

7. See previous letter, n. 2.

To Madame de Forcalquier, Monday 27 October 1766

Printed from the MS, a translation of HW's letter in English, in Jean-François Wiart's hand, now WSL. First printed, Toynbee vii. 58–60. For the history of the MS see *ante* 6 May 1766. Mme du Deffand wrote HW 5 Nov. 1766: 'J'ai fait traduire votre lettre à Mme de Forcalquier; elle est infiniment agréable, et j'ai eu beaucoup de plaisir à l'article qui me regarde; il m'est une nouvelle preuve de votre amitié' (DU DEFFAND i. 171). The original letter is missing; it is listed in HW's record of letters sent to Paris in 1766 (ibid. v. 383).

Londres, 27 octobre 1766.

JE ne pouvais pas concevoir, Madame, comment les eaux de Bath[1] pouvaient me faire du bien si subitement, mais actuellement le mystère est expliqué; vous me dites[2] que vous avez eu la bonté de faire des vœux pour le rétablissement de ma santé. Je souhaiterais que je l'eusse connu plutôt; cela m'aurait épargné un voyage désagréable; néanmoins, Madame, ma reconnaissance est si grande qu'au lieu de publier l'obligation que je vous ai, je la tiendrai secrète, autrement les infirmes et les goutteux seraient tous les jours à votre porte pour vous demander vos bonnes prières; et ce serait une chose indécente de voir à votre porte tant d'infirmes, au lieu de soupirants; ce doit être en effet un estropié qui vous regardera comme une madonna, et vous serez obligée de cacher vos attraits avant qu'on puisse rendre justice à vos vertus; on peut dire la même chose de votre esprit; soit que vous parliez parfaitement le français, ou moins parfaitement l'anglais. Le tout sera approuvé, quoique le vrai mérite de l'un ni de l'autre ne sera connu que quand on aura le temps de prêter son attention uniquement à ce que vous dites. Vous n'approuverez pas ce que je dis parce que vous négligez votre beauté, et que vous donnez toute votre attention à cultiver votre cœur et votre esprit. Mais, Madame, je dois dire la vérité, et n'ayant rien oublié de ce que j'ai vu d'admirable en France, est-il possible que tout ce que j'entends de vous efface tout ce dont je me souviens? Il n'est pas nécessaire, Madame, de me sommer de tenir ma promesse; je l'ai fait sincèrement, et j'aurai un trop grand plaisir à m'y conformer pour ne pas tenir strictement ma parole; rien ne m'empêchera d'être à Paris au mois de février;[3] notre ministère même, la

1. See *ante* 8 Sept. 1766, n. 5.
2. Mme de Forcalquier's letter is missing.

3. HW did not arrive in Paris until 23 Aug. 1767 ('Paris Journals,' DU DEFFAND v. 316).

chose la plus fragile du monde, durera vraisemblablement au delà de cette période; Milord Chatam est en très bonne santé à Bath,[4] quoique vous n'ayez pas, Madame, prié pour lui, et il pourra probablement amener de là quelques nouveaux amis—au moins le Duc de Bedfort[5] et lui y demeurent à deux portes l'un de l'autre.

Madame la Duchesse d'Aiguillon a eu la bonté de m'écrire au sujet de ma maladie;[6] puis-je vous prier, Madame, de lui faire mes très humbles remercîments et l'assurer de mes respects? J'aurai l'honneur de la remercier moi-même l'ordinaire prochain.

Le Marquis de Fitzjames[7] est ici; il parait aimer beaucoup Londres et il y est tres goûté. Nous vous avons envoyé une ambassadrice très gentille, Madame Rochefort;[8] cependant j'espère qu'elle n'effacera pas mes amies Madame de Hersfort et la Duchesse de Richemond.[9]

Madame du Deffand, suivant sa bonté ordinaire, a eu beaucoup d'égard pour Monsieur et Madame Fitzroy[10] qui en sont charmés et ne cessent de chanter ses louanges; je ne penserais pas aussi bien d'eux que je fais s'ils agissaient autrement. J'ai le plus grand plaisir du monde d'entendre dire que votre amitié l'une pour l'autre continue; j'espère la trouver aussi forte que jamais.

Je me flatte que la Duchesse de la Vallière[11] ne m'a pas tout à fait oublié; Monsieur de Guerchy m'assure que non,[12] et cela me

4. HW wrote Mann 26 Oct. 1766: 'I left Lord Chatham at Bath, in great health and spirits. . . . I am sure if the present administration does not hold, I don't know whither we are to go next!' (Mann vi. 462). Pitt had accepted the sinecure office of lord privy seal on 30 July 1766 and was raised to the peerage five days later. Early in 1767, after he had formed a new administration, ill health forced him to turn over leadership in the government to the Duke of Grafton.

5. John Russell, 4th D. of Bedford. He had arrived at Bath 9 Oct. (Conway iii. 76 n. 9). At this time negotiations between Chatham and Bedford were under way to bring Bedford and his followers into the new administration, but the negotiations broke down in early November because Bedford's demands were considered excessive (John Brooke, *The Chatham Administration 1766–1768*, 1956, pp. 38–42). For Chatham's further negotiations with Bedford see *post* 1 Dec. 1766.

6. Her letter is missing; for HW's reply see *post* 3 Nov. 1766.

7. Jean-Charles Fitzjames (1743–1805), son of the Duc de Fitzjames (ibid. i. 259 n. 7). HW had met him at Paris in 1765 ('Paris Journals,' ibid. v. 274).

8. Lucy Young (ca 1723–73), m. (1740) William Henry Nassau de Zuylestein, 4th E. of Rochford, 1738. Lord Rochford was the English ambassador to France 1766–8; he arrived at Paris 28 Oct. 1766 (Mann vi. 420 n. 5).

9. Lady Mary Bruce (1740–96), m. (1757) Charles Lennox, 3d D. of Richmond, 1750. Richmond was ambassador to France 1765–6; Lord Hertford had held the post 1763–5.

10. Charles Fitzroy (1737–97), cr. (1780) Bn Southampton; m. (1758) Anne Warren (d. 1807). They supped at Mme du Deffand's on 12 Oct. (du Deffand i. 152).

11. *Ante* 6 March 1766, n. 4.

12. HW had apparently seen Guerchy, the French ambassador, during his stay at Bath; see du Deffand i. 149.

cause un plaisir infini. Je souhaite ardemment de retrouver cette même compagnie à St-Joseph,[13] et je promets de ne pas jouer une seule fois à la grande patience quand cette agréable compagnie sera autour du feu après souper.

J'ai l'honneur d'être, Madame, votre très obligé, très obéissant, très dévoué, et très humble serviteur,

Horace Walpole

To the Duchesse de Choiseul, Monday 27 October 1766

Printed from the MS copy in Jean-François Wiart's hand, now WSL. First printed, Toynbee vii. 60–1. For the history of the MS copy see *ante* 6 May 1766. The original letter is missing; it is listed in HW's record of letters sent to Paris in 1766 (DU DEFFAND v. 383).

Endorsed by Wiart: Copie d'une lettre de Monsieur Walpole à Madame la D[uchesse] de Choiseul.

De Londres, ce 27 octobre 1766.

IL y a longtemps, Madame, que j'ai dû me jeter à vos pieds en reconnaissance des choses obligeantes qui me venaient de tous côtés sur le compte de vos bontés pour moi. Monsieur de Guerchy, Madame du Deffand, m'en parlaient continuellement, mes compatriotes ne cessaient de m'envier, mais étaient trop pénétrés de votre mérite, Madame, pour pouvoir s'en taire, et leur amour-propre fit que j'en susse une partie de la vérité. Une longue maladie, et encore plus la crainte de vous importuner, m'imposaient silence; mais la lettre[1] que Monsieur l'Ambassadeur[2] me rendit hier, autorise, ordonne même, l'effusion de ma sensibilité. La vie, Madame, à laquelle vous daignez vous intéresser me sera bien plus précieuse; nul philosophe ne tiendrait contre l'honneur de vous apporter ses hommages, et pour mourir content il aurait fallu avoir écrit quelque chose qui fut digne de transmettre votre nom à la postérité; mais, Madame, vous avez mal pris votre temps. Les Horaces d'aujourd'hui ne sont point donneurs d'immortalité, il faut vous fier à vos vertus.

---

13. The convent of Saint-Joseph, where Mme du Deffand lived in an apartment.

---

1. Missing; mentioned in Mme du Deffand to HW 27 Oct. 1766 (DU DEFFAND i. 163).

2. Comte de Guerchy.

Ce sera au mois de février que je me promets l'honneur de vous marquer, Madame, en personne la sensibilité extrême dont je suis pénétré.³ Mais il y a encore une grâce que j'oserai vous demander; c'est de m'accorder votre protection, Madame, auprès de Monsieur le Duc de Choiseul. C'est fâcheux que je ne saurais attribuer cette ambition uniquement à l'envie qui me possède de connaître ce qui vous est cher, mais Madame, il faut me le pardonner; les talents supérieurs et le caractère si respectable de Monsieur le Duc de Choiseul m'ont touché le cœur. Quoique mon peu de mérite et de considération m'ont empêchés jusqu'à cette heure de l'importuner trop de mes hommages, je suis persuadé qu'un homme pour qui vous daignez avoir de la bonté, ne peut que trouver un accueil favorable auprès de Monsieur le Duc.

J'ai l'honneur d'être, Madame la Duchesse, avec le plus profond respect,

Votre très humble, très obéissant
et très dévoué serviteur,

Horace Walpole

From David Hume, Thursday 30 October 1766

Printed from *Works* iv. 259, where the letter was first printed. Reprinted, in T. E. Ritchie, *An Account of the Life and Writings of David Hume, Esq.*, 1807, pp. 256–7 (closing and signature omitted); *The Letters of David Hume*, ed. J. Y. T. Greig, Oxford, 1932, ii. 98–9. The history of the MS and its present whereabouts are not known.

Edinburgh, 30th of Oct. 1766.

Dear Sir,

A FEW posts ago I had a letter from M. d'Alembert,¹ by which I learn, that he and my other friends at Paris had determined to publish an account of my rupture with Rousseau, in consequence of a general discretionary power which I had given them. The narrative² they publish is the same with that which I left with

---

3. See previous letter, n. 3.

1. His letter from Paris 6 Oct. 1766 is printed in Hume's *Letters*, ed. Greig, ii. 445.

2. *Exposé succinct de la contestation qui s'est élevée entre M. Hume et M. Rousseau*, published at Paris in Oct. 1766 (HW to Hume *ante* 26 July 1766, n. 4).

Lord Hertford, and which I believe you have seen.[3] It consists chiefly of original papers, connected by a short recital of facts. I made a few alterations, and M. d'Alembert tells me he has made a few more, with my permission and at my desire. Among the papers published is your letter to me,[4] justifying my innocence with regard to the King of Prussia's letter. You permitted me to make what use of it I pleased for my own apology; and as I knew that you could have no reason for concealing it, I inserted it without scruple in the narrative. My Parisian friends are to accompany the whole with a preface, giving an account of my reluctance to this publication, but of the necessity which they found of extorting my consent. It appears particularly, that my antagonist had wrote letters of defiance against me all over Europe, and said, that the letter he wrote me[5] was so confounding to me, that I would not dare to show it to anyone without falsifying it.[6] These letters were likely to make impression, and my silence might be construed into a proof of guilt. I am sure that my friends have judged impartially in this affair, and without being actuated by any prejudice or passion of their own; for almost all of them were at first as averse as I was to the publication, and only proceeded to it upon the apparent necessity which they discovered. I have not seen the preface; but the book will probably be soon in London,[7] and I hope you will find that the reasons assigned by my friends are satisfactory. They have taken upon them

3. Hertford and his brother Henry Conway had both advised Hume to publish a full account of his quarrel with Rousseau (Hume to Mme de Boufflers 15 July 1766, in Greig, op. cit. ii. 61). There is no evidence that HW had been shown the copy of the narrative given to Hertford, presumably in August, but he may well have seen it.

4. HW to Hume *ante* 26 July 1766 (*Exposé*, pp. 117–18).

5. See Hume to HW *ante* 26 July 1766, n. 4.

6. 'Mr Rousseau had addressed a letter to a bookseller at Paris; in which he directly accuses Mr Hume of having entered into a league with his enemies, to betray and defame him; and in which he boldly defies Mr Hume to print the papers he had in his hands. This letter was communicated to several persons in Paris, was translated into English, and the translation printed in the public papers in London' ('Advertisement of the French Editors,' *A Concise and Genuine Account of the Dispute between Mr Hume and Mr Rousseau*, 1766, pp. vi–vii). See Rousseau to Pierre Guy 2 Aug. 1766, printed in *Correspondance complète de Jean Jacques Rousseau*, ed. R. A. Leigh, Geneva, Banbury, and Oxford, 1965– , xxx. 196–200.

7. Hume received a copy of the *Exposé* 3 Nov. (*post* 4 Nov. 1766). He instructed William Strahan, the printer of the English edition, to send a copy of the *Exposé* to HW (Hume to Strahan Oct. 1766, in Greig, op. cit. ii. 97). HW's copy, bound with other tracts concerning the Hume-Rousseau controversy, is Hazen, *Cat. of HW's Lib.*, No. 1680.

the blame, if any appears to lie in this measure. I am, with great truth and sincerity,

> Dear Sir,

> Your most obedient and most humble servant,

> David Hume

To the Duchesse d'Aiguillon,
Monday 3 November 1766

Printed from a photostat of HW's MS draft in the Pierpont Morgan Library. First printed in *Extracts from the Journals and Correspondence of Miss Berry,* ed. Lady Theresa Lewis, 2d edn, 1866, ii. 30–2 (second paragraph omitted). Reprinted, Toynbee vii. 62–4. The MS draft was in the possession of Mary Berry, the editor of HW's *Works,* who bequeathed it to Sir Thomas Frankland Lewis, 1st Bt; on his death it passed to his daughter-in-law, Lady Theresa Lewis, who left it to her son by her first marriage, Sir Thomas Villiers Lister; acquired from Lister's widow by J. Pierpont Morgan. Preserved with the draft is an 'Extract of a letter to the Duchess Dowager D'Aiguillon' in HW's hand, beginning 'Mr Hume has, I own, surprised me' and ending 'Nor am I surprised, that a trifle, designed as a jest,' and omitting the fourth paragraph which HW crossed out in the draft (see n. 11 below). An extract of the letter, in French, in Jean-François Wiart's hand, endorsed 'Extrait d'une lettre de Monsieur Walpole à Madame la Duchesse D'aiguillon du 4 novembre 1766,' is now WSL; for the history of this MS see *ante* 6 May 1766. The original letter is missing; it is listed in HW's record of letters sent to Paris in 1766 (DU DEFFAND v. 383).

Endorsed by HW: To the Dowager Duchess d'Aiguillon.

Strawberry Hill, Nov. 3d 1766.

ONE cannot repine, Madam, at some portion of illness,[1] when it procures one such marks of goodness as I have experienced, especially from your Grace; indeed it grew a little too serious, and I began to think that I should not live to pay my debts of gratitude. My Lady Hervey, with all her kindness to me, and her partiality, her just partiality to France, is however in the wrong to attribute any part of my illness to my manner of living at Paris. I came from thence perfectly well; and to say the truth, I ascribe much

---

1. See *ante* 8 Sept. 1766, n. 6.

more to the damp air of England, than to any course of life. Yet I will not say too much against my own country, that I may not destroy any little merit I may have in returning to Paris this winter.[2] I neither deserve nor expect any sacrifice, but am ready to sacrifice anything both to your Grace and Madame du Deffand, who have both shown me so many marks of kindness and protection.

As I interest myself so much in whatever touches your Grace, I must condole with you, Madam, on the ill state of health of the Duchess of Fronsac.[3] Though I had the honour of seeing her but once, I heard enough in her praise to know that she deserves to be lamented on her own account. I hope, Madam, you will still have the satisfaction of seeing her recover.[4]

Mr Hume has, I own, surprised me, by suffering his squabble with Rousseau to be published.[5] He went to Scotland determined against it. All his friends gave him the same advice, but I see some philosophers can no more keep their resolution, than other philosophers can keep their temper.[6] If he has been over-persuaded from Paris, I suspect that the advice was not so much given him for his sake, as to gratify some spleen against Rousseau, and that his counsellors had a mind to figure in the quarrel; for men of letters delight in these silly altercations, though they affect to condemn them. It spreads their names, and they are often known by their disputes, when they cannot make themselves talked of for their talents. For my own part, I little expected to see my letter in print, as your Grace tells me it is; for I have not yet seen the book. I have neither been asked, nor given any consent to my letter being published. I do not take it ill of Mr Hume,[7] as I left him at liberty to show it to whom he pleased. I am however sorry it is printed; not that I am ashamed of any sentiment in it, especially since your Grace does me the honour of approving it: but I think all literary controversies ridiculous, impertinent, and contemptible. The world justly despises them, especially from the arrogance which modern

2. See HW to Mme de Forcalquier *ante* 27 Oct. 1766, n. 3.

3. Adélaïde-Gabrielle de Hautefort (1742–67), m. (1764) Louis-Antoine-Sophie Vignerot du Plessis-Richelieu, Duc de Fronsac. HW had met her in Paris on 20 Jan. 1766 ('Paris Journals,' DU DEFFAND v. 296).

4. She died 5 Feb. 1767 (ibid. i. 226).

5. See previous letter, n. 2.

6. The following two sentences are written on the last page of the draft, to be inserted at this point.

7. 'Who, I am sure, will neither do anything by me or anybody else that is unfriendly' crossed out in the draft.

authors assume. I don't know who the publishers are,[8] nor care; I only hope that nobody will think that I have any connection with them: nor have I, though I have played the fool in print, so much of the author as to think myself of consequence enough to trouble the world with my letters and quarrels. Authors by profession[9] may, at least they generally do, give themselves such airs of dignity; but they do not become me.[10] However, Madam, I only laugh at all this, for I am no philosopher, and therefore am not angry.

I[11] am told it is asserted that I have owned that the letter to Rousseau, was not mine;[12] I wish it was not, for then it would have been better. I told your Grace, I believe, what I told to many more, that some grammatical faults in it had been corrected for me,[13] for I certainly do not pretend to write French well; and it ought to be remarked too, that the letter was not written in the name of a Frenchman. I must have been vain indeed, if I had flattered myself that I could write French well enough to be mistaken for a Frenchman. The book too, I hear, says, that the real author ought to discover himself.[14] I was the real author, and never denied it. But is not it amusing, Madam, to hear an anonymous author[15] calling on somebody, he does not know whom, to name himself? and are not such authors very respectable? I shall not imitate him, nor ask to hear the publisher's name: I do not believe I should be much the wiser for knowing it.

I am told too that my letter to Rousseau is censured[16] in this book.[17] It is very mortifying to me to be sure, that, when so many persons of taste had been pleased with that letter, it should be condemned by higher authority; but it is not uncommon for men

8. HW had apparently not yet received Hume's letter *ante* 30 Oct. 1766, in which he reported d'Alembert's main responsibility for the publication of Hume's narrative.

9. HW first wrote 'An author in a garret,' crossed out 'in a garret,' then wrote 'that writes for subsistence' and crossed it out.

10. 'A gentleman' first crossed out, then 'anybody else' crossed out.

11. This paragraph is crossed out in the draft and does not appear in HW's 'Extract' (see headnote); it was presumably omitted in the letter sent to Mme d'Aiguillon.

12. For other rumours concerning the authorship of the letter see *post* 20 Nov. 1766, n. 16.

13. By Claude-Adrien Helvétius, the Duc de Nivernais, and Président Hénault (HW's 'Narrative of what Passed Relative to the Quarrel . . . ,' *Works* iv. 250).

14. See *post* 20 Nov. 1766, n. 15.

15. Having 'not yet seen the book,' HW was unaware that the 'Déclaration' at the end of the *Exposé succinct* is signed by d'Alembert.

16. 'As a *mauvaise plaisanterie et méchante*' crossed out in the draft.

17. See *post* 4 Nov. 1766, n. 4.

of taste and men of letters to be of a totally different opinion. Nor am I surprised that a trifle, designed as a jest, and certainly never intended to be made public, should be[18] anathematized by their Holinesses, the philosophers, and the enemies of Rousseau.[19] It looked like candour to blame me, when so real an injury was meditated against him[20] as the publication of his absurd letter to Mr Hume.[21] Philosophy is so tender, and so scrupulous!

I beg your Grace's pardon for troubling you so long. You find I am so much of an author, that I contradict myself, and think this very foolish controversy important enough to employ two pages. Indeed it is not; and if I were not alone in the country, I should not have thought it worth two lines. Such a real genius as Rousseau cannot appear, but he causes all the insignificant scribblers in Europe to overwhelm the public with their opinions of him and his writings. But he may comfort himself; his works will be admired, when the compilers of dictionaries and mercuries will be as much forgotten as your Grace's

Most obedient humble servant

Horace Walpole

From David Hume, Tuesday 4 November 1766

Printed from *Works* iv. 262, where the letter was first printed. Reprinted in T. E. Ritchie, *An Account of the Life and Writings of David Hume, Esq.*, 1807, pp. 257–8 (last paragraph, closing, and signature omitted); *The Letters of David Hume*, ed. J. Y. T. Greig, Oxford, 1932, ii. 100–1; extracts printed in *Letters of David Hume to William Strahan*, ed. G. B. Hill, Oxford, 1888, pp. 90, 94. The history of the MS and its present whereabouts are not known.

Edinburgh, 4th of Nov. 1766.

Dear Sir,

YESTERDAY I received by the post a copy of the edition, printed at Paris, of my narrative[1] of this ridiculous affair be-

---

18. 'Styled a *méchanceté*' first crossed out in the draft, then 'blamed' and 'condemned' both crossed out.

19. HW first wrote 'by Rousseau's enemies,' crossed it out, and inserted 'by their Holinesses, the philosophers, and the enemies of Rousseau.'

20. 'Rousseau' crossed out in the draft.

21. See Hume to HW *ante* 26 July 1766, n. 4.

---

1. See *ante* 30 Oct. 1766, nn. 2, 7.

tween Rousseau and me. There is an introduction in the name of
my friends,[2] giving an account of the necessity under which they
found themselves to publish this narrative; and an appendix in
d'Alembert's name,[3] protesting his innocence with regard to all the
imputations thrown on him by Rousseau. I have no objection with
regard to the first, but the second contains a clause which displeases
me very much, but which you will probably only laugh at: it is
that where he blames the King of Prussia's letter as cruel.[4] What
could engage d'Alembert to use this freedom, I cannot imagine.
Is it possible that a man of his superior parts can bear you ill will
because you are the friend of his enemy, Madame du Deffand?[5]
What makes me suspect that there may be something true of this
suspicion, is, that several passages in my narrative, in which I mention you and that letter, are all altered in the translation, and rendered much less obliging than I wrote them:[6] for my narrative sent
to Paris was an exact copy of that left in Lord Hertford's hands. I
would give anything to prevent a publication in London (for surely
the whole affair will appear perfectly ridiculous); but I am afraid
that a book printed at Paris will be translated in London, if there
be hopes of selling a hundred copies of it. For this reason, I fancy
it will be better for me to take care that a proper edition be pub-

2. 'Avertissement des Éditeurs' (*Exposé*,
pp. iii–xiv).

3. 'Déclaration adressée par M. d'Alembert aux Éditeurs' (ibid. 125–7); it is
signed by d'Alembert.

4. 'Je puis citer de cent personnes,
amies et ennemies de M. Rousseau, qui
m'ont entendu la désapprouver beaucoup,
par la raison qu'il ne faut point se mo-
quer des malheureux, surtout quand ils
ne nous ont point fait de mal' (ibid. 126).

5. For a discussion of the cause of the
enmity between d'Alembert and Mme du
Deffand see *Letters to and from Madame
du Deffand and Julie de Lespinasse*, ed.
W. H. Smith, New Haven, 1938, pp. xvii–
xix; see also Hume's *Letters*, ed. Greig, i.
469 and n. 1. Hume wrote John Craufurd
5 Nov. 1766: 'It has happened as you
foresaw; that I should at last, whether I
would or not, be obliged to give to the
public an account of the ridiculous affair
between Rousseau and me. D'alembert
has made use of the discretionary power
I gave him, and has printed the narrative

you saw, with a preface, giving an account of the necessity which he lay under
to do so. The only thing, that displeases
me is a declaration annexed, which is
very disobliging to Horace Walpole. There
is also a little squib thrown at Madame
du Duffand if I understand it right. Besides, some obliging things which I said,
from my sincere sentiments, of Mr Walpole, are expunged, which is a little unaccountable. Is it possible, that a man of
such parts and virtues as Dalembert can
bear an ill will to Mr Walpole merely
because the latter has a friendship for a
person whom the former hates? And does
philosophy serve us to so little purpose?
. . . I have wrote to Mr Walpole about
this affair of Dalembert's declaration; and
as he makes profession of being no philosopher, I doubt but I shall find him a
reasonable man' (MS in a private collection in Scotland, kindly communicated by
the owner).

6. See *post* 20 Nov. 1766.

lished, in which case I shall give orders that all the passages altered in my narrative shall be restored.[7]

Since I came here I have been told that you have had a severe fit of sickness, but that you are now recovered:[8] I hope you are perfectly so. I am anxious to hear of your welfare;[9] being with great sincerity,

Dear Sir,
Your most obedient and most humble servant,

DAVID HUME

7. At Hume's instigation, an English edition of the *Exposé* was printed by William Strahan and published by Thomas Becket. In October Hume instructed Strahan to 'follow the French and translate it: the reason of this is, that I allowed my friends at Paris to make what alterations they thought proper; and I am desirous of following exactly the Paris edition. All my letters must be printed verbatim, conformable to the manuscript I send you.' After seeing a copy of the French pamphlet and noting liberties which had been taken in the translation, he wrote Strahan 4 Nov.: 'Contrary to my former directions, I now desire you not to follow the Paris edition in my narrative; but exactly the English copy which I sent you in manuscript' (Hume's *Letters*, ed. Greig, ii. 96, 99–100). But Hume's second instruction ap-

parently came too late, and the narrative was 'retranslated, for the most part, from the French; the French editors having taken some liberties . . . with the English original' (*A Concise and Genuine Account of the Dispute between Mr Hume and Mr Rousseau*, 1766, p. vii n). HW's copy of the English edition is Hazen, *Cat. of HW's Lib.*, No. 1609 : 16 : 1.

8. See *ante* 12 Sept. 1766, n. 1.

9. About this time Hume wrote to an unknown correspondent, n.d.: 'I am a little uneasy at not hearing from Horace Walpole. It is not possible, that he can be angry at me for D'alembert's publishing a paper, which I never saw, till I read it in print' (MS now WSL; see *New Letters of David Hume*, ed. Raymond Klibansky and E. C. Mossner, Oxford, 1954, p. 153).

To David Hume, Thursday 6 November 1766

Printed from a photostat of the MS in the possession of the Royal Society of
Edinburgh, furnished through the good offices of Mr W. H. Rutherford. First
printed, *Works* iv. 260–1. Reprinted in T. E. Ritchie, *An Account of the Life
and Writings of David Hume, Esq.*, 1807, pp. 259–63 (signature omitted); Wright
v. 168–70 (closing incorrectly printed and signature omitted); Cunningham v.
23–5 (signature omitted); Toynbee vii. 66–8 (one sentence omitted); extracts
printed in J. H. Burton, *Life and Correspondence of David Hume*, Edinburgh,
1846, ii. 361; *Letters of David Hume to William Strahan*, ed. G. B. Hill, Oxford,
1888, pp. 90–1, 95–6. For the history of the MS see *ante* 15 July 1758.

This letter is HW's reply to Hume's letter *ante* 30 Oct. 1766.

Endorsed in an unidentified hand: Hor. Walpole (as to Rousseau).

Arlington Street, Nov. 6th 1766.

Dear Sir,

YOU have, I own, surprised me by suffering your quarrel with
Rousseau to be printed, contrary to your determination when
you left London,[1] and against the advice of all your best friends
here. I may add, contrary to your own nature, which has always
inclined you to despise literary squabbles, the jest and scorn of all
men of sense. Indeed I am sorry you have let yourself be over-
persuaded, and so are all that I have seen who wish you well: I
ought rather to use your own word *extorted:* you say, *your Parisian
friends extorted* your consent to this publication. I believe so. Your
good sense could not approve what your good heart could not refuse. You add, that they told you *Rousseau had sent letters of defiance against you all over Europe.*[2] Good God! my dear Sir, could
you pay any regard to such fustian! all Europe laughs at being
dragged every day into these idle quarrels, with which Europe only
wipes its backside.[3] Your friends talk as loftily as of a challenge
between Charles V and Francis the First. What are become of all
the controversies since the days of Scaliger and Scioppius,[4] of Bil-

---

1. Hume left London for Scotland in
late Sept. 1766 (*New Letters of David
Hume,* ed. Raymond Klibansky and E. C.
Mossner, Oxford, 1954, p. xxxiii).

2. See *ante* 30 Oct. 1766; HW is quoting
loosely from this letter.

3. 'Wipes its backside' omitted in
Wright.

4. Joseph Juste Scaliger (1540–1609)
and Kaspar Schoppe, called Scioppius
(1576–1649), scholars and polemicists, who
verbally attacked their adversaries in the
abusive manner of Billingsgate market.

lingsgate memory? why, they sleep in oblivion, till some Bayle[5] drags them out of their dust, and takes mighty pains to ascertain the dates of each author's death, which is of no more consequence to the world than the days of their birth. Many a country squire quarrels with his neighbour about game and manors, yet they never print their wrangles, though as much abuse passes between them, as if they could quote all the philippics of the learned.

You have acted, as I should have expected if you *would* print, with sense, temper and decency, and what is still more uncommon, with your usual modesty. I cannot say so much for your editors— but editors and commentators are seldom modest. Even to this day that race ape the dictatorial tone of the commentators at the restoration of learning, when the mob thought that Greek and Latin could give men the sense which they wanted in their native languages. But *Europe* is now grown a little wiser, and holds these magnificent pretensions in proper contempt.

What I have said, is to explain why I am sorry my letter[6] makes a part of this controversy. When I sent it to you, it was for your justification; and had it been necessary I could have added much more, having been witness to your anxious and boundless friendship for Rousseau. I told you, you might make what use of it you pleased. Indeed at that time I did not, could not think of its being printed, you seeming so averse to any publication on that head. However I by no means take it ill, nor regret my part, if it tends to vindicate your honour.

I must confess that I am more concerned that you have suffered my letter to be curtailed;[7] nor should I have consented to that, if you had asked me. I guessed that your friends consulted your interest less than their own inclination to expose Rousseau; and I think *their* omission of what I said on that subject, proves I was not mistaken in my guess. My letter hinted too my contempt of learned men and their miserable conduct. Since I was to appear in print, I should not have been sorry that that opinion should have appeared at the same time. In truth there is nothing I hold so cheap as the

5. Pierre Bayle (1647–1706), whose *General Dictionary*, 1734–41, ix. 104–8, 122–32, gives much space to the biographies of Scaliger and Scioppius.

6. HW to Hume *ante* 26 July 1766.

7. See ibid. n. 5. 'Gilly' Williams reported to George Selwyn 11 Nov. 1766: 'Horry Walpole is . . . in tolerable humour. He says they have castrated his letter to Hume, and spoiled it' (Selwyn 238).

generality of learned men; and I have often thought that young men ought to be made scholars, lest they should grow to reverence learned blockheads, and think there is any merit in having read more foolish books than other folks, which as there are a thousand nonsensical books for one good one, must be the case of any man who has read much more than other people.

Your friend Dalembert, who I suppose has read a vast deal, is it seems offended with my letter to Rousseau. He is certainly as much at liberty to blame it, as I was to write it. Unfortunately he does not convince me; nor can I think but that if Rousseau may attack all governments and all religions, I might attack him: especially on his affectation and affected misfortunes, which you and your editors have proved *are affected*. Dalembert might be offended at Rousseau's ascribing my letter to him;[8] and he is in the right. I am a very indifferent author, and there is nothing so vexatious to an indifferent author as to be confounded with another of the same class. I should be sorry to have his *éloges*[9] and translations of scraps of Tacitus[10] laid to me. However I can forgive him anything, provided he never translates me.

Adieu! my dear Sir; I am apt to laugh, you know, and therefore you will excuse me, though I do not treat your friends up to the pomp of their claims. They may treat me as freely; I shall not laugh the less; and I promise you I will never enter into a controversy with them.

Yours most sincerely

HOR. WALPOLE

---

8. Rousseau ascribed HW's 'King of Prussia' letter to d'Alembert in his letter to Hume 10 July 1766 (*The Letters of David Hume*, ed. J. Y. T. Greig, Oxford, 1932, ii. 393). He had earlier accused d'Alembert in a letter to Malesherbes 10 May 1766 (*Correspondance complète de Jean Jacques Rousseau*, ed. R. A. Leigh, Geneva, Banbury, and Oxford, 1965– , xxix. 191).

9. His eulogies pronounced at the French Academy over many years; one of the earliest to appear in print was translated into English as 'An Eulogium on President Montesquieu' in *Miscellaneous Pieces of M. de Secondat, Baron de Montesquieu*, 1759.

10. Later published as *Morceaux choisis de Tacite, traduits en françois avec le latin à côté. Par M. d'Alembert*, 2 vols, 1784.

To David Hume, Tuesday 11 November 1766

Printed from a photostat of the MS in the possession of the Royal Society of Edinburgh, furnished through the good offices of Mr W. H. Rutherford. First printed, *Works* iv. 263–5. Reprinted in T. E. Ritchie, *An Account of the Life and Writings of David Hume, Esq.*, 1807, pp. 263–8; Wright v. 170–4; Cunningham v. 25–8 (signature omitted in Ritchie, Wright, and Cunningham) ; Toynbee vii. 68–72. For the history of the MS see *ante* 15 July 1758.

This letter is HW's reply to Hume's letter *ante* 4 Nov. 1766.

Endorsed in an unidentified hand: Horace Walpole.

Arlington Street, Nov. 11th 1766.

INDEED, dear Sir, it was not necessary to make me any apology. Dalembert is certainly at liberty to say what he pleases of my letter; and undoubtedly you cannot think that it signifies a straw to me what he says. But how can you be surprised at his printing a thing that he sent to you so long ago? All my surprise consists in your suffering him to curtail my letter to you, when you might be sure he would print his own at length. I am glad however that he has mangled mine: it not only shows his equity; but is the strongest presumption that he was conscious I guessed right, when I supposed he urged you to publish, from his own private pique to Rousseau.

What you surmise of his censuring my letter, because I am a friend of Madame du Deffand, is astonishing indeed; and not to be credited unless you had suggested it. Having never thought him anything like *a superior genius* as you term him,[1] I concluded his vanity was hurt by Rousseau's ascribing my letter to him—but to carry resentment to a woman, to an old and blind woman, so far as to hate a friend of hers, *qui ne lui avait point fait de mal,*[2] is strangely weak and lamentable! I thought he was a philosopher, and that philosophers were virtuous, upright men, who loved wisdom, and were above the little passions and foibles of humanity. I thought they assumed that proud title as an earnest to the world that they intended to be something more than mortal; that they engaged themselves to be patterns of excellence, and would utter no opinion, would pronounce no decision, but what they believed the quintessence of truth; that they always acted without prejudice

1. Hume called d'Alembert 'a man of superior parts,' as he points out *post* 20 Nov. 1766.

2. HW is playing on d'Alembert's phrase concerning HW's treatment of Rousseau; see *ante* 4 Nov. 1766, n. 4.

and respect of persons. Indeed we know that the ancient philosophers were a ridiculous composition of arrogance, disputation and contradictions; that some of them acted against all ideas of decency; that others affected to doubt of their own senses; that some, for venting unintelligible nonsense, pretended to think themselves superior to kings: that they gave themselves airs of accounting for all that we do and do not see; and yet that no two of them agreed in a single hypothesis. That one thought fire, another water, the origin of all things; and that some were even so absurd and impious, as to displace God, and enthrone matter in his place. I do not mean to disparage such wise men, for we are really obliged to them: they anticipated and helped us off with an exceeding deal of nonsense, through which we might possibly have passed, if they had not prevented us. But when in this enlightened age, as it is called, I saw the term *philosophers* revived, I concluded the jargon would be omitted, and that we should be blessed with only the cream of sapience: and one had more reason still to expect this from any *superior genius*. But alas! my dear Sir, what a tumble is here! Your Dalembert is a mere mortal oracle. Who but would have laughed, if when the buffoon Aristophanes ridiculed Socrates, Plato had condemned the former, not for making sport with a great man in distress, but because Plato hated some blind old woman, with whom Aristophanes was acquainted?

Dalembert's conduct is the more unjust, as I never heard Madame du Deffand talk of him above three times in the seven months that I passed at Paris;[3] and never, though she does not love him, with any reflection to his prejudice. I remember the first time I ever heard her mention his name, I said I had been told he was a good mimic, but could not think him a good author. (Mr Crauford[4] recollects this, and it is a proof that I always thought of Dalembert as I do now.) She took it up with warmth, defended his parts, and said he was extremely amusing.[5] For her quarrel with him, I never troubled my head about it one way or other, which you will not wonder at. You know in England we read their works, but seldom or never take any notice of authors: we think them sufficiently paid if their works sell, and of course leave them to their colleges

3. 13 Sept. 1765 – 17 April 1766 ('Paris Journals,' DU DEFFAND v. 260, 314).
4. John ('Fish') Craufurd.

5. For Madame du Deffand's 'portrait' of d'Alembert see Appendix 5m, ibid. vi. 94–5.

and obscurity, by which means we are not troubled with their vanity and impertinence. I, who am an author, must own this conduct very sensible, for in truth we are a most useless tribe. In France they spoil us, but that was no business of mine.[6]

That Dalembert should have omitted passages, in which you was so good as to mention me with approbation, agrees with his peevishness, not with his philosophy. However, for God's sake don't reinstate the passages. I do not love compliments, and will never give my consent to receive any. I have no doubt of your kind intentions to me, but beg they may rest there. I am much more diverted with the philosopher Dalembert's underhand dealings, than I should have been pleased with panegyric, even from you.

Allow me to make one more remark, and I have done with this trifling business for ever. Your moral friend pronounces me ill-natured for laughing at an unhappy man who had never offended me. Rousseau certainly never did offend me. I believed from many symptoms in his writings, and from what I had heard of him, that his love of singularity made him choose to invite misfortunes, and that he hung out many more than he felt. I who affect no philosophy, nor pretend to more virtue than my neighbours, thought this ridiculous in a man, who is really a *superior genius;* and joked upon it in a few lines, certainly never intended to appear in print. The sage Dalembert reprehends this—and where? in a book published to expose Rousseau, and which confirms by serious proofs, what I had hinted at in jest. What! does a philosopher condemn me, and in the very same breath, only with ten times more ill-nature, act exactly as I had done? Oh! but you will say; Rousseau had offended Dalembert by ascribing the King of Prussia's letter to him—worse and worse! if Rousseau is unhappy, a philosopher should have pardoned. Revenge is so unbecoming the *regem regum,* the man who is *præcipue sanus—nisi cum pituita molesta est.*[7] If Rousseau's misfortunes are affected, what becomes of my ill-nature?—In short, my dear Sir, to conclude as Dalembert concludes his book,[8] I do

---

6. The last two sentences of this paragraph were reversed in all previous editions.

7. *Sapiens uno minor est Iove, dives / liber, honoratus, pulcher, rex denique regum / præcipue sanus, nisi cum pituita molesta est:* 'the wise man is less than Jove alone; he is rich, free, honoured, beautiful, in short a king of kings; above all, sound, except when troubled by the phlegm' (Horace, *Epistles* I. i. 106–8).

8. 'Je le plains bien sincerement de croire si peu à la vertu, et surtout à celle de M. Hume' (*Exposé succinct de la contestation qui s'est élevée entre M. Hume et M. Rousseau,* 1766, p. 127).

believe in the virtue of Mr Hume, but not much in that of philosophers. Adieu!

Yours ever

HOR. WALPOLE

PS. It occurs to me that you may be apprehensive of my being indiscreet enough to let Dalembert learn your suspicions of him on Madame du Deffand's account; but you may be perfectly easy on that head. Though I like such an advantage over him, and should be glad he saw this letter, and knew how little formidable I think him, I shall certainly not make an ill use of a private letter, and had much rather waive any triumph, than give a friend a moment's pain. I love to laugh at an impertinent *savant;* I respect learning, when joined to such goodness as yours, and never confound ostentation and modesty.

I wrote to you last Thursday, and by Lady Hertford's advice, directed my letter to Nine Wells near Berwick:[9] I hope you will receive it.

To JEAN CAPPERONNIER,[1] Monday 17 November 1766

Printed from a photostat of the MS in the Bibliothèque Nationale, bound in HW's presentation copy of Lucan's *Pharsalia*, SH, 1760 (Réserve g Yc 66). First printed in Paget Toynbee, 'Books of Horace Walpole: A Gift to Paris,' *The Times* 23 Aug. 1929, p. 15; extracts printed in Lucien Auvray, 'Horace Walpole et la Bibliothèque du Roi (1766–1792),' *Bibliothèque de l'École des chartes*, 1929, xc. 229–30. The MS was doubtless deposited in the Bibliothèque Nationale by Capperonnier himself.

Endorsed in an unidentified hand: À Monsieur Capperonnier, Garde des Livres imprimés de la Bibl[iothèque] du Roi.

De Londres ce 17 novembre 1766.

Monsieur,

ON ne peut pas être plus confus que je ne le suis, en vous donnant la peine de lire cette lettre, et qui vous annonce une peine encore plus grande. Monsieur Buckner,[2] chapelain de Mon-

---

9. Ninewells, the house of Hume's elder brother, John Home (1709–86), in Berwickshire, where Hume made occasional visits.

1. (1716–75), keeper of printed books in the Bibliothèque du Roi, 1760; classical scholar (DU DEFFAND i. 262 n. 6).

2. Rev. John Buckner (ca 1734–1824),

sieur le Duc de Richmond, et Monsieur Dutens[3] m'ont dit qu'on
me fit le trop grand honneur de demander mes faibles ouvrages et
la petite quantité d'autres livres que j'ai fait imprimer chez moi,
pour la Bibliothèque de sa Majesté le Roi de France.[4] Je me sentais
trop indigne d'une pareille distinction, et je resistais à la première
demande.[5] Un second refus aurait eu l'air d'une impertinence. La
modestie n'est plus de saison, quand il s'agit de l'obéissance. C'est
à votre porte donc, Monsieur, que je laisse mes misérables enfants.[6]
Ils ne méritent assurément pas la glorieuse place que votre bonté
leur destine; faites en ce que vous voudrez; mais soyez persuadé,
je vous en conjure, Monsieur, qu'une pareille ambition ne s'est jamais
soulevée dans mon âme. Cachez la faute que votre indulgence m'a
fait commettre.

J'adresse la caisse à Monsieur le Comte de St-Florentin[7] par les
conseils de Monsieur Dutens, qui, à ce que j'espère, vous rendra
compte, Monsieur, de ma répugnance. Il sera digne de la générosité
de votre pays, où l'on m'a comblé de bontés, d'y ajouter la justice
de me croire incapable d'une telle présomption, à moins qu'on

chaplain to the Duke of Richmond, 1762;
prebendary, 1768, archdeacon, 1792, and
bishop of Chichester, 1798 (John Le Neve
and T. D. Hardy, *Fasti Ecclesiæ Anglicanæ*, 1854, i. 254, 261, 276).

3. Vincent-Louis Dutens (1730–1812),
traveller, antiquary, and man of letters.
A Protestant refugee, he lived in England
at various times during his life (*Dict. de
biographie française* xii. 893–4; NBG). He
occasionally translated HW's letters for
Mme du Deffand (DU DEFFAND iv. 308,
310).

4. Dutens had written Capperonnier 7
Oct. 1766: 'En arrivant ici [London] je
n'ai rien eu de plus pressé que de m'ac-
quitter de la commission que vous m'aviez
donnée auprès de Monsieur de Walpole,
et j'ai obtenu de lui qu'il vous enverrait
tous ses ouvrages, et toutes les éditions
imprimées chez lui à Strawberry Hill. Il
a donné un exemplaire de chacun de ses
livres à relier, et il m'assure que le moment qu'ils seront prêts il me les remettra.'
A month later, on 4 Nov., Dutens wrote
Capperonnier from Newcastle: 'J'ai l'honneur de vous donner avis que Monsieur
de Walpole vous a expédié ses livres et
ses éditions dans une boîte à l'adresse de

Monsieur de St-Florentin, de qui vous
aurez la bonté de les demander' (MSS in
the Bibliothèque Nationale, bound in
HW's presentation copy of *Ædes Walpolianæ*, 2d edn, 1752).

5. The original request was doubtless
received by the Duke of Richmond when
he was ambassador to Paris in 1765–6 and
then relayed to HW by Buckner.

6. HW sent copies of the following
works printed at the SH Press 1757–64, as
well as copies of *Ædes Walpolianæ*, 2d
edn, 1752, and *The Castle of Otranto*,
1765: Gray's *Odes*; Hentzner's *Journey
into England*; *Royal and Noble Authors*,
2 vols; *Fugitive Pieces*; Whitworth's *Account of Russia*; Spence's *Parallel in the
Manner of Plutarch*; Lucan's *Pharsalia*;
Anecdotes of Painting, 3 vols; *Catalogue
of Engravers*; *Life of Edward Lord Herbert of Cherbury*. The fifteen volumes
are all handsomely bound in red morocco
with Walpole's arms stamped on the sides.

7. Louis Phélypeaux (1705–77), Comte
de Saint-Florentin, later (1770) Duc de la
Vrillière; adviser to Louis XV; minister
of foreign affairs 1770–1 (DU DEFFAND i.
262 n. 7). HW had met him at Paris and
disliked him.

ne se fût servi, Monsieur, de votre nom respectable.[8] Je n'ai pu y resister, ayant l'honneur d'être,

Monsieur
Votre très humble et très obéissant serviteur

Horace Walpole

From David Hume, Thursday 20 November 1766

Printed from *Works* iv. 266–9, where the letter was first printed. Reprinted in T. E. Ritchie, *An Account of the Life and Writings of David Hume, Esq.*, 1807, pp. 268–73 (closing and signature omitted); *The Letters of David Hume*, ed. J. Y. T. Greig, Oxford, 1932, ii. 108–11; extracts printed in *Letters of David Hume to William Strahan*, ed. G. B. Hill, Oxford, 1888, pp. 91–2, 98. The history of the MS and its present whereabouts are not known.

Edinburgh, 20th of Nov. 1766.

I READILY agree with you, my dear Sir, that it is a great misfortune to be reduced to the necessity of consenting to this publication;[1] but it had certainly become necessary. Even those who at first joined me in rejecting all idea of it, wrote to me and represented, that this strange man's defiances had made such impression, that I should pass universally for the guilty person, if I suppressed the story. Some of his greatest admirers and partisans, who had read my manuscript, concurred in the same sentiments with the rest. I never consented to anything with greater reluctance in my life. Had I found one man of my opinion, I should have persevered in my refusal. One reason of my reluctance was, that I saw this publication, if necessary at Paris, was yet superfluous, not to say worse, at London. But I hope it will be considered that the publication is not, properly speaking, my deed, but that of my friends, in consequence of a discretionary power which I gave them, and which it was natural for me to give them, as I was at too great a distance to form a judgment in the case.

I am as sensible as you are of the ridicule to which men of letters have exposed themselves, by running every moment to the public with all their private squabbles and altercations; but surely there

8. See *post* 21 Nov. 1766.   1. See *ante* 11 Nov. 1766.

has been something very unexpected and peculiar in this affair. My antagonist, by his genius, his singularities, his quackery, his misfortunes, and his adventures, had become more the subject of general conversation in Europe (for I venture again on the word) than any person in it. I do not even except Voltaire, much less the King of Prussia and Mr Pitt.[2] How else could it have happened, that a clause of a private letter, which I wrote somewhat thoughtlessly to a private gentleman at Paris,[3] should in three days time have been the only subject of conversation in that capital, and should thence have propagated itself everywhere as fast as the post could carry it? You know, that at first I was so little inclined to make a noise about this story, that I had entertained thoughts of giving no reply at all to the insult, which was really so ridiculous: but you very properly dissuaded me from this resolution; and by your advice I wrote that letter,[4] which certainly nobody will find fault with.

Having made this apology for myself (where, however, I expect to be absolved as much by your compassion as your judgment), I proceed to say something in favour of my friends. Allow me then to inform you, that it was not d'Alembert who suppressed that clause of your letter,[5] but me, who did not transcribe it in the copy I sent to Paris. I was afraid of engaging you needlessly in a quarrel with these litterati; and as that clause had no reference to the business in hand, I thought I might fairly secrete it. I wish I could excuse him as well on another head. He sent me above two months ago[6] something like that declaration, and desired me to convey it to Rousseau; which I refused to do, and gave him some reasons of my refusal:[7] but he replied to me, that he was sure my true secret reason was my regard to you.[8] He ought thence to have known, that it would be

2. See HW to Mme de Forcalquier *ante* 27 Oct. 1766, n. 4.

3. Presumably his letter of 27 June or of 1 July 1766 to Paul-Henri Thiry (1723–89), Baron d'Holbach. Both letters are missing, but in one of them Hume was reported to have written: 'You are quite right, Monsieur le Baron, Rousseau is a monster' (Jean-François Marmontel, *Mémoires*, 1891, ii. 258). Hume wrote Mme de Meinières 25 July 1766 that his letter to d'Holbach, 'which I never desired him to conceal,' was soon much talked about in Paris (Hume's *Letters*, ed. Greig, ii. 69).

4. Of 22 July 1766, in reply to Rousseau's long letter of 10 July; printed ibid.

ii. 66–8. This was the final exchange of letters between Hume and Rousseau.

5. See HW to Hume *ante* 26 July 1766, n. 5.

6. Enclosed in his letter to Hume 4 Aug. 1766, printed in Greig, op. cit. ii. 430–3. The enclosure is substantially the same as the 'Déclaration' which d'Alembert appended to the *Exposé succinct*.

7. Hume's letter of refusal is missing.

8. In his letter to Hume 6 Oct. 1766 d'Alembert urged Hume to admit 'que la véritable [raison] est que vous n'avez pas voulu faire connaître à Rousseau que je désapprouve votre ami Valpole' (ibid. ii. 445).

disagreeable to me to see such a piece annexed to mine. I have remarked also the omission of a phrase in the translation; and this
omission could not be altogether by accident: it was where I mention your suppressing the King of Prussia's letter, while we lived
together at Paris. I said it was *agreeable to your usual politeness
and humanity*.⁹ I have wrote to Becket¹⁰ the bookseller to restore
this passage,¹¹ which is so conformable to my real sentiments: but
whether my orders have come in time, I do not know as yet.¹² Before I saw the Paris edition, I had desired Becket to follow it
wherever it departed from my original.¹³ The difference, I find,
was in other respects but inconsiderable.

It is only by conjecture I imagine, that d'Alembert's malevolence
to you (if he has any malevolence) proceeds from your friendship
with Madame du Deffand; because I can find no other ground for
it.¹⁴ I see also, that in his declaration there is a stroke obliquely
levelled at her,¹⁵ which perhaps you do not understand, but I do;
because he wrote me that he heard she was your corrector.¹⁶ I found
these two persons in great and intimate friendship when I arrived
at Paris: but it is strange how intemperate they are both become

9. In the *Exposé succinct*, p. 27, the
passage reads: 'quoique je logeasse dans
le même hôtel que M. Walpole et que
nous nous vissions très souvent, cependant,
par attention pour moi, il avait soigneuse-
ment caché cette plaisanterie jusqu'après
mon départ.' The English translation in
the *Concise and Genuine Account*, p. 21,
reads: 'though we lodged in the same
hotel, and we were often together, Mr
Walpole, out of regard to me, carefully
concealed this piece of pleasantry till
after my departure.' Hume and HW both
lived in the Hôtel du Parc Royal, rue du
Colombier.

10. Thomas Becket (fl. 1760–76), bookseller in the Strand, in partnership with
Peter Abraham De Hondt (H. R. Plomer,
G. H. Bushnell, and E. R. McC. Dix, *A
Dictionary of the Printers and Booksellers . . . from 1726 to 1775*, Oxford,
1930, pp. 20–1).

11. 'I cannot imagine that a piece on so
silly a subject as mine will ever come to
a second edition; but if it should, please
order the following corrections to be
made. . . . Page 21 instead of *out of regard to me*, read, *agreeably to the usual
politeness and humanity of his character*'

(Hume to Becket n.d., in Greig, op. cit. ii.
116).

12. A second edition was never published.

13. See *ante* 4 Nov. 1766, n. 7.

14. D'Alembert's letters of 4 Aug. and
1 Sept. 1766 to Hume, commenting at
length on 'la Vipère,' as he called Mme
du Deffand, were doubtless chiefly responsible for Hume's 'conjecture'; see
Greig, op. cit. ii. 432, 439.

15. 'Il [Walpole] convient seulement
d'avoir été aidé, pour le style, par une
personne qu'il ne nomme point, et qui
devrait peut-être se nommer' (*Exposé*, p.
125).

16. 'On dit ici comme une chose très
certaine, que c'est Madame du deffand
qui lui a inspiré cette méchanceté . . . on
ajoute que c'est elle qui a revu et corrigé
la lettre pour le style' (d'Alembert to
Hume 4 Aug. 1766, in Greig, op. cit. ii.
432). Mme du Deffand had previously
written HW 20 Oct. 1766 concerning the
passage: 'il [d'Alembert] dit que vous
convenez de le devoir à une personne
que vous ne voulez pas nommer, mais
qu'elle devrait bien se faire connaître:
Mme de Luxembourg m'a dit que c'était

in their animosity; though perhaps it is more excusable in her, on account of her age, sex, and bodily infirmities. I am very sensible of your discretion in not citing me on this occasion; I might otherwise have a new quarrel on my hands.

With regard to d'Alembert, I believe I said he was a man of *superior parts,* not a *superior genius;* which are words, if I mistake not, of a very different import. He is surely entitled to the former character, from the works which you and I have read: I do not mean his translation of Tacitus, but his other pieces.[17] But I believe he is more entitled to it from the works which I suppose neither you nor I have read, his *Geometry* and *Algebra.*[18] I agree with you, that in some respects Rousseau may more properly be called a superior genius; yet he is so full of extravagance, that I am inclined to deny even him that appellation. I fancy d'Alembert's talents and Rousseau's united might fully merit such a eulogy.

In other respects, d'Alembert is a very agreeable companion, and of irreproachable morals. By refusing great offers from the Czarina[19] and the King of Prussia,[20] he has shown himself above interest and vain ambition. He lives in an agreeable retreat at Paris, suitable to a man of letters. He has five pensions: one from the King of Prussia, one from the French king, one as member of the Academy of Sciences, one as member of the French Academy, and one from his own family.[21] The whole amount of these is not 6000 livres a year; on the half of which he lives decently, and gives the other half to poor people with whom he is connected. In a word, I scarce know a man, who, with some few exceptions (for there must always be some exceptions), is a better model of a *virtuous* and *philosophical* character.

You see I venture still to join these two epithets as inseparable and almost synonymous; though you seem inclined to regard them almost as incompatible. And here I have a strong inclination to

apparemment moi qu'il voulait désigner' (DU DEFFAND i. 158).

17. HW owned a copy of d'Alembert's *Mélanges de littérature, d'histoire, et de philosophie,* 4 vols, Amsterdam, 1759, and also his *Sur la destruction des Jésuites en France,* Geneva, 1765, sent to him by Lord Hertford (Hazen, *Cat. of HW's Lib.,* No. 799; CONWAY ii. 537 n. 1).

18. D'Alembert's treatises on mathematical subjects were published in *Opuscules mathématiques, ou, mémoires sur différens sujets de géométrie, de mé-*

chanique, d'optique, d'astronomie, *etc.,* 8 vols, 1761–80.

19. Catherine the Great, Empress of Russia. In 1762 she had offered d'Alembert the post of tutor to her son, the Grand Duke Paul, at 100,000 livres a year (Ronald Grimsley, *Jean d'Alembert (1717– 83),* Oxford, 1963, pp. 172–3).

20. Frederick II of Prussia had offered d'Alembert the presidency of the Berlin Academy in 1752 (ibid. 157–8).

21. Frederick II granted d'Alembert a pension of 1200 livres in 1754; the French

say a few words in vindication both of myself and of my friends, venturing even to comprehend you in the number. What new pre-possession has seized you to beat in so outrageous a manner your nurses of Mount Helicon, and to join the outcry of the ignorant multitude against science and literature? For my part, I can scarce acknowledge any other ground of distinction between one age and another, between one nation and another, than their different prog-ress in learning and the arts. I do not say between one man and another; because the qualities of the heart and temper and natural understanding are the most essential to the personal character; but being, I suppose, almost equal among nations and ages, do not serve to throw a peculiar lustre on any. You blame France for its fond admiration of men of genius; and there may no doubt be, in par-ticular instances, a great ridicule in these affectations: but the senti-ment in general was equally conspicuous in ancient Greece, in Rome during its flourishing period, in modern Italy, and even per-haps in England about the beginning of this century. If the case be now otherwise, it is what we are to lament and be ashamed of. Our enemies will only infer, that we are a nation which was once at best but half civilized, and is now relapsing fast into barbarism, ignorance, and superstition. I beg you also to consider the great difference in point of morals between uncultivated and civilized ages.—But I find I am launching out insensibly into an immense ocean of commonplace; I cut the matter therefore short, by declar-ing it as my opinion, that if you had been born a barbarian, and had every day cooked your dinner of horseflesh by riding on it fifty miles between your breech and the shoulder of your horse, you had certainly been an obliging, good-natured, friendly man; but at the same time, that reading, conversation, and travel have detracted nothing from those virtues, and have made a considerable addition of other valuable and agreeable qualities to them. I remain, not with ancient sincerity, which was only roguery and hypocrisy, but very sincerely, dear Sir,

Your most obedient and most humble servant,

DAVID HUME

government, a 'small' pension in 1756. He received 500 livres a year from his ap-pointment to the Académie des Sciences in 1745 (increased in 1765), 1200 livres from the secretaryship of the Académie Française (1766), and 1200 livres from an annuity left to him by his father (ibid. 4, 90, 99–100, 158–9).

PS. The French translation of this strange piece of mine (for I must certainly give it that epithet) was not made by d'Alembert, but by one[22] under his direction.[23]

To Jean Capperonnier, Friday 21 November 1766

Printed from a photostat of the MS in the Bibliothèque Nationale, bound in HW's presentation copy of Lucan's *Pharsalia*, SH, 1760 (Réserve g Yc 66). First printed in Paget Toynbee, 'Books of Horace Walpole: A Gift to Paris,' *The Times* 23 Aug. 1929, p. 15. For the history of the MS see *ante* 17 Nov. 1766.

Address: À Monsieur Monsieur Capperonier, Garde de la Bibliothèque du Roi, rue de Richelieu à Paris. *Postmark:* JO.

De Londres ce 21 novembre 1766.

JE suis au désespoir, Monsieur, d'un petit dérangement qui a retardé l'arrivée des livres que j'ai eu l'honneur de vous annoncer.[1] Ils avaient été mal emballés, la caisse s'est rompue en chemin, et on me les a renvoyés à Londres. Ils n'arriveront que trop tôt pour mon honneur, et l'attente ne peut que leur[2] nuire.[3] Excusez, Monsieur, cette répétition de peine que je vous donne, et exercez toute votre candeur en faveur du zèle dont j'ai l'honneur d'être,

Monsieur,
Votre très humble
et très obéissant serviteur

Horace Walpole

22. Jean-Baptiste-Antoine Suard (1733–1817), journalist and translator; sometime editor of the *Gazette littéraire de France* (du Deffand i. 158 n. 6). Hume's letter to Suard 5 Nov. 1766 concerning the French translation of his narrative of the Hume-Rousseau quarrel is printed in Greig, op. cit. ii. 101–4.

23. HW's friend John Craufurd wrote Hume from London 29 Nov. 1766 that HW was well pleased with Hume and himself after receiving Hume's 'message' (J. Y. T. Greig and Harold Beynon, 'Calendar of Hume MSS. in the Possession of the Royal Society of Edinburgh,' *Pro-*ceedings of the Royal Society of Edinburgh*, 1932, lii pt i. 55).

1. *Ante* 17 Nov. 1766.
2. The MS reads 'les.'
3. Three months later, having received no acknowledgment of the books' arrival, HW asked Mme du Deffand to make inquiries. She reported to him 13 March 1767: 'J'envoyai chercher hier l'Abbé Boudot, c'est l'adjoint de M. Capperonnier. Il y a plus de six semaines qu'il a reçu vos livres. Ils ne doutaient pas tous les deux que M. de Saint-Florentin ne vous en eût accusé la réception, et qu'il ne

To the Duke of Grafton,[1]
Tuesday 25 November 1766

Printed from a photostat of the MS in the Bury St Edmunds and West Suffolk Record Office, Bury St Edmunds, Suffolk, kindly furnished by the late 10th Duke of Grafton (who deposited the MS in the Record Office before 1953) through the good offices of Mr M. P. Statham (Grafton MS 777). First printed in John Brooke, *The Chatham Administration 1766–1768*, 1956, p. 70 (salutation, closing, and signature omitted).

Dated by the reference to the 'debate and division' in the House of Commons 25 Nov. 1766 (see n. 2 below).

Endorsed by Grafton: NB. I believe in December 1766.

Address: To his Grace the Duke of Grafton, Grosvenor Square.

Tuesday night.

My Lord,

YOUR Grace has heard of today's debate and division,[2] and of the very obliging behaviour of Lord John Cavendish[3] and

vous eût fait les remercîments qu'un tel présent mérite.' Two days later she continued: 'M. de Saint-Florentin n'a nul tort, il ne lui sera fait aucun reproche, c'est MM. Capperonnier et Boudot qui sont très étourdis et négligents' (DU DEFFAND i. 262–3). In due course HW apparently received a letter of thanks from Boudot. See Le Fèvre d'Ormesson to HW *post* 5 April 1792.

———

1. Augustus Henry Fitzroy (1735–1811), 3d D. of Grafton, 1757; first lord of the Treasury July 1766 – Jan. 1770. Grafton wrote of HW: 'There was no one from whom I received so just accounts of the schemes of the various factions . . . than from Mr Horace Walpole. . . . His friendship, and attachment to Mr [Henry Seymour] Conway had been constant, and he was well known; and his zealous desire, that we two should be more closely united, urged him to sift out the designs of those who were counteracting his active endeavours: and no person had so good means of getting to the knowledge of what was passing, as himself' (*Autobiography and Political Correspondence of Augustus Henry Third Duke of Grafton*, ed. Sir William R. Anson, 1898, pp. 140–

1). HW's presentation copy of *The Castle of Otranto* to Grafton is in the Lilly Library, Indiana University.

2. On 25 Nov. 1766 a motion was made in the House of Commons that a committee be appointed to inquire into the state of the East India Company. The motion carried by a vote of 129 to 76; it was the first time that the Rockingham Whigs voted against Chatham's administration (*Journals of the House of Commons* xxxi. 25; Brooke, op. cit. 61). 'On the 25th . . . Alderman Beckford . . . moved to take into consideration the state of the East India Company's affairs. . . . Wedderburne and Charles Yorke opposed the motion. The Whigs deserted Mr Conway, who supported it, by the mouth of their spokesman, Lord John Cavendish, though he paid profuse compliments to the latter. Burke and Grenville appeared as opponents, too, and the violation of property was sounded high. Yet the motion was carried by 129 to 76, Charles Townshend speaking for it, and the Duke of Bedford's friends staying away' (*Mem. Geo III* ii. 279–80).

3. (1732–96), fourth son of the 3d Duke of Devonshire; lord of the Treasury July 1765 – July 1766; M. P. After serving in

that party to Mr Conway,[4] though varnished over with many compliments. May I take the liberty of begging your Grace to urge this home to him, and to show him how little they deserve the struggle he is making for them. Surely it dispenses him from trying it farther. I have just told him so, and that when they abandon him, he is free from all engagements with them. They have left him for George Grenville,[5] whom they had so much disclaimed; and the very cautious Mr Yorke[6] has stepped forth into strong opposition. I am sure that the more your Grace shall paint this to him as *factious* behaviour, the more impression it will make on him. If Lord Chatham would throw in a friendly word or two to him, it will make him feel their ill treatment more strongly.[7] I beg pardon for using so much freedom, but should be so hurt at seeing any separation between your Grace and Mr Conway, whose integrity was so made for each other, that I cannot resist any occasion of doing all in my power to preserve that connection, and of both with Lord Chatham.

I am my Lord

Your Grace's most obedient humble servant

Hor. Walpole

---

the Rockingham ministry, he declined Chatham's offer of a place in the new government, refusing to separate himself from the Rockingham Whigs.

4. Conway, who had agreed to serve under Chatham as secretary of state for the northern department, was offended by the recent dismissal of Lord Edgcumbe (the friend of Conway's late patron, the Duke of Devonshire) as treasurer of the Household, and hinted at resignation. At a meeting of the Rockingham party chiefs on 19 Nov., Lord John Cavendish and others argued for further resignations from the administration as a show of support for Conway. George Grenville's diary describes Lord John's speech in the Commons debate on the 25th as 'a farewell speech to the administration' (*The Grenville Papers*, ed. W. J. Smith,

1852–3, iii. 389; see also *Correspondence of William Pitt, Earl of Chatham*, ed. W. S. Taylor and J. H. Pringle, 1838–40, iii. 126–9; *Mem. Geo. III* ii. 266–8; Brooke, op. cit. 53–6).

5. The policies of Grenville and his followers are discussed in Brooke, op. cit. 262–75.

6. Hon. Charles Yorke (1722–70), second son of the 1st E. of Hardwicke; attorney-general 1762–3, Aug. 1765 – Aug. 1766; lord chancellor, 1770; M.P.

7. HW reported to Mann 8 Dec. 1766: 'Lord Chatham paid him [Conway] the greatest compliments, and declared how difficult it would be for him to go on without him. The Duke of Grafton was alarmed to the utmost from his affection for him, and Lord Hertford and I, seeing the factious and treacherous behaviour of

From Lord Holland, late November 1766

Printed for the first time from a photostat of Holland's MS fragment (which appears to be the second leaf of a draft of a letter) among the Holland House papers in the British Museum (Add. MS 51,404, f. 222). For the history of the MS draft see *ante* 20 Aug. 1753.

Dated approximately by the reference to Lord Kildare's creation as Duke of Leinster (see n. 9 below). The draft appears on the same sheet as the drafts of letters apparently to Lord Chatham and the King, which may have been enclosed for HW's consideration. There is no evidence that Holland sent any of these letters requesting an earldom for himself.

However it may from some, indeed many, circumstances seem strange, I don't dislike what I hear from England.[1] I'm above [the ingratitude of][2] Calcraft,[3] Shelburne,[4] Lord Gower[5] etc., all but

his friends, and thinking it full as proper that he should govern them, as they him, have done everything in our power to stop him' (MANN vi. 472). On 27 Nov. the Duke of Portland, Lords Scarbrough, Bessborough, and Monson resigned their employments. HW wrote of the event: 'This defection of the Rockingham party, of whom scarce a dozen remained in connection with the Court, reduced Lord Chatham, who had defeated his own purpose of dividing them, to look out for new strength' (*Mem. Geo. III.* ii. 280–1). For Chatham's reopened negotiations with the Bedford faction see *post* 1 Dec. 1766.

---

1. Holland had gone to Italy with his family to recover his health. He left England 23 Sept. 1766 and arrived at Naples 11 Nov. (Earl of Ilchester, *Henry Fox, First Lord Holland*, 1920, ii. 320; *Correspondence of Emily, Duchess of Leinster*, ed. Brian Fitzgerald, Dublin, 1949–57, i. 481).

2. Wording conjectural; 'ingratitude that' is an interlinear addition that appears above 'Lord Gower' in the MS.

3. John Calcraft (1726–72), M.P.; army agent and politician. Through his friendship with Henry Fox, Calcraft became agent for many regiments and acquired vast wealth and influence in army administration. In the spring of 1763, when Fox was manœuvring to succeed Lord Bute at the Treasury, Calcraft withdrew his support and approved Lord

Shelburne's attempts to make Fox relinquish his post as paymaster of the Forces. Their friendship ended on the question of whether Fox was obliged to quit the pay office when made a peer (he was created Bn Holland on 17 April 1763, but remained paymaster until May 1765). HW noted in *Mem. Geo. III* that Calcraft 'rose against him [Fox]' (quoted in Namier and Brooke ii. 172).

4. See *ante* 11 March 1766, n. 5. Shelburne, like Calcraft and Richard Rigby, had been Fox's intimate friend and ally in Parliament; he served as negotiator between Fox and Lord Bute. A documentary account of the rupture between Fox and Shelburne in 1763 is given in Lord Fitzmaurice, *Life of William Earl of Shelburne*, 2d edn, 1912, i. 146–67; see also *Mem. Geo. III* i. 203 and Ilchester, op. cit. ii. 238–57.

5. See *post* 1 Dec. 1766, nn. 6, 11. In March 1763 Fox had recommended Gower to Bute for a high place in the new administration (Fitzmaurice, op. cit. i. 142). Holland imputed his own dismissal as paymaster in May 1765 to the influence of his former allies, the Bedfords, and of Lord Gower in particular; he wrote Lord Bute 27 Aug. 1765: 'That tell-tale, the Duke of Bedford, has owned that Lord Gower impelled him to turn me out, by telling him . . . the dealings I had with you against them' (Ilchester, op. cit. ii. 294).

Rigby's.[6] Mr Mackenzie[7] restored, Lord North[umberlan]d made a duke,[8] and the Duke of Leinster[9] please me. This ministry will be honourable and lasting. How unlike the last![10] Indeed nothing was ever like them, afraid of making a friend, and so they did not make one.

I grow to like Pitt's different behaviour, and should have no scruple to ask of him and be obliged to him and declare myself,[11] and he might have mine and my sons'[12] cordial and avowed good wishes, so cheap; that perhaps (nothing as I am) he might give me what he has given Legonier,[13] an earldom, for the place the ungrateful Bedfords took from me.[14] But how to ask, unless I knew first how my request would be received? and how to know that without committing myself? If you approve of this and think it can be managed with absolute secrecy, especially from the Richm[on]ds,[15]

6. Richard Rigby (1722–88), M.P. Rigby, along with Calcraft and Shelburne, had pressed Fox to give up the pay office on receiving his peerage. 'The man he [Fox] most loved was Rigby; and though Fox had not crammed him with wealth in the same lavish guise with which he had enriched Calcraft, he had assisted in Rigby's promotions, and wished to push him forwards, and to be strictly connected with him in every political walk. In the height of his quarrel with Shelburne and Calcraft, Fox . . . met and stopped Rigby's chariot, and . . . began to vent his complaints; when the other unprovoked and unconcerned in the dispute, interrupted the other with these stunning sounds, "*You* tell your story of Shelburne; *he* has a damned one to tell of you; I do not trouble myself which is the truth"; and, pushing him aside, ordered his coachman to drive away. From that moment Rigby became the enemy of Fox' (*Mem. Geo. III* i. 208). Holland wrote HW 16 Aug. 1767: 'I am a weak old man, sensible to the jeers and taunts of Rigby . . . I am only laughed at. I am ashamed of this, but I can't help it' (Selwyn 248).

7. Hon. James Stuart Mackenzie (?1719–1800), younger brother of the 3d E. of Bute; Keeper of the Great Seal of Scotland 1763–5, Aug. 1766–1800. The King had reluctantly dismissed Mackenzie as lord privy seal (Scotland) at Grenville's

insistence in May 1765; he was reinstated immediately on the formation of the Chatham administration.

8. He was created Duke of Northumberland on 22 Oct. 1766.

9. James Fitzgerald (1722–73), 20th E. of Kildare; cr. (1761) M. of Kildare and (26 Nov. 1766) D. of Leinster. Holland apparently learned of Kildare's dukedom from his wife, who arrived at Naples 27 Nov. 1766. Lady Holland wrote the new Duchess of Leinster, her younger sister, 2 Dec. that 'Lady Hervey was so obliging as to notify this piece of news to me before it was public in London' (*Leinster Corr.* i. 482). HW refers to the 'patent of Duke . . . drawing for Lord Kildare' in his letter to Holland 14 Nov. (Selwyn 237).

10. The first Rockingham administration lasted from 10 July 1765 to 30 July 1766.

11. With regard to an earldom, which Holland had long desired; see below. 'And declare myself' is an interlinear addition that appears above 'obliged to him' in the MS.

12. Hon. Stephen Fox (1745–74), 2d Bn Holland, 1774; Charles James Fox (1749–1806); Henry Edward Fox (1755–1811).

13. Sir John Louis Ligonier (1680–1770), K.B., 1743; cr. (1757) Vct and (10 Sept. 1766) E. Ligonier; army officer; M.P.

14. See n. 5 above.

15. See *ante* 6 Aug. 1766 and nn. 5, 6.

but indeed from everybody whatever, go about it, dear Hori. But I must not ask to be refused. I must die with dignity. Not that I am going to die etc.

Sir,[16]

I BEG the favour of you to deliver the enclosed to his Majesty, at your leisure. And if you will contribute to his gracious reception of the request I have presumed to make in it, I shall ever declare myself to be your most obliged and faithful humble servant.

Letter enclosed

Sir,

WHEN you had it in view that you might want to dispose of my place, your Majesty told me you should not have done it without giving me what I should like as well.[17] With the most sincere humble thanks for these gracious words, do I presume too far in hoping this was almost saying you would give me an earldom when you took away my place? Your M[ajesty] knows how I lost that and I may venture to say, I did not lose it for offending, nor was it taken from me to please your Majesty, to whom I beg leave with all humility etc. etc.[18]

16. Probably Lord Chatham: 'I . . . should have no scruple to ask of him and be obliged to him and declare myself.'

17. On 30 Aug. 1766, before going abroad, Holland had written directly to the King soliciting an earldom for himself: 'Your Majesty, in the year 1763, was so gracious as to tell me that had you had occasion for my place [of paymaster] in July that year, you would not have taken it away without giving me what I should have liked as well' (Ilchester, op. cit. ii. 316). Lord Bute told Holland that he was 'unable to guess even at the consequences of your letter' (Bute to Holland 1 Sept. 1766, in *Letters to Henry Fox, Lord Holland*, ed. Lord Ilchester, Roxburghe Club, 1915, p. 270).

18. No reply by HW to Holland's letter has been found. At Holland's urging, he later (in August 1767) interceded with the Duke of Grafton in an effort to obtain the earldom for Holland, but Holland was never granted the title (SELWYN 245–9; *Mem. Geo. III* iii. 68–9).

To the Duke of Grafton, Monday 1 December 1766

Printed for the first time from a photostat of the MS in the Bury St Edmunds and West Suffolk Record Office, Bury St Edmunds, Suffolk, kindly furnished by the late 10th Duke of Grafton through the good offices of Mr M. P. Statham (Grafton MS 779A). An extract was printed in John Brooke, *The Chatham Administration 1766–1768*, 1956, p. 65. For the history of the MS see *ante* 25 Nov. 1766.

Dated by the attempted 'coalition' between Lord Chatham and the Duke of Bedford, concerning which negotiations broke down on this day (see n. 14 below).

Endorsed by Grafton: November or December 1766.

Monday morning.

My Lord,

AS your Grace allows me to trouble you, I think it necessary to tell you that Mr Grenville is endeavouring all he can to prevent the coalition with the Duke of Bedford,[1] particularly by Mr Brand[2] and Lady Waldegrave.[3] On the other hand the Duchess,[4] Lord Tavistock,[5] Lord Gower[6] and Lord Ossory[7] are eager for it.[8]

I should hope that whatever terms Lord Chatham means to grant,[9] may be given directly, for those that wish ill, hope to defeat

1. From the beginning of the Chatham administration, Grenville had advocated strong opposition, while Bedford and his followers wavered between opposition and negotiations for re-entering the government; see Namier and Brooke ii. 543.

2. Thomas Brand, HW's friend and correspondent, who had married Lady Caroline Pierrepont, half-aunt of the Duchess of Bedford. A former Whig adherent, Brand hoped to gain a peerage through the Duke of Bedford's interest.

3. Lady Elizabeth Leveson Gower (1724–84), younger sister of the Ds of Bedford; m. (1751) John Waldegrave, 3d E. Waldegrave, 1763.

4. Hon. Gertrude Leveson Gower (1715–94), m. (1737), as his second wife, John Russell, 4th D. of Bedford. She and her brother Lord Gower had for some time been hoping to return to Court.

5. Francis Russell (1739–67), styled M. of Tavistock; second surv. son and heir of John, 4th D. of Bedford; M.P. Unam-

bitious of office for himself, he had served as intermediary between Grafton and the Bedfords in Aug. 1766; see *Correspondence of John, Fourth Duke of Bedford*, ed. Lord John Russell, 1842–6, iii. 342–3.

6. Granville Leveson Gower (1721–1803), younger brother of the Ds of Bedford; styled Vct Trentham 1746–54; 2d E. Gower, 1754; cr. (1786) M. of Stafford.

7. Nephew of the Ds of Bedford.

8. 'It was thought that the Duchess, Lord Tavistock, Lords Gower and Ossory were earnest for the junction' (*Autobiography and Political Correspondence of Augustus Henry Third Duke of Grafton*, ed. Sir William R. Anson, 1898, p. 102).

9. On 27 Nov. Chatham conveyed the terms to Lord Gower, who went to Woburn the next day to report them to Bedford: "That Lord Gower should be appointed Master of the Horse, Lord Weymouth one of the postmasters, and Mr Rigby (though out of delicacy to him, as he showed some little inclination in this session [of Parliament] to

the treaty by rising in their demands.[10]

Above all things it will be prudent to get Lord Gower to kiss hands as quickly as possible. He is so charmed at coming in again,[11] that if once engaged, he may be made to overset all obstacles. Particular civilities and attentions to the Duchess from Lord and Lady Chatham will go a great way too.

The Duke has refused to listen to any objections, and said his resolution was fixed, but will be pleased the better the offer is to Mr Rigby.[12]

It was right your Grace should be precisely informed in the situation of the family;[13] and in that light only I submit these hints to your Grace and Lord Chatham, by no means presuming to dictate, or to think myself capable of giving advice.

> I am my Lord
> Your Grace's most obedient humble servant
>
> Hor. Walpole

PS. If I might venture to suggest anything, it would be to say, that it were better any explanations were avoided with Mr Rigby on anything that is passed. If a place is given to him, the Duke of Bedford will make him of course vote for whatever his Grace and Lord Gower shall vote, and I should think the Duke would take it kind to have no mention made of past transactions; and any altercations may produce difficulties, which considering the Duke's

oppose, he did not know what offer should be made to him) should likewise be provided for to my satisfaction' (Bedford to the Duke of Marlborough 29 Nov. 1766, *Bedford Corr.* iii. 355).

10. HW alludes particularly to Richard Rigby, who acted as spokesman for the Bedford group in Parliament. Grafton observed that 'Lord Chatham found the Duke rising in his demands on every attempt to provide suitably for his friends: which may be attributed in a great manner to the weight of Mr Rigby, who did not see that office within his reach which might answer his wants, as well as his ambition' (*Autobiography*, p. 102). Rigby had preceded Gower to Woburn on 27 Nov., but was for the moment unable to dissuade the Duke from accepting Chatham's terms (*The Gren-*

ville Papers, ed. W. J. Smith, 1852–3, iii. 391–2).

11. Gower's most recent employment was as lord chamberlain of the Household in the Grenville administration April 1763 – July 1765.

12. On 1 Dec., after Rigby had returned to London from Woburn, George Grenville visited him and was told 'it was true that the resolution was taken to accept [Chatham's offer], and that the Duke of Bedford was coming to town to settle the terms.' Rigby declared that the terms 'disgraced and dishonoured them for ever,' and that he had even told the Duke he would rather not accept any office until the end of the session (ibid. iii. 391).

13. That is, the Bedfords.

present amicable disposition are not likely otherwise to arise. Mr Rigby will be as good a courtier as anybody when once in place.[14]

To the DUKE OF GRAFTON, Saturday 17 January 1767

Printed from a photostat of the MS in the Bury St Edmunds and West Suffolk Record Office, Bury St Edmunds, Suffolk, kindly furnished by the late 10th Duke of Grafton through the good offices of Mr M. P. Statham (Grafton MS 786). First printed in John Brooke, *The Chatham Administration 1766–1768*, 1956, pp. 104–5 (salutation, second paragraph, closing, and signature omitted). For the history of the MS see *ante* 25 Nov. 1766.

Endorsed in an unidentified hand: January 17, 1767 Mr H. Walpole. *Endorsed in another hand:* Mr H. Walpole Jan. 17, 1767.

Arlington Street, Saturday, Jan. 17th.

My Lord,

AFTER the permission your Grace has given me of telling you anything particular that I hear, it becomes my duty to do so. Lord Gower told me last night, I thought with design, that he heard my Lord President[1] was at the point of death. I should not have taken so much notice of this, if I did not know from the best authority that the Duchess of Bedford and Lord Gower are still most desirous of connecting with Lord Chatham, and have fixed the Duke of Bedford to that point. I was myself on Thursday with the Duchess: George Grenville was with the Duke: She sent twice to

14. The negotiations broke down after Bedford met with Rigby and other supporters later in the day (1 Dec.) and, in an interview with Chatham (who offered to make Rigby cofferer), presented a long list of new demands which were unacceptable. See *Mem. Geo. III* ii. 283–4; *Bedford Corr.* iii. 358–60; *Grenville Papers* iii. 391–2; *Correspondence of William Pitt, Earl of Chatham,* ed. W. S. Taylor and J. H. Pringle, 1838–40, iii. 136–7; *The Correspondence of King George the Third from 1760 to December 1783,* ed. Sir John Fortescue, 1927–8, i. 419–22; John Brooke, *The Chatham Administration 1766–1768,* 1956, pp. 66–7. HW reported to Mann 8 Dec. 1766 that 'instead of modest demands, the Duke went to

Lord Chatham with a list of friends, large enough to fill half the places under the government. This was as flatly refused; the Duke went away in wrath. . . . The consequence of all this, is, the junction of Lord Chatham and Lord Bute, and the full support of the Crown being given to the former' (MANN vi. 472–3). See also the following letter.

───

1. Robert Henley (ca 1708–72), cr. (1760) Bn Henley and (1764) E. of Northington; lord chancellor 1761–6; lord president of the Council July 1766 – Dec. 1767. He had expressed a wish to retire in the spring of 1767 on account of his failing health, but at the King's request he remained in office until December.

know if he was gone, and three or four times repeated these words, *When once he gets into the House, there is no getting him out.*[2] This wanted no key: and yet she added, *I heard he was locked up by the snow, but I knew he would force his way to town.* In short, my Lord, they are so convinced of their error in having persuaded the Duke of Bedford to swell his terms last time,[3] that I believe they may be had very cheap at present. Above a fortnight ago, their language was, that if my Lord President should retire, and be succeeded by Lord Talbot,[4] the Steward's stick for Lord Gower, and a very few trifles would make everything else easy. My Lord Gower himself, I am persuaded, would open himself to your Grace: my taking the liberty to say I wish this accession, is, because I am aware that if we cannot persuade Mr Conway to stay,[5] the Bedfords (if they are not previously secured) will be more difficult afterwards.

The Cavendishes I have reason to think are dealing with George Grenville; and from some conversation that passed last night at White's[6] between Lord Frederic[7] and Lord Thomond,[8] it seemed to me that upon the occasion of the Sussex Election,[9] there had been intercourse between the Duke of Richmond and Lady Egremont.[10] In truth, my Lord, I am so zealous for the administration of your Grace and Lord Chatham, that I attend to the smallest particulars.

> I am my Lord
> Your Grace's most obedient humble servant
> HOR. WALPOLE

2. HW observed to Lord Holland 10 Feb. 1767 that 'even George Grenville has given over talking, and scarce goes to the House,—indeed he had talked everybody out of it first' (SELWYN 240).

3. See previous letter, n. 14.

4. William Talbot (1710–82), cr. (1761) E. Talbot; lord steward of the Household 1761–82.

5. That is, stay in office as secretary of state for the northern department and leader of the House of Commons.

6. 'Gilly' Williams reported to George Selwyn 5 Dec. 1766: 'Horry Walpole is more violent, I think, for the present arrangement than for any I have yet seen. He is forever abusing the white Cavendishes, who are whispering in every corner of White's, and declare their inten-

tion of storming the closet in a few months' (J. H. Jesse, *George Selwyn and His Contemporaries,* new edn, 1882, ii. 97).

7. Lord Frederick Cavendish (1729–1803), third son of the 3d D. of Devonshire; army officer; M.P.

8. Percy Wyndham (after 1741, Wyndham O'Brien) (?1723–74), younger brother of the 2d E. of Egremont; cr. (1756) E. of Thomond; M.P. George Grenville was Thomond's brother-in-law.

9. Following a by-election, the Duke of Richmond's brother, Lord George Henry Lennox (1737–1805), was returned as M.P. for Sussex on 3 Feb. 1767 (Namier and Brooke iii. 35–6).

10. See *ante* 14 April 1764, n. 20.

From the Duchesse de Choiseul,
Saturday 14 February 1767

Printed from the MS now WSL. First printed, Toynbee *Supp.* iii. 205–7.
Damer-Waller; the MS was sold Sotheby's 5 Dec. 1921 (first Waller Sale), lot
105, bought in; resold Christie's 15 Dec. 1947 (second Waller Sale), lot 55, to
Maggs for WSL.

The year of the letter is established by the reference to the approaching visit
of Mme de Choiseul's nephew to England (see n. 2 below).

À Versailles ce 14 février.

CETTE lettre, Monsieur, n'est point absolument uniquement
intéressée; il est certain que son objet, du moins son prétexte,
est de vous demander vos bontés pour mon neveu[1] pendant le séjour
qu'il fera à Londres.[2] L'amitié [et] la parenté doivent justifier cette
indiscrétion, et votre bonté dispense de la justification.[3] On n'est
jamais indiscret envers la vraie bonté, c'est lui rendre hommage que
l'employer; elle n'est une vertu passive que dans l'opinion des sots;
l'action est son essence. J'entends dire à tous vos amis, Monsieur, que
toute votre conduite, que tous vos procédés, prouvent cette opinion,
et vous me l'auriez fait naître, si je n'étais assez vieille pour l'avoir
eu avant d'avoir l'honneur de vous connaître.

Avec ses sentiments, vous pouvez juger qu'il ne m'était pas nécessaire d'avoir besoin de vous pour vous écrire; je n'en attendais que
l'occasion. J'avais bien envie de répondre à une réponse charmante
que vous m'aviez faite à la fin de l'année;[4] elle était courte, cette
réponse, mais elle me fournissait mille choses à vous dire. C'est le
propre des gens d'esprit de reveiller, de faire naître toutes les idées
de ceux à qui ils parlent, mais j'ai imaginé que vous n'aimiez pas les
longues lettres, et je me suis tue. Je vous prie par parenthèse de remar-
quer que celle-ci n'est longue que de rature;[5] je sais qu'il est impoli

1. Armand-Louis de Gontaut (1747–93),
Comte de Biron; Duc de Lauzun, 1766;
Duc de Biron, 1788 (DU DEFFAND i. 230
n. 3; MANN ix. 211 n. 9).
2. Lauzun had fallen in love with Lady
Sarah Bunbury during her visit to France
Dec. 1766 – Feb. 1767; he went to England
in pursuit of her, arriving in London by
22 Feb. (DU DEFFAND i. 234 and n. 4).
3. Mme du Deffand advised HW 20
Feb. 1767: 'ayez quelques attentions pour

lui, mais ne vous en gênez pas le moins
du monde. Laissez-le avec sa Milady, et
ne vous en embarrassez guère' (ibid. i.
242). We have found no evidence that
HW entertained Lauzun during his stay
in England.
4. HW to the Duchesse de Choiseul
ante 27 Oct. 1766.
5. The MS contains three short false
starts that have been crossed out.

d'envoyer une lettre raturée, mais ma politesse ne va pas jusqu'à faire une froide copie d'un détestable original. Mes lettres sont presque toutes raturées parce que je ne sais presque jamais ce que je vais dire, et souvent ce que je dis; mes amis veulent bien s'en contenter telles qu'elles sont; voulez-vous bien faire de même.

Vous êtes désiré et attendu ici avec impatience, non seulement de tous ceux qui vous connaissent mais encore de ceux qui ne vous connaissent pas. Ma petite-fille[6] et sa grand'mère[7] n'ont qu'un cri après vous, cela est tout simple, mais Monsieur de Choiseul est de même; il me gronde de ce qu'il n'a pas eu l'honneur de vous connaître à votre dernier voyage comme si c'était ma faute.[8] Il espère être plus heureux à votre retour, mais il dit que pour faire connaissance il ne faut pas que vous veniez le mardi avec les étrangers à Versailles,[9] mais les autres jours dans notre intérieur. Vous accommoderez-vous, Monsieur, de cette condition; je désire fort qu'elle vous plaise; je désire que celui qui vous l'a demandé réussisse auprès de vous, qu'il obtienne votre amitié et votre estime, et que votre liaison me donne de plus fréquentes occasions de vous renouveler l'assurance des sentiments avec lesquels j'ai l'honneur d'être, Monsieur, votre très humble et très obéissante servante,

La Duchesse de Choiseul[10]

---

6. Mme de Choiseul's nickname for Mme du Deffand.

7. Mme de Choiseul herself.

8. 'La grand'maman m'a dit tout le contenu de sa lettre . . . . elle désire passionnément que vous fassiez connaissance avec M. de Choiseul' (Mme du Deffand to HW 18 Feb. 1767, ibid. i. 239).

9. Choiseul apparently held a formal reception for foreign visitors on Tuesdays at Versailles, after the State Council had met; see Gaston Maugras, *Le Duc et la duchesse de Choiseul*, 1924, pp. 125-6.

10. HW's reply to this letter, dated 24 Feb., is missing; it is listed in HW's record of letters sent to France in 1767 (DU DEFFAND v. 384).

To the Rev. John Hutchins, Tuesday 17 February 1767

Printed from the MS now WSL. First printed in John Hutchins, *The History and Antiquities of the County of Dorset,* 3d edn, ed. William Shipp and J. W. Hodson, 1861–73, ii. 462. Reprinted, Toynbee vii. 86. The MS was *penes* Henry Sotheran and Co. in 1904; later acquired by C. Francis Gaskill, who sold it in a collection of Walpoliana to WSL, 1939.

Endorsed in an unidentified hand: Walpole.

Arlington Street, Feb. 17, 1767.

Sir,

IN the autumn I turned over Vertue's MSS to see if I could find anything satisfactory for you relating to Sir James Thornhill,[1] but indeed I could not. There is nothing, but some few notices relating to his works, the principal of which were the cupola of St Paul's[2] and his paintings at Greenwich.[3] I believe it would be your best way to apply to his daughter Mrs Hogarth,[4] widow of the famous painter. I believe she still lives at the Golden Head in Leicester Fields.[5] To be sure she would be glad to contribute to the illustration of her father's memory. I am sorry it is not in my power, Sir, to give you better information, and am

Sir

Your humble servant

Hor. Walpole

PS. I shall immediately send and subscribe, Sir, to your work.[6]

---

1. See *ante* 22 Sept. 1765 and 10 May 1766.

2. Monochrome paintings of eight scenes from the life of St Paul, commissioned after the completion of the Cathedral dome to decorate its interior (*A History of St Paul's Cathedral,* ed. W. R. Matthews and W. M. Atkins, 1957, pp. 204, 342; DNB).

3. Baroque murals and ceiling paintings in the Great Hall and upper hall and the cupola vestibule of the Royal Naval Hospital, executed 1705–27 ('The Royal Hospital for Seamen at Greenwich 1694–1728,' *Wren Society* 1929, vi. 77–9; see also *Connoisseur,* 1923, lxvi. 162–3, and 1926, lxxiv. 3–7).

4. Jane Thornhill (ca 1709–89), m. (secretly, 1729) William Hogarth (1697–1764).

5. In 1733 Hogarth took a house in Leicester Fields known as the Golden Head, its sign being a head of Vandyck. After his death in 1764, his wife continued to live there when in town, carrying on a lucrative trade in Hogarth prints (Ronald Paulson, *Hogarth: His Life, Art, and Times,* New Haven, 1971, i. 337–40, ii. 511).

6. See *ante* 22 Sept. 1765, n. 6.

To William Langley,[1] Friday 13 March 1767

Printed from a MS copy, in an unidentified hand, corrected by HW[2] and sent to Mme du Deffand ca May 1767 (DU DEFFAND i. 304). First printed, *St James's Chronicle* 26–8 May 1767. Reprinted, *Whitehall Evening Post* 28–30 May 1767; GM 1767; xxxvii. 293; *The Lynn Magazine*, 1768; pp. 23–5; *European Magazine*, 1797, xxxi. 300–1; John Almon, *Biographical, Literary, and Political Anecdotes*, 1797, i. 65; Cunningham v. 41–2; Toynbee vii. 92–4. Preserved with the MS copy is Jean-François Wiart's French translation of the letter made from the copy for Mme du Deffand; for the history of these MSS see *ante* 6 May 1766. The letter actually sent to Langley is missing. A copy of the letter in William Cole's hand is among Cole's papers in the British Museum (Cole MS 5824, f. 18).[3]

Endorsed in the same hand: The following copy of a letter was sent by the Hon. Mr Horace Walpole to Wm. Langley Esq., Mayor of Lynn, Norfolk.[4]

Arlington Street, March 13, 1767.

Sir,

THE declining state of my health, and a wish of retiring from all public business, have, for some time, made me think of not offering my service again to the town of Lynn, as one of their representatives in Parliament.[5] I was even on the point, about eighteen months ago, of obtaining to have my seat vacated by one of those temporary places, often bestowed for that purpose; but I thought it more respectful, and more consonant to the great and singular obligations I have to the Corporation and Town of Lynn, to wait till I had executed their commands to the last hour of the commission they had voluntarily entrusted to me.

Till then, Sir, I did not think of making this declaration; but hearing that dissatisfaction and dissensions have arisen amongst you[6]

1. (d. 1770), merchant; Mayor of King's Lynn 1755–6, 1766–7 (Hamon Le Strange, *Norfolk Official Lists*, Norwich, 1890, p. 196; GM 1770, xl. 190).

2. There are four small corrections, each involving the alteration of one word.

3. Cole's prefatory note reads: 'Letter from Horace Walpole Esq. to the Mayor of Lynn. In the *Whitehall Evening Post* of *May 30, 1767* is this *letter* following: which is agreeable to what *Mr Walpole* told me *three* or *four years* ago, that he never had any *trouble* or *expense* of any sort from his *Corporation of Lynn*, where

he was never expected to come and *feast* among them.'

4. HW recorded in 'Short Notes': 'March [1767]. Wrote to the Mayor of Lynn that I did not intend to come into Parliament again' (GRAY i. 42).

5. HW had represented King's Lynn since 1757.

6. Perhaps a reference to the quarrel in 1765 between Sir John Turner (1712–80), 3d Bt, who held the other seat at King's Lynn, and one of his chief supporters; this quarrel led to political opposition against Turner (Namier and

(of which I am so happy as to have been in no shape the cause), that a warm contest is expected,[7] and dreading to see in the uncorrupted town of Lynn what has spread too fatally in other places, and what, I fear, will end in the ruin of this constitution and country, I think it my duty, by an early declaration, to endeavour to preserve the integrity and peace of so great, so respectable, and so unblemished a borough.

My father was rechosen by the free voice of Lynn, when imprisoned and expelled by an arbitrary court and prostitute Parliament;[8] and from affection to his name, not from the smallest merit in me, they unanimously demanded me for their member, while I was sitting for Castle Rising.[9] Gratitude exacts what in any other light might seem vainglorious in me to say, but it is to the lasting honour of the town of Lynn I declare, that I have represented them in two Parliaments without offering or being asked for the smallest gratification by any one of my constituents. May I be permitted, Sir, to flatter myself they are persuaded their otherwise unworthy representative has not disgraced so free and unbiased a choice.

I have sat above five-and-twenty years in Parliament;[10] and allow me to say, Sir, as I am in a manner giving up my account to my constituents, that my conduct in Parliament has been as pure as my manner of coming thither. No man who is, or has been minister, can say that I have ever asked or received a personal favour.[11] 'My votes have neither been dictated by favour nor influence, but by the

---

Brooke i. 341). Turner's voting in favour of general warrants in 1764 had caused disfavour among some of his constituents.

7. On 29 Sept. 1766 Crisp Molineux (1730–92), High Sheriff of Norfolk 1767–8, had declared himself a candidate for the seat held by Turner; Turner announced his intention to stand for reelection on 9 March 1767 (*Lynn Magazine*, 1768, pp. [3]–5). Turner narrowly escaped defeat in the general election of 1768 (Namier and Brooke i. 341; R. W. Ketton-Cremer, *Norfolk Portraits*, 1944, pp. 127–32). In a letter to George Montagu 12 March 1768, HW speaks of sitting contentedly in Arlington Street 'instead of being at Lynn in the high fever of a contested election' (MONTAGU ii. 254).

8. 'He adhered steadily to the Whig party, and was so formidable to the Tory administration that they sent him to the Tower [in 1712]' (HW to Mann 13 April 1762, MANN vi. 26). Sir Robert Walpole represented King's Lynn 1702–12, 1713–42. He was committed prisoner to the Tower from 17 Jan. to July 1712, on a charge of 'notorious corruption' condemned on a party vote, which attached no stigma to his character (GEC x. 82).

9. In 1757.

10. HW first sat in Parliament for Callington 1741–54, then for Castle Rising 1754–7 and King's Lynn 1757–68, a total of 27 years. 'On the dissolution of the Parliament this year [11 March 1768], I refused to serve again, agreeably to a letter I had written to the Mayor of Lynn, and which was published in the newspapers' ('Short Notes,' GRAY i. 44).

11. See *ante* 25 Nov. 1752.

principles on which the Revolution was founded, the principles by which we enjoy the establishment of the present royal family, the principles to which the town of Lynn has ever adhered, and by which my father commenced and closed his venerable life.'[11a] The best and only honours I desire, would be to find that my conduct has been acceptable and satisfactory to my constituents.

From your kindness, Sir, I must entreat to have this notification made in the most respectful and grateful manner to the Corporation and Town of Lynn.[12] Nothing can exceed the obligations I have to them, but my sensibility to their favours: and be assured, Sir, that no terms can outgo the esteem I have for so upright and untainted a borough, or the affection I feel for all their goodness to my family and to me.[13] My trifling services will be overpaid, if they graciously accept my intention of promoting their union and preserving their virtue; and, though I may be forgotten, I never shall or can forget the obligations they have conferred on

Sir, their and your most devoted humble servant

Horace Walpole

11a. HW may be quoting from one of his earlier election addresses.

12. For the reply from the 'Independent Freemen of King's Lynn' see *post* 13 July 1767. HW was succeeded by his cousin, the Hon. Thomas Walpole (1727–1803), whose letter announcing his candidacy at King's Lynn is dated 18 March 1767 (*Lynn Magazine*, p. 6; Conway iii. 95–6).

13. HW wrote Mann 18 Nov. 1771: 'I was told I should regret quitting my seat in Parliament—but I knew myself better than those prophets did. Four years are past, and I have done nothing but applaud my resolution. When I compare my situation with my former agitated and turbulent life, I wonder how I had spirits to go through the former, or how I can be charmed with the latter without having lost those spirits' (Mann vii. 351).

To Andrew Coltee Ducarel, Saturday 25 April 1767

Printed from the MS now WSL. First printed, Nichols, *Lit. Anec.* iv. 706. Reprinted, Wright v. 177; Cunningham v. 48; Toynbee vii. 104. The MS was sold Sotheby's 29 March 1922 (Stobart Sale), lot 703, to Baker; *penes* Dobell in 1925, who sold it to Goodspeed; acquired from them by WSL, 1932.

Endorsed by Ducarel: 25 April 1767—Mr Walpole. Ans[were]d April 25, 1767.[1] Thanks for my *Anglo-Norman Antiquities.*

Address: To Dr Ducarel at Doctors Commons.

April 25, 1767.[2]

MR Walpole has been out of town,[3] or should have thanked Dr Ducarel sooner for the obliging favour of his most curious and valuable work,[4] which Mr Walpole has read with the greatest pleasure and satisfaction. He will be very much obliged to Dr Ducarel if he will favour him with a set of the prints[5] separate, which Mr Walpole would be glad to put into his volumes of English heads;[6] and shall be happy to have an opportunity of returning these obligations.

1. Ducarel's reply is missing. 'Ans^d April 25, 1767' is crossed out in the MS.

2. The date was added by Ducarel.

3. HW had been at SH since 5 April (MANN vi. 503).

4. *Anglo-Norman Antiquities Considered,* 1767, an expanded folio edition of his *Tour through Normandy,* 1754. HW's copies are, respectively, Hazen, *Cat. of HW's Lib.,* Nos 3274 and 668:6. HW confided to Dalrymple 26 Oct. 1768 that 'Ducarel's book is in truth very superficial' (DALRYMPLE 123).

5. Twenty-seven engraved plates of Norman historical and topographical subjects, many 'contributed' by fellow members of the Society of Antiquaries.

6. HW's collection of engraved English portraits in the Library at SH consisted of 'twelve large folios . . . bound in vellum, and ranged according to the reign of each king. Five larger of the reign of George III and an additional volume of heads of different reigns collected since' ('Des. of SH,' *Works* ii. 446–7). The collection was sold at auction in London on six successive days, 13–18 June 1842, in over 800 lots.

To the Duke of Grafton, Saturday 23 May 1767

Printed from a photostat of the MS in the Bury St Edmunds and West Suffolk Record Office, Bury St Edmunds, Suffolk, kindly furnished by the late 10th Duke of Grafton through the good offices of Mr M. P. Statham (Grafton MS 785). First printed in *Autobiography and Political Correspondence of Augustus Henry Third Duke of Grafton*, ed. Sir William R. Anson, 1898, pp. 141–2. Reprinted, Toynbee vii. 108–10. For the history of the MS see *ante* 25 Nov. 1766.

Endorsed in an unidentified hand: May 23d 1767 Mr H. Walpole. No. 51.

Arlington Street, May 23, 1767.

I MUST entreat your Grace to look upon the trouble I give you, with your usual indulgence; and as my zeal to serve you has been hitherto attended with success, I will beg you to hear me with patience, when things are come to such a crisis, that my endeavours to prevent Mr Conway's resignation[1] are almost exhausted. Your Grace knows his honour and delicacy, and I may be bold to tell you, who are actuated by the same motives, that it is the character I hope he will always maintain. I had much rather see him give up everything and preserve his honour, than stay with discredit. But in the present case, I think him too much swayed by men who consult nothing but their own prejudices, passions and interests, to which they would sacrifice him and the country.

I need not tell your Grace, that on the dismission of Lord Edgcumbe,[2] Mr Conway declared he would not remain long in the ministry.[3] With infinite pains I have prevailed to keep him in place to the end of the session. He now persists in quitting[4]—but the ex-

1. As secretary of state for the northern department and leader of the House of Commons, in Lord Chatham's administration.

2. George Edgcumbe (1720–95), 3d Bn Edgcumbe 1761; cr. (1781) Vct Mount Edgcumbe and (1789) E. of Mount Edgcumbe; M.P.; naval officer. Edgcumbe was dismissed from his post as treasurer of the Household in Nov. 1766 (*ante* 25 Nov. 1766, n. 4; MANN vi. 470 n. 1).

3. Conway protested the dismissal in a letter to Chatham 17 Nov. 1766, declaring that 'I cannot with honour continue long in the situation I am in, unless I can preserve that reputation of fairness and consistency which I think I

must forfeit by a seeming concurrence in such repeated injuries to those with whom I lately acted, and to whom I conveyed an engagement' (*Correspondence of William Pitt, Earl of Chatham*, ed. W. S. Taylor and J. H. Pringle, 1838–40, iii. 129 [misdated 22 Nov.]).

4. Thomas Bradshaw, reporting to Grafton 14 May 1767 the debate on American affairs in the House of Commons, refers to 'Mr Conway's intended resignation' (Grafton, *Autobiography*, p. 178). HW wrote Mann 24 May: 'Mr Conway, I think, will retire, not from disgust or into opposition, but from delicacy towards his old friends. . . . It is not decided yet, nor publicly known,

travagance and unreasonableness of his old friends,[5] I think ought
to discharge him from all ties to them. They have abused him in
print, reflected on him in Parliament, and I maintain have broken
all their engagements to him. I will name nobody, but was witness
in the summer, to repeated promises from them *that they would
(though taking liberties with Lord Chatham) distinguish Mr Conway, commend him, and openly in their speeches avow their abhor-
rence of Mr Grenville.* The world has seen how they have adhered
to these declarations. What is worse; when Mr Conway came over
to them in the American business[6] and professed publicly his disposition towards them, was it not notorious that they received him
with the utmost coldness and indifference? They not only avoided
a single expression of good will to him, but sat still and heard him
abused by Grenville and Rigby.[7] He was thoroughly hurt at this
behaviour, and I would beg your Grace to paint it strongly to him.

In many late conversations with him, they have shown the utmost
extravagance: they not only aim at everything, but espouse George
Grenville, and though they say they do not like him for first minister, would absolutely make him a part of their system.[8] Mr Conway
objected strongly, and I went so far as to reproach them with this

but I chose you should be apprised, and
not think there were any reasons more
disagreeable for it' (Mann vi. 521–2).
See John Brooke, *The Chatham Administration 1766–1768*, 1956, pp. 140–2.

5. The Rockingham party.

6. Proposals offered by Charles Townshend 13 May for dealing with disobedi-
ent colonial assemblies in America and
for raising new revenue there by imposing import duties on certain articles
(*Journals of the House of Commons*
xxxi. 358; Brooke, op. cit. 136–8; Sir
Lewis Namier and John Brooke, *Charles
Townshend*, 1964, pp. 178–9). Conway
joined the Rockinghams in supporting
Grenville's motion to amend the Mutiny
Act, but the Court succeeded in rejecting
the amendment by 180 votes to 98 (*Mem.
Geo. III* iii. 28).

7. 'Mr Grenville attacked Mr Conway
with great violence upon not having
transmitted to the colonies the resolution of the Lords; asked by what authority he had said that Parliament were
ready to forgive; animadverted upon his
changing his department. . . . Mr Con-

way defended himself against Mr Grenville's attack; lamented his misfortune
in differing from his friends. . . . Mr
Rigby renewed the attack upon Mr Conway with great vehemence; observed,
upon his having mentioned lenient measures, that Mr Conway had no business
to write lenitives to America, which the
Parliament did not prescribe' (Bradshaw
to Grafton 14 May, Grafton, *Autobiography*, p. 177). 'Conway was not at all
supported by his old friends, when attacked by Grenville. They were offended
at his agreeing with Wedderburn in
imputing all the late changes [in the
administration] to faction; yet had he
added that if there was a secret influence, nobody lamented it more than he
did' (*Mem. Geo. III* iii. 28–9; for HW's
account of the debate see ibid. iii. 21–8).

8. According to HW, Grenville was 'the
only man who had ever inspired him
[Conway] with animosity' (ibid. iii. 9).
For an analysis of Rockingham's position
at this time with regard to Grenville see
Brooke, op. cit. 124–6.

contradiction to all their declarations, and with adopting so arbitrary and unpopular a man.

Having stated these facts, I will now take the liberty of informing your Grace of my motives of writing you this letter. I told Mr Conway, *that if his friends would not come in, I could not conceive why he was to go out;*[9] and that I thought the question turned singly on this. When he made his declaration to them, he at the same time protested against entering into opposition.[10] If they therefore will not come in but by force, does not their refusal put an end to his connection with them? Nothing therefore seems left but to drive them to this refusal. Accordingly, I have begged Mr Conway to open his mind to your Grace, and I thought it right to apprise your Grace of what he will say to you, that you may not be surprised, and may be prepared with your answer. Your kindness to him, my Lord, has been invariable, and I am sure will continue so on this occasion, which I flatter myself may preserve the union of two men who have the strictest honour and most public spirit of any men in England. The more indulgence your Grace shows to his scruples and delicacy, the more he will feel the wildness and unreasonableness of his other connections. Pray, my Lord, forgive the extreme liberty I take of suggesting behaviour to your Grace; but knowing Mr Conway as I do better than anybody does, I am called upon to paint to your Grace the best method of treating with him. If you should be so good as to tell him that you are willing to assist his delicacy, and to contribute to bring in his friends upon reasonable terms, and that you hope he will not gratify them in any unreasonable hopes, it will open the door to a negotiation, in which I can venture to say they will be so immoderate in their demands, that it will not only shock him, but be a strong vindication of his Majesty's rejection of them, and what is most at my heart, may I hope conduce to retain Mr Conway in the King's service, when his other friends have shown that they mean nothing but to engross all

9. 'As to Conway, if you hear, that he stays in with the approbation of his *family* connections, your intelligence is certainly good. If with that of his old friendships, and political *connections* (if he will own the latter idea) you are extremely misinformed' (Edmund Burke to Charles O'Hara 15 Jan. 1767, *The Correspondence of Edmund Burke*, ed. T. W. Copeland, Chicago, 1958–78, i. 290–1).

10. HW nevertheless 'feared that Conway would go into opposition. He [Conway] would not, he said, . . . serve by turns under everybody. Yet was he ill content with his old friends, who persisted in a junction with Grenville for fear of Bute' (*Mem. Geo. III* iii. 36).

power in league with the worst men, or to throw the country into the last confusion.

If I can but prevail to keep Mr Conway united with your Grace and acting with you, it is the height of my ambition;[11] and if your Grace is so good as at least to accept my labours favourably, I shall be overpaid, for I have most undoubtedly no views for myself, but those of being approved by honest men; and as there is nobody I can esteem more than your Grace, I am not ashamed, my Lord, though you are a minister, of professing myself

Your Grace's most obedient and devoted humble servant

HOR. WALPOLE

To the DUKE OF GRAFTON, Thursday 4 June 1767

Printed for the first time from a photostat of the MS in the Bury St Edmunds and West Suffolk Record Office, Bury St Edmunds, Suffolk, kindly furnished by the late 10th Duke of Grafton through the good offices of Mr M. P. Statham (Grafton MS 778). An extract was printed in John Brooke, *The Chatham Administration 1766–1768*, 1956, pp. 141–2. For the history of the MS see *ante* 25 Nov. 1766.

Endorsed in an unidentified hand: Mr Hor. Walpole.

June 4th 1767.

I WAS yesterday morning, my Lord, with the Duke of Richmond, but avoided entering on politics, till he began the subject himself, and talked of accommodation.[1] This convinced me that their defeat the day before[2] had greatly lowered their spirits. I answered carelessly, that their expectations had appeared to me so unreasonable

11. 'Mr Conway and myself continued in our usual intimacy and friendship, though we differed in . . . our confidence in Lord Chatham. The General leaned to the Marquis of Rockingham and his friends, and had never been easy in his own situation since the fatal breach with them' (Grafton, *Autobiography*, pp. 127–8). See following letter.

1. Between the Rockingham party opposition and the faltering administration of Lord Chatham and Grafton.

2. On 2 June Richmond moved resolutions concerning Quebec's need for 'further regulations and provisions, relating to its civil government' (*Journals of the House of Lords* xxxi. 628). The resolutions were rejected by 73 to 61. 'It was not expected, that the majority would have been so large; but the Court had exerted themselves to draw their strength together' (Cobbett, *Parl. Hist.* xvi. 361, quoted from the Hardwicke papers; see also *Mem. Geo. III* iii. 40).

when we talked last on the subject,[3] that finding I could do no good, I had determined to meddle no farther. He said, Mr Conway and I had taken it into our heads, that they were much more connected with the Grenvilles etc. than they are—and in fact, my Lord, I can assure your Grace that I believe that connection very slight indeed, from two reasons. In the first place, I know from very good authority that the Bedfords do not believe a word of Mr Conway's intention of resigning, which proves there is no confidence, for as Lord Rockingham and Duke of Richmond know it, the others would if there was communication of councils between them. In the next place, I asked the Duke why, before they stipulated for the other faction, they did not learn what their demands would be, and whether they would accede or not? Oh no! said the Duke, that would be giving them the lead; whereas we intend to tell them expressly, that we intend to govern, but will admit them to a degree if they are reasonable.

This was all that passed then, but the Duke desiring me to sup with him, I went again at night, when he renewed the conversation eagerly, and said Mr Conway had told him the night before that it was possible they might receive offers next week. I wish that had not been carried so far, because I see more and more, my Lord, that their former impracticability was founded on their vain hopes of majorities. The disappointment of those hopes, and the distance of another session has much altered the tone; and *that* in a very material point; for a fortnight ago, they talked of declining the administration if Grenville and the Bedfords should refuse. Last night the Duke spoke of a possibility of getting the Bedfords even if Grenville should refuse; but what was more explicit, his Grace made the following distinction: if, said he, they (Grenv[ille] and Bedfords) join us, we shall be strong enough to make removals of some of Lord Bute's friends—if they do not, it will be prudent to temporize, and keep the latter.

I pressed the Duke to give me some idea of their arrangement; he said, they had formed none. I named over the places, but found they

---

3. Presumably on 2 May, when HW went to the Duke 'to ask, in case Lord Chatham's health should not permit him to go on, and the King should order Conway to form an administration, whether his Grace and his friends would take on?' Richmond 'insisted on Conway's resigning before the end of the session' and said that the Rockingham party would demand 'the dismission of two or three of Lord Bute's friends' (ibid. iii. 13–14).

had settled nothing even in their own minds. He said he was indifferent about himself, and named Lord Dartmouth[4] and Lord Gower[5] for secretaries of state, and Saunders[6] for the Admiralty. I asked whom they thought on for Ireland.[7] He said he supposed Lord Weymouth.[8] I objected and told him such a choice would fling that country into a flame—and I added, I hoped they would not think of Lord Sandwich[9] too. He replied, no, for nothing considerable; but something he must have. Well, my Lord, said I, and what will you do with Yorke?[10] Oh! Chancellor! said he. Chancellor! my Lord, would you make such a timid trimming fellow Chancellor, and who has lost all character even for abilities? and would you lose such an able brave man as Lord Camden[11]—sure, President[12] would be a great thing for Yorke; and very great, if you threw in a peerage too! Faith, said the Duke, my Lord Rockingham has such a leaning to Yorke, that I believe he would insist on the seals for him—but his Grace did not seem very partial to him himself. I said, Well! My Lord, do you think Lord Temple would suffer Geo. Grenville to accede to this plan? Oh! said the Duke laughing, we might send Lord Temple to Ireland. What I most fear, said the Duke, is, that Lord Temple and Grenville, seeing they cannot have the Treasury, and averse to Lord Rockingham having it, should propose that both Lord Rockingham and Grenville should waive it and (as the Duke of Newcastle is now given up to the Grenvilles[13]) should name his Grace—who would take it, said the Duke, though he declares he will take nothing, and we encourage him, said the Duke, and commend him for his moderation.

This, my Lord, was the chief of what passed last night. Your Grace, I think, must not depend entirely upon the same tractability everywhere. The Cavendishes, especially Lord John,[14] will certainly

4. William Legge (1731–1801), 2d E. of Dartmouth, 1750. See Selwyn 229 n. 8.

5. See *ante* 1 Dec. 1766, n. 6.

6. Sir Charles Saunders (ca 1713–75), K.B., 1761; first lord of the Admiralty Aug.–Dec. 1766; naval officer; M.P. He was a follower of Lord Albemarle, a Rockingham party chief.

7. That is, Lord Lieutenant of Ireland.

8. Thomas Thynne (1734–96), 3d Vct Weymouth, 1751; cr. (1789) M. of Bath; Lord Lieutenant of Ireland May–July 1765; secretary of state for the northern department Jan.–Oct. 1768, for the southern department 1768–70 and 1775–9.

9. Sandwich, like Weymouth, was one of the leaders of the Bedford group in Parliament.

10. See *ante* 25 Nov. 1766, n. 6.

11. Lord chancellor July 1766–Jan. 1770.

12. Lord president of the Council.

13. For evidence of this see Brooke, op. cit. 180–1.

14. 'The intractable man of all was, as usual, Lord John Cavendish' (*Mem. Geo. III* iii. 15).

not be so moderate as the Duke of Richmond. Yorke and Lord Albemarle[15] will throw every impediment in the way, unless their expectations are fully satisfied. I have little notion that Grenville will acquiesce. But it is plain to me, that the Rockinghams find themselves so inefficient, that with proper management they may be beaten down in many of their demands.

What I have done, has been in obedience to your Grace's commands. It does not become me, my Lord, to advise, or I should wish to see the Parliament up before the treaty is begun—Perhaps some overtures flung out separately to Lord Gower, distinct both from Grenville and Rockingham, might be of use, as it would prevent their leaguing together, which may happen if only one party is dealt with.[16]

But, my Lord, forgive me if I say, that there is a point I have more at heart than all; and that is, to have the fittest man remain in the administration. I do not mean to flatter your Grace, it is not my turn; but the great abilities your Grace displayed on Tuesday, the admiration you raised in men of all parties, your former conduct and talents, your firmness, and above all, your strict honour, are absolutely necessary to the King's and nation's service, and you must not, my Lord, you cannot in justice to the public, give yourself up to your ease and pleasures, when such men are so much wanted, and so very few such to be found. You can moderate, my Lord, if you will not command. And how unhappy is the country, if your Grace and Mr Conway, at the moment when you may govern, with the approbation of the nation, persist in leaving it to the direction of weak though well-meaning men, or to the very worst men in it![17]

15. George Keppel (1724–72), styled Vct Bury 1724–54; 3d E. of Albemarle, 1754; army officer; M.P. His sister, Lady Elizabeth Keppel, had married the Duke of Bedford's son, Lord Tavistock, who died 22 March 1767. A Rockingham party leader (see n. 6 above), Albemarle favoured an alliance with the Bedfords.

16. Richard Rigby reported to Grenville that 'many conversations' passed between Grafton and Gower, in which Grafton 'expressed a desire that the King should send to the Duke of Bedford and Lord Temple to make a part in a new administration' (*The Grenville Papers*, ed. W. J. Smith, 1852–3, iv. 228). According to HW, Grafton 'offered Lord Gower any terms for himself and his friends,

only with the exclusion of Grenville' (*Mem. Geo. III* iii. 42). Chatham, though seriously ill, had seen Grafton at the King's request on 31 May and 4 June; Grafton told him that 'a junction with the Bedfords or the Rockinghams appeared to me [Grafton] to be the only steps that could now be effectual: to which his Lordship assented, though he inclined to prefer entering into negotiation with the former' (*Autobiography and Political Correspondence of Augustus Henry Third Duke of Grafton*, ed. Sir William R. Anson, 1898, p. 138).

17. HW later observed in *Mem. Geo. III* ii. 272: 'Wearisome contests it cost me for six months to prevent Mr Conway's resignation; and though I suc-

Forgive me, my Lord, but the freedoms your Grace has indulged me in, make it my duty to speak plainly, though perhaps not with all the respect due to your Grace from

> My Lord
>> Your Grace's most obedient humble servant

>>>>> Hor. Walpole

PS. I ought to tell your Grace, that in the conversation with the Duke of Richmond, there was no hint of Lord Chatham's remaining in power, because I knew it would break off the discussion, and I thought it most prudent to fathom their whole views, without disgusting them.

I should tell your Grace too, my Lord, that the principal reason they give for admitting the Grenvilles etc. to a participation, is, to leave themselves as little opposition as possible—the context of that wish, I have no doubt, is my Lord Rockingham's consciousness that he is unable to cope with opponents in the House of Lords.

Your Grace will see from all I have said, my Lord, that my opinion, if it is worth mentioning, is, that the present administration may stand, at least till it can treat with more advantage, or till it is seen whether Lord Chatham is able to come forth again. If he should, I see nothing to hinder his continuation.[18]

May I venture one word more, my Lord? The more your Grace and Lord Camden see him, the better. Lady Chatham, if she despairs of my Lord's recovery, must naturally lean towards her brothers.[19]

I am going out of town, but shall be back tomorrow night, if your Grace has any commands for me.

---

ceeded, and afterwards shut the door both on Grenville and Lord Rockingham, the person [Grafton] who profited of my fatigues, and of the credit I had with Mr Conway, proved so unworthy; and so sick did I grow both of that person and of the fatigues I underwent, that I totally withdrew myself from the scene of politics.'

18. Concerning the failure of the negotiations to form 'a comprehensive plan of administration' see Brooke, op. cit. 162–217.

19. Lord Temple, George Grenville, and the Hon. James Grenville (1715–83), M.P.

From the Independent Freemen of King's Lynn, Monday 13 July 1767

Printed from *The Lynn Magazine,* 1768, pp. 26–8. 'The Independent Free-men of King's Lynn' is probably the *nom de guerre* of Richard Gardiner (*ante* 12 March 1762, n. 12), who was directing propaganda on behalf of Crisp Molineux, candidate for the parliamentary seat at King's Lynn then held by Sir John Turner. According to the *Lynn Magazine* (a collection of election papers compiled by Gardiner), p. 25n, this reply to HW's letter *ante* 13 March 1767 was 'published' in July 1767; neither this printing nor any MS text has been found. The reply was doubtless never sent to HW, being intended for publication in a newspaper.

Lynn, July 13, 1767.

Sir,

YOUR favour to our very respectable chief magistrate[1] having been lately communicated in public to us, we take this first opportunity to return you our thanks for your steady, upright, and untainted conduct in Parliament; and for your invariable and firm support of the principles on which the Revolution was founded; the principles, by which we are so happy as to enjoy the establishment of the present royal family; the principles, to which the Town of Lynn has ever adhered, and which were so inflexibly maintained on all occasions throughout the whole of his life by your illustrious father.[2]

Your public-spirited behaviour within the House, your unimpeached integrity without, as they loudly call for universal applause and imitation, so have they conferred such lasting obligations upon your constituents, as will be forever fresh in our memories, and make the loss of so valuable and disinterested a representative, a loss sincerely and generally felt amongst us.

Permit us, Sir, at the same time, and with the same freedom with which we express our acknowledgments for your very honourable services in Parliament, and particularly in the late flagrant attack upon our liberties;[3] permit us, Sir, to express our concern that any

1. HW to William Langley, Mayor of Lynn, *ante* 13 March 1767.

2. These phrases follow closely the wording of HW's letter (ibid.).

3. In the Commons debate on the legality of general warrants, 14–17 Feb. 1764. The motion that the debate be postponed was passed by a majority of fourteen, HW voting with the Opposition (Mann vi. 207–8; *Mem. Geo. III* i. 287–302). Those, like HW, who voted with the minority were considered to be against general warrants, upholders of the principles of English liberty.

dissatisfaction or dissensions that have arisen amongst us, should unfortunately be the occasion of a more early declaration of your intentions to decline our representation; though other motives, you obligingly tell us, influenced those intentions (one of which, your ill state of health, creates in us great pain to be acquainted with), yet the bare mention of dissatisfaction and dissensions by you, however politely and tenderly introduced, does still, in some degree, convey a distant implication, as if we were acting in a manner not altogether so agreeable to your sentiments. What makes it more the object of our concern, is, that such implication must particularly affect those very gentlemen who would most gladly have continued their favours to you, and who are now actually exerting their utmost power in the support of the same interest in your name and family.[4]

All opposition, Sir, in every community, must naturally breed division, and division is too certainly the parent of dissension. We own the fact, and we lament the consequence, and should be proud to accept the assistance you offer to prevent them; but we humbly apprehend that there is one only possible method of prevention, and that we flatter ourselves you would not, nay you could not, consistently with your own principles, recommend to us to elect a man whose conduct has been the very reverse of your own. For instance, can you, Sir, whose honour it is, never to have received a personal favour from any minister whatever, think it justifiable in us to choose a candidate (should any such offer) who in the late violent encroachments upon the liberty of the subject, acted in favour of them all, abetted the most arbitrary men, and most unconstitutional measures; and who, instead of defending the freedom and independency of his constituents, actually sold and bartered his own?[5] Is this the method of preserving our virtue? Or could we any longer be called an upright and untainted borough (a title you have been pleased to confer upon us, and which we presume we shall never forfeit) when, by supporting such barefaced ministerial influence and corruption, we should, in effect, become tainted and corrupt ourselves?

4. HW's cousin Thomas Walpole had been nominated by the Walpole 'interest' to succeed him as representative for King's Lynn.

5. Sir John Turner, the other representative for King's Lynn, had voted with the majority in favour of general warrants (see n. 3 above). 'Sold and bartered' probably refers to the fact that after Lord Bute appointed Turner to the Treasury Board in May 1762, Turner supported administration measures and continued to do so when kept in office under George Grenville (Namier and Brooke iii. 570).

A candidate[6] has offered himself, a gentleman of independent fortune, a man of abilities, very active, very indefatigable, and strongly attached to Revolution principles. In a member professing these principles we can alone expect a steady protector of our rights and properties. But had not this gentleman declared himself, some other friendly advocate would have started up in defence of an injured community, long galled with the tyranny of one proud family[7] and its most arrogant adherents; a yoke it has at last bravely resolved to shake off.

You, Sir, have no share in our dissatisfactions or dissensions; as you truly observe, you have given no cause for them. Let those, therefore, who have ruled us with a rod of iron,[8] and whose continued oppressions have raised this spirit of self-defence and preservation; let the men who ridicule all public virtue, and private honour, and who would gladly give up their own liberties to trample upon those of others; let their deluded abettors, who are taught to prefer slavery and general warrants to freedom and independency, be answerable (for they only are answerable) for all the ill consequences of dissatisfaction and dissension which unhappily prevail amongst us. These are the men who have disturbed the peace of the town, and not

Sir,
    Your most faithful and obliged humble servants,

THE INDEPENDENT FREEMEN OF KING'S LYNN

---

6. Crisp Molineux.
7. The family of Lord Bute.
8. In the case of John Wilkes v. Robert Wood, in the Court of Common Pleas 6 Dec. 1763, Lord Chief Justice Pratt is said to have declared that the general warrant used to seize Wilkes's papers was illegal and that 'If jurisdictions should declare my opinion erroneous, I submit as will become me, and kiss the rod; but I must say, I shall always consider it as a rod of iron for the chastisement of the people of Great Britain' (*Lynn Magazine*, p. 13, in a letter of 18 April 1767 signed 'A Freeman' but probably written by Richard Gardiner). These words are not recorded in T. B. Howell's *A Complete Collection of State Trials*, 1816–26, xix. 1166–8, but Pratt's opinion that a general warrant is 'a practice in itself illegal, and contrary to the fundamental principles of the constitution' is printed there.

From JOSEPH EDMONDSON,[1] Saturday 25 July 1767

Printed for the first time from the MS now WSL. The MS was sold SH vi. 126 (in a portfolio of letters, proof sheets, and documents relating to HW's *Historic Doubts on . . . Richard III*, 1768) to Boone for the 13th Earl of Derby; resold Christie's 24 March 1954 (Derby Sale), lot 345, to Maggs for WSL. See Hazen, *Cat. of HW's Lib.*, No. 2620.

July 25th fell on Saturday in 1767, the year HW was engaged in writing *Historic Doubts,* the subject of this letter.

Address: To the Honourable Horratio Walpole.

Saturday morning, 11 o'clock, July 25.

Sir,

ACCORDING to your commands,[2] I made a strict search through the Rolls of Parl[iament] of Hen. VII with Mr Rooke.[3] In the act for attainting the followers of Richard III, which are numerous, the name of *Tirrel*[4] does nowhere appear.[5] Then Mr Rooke took down the Roll for the third Parl[iament] of Henry VII, where there is an act of attainder against the Earl of Lincoln[6] and his followers for conspiring against his King. The name of *Tirrel* does not appear there, although there is also a numerous body of people mention[ed].[7] These are the only two acts of attainder on the Rolls.[8] I

1. Joseph Edmondson (d. 1786), herald and genealogist. HW owned several works by him, including *Baronagium Genealogicum*, 6 vols, [1764]–84, and *A Complete Body of Heraldry*, 2 vols, 1780 (Hazen, *Cat. of HW's Lib.*, Nos 527, 528).

2. No letter from HW to Edmondson has been found. HW had begun writing *Historic Doubts on the Life and Reign of King Richard the Third* 'in the winter of 1767; continued it in the summer, and finished it after my return from Paris' ('Short Notes,' GRAY i. 43).

3. Henry Rooke (d. 1775), clerk of the Rolls Chapel and later also chief clerk to the Keeper of Records in the Tower (DALRYMPLE 1 n. 1a).

4. Sir James Tyrell (1445–1502), Kt, 1471; alleged murderer of the two princes, sons of Edward IV, in the Tower.

5. Tyrell's name does not appear in the Act of Attainder 7 Nov. 1485, but it does appear among those 'convicted, adjudged,

and attainted of high treason' in 1503 (19 Henry VII, *Rotuli parliamentorum,* 1767–77, vi. 545). HW stated in *Historic Doubts* that 'Tirrel is not named in the act of attainder to which I have had recourse' (*Works* ii. 142).

6. John de la Pole (ca 1462–87), cr. (1467) E. of Lincoln. Lincoln was bearer of the orb at the coronation of his uncle Richard III, 1483, and in 1485 was declared by Richard to be the next heir to the throne, failing issue to himself. But Lincoln submitted to the crowning of Henry VII and remained temporarily in his service. In early 1487 he fled to Flanders to join the cause of Lambert Simnel.

7. Sir Thomas Broughton, Thomas Haryngton, Robert Percy of Knaresborough, and Richard Harleston are among those named in the Act of Attainder in 1487 (3 Henry VII, *Rotuli parliamentorum* vi. 397).

8. Among the other documents in the portfolio relating to *Historic Doubts* (see

hope you will excuse me for taking the liberty in sending two covers. That I had will not enclose the table[9] to Sir Charles;[10] therefore beg the favour of you to direct these two: one for Sir Charles Townley, Knight, at Lenton Abbey[11] near Nottingham, and the other for Joseph Edmondson, Warwick Street, Golden Square, London, to have the table returned again.

> I am, Sir, with all respect,
> Your most obedient humble servant to command,
>
> JOSEPH EDMONDSON

From MADAME DE FORCALQUIER, early August 1767

Printed for the first time from the MS now WSL. For the probable history of the MS see *ante* 6 May 1766.

Dated approximately by the reference to Lady Suffolk's death (see n. 1 below).

Endorsed by HW: De Mad[ame] la Comtesse de Forcalquier.

QUE penserez-vous de moi, Monsieur? Je ne vous ait point fait moi-même mon compliment sur la perte d'une personne[1] que je savais que vous aimiez. M'en croiriez-vous moins sensible à ce qui vous touche? Assurément vous auriez tort; nul ne plaint davantage les chagrins de l'amitié; nul ne partage, plus que je fais, la douleur que vous avez eue, mais dans les premiers moments j'ai voulu vous épargner les civilités qu'on trouve importunes dans la première amertume d'une perte qui nous touche. Néanmoins, j'espère que vous n'auriez pas mis au rang d'une simple politesse ce que

headnote) is a transcript on seven folio leaves, with the heading 'Rotulus Parliamenti de Anno Regni Regis Ricardi tertii primo,' affirming the legitimacy of Richard's sovereignty. The last page is endorsed: 'This is copied as near as could be from the original record in the Chapel of the Rolls. Hen. Rooke.'

9. Presumably a genealogical table, but not further identified.

10. Sir Charles Townley (1713–74), Kt, 1761; Clarenceaux king of arms, 1755; Garter principal king of arms, 1773.

11. A country seat about a mile and a half from Nottingham overlooking the Trent Vale. Townley, whose son John was baptized in Lenton parish in 1757, appears to have leased the property on which the Abbey House then stood (J. T. Godfrey, *The History of the Parish and Priory of Lenton, in the County of Nottingham,* 1884, p. 283; information from Professor Maurice W. Barley, Univ. of Nottingham).

---

1. Lady Suffolk, who died at her house Marble Hill, near Twickenham, 26 July 1767. HW's (missing) letter of 28 July 1767 to Mme du Deffand doubtless contained the news of her death, which was then communicated to Mme de Forcalquier; see DU DEFFAND i. 331.

j'aurais pu vous mander, et que vous auriez démêlé avec justice que j'étais véritablement fâchée que la mort vous eût enlevé une amie, le plus grand des maux, sans doute.

Je veux quitter un sujet douloureux et l'adoucir par une question: ne voudrez-vous point voir, et le plus tôt que faire ce pourra, quelqu'un[2] qui, je crois, ne le cède à personne en attachement, estime, amitié pour vous, et, après elle, un grand nombre d'autres qui vous souhaite et vous estime? J'avais cru, par ce que vous m'aviez fait l'honneur de me mander,[3] que vous seriez incessament à Paris.[4] J'espère, Monsieur, qu'enfin vous réaliserez des espérances aimables, et dont je vous déclare que je ne veux pas me dépouiller.

Cette personne dont je vous ai parlé ci-dessus doit vous causer quelque importunité en ma faveur. C'est à l'égard de quelques recherches sur quelques personnes de mon nom[5] qui ont passé jadis en Angleterre. Peut-être me trouverez-vous présomptueuse de m'être adressé à vous pour vous causer cette peine; il faut dire vrai aussi, connaissant votre goût pour l'antiquité, ce penchant m'a inspiré plus de confiance, et j'ai une double joie, Monsieur, de n'être pas d'une noblesse de fraîche date, dans l'espérance que je vous en serai moins indifférente. Traitez-moi comme une vieille vitre de Strabery [H]ill. Tout ce qui me rendra à vos yeux plus méritoire me paraîtra bien digne d'être envié. Sans me faire un mérite du cas infini que je fais de vous, Monsieur, ne l'oubliez pourtant point, et soyez de même persuadé des sentiments bien vrais avec lesquels j'ai l'honneur d'être, Monsieur, votre très humble et très obéissante servante,

CARBONNEL DE CANISY, COMTESSE DE FORCALQUIER

---

2. Mme du Deffand.
3. See HW to Mme de Forcalquier 27 Oct. 1766.
4. HW arrived at Paris 23 Aug. 1767

for a visit lasting seven weeks ('Paris Journals,' DU DEFFAND v. 316, 324).
5. Not identified; we do not know if HW undertook these 'recherches.'

To Thomas Astle,[1] Monday 3 August 1767

Printed from a copy kindly supplied by the late Sir Shane Leslie, Bt, in 1941 from the MS then in the possession of the Hon. Mrs Clive Pearson, Parham Park, Pulborough, Sussex. First printed, Toynbee vii. 126. The MS was sold Sotheby's 6 July 1900 (Autograph Letters and Historical Documents Sale), lot 379, to Cater; *penes* Frederick Barker in 1904; later acquired by Sir Herbert H. Raphael, Bt, who inserted it in an extra-illustrated copy of Cunningham's edition of HW's *Letters*, 18 vols, folio; this copy was sold Sotheby's 4 Feb. 1919 (Raphael Sale), lot 311, to Bumpus for Lord Cowdray, the father of the Hon. Clive Pearson; bequeathed by his widow, the Hon. Mrs Pearson, to her daughter, Mrs P. A. Tritton, of Parham Park, in 1974.

Address: To Thomas Astle, Esq. at South Lambeth Surry. *Frank:* Free Hor. Walpole.

Arlington Street, Aug. 3d, 1767.

Dear Sir,

I HAVE been so long confined by my brother's illness,[2] that I have not been able to give myself the pleasure of asking you to bestow a day on me. I am now at liberty, and if you have nothing else to do next Sunday, I shall be very happy if you will dine with me at Strawberry Hill, where a bed will be at your service.[3] I want to show you what use I have made of the papers and books with which you was so kind as to furnish me:[4] it will take up some time to read it to you.

> I am Sir
>   Your much obliged and most obedient servant

HOR. WALPOLE

1. (1735–1803), F.S.A., 1763; F.R.S., 1766; chief clerk of the Record Office in the Tower, 1775; Keeper of the Rolls and Records, 1783; antiquary, paleographer, and collector of books and MSS. HW wrote of him to Mason 21 Dec. 1775: 'In the [state] paper-office there is a wight, called Thomas Astle, who lives like moths on old parchments. It was he who lent me the coronation roll, and to whom I communicated my book on Richard III, to every tittle of which he agreed' (MASON i. 238).

2. Sir Edward Walpole had been seriously ill with a fever in July, causing great concern to his family. The Duchess of Gloucester, Sir Edward's second daugh-

ter, wrote to her aunt Jane Clement 3 July 1767, 'Pray write me an exact account of my father, for if he is worse I will go up to town, as soon as I get your letter'; again on 28 July, 'I hope my father is quite recovered'; and on 9 Aug., 'I am very glad my father's fever is become intermittent as that was what Mr Roberts wished for when I was in town' (MSS now WSL).

3. No record of this visit has been found.

4. Doubtless materials used in writing *Historic Doubts on . . . Richard III*, which HW had been working on during the summer (*ante* 25 July 1767, n. 2). See *post* 26 Jan. 1768.

From the Rev. John Soley,[1] Saturday 22 August 1767

Printed for the first time from a photostat of the MS at Nostell Priory, Wakefield, Yorks, kindly furnished by the late Hon. Charles Winn. For the history of the MS see *ante* ?1762.

Address: To the Honourable Horace Walpole Esq. at Strawberry Hill, Middlesex. *Postmark:* 24 AV. FREE.

Suffolk, Bungay,[2] August the 22d 1767.

Sir,

IN the 66th page of the third volume of your *Anecdotes of Painting* etc. is an account of Dixon, a scholar of Sir Peter Lely, upon which I shall take the liberty to make the following remarks. His Christian name and the place of his residence in London are mistaken, and the time of his death not very accurately determined.[3] His name was Matthew;[4] he lived with his father in Chancery Lane, and died in October 1710. In the year 1684 (14 years before the bubble lottery)[5] and the 29th of his age he retired from business and London, contrary to the earnest solicitations of his friends, who were very unwilling he should leave the town, where he began to meet with encouragement, and had a fair prospect of advancing his fortunes. His

1. Probably the Rev. John Soley (d. 1780), rector of Worlingham, Suffolk (GM 1780, l. 153; Venn, *Alumni Cantab.*). John Soley, senior and junior, were both rectors of various parishes in East Suffolk and southeastern Norfolk; see Francis Blomefield, *An Essay towards a Topographical History of the County of Norfolk*, 2d edn, 1805–10, ii. 363, v. 295, vi. 108.

2. A village in East Suffolk, about six miles west of Beccles.

3. In his account of 'John Dixon' in *Anecdotes of Painting*, SH, 1762–3, iii. 66, HW confuses the painter of that name (d. 1721) with Nicholas Dixon (fl. 1667–1708), who succeeded Samuel Cooper as King's Limner in 1672. John Dixon, a crayon-painter, was a student of Sir Peter Lely (J. J. Foster, *A Dictionary of Painters of Miniatures*, 1926, pp. 91–2; Basil S. Long, *British Miniaturists*, 1929, pp. 127–8; R. W. Goulding, 'The Welbeck Abbey Miniatures,' *Walpole Society* 1914–15, iv. 25–6; C. H. Collins Baker, *Lely and the Stuart Portrait Painters*, 1912, ii. 185, 193–4; Thieme and Becker ix. 341, 343). HW

wrote that 'Dixon, falling into debt, removed for security from St Martin's Lane, where he lived, to the King's Bench Walks in the Temple, and latterly to a small estate he had at Thwaite near Bungay in Suffolk, where he died about 1715; and where his widow and children were living in 1725.'

4. Soley likewise confuses his grandfather Matthew Dixon (d. 1710), brother of John Dixon and also a student of Lely, with Nicholas Dixon (Thieme and Becker ix. 342).

5. Nicholas Dixon was concerned in a lottery called 'The Hopeful Adventure' in 1698. There were 1214 prizes ranging from £20 to £3,000, besides one prize consisting of 'a collection of limnings' which was on view at Dixon's house in St Martin's Lane (*Anecdotes* iii. 66; see also Vertue Note Books IV, *Walpole Society* 1935–6, xxiv. 50, 144). The scheme apparently failed and Dixon was forced to mortgage many of his miniature paintings, which were later acquired by the Duke of Newcastle (ibid. xxiv. 193; Long, loc. cit.).

reasons for taking the step were an ill state of health and a strong propensity to a country life; these he himself always alleged, and my mother,[6] his youngest daughter, has heard the same confirmed since his death by the concurring testimony of his sister (the late Mrs Birkhead of Knightsbridge) and other persons of credit, who knew him while he lived in London.

From the time he left London to his death he resided in Thwait and a neighbouring parish, in very comfortable circumstances, going to town about once a year upon a visit of a few days to his father (while he lived) and sister; entirely neglecting the art in which he had been educated; and without being concerned in the bubble lottery; unless it can be supposed that he engaged in that scheme, and was involved in the difficulties, which are said to have ensued without the knowledge of his family and acquaintance, and particularly of his wife, to whom he had been married six years at the time fixed for the lottery, and who I am very confident never heard of that affair, and, were she now living, would be deeply affected with the injury done to his memory.

Nor can I more readily acquiesce in the account of his being keeper of the King's Picture Closet, and that lucky incident of the picture sold to the Duke of Devonshire.[7] These are events never heard of in his family, which, had they been real, could not possibly have been the case.

It is some time since I saw your volumes of *Anecdotes,* and I have not at present an opportunity of consulting them; but, if I am not mistaken, there is somewhere a passage to this purport, 'that such of Mr Vertue's labours, as are of doubtful authority, are distinguished by a *Quære;*'[8] I should be glad to know whether the above-mentioned anecdotes of Dixon are not of that number.

His family now possesses some of his works in crayons, particularly his own head, and those of the Duchesses of Cleveland[9] and Portsmouth,[10] who lived in the reign of Charles the Second. Sir Peter

---

6. Neither Soley's great-grandfather nor his mother has been identified.

7. According to Vertue, Nicolas Dixon 'was keeper of the pictures in the King's Closet' and 'bought once a picture at a broker's at a very small price and sold it to the Duke of Devonshire for £500' (Vertue Note Books IV, op. cit. xxiv. 50–1). HW included this information in his account of 'John Dixon.'

8. 'In his [Vertue's] memorandums he always put a quære against whatever was told him of suspicious aspect; and never gave credit to it 'till he received the fullest satisfaction' (Preface, *Anecdotes* i. viii).

9. Barbara Villiers (ca 1641–1709), m. 1 (1659) Roger Palmer, cr. (1661) E. of Castlemaine; m. 2 (1705) Robert Feilding; cr. (1670) Ds of Cleveland; Charles II's mistress.

10. See *ante* 9 Aug. 1764, n. 3.

Lely once sat to him for his picture in crayons, which, when finished, was honoured with the approbation of that great master, who also desired that some improvement might be made in the drapery: before that could be done Sir Peter died, and the picture, which was designed to be a present to him, after continuing in our family many years, was given by my grandmother to the lady of John Fowle, Esq.[11] of Broome in Norfolk, by whom I hear it was afterward presented to the late Earl of Orford.[12] I cannot describe it better than by saying that the print of Sir Peter Lely in your valuable work above-mentioned is believed to be an exact resemblance of it.[13]

I hope this will not be deemed impertinent: if it be thought worthy of an answer,[14] I shall be truly sensible of the honour conferred on

Your most obedient humble servant,

JOHN SOLEY

11. John Fowle (d. 1772), of Broome, Norfolk; bencher of Gray's Inn, and auditor of excise 1750–72; m. Elizabeth Turner (d. 1763), dau. of Sir Charles Turner and Mary Walpole (HW's aunt) (GRAY ii. 198 n. 24).

12. Sir Robert Walpole, 1st E. of Orford, was Elizabeth Fowle's uncle.

13. The engraving by Alexander Bannerman in *Anecdotes* iii. 15 is after a self-portrait by Lely.

14. No reply has been found.

To Pierre-Jean Mariette, ca Thursday 8 October 1767

Printed from a photostat of the MS inserted in the first volume of Mariette's MS translation of HW's *Anecdotes of Painting* ('Anecdotes sur l'état de la peinture en Angleterre . . . par Monsieur Horace Walpole'[1]) in the Bibliothèque Nationale (MSS français 14650-2). First printed in Ruth Clark, 'Horace Walpole and Mariette,' *Modern Language Review*, 1914, ix. 522. Reprinted, Toynbee *Supp.* iii. 12-13; Musée du Louvre, *Le Cabinet d'un Grand Amateur: P. - J. Mariette 1694-1774*, 1967, p. 186, No. 333; Barbara Scott, 'Pierre-Jean Mariette, Scholar and Collector,' *Apollo*, 1973, xcvii. 57. The MS, along with the three volumes of Mariette's translation, was acquired from the widow of Adrien-Jacques Joly (1756-1829), art historian and curator of prints in the Bibliothèque du Roi, in April 1830.

Dated approximately by the reference to the 'nouvelle édition' of *Anecdotes of Painting* and by HW's departure from Paris for England (see nn. 2, 3 below). HW left Paris the day before 9 Oct. 1767, the date assigned to the letter by Toynbee.

MONSIEUR Walpole est très mortifié de quitter Paris,[2] sans avoir eu la satisfaction de voir son bon ami Monsieur Mariette. M. Walpole le prie de vouloir bien accepter ces estampes, ajoutées à la nouvelle édition de ses *Anecdotes* etc.[3] et surtout, le conjure de lui conserver son amitié.

1. In his late sixties Mariette learned English so that he could translate into French the first edition of *Anecdotes of Painting*. The MS of his translation comprises three quarto volumes, with his extensive marginal annotations. Mariette wrote Giovanni Gaetano Bottari, the librarian of the Vatican, 3 Aug. 1764: 'Il a été publiée à Londres et en anglais un ouvrage en quatre volumes in-4o, qui contient des anecdotes sur les peintres, les sculpteurs, les architectes et les graveurs, qui ont exercé ces différents arts en Angleterre. Je me suis amusé à le traduire, et je suis déjà à la fin du troisième volume. Mais ce travail sera sans doute pour moi seul; car je n'y trouve rien d'assez important pour qu'il en soit fait part au public dans notre langue. Je voudrais au moins que cet ouvrage pût faire honneur à la nation anglaise; mais si l'on en retranche tout ce qui concerne les artistes étrangers, le reste ne contient presque rien autre chose que des peintres de peu de réputation, et presque tous

portraitistes. L'auteur, néanmoins, est un homme de beaucoup d'esprit, et qui a mis dans son livre tout l'esprit que son livre pouvait comporter. C'est M. Horace Walpole, fils du ministre qui a gouverné longtemps l'Angleterre: cet ouvrage est enrichi de près de cent portraits, et l'impression en est véritablement magnifique' (A.-J. Dumesnil, *Histoire des plus célèbres amateurs français*, 1857-8, i. 211-12; see also G. G. Bottari, *Raccolta di Lettere sulla Pittura, Scultura ed Architettura*, Milan, 1822-5, iv. 570-1).

2. HW 'set out from Paris at half an hour after four' on 8 Oct., after a seven-week visit there ('Paris Journals,' DU DEFFAND v. 324).

3. The second edition of *Anecdotes of Painting*, dated 1765 but published in June 1767, contains four additional plates. These are engraved portraits of (1) Henry Giles (*ante* 4 March 1762, n. 4); (2) George Jamesone (*ante* 11 Sept. 1762, n. 6); (3) Jean Petitot, Sir Tobie Matthew (*ante* 24 April 1764, nn. 10, 11),

To the Duchesse de Choiseul, Friday 16 October 1767

Printed from the MS copy in Jean-François Wiart's hand, now WSL. First printed, Toynbee vii. 139–40. For the history of the MS copy see *ante* 6 May 1766. The original letter is missing; it is listed in HW's record of letters sent to Paris in 1767 (DU DEFFAND v. 386).

Dated by the endorsement.

Endorsed by Wiart: Copie d'une lettre de Monsieur Walpole à Mad. la D. de Choiseul du 16 octobre 1767.

VOICI, chère grand'maman,[1] le numéro de votre billet de loterie, c'est 17138. J'y ai écrit votre nom et je vous en dois six francs de reste. Ah que je souhaite que cela soit le gros lot! Non pas pour vous, chère grand'maman, car vous n'aimez pas l'argent, mais pour tous ceux que vous rendrez heureux.[2] Ne voulez-vous pas me mander comment va votre santé? Montez-vous à cheval? Dormez-vous? Vous ménagez-vous? Ou bien allez-vous vous tuer? Préférez-vous toujours les devoirs et même la politesse à la vie? Eh, mon Dieu! et pour qui vous assujettissez-vous à cette contrainte? Pour des courtisans, pour des femmes qui ne vous ressemblent point, et oubliez-vous que vous avez des amis qui s'intéressent à votre santé, que vous êtes la grand'maman de tous les pauvres, et que le Roi a des sujets qui sont honnêtes gens et à qui vous devez l'exemple et la protection. Je ne veux pas demander de vos nouvelles à ma pauvre femme,[3] car véritablement la tête lui tourne. Elle a si horriblement peur que vous ne devinssiez sérieusement malade, qu'elle ne fera que me communiquer ses agitations. C'est au bon Abbé[4] à qui je m'adresse,[5] et qui je supplie de me dire la vérité.

and Johannes Symoonisz van der Beeck, called Torrentius; and (4) Anthoni Schoonjans, called Sevonyans by HW. See Hazen, *SH Bibl.* 62–3.

---

1. Mme de Choiseul wrote Mme du Deffand 24 Oct. 1767: 'M. Walpole m'a écrit une lettre charmante où il m'appelle aussi sa grand'maman, parce qu'il est votre mari. Je vous l'envoie pour que vous en ayez aussi le plaisir. Vous me la rendrez lundi, afin que j'y réponde. Il me semble qu'il commence réellement à se mettre à son aise avec moi. C'est comme cela que je l'aime; pour cette fois, j'en suis très-contente' (*Correspondance complète de Mme du Deffand,* ed. the Marquis

de Sainte-Aulaire, 1866, i. 142). Mme du Deffand reported to HW 27 Oct.: 'Je soupai hier avec la grand'maman; je lui remis votre lettre qu'elle m'avait envoyée sur-le-champ; elle en est charmée; elle la fit lire tout haut par l'Abbé Barthélemy, en présence du [George] Selwyn et du Président [Hénault] . . . . Vous ferez très bien de continuer à lui écrire du même style' (DU DEFFAND i. 358).

2. The MS reads 'heureux heureux.'

3. Mme du Deffand.

4. Jean-Jacques Barthélemy (1716–95), Abbé; writer, antiquary, and numismatist. Barthélemy was a close friend of the Choiseuls and a permanent member of their household. 'Besides great learning,

Ma grand'maman, vous m'avez si bien persuadé que vous avez la bonté de vous intéresser à moi que je ne crois pas vous importuner en vous parlant de ce qui me regarde. J'ai eu un bien mauvais passage,[6] mais je me porte bien, et on veut même que je sois engraissé, mais je crois que ces gens-là me regardent à travers leurs lunettes comme l'ambassadeur de Naples[7] quand il croyait ses jambes si prodigieusement enflées.

Voilà, chère grand'maman, comme j'ai perdu la timidité. Mais le véritable respect, la plus parfaite reconnaissance, voici ce que je ne perdrais jamais. Conservez-nous vos bontés, à moi et à ma petite femme, et donnez-nous des oncles et des tantes. Je vous jure que nous n'en serons jamais jaloux, encore ne vous seront-ils pas plus attachés que votre très affectionné petit-fils,

HORACE WALPOLE

he has infinite wit and *polissonnerie,* and is one of the best kind of men in the world' (HW to Conway 31 Dec. 1774, CONWAY iii. 236).

5. The only recorded letter from HW to Barthélemy is that of 2 Feb. 1768; the letter is missing ('Paris Journals,' DU DEFFAND v. 386).

6. HW crossed the Channel 11 Oct. on his return from France to England. He wrote in 'Paris Journals': 'embarked at two, great storms of rain, and squalls;

very sick; did not land till ten at night' (ibid. v. 324).

7. Probably Domenico Caracciolo (1715–89), Neapolitan ambassador to England 1764–71, to Paris 1771–81; Viceroy of Sicily 1781–6 (MONTAGU ii. 216 n. 8). He was described by Jean-François Marmontel as having 'au premier coup d'œil . . . l'air épais et massif avec lequel on peindrait la bêtise' (Marmontel, *Mémoires,* 1891, ii. 98).

To the Rev. Jeremiah Milles,[1]
Tuesday 20 October 1767

Printed for the first time from a copy of the MS in the possession of the Dean and Chapter of Exeter Cathedral, kindly furnished by Mr L. J. Lloyd, Librarian of the University of Exeter, which administers the Cathedral Library (D. & C. Exeter MS 4670/1). The MS, part of Milles's official correspondence as Dean of Exeter Cathedral, was left by him among the Cathedral records.

Strawberry Hill, Oct. 20, 1767.

Sir,

AT my return last week from Paris to London,[2] I found your two packets,[3] one of which I have sent to Mr Bateman,[4] and for the other, I should have thanked you immediately, if I had not had a good deal of business, which my absence occasioned. I am indeed, Sir, much obliged to you for this favour, and shall be still more so if you will be so good as to subscribe for me to the plate, for which I will pay you when I have the pleasure of seeing you in town.

I am very glad to hear that Peckitt[5] improves so fast, and that he meets with so much encouragement.

I am Sir

Your obedient humble servant

Hor. Walpole

1. (1714–84), D.D., 1747; Dean of Exeter 1762–84; president of the Society of Antiquaries 1768–84. He used HW 'scurvily' by replying to part of *Historic Doubts* in 'Observations on the Wardrobe Account for the Year 1483,' read at the Society of Antiquaries 8 March 1770 and published the same year in *Archæologia* i. 361–83 (Cole to HW 28 Nov. 1770, Cole i. 203; see also Gray i. 46 n. 318).

2. HW returned to London 12 Oct. after a seven-week visit to Paris ('Paris Journals,' du Deffand v. 324).

3. Presumably brochures inviting subscriptions to pay for the Great West Window of Exeter Cathedral. The window was completely reglazed by Peckitt of York (see n. 5 below) and completed in 1767. Two subscription lists were opened towards the cost of this work: one, for sums of five or six guineas, from persons whose coats of arms were included in the window (the money to be used for painting each armorial); the other, for one guinea, from those who would receive a print of the window engraved by Richard Coffin of Exeter. HW had been invited to subscribe for the print, which was described as 'neatly engraved on copper plate, of a size to admit of the whole length figures being about two inches and [a] half, and the noblemen's coats of arms near one inch, which will be finished with accuracy equal to any print of larger size.' Milles was responsible for both subscription lists, which have not survived (information from Mr L. J. Lloyd, Librarian of the University of Exeter). See Cole i. 146–7.

4. See *ante* ca March 1745, n. 4.

5. William Peckitt (1731–95), glass painter of York, who executed work for HW at SH in 1762 and 1773 (*ante* 31 March 1764 *bis*, n. 7; Mason i. 213 n. 21).

From the Rev. John Cullum,[1]
Monday 23 November 1767

Printed for the first time from the MS now WSL. For the history of the MS see *ante* 25 July 1767.

Address: To the Honourable Mr Walpole.

Hardwick House,[2] near Bury, Suffolk,
Nov. 23d 1767.

Sir,

THOUGH I have not the honour of being known to you even by name, yet a fondness for the same kind of inquiries as the polite author of *Anecdotes of Painting in England* has made his amusement, may perhaps plead my excuse for giving you the present trouble.

You have already given me some information with respect to the monument of Sir Robert Drury in the church of Hawsted,[3] of which I am rector: but there is in the same church another monument, which an inquisitiveness (natural to most persons) into whatever relates to family concerns, makes me wish to know as much as I can about. It is a large elaborate piece of stucco work, painted in imitation of marble, and adorned with flowers etc. to the memory of Sir Thomas Cullum, Bart.,[4] who died in 1664. Family tradition has always ascribed this performance to an Italian;[5] and it would be well were tradition never more mistaken: for among a large trunkful of old papers which have lately fallen into my hands, in the steward's

1. Rev. Sir John Cullum (1733–85), 6th Bt, 1774; rector of Hawstead, 1762, and vicar of Great Thurlow, Suffolk, 1774; F.S.A., 1774; F.R.S., 1775; antiquary, botanist, and divine.

2. The seat of Sir John Cullum, about two miles south of Bury St Edmunds.

3. 'Sir Robert Drury at Hasteed by Bury, £140' (*Anecdotes of Painting*, SH, 1762–3, ii. 28n). The tomb of Sir Robert Drury (1575–1615), Kt, 1591, was the work of Nicholas Stone. Drury's widow erected the monument ·to the joint memory of her husband and father-in-law in 1617 (W. L. Spiers, 'The Note-book and Account book of Nicholas Stone,' *Walpole Society* 1918–19, vii. 45; John Cullum, *The History and Antiquities of Hawsted,*

in the *County of Suffolk*, 1784, pp. 54–6, 145, in *Bibliotheca Topographica Britannica*, vol. V [citing HW's note in *Anecdotes*, quoted above]).

4. Thomas Cullum (ca 1587–1664), cr. (1660) Bt.

5. Jacinthe de Coucy (fl. 1675), an Italian employed by Sir Thomas Cullum, 2d Bt, for the interior decorations at his seat, Hawstead Hall, in Suffolk. The monument to Sir Thomas Cullum, 1st Bt, is signed by him and dated 1675 (ibid. 56–8; Rupert Gunnis, *Dictionary of British Sculptors 1660–1851,* Cambridge, Mass., 1954, p. 125; C. L. S. Linnell, 'Suffolk Church Monuments,' *Proceedings of the Suffolk Institute of Archæology*, 1955–7, xxvii. 12, 20).

accounts for the year 1674, I find at different times, money 'advanced to the Italian on account of the monument'—the steward, I suppose, either did not know, or could not spell his name, but from his cypher[6] on a sarcophagus which makes part of the monument, you most probably will be able to discover it. I have sent it you as exactly as I could draw it—

Is this artist among yours of Charles II? or is he a new one, whose right to a place in your catalogue may perhaps depend on this single work? though in the church of Mildenhall in this county, there is a small mural monument[7] in much the same style for one of the North family, with whom we were about that time connected by marriage.[8] If you should not think this inquiry entirely beneath your notice, you would confer a great favour on, Sir,

Your obedient humble servant,

JOHN CULLUM

6. The cypher appears to be that of Sir Thomas Cullum rather than that of the sculptor.

7. 'There is another monument, evidently of the same artist, but upon a much smaller scale, in the chancel of Mildenhall Church, for Sir Henry North, Bart., who died in 1671. The Norths and Cullums were at that time closely connected by marriage' (Cullum, op. cit. 57n).

8. Sir Thomas Cullum (1628–80), 2d Bt, 1664; m. (1656) Dudleia North (1637–80), dau. of Sir Henry North (d. 1671), 1st Bt, of Mildenhall, Suffolk.

To the Rev. John Cullum,
Thursday 26 November 1767

Printed from a photostat of the MS in Trinity College Library, Cambridge (MS Cullum Q. 78). First printed in R. S. Woof, 'Some Horace Walpole Letters,' N & Q, 1965, ccx. 26. The MS is among a collection of family papers which descended to Cullum's great-great-nephew, George Gery Milner-Gibson-Cullum, who bequeathed the papers to Trinity College, Cambridge in 1921.

This is the only letter from HW to Cullum known to have survived, but there were others included in a collection of Cullum correspondence sold Evans 22 Dec. 1835 (Earl of Guilford Sale), lot 1153, to Dilke; not further traced. See also *post* 18 Dec. 1768, n. 5.

Arlington Street, Nov. 26, 1767.

Sir,

YOU do me justice in supposing that I should be very ready to give any information in my power to a gentleman, who, like yourself, Sir, applies to me on a difficulty he wishes to have cleared up. I am sorry my lights do not go so far as my readiness to oblige. I have turned over my *Anecdotes*, but can fix on no artist who seems exactly to answer the marks on the tomb. I have mentioned one Roberti,[1] an Italian, who in the reign of Queen Anne built the staircase at Coudray,[2] and he might have come over as early as 1674: but I do not know his Christian name, nor can I say that I discover an *R* in the cypher. It would be going too far back to ascribe it to Theodore Haveus,[3] whom I have mentioned at the end of my first volume,[4] though I discern most of the letters of his name, and the whole cypher has more the air of an artist who had worked in remoter times, than of one who lived down to ours. But, Sir, this is only telling you how many wrong guesses I have made: and yet I will add another, because the person in question lived nearer to the year 1674,

---

1. '— Roberti, an architect who built the staircase at Coudray, the Lord Montacute's; Pelegrini painted it' (*Anecdotes of Painting*, SH, 1762–3, iii. 154).

2. Cowdray, near Midhurst, Sussex, the seat of Anthony Joseph Browne (1728–87), 7th Vct Montagu, 1767. HW visited Cowdray in 1749 and again in 1774 (Montagu i. 98–9; *Country Seats* 76). The house, built ca 1535–45, was destroyed by fire in 1793. The great staircase, on the eastern side of the Buck Hall, had wide, shallow steps and a handsome balustrade (Mrs Charles Roundell, *Cowdray*, 1884, p. 114; S. D. Scott, 'Cowdray House, and its Possessors,' *Sussex Archæological Collections*, 1852, v. 182).

3. Theodore Haveus, Dutch painter, sculptor, and architect who worked in England during the reign of Elizabeth I (Thieme and Becker xvi. 163).

4. *Anecdotes* i. 167.

than Haveus, and actually did use such a sort of cypher; it was Gerard Chrismas,[5] who, Vertue supposed, built the gateway of Northumberland House.[6] But then, as *T* is one of the predominant letters in your cypher, he must have spelt his name like the festival, and not without the T as I found it in Vertue's MSS.

I beg your pardon, Sir, for taking up your time with vague conjectures, which are not intended to veil my own ignorance, a defect I am always very free to avow, but to show you that I have tried·to give you satisfaction.

May I ask if there is no date on the tomb at Mildenhall, which may help one to the discovery whether the period of the artist's life reached more backward or more forward than 1674, the knowledge of which would circumscribe our conjectures within a narrower compass.

I am Sir
Your obedient humble servant

HOR. WALPOLE

From PRÉSIDENT HÉNAULT, Friday 27 November 1767

Printed from *Cornélie Vestale,* SH, 1768, pp. [iii]–iv ('À Mons. Horace Walpole'), where the letter was first printed. Reprinted in *Œuvres inédites de M. le Président Hénault,* ed. [A. Sérieys], 1806, pp. 49–51. The history of the MS and its present whereabouts are not known.

Paris, ce 27 novembre, 1767.

CORNÉLIE *Vestale,* tragédie, fut représentée, Monsieur, à la Comédie-Française en 1713;[1] j'étais bien jeune alors, et c'était mon excuse: elle fut assez bien reçue, et j'eus du moins la sagesse de

5. Gerard Christmas (d. 1634), sculptor and woodcarver.

6. 'Before the portal of that palace [Northumberland House] was altered by the present Earl of Northumberland, there were in a frieze near the top in large capitals C. Æ. an enigma long inexplicable to antiquarians. . . . Till a clearer explication of those letters are given, I shall conclude with Vertue that they signified, Chrismas ædificavit' (ibid. ii. 35). Although the tomb in question was the work of Jacinthe de Coucy, there

is another monument in Hawstead Parish Church that was executed by Christmas in 1613; it is an effigy commemorating Elizabeth Drury, daughter of Sir Robert Drury (C. L. S. Linnell, 'Suffolk Church Monuments,' *Proceedings of the Suffolk Institute of Archæology,* 1955–7, xxvii. 5).

1. *Cornélie Vestale,* a verse tragedy in five acts by Hénault, was first produced at the Comédie-Française on 27 Jan. 1713, and had four subsequent performances. Hénault used the name of Louis Fuzelier

ne la pas faire imprimer: cependant j'y pensais souvent, comme on fait à une première passion.[2] On me flattait sur les détails de cette pièce: en effet c'était le premier ess[ai] d'une âme toute étonnée des sentiments qu'elle éprouve la première fois, la pure fleur du sentiment qui paraît exagéré quand on ne l'a pas connu, et qui est pourtant l'amour. On s'en moquera tant que l'on voudra, le reste de la vie n'est que de la galanterie, de la convenance, des traités, dont la condition secrète est de songer à se quitter au moment que l'on se choisit, comme l'on dit que l'on parle de mort dans les contrats de mariage. Je regrettais de temps en temps le sort de cette orpheline qui ne trouvait pas d'établissement. J'en causai avec vous, Monsieur, et je ne pouvais mieux m'adresser; vous comprîtes mes regrets, et vous finîtes par exiger de mon amitié de vous la donner pour la faire imprimer à cette presse que vous avez à votre campagne,[3] et d'où l'on a vu sortir l'édition magnifique de Lucain.[4] *Cornélie* n'aura pas perdu pour attendre. C'est pour elle un magnifique établissement, et assurément c'était un honneur auquel elle n'aurait jamais osé prétendre. Je vous l'abandonne, vous faites sa fortune; après avoir été l'accident de l'amour, elle finira bien plus noblement par être le prix de l'amitié dont vous m'honorez.[5] Je garde toujours l'incognito.[6]

(ca 1672–1752), a well known playwright, as a pseudonym (H. C. Lancaster, 'The Comédie Française 1701–1774,' *Transactions of the American Philosophical Society*, 1951, new series, xli. 638; Henri Lion, *Le Président Hénault 1685–1770*, 1903, p. 6; du Deffand i. 376 n. 19).

2. Hénault once called the play a 'déclaration en quinze cents vers, où quatre auraient suffi' (Lion, loc. cit.).

3. HW wrote George Montagu 15 April 1768: 'My press is revived, and is printing a French play written by the old President Hénault. . . . I print it to please the old man, as he was exceedingly kind to me at Paris; but I doubt whether he will live till it is finished" (Montagu ii. 260). HW printed 200 copies of *Cornélie Vestale* at the SH Press 11 April–11 June 1768; he sent 150 copies to Paris, keeping

only 50 for himself (Hazen, *SH Bibl.* 77; du Deffand ii. 100). A copy of the play said to be Hénault's own copy is now wsl (Hazen, *SH Bibl.*, 1973 edn, p. xix, copy 10).

4. See *ante* 17 Aug. 1766 and n. 2.

5. On 3 July 1768 Mme du Deffand sent a copy of the play to Voltaire, who replied 13 July: 'Je vous remercie d'abord de *Cornélie Vestale*. Je me souviens de l'avoir vu jouer, il y a plus de cinquante ans. Puisse l'auteur la voir représenter encore dans cinquante ans d'ici! Mais malheureusement ses ouvrages dureront plus que lui, c'est la seule vérité triste qu'on puisse lui dire' (*Voltaire's Correspondence*, ed. Theodore Besterman, Geneva, 1953–65, lxix. 249; see also du Deffand ii. 99–100).

6. See n. 1 above.

To the Duchesse de Choiseul,
Tuesday 8 December 1767

Printed from extracts quoted in Mme de Choiseul's reply *post* 19 Dec. 1767.
The original letter is missing; it is listed in HW's record of letters sent to
Paris in 1767 (du Deffand v. 386).[1]

[Je préfère votre] alliance à la fille d'un nabab, à un muid de
diamants et à un collier de perles gros comme des œufs de dindons.
. . . Le Roi d'Angleterre [est] le plus vertueux prince du monde
parce qu'il [a] acheté deux ou trois fois toutes les vertus des deux
chambres.

From the Duchesse de Choiseul,
Saturday 19 December 1767

Printed from a photostat of the MS in the possession of Mr H. R. Creswick,
Upper Bank, Gifford, East Lothian. First printed (with Mme de Sévigné to
Mme de Grignan 13 Sept. 1679 and Mme de Choiseul to Mme du Deffand
19 Dec. 1767) in *Lettres de Madame de Sévigné, de sa famille et de ses amis*,
ed. L.-J.-N. Monmerqué, 1862–8, xi. xiii-xv. Mme de Choiseul wrote to Mme
du Deffand 19 Dec. 1767, enclosing her letter to HW, also dated 19 Dec.,
along with the letter of Mme de Sévigné intended for him; Mme du Deffand
sent all three letters to HW. All three MSS belonged to 'Mr and Mrs Payne
of London' in 1865 and came into Mr Creswick's possession before 1934.
Endorsed by Mary Berry: To Horace Walpole.
Address (from *Lettres de Madame de Sévigné*): À Monsieur, Monsieur Horace Walpole, en son hôtel. À Londres.

À Versailles, ce 19.

J'IMAGINE qu'en Angleterre comme en France on donne du
bonbon aux petits enfants qui sont jolis, bien sages, qui ont bien
dit leurs leçons, et dont on est bien content. Or, comme vous êtes
mon petit-fils,[1] Monsieur, que je vous trouve un fort joli enfant, que
vous m'avez écrit une fort jolie lettre,[2] et que je suis fort contente de

1. Mme du Deffand wrote HW 11 [15]
Dec. 1767: 'La grand'maman m'envoya
hier votre lettre, et comme je ne suis pas
en train d'écrire je vous envoie la sienne.
Vous jugerez si elle est contente de vous
et si vous devez l'être d'elle' (du Deffand
i. 396).

1. See *ante* 16 Oct. 1767, n. 1.
2. In her letter to Mme du Deffand 13
Dec. 1767, Mme de Choiseul called HW's
letter of 8 Dec. 'infiniment jolie' (Appendix 16, du Deffand vi. 135).

vous, je vous envoie pour votre bonbon une lettre de Mme de Sévigné.[3] J'entends dire cependant que vous êtes fort épris des charmes de cette belle habitante des Champs-Élysées, et ce n'est pas un trop joli rôle à jouer pour une grand'mère de favoriser les passions amoureuses de son petit-fils; d'ailleurs, je crains que cet amour ne fasse tort à votre petite femme;[4] mais comme c'est elle qui m'a obligée à rechercher cette lettre et à vous l'envoyer,[5] je lui dois de vous faire connaître ce sublime effort de l'amour conjugal, pour que vous lui rapportiez toute la reconnaissance et les remerciements qu'elle mérite.

C'est du Marquis de Castelanne,[6] qui avait épousé l'arrière-petite-fille de Mme de Sévigné, que je tiens ces lettres. Il ne m'a été permis de vous en donner qu'une; mais je garde les autres, pour vous les faire lire à votre retour; et vous choisirez entre elles celle qui vous plaira le plus.[7] Celle-ci est du choix de ma petite-fille. Je voulais vous en envoyer une autre[8] qu'elle a dédaignée parce qu'elle est fort longue, et qu'elle traite d'une tracasserie fort obscure et à la vérité fort ennuyeuse; mais le commencement et la fin en sont si touchants pour sa fille, que je me suis écriée en les entendant: 'Ah! si ma mère[9] m'avait jamais dit la millième partie de cela!' C'était le Marquis qui lisait, et les glaces apparentes de son austérité se sont fondues à cette exclamation; il a presque pleuré avec moi, car il connaissait ma mère; elle avait toutes les vertus, tous les esprits, tous les agréments; mais elle ne me soupçonnait pas de connaître le prix de tout cela. Mme de Sévigné me fait regretter de n'avoir point de mère pour avoir le plaisir d'en être aimée; Mme de Sévigné me fait encore plus régretter de n'être pas mère pour avoir le plaisir encore plus grande d'aimer mes enfants. Que les liens, que les attachements de la nature sont doux! quelle béatitude de s'y livrer! quelle paix les accompagne! Ceux qui en sont privés sont les réprouvés sans doute.

---

3. Mme de Sévigné's letter to her daughter, Mme de Grignan, 13 Sept. 1679.

4. Mme du Deffand.

5. 'Mandez-moi je vous prie si la lettre de Mme de Sévigné vous aura fait plaisir; il y a deux mois que la grand'maman et moi, nous nous sommes occupées de cette grande affaire' (Mme du Deffand to HW 21 Dec. 1767, ibid. i. 402).

6. Jean-Baptiste de Castellane (d. 1790), Marquis d'Esparron et de la Garde; m. (1725) Julie-Françoise de Simiane (1704–28), great-granddaughter of Mme de Sévigné.

7. Four letters of Mme de Sévigné were in the SH sale (vi. 113), but that of 13 Sept. 1679 was apparently the only one which came from Mme de Choiseul.

8. This letter to Mme de Grignan has not been further identified.

9. Marie-Thérèse-Catherine Gouffier (d. 1758), m. (1722) Louis-François Crozat, Marquis du Châtel (ibid. ii. 416 n. 13). For Mme du Deffand's 'portrait' of her see Appendix 5x, ibid. vi. 109–11.

Le sentiment seul est la vie de l'âme; et pourtant tout l'effort de ma raison, tout le fruit de ma philosophie (car chacun a la sienne) ne tend journellement qu'à dessécher mon cœur. Aussi ma petite-fille me reproche-t-elle tous les jours de n'aimer rien. Ah! si j'étais insensible, travaillerais-je autant à le devenir? Mais parlons d'autres choses.

Rassurez-vous, mon cher petit-fils. J'espère que votre ménage n'ira point en décadence, on me l'a promis trop positivement pour n'y point compter, et je me flatte que vous n'aurez jamais à regretter *d'avoir préféré mon alliance à la fille d'un nabab, à un muid de diamants et à un collier de perles gros comme des œufs de dindons.*[10]

Pardon! je vous ai fait une infidelité; j'ai tant ri de ce que le *Roi d'Angleterre était le plus vertueux prince du monde parce qu'il avait acheté deux ou trois fois toutes les vertus des deux chambres,*[11] que je n'ai pu m'empêcher de le dire à M. de Choiseul, qui a ri aussi, et qui prétend que vous devez mieux le savoir que personne, parce que c'est Monsieur votre père qui a appris ce secret aux rois d'Angleterre. Il me tarde d'avoir des nouvelles du succès de l'opération que l'on a faite au Duc de Bedfort.[12] Si vous le rencontrez, dites-lui, je vous prie, combien j'y ai pris part.

Je ne veux point vous parler de mon voyage à Londres,[13] parce que j'en écris à Milady Charlotte,[14] et que je n'aime pas les rabachages; mais j'approuve fort assurément les arrangements du retour.

J'ai lu à l'Abbé[15] l'article de votre lettre qui le regarde; je pourrais

10. See previous letter.

11. That is, the two houses of Parliament.

12. Bedford had come to London 20 Nov. for the purpose of undergoing an operation for cataracts in his eyes. The operation took place on 5 Dec.; see MANN vi. 567 and n. 12. Richard Rigby wrote from Bedford House 8 Dec. to Newcastle: 'I should have taken the liberty of writing to your Grace last Saturday to have given you an account of the operation performed on the Duke of Bedford's eyes, but . . . determined to wait a day or two in order to inform you of the progress of the cure, which I have the infinite satisfaction now to tell your Grace is in as fair a way as the nature of the case can possibly admit. There is not the least degree of inflammation and all pain in a manner removed; it is uncertain how many days the bandages may yet be con-

tinued; but the person who performed the operation [Baron Wentzel] . . . has such confidence in his success, that the Duke of Bedford's friends have all the reason in the world to be satisfied' (Add. MS 32,987, ff. 212–13). Lady Mary Coke mentions the Duke's operation 11 Dec. and his recovery 31 Dec. in her *Journals* ii. 164, 172.

13. Mme de Choiseul never visited England.

14. Lady Charlotte Stanley (1728–76), m. (ca 1751) Gen. John Burgoyne (James Lunt, *John Burgoyne of Saratoga,* New York, 1975, pp. 12–14). Her friendship with the Choiseuls dated from about 1751, when she and her husband, encumbered by debts, went to live for several years in France (ibid.).

15. The Abbé Barthélemy (*ante* 16 Oct. 1767, n. 4).

vous dire qu'il a été fort touché de votre souvenir, mais je ne veux pas vous parler de lui, parce qu'il est assez grand pour parler tout seul.

Je ne veux pas vous parler de moi non plus, parce que je ne sais jamais qu'en dire. N'est-ce pas assez de vous avoir parlé de feue ma mère, que vous n'avez ni vue ni connue? Joignez à cela une lettre de Mme de Sévigné, morte depuis cent ans,[16] et vous trouverez que je vous ai traité comme M. Silvin,[17] qu'on dit qui n'aime que les morts. J'espère cependant, mon cher petit-fils, qu'il vous restera quelque peu d'amitié pour les vivants, qui vous chérissent et vous honore[n]t, vous chériront et vous honoreront toujours, comme votre grand'-maman,

La Duchesse de Choiseul[18]

From UNKNOWN, Tuesday 29 December 1767

Printed for the first time from the MS now wsl. For the history of the MS see *ante* 25 July 1767.

Address: To the Honourable Hor.[1] Walpole Esq. at Strawberry Hill, Middlesex. *Postmark:* 29 ⟨D⟩E. FREE. JJ.

December 29th 1767.

Sir,

IT is with pleasure that I read in the papers that you intended to publish your *Doubts on the Reign of Richard III.*[2] I have long doubted—or rather been certain that it is full of falsities, and that no truth durst be published which favoured the House of York through the severe reign of that crafty tyrant Henry VII or through the boisterous reign of Henry VIII, when all anecdotes relating to Richard must be forgotten and the falsities against him firmly es-

---

16. Mme de Sévigné died in 1696.

17. George Selwyn, HW's friend and correspondent.

18. The two letters enclosed with this letter are printed in Monmerqué, op. cit. xi. ix–xii.

---

1. 'Edward' has been crossed out and 'Hor.' written above it in a different hand. The date-line appears to have been altered from January 29th 1768 to December 29th 1767.

2. Dodsley's advertisement ('Soon after Christmas will be published, *Historic Doubts on the Life and Reign of King Richard the Third.* By Mr Horace Walpole') appeared in the *London Chronicle* 22–4, 24–6 Dec., xxii. 607, 611; also in the *Public Advertiser* 24, 25 Dec. The book was published 1 Feb. 1768 (Hazen, *Bibl. of HW* 71).

tablished. Some of them which are recorded in every history are absolutely impossible. He could not have a withered arm, for his bitterest enemies allow that he was one of the bravest men of his time, that he killed Sir Edward Brandon[3] and fought like a lion at his death; battles on horseback and in armour required two arms and pretty strong ones, whereas a withered arm is always a weak one: therefore whatever Lord Hastings[4] was beheaded for, it could not be for Jane Shore[5] and the Queen's[6] bewitching his arm,[7] except it meant in an allegorical sense that their advice to Hastings obstructed his power. The melancholy death of Jane Shore, who he is said to have starved to death, is entirely a fiction, for Sir Thomas Moor,[8] who would by no means have exculpated the House of York, knew her when she was an old woman. As to Richard's shape, the Countess of Desmond's evidence[9] is from her own knowledge and is confirmed by the picture you mention at Lambeth,[10] which I could wish to have seen. Phillip of Commines mentions his seeing Edward IV and

3. Doubtless Sir William Brandon, Kt, 1485, who was killed by Richard in the Battle of Bosworth Field 22 Aug. 1485.

4. Sir William Hastings (ca 1431–83), Kt, 1461; cr. (1462) Bn Hastings. Alleging a conspiracy of Hastings and the Woodvilles against him, Richard accused them of treason at a meeting of the council in the Tower in June 1783 and ordered Hastings's immediate execution (P. M. Kendall, *Richard the Third*, New York, 1956, pp. 243–8; Alison Hanham, 'Richard III, Lord Hastings and the Historians,' *English Historical Review*, 1972, lxxxvii. 233–48).

5. Jane Shore (née ?Wainstead) (d. ?1527), m. (before 1483) William Shore; mistress of Edward IV and of Thomas Grey, 1st M. of Dorset.

6. Elizabeth Woodville (1437–92), m. 1 (ca 1452) Sir John Grey; m. 2 (1464) Edward IV of England.

7. The evidence for Richard's having a withered arm is slight; the story of his accusing the Queen and Jane Shore of having withered it 'by their sorcery and witchcraft' is told by Sir Thomas More in his *History of King Richard the Third* (*The Complete Works of St Thomas More*, New Haven, 1963– , ii. ed. R. S. Sylvester, 48). Richard probably suspected Jane Shore of serving as in-

termediary between Hastings and the Queen (Kendall, op. cit. 549–50).

8. Sir Thomas More (1478–1535), historian and philosopher; canonized 1935. HW cited More frequently in *Historic Doubts*, accusing him of 'palpable and material falsehoods' (*Works* ii. 121; see also DAL-RYMPLE 177). HW's copy of More's *History of . . . Edward the Fifth, with the Troublesome and Tyrannical Government of Richard the Third*, 1641, is Hazen, *Cat. of HW's Lib.*, No. 2247.

9. See *ante* 17 Sept. 1757 and n. 3. 'The old Countess of Desmond, who had danced with Richard, declared he was the handsomest man in the room except his brother Edward, and was very well made' (*Historic Doubts, Works* ii. 166).

10. 'Earl Rivers presenting his book and Caxton his printer to Edward IV, the Queen and Prince; from a curious MS in the Archbishop's library at Lambeth.' This caption appears in the engraved frontispiece to the first volume of HW's *Catalogue of the Royal and Noble Authors*, SH, 1758. 'The person in a cap and robe of state is probably Richard D. of Gloucester.' The Lambeth MS is fully documented in Pamela Tudor-Craig, *Richard III* (National Portrait Gallery catalogue), 1973, p. 31, No. 66.

Richard at the Duke of Burgundy's[11] court and he expatiates much upon Edward's beauty.[12] The second time that he saw him he says he was the handsomest man by far in either the French or English armies, though he was then grown fat and nothing so handsome as what he remembered him before.[13] If Richard had been so deformed as he is represented it would have been impossible for Phillip of Commines not to have taken notice of the very great contrast between the two brothers: I should think that if Richard had not been a very handsome man that he could scarce have failed to have mentioned his being unlike his brother, as he says so much of Edward's beauty. In regard to his murdering his nephews[14] in the Tower, it does not seem likely that if he had he would have spared young Warwick,[15] his elder brother Clarence's[16] son, whom Henry did not spare,[17] for though Clarence was attainted by Act of Parliament,[18] one Act of Parliament can repeal another. Sir Richard Brackenbury,[19] who it's said was turned out from the government of the Tower because he would not murder the Princes, if it had been so would scarce have lost his life for Richard in Bosworth field. Sir James Tyrrel,[20] who it is said caused them to be murdered, denied it at his death,[21] and had been ambassador from Henry, which would have been a very poor compliment to his Queen[22] to employ as his own representative the murderer of her brothers. It seems

11. Charles (1433–77) the Bold, D. of Burgundy.

12. See *ante* 17 Sept. 1757, nn. 17, 18.

13. 'He was young, and the most beautiful man of his time, I mean when he was in his adversity, for afterwards he grew very corpulent' (Philippe de Commines, *Memoirs*, trans. Thomas Uvedale, 1712, i. 257).

14. Edward V (1470–83), and Richard (1473–83), D. of York.

15. Edward (Plantagenet) (1475–99), 17th E. of Warwick; nephew of Richard III.

16. George (Plantagenet) (1449–78), cr. (1461) D. of Clarence and (1472) E. of Warwick and Salisbury.

17. In 1485 Henry VII imprisoned Warwick in the Tower, where he remained until he was executed for his supposed complicity with Perkin Warbeck (n. 23 below).

18. See *post* 19 Dec. 1775 and DALRYM-

PLE 176 n. 1. In 1478 Clarence was found guilty of high treason and was executed.

19. Doubtless Sir Robert Brackenbury (d. 1485), Kt, ?1485, Master of the Monies and constable of the Tower, 1783 (DNB, Supplement). He remained loyal to Richard and died with him at Bosworth Field.

20. See *ante* 25 July 1767, n. 4.

21. More's *Richard III* is the chief authority for the story of Tyrell's murdering the two princes. In 1501 Tyrell became involved in the conspiracy of Edmund de la Pole, Earl of Suffolk, and was imprisoned in the Tower. There, according to More, he was 'examined, and confessed the murther' before he was executed 6 May 1502 (Sylvester, op. cit. 86). The report of Tyrell's 'confession' was probably fabricated by Henry VII (Kendall, op. cit. 474–81). See *Historic Doubts, Works* ii. 138–42.

22. Elizabeth (1466–1503) of York, m. (1486) Henry VII.

very plain that Perkin Warbeck[23] was the real Duke of York. The
Duchess of Burgundy[24] must have had strong reasons to believe so,
for she never would have set up a phantom to dethrone her own
niece[25] and her family. Henry's own behaviour confirms who he was
by always sticking to his claim from the House of Lancaster, than
which nothing could be weaker, for though John of Gaunt[26] had
interest sufficient to get his natural children[27] legitimated by[28] Act
of Parliament, yet that very Act particularly excepts to their in-
heriting the Crown[29] and it is from one[30] of them that Henry was
descended, whereas his claim by his Queen was clear; she was the
eldest daughter of Edward IV, but he knew she had a brother
and when he made his appearance that claim would stand for
nothing. It is not sufficiently explained in history what could be the
reason why Henry found so strong a party for him against so valiant
and able a prince as Richard's laws testify him to have been. For my
own part, I think that these might be some of the reasons. Though
the Queen had many enemies on account of her raising her relations
who had been Lancastrians to the first posts, which were expected by
such as had ventured their lives and large estates in the most dangerous times for the House of York, and now found themselves sup-
planted by their old enemies that they had vanquished, yet notwithstanding their disappointments there were many friends to the
hereditary line of Edward, and who, upon seeing the right heir set
aside, might do anything for revenge against the usurper, as Lord
Hastings and others, who I cannot suppose to have been beheaded
but for some treason very sufficiently proved, as he and his family had
been such constant enemies to the House of Lancaster. There is

23. (ca 1474–99), pretender to the English throne. HW was convinced that
he was the true Duke of York; see ibid.
ii. 152–61.

24. Margaret (Plantagenet) (1446–1503),
sister of Richard III; m. (1468) Charles
the Bold, D. of Burgundy. She espoused
the cause of Perkin Warbeck, receiving
him at the court in the Netherlands as
her nephew Richard, Duke of York, and
writing in his favour to other princes.

25. See n. 22 above.

26. John (1340–99) of Gaunt, son of
Edward III; cr. (1362) D. of Lancaster.

27. Three sons and a daughter, all illegitimate; see GEC xii pt i. 39n.

28. 'My' in the MS.

29. His three sons were legitimated,
with the assent of Parliament, by letters
patent 9 Feb. 1397, 20 Richard II. The
patent of legitimation was confirmed 10
Feb. 1407 by Henry IV, but with the introduction of the clause *excepta dignitate
regali*, which was not in the original
patent (ibid. xii pt i. 40–1).

30. John Beaufort (ca 1371–1410), eld-
est son of John of Gaunt; cr. (1397) E. of
Somerset. He was a great-grandfather of
Henry VII.

another still stronger reason: the priests had a great share in the revolutions of those times, for they had vast influence over the people and large possessions, and Richard made no scruple of declaring that he hated those drones, the monks. The House of Lancaster had always favoured them. Henry IV was the first English King that burnt heretics, for which he is recorded as a merciful prince. Henry V persecuted the Lollards most furiously. Henry VI was notoriously superstitious and this Henry was reputed to be a very pious prince. There is likewise another reason, and that is the great severity of the House of York to their enemies; and as the numerous friends of the Earl of Warwick[31] had been involved in the ruin of the Lancastrians, it must have greatly swelled the account of the oppressed and dissatisfied throughout the Kingdom against a prince as relentless as his brother had been, who spared nobody. Some histories are so absurd as to say that Richard represented his mother[32] as a whore in order to prove that he himself was the only son to the Duke of York: he would have been as short in common sense as in common honesty. I write not these hints to inform you of what you knew before, but to show you there are others that think as you do and that your book will be read with great pleasure by strangers, as all your books have been, and particularly by, Sir,

Your most obedient servant

31. Sir Richard Nevill (1428–71), 16th E. of Warwick, 1449; called the 'king-maker.' His younger daughter, Lady Anne Nevill, married Richard, D. of Gloucester, in 1472.

32. Lady Cecily Nevill (1415–95), m. (1424) Richard, 3d D. of York.

From HANS STANLEY,[1] Monday 11 January 1768

Printed for the first time from the MS now WSL. For the history of the MS see *ante* 25 July 1767.

Althorpe,[2] Jan. 11th 1768.

Dear Sir,

AS you were pleased upon my mentioning to you that the widow[3] of Perkin Warbeck married again, had issue,[4] and died and was buried in Glamorganshire, to express some curiosity with regard to those facts, I wrote to a gentleman[5] in that neighbourhood, whose answer I received only last post, on account of his having been detained from home and sick. He tells me he shall send me farther particulars very soon.

The tomb is in what is called the Herbert's [A]isle in Swansea church.[6] The enclosed inscription[7] is round the edges of it in the old manner; it is shown people who come into that country as a curiosity. The singular event of Lady Catherine made me recollect it though it is above 20 years ago, and though I had entirely forgot that Sir Mathew Cradock was her second husband.

1. (1721–80), lord of the Admiralty 1757–65; chargé d'affaires, Paris, 1761; governor of the Isle of Wight 1764–6, 1770–80; ambassador designate to Russia, 1766; cofferer of the Household 1766–74, 1776–80; M.P.

2. Althorp, the seat of Stanley's friend Lord Spencer, near Northampton.

3. Lady Catherine Gordon (d. 1537), m. 1 (1496) Perkin Warbeck, remaining after his execution (1499) at the English court; m. 2 (ca 1512) James Strangways (d. 1515); m. 3 (1517) Sir Matthew Cradock (ca 1468–1531); m. 4 Christopher Assheton, of Fyfield, Berks (DALRYMPLE 121 n. 7).

4. Lady Catherine had no children in her four marriages (*Scots Peerage* iv. 530–1).

5. Not identified.

6. The tomb in the Cradock chapel of St Mary's Church, Swansea, was doubtless erected in the lifetime of Sir Matthew Cradock, with the effigies of both Sir Matthew and Lady Catherine upon it. She survived him, however, to marry Christopher Assheton, of Fyfield, near Abington, Berks. By her will, proved 5 Nov. 1537, she directed that her body 'be buried in the parish church of Fifield' (*Proceedings of the Society of Antiquaries of London*, 1847, 1st ser., i. 208; *Quarterly Journal of the Berks Archæological and Architectural Society*, 1893, iii. 48; J. M. Traherne, *Historical Notices of Sir Matthew Cradock, Knt*, Llandovery, 1840, pp. 6–10, 24; Thomas Nicholas, *Annals and Antiquities of the Counties and County Families of Wales*, 1872, ii. 575; *Vict. Co. Hist. Berks*, 1924, iv. 288, 346, 347–8).

7. Missing; see HW's notes on Stanley's letter below. HW printed the inscription 'obligingly communicated to me by Mr Stanley' in the 'Addition' to *Historic Doubts*, 1768, p. [135] (*Works* ii. 184). See also Traherne, op. cit. 12.

Mr Rice[8] and I inherit the Manor of Cadoxton[9] as being the heirs general of this marriage.[10] The estate passed by a daughter[11] to the Herberts, and by a daughter of theirs to the Hobys,[12] which branch ended in three coheiresses.[13] The second was married to Mr Rice's grandfather; the youngest was my grandmother. I have endeavoured to make this more intelligible by a little scratch of the descent,[14] but as it is my first attempt of the kind, I do not know whether you will understand it.

As I see by an advertisement,[15] you are going very soon to publish those very interesting historical inquiries you did me the honour to mention to me, I was unwilling to delay sending you the inscription. I do not understand the meaning of the words R. Morg.R.[16]

I shall be very soon in town, for which reason, as well as to save you trouble, I beg you would not think of answering this letter.[17]

I have the honour to be with a very respectful attachment,

> Dear Sir,
>   Your most obedient and most humble servant,
>
>   H. STANLEY

8. George Rice (?1724–79), of Newton Castle, Carmarthenshire; Treasurer of the Chamber 1770–9; M.P. He was a first cousin once removed of HW's friend George Montagu (MONTAGU i. 85 n. 40).

9. Cadoxton-juxta-Neath, Glamorganshire, South Wales. HW refers to the 'small estate in Wales' in his letter to Lady Ossory 17 Jan. 1780 reporting Hans Stanley's suicide (OSSORY ii. 162). By Stanley's will made in July 1779, this estate was left to Rice, but Rice's predecease (2 Aug. 1779) made it a lapsed legacy (ibid.).

10. See n. 3 above.

11. Margaret Cradock, m. 1 John Malefant, of St George's Castle, Glamorganshire; m. 2 Sir Richard Herbert (d. 1510), of Ewyas, Herefordshire. She was the daughter of Sir Matthew Cradock by his first marriage (1488) to Alice, daughter of Philip Mansel, of Oxwich Castle. George Rice and Hans Stanley were descended from her (Traherne, op. cit., 'Pedigree of Sir Matthew Cradock, Knt').

12. Mary Herbert, great-great-granddaughter of Sir Richard Herbert, of Ewyas, married Sir William Doddington; their daughter Catherine married Peregrine Hoby, of Bysham Abbey, Berks (ibid.).

13. Elizabeth, Catherine, and Anne, daughters of Philip Hoby (d. 1678), of Neath Abbey, Glamorganshire (son of Peregrine Hoby). Catherine, the second daughter, married Griffith Rice (1667–1729), of Newton Park, paternal grandfather of George Rice. Anne Hoby was married to William Stanley, Hans Stanley's paternal grandfather (ibid.; Collins, Peerage, 1812, vii. 507).

14. Printed below. The pedigree omits several generations and otherwise contains various errors; see post 10 Feb. 1768.

15. See previous letter, n. 2.

16. A misreading of the inscription on the tomb: '& Morgān' (Traherne, op. cit. 12).

17. No reply has been found.

[Enclosure]

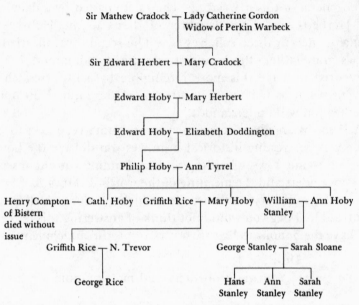

[HW's Notes on Stanley's Letter][18]

After the death of Perkin Warbeck, the Lady Katherine Gordon his widow, who from her marriage and exquisite beauty was called the White Rose of Scotland, was married to Sir Matthew Cradock, and is buried with him at Swansea in Wales, where their tomb still remains with this inscription in ancient characters

Here lies Sr Mathie Cradok Knight, some time Deputie unto the right honorable Charles Erle of Worcets in the Countie of Glamorgan R. Attor. G. R. Chauncelor of the same, Steward of Gower and Hilvie, and mi Ladie Katerin his Wife.

From this match are descended Mr Stanley and Mr Rice, as appears by the following table;

---

18. These notes, which were later revised for the 'Addition' to *Historic Doubts* (n. 7 above), appear on the verso of the blank leaf of Stanley's letter. See also n. 14 above.

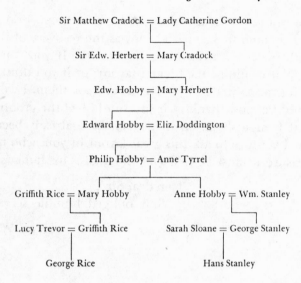

To Thomas Astle, Saturday 16 January 1768

Printed from the MS now WSL. First printed (with omissions), Toynbee vii. 155. Reprinted, Toynbee xv. 453. The MS was sold Sotheby's 23 Dec. 1896 (Autograph Letters and Historical Documents Sale), lot 275, to Boothe; resold Sotheby's 15 April 1899 (Autograph Letters and Historical Documents Sale), lot 198, to Maggs; resold Sotheby's 18 July 1904 (property of F. Clarke), lot 125, to Ellis, who sold it to E. Percival Merritt, of Boston; sold from the Merritt collection by Goodspeed's to WSL, May 1943.

Endorsed in an unidentified hand: 307.

Address: To Thomas Astle Esq. inquire at Mr Ancel's[1] at the Treasury or at the Bishop of Carlisle's.[2] [Not sent through the post.]

Saturday night Jan. 16th 1768.

Dear Sir,

MR Hume[3] has told me today that you have been so very kind as to say that Mr Duane[4] is possessed of my father's papers, which we have reckoned so invaluable a loss to our family, and that you

---

1. Not identified.
2. HW's friend Charles Lyttelton, Bishop of Carlisle, had a house in Clifford Street, where he died 22 Dec. 1768 (Nichols, *Lit. Anec.* v. 380).

3. 'David Hume the historian' (MS note in an unidentified hand on the letter).
4. See *ante* 20 May 1762, n. 3.

thought he would not be averse to let me have them. I do not know the thing that could make me so happy as the recovery of them,[5] nor which would be so great an obligation to me. If you could obtain them for me, it would be the highest favour; or if you think it would be proper for me to write to Mr Duane and ask them, I would do it. Still I should be most thankful if you would feel the ground for me, and learn if I might hope for them. You have already been so kind to me, that I venture to ask this great favour of you, who may judge what a treasure it must be to a son who adores his father's memory.

I am dear Sir
Your obliged humble servant

HOR. WALPOLE

5. William Coxe, in his *Memoirs of the Life and Administration of Sir Robert Walpole, Earl of Orford,* 1798, i. xvi, xxii–xxiii, mentions papers of Sir Robert which were in HW's possession, but it is unlikely that they were the papers referred to in this letter. We have found no evidence that Duane ever had in his possession or turned over to HW any of Sir Robert's papers; almost all of those which survived were among the Cholmondeley MSS (G. A. Chinnery, *A Handlist of the Cholmondeley (Houghton) MSS, Sir Robert Walpole's Archive,* Cambridge, 1953, p. 5).

From Thomas Astle, Tuesday 26 January 1768

Printed for the first time from the MS now WSL. For the history of the MS see *ante* 25 July 1767.

HW must have been sent this letter concerning Richard III when he was engaged on *Historic Doubts;* 26 January fell on Tuesday in 1768, less than a week before publication of the book.

Address: To the Honourable Mr Walpole. [Not sent through the post.]

Treasury, Tuesday, Jan. 26th.

Dear Sir,

ON the other side I send you a transcript of the letter[1] I mentioned to you when I had the honour of seeing you last. I am with great truth,

Your obedient humble servant,

THOS. ASTLE

[Enclosure]

Richard the 3d to the Mayor of Windsor.[2]
By the King.

R Rex

TRUSTY & well beloved We greet you well, And forasmuch, as wee *are* credibly informed yt our Rebells & Traitours now Confedered with our Ancyent Enemyes of France, by many & sundry ways conspire & study the means to yr Subversion of this our Realme, & of Unity amongst our Subjects, as in sending Writings by seditious Persons, which counterfeyt & contrive Invenc̄ons tydings & rumours, to th'intent, to provoke & stirre Discord & Division betwixt us & our Lds which be as faithfully disposed as any subjects can suffice, We

1. Richard III to the Mayor of Windsor 6 Dec. 1484, printed below. Astle transcribed the letter from BM Harleian MS 787, f. 2b, which is itself a much later transcript of the original (not located). Astle compiled the index to the *Catalogue of the Harleian Collection of Manuscripts,* 2 vols, 1759, in which the letter is listed as follows (vol. I, p. 438, No. 6): 'K. Richard III to the Mayor of Windsor; commanding him to inquire after apprehend, and punish, the first shewers and utterers of false rumours, i.e. of news touching the then Earl of Richmond' (information kindly communicated by Mr Albert Makinson). HW's 'Memoranda, from Catalogue of the Harleian MSS' used in writing *Historic Doubts* is now WSL; his annotated copy of the *Catalogue* is also at Farmington (Hazen, *Cat. of HW's Lib.,* No. 218).

2. Astle's transcript, which follows closely Harleian MS 787, f. 2b, has not been normalized.

therefore will & command you streightly yt in eschewing of ye In-
convenients above said you put you in your utmost desire if any
such rumours or writings come amongst you to search & enquire ye
first shewers & utterers thereof and them yt ye shall so find ye doe
commit unto sure ward, & after proceed to their sharp punishment
in example & fears of all other, not failing hereof in any wise as ye
entend to please us & will answer unto us at your Perils.

Geoven under our Signet at our Palace of Westminster ye 6th
day of Decr.

To GEORGE ONSLOW,[1] Sunday 31 January 1768

Printed for the first time from a photostat of the MS in the Henry E. Huntington Library, inserted in HW's presentation copy of *Historic Doubts* to
George Onslow. For the history of this copy see Hazen, *Bibl. of HW* 74, copy
12.

Jan. 31, 1768.[2]

MR Walpole is ashamed to trouble Mr Onslow at such a time
with the enclosed work,[3] but does it in obedience to the commands of Mr Onslow's father,[4] who desired it might be sent as soon
as possible; and Mr Walpole cannot omit any opportunity of paying
regard where he feels so much. Mr Walpole has not troubled Mr
Onslow with inquiries, choosing to inform himself by others to
avoid giving Mr Onslow that pain, and is very unhappy at receiving
no better accounts.

1. (1731–1814), 4th Bn Onslow, 1776;
cr. (1801) E. of Onslow; M.P.
2. Not in HW's hand; presumably
added by George Onslow.
3. A copy of HW's *Historic Doubts on
the Life and Reign of King Richard the
Third*, 1768; see headnote.

4. Arthur Onslow, HW's occasional
correspondent, who died 17 Feb. 1768.
'His death was long and dreadfully painful, but he supported his agony with
great patience, dignity, good humour, and
even good breeding' (HW to Mann 26
Feb. 1768, MANN vi. 585).

From Andrew Coltee Ducarel,
Saturday 6 February 1768

Printed from the MS now WSL. First printed, Nichols, *Lit. Anec.* iv. 706 (enclosure omitted). For the history of the MS see *ante* 25 July 1767. Ducarel's MS draft of this letter is also now WSL; for its history see *ante* 23 Feb. 1762.

Doctors Commons, Feb. 6, 1768.

Sir,

I AM greatly obliged to you for your very kind present of the *Historic Doubts*. That learned work has afforded me much instruction and a singular satisfaction.

The coronation roll mentioned p. 65[1] I had seen, with astonishment, seven or eight years ago; and have long since been convinced that a true history of England can only be drawn from records.

On this occasion, Sir, I have examined the register book of Archbishop Bourchier[2] under my custody at Lambeth,[3] and hope the enclosed extracts therefrom[4] will not prove unacceptable to you. I have the honour to remain with great esteem,

Sir,
Your most obliged and faithful humble servant,

AND. COLTEE DUCAREL

Hon. Horace Walpole Esq.

---

1. 'This singular curiosity was first mentioned to me by the Lord Bishop of Carlisle. Mr Astle lent me an extract of it, with other useful assistances; and Mr Chamberlain of the Great Wardrobe obliged me with the perusal of the original' (*Historic Doubts on the Life and Reign of King Richard the Third*, 1768, p. 65n; *Works* ii. 146n). HW later admitted that the document was a wardrobe account and not a coronation roll; see GRAY i. 46 n. 318 and MASON i. 238 n. 13.

2. Thomas Bourchier (ca 1404–86), cardinal, 1467; Abp of Canterbury 1454–86. See n. 7 below.

3. Ducarel was Keeper of the Archiepiscopal Library at Lambeth.

4. Printed below. Ducarel also sent HW three pages of 'Extracts relating to Kings Edward IV, Edward V, and Richard III, taken from a register book at Lambeth called *Morton, Dene, Bourchier, and Courtney*.' This MS, now WSL, was endorsed by Ducarel: 'Doctors Commons, March 3d 1768 / For the Hon. Horace Walpole.' Some of these extracts were later printed by John Nichols; see n. 16 below.

[Enclosure]

Extracted from a register book at Lambeth, called *Morton,*[5] *Dene,*[6] *Bourchier, Courtney.*[7]

Commissio d[omi]ni Archiep[iscop]i (Bourchier) directa d[omi]no Thom[a]e,[8] Ebor[acensis] Archiep[iscop]o et D[omi]nis Joh[ann]i[9] Lync[olniensis], Edwardo[10] Cycestren[sis], et Joh[ann]i[11] Elien[sis] Episcopis; necnon D[omi]nis Will[ilmi] Hastynges[12] d[omi]no de Hastynge, Tho[mæ] Stanley[13] d[omi]no de Stanley, ac Tho[mæ] Mongomery[14] militi, Executoribus in Testamento et ultima voluntate felicis memori[a]e Edwardi quarti nuper Regis Angli[a]e et Franci[a]e nominat. Pro Funeralium[15] expensis dicti Regis Solvendis, quæ ad estimationem MCCCCLXXXXVI libr. XVII sol. II den. se extendunt. Dat[um] apud Knoll 23 die Maii A.D. 1483. fol. 175b.[16]

Juramentum et Professio d[omi]ni Ricardi Regis Angli[a]e tempore Coronationis Sue. ibid. fol. 1772a.

Thomas Rotheram, Archbishop of York
John Russell, Bishop of Lincoln
Edward Story, Bishop of Chichester   A.D. 1483
John Morton, Bishop of Ely

5. John Morton (ca 1420–1500), Bp of Ely 1479–86; Abp of Canterbury 1486–1500.

6. Henry Deane (d. 1503), Abp of Canterbury 1501–3.

7. William Courtenay (ca 1342–96), Abp of Canterbury 1381–96. The book is one of two registers kept by Archbishop Courtenay during his primacy, a 'folio volume containing also registers of the archbishops Bourgchier, Morton, and Deane' ([H. J. Todd,] *A Catalogue of all the Archiepiscopal Manuscripts in the Library at Lambeth Palace. With an Account of the Archiepiscopal Registers and Other Records There Preserved,* 1812, p. 266).

8. Thomas Rotherham (1423–1500), Abp of York 1480–1500.

9. John Russell (d. 1494), Bp of Rochester 1476–80, of Lincoln 1480–94.

10. Edward Story (d. 1503), Bp of Carlisle 1468–78, of Chichester 1478–1503.

11. See n. 5 above.

12. See *ante* 29 Dec. 1767, n. 4.

13. Sir Thomas Stanley (ca 1435–1504), 2d Lord Stanley, 1459; Kt, 1460; cr. (1485) E. of Derby.

14. Sir Thomas Montgomery (d. 1495), Kt, 1461.

15. 17–20 April 1483.

16. This 'extract' from the register book of Archbishop Bourchier is actually a summary made by Ducarel of the original document, which is a letter from Bourchier to the executors of Edward IV; the complete text of the letter is printed in *Registrum Thome Bourgchier,* ed. F. R. H. Du Boulay, Oxford, 1957, pp. 54–5 (Canterbury and York Society series, vol. liv). The executors named in the letter are not the same as those named in Edward's will dated 20 June 1475 (transcribed by Rymer in [Samuel Bentley], *Excerpta historica, or, Illustrations of English History,* 1831, pp. 366–79). Apparently Ed-

From the COMTE DU CHÂTELET,[1]
Sunday 7 February 1768

Printed from Toynbee *Supp.* iii. 208, where the letter was first printed. Damer-Waller; the MS was sold Sotheby's 5 Dec. 1921 (first Waller Sale), lot 117, to Maggs; not further traced.

Great George Street, ce 7 février 1768.

LE Comte du Châtelet présente ses compliments à Monsieur Horace Walpole, et comme il n'a peut-être pas encore reçu la pièce intitulée *Les Trois empereurs,*[2] M. du Châtelet pense qu'elle pourrait lui faire plaisir. Il a l'honneur de la lui envoyer et de le prier de la garder à sa disposition soit pour la lire soit pour la faire copier.

From LORD CAMDEN, Monday 8 February 1768

Printed for the first time from the MS now WSL. For the history of the MS see *ante* 25 July 1767.

Lincoln's Inn Fields, February 8, 1768.

Dear Sir,

I HAVE deferred thanking you for your book[1] till I had read it, because I was desirous of knowing the value of your present, first that I might proportion my acknowledgment to the merit of the

ward made another will after 1475 or added codicils to his 1475 will; see *The Usurpation of Richard the Third,* ed. C. A. J. Armstrong, 2d edn, Oxford, 1969, p. 107, n. 7. Ducarel later communicated the same letter to John Nichols, who printed it in *A Collection of All the Wills, now Known to be Extant, of the Kings and Queens of England,* 1780, pp. 347–8. Nichols, who was unaware of the existence of the 1475 will, argued that Edward had clearly made a will but that 'probably it was intentionally destroyed during the usurpation of his brother Richard III' (ibid. 345). Ducarel's own extracts from Bourchier's register book are in Lambeth Palace Library MS 1351, ff. 78–83.

1. Louis-Marie-Florent (1727–93), Comte (Duc, 1777) du Châtelet; French ambassa-

dor to England 1767–70 (DU DEFFAND i. 237 n. 8; *Dict. de biographie française* xi. 1197–9). HW entertained him at SH in May 1769 (MONTAGU ii. 278); he later described Du Châtelet as 'the most peevish, and insolent of men, our [England's] bitter enemy' (HW to Mann 29 Dec. 1770, MANN vii. 258).

2. *Les Trois empereurs en Sorbonne,* [Geneva], 1768, a satirical poem by 'M. l'Abbé Caille' (a pseudonym used by Voltaire; see Georges Bengesco, *Voltaire: Bibliographie de ses œuvres,* 1882–90, i. 198–9, No. 695). This title does not appear in the SH records.

1. *Historic Doubts on the Life and Reign of King Richard the Third,* published 1 Feb. 1768.

work. I have perused it, am delighted with the composition and accede to the argument. I always had my doubts concerning the real person of Perkin Warbeck,[2] and now have much stronger reason to suspect him to be a true Plantagenet than ever. Your note of our three chancellors[3] is just: Sir Thomas Moore was a boy when he wrote his history;[4] the other two were arrant knaves. I shall avoid the rock of history, and confine myself to the honest pale of my own profession. Now I have perused the work, I can with a safe conscience and without flattery not only thank you for your civility, but put a price upon the present by declaring that the worth of the gift is more valuable than the courtesy of giving.

I have the honour, dear Sir, to be with the truest respect and esteem,

Your most obedient faithful servant,

CAMDEN

From HANS STANLEY, Wednesday 10 February 1768

Printed for the first time from the MS now WSL. For the history of the MS see *ante* 25 July 1767.

Privy Garden, Feb. 10th 1768.

Dear Sir,

I RECEIVED from Wales by last post an inscription[1] upon a monument in the Herbert's [A]isle in Swansea church in Glamorganshire; it contains nothing relative to the person of Perkin Warbeck's

2. See *ante* 29 Dec. 1767, n. 23.

3. 'And here let me lament that two of the greatest men in our annals have prostituted their admirable pens, the one to blacken a great prince, the other to varnish a pitiful tyrant. I mean the two chancellors, Sir Thomas More and Lord Bacon. . . . It is unfortunate, that another great chancellor should have written a history with the same propensity to misrepresentation, I mean Lord Clarendon. It is hoped no more chancellors will write our story, till they can divest themselves of that habit of their profession, apologizing for a bad cause'

(*Historic Doubts*, p. 63 and n; *Works* ii. 144–5).

4. More was born in 1478; he probably began to write his *History of King Richard the Third* between 1514 and 1518 and may have continued to work on it intermittently until the 1530s (*The Complete Works of St Thomas More*, New Haven, 1963– , ii. ed. R. S. Sylvester, lxiii–lxv; Alison Hanham, *Richard III and His Early Historians 1483–1535*, Oxford, 1975, pp. 217–19).

1. Enclosed with the letter and printed below.

widow, but it sets right some errors with regard to her descendants, which I committed in that abstract which I sent you[2] merely upon my imperfect recollection when I was at Althorpe, where I had no papers by me.

If they could never have affected any other point but the descent of so inconsiderable a person as myself, I should not have given you a second trouble by correcting them, but as you sometimes amuse yourself with disquisitions of this kind, I was afraid that some error in which I might have led you, might at a future time embarrass you in other points.

The pedigree at present enclosed[3] is, I believe, free from mistakes. I had occasion to trace it pretty far back in a lawsuit some years ago, and it was conformable to the title deeds of the Cadoxton estate, which Mr Rice and I inherit from Sir M. Cradock.

It is with a great deal of diffidence, that I propose a doubt to you, with regard to the obliging note you have pleased to insert at the end of your *Historic Doubts,* in which you do me the honour of mentioning me.

You say that Sir Edward Herbert[4] was the son of the first Earl of Pembroke;[5] some papers I have mention him to have been Comptroller of the Household to Henry VIII. I have not the *British Compendium*[6] by me, but in the list of the Peerage,[7] I find the creation of that title to have been in 1551 Temp. Ed. VI.

It appears that the elder branch of the family ended in Mary Herbert, the mother of Sir William Doddington,[8] and that she was the heir general to the estate.

2. *Ante* 11 Jan. 1768.

3. Printed below; it corrects some of the errors contained in the pedigree sent previously, but it is not 'free from mistakes.' Cf. the 'Pedigree of Sir Matthew Cradock, Knt' in J. M. Traherne, *Historical Notices of Sir Matthew Cradock, Knt,* Llandovery, 1840.

4. (d. 1595), of Powis Castle; Kt, 1574; second son of William Herbert (ca 1506–70), cr. (1551) E. of Pembroke; m. Mary Stanley, dau. of Thomas Stanley, of Standon, Herts. His eldest son and heir was William Herbert (ca 1573–1656), cr. (1629) Bn Powis (GEC *sub* Powis; *Collections Historical and Archæological Relating to Montgomeryshire,* 1872, v. 170–5).

5. 'They [Sir Matthew Cradock and his wife] had a daughter Mary, who was married to Sir Edward Herbert, son of the first Earl of Pembroke; and from that match are descended the Earls of Pembroke and Powis, Hans Stanley, Esq.; George Rice, Esq.; etc.' ('Addition' to *Historic Doubts,* 1768, p. [135]).

6. [Francis Nichols], *The British Compendium: Or, Rudiments of Honour,* 3 vols, 1725–7. HW's copy, now WSL, is Hazen, *Cat. of HW's Lib.,* No. 755.

7. See *Court and City Register,* 1768, p. 4.

8. Mary Herbert was the wife of Sir William Doddington; see *ante* 11 Jan. 1768, n. 12. On the death of her father, Sir John Herbert, in 1617, the manor

My difficulty is how Sir Edward and Sir George Herbert[9] came not to have the title, if the one was the son and the other the grandson of the first Earl of Pembroke?[10] and why the creation is placed at so much a later date?

I do not mean to give you the trouble of writing me an answer to a question so very immaterial, but if you happen to remember it, you will be so good as to satisfy this idle curiosity when I have the pleasure of meeting you.

I have the honour to be with the most respectful and affectionate esteem,

Dear Sir,
Your very obedient and most humble servant,

H. STANLEY

[Enclosures]

Endorsed by Stanley on the verso: Inscription on a monument in the church of Swansea.

Inscription on a Monument in Swansea Church

Here
Lyeth The Body of
Philip Hoby of the Abby of Neath, in this County Esqr, Fourth Son to Peregrine Hoby of Bisham in the County of Berks Esqr, by Catherine Daughter to Sir William Dodington of Breymore in the County of Southampton Knight by Mary the Daughter and sole Heir of Sir John Herbert[11] Knight, and Secretary of State to Queen Elizabeth.

Who departed this Life the 15th of June 1678 and the first Day of July following was brought to this place to be interred with one

estate was divided between Mary and her first cousin, William Herbert, son of Sir John's brother, Nicholas (J. S. Corbett, *Glamorgan: Papers and Notes on the Lordship and its Members,* Cardiff, 1925, pp. 100–1 [*Transactions of the Cardiff Naturalists' Society,* vol. lvi]).

9. (d. 1570), of Swansea; younger brother of William, 1st E. of Pembroke (Traherne, loc cit.).

10. Sir Edward Herbert had a second son who was also named George (*Montgomeryshire Collections* v. 174), but the title passed to the eldest sons of the 1st and 2d Earls of Pembroke, respectively.

11. (ca 1550–1617), Kt, 1617; Master of Requests; second secretary of state, 1600 (Traherne, loc. cit.; *Calendar of State Papers, Domestic Series . . . 1598–1601,* 1869, p. 437; W. A. Shaw, *The Knights of England,* 1906, ii. 160).

of his Ancestors, Sir Mathew Cradock Knight, Grandfather to Sir George Herbert Knight, The Father of the said, Sir John, and eldest brother to William the First Earl of Pembroke[12] of this Family of the House of Pembroke now in being.

On the North Side of the same Tomb.

He was married to
Elizabeth[13]

Eldest Daughter of Sir Timothy Tyrrell of Shottover in the County of Oxford Knight by Elizabeth[14] the sole and only Daughter of the most Reverend Father in God James Usher of famous Memory late Ld Archbishop of Armagh, and Primate of all Ireland by whom he left behind him three Daughters to inherit the Antient Monastery of the Abby of Neath, and the Lordship and Manor of Cadoxton which Monastery, Lordship, and Manor was given to their Father by his Uncle Edward Dodington Esqr Son to the said Sir William to whom it descended by Mary his Mother, Daughter to Sir John Herbert aforesaid.

On the Top of the Tomb.

Here also lyeth the Body of Elizabeth the Widow, and Relict of Philip Hoby Esqr who departed this life the 27th Day of August. An. Dom. 1699.

Endorsed by Stanley on the verso: Pedigree of some of the descendants of Sir Mathew Cradock and Lady Catherine Gordon, widow of Perkin Warbeck. From a monument in the church of Swansea in Glamorganshire.

---

12. Sir John Herbert was the son of Matthew Herbert, of Swansea, and a grandson of Sir George Herbert, who was a younger brother of the 1st Earl of Pembroke (Traherne, loc. cit.).

13. Elizabeth Tyrrell (d. 1699), dau. of Sir Timothy Tyrrell (ca 1618–1701), of Oakley, Bucks, and (later) Shotover, Oxfordshire; m. Philip Hoby.

14. Elizabeth Ussher (ca 1619–93), only child of James Ussher (1581–1656), Abp of Armagh, 1625; m. (1641) Sir Timothy Tyrrell (DNB *sub* James Ussher).

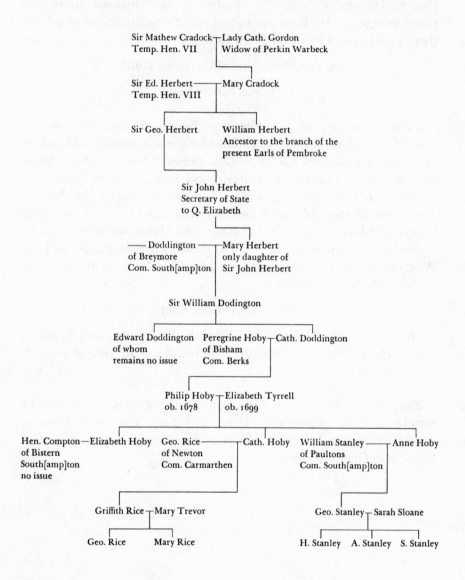

Sir Mathew Cradock — Lady Cath. Gordon
Temp. Hen. VII   Widow of Perkin Warbeck

Sir Ed. Herbert ——— Mary Cradock
Temp. Hen. VIII

Sir Geo. Herbert   William Herbert
                     Ancestor to the branch of the
                     present Earls of Pembroke

Sir John Herbert
Secretary of State
to Q. Elizabeth

—— Doddington ——— Mary Herbert
of Breymore   only daughter of
Com. South[amp]ton   Sir John Herbert

Sir William Dodington

Edward Doddington   Peregrine Hoby — Cath. Doddington
of whom   of Bisham
remains no issue   Com. Berks

Philip Hoby — Elizabeth Tyrrell
ob. 1678   ob. 1699

Hen. Compton — Elizabeth Hoby   Geo. Rice ——— Cath. Hoby   William Stanley ——— Anne Hoby
of Bistern   of Newton   of Paultons
South[amp]ton   Com. Carmarthen   Com. South[amp]ton
no issue

Griffith Rice — Mary Trevor   Geo. Stanley — Sarah Sloane

Geo. Rice   Mary Rice   H. Stanley   A. Stanley   S. Stanley

From ? SIR BROOK BRIDGES,[1]
Wednesday 10 February 1768

Printed for the first time from the MS now WSL. For the history of the MS see *ante* 25 July 1767.

The postmark 'FREE' on the letter indicates that HW's anonymous correspondent is a peer or M.P. The close proximity of Wingham and Lee Priory (the seat of 'Mr Barret, my neighbour') to Goodnestone Park suggests that the writer is Sir Brook Bridges, who was M.P. for Kent 1763–74.

Address: To the Honourable Mr Horace Walpole, Arlington Street, London.
Postmark: 10 FE. FREE.

Wingham in Kent, Feb. 10, 1768.

THIS picture is in the possession of a Kentish gentleman and has been in his family time out of mind, something damaged and rubbed, and is on boards, in bad condition.

Kinge Rychard The III

A small half length, i.e. to the waist—small life.

23 inches high ⎫
17 inches wide ⎭ the painted part only

A wize[n]ed withered shrunk face, greyish eyes, thin lips, an out-under jaw and chin, more than the proportion dark reddish hair, short and lank, a little turned up in a curl at the tips, sour ill look. The left hand is taking off a ring from the little finger of the right. The next finger has another ring, and likewise the thumb, long small fingers. Complexion pale, owing perhaps to length of time. A cap much like the cut before his history in Rapin.[2] I have mislaid Mr H. W. *Painters.*[3] His body turned the different way, so that his

---

1. (1733–91), of Goodnestone Park, Kent; 3d Bt, 1733; M.P.

2. Paul de Rapin-Thoyras, *The History of England*, trans. Nicholas Tindal, 3d edn ('Illustrated with . . . the Heads and Monuments of the Kings'), 4 vols in 5, 1743–7. George Vertue's engraving of Richard III, 'From an Ancient Original Painting on Board at Kensington Palace,' appears in vol. I, facing p. 637, at the beginning of the account of Richard's reign. HW did not own a copy of this edition, but he did have Vertue's *Heads of the Kings of England proper for Mr Rapin's History*, 1736, in which the en-graving of Richard was first published (Hazen, *Cat. of HW's Lib.*, No. 3663). The original painting is doubtless that in the Royal Collection at Windsor, which is among the earliest surviving portraits of Richard and the prototype for many later copies. The picture described here has not been located, but it was clearly of the Windsor type; see Pamela Tudor-Craig, *Richard III* (National Portrait Gallery catalogue), 2d edn, 1977, esp. p. 93, No. P44.

3. 'Richard III . . . appears in another old picture at Kensington' (*Anecdotes of Painting*, SH, 1762–71, i. 44).

right shoulder is the part advanced. The robe seems to have been purple, plaited, lined with fur, underneath cloth of gold, striped and spotted, discovered by slashed sleeves. The cap with the gold scalloped buckle or button, like Rapin's cut, the countenance resembling this picture very much. The gold collar over the shoulder exactly the same, the shape of the hair etc. And as I find that was engraved by Virtue, and probably from the drawing mentioned by Mr W.,[4] I believe this picture produced that drawing.[5] It is very ancient and came into possession of the forenamed family when a very learned and curious antiquary[6] was at the head of it above 100 years ago. There are thoughts of sending it up to be secured, either by Anderson[7] or some other painter. I imagine the cut in Rapin is the different position from the drawing.

I think if Richard's right shoulder was visibly out of proportion, the painter would not have placed his body so as to render it most perspicuous, unless it was to show how little the disproportion is, which is scarce discernable.

Mr Barret,[8] my neighbour, admired this picture for its antiquity and because he said he never saw or knew of any portrait of Richard III.

Upon recollection, the drawing cannot be connected with this picture, because of the hands[9]—what the meaning of his taking off his ring I do not know.

4. 'Among the drawings which I purchased at Vertue's sale was one of Richard and his queen, of which nothing is expressed but the outlines. There is no intimation from whence the drawing was taken; but . . . if not copied from a picture, it certainly was from some painted window; . . . I have given two prints of this drawing, which is on large folio paper, that it may lead to a discovery of the original, if not destroyed' (*Historic Doubts on the Life and Reign of King Richard the Third*, 1768, pp. 103–4). The two prints appear as the frontispiece to *Historic Doubts* and facing p. 103. Vertue's drawing was sold SH xi. 112 and is now WSL (see illustration); the whereabouts of the original is not known.

5. See n. 9 below.

6. Possibly Sir John Marsham (1602–85), of Cuxton, Kent; Kt, 1660; cr. (1663) Bt; M.P.; author of *Chronicus canon ægyptiacus, ebraicus, græcus et disquisitiones*, 1672, and other works on chronology. His granddaughter, Margaretta Marsham (1684–1719), married Sir Brook Bridges, 1st Bt, in 1707.

7. Not identified.

8. Thomas Barret (?1743–1803), M.P.; HW's friend and occasional correspondent. His seat, Lee Priory, near Canterbury, was about three miles from Goodnestone Park.

9. In Vertue's drawing Richard holds the sword of state in his right hand and the orb in his left hand, whereas in the painting Richard is playing with the ring on the little finger of his right hand.

Ricardus tertius Rex
anglie & francie & Dns hibnie

VIII.

Dna anna filia Rici Comitis Warici
Dei gra Regina anglie & francie &
Dna hibnie

**VERTUE'S DRAWING OF RICHARD III
AND QUEEN ANNE**

From the REV. JAMES GRANGER,
Thursday 11 February 1768

Printed from a photostat of the MS in the British Museum (Add. MS 28,104, f. 42). First printed in *Letters between the Rev. James Granger . . . and Many of the Most Eminent Literary Men of his Time*, ed. J. P. Malcolm, 1805, pp. 18–19. The MS was acquired by the BM in 1869; for its probable earlier history see *ante* 24 April 1764.

Endorsed in an unidentified hand: Lot 410.

Shiplake, 11th Feb. 1768.

Honoured Sir,

I YESTERDAY received your very kind and much esteemed present of the *Historical Doubts of the Life and Reign of King Richard the Third,* for which I return you my sincerest thanks. I am not only grateful for that favour, but also proud of the distinction which it confers. I opened the book with all the eagerness with which I had before entered upon the perusal of your works; but being soon after called away in business was obliged to suspend that appetite which a partial reading of so interesting a history must necessarily excite. Thus much, Sir, I have collected in general, concerning your subject, that it required great labour, as well as the nicest judgment, to wash away the false daubing which was so intimately blended with the character of Richard: and that to have discovered the real person of the Duke of York in that of Perkin Warbec,[1] was fetching up truth from the bottom of her well, and must have required a chain of many links. I shall, Sir, upon your authority, make an alteration in that part of my book[2] which relates to Richard the Third.[3] Sir William Musgrave[4] tells me, that

1. See *ante* 29 Dec. 1767, n. 23.

2. *A Biographical History of England*, 2 vols in 4, 1769. See *ante* 3 April 1764, n. 2.

3. Granger added the following note to his account of Richard III: "Mr Walpole, who is well known to have struck new light into some of the darkest passages of English history, has brought various presumptive proofs, unknown to Buck, that Richard was neither that deformed person, nor that monster of cruelty and impiety, which he has been represented by our historians. But it must be acknowledged, that though this

gentleman has done much towards clearing up the character of Richard, that he has left the matter still problematical. His arguments to prove that Perkin Warbeck was the real Duke of York, appear more conclusive. I am assured by a good hand, that the Lord Treasurer Oxford, who read as much of our history, and with as much judgment, as any man of his time, was entirely of that opinion' (*Biographical History* i. 18n).

4. Through Musgrave's offices Granger had obtained HW's 'protection . . . assistance and advice' for the *Biographical History* (*ante* 3 April 1764).

he has received that 'great pleasure' which I speedily promise myself from the entire perusal of your work.

I am, Sir, with the greatest respect,
Your most obliged and truly grateful humble servant,

JAMES GRANGER

From LORD SANDWICH, Wednesday 17 February 1768

Printed for the first time from the MS now WSL. For the history of the MS see *ante* 25 July 1767.

Kimbolton,[1] Feb. 17, 1768.

Dear Sir,

LOOKING over some old papers which the Duke of Manchester has in his possession, I saw a very curious pedigree drawn in the time of King Richard the Third,[2] in which is a drawing[3] of himself, his wife Lady Anne,[4] and his son Edward Prince of Wales.[5] The drawing is extremely fresh and well done, and Richard is drawn as a straight and comely person; there is also an inscription under his figure, which I send you herewith.[6]

1. Kimbolton Castle, Hunts, the seat of George Montagu (1737–88), 4th D. of Manchester, 1762. Manchester and Sandwich were fifth cousins.

2. The English version of the so-called Rous Roll, one of two armorial roll chronicles executed by the antiquary John Rous (?1411–91) to celebrate the history of the earls of Warwick; it was acquired by the British Museum in 1955 and is now BM Add. MS 48,976. The roll, twenty-four feet long, contains sixty-four pen-and-ink portraits of the earls of Warwick and of their royal and other benefactors, including Richard III, his queen, and their son. Above each figure is a painted coat of arms, with a brief biographical notice in English below. This 'Yorkist' roll in English was completed sometime before the Battle of Bosworth Field 22 Aug. 1485; the 'Lancastrian' version in Latin, apparently altered by Rous after Bosworth, has been

in the possession of the College of Arms since 1786 (C. E. Wright, 'The Rous Roll: The English Version,' *British Museum Quarterly*, 1955–6, xx. 77–81).

3. Illustrated ibid. pl. XXVII, following p. 96. HW later 'had some of the portraits not only copied but engraved for a second edition of my *Historic Doubts*' (HW to George Nicol *post* 6 July 1790); see *Works* ii. following p. 166.

4. Lady Anne Nevill (1456–85), m. 1 (1470) Edward (1453–71), P. of Wales, son of Henry VI; m. 2 (1472) Richard, D. of Gloucester, afterwards K. of England as Richard III.

5. (1473–84), only son of Richard III.

6. Printed below; HW quoted the inscription in the 'Supplement to the Historic Doubts,' *Works* ii. 217. George Hardinge also communicated the inscription to HW in his letter of 17 July 1780 (CHUTE 607).

If these materials are of any use to you his Grace of Manchester will I dare say very readily give you a sight of the original.[7]

I am with great truth and regard,
Your most obedient and most humble servant,

SANDWICH

If you favour me with an answer be so good as to direct to me at Hinchingbrook.

[Enclosure][8]

The moost myghty prynce Rychard by the grace of god Kynge of Yngland and of fraunce and Lord of Yreland by verrey matrymony w^{t}out dyscontynuans or any defylinge yn the lawe by eyre male lineally dyscending fro kyng harre the second [all avaryce] set a syde [rewled] hys subjettys. In his realme ful commendably punyshynge offenders of his Laws specyally extortioners and oppressers of hys comyns & chereshynge tho' yat were virtues by the whych dyscrete guydynge he gat grete thank of god & love of all hys subjettys ryche and pore and gret laud of the people of all othyr landys abowt hym.

N.B. The blanks I cannot well fill up, but I dare say you will be able to do it the moment you see the original.

7. HW wrote Gray 26 Feb. 1768: 'Lord Sandwich . . . very obligingly sent me an account of the roll at Kimbolton; and has since, at my desire, borrowed it for me and sent it to town. . . . Mr Astle is to come to me tomorrow morning to ex-

plain the writing' (GRAY ii. 177–8). See also COLE i. 133–4 and *post* 22 April 1768.
8. The blanks in Sandwich's transcript have been filled up within brackets.

To the Duchesse de Choiseul,
Tuesday 23 February 1768

Printed from the MS copy in Jean-François Wiart's hand, now WSL. First printed, Toynbee vii. 165–7. For the history of the MS copy see *ante* 6 May 1766; Mme du Deffand mentions the copy in her letter to HW 29 April 1768 (DU DEFFAND ii. 61). The original letter is missing; it is listed in HW's record of letters sent to Paris in 1768 (ibid. v. 387).

Endorsed by Wiart: Copie d'une lettre de Monsieur Walpole à Mad. la D[uchesse] de Choiseul.

De Londres, ce 23 février 1768.

AH, Madame, que vous m'avez comblé de surprise, de joie et de reconnaissance, et cependant que je suis mécontent! Votre petite-fille[1] qui cherche toujours à faire adorer vos bontés, m'avait annoncé par M. l'Ambassadeur[2], le tableau[3] qu'il m'apportait, en m'ordonnant de l'envoyer demander au moment de son arrivée. Jugez de mon impatience, Madame, et de ma mortification en apprenant que ce cher tableau était déposé à Calais. Ce délai augmentait la persuasion où j'ai été qu'au moins après quelques jours, mais quels jours, je vous retrouverais exactement comme ma très fidèle mémoire vous conserve trait pour trait.

Enfin, ce jour tant désiré arrive; je déchire le ballot plutôt que je ne l'ouvre! Oh! ma chère grand'maman, je tombe des nues; je n'aurais pas été plus pétrifié en y trouvant ma véritable aïeule; il n'y a pas la moindre ressemblance. Non, non, il n'y a que le souvenir de la grâce que vous avez bien voulu me faire qui reste et qui m'empêche de me désespérer; grâce si inattendue, et que jamais je n'aurais eu la présomption de demander. M. de Carmontel, où a-t-il pris que vous avez une figure comme le reste du monde?[4] Je

1. Mme du Deffand.
2. See *ante* 7 Feb. 1768, n. 1.
3. A watercolour drawing of Mme du Deffand and Mme de Choiseul by Louis Carrogis (1717–1806), called Carmontelle; it hung in the Breakfast Room at SH. 'Every part of the room is exactly represented, and Madame du Deffand most exactly like, which the Duchesse is not' ('Des. of SH,' *Works* ii. 425). Mme du Deffand wrote HW 26 Jan. 1768: 'Il faut que je me justifie du mystère que

je vous ai fait du tableau que vous recevrez; la grand'maman l'avait exigé, et ce n'a été que pour lui obéir que je vous en ai gardé le secret' (DU DEFFAND ii. 13; see also ibid. i. 392 and illustration).
4. 'Pour la chère grand'maman, rien de plus manqué. Jamais, non jamais je ne l'aurais devinée. C'est une figure des plus communes' (HW to Mme du Deffand 18 Feb. 1767, ibid. ii. 27).

crois que s'il avait à peindre votre âme, il ne la peindrait pas plus belle que celle de Marc Aurèle. Que lui avez-vous fait, Madame, vous qui n'avez fait de mal à personne; et de ce que vous ne vous souciez pas de votre figure, lui est-il permis à lui de n'y prendre pas garde? J'aurais beau faire, si nous étions au temps de la chevalerie, de promener ce joli portrait par tous les pays de la terre, pour faire avouer que vous êtes la plus parfaite personne du monde; le premier géant de rencontre se moquerait de moi, et ce ne serait qu'après l'avoir vaincu et envoyé vous baiser la main à Paris, qu'il conviendrait que j'eusse raison.

M. le Duc de Bedford, qui était au comble de sa joie d'avoir regagné la vue quand je lui ai annoncé le charmant portrait qui devait m'arriver, croira qu'on ne lui a pas fait l'opération[5] tout de bon, et pour votre amie Milady Charlotte, il faudra absolument à cette heure, que votre voyage en Angleterre ait lieu,[6] pour la persuader que vous n'êtes pas devenue actuellement grand'mère! Ah, Madame, il n'y a que le premier pas vers cet événément qui pourrait me consoler du changement qu'a opéré cet abominable M. de Carmontel. Mais non, Madame, vous n'êtes point changée, témoin la grâce de votre intention. Les peintres n'ont point de pouvoir sur ma reconnaissance, que vous voit telle que vous êtes, elle retouche ce tableau et vous rend toutes vos grâces.

Eût-il réussi comme au portrait de Mme du Deffand, encore y manquerait-il ce que j'eusse cherché inutilement; l'éloquence, l'élégance, la saine raison, la bonté, l'humilité et l'affabilité, sont-elles du ressort de la peinture? Voilà ce que vous eussiez possédé, Madame, avec une figure tout comme celle du tableau; cependant, tout n'est pas perdu. Sous le joli badinage de la poupée[7] on découvre cette unique duchesse, femme de premier ministre, qui quitte les plaisirs et la grandeur pour amuser les tristes moments d'une digne amie. Voilà cette âme qui, en dépit de la maladresse du peintre, se peint elle-même. Voilà d'où vient, Madame, que j'adore ce précieux monument de votre bon cœur; voilà d'où vient que je dis et que je dirai toujours, je suis content. J'ai l'honneur d'être, Madame la Duchesse votre très reconnaissant et très fidèle serviteur

H. Walpole

5. See *ante* 19 Dec. 1767, n. 12.
6. See ibid., nn. 13, 14.
7. Carmontelle's drawing shows Mme de Choiseul giving a doll to Mme du Deffand, an allusion to Mme du Deffand's playful use of the nickname 'grand'maman' for the Duchesse.

From JAMES BOSWELL, Tuesday 23 February 1768

Printed from a photostat of the MS in the Hyde Collection, Sommerville, New Jersey. First printed, Toynbee *Supp.* ii. 138–9. Reprinted in *Letters of James Boswell*, ed. C. B. Tinker, Oxford, 1924, i. 146–7 (misdated '28 February 1768'); *The R. B. Adam Library Relating to Dr Samuel Johnson and his Era*, 1929–30, vol. I ('Letters of James Boswell, Esq.'), pp. 48–9; *Boswell in Search of a Wife 1766–1769*, ed. Frank Brady and F. A. Pottle, New York, 1956, p. 132 (misdated '26 February 1768'). Damer-Waller; the MS was sold Sotheby's 5 Dec. 1921 (first Waller Sale), lot 94, to Maggs; acquired before 1929 by R. B. Adam; sold with the Adam collection to Donald F. Hyde, 1948.

Edinburgh, 23 February 1768.

Sir,

I BEG your acceptance of a copy of my *Account of Corsica*[1] to which you have a better claim than you perhaps imagine as I dare say you have forgotten what you said to me at Paris[2] when I had the honour of giving you a few anecdotes of what I had just come from seeing among the brave islanders. In short, Sir, your telling me that I ought to publish something in order to show the Corsicans in a proper light, was my first incitement to undertake the work which has now made its appearance.

If it gives any pleasure to Mr Horace Walpole, I shall be particularly happy.[3] I shall think that I have been able to make him some small return for the pleasure which his elegant writings have afforded me.

I have the honour to be,

Sir,

Your most obedient humble servant,

JAMES BOSWELL

1. *An Account of Corsica, the Journal of a Tour to that Island; and Memoirs of Pascal Paoli*, published at Glasgow 18 Feb. 1768 (F. A. Pottle, *The Literary Career of James Boswell, Esq.*, Oxford, 1929, p. 61, n. 1). HW may have owned more than one copy of the book; he wrote Gray 18 Feb. 1768: 'Pray read the new *Account of Corsica*. What relates to Paoli will amuse you much. There is a deal about the island and its divisions that one does not care a straw for. The author, Boswell, is a strange being, and

... has a rage of knowing anybody that ever was talked of. He forced himself upon me at Paris in spite of my teeth and my doors, and I see he has given a foolish account of all he could pick up from me about King Theodore' (GRAY ii. 170). See Hazen, *Cat. of HW's Lib.*, No. 3069.

2. On 21 Jan. 1766; see *ante* ca 20 Jan. 1766 and n. 4.

3. Boswell wrote his friend the Rev. William Temple 24 March 1768 that 'Lord Lyttelton, Mr Walpole, Mrs Ma-

From the REV. THOMAS WILSON,[1]
Tuesday 1 March 1768

Printed for the first time from the MS now WSL. For the history of the MS see *ante* 25 July 1767.

Little Cloysters, West[minste]r Abbey,
March 1st 1768.

Sir,

I HAVE been reading with great pleasure your *Historic Doubts,* as you modestly call them; to me they most of them appear certainties.

As I have for some time past been collecting materials for writing the life of William Patten de Waynfleete,[2] Bishop of Winchester and Lord Chancellor, the munificent founder of Magdalen College, Oxford,[3] and one of the best and most learned men of those times, from whose father, by my mother,[4] I am descended in a direct line.

There is a long and minute account of the founder's reception and entertainment of Richard III at his college 22 July A.D. 1483, where the greatest honours were shown that prince by the university, and the noblemen who attended him there. I do not know that any of our historians have taken notice of this, and as I am sure your book will have many impressions,[5] you will not be displeased if I refer you to this account, taken from the register and archives of Magdalen College,[6] which must be authentic, and printed by Wood,

---

caulay, Mr Garrick have all written me noble letters about it' (Boswell's *Letters,* op. cit. i. 148). HW's letter to Boswell is missing.

---

1. (1703–84), D.D., 1739; rector of St Stephen's, Walbrook, 1737–84 and of St Margaret's, Westminster, 1753–84; prebendary of Westminster 1743–84. Writing to Mason 16 March 1778, HW referred to him as 'that dirty disappointed hunter of a mitre, Dr Wilson' (MASON i. 372).

2. William (ca 1395–1486) of Waynflete, son of Richard Patyn (or Patten), of Wainfleet, Lincs; Bp of Winchester 1447–86; lord chancellor 1456–60.

3. Waynflete obtained letters patent, dated 6 May 1448, for the foundation of St Mary Magdalen Hall at Oxford for

the study of theology and moral philosophy (Anthony à Wood, *The History and Antiquities of the Colleges and Halls in the University of Oxford,* ed. John Gutch, Oxford, 1786, pp. 307–11).

4. Mary Patten (1674–1705), dau. of Thomas Patten; m. (1698) Thomas Wilson (1663–1755), Bp of Sodor and Man, 1697.

5. The first edition of 1200 copies sold so rapidly that a second edition of 1,000 copies was immediately called for and published 12 Feb. 1768 (Hazen, *Bibl. of HW* 71–2).

6. The account of Richard's reception at Magdalen College 24–5 July 1483 is given in Register A, f. 27b, of the College records (printed in W. D. Macray, *A Register of the Members of St Mary*

Historia et antiquitates universitatis Oxon., Lib. I, p. 233.[7] This fills up the vacancy of his journey from London to Gloucester. If it be of any use to you I shall think myself happy in communicating what none of our historians, that I know of, have taken notice of.

If you had your education at Eton,[8] you will be pleased to see the life of Will. Waynfleete, the first master and provost of that college, and before that time, Master of Winchester School.[9] Perhaps you may have something curious relating to this great man, and your love of history is my excuse for my entreating the favour of you to communicate any anecdotes relating to him.

If I had your pen and uncommon abilities, my intended history of his life[10] would be received with applause. But I despair of this. It will be an honest narration drawn from all the records I can meet with, and that is all I can say of it.

I am, Sir,
Your most obedient and most humble servant,

THO. WILSON

PS. If you honour me with a letter, pray direct to Dr Wilson, Prebendary of West[minste]r.

Our historians differ about the time when Waynfleete, the Bishop of Winchester, had the seals of Lord Chancellor of England, and when he resigned them into the hands of Hen. VI.[11] This, I know, you can ascertain with certainty.

Magdalen College, Oxford, new series, 1894–1915, i. 11–12). Waynflete arrived at Oxford 22 July to prepare for the royal visit.

7. Anthony à Wood's *Historia et antiquitates universitatis Oxoniensis*, Oxford, 1674, i. 233, correctly refers to '*Reg. Magd. A. ut supra fol.* 27.*b*.' as the source of the account.

8. HW was at Eton 1727–34 ('Short Notes,' GRAY i. 4–5).

9. Waynflete was headmaster of Winchester 1429–41, and tradition accords

him the rôle of first headmaster of Eton 1441–2. He became provost of Eton on 21 Dec. 1442, succeeding Henry Sever, and held that position until ca July 1447 (T. F. Kirby, *Winchester Scholars*, 1888, pp. 52, 61; *Eton Coll. Reg.* xv–xvi, xxviii, xxxii).

10. Never published.

11. Waynflete was appointed lord chancellor by Henry VI on 11 Oct. 1456 and resigned the office on 7 July 1460, shortly before the Battle of Northampton.

From the REV. THOMAS WILSON,
Tuesday 1 March 1768 *bis*

Printed for the first time from the MS now WSL. For the history of the MS see *ante* 25 July 1767.

West[minste]r Abbey, March 1st 1768.

Sir,

I AM much honoured by your obliging letter,[1] and that I may not let the world lose a moment of your time in the inquiry about Waynfleet's resignation, Dr Ducarel[2] has been so kind as to fix the dates from the Close Roll of Hen. VI amongst the Tower records. You have, Sir, obliged the sensible part of mankind to own that they have been grossly mistaken, and I have not so ill an opinion of the world as to think the second impression[3] will be long unsold. What I sent you from Wood's *Hist. et Antiq. Univer. Oxon.*,[4] when applied by so masterly a hand, will in my opinion, please you. There can be no mistakes, because the account is extracted from the College Register, and I have sent for the particulars; when I have them, I shall communicate them to you.[5] Richard III you will find went from Windsor to Oxford, stayed there two or three days, from thence, attended by a great number of persons of rank, to Woodstock, where he might probably stay a day or two, before he set out to Gloucester.[6] *Ratcliffe*[7] is mentioned as being with him at Oxford. Public exercises were performed before the King, and he did some particular favours to both universities at the same time. I am well convinced, that he never thought of assassinating his nephews[8] at that or any other time. If W. G.[9] be the man who gave me so much

---

1. Missing.
2. Andrew Coltee Ducarel, HW's correspondent.
3. See previous letter, n. 5.
4. See ibid., n. 7.
5. No later communication from Wilson has been found.
6. For details of the royal progress see P. M. Kendall, *Richard the Third*, New York, 1956, pp. 301–2.
7. Sir Richard Ratcliffe (or Radcliffe) (d. 1485), Kt, 1471; adviser to Richard III.

8. See *ante* 29 Dec. 1767, n. 14.
9. Wilson had apparently seen the newspaper advertisement for *An Answer to Mr Horace Walpole's late Work*, entitled, *Historic Doubts on the Reign and and Life of King Richard the Third; or, An Attempt to Confute Him from his Own Arguments. By F. W. G.* [Frederick William Guydickens] *of the Middle Temple*, published 10 March 1768. The advertisement appeared in the *Daily Adv.* 17 Feb. (GRAY ii. 172 n. 7).

plague in wading through what he called a history,[10] unless it be very short, I shall hardly read his remarks upon your book. It may possibly make you laugh, and your bookseller rejoice, but you will not reply to it.[11]

I can convince you that I have neither your style nor abilities, if you have read *The Ornaments of Churches Considered*,[12] published by Dodsley some years ago. I gained the point I aimed at—the putting an end to a lawsuit carrying on against a fine painted window in St Margarett's Church.[13] And as you are an admirer of *stained glass,* you will overlook many faults in the book. Waynfleete laid the foundation of learning at Eton, which has since produced some of the greatest men in this kingdom: so far you will honour his memory.

I have great reason to ask your pardon for so long a letter; you have given me so much pleasure in everything that you have favoured the world with, that I should not know where to stop in expressing my grateful thanks. Go on, Sir, in obliging the world with more.

I am, with the highest regard,
Sir,
Your most obedient and most humble servant,

THO. WILSON

On or about 3 March Andrew Coltee Ducarel sent HW 'Extracts relating to Kings Edward IV, Edward V, and Richard III, taken from a register book at Lambeth . . .' These 'Extracts' are contained in a

10. *A General History of England,* 3 vols, 1744–51, by William Guthrie (*ante* 5 June 1764, n. 14). In the *Critical Review,* Feb. 1768, xxv. 116–26, Guthrie severely criticized HW for taking no notice of his *History* in *Historic Doubts;* the review is unsigned.

11. HW replied to Guthrie in the 'Supplement to the Historic Doubts,' *Works* ii. 187–91; Guydickens's book was passed over in two sentences (ibid. ii. 191). See also MONTAGU ii. 254–5 and GRAY ii. 176.

12. [William Hole], *The Ornaments of Churches Considered, with a Particular View to the late Decoration of the Parish Church of St Margaret Westminster,* ed. [Thomas Wilson], Oxford, 1761. Wilson wrote the Preface, the 'Appendix, containing the history of the said church; an account of the altar-piece, and stained glass window erected over it; a state of the prosecution it has occasioned; and other papers,' and the Postscript (1762). HW did not own a copy of this work.

13. The Eastern Window is described in the 'Appendix,' pp. 4–6; the lawsuit in the Ecclesiastical Court is discussed in the Preface, pp. v–xiv.

three-page MS, now WSL, which was endorsed by Ducarel: 'Doctors Commons, March 3d 1768 / For the Hon. Horace Walpole' (*ante* 6 Feb. 1768, n. 4). For the history of the MS see *ante* 25 July 1767.

From the COMTE DE GRAVE,[1] Wednesday 20 April 1768

Printed from a photostat of the MS in the Bodleian Library (MS Toynbee d. 3, pp. 135–8). First printed in *Lettres de la Marquise du Deffand à Horace Walpole (1766–1780)*, ed. Mrs Paget Toynbee, 1912, i. 630. Grave wrote to Mme du Deffand 20 April 1768, enclosing his letter to HW, also dated 20 April, along with an original letter of Mme de Sévigné intended for him; Mme du Deffand sent all three letters to HW on 30 April (DU DEFFAND ii. 63; Appendix 19, vi. 139–40). The MS was among the Du Deffand letters sold SH vi. 107 to Dyce-Sombre, whose widow (later Lady Forester) died in 1893 leaving them to her nephew, W. R. Parker-Jervis; resold Sotheby's 12 March 1920 (Parker-Jervis Sale), lot 387, to Hobbs for Paget Toynbee; given by him to the Bodleian Library, Oct. 1920.

Endorsed by HW: From the Comte de Grave.

À Montpellier, le 20 avril 1768.

DEPUIS six mois, Monsieur, je suis occupé à vous faire avoir de l'écriture de cette femme[2] dont vous admirez avec tant de raison le style. Ce n'est pas ma faute, je vous assure, si je ne vous en envoie pas de quoi faire un volume. Mais ces lettres sont en la possession de deux demoiselles[3] qui ont 80 ans passés, et à cet âge-là on se détache difficilement de ce qu'on tient. Je leur ai fait ma cour avec plus d'assiduité qu'on ne la fait à une jeune personne, de qui on veut obtenir un billet-doux. Il me semble que vous nous fîtes espérer l'année dernière le plaisir de vous voir celle-ci.[4] Je suis d'abord après Madame du Defand pour la vivacité des sentiments

---

1. Charles-François (1726–88), Comte de Grave. Like Mme du Deffand, he had an apartment in the convent of Saint-Joseph. HW met him frequently during his visits to Paris in 1767 and 1769.

2. Mme de Sévigné.

3. The Mlles Girard (d. 1772), the 'vieilles demoiselles' of Montpellier (DU DEFFAND ii. 74 n. 3). Their grandfather,

the Président de Moulceau, had been one of Mme de Sévigné's correspondents; the letter procured by Grave for HW was apparently one of thirty-four letters in their possession at this time (ibid. vi. 139, Appendix 19).

4. HW visited Paris again from 21 Aug. to 5 Oct. 1769 ('Paris Journals,' ibid. v. 324–5, 333).

que vous inspirez à tous ceux qui ont l'honneur de vous connaître.
C'est, je crois vous dire, Monsieur, bien positivement et avec la
franchise qui vous convient et que vous m'avez permise, que personne ne désire plus que moi de trouver souvent les occasions de
vous assurer du très sincère attachement que je vous ai voué pour
ma vie.[5]

To Thomas Astle, Friday 22 April 1768

Printed from the MS now WSL, removed from a copy of the SH sale catalogue,
1842. First printed, Toynbee vii. 184. The MS was sold Sotheby's 6 July 1900
(Autograph Letters and Historical Documents Sale), lot 380, to Cater; *penes*
Frederick Barker in 1904; resold Parke-Bernet 30 Oct. 1945 (Hartshorne Sale),
lot 397, to Brick Row for WSL.

Endorsed in an unidentified hand: Rigby's.

Address: To Thomas Astle Esq. at South Lambeth. *Postmarks:* PENNY
POST PAID W FR. 5 O'CLOCK.

Arlington Street, April 22d 1768.

Dear Sir,

YOU was so good as to say you would procure a person for me,
who could transcribe the inscriptions on the Duke of Manchester's roll of the Earls of Warwick:[1] but as you thought the expense would be considerable, I wish, Sir, I could see such a person,
that I might know what he would ask for that work. I shall be much
obliged to you, Sir, if you can send any such person to me, or will
only inform me where I may meet with him. You will excuse, I
hope, the trouble I give you, though it is not for myself, to whom
you have always been most obliging.

I am Sir
Your obedient humble servant

HOR. WALPOLE

5. HW wrote Grave 20 May, presumably thanking him for the letter of Mme
de Sévigné; HW's letter (missing) is
listed in his record of letters sent to
France in 1768 (ibid. v. 387).

1. See *ante* 17 Feb. 1768 and nn. 2, 7.

From Dr Charles Chauncey,[1] Thursday 28 April 1768

Printed for the first time from the MS now wsl, pasted by HW in the first volume of his *Collection of Prints, Engraved by Various Persons of Quality*. For the history of this volume see Hazen, *Cat. of HW's Lib.*, No. 3588.

Austin Fryers, April 28, 1768.

DR Chauncy presents his best respects to Mr Walpole, and has sent him by Mr Bathoe[2] four etchings[3] by the Earl of Sunderland,[4] which is all he finds he is possessed of. They were bought at Mr Pond's[5] sale of prints etc.[6] He had them (as he told the Dr) from Mr Goupy,[7] as done by Lord Sunderland, who at that time was learning of him. The writing at the bottom[8] is Mr Pond's.

1. (or Chauncy) (1706–77), M.D., 1739; F.R.S., 1740; physician, antiquary, and collector.

2. William Bathoe (d. 2 Oct. 1768), bookseller.

3. Four small etchings of landscapes, one of them signed in the plate 'G and S sculpserunt.' Chauncey's letter is pasted on the verso of the previous page, facing the etchings (see headnote).

4. Robert Spencer Earl of Sunderland d. at Paris 1729. He was elder brother of Charles Duke of Marlborough (HW). Robert Spencer (1701–29), styled Lord Spencer 1702–22; 4th E. of Sunderland, 1722.

5. Arthur Pond (ca 1705–58), F.R.S., 1752; F.S.A., 1752; painter and engraver.

6. 'He had formed a capital collection of etchings by the best masters, and of prints, all of which he disposed of to a gentleman in Norfolk: they have since been sold by auction, as were his cabinet of shells after his death' (HW's *Catalogue of Engravers, Works* iv. 113). The Pond collection owned by Sir Edward Astley (1729–1802), 4th Bt, of Melton Constable, Norfolk, was sold 27 March–25 April 1760 (Frits Lugt, *Répertoire des catalogues de ventes publiques*, The Hague, 1938, vol. I, No. 1090). Prints from Pond's collection were also sold 25 April–3 May 1759 (ibid., No. 1048).

7. Probably Lewis Goupy (d. 1747), painter and drawing master; uncle of Joseph Goupy (d. 1769 or 1770), painter and miniaturist (*Walpole Society* 1920–21, ix. 77–87; Catalogue of Joseph Goupy's sale, Langford and Son, 3 April 1770).

8. 'Earl of Sunderland fecit.'

From VOLTAIRE,[1] Monday 6 June 1768

Printed from the MS now WSL. First printed, *Works* v. 629–30. Reprinted in *Œuvres complètes de Voltaire*, ed. L.-E.-D. Moland, 1877–85, xlvi. 57 (signature omitted); *Voltaire's Correspondence*, ed. Theodore Besterman, Geneva, 1953–65, lxix. 178–9; extract printed in M. B. Finch and E. A. Peers, 'Walpole's Relations with Voltaire,' *Modern Philology*, 1920–1, xviii. 192, n. 1. Damer-Waller; the MS was sold Sotheby's 5 Dec. 1921 (first Waller Sale), lot 188, to Quaritch; later acquired by Sir R. Leicester Harmsworth, Bt; sold Sotheby's 22 Feb. 1949 (Harmsworth Trust Library Sale, Part XVII), lot 5909, to Maggs for WSL. A MS copy in Jean-François Wiart's hand is also now WSL; for its history see *ante* 6 May 1766.

À Ferney près de Genève, 6 juin 1768.[2]

Monsieur,

J'APPRENDS dans ma retraite que vous avez fait un excellent ouvrage[3] sur le pyrrhonisme de l'histoire,[4] et que vous avez répandu une grande lumière sur l'obscurité qui couvre encore les temps des Roses blanche et rouge, toutes [les] deux sanglantes et fanées.

Il y a cinquante ans que j'ai fait vœu de douter. J'ose vous supplier, Monsieur, de m'aider à accomplir mon vœu. Je vous suis peut-être inconnu, quoique j'aie été honoré autrefois de l'amitié of the two brothers.[5]

Je n'ai d'autre recommandation auprès de vous que l'envie de m'instruire. Voyez si elle suffit. Voulez-vous avoir la bonté de m'envoyer votre ouvrage par la poste sous l'enveloppe de M. le chef du bureau des interprètes à Versailles.[6] Ma témérité va plus loin encore, Monsieur, j'ai toujours douté de l'assassinat de M. de

1. (François-Marie Arouet) (1694–1778).
2. The date, closing, and signature are in Voltaire's hand; the rest of the letter is in the hand of Voltaire's amanuensis Simon Bigex.
3. *Historic Doubts on . . . Richard the Third*, 1768.
4. Voltaire was at work on *Le Pyrrhonisme de l'histoire*, which was published probably at the beginning of 1769.
5. 'Sir Robert Walpole and his brother Horace' (MS note in Mary Berry's hand on the MS). During his visit to England 1726–8, Voltaire received invitations to Sir Robert's house. Horatio Walpole, 1st Bn Walpole of Wolterton, who was then the English ambassador in Paris, had given

him letters of introduction to the Duke of Newcastle and others at Court (Theodore Besterman, *Voltaire*, New York, 1969, p. 111).
6. 'Though Voltaire with whom I had never had the least acquaintance or correspondence, had voluntarily written to me first and asked for my book, he wrote a letter to the Duchesse de Choiseul, in which, without saying a syllable of his having written to me first, he told her I had officiously sent him my works and declared war with him' (HW's 'Short Notes,' GRAY i. 45). Voltaire's letter to Mme de Choiseul 15 July 1768 is printed in DU DEFFAND vi. 144; see also CHATTERTON 199.

VOLTAIRE, BY JEAN HUBER

Genonville,[7] qui a produit en France plus de mauvais vers[8] que de représailles. Je vois que dans aucune pièce juridique, dans aucun manifeste, dans aucun écrit des ministres respectifs, il n'est question de cet assassinat prétendu. Si cependant il est vrai que vos soldats aient commis cette barbarie sauvage ou chrétienne en Canada, je vous prie de me l'avouer; s'ils n'en sont pas coupables, je vous prie de les justifier par un mot de votre main. Tout ce que la renommée m'apprend de vous, me persuade que vous pardonnerez à toutes les libertés que je prends.

Vous pardonnerez encore plus à mon ignorance de vos titres; je n'en respecte pas moins votre personne. Je connais plus votre mérite que les dignités dont il doit être revêtu.

Je suis avec l'estime la plus respectueuse,

    Monsieur,

        Votre très humble et très obéissant serviteur,

                                VOLTAIRE

7. Joseph Coulon de Villiers (1718–54), sieur de Jumonville; French army officer. On 28 May 1754 Jumonville and nine other French soldiers were killed during a skirmish between British and French troops in woods near the site of Fort Necessity, about 50 miles south of the forks of the Ohio River. Jumonville was carrying a diplomatic summons demanding the withdrawal of any British forces found on territory claimed by France, but his primary mission was apparently to gain military intelligence. The British detachment, commanded by Lt-Col. George Washington, surprised the French, whom they suspected of spying. News of Jumonville's death created a sensation in France and publicized the conflict of British and French interests in the Ohio valley. The French government later maintained that Jumonville had been 'assassinated,' although eyewitness accounts of the engagement disagreed about what had actually happened (Marcel Trudel, 'L'Affaire Jumonville,' Revue d'histoire de l'Amérique française, 1952–3, vi. 331–73; G. F. Leduc, Washington and 'The Murder of Jumonville,' Boston, 1943, pp. 75–101).

8. Antoine-Léonard Thomas, Jumonville. Poëme, 1759; Voltaire may also have had in mind François-Antoine Chevrier's L'Acadiade; ou, proüesses angloises en Acadie, Canada etc., Cassel, 1758.

To Voltaire, Tuesday 21 June 1768

Printed from the MS now wsl, which is apparently the original letter (see n. 4 below). First printed, *Works* v. 630–1. Reprinted in *Elegant Extracts . . . Originally Compiled by the Rev. Vicesimus Knox,* ed. J. G. Percival, Boston [?1826], iv. 285–6; Wright v. 208–10; Cunningham v. 108–10 (signature omitted in Percival, Wright, and Cunningham); Toynbee vii. 199–202; *Voltaire's Correspondence,* ed. Theodore Besterman, Geneva, 1953–65, lxix. 203–4; extracts printed in Archibald Ballantyne, *Voltaire's Visit to England,* 1893, p. 264; M. B. Finch and E. A. Peers, 'Walpole's Relations with Voltaire,' *Modern Philology,* 1920–1, xviii. 194–5; Theodore Besterman, *Voltaire,* 1969, p. 475. The MS was sold by Charavay at Paris 12 March 1855, lot 243, to Julien; resold in Paris 24 April 1876 (Rathery Sale), lot 963, to unknown; resold at the Hôtel Drouot, Paris, 21 April 1948 ('Lettres, autographes, documents littéraires et manuscrits'), lot 192, to Arthur Rau for wsl. Jean-François Wiart's MS copy of HW's translation (sent to Mme du Deffand 21 June 1768) is also now wsl; for its history see *ante* 6 May 1766.

Strawberry Hill, June 21st 1768.

Sir,

YOU read English with so much more facility, than I can write French, that I hope you will excuse my making use of my own tongue to thank you for the honour of your letter.[1] If I employed your language, my ignorance in it might betray me into expressions that would not do justice to the sentiments I feel at being so distinguished.

It is true, Sir, I have ventured to contest the history of Richard the Third, as it has been delivered down to us: and I shall obey your commands, and send it to you, though with fear and trembling; for though I have given my work to the world, as it is called, yet as you have justly observed, Sir, *that* world is comprised within a very small circle of readers; and undoubtedly I could not expect that you would do me the honour of being one of the number. Nor do I fear you, Sir, only as the first genius in Europe, who have illustrated every science: I have a more intimate dependence on you than you suspect. Without knowing it, you have been my master: and perhaps the sole

1. 'June 20, received a letter from Voltaire desiring my *Historic Doubts.* I sent them, and *The Castle of Otranto,* that he might see the preface, of which I told him. He did not like it, but returned a very civil answer [*post* 15 July 1768], defending his opinion. I replied [*post* 27 July 1768] with more civility, but dropping the subject, not caring to enter into a controversy; especially on a matter of opinion; on which, whether we were right or wrong, all France would be on his side, and all England on mine' ('Short Notes,' Gray i. 43).

merit that may be found in my writings, is owing to my having studied yours; so far, Sir, am I from living in that state of barbarism and ignorance, with which you tax me, when you say *que vous m'êtes peut-être inconnu.* I was not a stranger to your reputation very many years ago, though I was at school and had not the happiness of seeing you, but I remember to have thought you honoured our house by dining with my mother;[2] and yet my father was in a situation[3] that might have dazzled older eyes than mine.[4] The plain name of that father, and the pride of having had so excellent a father, to whose virtues truth at last does justice, is all I have to boast. I am a very private man, distinguished by neither dignities nor titles, which I have never done anything to deserve. But as I am certain that titles alone would not have procured me the honour of your notice, I am content without them.

But, Sir, if I can tell you nothing good of myself, I can at least tell you something bad: and after the obligation you have conferred on me by your letter, I should blush if you heard it from anybody but myself. I had rather incur your indignation than deceive you. Some time ago I took the liberty of finding fault in print with the criticisms you had made on our Shakespeare.[5] This freedom, and no wonder, never came to your knowledge. It was in a preface to a trifling romance,[6] much unworthy of your regard, but which I shall send you,[7] because I cannot accept even the honour of your correspondence, without making you judge whether I deserve it. I might retract; I might beg your pardon: but having said nothing but what

---

2. Presumably in 1727 or 1728, during Voltaire's visit to England, when HW was at Eton.

3. As Prime Minister.

4. The text in *Works* reads: 'I was not a stranger to your reputation very many years ago, but remember to have then thought you honoured our house by dining with my mother—though I was at school, and had not the happiness of seeing you: and yet my father was in a situation that might have dazzled eyes older than mine.' All later editions follow *Works*, but Wiart's MS copy of HW's translation conforms to the text printed here from the MS now WSL.

5. See *ante* 5 Feb. 1765, n. 13. All of Voltaire's writings on Shakespeare are collected in Theodore Besterman, 'Voltaire on Shakespeare,' *Studies on Voltaire and the Eighteenth Century*, Geneva, 1955– , liv.

6. The Preface to *The Castle of Otranto*, 2d edn, 1765 (*Works* ii. 9–11). Voltaire may have already known of it through a French translation of the second edition that was published at Paris and Amsterdam in 1767; see DU DEFFAND i. 256 and n. 7.

7. Voltaire's copy of the third edition, 1766, is now in the Leningrad Public Library; see G. R. Havens and N. L. Torrey, 'Voltaire's Catalogue of his Library at Ferney,' *Studies on Voltaire and the Eighteenth Century*, Geneva, 1955– , ix. 256, No. 3238. The third edition includes the prefaces to both the first and second editions.

I thought, nothing illiberal or unbecoming a gentleman, it would be treating you with ingratitude and impertinence, to suppose that you would either be offended with my remarks, or pleased with my recantation. You are as much above wanting flattery, as I am above offering it to you. You would despise me, and I should despise myself; a sacrifice I cannot make, Sir, even to you.

Though it is impossible not to know *you*, Sir; I must confess my ignorance on the other part of your letter. I know nothing of the history of M. de Genonville, nor can tell whether it is true or false, as this is the first time I ever heard of it: but I will take care to inform myself as well as I can; and if you allow me to trouble you again, will send you the exact account as far as I can obtain it. I love my country, but I do not love any of my countrymen, that have been capable, if they have been so, of a foul assassination. I should have made this inquiry directly, and informed you of the result of it in this letter, had I been in London; but the respect I owe you, Sir, and my impatience to thank you for so unexpected a mark of your favour, made me choose not to delay my gratitude for a single post.[8] I have the honour to be, Sir,

Your most obliged and most obedient humble servant

HORACE WALPOLE

8. HW wrote to Mme du Deffand the same day, enclosing Voltaire's letter to him of 6 June and a translation of his reply; for her comments on the reply see DU DEFFAND ii. 95–7.

From VOLTAIRE, Friday 15 July 1768

Printed from HW's MS copy, now WSL. First printed in *Mercure de France*, May 1769, pp. 134–43. Reprinted in Voltaire's *Commentaire historique sur les œuvres de l'auteur de la Henriade*, Basle, 1776, pp. 199–209; *London Chronicle* 16–18 Jan. 1777, xli. 61–2 (an English translation); *Œuvres complètes de Voltaire*, ed. Beaumarchais, Condorcet, and Decroix, [Kehl], 1784–9, lx. 505–12; *Works* v. 632–6; *Œuvres de Voltaire*, ed. A.-J.-Q. Beuchot, 1829–40, lxv. 132–40; *Œuvres complètes de Voltaire*, ed. L.-E.-D. Moland, 1877–85, xlvi. 78–84; *Voltaire in His Letters*, ed. and trans. S. G. Tallentyre, 1919, pp. 216–22; *Voltaire's Correspondence*, ed. Theodore Besterman, Geneva, 1953–65, lxix. 251–6; *The Selected Letters of Voltaire*, ed. and trans. R. A. Brooks, New York, 1973, pp. 271–5; extracts quoted in Wright v. 213 n. 1; Cunningham v. 114 n. 1; M. B. Finch and E. A. Peers, 'Walpole's Relations with Voltaire,' *Modern Philology*, 1920–1, xviii. 195–6; Theodore Besterman, 'Voltaire on Shakespeare,' *Studies on Voltaire and the Eighteenth Century*, Geneva, 1955– , liv. 158–9. HW's MS copy was among the papers bequeathed by Mme du Deffand to HW on her death in 1780; sold SH vi. 107 to Dyce-Sombre, whose widow (later Lady Forester) died in 1893 leaving them to her nephew, W. R. Parker-Jervis; resold Sotheby's 12 March 1920 (Parker-Jervis Sale), lot 393, to Maggs; bought by Henry C. Folger for the Folger Shakespeare Library, from which WSL acquired it by exchange, June 1950. A copy in the hand of Jean-Louis Wagnière, Voltaire's secretary, is also now WSL; it was offered by Emily Driscoll, Cat. No. 15 (1955), lot 459 (with drafts of other letters of Voltaire); sold by her to James M. Osborn, who gave it to WSL, Dec. 1955. The texts of the copies by HW and Wagnière are almost identical, but differ substantially from those of the earliest and later printings; the variants are listed in *Voltaire's Correspondence*, ed. Besterman, lxix. 256–7 (Textual Notes). The original letter was sent by Voltaire to Mme de Choiseul, who passed it on to Mme du Deffand, who forwarded it to HW; its present whereabouts is not known.

Du château de Ferney,[1] pays de Gex par Versoi[x] et
Lyon, 15 juillet 1768.

Monsieur,

IL Y a quarante ans que je n'ose plus parler anglais, et vous parlez notre langue très bien.[2] J'ai vu des lettres de vous écrites comme

1. In 1758 Voltaire had purchased the Château de Ferney, situated on the northern shore of Lac Léman in the district of Gex, about three and a half miles from Geneva (Theodore Besterman, *Voltaire*, New York, 1969, p. 391).

2. 'Voltaire's English would be good English in any other foreigner—but a man who gave himself the air of criti-

cizing our—and I will say, the world's, greatest author, ought to have been a better master of our language, though both this letter and his commentary prove that he could neither write it nor read it accurately and intelligently' (HW to Joseph Warton *post* 9 Dec. 1784).

2a. Voltaire was then seventy-four.

vous pensez. D'ailleurs, mon âge[2a] et mes maladies ne me permettent pas d'écrire de ma main. Vous aurez donc mes remerciements dans ma langue.

Je viens de lire la préface de votre histoire de Richard Trois; elle me parait trop courte. Quand on a [si][3] visiblement raison, et qu'on joint à ses connaissances une philosophie si ferme, et un style si mâle, je voudrais qu'on me parlât plus longtemps. Votre père était un grand ministre, et un bon orateur, mais je doute qu'il eût pu écrire comme vous. Vous ne devez pas dire, *quia pater major me est*.[4]

J'ai toujours pensé comme vous qu'il faut se défier de toutes les histoires anciennes. Fontenelle, le seul homme du siècle de Louis XIV qui fut à la fois poète, philosophe, et savant, disait, qu'elles étaient des fables convenues.[5] Et il faut avouer que Rolin[6] a trop compilé de chimères et de contradictions.

Après avoir lu la préface de votre histoire, j'ai lu celle de votre roman. Vous vous y moquez un peu de moi. Les Français entendent raillerie, mais je vais vous répondre sérieusement.

Vous avez fait accroire à votre nation, que je méprise Shakespear. Je suis le premier qui ait fait connaître Shakespear aux Français. J'en ai traduit des passages il y a quarante ans,[7] ainsi que de Milton,[8] de Waller, de Rochester, de Driden et de Pope.[9] Je peux vous assurer qu'avant moi presque personne en France ne connaissait la poésie anglaise; à peine avait-on même entendu parler de Loke. J'ai été persecuté pendant trente ans par une nuée de fanatiques pour avoir dit que Loke est l'Hercule de la métaphysique, qui a posé les bornes de l'esprit humain.[10]

3. *Sic* in Wagnière's copy, but not in HW's copy.

4. 'For my father is greater than I' (John 14.28).

5. 'Toute l'ancienne histoire d'un peuple . . . n'est qu'un amas de chimères, de rêveries et d'absurdités' (Fontenelle, *De l'Origine des Fables*, ed. J.-R. Carré, 1932, p. [11]).

6. Charles Rollin (1661–1741), historian, author of *Histoire ancienne des Égyptiens*, 1730–8.

7. A translation of Hamlet's soliloquy 'To be, or not to be' is included in Letter XVIII of the *Lettres philosophiques*, 1734, written ca 1728–30 and first published in English as *Letters Concerning the English Nation*, 1733 (*Œuvres*, ed. Moland, xxii. 150–2).

8. In the *Essai sur la poésie épique*, 1733, chapter ix, 'Milton' (ibid. viii. 354).

9. Translations of passages by Waller and by Rochester are included in Letter XXI, 'Sur le Comte de Rochester et M. Waller,' of *Lettres philosophiques;* by Dryden in Letter XVIII, 'Sur la tragédie'; and by Pope in Letter XXII, 'Sur M. Pope et quelques autres poètes fameux' (ibid. xxii. 165–7, 152–3, 176–7).

10. Voltaire did not say exactly that in Letter XIII 'Sur M. Locke' of the *Lettres philosophiques* (ibid. xxii. 121–7), but see his note on Locke in his *Poème sur la loi naturelle*, 1752 (ibid. ix. 454–5).

Ma destinée a encore voulu que je fusse le premier qui ait expliqué à mes concitoyens les découvertes du grand Neuton,[11] que quelques sots parmi nous appellent encore des systèmes. J'ai été votre apôtre et votre martyr. En vérité il n'est pas juste que les Anglais se plaignent de moi.

J'avais dit il y a très longtemps que si Shakespeare était venu dans le siècle d'Adisson, il aurait joint à son génie l'élégance et la pureté qui rendent Adisson recommandable. J'avais dit, que *son génie était à lui,* et que *ses fautes étaient à son siècle.*[12] Il est précisément, à mon avis, comme le Lopes de Vega[13] des Espagnols, et comme le Caldéron.[14] C'est une belle nature, mais sauvage, nulle régularité, nulle bienséance, nul art: de la bassesse avec de la grandeur, de la bouffonnerie avec du terrible; c'est le chaos de la tragédie, dans lequel il y a cent traits de lumière.

Les Italiens, qui restaurèrent la tragédie un siècle avant les Anglais et les Espagnols, ne sont point tombés dans ce défaut; ils ont mieux imité les Grecs; il n'y a point de bouffons dans l'*Œdipe* et dans l'*Électre* de Sophocle. Je soupçonne fort que cette grossièreté eut son origine dans nos fous de cour. Nous étions un peu barbares tous tant que nous sommes en deçà des Alpes. Chaque prince avait son fou en titre d'office. Des rois ignorants élevés par des ignorants ne pouvaient connaître les plaisirs nobles de l'esprit; ils dégradèrent la nature humaine au point de payer des gens pour leur dire des sottises. De là vint notre *mère sotte;*[15] et avant Molière il y avait un fou de cour dans presque toutes les comédies. Cette méthode est abominable.

J'ai dit, il est vrai, Monsieur, ainsi que vous le rapportez,[16] qu'il y a des comédies sérieuses, telles que le *Misantrope,* qui sont des chefs-d'œuvre; qu'il y en a de très plaisantes, comme *George*

---

11. *Éléments de la philosophie de Newton* was published between 1738 and 1741.

12. In the 'Discours sur la tragédie,' prefixed to his tragedy *Brutus,* 1730, Voltaire remarked on Shakespeare's *Julius Caesar:* 'Je ne prétends pas assurément approuver les irrégularités dont elle est remplie; il est seulement étonnant qu'il ne s'en trouve pas davantage dans un ouvrage composé dans un siècle d'ignorance, par un homme qui même ne savait pas le latin, et qui n'eut de maître que son génie' (Moland, op. cit. ii. 316–17). Voltaire considered Addison's *Cato*

to be the best English model for tragedy.

13. Lope Félix de Vega Carpio (1562–1635).

14. Pedro Calderón de la Barca (1600–81).

15. In *Le Jeu du prince des sots et mère sotte,* 1511, by Pierre Gringore (or Gringoire) (ca 1475–1538).

16. In the Preface to the second edition of *The Castle of Otranto* (*Works* ii. 9–10), HW quotes from Voltaire's preface to *L'Enfant prodigue,* 1738 (Moland, op. cit. iii. 443).

Dandin;[17] que les plaisanteries, le sérieux, l'attendrissement, peuvent très bien s'accorder dans la même comédie.

J'ai dit que tous les genres sont bons hors le genre ennuyeux.[18] Oui, Monsieur, mais la grossièreté n'est point un genre. Il y a beaucoup de logements dans la maison de mon père;[19] mais je n'ai jamais prétendu qu'il fut honnête de loger dans la même chambre Charles Quint[20] et Don Japhet d'Arménie,[21] Auguste et un matelot ivre, Marc Aurèle et un bouffon des rues. Il me semble qu'Horace pensait ainsi dans le plus beau des siècles; consultez son art poétique.[22] Toute l'Europe éclairée pense de même aujourd'hui; et les Espagnols commencent à se défaire à la fois du mauvais goût comme de l'Inquisition; car le bon esprit proscrit également l'un et l'autre.

Vous sentez si bien, Monsieur, à quel point le trivial et le bas défigurent la tragédie, que vous reprochez à Racine de faire dire à Antiochus dans *Bérénice:*

> De son appartement cette porte est prochaine,
> Et cette autre conduit dans celui de la Reine.[23]

Ce ne sont pas là certainement des vers héroïques. Mais ayez la bonté d'observer qu'ils sont dans une scène d'exposition, laquelle doit être simple. Ce n'est pas là une beauté de poésie; mais c'est une beauté d'exactitude, qui fixe le lieu de la scène, qui met tout d'un coup le spectateur au fait, et qui l'avertit que tous les personnages paraîtront dans ce cabinet, qui est commun aux autres appartements, sans quoi il ne serait point du tout vraisemblable que Titus, Bérénice et Antiochus parlassent toujours dans la même chambre.

> Que le lieu de la scène y soit fixe et marqué,

dit le sage Despréaux, l'oracle du bon goût, dans son art poétique,[24] égal pour le moins à celui d'Horace. Notre excellent Racine n'a presque jamais manqué à cette règle: et c'est une chose digne d'admiration qu'Athalie paraisse dans le temple des Juifs,[25] et dans la même

17. Both plays by Molière.

18. 'Encore une fois, tous les genres sont bons, hors le genre ennuyeux' (Preface to *L'Enfant prodigue,* ibid. iii. 445).

19. 'In my Father's house are many mansions ' (John 14.2).

20. *Sic* in Wagnière's copy; HW's MS copy reads 'Charlequint.' Charles V (1500–58), Holy Roman Emperor 1519–58; King of Spain (as Charles I) 1516–56.

21. The title-rôle of the comedy by Paul Scarron, first published in 1653.

22. See *Ars poetica,* ll. 89–98.

23. Racine. *Bérénice* I. i. 7–8.

24. Nicolas Boileau-Despréaux, *L'Art poétique* iii. 38.

25. *Athalie* V. v.

place où l'on a vu le grand prêtre, sans choquer en rien la vraisemblance.

Vous pardonnerez encore plus, Monsieur, à l'illustre Racine, quand vous vous souviendrez que la pièce de *Bérénice* était en quelque façon l'histoire de Louis XIV et de votre princesse anglaise,[26] sœur de Charles Second. Ils logeaient tous deux de plein pied à St-Germain, et un salon séparait leurs appartements.

Vous n'observez vous autres libres Bretons, ni unité de lieu, ni unité de temps, ni unité d'action. En vérité vous n'en faites pas mieux: la vraisemblance doit être comptée pour quelque chose. L'art en devient plus difficile; et les difficultés vaincues donnent en tout genre du plaisir et de la gloire.

Permettez-moi, Monsieur, tout Anglais que vous êtes, de prendre un peu le parti de ma nation. Je lui ai dit si souvent ses vérités, qu'il est bien juste que je la caresse quand je crois qu'elle a raison. Oui, Monsieur, j'ai cru, je crois, et je croirai que Paris est très supérieur à Athène en fait de tragédies et de comédies. Molière, et même Regnard[27] me paraissent l'emporter sur Aristophane, autant que Demosthène l'emporte sur nos avocats. Je vous dirai hardiment, que toutes les tragédies grecques me paraissent des ouvrages d'écoliers en comparaison des sublimes scènes de Corneille, et des parfaites tragédies de Racine. C'était ainsi que parlait Boileau lui-même, tout admirateur des anciens qu'il était. Il n'a fait nulle difficulté d'écrire au bas du portrait de Racine, que ce grand homme avait surpassé Euripide et balancé Corneille.[28]

Oui, je crois démontré qu'il y a beaucoup plus d'hommes de goût à Paris que dans Athène, parce qu'il y a plus de trente mille âmes à Paris uniquement occupées des beaux arts, et qu'Athène n'en avait pas dix mille; parce que le bas peuple d'Athène entrait au spectacle, et qu'il n'y entre point chez nous; parce que ceux qui parmi nous jugent des beaux arts n'ont guère que cette occupation; parce que notre commerce continuel avec les femmes a mis dans nos sentiments beaucoup plus de délicatesse, plus de bienséance dans nos mœurs, et plus de finesse dans notre goût. Laissez-nous notre théâtre; laissez aux Italiens leurs *favole boscareccie;*[29] vous êtes assez riches d'ailleurs.

26. Henrietta Anne (1644–70) of England, m. (1661) Philippe, Duc d'Orléans; sister-in-law of Louis XIV.

27. Jean-François Regnard (1655–1709), comic dramatist and disciple of Molière.

28. Boileau, *Vers pour mettre au bas du portrait de Monsieur Racine:*

Du Théâtre François l'honneur et la merveille,
Il scût ressusciter Sophocles en ses écrits,
Et dans l'art d'enchanter les cœurs et les Esprits,
Surpasser Euripide et balancer Corneille.

29. That is, pastoral dramas.

De très mauvaises pièces, il est vrai, ridiculement intriguées, barbarement écrites, ont pendant quelque temps à Paris des succès prodigieux, soutenus par la cabale, l'esprit de parti, la mode, la protection passagère de quelques personnes accréditées; mais en très peu d'années l'illusion se dissipe, les cabales passent, et la vérité reste.

Permettez-moi de vous dire encore un mot sur la rime que vous nous reprochez. Presque toutes les pièces de Driden sont rimées. C'est une difficulté de plus. Les vers qu'on retient de lui, et que tout le monde cite, sont rimés. Et je soutiens encore que *Cinna, Athalie, Iphigénie*,[30] étant rimés, quiconque voudrait secouer ce joug en France serait regardé comme un artiste faible, qui n'aurait pas la force de le porter.

En qualité de vieillard, il faut que je vous dise une anecdote. Je demandais un jour à Pope pourquoi Milton n'avait pas rimé son poème[31] dans le temps que les autres poètes rimaient leurs poèmes à l'imitation des Italiens: il me répondit, *because he could not*.[32]

Je vous ai dit, Monsieur, tout ce que j'avais sur le cœur. J'avoue que j'ai fait une grosse faute en ne faisant pas attention que le Comte de Leicester s'était d'abord appelé Dudley;[33] mais si vous avez la fantaisie d'entrer dans la chambre des pairs et de changer de nom,[34] je me souviendrai toujours du nom de Walpole avec l'estime la plus respectueuse.

Avant le départ de ma lettre, j'ai eu le temps, Monsieur, de lire votre *Richard Trois*. Vous seriez un excellent attorney-general; vous pesez toutes les probabilités; mais il paraît que vous avez une inclination secrète pour ce bossu. Vous voulez qu'il ait été beau garçon,

30. Wagnière's copy reads 'Cinna, Athalie, Phèdre, Iphigénie.' The first play is by Corneille, the others by Racine.

31. Doubtless *Paradise Lost*. In the preface Milton defended his use of blank verse for a heroic poem: 'This neglect then of rhyme so little is to be taken for a defect, though it may seem so perhaps to vulgar readers, that it rather is to be esteemed an example set, the first in English, of ancient liberty recovered to heroic poem from the troublesome and modern bondage of rhyming.'

32. Voltaire quoted this remark in the *Gazette littéraire* 2 May 1764 (Moland, op. cit. xxv. 175 and n. 1).

33. Robert Dudley (1532 *or* 1533–88),

cr. (1564) E. of Leicester. In the preface to his *Remarques sur Le Comte d'Essex*, a tragedy by Thomas Corneille, Voltaire had written: 'Le comte de Leicester succéda dans la faveur [d'Élisabeth] à Dudley, et enfin, après la mort de Leicester, Robert d'Évreux, comte d'Essex, fut dans ses bonnes grâces' (ibid. xxxii. 325). HW added a long footnote in the Preface to *The Castle of Otranto*, pointing out Voltaire's ignorance 'that Robert Dudley and the Earl of Leicester were the same person' (*Works* ii. 9n).

34. HW became fourth Earl of Orford in 1791, on the death of his nephew, but never took his seat in the House of Lords.

et même galant homme. Le Bénédictin Calmet[35] a fait une dissertation[36] pour prouver que Jesus-Christ avait un fort beau visage. Je veux croire avec vous que Richard Trois n'était ni si laid ni si méchant qu'on le dit; mais je n'aurais pas voulu avoir à faire à lui. Votre rose blanche et votre rose rouge avaient de terribles épines pour la nation;

> Those gracious kings are all a pack of rogues.[37]

En lisant l'histoire des York et des Lancastre, et de bien d'autres, on croit lire l'histoire des voleurs de grand chemin. Pour votre Henri Sept, il n'était que coupeur de bourses.

Be a minister or an anti-minister, a lord or a philosopher, I will be with an equal respect,

Sir,
Your most humble obedient servant,

VOLTAIRE

Be so kind as to tell me frankly if Jumonville was assassinated near the river called Oyo.[38]

35. Dom Augustin Calmet (1672–1757), Benedictine monk and theologian.

36. 'Dissertation sur la beauté de Jésus-Christ,' included in Calmet's *Dissertations qui peuvent servir de prolégomènes de l'Écriture Sainte*, 1720, iii. 422–36.

37. The source of this quotation has not been found.

38. Ohio; see *ante* 6 June 1768, n. 7, and the following letter. For HW's comments on this letter see DU DEFFAND ii. 119–20, 129.

To Voltaire, Wednesday 27 July 1768

Printed from *Works* v. 637–8, where the letter was first printed. Reprinted in *Elegant Extracts . . . Originally Compiled by the Rev. Vicesimus Knox,* ed. J. G. Percival, Boston, [?1826], iv. 286–7; Wright v. 211–13; Cunningham v. 112–14 (signature omitted in Percival, Wright, and Cunningham); Toynbee vii. 206–7; *Letters of Horace Walpole,* ed. C. B. Lucas, [?1904], pp. 494–5; *Voltaire's Correspondence,* ed. Theodore Besterman, Geneva, 1953–65, lxix. 281–3; extracts printed in Archibald Ballantyne, *Voltaire's Visit to England,* 1893, p. 265; M. B. Finch and E. A. Peers, 'Walpole's Relations with Voltaire,' *Modern Philology,* 1920–1, xviii. 198. The history of the MS and its present whereabouts are not known. Jean-François Wiart's MS copy of HW's translation (sent to Mme du Deffand 28 July 1768) is now WSL; for its history see *ante* 6 May 1766.

Strawberry Hill, July 27, 1768.

ONE can never, Sir, be sorry to have been in the wrong, when one's errors are pointed out to one in so obliging and masterly a manner. Whatever opinion I may have of Shakespeare, I should think him to blame, if he could have seen the letter you have done me the honour to write to me, and yet not conform to the rules you have there laid down. When he lived, there had not been a Voltaire both to give laws to the stage, and to show on what good sense those laws were founded. Your art, Sir, goes still farther; for you have supported your arguments, without having recourse to the best authority, your own works. It was my interest perhaps to defend barbarism and irregularity. A great genius is in the right, on the contrary, to show that when correctness, nay when perfection is demanded, he can still shine, and be himself, whatever fetters are imposed on him. But I will say no more on this head; for I am neither so unpolished as to tell you to your face how much I admire you, nor, though I have taken the liberty to vindicate Shakespeare against your criticisms, am I vain enough to think myself an adversary worthy of you.[1] I am much more proud of receiving laws from you, than of contesting them. It was bold in me to dispute with you even before I had the honour of your acquaintance; it would be ungrateful now when

1. '[Voltaire] wrote a letter to the Duchesse de Choiseul, in which . . . he told her I had officiously sent him my works and declared war with him, in defence *de ce bouffon de Shakespeare,* whom in his reply to me, he pretended so much to admire. The Duchess sent me Voltaire's letter, which gave me such contempt for his disingenuity that I dropped all correspondence with him' ('Short Notes,' GRAY i. 45).

you have not only taken notice of me, but forgiven me. The admirable letter you have been so good as to send me, is a proof that you are one of those truly great and rare men, who know at once how to conquer and to pardon.

I have made all the inquiry I could into the story of M. de Jumonville;[2] and though your and our accounts disagree, I own I do not think, Sir, that the strongest evidence is in our favour. I am told we allow he was killed by a party of our men, going to the Ohio. Your countrymen say he was going with a flag of truce. The commanding officer[3] of our party said M. de Jumonville was going with hostile intentions; and that very hostile orders were found after his death in his pocket. Unless that officer had proved that he had previous intelligence of those orders, I doubt he will not be justified by finding them afterwards; for I am not at all disposed to believe that he had the foreknowledge of your hermit, who pitched the old woman's nephew into the river, because *ce jeune homme aurait assassiné sa tante dans un an.*[4]

I am grieved that such disputes should ever subsist between two nations who have everything in themselves to create happiness, and who may find enough in each other to love and admire. It is your benevolence, Sir, and your zeal for softening the manners of mankind; it is the doctrine of peace and amity which you preach, that have raised my esteem for you even more than the brightness of your genius. France may claim you in the latter light, but all nations have a right to call you their countryman *du côté du cœur.* It is on the strength of that connection that I beg you, Sir, to accept the homage of,

Sir, your most obedient humble servant,

Hor. Walpole[5]

---

2. See *ante* 6 June 1768, n. 7.

3. George Washington. His account of the affair is given in letters to Governor Dinwiddie and in his own journal; see *The Writings of George Washington*, ed. J. C. Fitzpatrick, Washington, D. C., 1931–44, i. 63–6, 68–9; Hugh Cleland, *George Washington in the Ohio Valley*, Pittsburgh, 1955, pp. 79–83.

4. 'Ce jeune homme dont la Providence a tordu le cou aurait assassiné sa tante dans un an' (*Zadig*, chapter 20; *Œuvres complètes de Voltaire*, ed. Moland, 1877–85, xxi. 89).

5. For Mme du Deffand's comments on this letter see du Deffand ii. 122–3.

From PAUL PANTON,[1] Monday 8 August 1768

Printed for the first time from a photostat of ·the MS at Nostell Priory, Wakefield, Yorks, kindly furnished by the late Hon. Charles Winn. For the history of the MS see Unknown to HW ?1762.

Address: To the Honourable Horace Walpole Esq. at Strawberry Hill near London. *Postmark:* BANGOR 13 AV.

Plasgwyn in Anglesey, August 8, 1768.

Sir,

LOOKING over an old account of Sir Richard Wynn's[2] of Gwidir in Caernarvonshire, who was Treasurer and Receiver-General to Henriette Marie, consort to Charles I, settled from Michaelmas 1640 to Michaelmas 1641, I find the following articles relating to persons mentioned by you in your very judicious and highly entertaining *Anecdotes of Painting* etc.[3]

Pd Nicholas Lanier Esq.[4] as well for his wages at £53.6s.8d. as for his livery at £6.13.4 p. ann. due for the same time as by his acquittances remaining may appear.[5]

Inigo Jones[6] Surveyor of her Majesty's Works for his pension at £40 p. ann. due for the same time as by his acquittance etc.

Jeoffrey Hudson[7] her Majesty's dwarf for his diet and his man at £50 p. ann.

In the above are also the following allowances—

1. (1727–97), of Plas Gwyn, Anglesey, North Wales; barrister and antiquary (*Dictionary of Welsh Biography*, 1959, p. 728). 'A character distinguished . . . for his acquaintance with the history and antiquities of his native country; and who left behind him a valuable collection of Welsh manuscripts; but who was more particularly conspicuous for his liberality in aiding others, who pursued a similar track with himself' (Nicholas Carlisle, *A Topographical Dictionary of the Dominion of Wales*, 1811, *sub* Llan Edwen).

2. Sir Richard Wynn (ca 1588–1649), of Gwydir, Carnarvonshire; 2d Bt, 1626; M.P. He was gentleman of the Privy Chamber to Charles, P. of Wales, whom he accompanied to Spain; after Charles I's accession in 1625, he was treasurer to the

Queen Consort Henrietta Maria (1609–69).

3. Panton's annotated copy of the first edition of *Anecdotes*, lacking the fourth volume, is now WSL; see Hazen, *SH Bibl.*, 1973 edn, p. xvii, copy 27. See also *post* 24 June 1789.

4. (or Laniere) (1588–1666), Master of the King's Music, 1626; singer, composer, and amateur artist (*Grove's Dict. of Music and Musicians*, 5th edn, ed. Eric Blom, 1954–61, v. 51; COLE i. 24 n. 11). See *Anecdotes of Painting*, SH, 1762–3, ii. 115–16.

5. In the MS 'Groom of the Privy Chamber' is written opposite the entry on Lanier.

6. See ibid. ii. 142–54.

7. Jeffrey Hudson (1619–82), a dwarf. As a child he was in the service of the Duke of Buckingham; the Duchess pre-

John Launier Esq.[8] as well as for his wages £53.6.8 p. ann. as for his livery at £6.13.4 due for the same time etc.

Thos. Alexander in the room of Jeremy Criquitt servant to Jeoffrey her Majesty's dwarf for his pension at £20 p. ann.

Sara Hudson[9] her Majesty's dwarf for her own diet and her maids at £50 p. ann.

Elizabeth Alexander servant to little Sara her Majesty's dwarf for her pension at £12 p. ann.

I hope you will excuse this impertinence in, Sir, a constant purchaser and admirer of all your works.

P. P.

From MADAME DE FORCALQUIER, mid-August 1768

Printed from the MS now WSL. First printed, Toynbee *Supp.* iii. 209–11. Damer-Waller; the MS was sold Sotheby's 5 Dec. 1921 (first Waller Sale), lot 124, bought in; resold Christie's 15 Dec. 1947 (second Waller Sale), lot 55 (with other letters), to Maggs for WSL.

Dated approximately by Mme du Deffand's reference in her letter to HW 23 Aug. 1768: 'La belle Comtesse est charmée de votre lettre, elle y a fait sur-le-champ la réponse que je vous envoie' (DU DEFFAND ii. 132–3).

Endorsed in an unidentified hand: A letter from Madame de Forcalquier written in English.

Sir,

NOTHING may compensate the want of your return hither if not you make me hoping you grieve for not being here; but frankly, it's a poor compensation: and I am very sorry. I ought to thank you for one thing, while I am so displeased for another. Don't so polite, Sir, and be more a traveller.

The description you make of the King of the Danmark[1] is like the

sented him to Henrietta Maria, Queen Consort of Charles I, shortly after their marriage. The Queen kept him as her dwarf for the entertainment of the Court, where he became a favourite. See ibid. ii. 8–10.

8. Possibly John Lanier (d. 1650), who was a musician in the service of the Crown; he was a son of Nicholas Lanier (d. 1612), who was probably the uncle of Nicholas Lanier (1588–1666) (DNB *sub* Nicholas Lanier). In the MS 'Groom of

the Privy Chamber' is written opposite this entry.

9. Originally 'Hudson' in the MS; changed to read 'Holton.'

1. Christian VII (1749–1808), King of Denmark 1766–1808. He arrived in London 11 Aug. For HW's accounts of his reception see MONTAGU ii. 264–5; MANN vii. 41–2; CHUTE 325–8; *Mem. Geo. III* iii. 159–61.

picture made to me by others. I am of the same opinion upon kings as some philosophers were on death. I aspect them without wishing or fearing them; you do better, you Anglishmen! Ye make them tremble.

The favourite[2] of the little King (giving trust to the report) is a great favourite, but commonly a great favourite is a little man, God bless all. You mention my indifference, Sir, will it last? I don't know: your little King[3] perhaps will destroy it; however, I hate despotical personage and for my repose I'll shun him.

I find my Lady Rochefort[4] witty, she has humour certainly. For your good friend Mme du Deffand, she is good indeed to me, as much as one can be; she praises me, but without subject; she is happily partial towards me, for all who know her must do justice to her, as much as I do.

Yesterday I supped with her; the evening was gentle, quiet; if you had been, nothing amiss.

I have made acquaintance since some times with the General Irwine;[5] he seems to me the best, and honest man in the world—at less, he speaks likely, and we not must injure men by doubts when they appear in good sight; then, I account Mr Irwine in the little numbers of those who do honour to mankind. You, Sir, who are also a fleuron to humanity, lives as long as you deserve, never preachers wishing immortal life had no so good hopes to obtain't for his auditory, so great advantage for calculating on merits they will see, than 〈   〉[6] dyings, but my wows are directed on you, and some others only.

I will make your compliments to the Duchess of Ruel,[7] and surely she will receive its very sensibly and gratefully. Mme de la Vallière[8] has charged me with thousands things of the more gallant sort, but, Sir, I am very awkward. Then come, Sir, to hear so pretty sounds of her own mouth! I finish my epistle, with the usual esteem and true

2. Frederik Vilhelm Conrad Holck (1745–1800), Count (Greve) Holck (MONTAGU ii. 265 n. 5). He fell from favour in 1770 on the rise of Struensee.

3. 'He is as diminutive as if he came out of a kernel in the fairy tales' (HW to Montagu 13 Aug. 1768, ibid. ii. 264).

4. Rochford. See *ante* 27 Oct. 1766, n. 8.

5. John Irwin (ca 1728–88), Maj.-Gen.;

K.B., 1775; M.P. He lived in Paris in 1768–9 (DU DEFFAND ii. 93 n. 6, ii. 133).

6. Word illegible in the MS.

7. The Duchesse douairière d'Aiguillon. She often stayed at Rueil, the country seat of her son, the Duc d'Aiguillon. HW wrote verses at her request expressing her 'love of retirement' there; see ibid. v. 363.

8. See *ante* 6 March 1766, n. 4.

consideration you have inspired to me and with which I have the honour to be, Sir,

Your most humble most obedient servant,

COMTESSE DE FORCALQUIER

To THOMAS WARTON, Tuesday 20 September 1768

Printed from John Wooll, *Biographical Memoirs of the late Reverend Joseph Warton, D.D.*, 1806, pp. 335–6, where the letter was first printed. Reprinted, Cunningham v. 127–8; Toynbee vii. 227–8. The history of the MS and its present whereabouts are not known.

Strawberry Hill, Sept. 20th 1768.

Sir,

I RETURNED hither but last night from a tour into Yorkshire, Derbyshire, etc.[1] and found your letter,[2] from the date of which I fear you will have thought me very rude, and forgetful of the civilities I received from you. You do me great justice, Sir, in thinking I should be happy to be of use to you, if it was in my power; and I may add that nobody can think what you desire more proper for you than I do. Your merit is entitled to that and greater distinction, and were the place[3] in my gift, I should think you honoured it by accepting it. But, alas! Sir, my opinion and my wishes are both very fruitless. I should not deserve the honour you have done me, if I did not speak sincerely and frankly to you. I have no interest with the ministry, I desire none, and have shown by my whole life that I will cultivate none.[4] I have asked no favour for myself or my friends. Being now out of Parliament by choice,[5] I doubt it would not help my interest. Mr Gray's preferment[6] gave me great pleasure;

1. The tour began on 2 Sept. with a visit to Weston in Warwickshire (*Country Seats* 62–7).

2. Missing.

3. The Regius professorship of modern history at Oxford.

4. For HW's account of his relations with government ministers, see his 'Account of my Conduct . . . towards Ministers' (*Works* ii. 364–70).

5. HW declined to stand again for King's Lynn (*ante* 13 March 1767) and at the dissolution of Parliament 11 March ceased to be a member.

6. Thomas Gray had been appointed Regius professor of modern history at Cambridge by the Duke of Grafton, the prime minister, at the King's command 28 July 1768 (*Correspondence of Thomas Gray*, ed. Paget Toynbee and Leonard Whibley, Oxford, 1935, iii. 1033–5, 1038–9).

but I assure you upon my honour, Sir, that I knew not a word of its being intended for him, till I saw in the papers that he had kissed hands.[7] I believe, Sir, you are acquainted with him, and he would confirm this to you. It would therefore, Sir, be giving myself an air of importance which I have not, if I pretended I could either serve you, or would try to serve you in this case; I had much rather you should know how insignificant I am than have you think me either vain of favour I have not, or indifferent to your interest. I am so far from it, that I will tell you what I think might be a method of succeeding, though I must beg you will not mention my name in it in any shape. Mr Stonehewer[8] is a great favourite of the Duke of Grafton, and the person that recommended Mr Gray.[9] If you are acquainted with Mr Stonehewer, who is a very worthy man, he might possibly be inclined to name you to the Duke, if the place is not promised, nor he unwilling to recommend a second time.[10] Lord Spencer[11] or Lord Villiers,[12] if you know either of them, might be useful too. Excuse my hinting these things, but as I should be happy to promote such merit, Sir, as yours, you will interpret them as marks of the regard with which I am, Sir,

Your obedient humble servant,

Hor. Walpole

PS. The Duke of Marlborough[13] might assist you, Sir, too.

7. HW wrote to H. S. Conway 9 Aug. 1768: 'Yes, it is my Gray, Gray the poet, who is made professor of modern history; . . . I knew nothing of it till I saw it in the papers; but believe it was Stonehewer that obtained it for him' (Conway iii. 106). 'On Friday last [29 July], Thomas Gray, Esq. kissed his Majesty's hand on being appointed professor of history and modern languages in the University of Cambridge' (*St James's Chronicle* 30 July – 2 Aug.).

8. Richard Stonhewer (ca 1728–1809), under-secretary of state 1765–6; auditor of excise 1772–89; friend of Gray (*post* 16 Sept. 1771, n. 1).

9. Stonehewer was appointed private secretary to Grafton in 1766. It was generally believed that Gray's appointment was due to Stonhewer's influence with Grafton (*Corr. of Thomas Gray* iii. 1038 n. 9). See also HW to Stonehewer *post* 16 Sept. 1771.

10. Warton apparently followed HW's suggestion, as Grafton wrote to him 22 Sept.: 'I should with great pleasure have laid before the King your request to succeed to the professorship of modern history at Oxford, if I had not known that it was his Majesty's intention to confer it on another gentleman' (Wooll, op. cit. 337). This 'gentleman' was the Rev. John Vivian (ca 1729–71), who was appointed Regius professor the same year and held the post until his death (Foster, *Alumni Oxon.*). Warton's applications came to nothing.

11. John Spencer (1734–83), cr. (1765) E. Spencer; M.P.

12. George Bussy Villiers (1735–1805), styled Vct Villiers 1742–69; 4th E. of Jersey, 1769; vice-chamberlain of the Household 1765–9; M.P.

13. George Spencer (1739–1817), 3d D. of Marlborough; lord chamberlain of the Household 1762–3; lord privy seal 1763–5.

To Horace-Bénédict de Saussure,[1]
ca November 1768

Printed from a photostat of the MS in the Archives de Saussure, Bibliothèque publique et universitaire, Geneva (MS Saussure 10, f. 120). First printed in Claire-Eliane Engel, *La Suisse et ses amis*, Neuchâtel, [1943], pp. 106–7. The MS is among the Saussure family archives which were deposited in the Bibliothèque publique et universitaire by MM. Jacques and Raymond de Saussure in 1941.

Dated approximately by Saussure's residence in London and the reference to HW's 'long accès de goutte' (see n. 2 below).

MONSIEUR Walpole est infiniment sensible aux bontés de M. de Saussure; et l'assure qu'il a été au désespoir de n'avoir pas été assez heureux d'être au logis quand M. de Saussure lui a fait l'honneur de passer à sa porte. M. Walpole était à la campagne la dernière fois, ayant eu un long accès de goutte[2] depuis leur rencontre à Chatsworth.[3] Il a cherché M. de Saussure en Pall Mall, et n'a pas pu trouver son logis, mais actuellement il ne manquera pas de lui rendre ses devoirs; et il s'informera si Madame la Duchesse de Portland[4] est en ville pour prendre une heure avec elle, afin que M. de Saussure voie son cabinet.[5] Comme M. Walpole n'est pas en état encore de sortir que très tard le matin, il sera charmé de voir M. de Saussure quand il lui plaira entre les onze et une heures.

1. (1740–99), Swiss naturalist and traveller; author of *Voyage dans les Alpes*, Geneva and Neuchâtel, 1779–96, and other works on geology and natural history. Saussure and his wife visited England in 1768–9; his unpublished travel diary (MS Saussure 26, Bibliothèque publique et universitaire, Geneva) records his chance meeting on 8 Sept. 1768 with HW and General Conway at Chatsworth, where they were received by Lord John Cavendish. HW, who is described as 'auteur de la lettre du Roi de Prusse à Rousseau, un peu francisé, un peu languissant,' promised to introduce Saussure to the Duchess of Portland, so that he could see her celebrated collection (n. 5 below). He dined with HW and Conway at Chatsworth the following day. For further details of Saussure's visit to England see D. W. Fresh-

field, *The Life of Horace Benedict de Saussure*, 1920, pp. 11–19; Claire-Eliane Engel, 'Horace-Bénédict de Saussure à Londres,' *Alma Mater: Revue universitaire de la Suisse romande*, 1944–5, i. 329–40.

2. 'I have been laid up with a fit of the gout in both feet and a knee; at Strawberry for an entire month, and eight days here [Arlington Street]' (HW to Montagu 10 Nov. 1768, MONTAGU ii. 266).

3. The Duke of Devonshire's seat, in Derbyshire.

4. Margaret Cavendish Harley (1715–85), m. (1734) William Bentinck (1709–62), 2d D. of Portland, 1726.

5. Her 'museum' of virtu, gems, and shells in her house in the Privy Garden; for HW's description of it see *The Duchess of Portland's Museum*, ed. W. S. Lewis, New York, 1936. See following letter.

To Horace-Bénédict de Saussure,
ca November 1768 *bis*

Printed from a photostat of the MS in the Archives de Saussure, Bibliothèque publique et universitaire, Geneva (MS Saussure 10, f. 121). First printed in Claire-Eliane Engel, *La Suisse et ses amis*, Neuchâtel, [1943], p. 106. For the history of the MS see *ante* ca November 1768.

Dated approximately by the previous letter.

MONSIEUR Walpole fait bien ses compliments à Monsieur de Saussure, et est très fâché de lui faire savoir, que s'étant plusieurs fois informé de Madame la Duchesse de Portland, il vient d'apprendre, qu'elle ne sera en ville qu'après Noël.[1]

From David Hume, Friday 11 November 1768

Printed from Toynbee *Supp.* ii. 76, where the letter was first printed. Reprinted in *The Letters of David Hume,* ed. J. Y. T. Greig, Oxford, 1932, ii. 193. Damer-Waller; the MS was sold Sotheby's 5 Dec. 1921 (first Waller Sale), lot 150, to Oppenheim; not further traced.

Brewers Street,[1] 11 of November 1768.

Dear Sir,

THIS letter will be delivered to you by M. Deyverdun,[2] a Swiss gentleman, a man of letters and of merit, whom I had occasion to know particularly, because he was in the Secretary's office, and in Mr Conway's department.[3] He has undertaken a work, of which he has published only one number, under the title of *Mémoires lit-*

1. Saussure and his wife were subsequently introduced to the Duchess of Portland by HW, and they saw her collection (Engel, op. cit. 107).

1. Hume lodged at 'Miss Elliot's' in Brewer Street, Golden Square (Hume's *Letters*, ed. Grieg, ii. 132).

2. Jacques-Georges Deyverdun (ca 1734–89), a Swiss employed as clerk in the secretary of state's office, first (1766–8) in the northern department under Henry Conway and later (1768–9) in the southern department; friend of Edward Gibbon, who was his collaborator in the *Mémoires littéraires de la Grande Bretagne* (GRAY i. 44 n. 302). Deyverdun had contributed two newspaper squibs on the Hume-Rousseau quarrel published in the *St James's Chronicle* in 1766; see F. A. Pottle, 'The Part Played by Horace Walpole and James Boswell in the Quarrel between Rousseau and Hume: A Reconsideration,' in *Horace Walpole: Writer, Politician, and Connoisseur,* ed. W. H. Smith, New Haven, 1967, pp. 277–8.

3. Hume was under-secretary to Conway in 1767–8.

téraires de la Grande Bretagne; and he has a second in hand. He
wishes to enrich it by an account of Lord Herbert's *Life;*[4] but not
knowing where to find a copy, he uses the freedom, through my
recommendation, to apply to you: I hope you will have no objection
to the supplying him with one.[5] I am, dear Sir,

Your most obedient and most humble servant,

DAVID HUME

From the DUCHESS OF NORFOLK,[1]
Sunday 20 November 1768

Printed from the MS now WSL. First printed, Toynbee *Supp.* iii. 212. For the
history of the MS see *ante* ?19 March 1759.

Worksop Manor,[2] Nov. 20, 1768.

Sir,

I HAVE but this moment received the picture[3] of which an obliging letter[4] from you had given me notice near three weeks ago; I
have waited with no small impatience for its arrival, unwillingly delaying to make the Duke of Norfolk's and my best acknowledgment
for so valuable a present, and yet desirous to be able at the same time

4. *The Life of Edward Lord Herbert
of Cherbury, Written by Himself,* SH,
1764 (Hazen, *SH Bibl.* 68–72).
5. HW supplied him with a copy as
requested. In the *Mémoires* for 1768 an
unfavourable review of HW's *Historic
Doubts* appeared, with notes by Hume
appended to it. HW assumed that the
review was written by Deyverdun, but
it was actually by Gibbon. His annoy-
ance at the conduct of Hume and Deyverdun is recorded in 'Short Notes' *sub*
May 1769 (GRAY i. 44–5).

1. Mary Blount (ca 1702–73), m. (1727)
Edward Howard (1686–1777), 9th D. of
Norfolk, 1732.
2. The Duke of Norfolk's seat, in Not-
tinghamshire. The original Elizabethan
house, which HW saw in 1756, was destroyed by fire in 1761. Construction of a
new house on the old site was begun in

1763; during his visit in mid-September
1768, HW recorded that it had a 'magnificent new front 301 feet long already
built and near furnished' (CHUTE 270;
Country Seats 65). 'The present Duchess
has reassembled all she could [of the
Arundelian collection]—but I doubt, much
even of that was burnt at Worksop' (HW
to Dalrymple 8 Nov. 1767, DALRYMPLE
114).
3. Apparently a portrait of Henry
Frederick Howard (1608–52), second but
oldest surviving son of Thomas Howard
(1585–1646), 14th E. of Arundel; styled
Lord Maltravers 1624–40, after the death
of his older brother, Sir James Howard
(1607–24); 15th E. of Arundel, 1646. Both
he and his brother were made K.B. at the
creation of Charles, P. of Wales, in 1616.
See n. 5 below.
4. Missing.

to inform you that it was safe in our hands. I am charged by the Duke of Norfolk to assure you of the very grateful sense he has of your obliging and polite remembrance of him on this occasion, and of the great pleasure with which he receives the honour you have done him in this mark of your attention. He has no single portrait of a Lord Maltravers, son to the Earl of Arrundel. There is a Henry Lord Maltravers in the family picture of the Earl of Arrundel done by Vandyke at Antwerp; that Henry was a Knight of the Bath, and in that is called eldest son to the Earl of Arrundel: there is a great resemblance between the portrait I here mention and that you have honoured us with.[5] I must again repeat our joint thanks, and am,

Sir,

Your most humble servant,

M. NORFOLK

To the DUCHESSE DE CHOISEUL,
Tuesday 13 December 1768

Printed from an extract quoted in Mme de Choiseul's reply *post* 7 Feb. 1769. The original letter (apparently misdated '13 février') is missing; it is listed in HW's record of letters sent to Paris in 1768 (DU DEFFAND v. 388).[1]

[Vous êtes une femme] supérieure à la fortune, qui n'en craint que les faveurs et non les revers.

---

5. A portrait of 'Henry, Earl of Arundel, ob. 1652' is listed as one of the principal pictures at Worksop Manor in J. P. Neale, *Views of the Seats of Noblemen and Gentlemen*, 1st Series, 1818–23, iii. *sub* Worksop Manor.

1. Mme du Deffand wrote HW 27 [28] Dec. 1768: 'La grand'maman avait laissé votre lettre à Versailles, elle croyait me l'avoir envoyée, elle me l'enverra, elle m'a dit en être fort contente; je lui ai demandé si elle était sans prétentions: "Oh! oui," m'a-t-elle dit, "fort naturelle"' (DU DEFFAND ii. 174). On 12 Jan. 1769 she reported: 'La grand'maman me recommanda bien hier de lui rapporter votre lettre, parce qu'elle y veut répondre incessamment' (ibid. ii. 184).

From Lord Bristol,[1] Sunday 18 December 1768

Printed from Toynbee *Supp.* i. 179, n. 3, where the letter was first printed. Reprinted in *Horace Walpole's Fugitive Verses*, ed. W. S. Lewis, 1931, p. 150 (date, salutation, closing, and signature omitted). Damer-Waller; the MS was sold Sotheby's 5 Dec. 1921 (first Waller Sale), lot 97, to Dobell; not further traced.

St James's Square, 18th of December 1768.

Sir,

ALLOW me to return you my thanks as grateful as they are sincere for the very obliging letter[2] I had the honour of receiving last night from you enclosing an extreme perfect elegy to the memory of my mother;[3] I liked the first, and I am pleased with this. You must permit me to put your name at the bottom on the tomb stone.[4] I agree entirely with you in thinking too much could not be said of my deceased parent; she deserved the character you have given of her. I can add nothing more; even an indifferent person must admire the composition.[5]

I am with the truest regard, respect, and attachment,

Your most obedient faithful and obliged humble servant,

BRISTOL

1. George William Hervey (1721–75), styled Lord Hervey of Ickworth; 2d Bn Hervey of Ickworth, 1743; 2d E. of Bristol, 1751; son of HW's friend and correspondent Mary Lepell, Lady Hervey.

2. Missing.

3. 'Nov. 18, [1768] at the desire of her son George William Hervey Earl of Bristol, I wrote the elegy for the monument of Mary Lepelle Lady Hervey, to be erected in the church at Ickworth in Suffolk' ('Short Notes,' GRAY i. 43). HW sent a copy of the elegy, a poem of 36 lines, to Sir Edward Walpole 28 April 1769 (FAMILY 51); for the text see *Horace Walpole's Fugitive Verses*, pp. 149–50.

4. HW had apparently revised an earlier version of the poem submitted to Bristol for his consideration. The elegy inscribed on the tombstone in Ickworth Church is signed 'Hon. Horace Walpole Esq. fecit.' See also GRAY i. 43 n. 296.

5. In a letter from HW's occasional correspondent the Rev. Sir John Cullum (*ante* 23, 26 Nov. 1767) to the Duchess of ——, Cullum writes '. . . your Grace expressed an inclination to see Mr Hor. Walpole's Inscription upon the late Lady Hervey. I am happy to have it in my power to show at least a desire of making some return for the favours your Grace has bestowed upon me, by sending you the following exact copy of it. . . . This your Grace will allow to be lamentable indeed, but Mr Walpole is rather unfortunate when he attempts to be touching and pathetic' (MS in the Osborn Collection, Yale University Library).

From 'F. W.,'[1] 1769

Printed for the first time from a photostat of the MS in the Harvard College Library, inserted in the presentation copy of *Friendship: A Poem* in HW's 'Poems of George III.' For its history see Hazen, *Cat. of HW's Lib.*, No. 3222.

Dated approximately by the publication of *Friendship: A Poem* (see n. 2 below).

Endorsed by HW: Letter from the author of *Friendship, a poem.*

Sir,

I TAKE the liberty of presenting this trifle[2] to you, as a testimony of my great respect and esteem of your character; and as an acknowledgment of my obligations, for the pleasure and improvement I have received from those literary productions with which you have obliged the world. *The Castle of Otranto* has particularly pleased me: and if it be not presuming too far, I should be obliged, Sir, for your opinion, as to its being the subject for a dramatic performance, with such alterations as the present state of manners and the stage may demand.[3]

I am, Sir, with the greatest respect,

Your most humble servant,

THE AUTHOR

PS. A line directed to F. W. to be left with the publisher[4] will soon reach the author.

---

1. Not identified.

2. A copy of *Friendship: A Poem Inscribed to a Friend: To which is Added, an Ode*, 1769, 4to (Hazen, *Cat. of HW's Lib.*, No. 3222:9:4).

3. *The Castle of Otranto* was adapted for the stage by Robert Jephson as *The*

Count of Narbonne and had its first performance at Covent Garden on 17 Nov. 1781. See *post* 27 Jan. 1780 and 7 Nov. 1781.

4. The title-page reads: 'Printed for G[eorge] Kearsly, in Ludgate Street, and Johnson and Payne, in Paternoster Row.'

From the Duchesse de Choiseul, Tuesday 7 February 1769

Printed from the MS now wsl. First printed in *Correspondance complète de Mme du Deffand,* ed. the Marquis de Sainte-Aulaire, 1866, i. 191–2. The MS was in the possession of Sainte-Aulaire in 1866; not further traced until acquired (in three volumes of Mme du Deffand's correspondence with her friends, 1763–73) from an anonymous French owner by Arthur Rau, Paris, who sold the volumes to wsl, Sept. 1950. Mme du Deffand wrote HW 22 Feb. 1769: 'La grand'maman m'a dit vous avoir écrit de Tugny' (DU DEFFAND ii. 205).

Endorsed by Mary Berry: Mme la D[uche]sse de Choiseul à M. Walpole 7th février 1769.

À Tugny,[1] ce 7 février 1769.

J'AI reçu une lettre[2] charmante de mon Horace, de mon cher petit-fils;[3] mais comment cela se fait-il? Elle est datée du 13 février et nous ne sommes encore qu'au 7; il est vrai qu'elle marque aussi 68 et que nous sommes en 69. Elle a donc un an d'antiquité. Cependant je ne l'ai reçue qu'il y a environ trois semaines; elle est en réponse à une lettre que j'ai écrite, il y en a environ six, au Général Irwin.[4] Mon petit-fils est-il donc comme l'*Éternel* qui réunit tous les temps? J'aimerais bien mieux qu'il lui ressemblât par le don de remplir l'espace, je l'aurais auprès de moi. En vérité, Monsieur, votre présence me serait assez due, il y a assez longtemps que l'on vous désire, vous avez beau écrire des galanteries à votre jeune femme[5] et à votre vieille grand'mère, je ne puis croire que vous les aimiez quand vous êtes deux ans sans les voir.[6] Malgré votre absence, malgré votre indifférence, je ne me repens cependant point de vous avoir fait des agaceries dans ma lettre au Général, puisqu'elles m'en ont procuré une si jolie de votre part; on a beau être vieille et grand'mère, on n'en aime pas moins les douceurs et j'aime particulièrement les vôtres. Trêve donc de reproches, votre lettre vous a tout fait pardonner (hors une si longue absence); on est toujours sûr du retour d'une femme dont on a su flatter la vanité. Croyez-vous cependant que la mienne m'ait assez aveuglée pour m'attribuer un portrait qui

1. Mme de Choiseul was visiting her uncle, the Baron de Thiers, at Thugny, near Rethel.
2. *Ante* 13 Dec. 1768; HW apparently misdated the letter '13 février.'
3. See *ante* 16 Oct. 1767, n. 1.

4. See *ante* mid-August 1768, n. 5.
5. Mme du Deffand.
6. HW had last visited Paris 23 Aug.– 8 Oct. 1767; he returned in Aug. 1769 ('Paris Journals,' DU DEFFAND v. 316, 324).

ne me ressemble point? Je ne connais pas cette femme *supérieure à la fortune, qui n'en craint que les faveurs et non les revers.* J'en connais une qui tâche d'en jouir sans s'en laisser éblouir, qui cherche à en prévoir les revers pour apprendre d'avance à les supporter, mais je ne connais pas la merveille dont vous me parlez; si je la trouve, je vous l'indiquerai pour que vous l'aimeriez mieux que moi. En attendant, Monsieur, aimez-moi comme la femme du monde qui vous rend le plus de justice et qui est la plus pénétrée de tous les sentiments que vous méritez.

Mille choses pour moi, je vous prie, au Général, si vous le rencontrez.

To Grosvenor Bedford, Friday 24 March 1769

Printed from Cunningham v. 150, where the letter was first printed. Reprinted, Toynbee vii. 262. The history of the MS and its present whereabouts are not known.

March 24, 1769.

IF Mr Palmer[1] will not give in his accounts, I order Mr Bedford to give in my accounts without them. I will connive at nothing, nor have any underhand dealings with Mr Palmer or anybody else; but will have the business of my office[2] done openly, fairly, and regularly, as it is my duty to do, and as I can justify to the Lords of the Treasury and to the public.

Hor. Walpole

1. Doubtless Charles Palmer (d. 26 Oct. 1769), office-keeper in the Treasury (*Court and City Register*, 1769, p. 113; *London Magazine*, 1769, xxxviii. 592).
2. 'You must remember how strongly I rejected old Palmer's pretensions, and was firm that I would lose the perquisites due on what he was entitled to take at the office, rather than enter into any bargain with him' (HW to Grosvenor Bedford *post* 27 Feb. 1771).

From Madame Élie de Beaumont,[1]
Wednesday 26 April 1769

Printed from the MS now wsl. First printed, Toynbee *Supp.* iii. 214–17. Damer-Waller; the MS was sold Sotheby's 5 Dec. 1921 (first Waller Sale), lot 121, to Wells; given by him to Thomas Conolly, of Chicago, from whom wsl acquired it in 1937.

À Paris ce 26 avril 1769.

JE VOUS dois bien des remerciements, Monsieur; vous m'avez fait connaître Madame Cholmondelei.[2] Les éloges que vous m'en avez faits sont si moderés qu'en vérité si vous n'étiez pas son parent j'oserais vous en faire des reproches. Cette dame joint les grâces aux vertus; elle est en même temps aimable et charmante. Je regrette bien de n'être pas à portée de cultiver ses bontés aussi souvent que je le désirerais; l'éloignement, les embarras d'aller quand on n'a pas de carrosse, toutes ces choses sont de grands obstacles, surtout pour les femmes. Malgré l'envie que j'en aurais, je ne vois presque pas Madame du Deffand par ces raisons-là; elle veut bien les entendre, Madame Cholmondelei a la même indulgence; je leur en suis bien obligée, mais je n'en suis pas moins à plaindre.

À travers les événements qui font nouvelle, il s'en trouve quelquefois de frappants. L'autre jour que Madame votre parente, Monsieur, me faisait l'honneur d'être chez moi, on conta en sa présence la mort de M. Gilbert de Voisins,[3] conseiller d'état et du conseil des dépêches, l'un de nos plus grands magistrats. Les détails de la mort[4] de cet honnête homme marquent tant de grandeur, de fermeté et de simplicité que Madame Cholmondelei, qui en fut frappée d'admiration, me pria de vous les écrire. Je la pressai beaucoup de faire elle-même cette commission; elle insista, j'obéis.

M. Gilbert de Voisins, toujours très pieux, âgé de 85 ans, et travaillant à juger les affaires les plus importantes du royaume du matin au soir depuis l'âge de 30 ans, se trouva malade le dimanche

1. Anne-Louise Morin-Dumesnil (1729–83), m. (1750) Jean-Baptiste-Jacques Élie de Beaumont. See *ante* 18 March 1765.

2. Mary Woffington (ca 1729–1811), sister of Peg Woffington, the actress; m. (1746) the Rev. Hon. Robert Cholmondeley (1727–1804), HW's nephew. She was living in Paris at this time; HW had introduced her to Mme du Deffand (Family 49 n. 1).

3. Pierre Gilbert de Voisins (1684–1769), avocat général, 1718; conseiller d'État, 1740; premier président au Grand Conseil, 1744; membre du Conseil des Dépêches, 1757 (nbg).

4. He died at Paris on 20 April 1769.

16 de ce mois. Il dit à M. Le Beau,[5] un savant d'ici, son ami qui
venait dîner avec lui, 'Je me sens défaillir, je n'irai pas loin, je
mourrai vendredi ou samedi, j'en suis sûr; n'en dites rien ici, à
cause de mes enfants.' Il fut ce jour-là en présence de sa famille
comme à l'ordinaire. Le lundi on fît venir son médecin qui après
l'avoir examiné convint qu'il n'était pas bien, mais ajouta cependant
qu'il était probable que ce ne serait rien. 'Mon ami,' dit le malade,
'je n'ai jamais donné dans le probabilisme.' Le mardi, son médecin
revint encore. 'Eh bien,' lui dit-il, 'je vous l'avais bien dit, je me sens
bien.' Il fut au conseil le mercredi, il opina deux heures dans une
affaire très importante; les papiers tombèrent de ses mains, il eut
une faiblesse; il se remît et continua. Il dît aux autres conseillers
d'état: 'Messieurs, il serait important que je fusse au jugement de
cette affaire, beaucoup de détails venus à ma connaissance et qui
doivent y influer sont connus de moi et ignorés de vous. Mais je me
sens mal, il faut se dépêcher. Je ne pourrai demain revenir au conseil,
mais, si vous voulez venir chez moi, j'espère être encore en état
demain matin de conférer avec vous.' Ces messieurs se rendirent chez
lui le jeudi à 10 heures. Cette séance dura jusqu'à midi sans que
l'affaire fut terminée; 'Cela devient bien long,' dit-il, 'il faut que je
me remette un peu. Revenez, je vous prie, à 6 heures ce soir, je crois
que je pourrai encore travailler avec vous.' Ces messieurs partirent. Il
monta en carrosse et fut se promener seul dans sa voiture jusqu'à une
heure et demie, afin de prendre des forces. Il revint chez lui, trouva
sa famille à table, s'assit au bout de cette table sans manger et causa
avec ses enfants. À trois heures on le porta dans sa chambre assis dans
son fauteuil, et ce fut là qu'il fut administré, il en avait donné l'ordre
le matin; il reconduisit le viatique jusque sur son escalier à l'aide de
deux bras. Il rentra dans son cabinet; il s'y recueillit jusqu'à 6 heures,
alors il demanda si ces messieurs étaient venus. Comme ils avaient vu
son état le matin, ils s'étaient fait excuser sous différents prétextes
pour ne le pas fatiguer; on lui dît donc qu'ils n'y étaient pas. 'J'en
suis fâché,' dit-il, 'au reste ce n'est pas ma faute.' Il resta avec ses
enfants jusqu'à 8 heures qu'il se coucha. Son valet de chambre voulut,
comme à l'ordinaire, rouler ses cheveux en papillottes sous son bonnet
de nuit. 'Oh!' dit-il, en souriant, 'cela est par trop inutile.' On lui

5. Charles Le Beau (1701–78), secretary
of the Académie des Inscriptions, 1755;
French historian. Le Beau wrote the epitaph for Gilbert de Voisins in the church
of St Séverin de Paris.

demanda plusieurs fois comment il se trouvait. 'Je remercie Dieu,' répondit-il, 'de ne pas souffrir davantage. Ma tête est libre, je n'éprouve point de douleur, mais du mal-aise.' Cela va bientôt finir, effectivement à deux heures après minuit il expira doucement et sans aucun effort.

Le peu de faste de cette mort, les devoirs de l'état remplis jusqu'au dernier instant, sans faiblesse, sans superstition, avoir passé le dernier jour de sa vie comme tous les autres, en sachant bien que c'était le dernier; ce sont là des traits qui ne vous échapperont pas, Monsieur; ils n'ont pas échappé à Madame Cholmondelei non plus. Je suis fâchée seulement que la matière de mon histoire soit triste.

J'ai l'honneur d'être avec la plus grande considération,

> Monsieur,
> Votre très humble et très obéissante servante,
>
> Morin Élie de Beaumont

Recevez, je vous supplie, Monsieur, les assurances du respect de mon mari.

To Robert Wood,[1] Sunday 19 November 1769

Printed for the first time from a photostat of the MS in the possession of Mr Robert W. Wood, Field's End, Roman Road, Lyme Regis, Dorset, kindly supplied by Mr Wood's father, the late Canon G. Robert Wood. Mr Wood, a great-great-great-grandson of Robert Wood, acquired the MS by family descent.
Endorsed by Mrs Robert Wood: 19 November 1769 Mr Ho. Walpole.

Arlington Street, Nov. 19, 1769.

I AM extremely sorry, Sir, not to have been at home when you did me the honour to call; you would have seen how much I am flattered by the particular distinction with which your partiality has favoured me; though my vanity is not so seduced by it as to make me think myself capable of correcting one of the best and purest authors we have ever had.[2] It is only as your admirer, Sir, that I

---

1. (ca 1717–71), M.P.; undersecretary of state 1756–63, 1768–70; groom porter 1764–6; traveller and antiquary; author of *The Ruins of Palmyra*, 1753, and *The Ruins of Balbec*, 1757. HW's copies are, respectively, Hazen, *Cat. of HW's Lib.*, Nos 3548 and 3547.

2. In the Preface to *Anecdotes of Painting* HW wrote: 'But of all the [architectural] works that distinguish this age,

can presume to think myself entitled to a preference in seeing your work³ before it is made public. I am just going out of town, and with your permission will carry it with me, that I may have time to read it as carefully as I am sure it deserves. If your Homer by a strange accident, or by your other avocations, *aliquando dormitat*,⁴ I will take the liberty you allow me, Sir, to give him a little jog, not from self-sufficience, but as a proof that I think Mr Wood above flattery, that I never have flattered him, and that I am his

Very obedient humble servant

Hor. Walpole

To Robert Wood, Thursday 23 November 1769

Printed for the first time from a photostat of the MS in the possession of Mr Robert W. Wood, Field's End, Roman Road, Lyme Regis, Dorset, kindly supplied by Mr Wood's father, the late Canon G. Robert Wood. For the history of the MS see *ante* 19 Nov. 1769.

Strawberry Hill, Nov. 23d 1769.

I HAVE read, Sir, with the greatest satisfaction, delight and information the book¹ you was so good as to send me; and I wish I could find words that had not been prostituted in compliments to au-

none perhaps excel those beautiful editions of Balbec and Palmyra . . . undertaken by private curiosity and good sense, and trusted to the taste of a polished nation. . . . The modest descriptions prefixed are standards of writing: the exact measure of what should and should not be said, and of what was necessary to be known, was never comprehended in more clear diction, or more elegant style' (*Works* iii. 8–9).

3. *An Essay on the Original Genius of Homer*, 1769. Only seven copies of this edition were printed. Wood apparently sent HW one of the copies for his criticisms, and HW returned it; see Mason i. 212 n. 13. William Bowyer, the printer of the 1769 edition, retained one copy in which he entered all of Wood's later additions and corrections; these were incorporated in the edition of the *Essay* pub-

lished posthumously in 1775 (Nichols, *Lit. Anec.* iii. 81–5). See following letter and HW to Mrs Wood *post* 7 July 1775.

4. Doubtless an allusion to Horace's *Ars poetica*, l. 359: *quandoque bonus dormitat Homerus* ('whenever good Homer "nods" ').

———

1. *An Essay on the Original Genius of Homer*, 1769, 4to. This edition, of which only seven copies were printed, is only 70 pages long. A greatly expanded and corrected edition was published posthumously in 1775, entitled *An Essay on the Original Genius and Writings of Homer: With a Comparative View of the Ancient and Present State of the Troade*, 4to; it consisted of 342 pages, not including an eleven-page preface 'To the Reader.' All notes below refer to the 1775 edition of the *Essay*.

thors, to tell you my real sentiments, without suspicion of flattery. The discoveries you have made by the exercise of your judgment, must convince you, that when I point out some of them, I am not merely repaying the honour you have done me in asking my opinion. Amongst others, nothing struck me more than that totally new method of criticism, by which you have ascertained Homer's country, from considering the perspective, and proving what was his position when he wrote. If that sagacity was happy, the knowledge with which you have illustrated it, is as great as it was necessary.

The observation in page xv on the various reasons that influenced Nestor etc. formerly, and you in your modern voyage,[2] is not less judicious.

I was extremely pleased too with your reasoning in p. xix at the end of the chapter, on the voyage of Antenor.[3] I should call it obvious, if all the commentators had not missed it; but you have shown the difference between good sense and writing comments; or in other words, between good sense and conjectures.

The chapter on the Winds[4] is very new and consequently very instructive: but nothing is more amazing than Pope's map being a map reversed.[5] With all your mercy to him, I fear you have proved what his enemies asserted, that[6] he little understood the original; I do not mean merely from that map, which he not only in all probability left to the execution of others, but never cast his eye upon.

If a poet has not done justice to a poet, you have, Sir. Your vindication of him in the danger of the coast of Egypt[7] is unanswerable.

On the Egyptians and the panegyrics so unjustly bestowed on them, you have given me much satisfaction.[8] Voltaire had weakened my faith on that head.[9] That you could glean new objections is very extraordinary; and as they are ascertained by your own experience and observation, I give them much more credit than I often do to his hypotheses.

The confutation of the Romans being descended from Æneas,[10] and the nice and accurate observations on Virgil's expressions in

2. *Essay*, pp. 40–1.
3. Ibid. 58–61.
4. 'Homer's Winds,' ibid. 62–71.
5. Ibid. 87–9.
6. The MS reads 'than.'
7. Ibid. 109–15.
8. Ibid. 120–4.

9. For example, in the 'Troisième Diatribe de l'Abbé Bazin,' 'Sur l'Égypte,' in *La Défense de mon oncle*, 1767 (*Œuvres complètes de Voltaire*, ed. Moland, 1877–85, xxvi. 420–2).
10. *Essay*, pp. 196–8.

p. lii,[11] by which you give infinitely more meaning to his words than had yet been discovered, are admirable; in short, as full of penetration, as the remarks at the beginning on the perspective from Homer's position. In the same style, Sir, you have doubled the force of the propriety with which the Ancients called the Muses, Daughters of Memory; [12] the want of letters making it as necessary for the Muses to remember what their votaries should produce, as what they had dictated to those poets.

If I ventured to disagree with you, Sir, on any point, it would be in the supposition that for some centuries the *Iliad* and *Odyssey* were preserved only by oral tradition.[13] I doubt whether Homer himself could have retained them by heart—and though this supposition does not demand such extravagant credulity as *Fingal* [14] does, I own I cannot conceive the preservation of such voluminous works solely by memory. If the fact is true, and I certainly am not learned enough to confute you, the fact itself is a full answer to all the faults that have been found with Homer. It would account for his tautology and repetitions, and a man would be very excusable to make use of the answer, which divines and commentators have so often urged on other occasions, with far less foundation, that his faults are interpolations or corruptions. But this being a matter of private opinion I will not trouble you with cavils, nor even with pointing out many other beauties and criticisms which have charmed me in your work. Much less have I any occasion to offer corrections. Some errors of the press, as a printer myself, I have marked in the copy. In the style I see nothing but clearness, precision, and singular merit, yet to prove that I was ready to find fault even on this head, allow me to point out three trifling slips.

In the very first page (to the reader) at the beginning of the second paragraph, I would not repeat twice in three lines, *as to* the manner, *as to* the choice.[15]

In page xx, forgive me if I dislike the words *in the jockey phrase*.[16] They are not of a piece with the dignity and gravity of all the rest.

The third is still more unimportant. In p. xxix, line 21, I would say India*n*, not India commodities.[17] In English we are too apt to

11. Ibid. 198–209.

12. Ibid. 260–2.

13. Ibid. 249–60.

14. The Ossianic epic published by James Macpherson in 1761. HW doubted its authenticity; see Montagu i. 407–8.

15. The 1775 edition, p. [v], retains 'as to the manner of' but omits 'as to the choice.'

16. These words were later omitted.

17. The 1775 edition, p. 101, reads 'Indian commodities.'

turn all substantives into adjectives, to the prejudice of our language's purity.

I cannot finish this abstract of my sentiments and content, without expressing my impatience, Sir, to see your larger work and your travels.[18] Such observation and acute penetration must have made remarks that could not properly find a place in your dissertation on Homer. Remember that you have interested me as much about yourself, as you [have][19] about what relates to him: and though that can be no inducement to you to humour me, it is at least a reason why I should prefer my request. I grow old, and as my taste for poetry abates, the passion for excellent sense increases. You have opened a mine to me, and told me you have more of the ore in your burrow. If begging would do, is this an age in which one should not be rich? Pray bestow your charity, for I am not young enough to expect a legacy. I am Sir

> Your much obliged and obedient humble servant
>
> Hor. Walpole

From the Duchesse de Choiseul, Thursday 30 November 1769

Printed from *Correspondance complète de Mme du Deffand,* ed. the Marquis de Sainte-Aulaire, 1866, iii. 376–7, where the letter was first printed. The letter was apparently in the possession of Sainte-Aulaire in 1866; not further traced.

De Paris, ce 30 novembre 1769.

C'EST la petite-fille,[1] Monsieur, qui, loin d'avoir la soumission d'un enfant vis-à-vis de sa grand'maman, a pour moi la dureté d'une marâtre; c'est elle qui m'a empêchée jusqu'à ce jour de répondre à votre aimable et très aimable lettre.[2] Oui, Monsieur, elle m'a fait un plaisir infini; elle est pleine d'affection et de sensibilité pour moi; j'en ai été touchée; j'ai ri en même temps de la tournure que vous donnez à vous inquiétudes et même de vos injustices. Oh!

---

18. Apparently a reference to Wood's plan of expanding the *Essay* and including the *Comparative View of the Ancient and Present State of the Troade* (n. 1 above). See HW to Mrs Wood *post* 7 July 1775.

19. The MS reads 'are.'

---

1. Mme du Deffand.
2. HW's letter to Mme de Choiseul 3 Nov. 1769 is missing.

la jolie lettre! la jolie lettre que celle de mon aimable petit-fils! la petite-fille a dû vous dire au moins combien elle m'avait fait de plaisir.[3]

Je vois que vous m'avez crue beaucoup plus malade que je ne l'ai été, et que vous croyez que je me conduis beaucoup moins bien que je ne me suis conduite. Sachez que j'ai été fort peu malade, et que je me suis conduite à merveille; mais sachez, ce qui est bien plus extraordinaire, que je ne pourrais pas payer de toute ma fortune le plaisir, le bonheur, les délices que m'a procurés cette petite maladie. J'ai éprouvé de la part du public, en général, une bienveillance faite pour flatter ma vanité; mais ce n'est rien que la vanité, j'ai éprouvé de mes amis les soins les plus tendres, les plus aimables, les plus sensibles, et de la part du grand-papa[4] surtout, une tendresse qui pénétrait mon cœur. Non, j'ai été trop heureuse, je le suis trop encore, je ne voudrais pas pour rien au monde n'avoir pas fait cette délicieuse épreuve. Pardonnez ces puérilités qui vous paraîtront peut-être fades; vous pensez peut-être, comme bien d'autres, que la sensibilité des femmes n'est que faiblesse; mais qu'importe comme quoi je sois heureuse, pourvu que je le sois? et je le suis à un degré dont je ne pouvais pas même concevoir l'idée. Conservez votre amitié à la grand'maman, mon cher petit-fils, elle importe infiniment au bonheur dont elle se vante.

Je vous quitte pour aller joindre la petite-fille et lui parler de vous; je me flatte d'être fort joliment avec la nièce[5] que j'aime beaucoup.

---

3. 'La grand'maman a été charmée de votre lettre, elle aime son petit-gendre, et toute sa petite cour suit son exemple' (Mme du Deffand to HW 12 Nov. 1769, du Deffand ii. 304).

4. The Duc de Choiseul.

5. Mrs Robert Cholmondeley, wife of HW's nephew (ante 26 April 1769, n. 2).

From DAVID GARRICK, Tuesday 26 December 1769

Printed from a photostat of the MS in the Library of the Cathedral of St Asaph. First printed in *The Letters of David Garrick*, ed. D. M. Little and G. M. Kahrl, Cambridge, Mass., 1963, ii. 678. The MS was probably that sold SH vi. 127 to Payne and Foss; not further traced until acquired by the Cathedral of St Asaph.

The year of the letter is established by the reference to *The Jubilee* (see n. 4 below).

Address: To the Honourable Mr Walpole, Arlington Street.

December 26.

MR GARRICK presents his respects to Mr Walpole. He returned from Hertfordshire last night, and found his note[1] upon the table. He immediately sent to the Housekeeper,[2] and Madame de Châtelet[3] may have the stage box opposite to the King's, either the 2d or 3d of January, and Mr Garrick will take care to have the *Jubilee*[4] on that night Madame Châtelet pleases to appoint.

To the REV. THOMAS PERCY, 1770

Printed from a photostat of the MS in the British Museum (Add. MS 32,329, f. 70). First printed, Toynbee xv. 446–7. For the history of the MS see *ante* 5 Feb. 1765.

Dated approximately by the reference to 'the valuable book' published in 1770 (see n. 1 below).

Address: To the Reverend Dr Percy at Northumberland House.

MR Walpole sends his best compliments to Dr Percy, and gives him a thousand thanks for the valuable book[1] he has received from him, and for which Mr W. begs Dr Percy will be so kind as to

1. Missing.
2. Of Drury Lane theatre.
3. Diane-Adélaïde de Rochechouart (d. 1794), m. (1751) Louis-Marie-Florent, Comte (Duc, 1777) du Châtelet, French ambassador to England 1767–70. They arrived in London 9 Dec. (*Public Adv.* 11 Dec. 1769). 'Madame du Châtelet is returned with her husband; but take notice, Madam, I do not announce this to you as good news' (HW to Lady Mary Coke 14 Dec. 1769, MORE 144).

4. Garrick's dramatic entertainment *The Jubilee* was a stage adaptation of the Shakespearian pageant at Stratford which had been prevented by rain. It was first performed at Drury Lane 14 Oct. 1769; the fifty-sixth performance was given on 3 Jan. 1770 (*London Stage* Pt IV, iii. 1419, 1429–30, 1446).

1. 'Northumberland Household-book' (MS note in an unidentified hand on the letter). Percy edited *The Regulations and*

make his acknowledgments to the Duke of Northumberland.[2]

Mr W. takes the liberty of troubling Dr Percy with a very inadequate return, the enclosed pieces;[3] one of which he is begged to accept, and to have the goodness of offering the other to his Grace in Mr Walpole's name.

To Lord Camden, Wednesday 17 January 1770

Printed from HW's MS draft, now WSL. First printed, Toynbee *Supp.* i. 182–3. For the history of the MS draft see *ante* 2 Feb. 1754. The original letter sent to Camden is missing.

Endorsed by HW: To Lord Camden.

Jan. 17, 1770.

My Lord,

THE less I paid attendance on your Lordship, when in place,[1] the more I think it my duty to give every mark of respect and esteem to your Lordship's virtues, when no interest but those of truth and gratitude can dictate the expression of my sentiments. I can never forget, my Lord, the defence the constitution owed to your firmness;[2] and I must put your Lordship in mind that nothing could be more obliging than the manner in which you granted at my request a preferment to Mr Chute's nephew.[3] But, my Lord, neither gratitude for public or private benefits, however strongly I feel both, are the sole motives of my troubling you with this letter. I lament the loss the country feels in being deprived of your Lordship's integrity

Establishment of the Household of Henry Algernon Percy, the fifth Earl of Northumberland, privately printed, 1770. HW's copy, inscribed 'Presented to Horace Walpole, Esq. (by command of the Duke of Northumberland) with his best respects by the Editor,' is now WSL; it is Hazen, *Cat. of HW's Lib.,* No. 2436.

2. Sir Hugh Smithson (after 1750, Percy) (1715–86), 4th Bt, 2d E. of Northumberland, n. c.; cr. (1766) D. of Northumberland. Percy had been appointed domestic chaplain and secretary to Northumberland in 1765.

3. Doubtless one of the SH Press's productions.

1. Camden had been dismissed as lord chancellor on 12 Jan. but retained the seal of office until 17 Jan., when it was transferred to Charles Yorke; see DALRYMPLE 130 n. 2.

2. HW doubtless refers to Camden's conduct in 1758, when (as attorney-general) he introduced a bill 'for explaining and extending the Habeas Corpus, and ascertaining its full operation' (*Mem. Geo. II* iii. 100–4, 112–21).

3. John Tracy Atkyns (1706–73), barrister, son of John Chute's half-brother John Tracy, was in 1755 appointed cursitor baron of the Exchequer (DNB).

and wisdom at the head of its laws and councils; and I lament the wound the constitution receives in your being removed on the difference of opinion,[4] a reason I never have approved nor can approve, when I am persuaded that a conscience so sound as your Lordship's inspired that opinion. I know myself too inconsiderable, my Lord, to think my sentiments of any importance, if I did not believe that a mind like yours would be pleased with the testimony borne to its virtues by any disinterested man. I have never had any personal views, and am indifferent to all parties. I wish the good of my country, and as a friend to it, must love those whom I have seen attached to its interests. As your Lordship is one of the brightest in that number, give me leave to assure you that nobody can be with greater respect and admiration than I am

> My Lord
> Your Lordship's most grateful
> and most obedient humble servant

> HOR. WALPOLE

From Lord Camden, Saturday 27 January 1770

Printed from the MS now WSL. First printed, Toynbee *Supp.* i. 183–4. For the history of the MS see *ante* 2 Feb. 1754.

> Lincoln's Inn Fields,
> January 27, 1770.

Sir,

THE hurry of various business which the great change of my affairs has brought upon me by my dismission,[1] has prevented me from taking notice of your most obliging letter. But give me leave to assure you that though I have received upon the present occasion some very flattering compliments sufficient almost to compensate the loss of my office, yet I esteem none of all these so honourable or valuable as your favourable testimony of my conduct; for I prefer the private praise of one gentleman of distinguished worth, disinterested (as you must be), and attached to no party, to the noisy applause of

4. Camden had joined Lord Chatham in his attack 9 Jan. on the King's speech to Parliament (*Mem. Geo. III* iv. 23–4).

1. See previous letter, n. 1.

multitudes. Your letter therefore must be my epitaph, unless I should happen by some change of conduct hereafter to undeserve it. In that case you will have a right to recall your good opinion as a thing forfeited by my own unworthiness. But I am sure that temptation must be very strong that should induce me to part with this fair monument of my own character, which my posterity will read with as much pride, as I did with pleasure.

As every station of life brings some good as well as evil with it, I reckon the possession of leisure and the command of my own time among the principal comforts of my present situation, being now [for][2] the first time emancipated from the slavery of my profession. The best use of this leisure will be to cultivate the conversation of my friends, and if you will honour me so far as to enlist me in the number of yours and open your door to me, I shall make it my business to renew our long interrupted acquaintance.[3]

I have the honour to be, with the most perfect esteem and sincerity,

Your most obliged and obedient servant,

CAMDEN

To LADY JERSEY,[1] after 26 March 1770

Printed for the first time from the MS now WSL. The MS was sold Sotheby's 23 April 1934 (property of the late Walter Sneyd), lot 169, to Maggs for WSL; its earlier history is not known.

Frances Twysden became Lady Jersey on 26 March 1770.

Address: To the Countess of Jersey, Grosvenor Square.

Memoranda (presumably by Lady Jersey):

    Nantwich

    Gregory

    Castle Dublin

I AM much honoured, Madam, by the message[2] your Ladyship was so good as to leave for me yesterday; and I would fly to obey it, if, as I have almost lost the use of my feet, I had got any wings in their

2. The MS reads 'from.'

3. At Eton and King's College. See Nichols, *Lit. Illus.* i. 500–5.

———

1. Frances Twysden (1753–1821), m. (26 March 1770) George Bussy Villiers (1735–1805), 4th E. of Jersey, 1769. See BERRY ii. 138 n. 3.

2. Missing.

room. I have been confined this month by the gout, and though I just crawl out again a little, I am forced to be led, and own I have not courage enough yet to come into your room like an old beggar. If I am more heroic in two or three days, and you will allow me to call about eight o'clock, before you have company, I think I shall venture, as it is the only mark I can give you, Madam, of the respectful regard of

Your Ladyship's most devoted humble servant

HOR. WALPOLE

From LORD DACRE, Monday 30 April 1770

Printed from the MS now WSL. First printed, Toynbee *Supp.* iii. 219. Damer-Waller; the MS was sold Sotheby's 5 Dec. 1921 (first Waller Sale), lot 115 (with lot 116), to Wells; given by him to Thomas Conolly, of Chicago, from whom WSL acquired it in 1937.

April 30 fell on Monday in 1764 and 1770. Dacre would hardly have troubled HW with a 'recommendation to General Conway' on 30 April 1764, only ten days after Conway had been dismissed from his regiment and from the Bedchamber (CONWAY ii. 376); 1770 is doubtless the correct year.

Endorsed by HW: From Thomas Lennard Barret Lord Dacre.
Address: To the Honourable Horatio Walpole.

Monday, April 30th.

Dear Sir,

AS YOU were so good as to say that you would honour Mr Roper[1] with your recommendation to General Conway,[2] I have advised him to postpone waiting on the General till he had had that advantage. However, that his delay may not appear want of due attention and respect, I beg that you will mention the reason of it when you speak to Mr Conway.

As I am obliged to go into Essex[3] this evening upon business and shall not return till Wednesday evening, it will be Thursday at soonest before I can bring Mr Roper to wait upon you, as you were so

---

1. Trevor Charles Roper (1745–94), 18th Bn Dacre, 1786; Lord Dacre's nephew.

2. Conway was at this time Lieutenant-General of the Ordnance. The 'recommendation' may have concerned army

business, although Roper does not appear to have ever served in the military.

3. Belhus, Dacre's seat, was near Aveley, Essex.

good to permit me to do. When he has had that happiness and under your protection he will be impatient to pay his respects to the General. I am, dear Sir,

Your most obedient and obliged servant,

DACRE

From the REV. JAMES GRANGER, ca May 1770

Printed from *Letters between the Rev. James Granger . . . and Many of the Most Eminent Literary Men of his Time*, ed. J. P. Malcolm, 1805, pp. 20–1, where the letter was first printed. For the history of the MS see *ante* 24 April 1764. Granger's MS draft of the letter is in the possession of Mrs P. A. Tritton, of Parham Park, Pulborough, Sussex; it formerly belonged to Mrs Tritton's mother, the Hon. Mrs Clive Pearson, who bequeathed it (1974) to her daughter.

Dated approximately by Granger to HW *post* 19 May 1770.

Honoured Sir,

I BELIEVE there was never yet an infallible author, or a book published withont an error. I have, even in your works, where I least expected to find any, met with here and there one. May I, Sir, take the liberty (with all humility I ask it) to mention them,[1] as they may be corrected in a table of errata, or in a subsequent edition? It was with the greatest difficulty I prevailed upon myself to use this freedom, which perhaps may be thought a preposterous way of expressing my great veneration for the author of the *Anecdotes;*[2] but, if I have done wrong, it was from an error of judgment, not from any fault of my will. I, indeed, very naturally concluded that what would be the greatest condescension in you, with respect to my blundering performance,[3] would be the height of presumption in me with regard to your work;[4] which, notwithstanding a few escapes, is, among its other excellencies, to be admired for its correctness.

But Tom Pidgeon,[5] my parish clerk, got the better of this reasoning: he told me, the other day, before the congregation, that I had named the wrong Psalm;[6] such is my love of truth, that, though

1. Granger's list of errata is missing.
2. *Anecdotes of Painting in England.*
3. *A Biographical History of England*, 1769. See *ante* 3 April 1764, n. 2.
4. *Historic Doubts on the Life and* *Reign of King Richard the Third*, 1768. For Granger's opinion of the book see *ante* 11 Feb. 1768, n. 4.
5. Not further identified.
6. Granger was vicar of Shiplake, Oxon.

Tom is a great blunderer himself, I could not find in my heart to be angry with him. This incident at once overcame my timidity, and I reasoned thus with myself. Surely Mr Walpole, as the disparity is greater betwixt us, will no more be displeased with me, than I was with Tom Pidgeon.

I have, together with the errata, taken occasion to mention a few other particulars, as they occurred to me. I hope, Sir, you will not think of returning the prints,[7] which are much at your service.

I am, Sir, with the greatest respect,

Your most obedient humble servant,[8]

JAMES GRANGER

From the REV. JAMES GRANGER, Saturday 19 May 1770

Printed from the MS now WSL. First printed in *Letters between the Rev. James Granger . . . and Many of the Most Eminent Literary Men of his Time,* ed. J. P. Malcolm, 1805, pp. 21–2 (closing omitted). Reprinted, Toynbee *Supp.* iii. 219–20. Damer-Waller; the MS was sold Sotheby's 5 Dec. 1921 (first Waller Sale), lot 133, to Maggs; offered by them, Cat. No. 433 (Christmas 1922), lot 3287; sold by Maggs to Capt. Frank L. Pleadwell, M. D., USN, before 1935; given by him to WSL, 1947.

Shiplake, 19 May 1770.

Sir,

I RETURN you a thousand and a thousand thanks for your last letter.[1] The great excellence of your understanding, and the goodness and gentleness of your nature are apparent in every line of it. For this and your other favours, which are all of an extraordinary kind, I shall ever love, esteem, and honour you. Permit me, good and worthy Sir, to assure you that not a syllable of that impertinent letter[2] to which you vouchsafed an answer, was dictated by spleen or resentment. It was the effect of *timidity;* and, I fear, of a little un-

7. Probably engraved 'heads' of persons included in Granger's *Biographical History,* but not otherwise identified.

8. The closing is supplied from Granger's MS draft (see headnote).

1. Missing.

2. *Ante* ca May 1770.

subdued *vanity*, which was scarce known to myself. I shall endeavour to root out every fibre of these ill weeds from my nature, which if permitted to grow, must not only render me unhappy, but ridiculous; though I am in more danger from the latter than ever, from your abundant candour in favour of my work.[3] I hope, Sir, that you will, as you see occasion, be so much my friend as to continue to inform me of my errors of any kind.[4] I shall ever listen to you with the utmost attention, and shall thank and bless you for your kind and gentle reproofs. That every blessing here and hereafter may attend you, is the ardent wish and prayer of,

Honoured Sir,
    Your ever obliged, and most grateful humble servant,

JAMES GRANGER

To MARY DEWES,[1] ca Friday 8 June 1770

Mary Dewes wrote to her future husband, John Port, 9 June 1770: 'I yesterday received a very polite note from Mr Walpole to invite me to Strawberry Hill on Monday next "to meet the Duchess of Portland and Mrs Delany," but I am engaged, so have sent an excuse' (*The Autobiography and Correspondence of Mary Granville, Mrs Delany*, ed. Lady Llanover, 1861–2, iv. 267). The whereabouts of HW's letter is not known.

---

3. See ibid. n. 3.
4. See *post* 30 Jan. 1772.

———

1. (1746–1814), dau. of John Dewes, of Welsbourne, Warwickshire; m. (4 Dec. 1770) John Port (ca 1736–1807), of Ilam Hall, Staffs; Mrs Delany's niece (*Delany Corr.* iv. 312 n. 1; GM 1814, lxxxiv pt i. 699–700).

THE GALLERY AT STRAWBERRY HILL

To Paul Sandby,[1] Sunday 24 June 1770

Printed for the first time from a photostat of the MS bound in a copy of George Baker's *Catalogue of Books, Poems, Tracts, and Small Detached Pieces, Printed at the Press at Strawberry-Hill*, 1810, now in the Brighton Public Library. The history of this copy is not known.

Address: To Paul Sandby Esq. in Poland Street, London.

Strawberry Hill, June 24, 1770.

Sir,

AS YOUR brother[2] was so obliging as to promise to come and draw the perspective of my Gallery,[3] and as I do not know where to write to him,[4] I must beg the favour of you to put him in mind; and I should take it kindly if you or he would be so good as to let me know how soon it would be convenient to him to come hither, because I shall be absent all the month of August.[5]

I am Sir
Your obedient humble servant,

Hor. Walpole

1. (1725–1809), painter.

2. Thomas Sandby (1721–98), architect; elder brother of Paul Sandby.

3. Thomas Sandby's drawing of the Gallery at SH was finished by Edward Edwards. Writing to Cole 16 June 1781, HW refers to 'T. Sandby's fine view of the Gallery, to which I could never get him to put the last hand' (Cole ii. 274). HW pasted the drawing in his extra-illustrated copy of the 1784 *Description of SH*, now wsl (Hazen, *Cat. of HW's Lib.*, No. 3582). The drawing was engraved by Thomas Morris for the *Description*.

4. His address in 1770 was Windsor Great Park (Algernon Graves, *The Royal Academy of Arts*, 1905–6, vii. 13).

5. HW planned to visit Lord Strafford at Wentworth Castle in Yorkshire and the Duke of Richmond at Goodwood House in Sussex. He wrote Conway 12 July 1770: 'I entreat that the journey to Goodwood may not take place before the 12th of August, when I will attend you. But this expedition to Stowe [in early July] has quite blown up my intended one to Wentworth Castle. I have not resolution enough left for such a journey' (Conway iii. 128). HW was in Sussex in mid-August, but was apparently forced to curtail his visit due to an attack of gout (*Country Seats* 68; *post* 20 Oct. 1770).

To Lord Charlemont,[1] Saturday 20 October 1770

Printed from a photostat of the MS in the Royal Irish Academy, Dublin. First printed (with omissions) in Francis Hardy, *Memoirs of the Political and Private Life of James Caulfield, Earl of Charlemont*, 2d edn, 1812, i. 313–15 (misdated 'October 17th'). Reprinted (signature omitted), Wright v. 287–8 and Cunningham v. 263–4; Hist. MSS Comm., 12th Report, App. Part x (*Charlemont MSS*), 1891, p. 302 (closing and signature omitted); Toynbee vii. 416–18 (misdated 'Oct. 17' in Wright, Cunningham, and Toynbee). The MS descended in the Caulfeild family to the 3d Earl of Charlemont, who deposited his grandfather's papers in the Royal Irish Academy between 1882 and 1891.

Arlington Street, Oct. 20, 1770.

My Lord,

I AM very glad your Lordship resisted your disposition to make me an apology for doing me a great honour, for if you had not, the Lord knows where I should have found words to have made a proper return. Still you have left me greatly in your debt. It is very kind to remember me, and kinder to honour me with your commands; they shall be zealously obeyed to the utmost of my little credit, which will probably appear much greater than it is, for an artist that your Lordship patronizes, will, I imagine, want little recommendation besides his own talents.

It does not look indeed like very prompt obedience, when I am yet guessing only at Mr Jervais's[2] merit; but though he has lodged himself within a few doors of me, I have not been able to get to him, having been confined, my Lord, near two months with the gout, and still keeping my house.[3] My first visit shall be to gratify my duty and curiosity.

I am sorry to say, and beg your Lordship's pardon for the confession, that however high an opinion I have of your taste in the arts, I do not equally respect your judgment in books. It is in truth a defect you have in common with the two great men who are the respective models of our present parties,

1. James Caulfeild (1728–99), 4th Vct Charlemont, 1734; cr. (1763) E. of Charlemont; collector.

2. Thomas Jervais (or Jarvis) (d. 1799), glass painter, who executed Sir Joshua Reynolds's design for the great west window of New College Chapel. Charlemont had presumably asked HW to oversee a commission given to Jervais.

3. In late August HW was attacked by gout; he was 'perfectly recovered' and without 'the smallest symptom . . . of lameness or weakness' by late November (MANN vii. 236, 251–2).

The Hero William and the Martyr Charles.[4]

You know what happened to them after patronizing Kneller[5] and
Bernini—[6]

One knighted Blackmore[7] and one pensioned Quarles.[8]

After so saucy an attack, my Lord, it is time to produce my proof.
It lies in your own postscript,[9] where you express a curiosity to see a
certain tragedy,[10] with a hint that other works of the same author
have found favour in your sight, and that the piece ought to have
been sent to you. But, my Lord, even your approbation has not made
that author vain—and for the play in question, it has so many perils
to encounter, that it never thinks of producing itself.[11] It peeped out
of its lurking corner once or twice, and one of those times by the negligence of a friend[12] had like to have been, what is often pretended in
prefaces, *stolen and consigned to the press*.[13] Whenever your Lordship comes to England,[14] which, for every reason but that, I hope will
be soon, you shall certainly see it, and will then allow I am sure how
improper it would be for the author to risk its appearance in public.
However, unworthy as that author may be from his talents of your

---

4. Pope, 'Imitations of Horace' (Epistles
II. i), ll. 380–7:
Charles, to late times to be transmitted
fair,
Assign'd his figure to Bernini's care;
And great Nassau to Kneller's hand de-
creed
To fix him graceful on the bounding
steed:
So well in paint and stone they judg'd
of merit:
But Kings in Wit may want discerning
Spirit.
The Hero William, and the Martyr
Charles,
One knighted Blackmore, and one pension'd Quarles.
5. Sir Godfrey Kneller (1646–1723),
painter. His equestrian portrait of William III, now at Hampton Court, was
painted in 1701 to commemorate William's return to England after signing
the peace of Ryswick in 1697.
6. Giovanni Lorenzo Bernini (1598–
1680), Italian sculptor. His bust of Charles
I, executed 1636 in Rome, was destroyed
by fire at Whitehall in 1698.

7. Sir Richard Blackmore (d. 1729),
physician and poet. In 1697 he was appointed physician to William III and
knighted for his services.
8. Francis Quarles (1592–1644), poet.
He dedicated many of his works to
Charles I, but nothing is known of the
pension alluded to by Pope.
9. Charlemont's letter is missing.
10. HW's *The Mysterious Mother*, first
printed at the SH Press, 1768, in an
edition of 50 copies. HW carefully distributed only a few copies to friends.
11. 'I am not yet intoxicated enough
with it, to think it would do for the
stage, though I wish to see it acted' (HW
to Montagu 15 April 1768, Montagu ii.
259).
12. Not identified.
13. Concerning the unauthorized publication of the play at Dublin in 1791,
see HW to Charlemont *post* 17 Feb.
1791.
14. From Ireland.

Lordship's favour, do not let his demerits be confounded with the esteem and attachment with which he has the honour to be

My Lord
Your Lordship's most devoted humble servant

HORACE WALPOLE

From Madame du Deffand,[1]
Wednesday 26 December 1770

Printed from the Earl of Ilchester, 'Madame du Deffand to Walpole,' *Times Literary Supplement,* 19 June 1948, xlvii. 348, where the letter was first printed. The MS in Jean-François Wiart's hand (listed as missing in DU DEFFAND ii. 497) was found by the 6th Earl of Ilchester while rearranging the papers evacuated from Holland House during World War II; not further traced (not among the Holland House papers acquired by the British Museum in 1963). Wiart's spelling of proper names has been normalized, and a few obvious errors in the printed text have been silently corrected.

Memorandum (by HW, on the verso): Letter from Mme la Marquise du Deffand to Mr Horace Walpole, with an account of the Duc de Choiseul's disgrace.[2]

Mme du Deffand's grandmother was a Duchess of Choiseul, for which reason as the Duchess of the same name, wife of the prime minister, had a great friendship for Madame du Deffand. Though near forty years older, the latter called the Duchess *grand'maman,* and the Duchess called her *sa petite-fille.* These sobriquets became so familiar, that in their society the Duke was called *le grand-papa,* and Mme du Deff[and] named them together, *ses parents.*

Madame la Maréchale de Mirepoix was a very old friend of Mme du Deffand, and had been so of the Duc de Choiseul, but had quarrelled with him and was at the time of his disgrace leagued with Mme du Barry,[3] the King's mistress, the Marshal de Richelieu[4] and the Duke's enemies. Whether it was from friendship for Mme du Deff[and] or to keep some appearance of decency towards Choiseul, or to please her brother the Prince de Beauvau, who was particularly attached to Choiseul, as his wife the Princesse de Beauvau was to the Duchesse de Gram-

1. Marie de Vichy-Champrond (1696–1780), m. (1718) Jean-Baptiste-Charles du Deffand de la Lande, Marquis de Chastres.

2. Choiseul's resignation as secretary of state for war and minister for foreign affairs was ordered by Louis XV on 24 Dec. 1770; see Henri Verdier, *Le Duc de Choiseul,* 1969, pp. 197–228.

3. Jeanne Bécu (1743–93), m. (1768) Guillaume, Comte du Barry; mistress of Louis XV. She was chiefly responsible for Choiseul's removal from office.

4. Louis-François-Armand Vignerot du Plessis (1696–1788), Duc and Maréchal de Richelieu; first gentleman of the Bedchamber (DU DEFFAND i. 154 n. 4).

mont,[5] Choiseul's sister, I cannot tell. The Duchesse douairière d'Aiguillon lived on the best of terms with the Choiseuls, and with almost all the nobility, would not visit Madame du Barry. However, after her son[6] became minister, he insisted on his mother's visiting the mistress, and she did, though with extreme repugnance.[7]

The Abbé Barthélemi, keeper of the King's medals and known by some publications, was a.Provençal and the chief friend and confidant of the Duchesse de Choiseul. Gatti,[8] a Florentine was her physician. M. de Castellane was another of her particular friends, as was the Prince de Bauffremont.[9] The Marquise de Boufflers was mother of the witty Chevalier,[10] and was sister of Mme de Mirepoix and the Prince de Beauvau. M. de Lisle[11] was attached to M. de Choiseul, was in England with M. du Châtelet, and wrote verses, but was a different person from Abbé de Lisle[12] the poet.

This letter is very valuable.

The Duc de Liancour,[13] the Marquis de Conflans,[14] and Monsieur Esterhasi[15] were in England with the Comte du Châtelet ambassador from France, and great friend of Choiseul; as all three were at different times afterwards.

Paris, ce mercredi 26 décembre 1770, à 10 heures du matin.

ON m'assure que je puis écrire en toute sûreté; je vais donc hasarder de vous raconter tout ce qui s'est passé depuis huit jours. Il faut vous dire d'abord que le lundi 17, une de mes amies[16] (dont je n'ose hasarder le nom, malgré l'assurance qu'on me donne) vint me trouver à 2 heures après minuit—j'avais donné à souper; elle attendit d'être seule. 'Jamais,' me dit-elle, 'vos amis n'ont été en si grand danger; le voyage de Choisy[17] est rompu' (on y devait aller le lendemain pour deux jours) 'et l'on compte bien employer le temps. M. d'Aiguillon en sortant de chez le Roi a dit tout bas à un de ses amis *nous avons gagnés deux précieux jours et nous espérons tout.*

5. Béatrix de Choiseul-Stainville (1730–94), m. (1759) Antoine-Antonin, Duc de Gramont (ibid. i. 30 n. 8).

6. Emmanuel-Armand Vignerot du Plessis-Richelieu (1720–88), Duc d'Aiguillon; governor of Brittany (ibid. i. 65 n. 11).

7. See ibid. iii. 110.

8. Angelo Giuseppe Maria Gatti (1730–98), Florentine physician, whom HW often met at Paris (ibid. i. 241 n. 5).

9. Charles-Roger de Bauffremont (1713–95), Chevalier de Listenois; Prince de Bauffremont, 1769 (ibid. i. 404 n. 3).

10. Stanislas-Jean de Boufflers (1737–1815), Chevalier de Boufflers; Marquis de Remiencourt (ibid. i. 13 n. 21).

11. Chevalier Jean-Baptiste-Nicolas de l'Isle (d. 1784), poet (ibid. ii. 24 n. 5).

12. Jacques Delille (1738–1813), abbé.

13. François-Alexandre-Frédéric (1747–1827), cr. (1765) Duc de Liancourt; Duc de la Rochefoucauld-Liancourt, 1792 (CHATTERTON 225 n. 5).

14. Louis-Gabriel de Conflans d'Armentières (1735–89), Marquis de Conflans (DU DEFFAND i. 237 n. 7).

15. Valentin-Ladislas (1740–1805), Comte Eszterházy (ibid. iv. 30 n. 3).

16. Madame de Mirepoix (HW).

17. A royal residence often visited by Louis XV, situated on the Seine southeast of Paris (DU DEFFAND i. 122 n. 9).

Faites usage de cet avis.' 'Que puis-je faire,' repartis-je, 'et quel partie faut-il prendre?' Je n'en sais rien mais je les tiens perdus. Jugez de mon embarras; le mardi dès les 7 heures du matin j'écrivis à l'Abbé[18] de venir me trouver et je lui envoyai mon carrosse; il vint. Nous écrivîmes au grand-papa;[19] c'était jour d'ambassadeurs,[20] il ne devait pas souper chez lui le mardi ni le mercredi. L'Abbé fut à onze heures chez la grand'maman qui envoya mon billet; nous soupâmes en très petite compagnie. Le grand-papa vint après souper; il me parût qu'il ne recevait point mon avis comme il devait; il disait qu'il était tranquille, qu'il ne craignait rien, mais avec une voix oppressée. Je me repentis presque de ma démarche. En me quittant il me demanda s'il ne me verrait pas le lendemain, qu'il ne souperait pas chez lui, mais qu'il reviendrait de très bonne heure. Le mercredi il y eut à souper Mme d'Anville,[21] la Comtesse[22] de Choiseul[23] qu'on appelle la petite sainte, l'Archev[êque] de Cambrai,[24] le Prince de Beauffremont, l'Abbé et moi. On vint apporter à l'Archevêque un petit billet, il le lut sans rien dire, mais quand il s'en alla il approcha de la grand'maman[25] et lui [dit] tout bas, 'Je viens de recevoir l'avis que mon frère sera renvoyé incessamment.' Dès qu'il fut sorti la grand'maman nous confia ce secret. Le grand-papa[26] arriva l'instant d'après, plus gai, plus amiable que jamais. On lui dit le billet; nous raisonnâmes on ne conclut rien; il était, disait-il, sans inquiétude, non qu'il ne prévît l'événement, mais il ne le craignait pas. Le jeudi il alla à Versailles dont il ne devait revenir que le jour de Noël. La veille de Noël la grand'maman devait souper chez moi avec Mme de Chabot,[27] M. de la Rochefoucault,[28] l'Év[êque] de Rodez,[29] le Prince de

18. Barthélemi (HW).

19. Duc de Choiseul (HW).

20. See *ante* 14 Feb. 1767, n. 9.

21. La Duchesse d'Anville (HW); Wiart wrote 'Mad. d'Emville.' Marie-Louise-Nicole-Élisabeth de la Rochefoucauld (1716–94), m. (1732) Jean-Baptiste-Louis-Frédéric de la Rochefoucauld de Roye, Duc d'Anville (DU DEFFAND i. 399 n. 2).

22. Wiart wrote 'la C.'; expanded by HW to 'Csse.'

23. Marie-Françoise Lallemant de Betz (d. 1793), m. (1749) Marie-Gabriel-Florent, Comte de Choiseul-Beaupré (ibid. i. 289 n. 10). She was often referred to as 'la petite sainte' because of her religious practices.

24. Frère du D[uc] de Choiseul (HW). Léopold-Charles de Choiseul-Stainville

(1724–74), Abp of Cambrai (ibid. i. 240 n. 4).

25. Wiart wrote 'g. m.'; expanded by HW to 'Maman.'

26. Wiart wrote 'G. P.'; expanded by HW to 'Grand Papa.'

27. Élisabeth-Louise de la Rochefoucauld (1740–86), dau. of the Duchesse d'Anville; m. (1757) Louis-Antoine-Auguste de Rohan-Chabot, Comte (Duc, 1775) de Chabot, Duc de Rohan, 1791 (ibid. ii. 318 n. 5).

28. Louis-Alexandre de la Rochefoucauld d'Anville (1743–92), son of the Duchesse d'Anville; Duc de la Rochefoucauld.

29. Jérôme-Marie Champion de Cicé (1735–1810), Bp of Rodez, 1770 (ibid. ii. 469 n. 5).

Beauffremont, l'Abbé, votre cousin,[30] l'envoyé palatin,[31] Gatti[32] et
M. de Stainville.[33] Le jeudi, le vendredi se passèrent sans événement,
le samedi je ne vis point la grand'maman. C'est le jour où je donne
à souper; j'eus comme à l'ordinaire Mesdames d'Aiguillon,[34] de
Mirepoix, la Marquise[35] de Boufflers et plusieurs hommes. Je ne me
portais pas bien—je ne me mis pas à table, je pris ma casse; tout le
monde s'en alla à une heure. Je restai un peu de temps seule avec
une personne[36] qui me confirma dans mes craintes, et qui me dit que
l'événement était bien prochain, et que[37] ce qu'il y aurait de mieux à
faire ce serait que M. de Praslin[38] fût parlé au Roi. Cela était impossible parce qu'il est pris de la goutte depuis la tête jusqu'aux
pieds. Le lendemain dimanche je passai la soirée chez la grand-
maman.[39] Il n'y avait que la petite sainte, M. de Stainville, quelqu'autres personnes dont je ne me souviens pas, mais devant qui on
pouvait parler librement; nous conclûmes de tous nos raisonnements
que la disgrâce était certaine mais qu'elle n'arriverait pas avant la
conclusion des négociations[40] soit paix, soit guerre, et effectivement
le grand-papa[41] avait pris son partie, il se serait alors retiré s'il n'avait
été renvoyé.

Nous nous séparâmes à une heure. Le lendemain, lundi, je m'oc-
cupai à ordonner mon souper. À 4 heures après midi comme je finis-
sais ma toilette Pont-de-Veyle[42] arriva chez moi, et avec une voix
très étouffée, 'N'avez-vous rien appris?' me dit-il. 'Non; il y a quel-

30. Robert Walpole (HW). Hon. Robert
Walpole (1736–1810), son of HW's uncle
Horatio Walpole, 1st Bn Walpole of
Wolterton; secretary of embassy 1768–9
and minister plenipotentiary 1769–71 at
Paris; envoy extraordinary and plenipo-
tentiary to Portugal 1771–80 (MANN vii.
141 n. 2).

31. Karl Heinrich Joseph (1737–91),
Reichsgraf von Sickingen; minister from
the Elector Palatine to France (DU DEF-
FAND ii. 442 n. 13).

32. Médecin (HW).

33. Frère du Duc de Choiseul (HW).
Jacques-Philippe de Choiseul (d. 1789),
Comte de Stainville (DU DEFFAND i. 217
n. 3a).

34. La Duchesse douairière, mère du
Duc (HW).

35. Expanded by HW from Wiart's 'M.'

36. Madame de Mirepoix (HW).

37. 'Que' added by HW in the MS.

38. César-Gabriel de Choiseul (1712–85),

Duc de Praslin; secretary of state; the
Duc de Choiseul's cousin and political
ally (DU DEFFAND i. 55 n. 3).

39. Grand Maman, Duchesse de Choiseul (HW); Wiart wrote 'la G. M.'

40. Negotiations to settle the dispute
between England and Spain concerning
the Falkland Islands. The English garri-
son there had been expelled by Spanish
forces, bringing the two nations to the
verge of war. France was sympathetic to
Spain, and Choiseul apparently believed
his position would be strengthened by
involving France in a naval war with
England. Peace was finally confirmed on
18 Jan. 1771 (DU DEFFAND ii. 482; MANN
vii. 244, 258).

41. Expanded by HW from Wiart's
'g. p.'

42. Antoine Ferriol (1697–1774), Comte
de Pont-de-Veyle. Pont-de-Veyle, a po-
etaster, was one of Mme du Deffand's
oldest friends (DU DEFFAND i. 11 n. 8).

que chose?' 'Oui.' 'Cela est-il fâcheux?' 'Sans doute.' 'Le grand-papa est-il exilé?' 'Oui.' Je fus saisie comme si je n'avais pas été prévenue. L'instant d'après je reçûs un petit billet de la grand'maman conçu en ces termes: 'Tout est fini, ma chère petite-fille. Je ne souperai pas chez vous ce soir mais vous souperez chez moi dans le sein de votre famille qui a bien de la tendresse pour vous.'

Il est superflu de vous dire l'état où j'étais. Je restai avec Pont-de-Veyle, je pris mon thé pendant qu'on mettait mes chevaux. J'écrivais un billet à l'Hôtel de la Rochefoucault pour dire qu'il n'y avait point de souper chez moi, et puis je courus chez la grand'maman. Je la trouvai avec la petite sainte, l'Abbé. La porte était fermée excepté pour la famille et un très petit nombre d'amis. Je ne puis vous peindre la tranquillité et même la gaîté de la grand'maman, mais sans affectation, sans fausseté, sentant l'indignité et la singularité du procédé, dans le moment où se devait décider et terminer une négociation dont le succès tenait et dépendait de l'estime et de la confiance qu'on[43] avait pour le grand-papa. Lui de son côté était dans son appartement occupé à arranger ses affaires. À chaque personne qui envoyait en haut pour demander à voir la grand'maman, elle prenait les ordres de son mari; elle ne laissa pas de voir assez de monde, il y eut bien 12 ou 13 personnes qui restèrent à souper. J'étais trop saisie pour pouvoir manger. Je ne me mis point à table, et quand tout le monde en fut sorti il me fut impossible de rester davantage; je partis avec le Prince.[44] Je revins chez moi, où je trouvai dans ma tribune la personne qui m'avait donné le premier avis. Elle me marqua infiniment d'amitié, et sans y compter beaucoup je ne laisse pas de m'applaudir de m'être maintenue bien avec elle; ce que je n'ai fait qu'avec l'agrément de mes parents,[45] qui lui savent gré de sa conduite dans cette occasion-ci.

Il faut vous dire présentement toutes les circonstances de la disgrâce. Le lundi à onze heures du matin M. de la Vrillière[46] arriva chez le grand-papa, et en répandant des larmes—comme c'est sa coutume depuis 50 ans qu'il est exercé cet office—il lui remet la lettre du Roi sans être cachetée, écrite de sa main et dont voici à peu près la teneur:

'J'ordonne à mon cousin le Duc de Choiseul de donner sa démis-

---

43. En Espagne (HW).
44. The Prince de Bauffremont.
45. Les Choiseuls (HW).

46. Ci-devant Comte de St-Florentin, secrétaire d'état (HW). See *ante* 17 Nov. 1766, n. 7.

sion de sa charge de secrétaire d'état et de la surintendance des postes. Je lui ordonne de se rendre à Chanteloup[47] et d'y rester jusqu'à nouvel ordre.'

Le grand-papa demanda s'il lui était permis de ne partir que le mercredi pour qu'on eût le temps d'échauffer le château; et comme de la Vrillière parut embarrassé de se charger de cette demande, le grand-papa écrivit au Roi et chargea le ministre de rendre son lettre. Ce fut pendant le souper de lundi qu'il reçut la réponse, qui fut de partir le mardi avant midi. Il dit après avoir lu, *Ah, c'est la goutte d'eau qui fait verser le verre.* Quand je sus cette réponse mon saisissement augmenta et je ne pus plus rester. Leur courage, leur fermeté, leur gaîté même me perçait l'âme, et quelque effort qu'ils fissent pour me retenir, je partis, et ce fut comme je vous ai dit qu'en rentrant chez moi je trouvai cette personne. Vous croyez bien que je ne dormis point de la nuit. Je me levai avant dix heures et je fus chez la grand'maman qui prétendait avoir bien dormi, se bien porter; mais tout le courage qui lui fait renfermer en elle-même son émotion et sa douleur ne peut manquer de bien nuire à sa santé. Je ne vis point le grand-papa. Il m'envoya des porcelaine[s] pour mes étrennes, et puis un moment après il fit dire à sa femme de descendre; nous fondions tous en larmes. Jamais non jamais il n'y eu de séparation plus touchante. Vous en auriez été pénétré, ils partirent à midi précises, eux deux avec Gatti. L'après-midi à 5 heures De L'Isle vint chez moi et surprit beaucoup en me disant qu'il venait de la grand'maman me donner de ses nouvelles; qu'il avait été à Longjumeau[48] les attendre, et que Messieurs de Liancourt,[49] de Conflans et d'Eszterházy y étaient venus dans le même dessein. Que le grand-papa leur avait demandé pourquoi ils étaient là, qu'ils étaient fondus en larmes pour toute réponse, ce qui avait émue le grand-papa au point de lui en faire répondre. Ils ont couchés cette nuit à Orléans et seront de bonne aujourd'hui à Chanteloup.[50] L'Abbé sollicite la permission d'aller les trouver. Je ne doute pas qu'il ne l'obtienne, mais si on la refuse c'est fait de la grand'maman. Mme de Grammont part aujourd'hui, M. de Cambrai vendredi, Mme de Beauvau samedi, et M. de Stainville dimanche. Le Prince de Beauffremont demandera la permission

47. Choiseul's estate, near Amboise.
48. About 12 miles south of Paris, on the road to Orléans.
49. Duc de Liancour (HW).
50. Mme de Choiseul's letter to Mme du Deffand written from Chanteloup 26 Dec. is printed in *Correspondance complète de Mme du Deffand,* ed. the Marquis de Sainte-Aulaire, 1866, i. 296.

d'y aller. La petite sainte qui ne se porte pas bien ira le plus tôt qui lui sera possible; et M. de Castellane qui est en Dauphiné et qui devait revenir à Paris le mois prochain, obtiend[r]a peut-être la permission d'aller les trouver.

J'oubliais de vous dire que dans les instructions que le Roi a donné par écrit à M. de la Vrillière, il dit que s'il n'a pas envoyé le grand-papa plus loin c'est par rapport à la grand'maman; mais que bien qu'il se trouve exilé dans son gouvernement ce sera comme s'il n'y était pas parce qu'il n'y aura aucune autorité de gouverneur; qu'ils ne recevront que leur famille et ceux qui auront la permission d'y aller.

Il me reste à vous parler de M. de Praslin—qui est exilé à Praslin. On lui a accordé un delai jusqu'à samedi pour s'y rendre,[51] mais avec la défense de recevoir chez lui autre personne que sa famille.

Je ne puis vous peindre la consternation et la douleur que cette disgrâce cause à tout le monde. Je vis hier prodigieusement de monde de tout espèce, étrangers, compatriotes, gens de la Cour, gens de la ville; chacun disait qu'il semblait qu'il n'y eut plus personne dans le monde, tout était réuni à lui. La noblesse, la fermeté, la franchise de sa conduite, l'horreur, le mépris qu'on a pour ses ennemis tout a concouru à le faire aimer et adorer. Qu'allons-nous devenir? Je n'en sais rien. Je tiens de l'eau dans ma bouche. Je n'ai nulle curiosité de savoir qui lui succédera, cela m'est d'une indifférence parfaite. On contait hier, et cela est certain que le Comte de Muy[52] a refusé sa place de secrétaire d'état de la guerre;[53] il est extrêmement dévot, et il a donné pour raison de son refus qu'il ne pourrait jamais rien faire qui fut contre ses principes, qu'il ne pourrait agir en courtisan, et qu'ainsi il y aurait beaucoup d'indiscretion à lui d'accepter une place dont il serait chassé au bout d'un an.

Voilà tout ce que vous aurez de moi aujourd'hui. On me répond que ma lettre ne sera point ouverte et je la mets en bonne main—je viens de faire un effort dont je ne me croyais pas capable.

Je reprends une demie feuille pour vous prier de dire ou de faire savoir à votre nièce[54] que je suis pas en état de lui écrire, en effet

---

51. See MANN vii. 257 and n. 3.

52. Louis-Nicolas-Victor de Félix (1711–75), Comte du Muy; Maréchal de France, 1775 (ibid. vii. 258 n. 8).

53. Du Muy declined the office of secretary of state for war at this time, but filled it in 1774–5. The Marquis de

Monteynard succeeded Choiseul in this post, and the Duc d'Aiguillon succeeded him as minister for foreign affairs (ibid. vii. 258 nn. 8–9, 265, 283 n. 33).

54. Mme Cholmondeley (HW). See *ante* 26 April 1769, n. 2.

c'est un effort que je ne pouvais faire que pour vous, mon corps est trop faible pour soutenir les secousses que reçoit mon âme. Vous me ferez plaisir de me donner l'adresse de votre nièce. J'ignore si elle est à la ville ou à la campagne.

Je n'entends point parler du petit Crauford.[55] Je ne serais pas étonnée d'apprendre qu'il s'est débarrassé de la vie. Il est bien profondément triste. Je comprends que sa compagnie ne vous convient guère.

J'ai reçu ces jours-ci une lettre de Voltaire,[56] qui sous prétexte d'être indigné de ce que le Président[57] ne m'a pas donné une marque de souvenir dans son testament[58] se délecte à m'en faire un portrait des plus satiriques; il traite sa chronologie d'almanach d'étrennes mignonnes;[59] il dit qu'il avait l'âme molle et le coeur dur; il tourne toute sa vie et ses occupations en ridicule. Quand je serais plus tranquille je lui écrirai que je [ne] suis pas contente de sa lettre;[60] mais je ne suis pour le présent en état d'écrire à personne, pas même à M. de Beauvau qui sera bien consterné de cet événement-ci. Pour moi je le suis au delà de toute expression, et l'idée de ne plus revoir la grand'maman n'est pas supportable, car, puis-je faire des projets de voyage à mon âge? Et puis dois-je me méprendre et ne pas sentir la différence qu'il y a entre la bonté et la tendresse? Pourrais-je consentir à devoir à la compassion ce que je ne veux devoir qu'à l'amitié? La reconnaissance qu'on aurait de la mienne ne me suffirait pas. Non, non il faut se dire ses vérités à soi-même; elles sont moins dures que de les entendre par la bouche des autres.

Je vous prie de faire tenir à votre nièce ces deux petits papiers.[61] C'est une lettre de Mme de Jonzac[62] et un mémoire de M. de Grave.

Je veux égayer cette lettre par ce petit couplet sur l'air de Joconde:[63]

Madame on ne saurait dit-on
vous voir et vous séduire
qu'on ne soit faux, lâche et fripon

55. John ('Fish') Craufurd, HW's friend and occasional correspondent.

56. Voltaire to Mme du Deffand 16 Dec. 1770, printed in *Voltaire's Correspondence*, ed. Theodore Besterman, Geneva, 1953–65, lxxvii. 167–8.

57. Hénaut (HW).

58. See du Deffand ii. 486 n. 2.

59. *Étrennes mignonnes* was the name of an almanac in very small format published at Paris from 1716 to 1845. Hénault's

Nouvel abrégé chronologique de l'histoire de France, 1744, was an octavo; the edition published in 1768 was a large quarto.

60. See Mme du Deffand to Voltaire 28 Dec. 1770, in Besterman, op. cit. lxxvii. 204.

61. Missing.

62. Hénault (HW). The Marquise de Jonzac, Hénault's niece (*ante* 17 Aug. 1766, n. 9).

63. À Madame du Barry (HW).

> et toujours prêt à nuire.
> Du mariage étrange effet!
> douce franche et gentille,
> c'est ce chacun vous trouvait
> lorsque vous étiez *fille*.

Vraiment j'oubliais de vous dire que celui qui a porté les derniers coups c'est M. le Prince de Condé. L'on craint qu'il n'en reste par là; on tremble pour les Suisses.[64]

> À 5 heures après midi.

Vous ne tomberez pas à la renverse quand vous apprendrez que M. de Muy a accepté. Il s'est rendu au réiteratives instances qu'on lui a fait d'accepter; il alléguait[65]

To the DUCHESSE DE CHOISEUL,
Monday 28 January 1771

Printed from a photostat of HW's MS copy in the Pierpont Morgan Library. First printed in *Extracts from the Journals and Correspondence of Miss Berry*, ed. Lady Theresa Lewis, 2d edn, 1866, ii. 35–6 (undated). Reprinted, Toynbee viii. 10-11. The history of the MS copy is not known. The original letter was sent by HW to Madame du Deffand to be forwarded to Mme de Choiseul; Mme du Deffand suppressed it, although she quoted a fragment of it in her letter to Mme de Choiseul 10 Feb. 1771 (see n. 3 below). Mme du Deffand wrote HW 1 Feb. 1771: 'Cette lettre ne sera pas fermée que je jetterai la vôtre au feu, et celle que vous écrivez à la grand'maman; elle n'est assurément pas du style que je vous avais conseillé' (DU DEFFAND iii. 21). The original is listed in HW's record of letters sent to Paris in 1771, 'par M. Francès' (ibid. v. 392).

Endorsed by HW: To the Duchess of Choiseul.

PENDANT que la France entière vous marquait ses regrets, Madame, je n'osais pas vous importuner des miens.[1] Mais le triomphe de la vertu doit-il se borner à un seul pays? La reconnaissance et la plus parfaite estime ne trouveront-elles pas un moment à se faire entendre? Oui, chère grand'maman, je perds le respect, qui vous est dû à tant d'égards, pour épancher mon cœur avec plus de liberté et de

---

64. It was alleged that the Prince de Condé wished to succeed Choiseul as Colonel-General of the Swiss; see *Mem. Geo. III* iv. 167–9, where HW describes Choiseul's downfall.

65. The rest of the MS is missing.

---

1. HW wrote Mann 29 Dec. 1771 concerning the Duc de Choiseul's fall from power: 'Thus Abishag [Mme du Barry] has strangled an administration, that had lasted fourteen years! I am sincerely grieved for the Duchess de Choiseul, the most perfect being I know of either sex. I cannot possibly feel for her husband; Corsica is engraved in my memory, as I believe it is on your heart' (MANN vii. 258).

tendresse. Je me réjouis avec vous, car de quoi vous plaindre? Avez-vous été ambitieuse, avare, insolente? Sont-ce des créatures qui vous regrettent, ou des malheureux? Monsieur le Duc de Choiseul est-il condamné de sa patrie, et de vous, ou approuvé, et comblé de louanges? Est-il plus doux de deviner ce que la postérité dira de nous, ou de l'entendre de la bouche de sa patrie et de toute l'Europe? Oh! vraiment je bénis le ciel de m'avoir donné un père et un grand-père dont la gloire ne fait qu'accroître tous les jours, et à qui il ne manquait que la disgrâce pour fixer l'immortalité. Oui, oui, belle maman, il faut vous conter ce qu'on dit de papa Choiseul—et cela ne vient pas d'une voix suspecte. My Lord Chatham a dit en plein parlement, que depuis M. le Cardinal de Richelieu la France n'avait point possédé un aussi grand ministre que M. le Duc de Choiseul, et qu'il avait emporté les regrets de tous les ordres de l'état[2]—voilà comme parlent les véritables grands hommes, qui s'y entendent. Notre peuple, qui ne connaît M. de Choiseul que par la peur qu'il leur avait faite, a une manière de louer toute différente, et se félicite de sa chute. Ce n'est pas un éloge à mépriser.[3]

Votre fermeté et la noblesse de votre âme, Madame, m'assurent, que parmi tant de sujets de gloire, vous[4] n'oublierez pas entièrement un homme que vous avez comblé de bontés, et qui vous est attaché par la reconnaissance et par l'admiration de toutes vos belles qualités. Permettez-moi de conserver le doux titre de votre petit-fils: et laissez-moi m'en orgueillir, comme si j'étais grand prince, sans mérite des vertus de mes ancêtres. Ma foi, je ne les troquerais pas contre un Cardinal de Richelieu; trop flatté si j'ose me signer

> Madame
>> Votre très affectionné et très fidèle serviteur

>>> HORACE WALPOLE DE CHOISEUL

2. Chatham's speech in the House of Lords on 25 Jan.: 'On the Duc de Choiseul he made a strained panegyric, pronouncing him the greatest minister that had appeared in France since Cardinal Richelieu—that he was regretted by all ranks of people in that country, and would (he would venture to prophesy) be recalled!' (*Mem. Geo. III* iv. 177).

3. 'My Lord Chatham a dit . . . mépriser' is quoted by Mme du Deffand in her letter to Mme de Choiseul 10 Feb. 1771 (*Correspondance complète de Mme du Deffand*, ed. the Marquis de Sainte-Aulaire, 1866, i. 340). Mme de Choiseul replied 12 May: 'Vous n'aurez pas une moindre querelle avec moi, ma chère petite, pour m'avoir privée de la lettre que m'a écrite M. de Walpole, que vous ne l'avez eue avec lui pour avoir refusé de me l'envoyer. J'aurais été charmée de recevoir de lui-même des marques de son intérêt et de son amitié pour le grand-papa et pour moi, et d'avoir une occasion de lui marquer directement combien nous y sommes sensibles' (ibid. i. 423).

4. The MS reads 'votre.'

To the Rev. William Huddesford,[1]
Tuesday 19 February 1771

Printed from a photostat of the MS in the Bodleian Library (MS Ashmole 1822, f. 206). First printed, Toynbee *Supp.* iii. 328. The MS, in a volume of Huddesford's correspondence, was transferred from the Ashmolean Library to the Bodleian ca 1866.

Endorsed in an unidentified hand: CCVI.

Address: To the Reverend Mr Huddesford at Trinity College, Oxford.

Arlington Street, Feb. 19, 1771.

Sir,

I WOULD not delay thanking you by the first post for the favour of your obliging letter,[2] which I received later than I should have done, if it had not been directed to my house in the country. The paper[3] you was so kind as to send me, is a curiosity to me, and I am glad to possess it; but as I have not the pleasure of knowing you, I am still more indebted to you, Sir, for the civility than for the paper itself, and beg you will believe that I am very grateful for the trouble you have given yourself, and am Sir,

Your most obliged and obedient humble servant

Hor. Walpole

1. (1732–72), B.D. (Oxon.), 1767; fellow of Trinity College, Oxford, 1757; keeper of the Ashmolean Library 1755–72; antiquary.

2. Missing.

3. Possibly Huddesford's 'Short Account of Osney Abbey, and of the Print annexed,' an unsigned piece which appeared in GM 1771, xli. 153. HW also owned Huddesford's *The Lives of those Eminent Antiquaries, John Leland, Thomas Hearne, and Anthony à Wood,* 2 vols, 1772 (Hazen, *Cat. of HW's Lib.,* No. 2875).

From the CONTESSA DI VIRY,[1] Monday 25 February 1771

Printed from the MS now WSL. First printed, Toynbee *Supp*. iii. 221–2. Damer-Waller; the MS was sold Sotheby's 5 Dec. 1921 (first Waller Sale), lot 187, to Wells; given by him to Thomas Conolly, of Chicago, from whom WSL acquired it, 1937.

Madrid, February the 25th 1771.

MADAME de Viry with her best compliments to Mr Walpole sends the enclosed verses which the Marquis d'Ossun[2] (the French ambassador at this Court) presented from Voltaire to the Comte d'Aranda[3] (the President of Castile who banished the Jesuits from Spain), accompanied with a watch made in the village of Ferney, and on which was enamelled Comte d'Aranda's picture.[4] Madame de Viry flatters herself Voltaire is a better poet than he is a prophet.[5]

In return for this mark of Madame de Viry's remembrance, she begs Mr Walpole would send her Lady Mary Churchill's direction,[6] and likewise inform her how he does. She hopes he has not been tormented with the gout,[7] and desires to be remembered to all Pam's coterie[8] and particularly to Lord and Lady Hertford, Lady Holderness[9] and Lady Charlotte Burgoyne.[10]

---

1. Henrietta Jane Speed (1728–83), m. (1761) Francesco Maria Giuseppe Giustino, Barone di la Perrière, Conte di Viry, 1766; friend of Thomas Gray (OSSORY i. 254 n. 17, 256 n. 42).

2. Pierre-Paul (1713–88), Marquis d'Ossun; French ambassador to Spain 1759–77; minister of state, 1778 (MANN v. 275 n. 13).

3. Pedro Pablo Abarca de Bolea (1719–98), Conde de Aranda; Spanish ambassador to France 1773–80; president of the Council of Castile 1766–73 (*Enciclopedia de la Cultura Española*, Madrid, 1963, i. 431–2). Aranda had been in charge of the official inquiry which led to the expulsion of the Jesuits from Spain by royal decree 27 Feb. 1767.

4. Voltaire's letter to the Marquis d'Ossun 16 July 1770 concerns 'une montre à répétition fort belle, avec le portrait de

M. le Comte d'Aranda,' made by the firm of Dufour, Céret, et Cie. in Ferney (*Voltaire's Correspondence*, ed. Theodore Besterman, Geneva, 1953–65, lxxvi. 45–6). The letter was accompanied by the verses printed below.

5. In the last two verses.

6. HW's half-sister Lady Mary Churchill and her family were in Paris at this time; see DU DEFFAND iii. 31.

7. See *ante* 20 Oct. 1770 and n. 3.

8. That is, the circle of friends who played the game of loo together. In loo Pam is the knave of clubs, the highest ranking card in the pack; see MONTAGU i. 238 and n. 5.

9. Mary Doublet (ca 1720–1801), m. (1743) Robert Darcy, 4th E. of Holdernesse, 1722.

10. See *ante* 19 Dec. 1767, n. 14.

[Enclosure][11]

M. le Marquis d'Ossun m'a flatté que V[otre] E[xcellence] ne dédaignerait pas d'accepter l'hommage de ma petite colonie de Fernay.

> Le Barbouilleur de mon village
> A très mal peint je l'avouerai
> Les traits du héros de notre âge
> Il est un peu défiguré:
> Mais dans les cœurs est son image
> C'est lui, c'est D'ARANDA dit-on
> Par qui l'Espagne est florissante;
> Qui sçut avec religion
> Dompter la superstition
> Et chasser l'horde puissante
> Des docteurs de l'attrition
> Et de la grâce suffisante.
> C'est lui qui dans ses grands projets
> Dont nous verrons un jour les suites
> Sçaura triompher des Anglais
> Comme il triomphe des Jésuites.

J'ai l'honneur d'être sans que vous le sachiez, Monseigneur de V[otre] E[xcellence],

> L'admirateur et le bien humble
> et très obéissant serviteur,

VOLTAIRE

11. A copy in Contessa di Viry's hand of Voltaire's letter to the Conde de Aranda, n.d. [July 1770].

To the Rev. John Hutchins,
Tuesday 26 February 1771

Printed from the MS now WSL. First printed in John Hutchins, *The History and Antiquities of the County of Dorset,* 3d edn, ed. William Shipp and J. W. Hodson, 1861–73, ii. 462. The MS was sold Puttick and Simpson 12 March 1862 (Extraordinary Collection of Autograph Letters Sale), lot 713, to Boone; not further traced until resold Christie's 29 July 1971 (property of the Trustees of the 7th Duke of Newcastle), lot 526, to Seven Gables for WSL.

Arlington Street, Feb. 26, 1771.

Sir,

AS I had not heard any more of your work[1] for so long a time, I had concluded you had dropped all thoughts of it. I am glad to find on the contrary that it is in so much forwardness. I hope it will not be too late, if there should be any information worth your transcribing in the enclosed paper,[2] which is part of the last volume of my *Anecdotes,* now almost printed and to be published in a short time. It contains all I have found in Mr Vertue's papers relative to Sir James Thornhill.[3] I shall subscribe Sir to your book with pleasure, and am

Your obedient humble servant

Hor. Walpole

---

1. See *ante* 22 Sept. 1765, n. 6, and 17 Feb. 1767.
2. Missing.
3. See HW to Onslow *ante* 31 March 1764, n. 6. Hutchins appears not to have used HW's information in the brief notice on Thornhill in his *History and Antiquities of the County of Dorset,* 1774, i. 410.

To Grosvenor Bedford, Wednesday 27 February 1771

Printed from *Works* ii. 380–2, where the letter was first printed. Reprinted, Cunningham v. 284–5; Toynbee viii. 14–16. The history of the MS and its present whereabouts are not known.

Arlington Street, Feb. 27, 1771.

Dear Sir,

INQUIRING of your son[1] today why my new clerk[2] was not more instructed, he said, there were circumstances which some persons of the Treasury would not like to have communicated; which much surprising me, your son said Mr Rowe[3] had had some cloth, which he chose to have entered as some other article. This notice did and could not but greatly astonish me, who have always told you in the most positive manner that I never would connive at the smallest collusion, nor upon any account receive the least profit that was not strictly and justly my due. You know I have repeatedly declared to you that I would not suffer the benefits of my office to be raised by any indirect practices on my part; and you must remember how strongly I rejected old Palmer's[4] pretensions, and was firm that I would lose the perquisites due on what he was entitled to take at the office, rather than enter into any bargain with him.

When I talked to you last at Brixton Causeway,[5] you desired me not to let anybody into the secrets of my office. I replied with dissatisfaction that *I would have no secrets in my office,* nor would receive a shilling from it that I was not willing all the world should know—and I appeal to yourself if this has not been my constant rule.

1. Charles Bedford, clerk in the office of usher of the Exchequer (*ante* 23 Sept. 1761, n. 2). Grosvenor Bedford died 4 Nov. 1771 and was succeeded by Joseph Tullie as HW's deputy in the Exchequer; on Tullie's death 20 Nov. 1774 Charles Bedford became deputy usher (Ossory i. 217 n. 1; *Court and City Register,* 1775, p. 95; 1776, p. 97).

2. William Harris (d. *post* 1793), HW's clerk in the Exchequer, 1771; yeoman usher of the Exchequer, 1772 (*Court and City Register,* 1773, p. 104; Gray ii. 256). The text in Cunningham reads 'my new clerk Mr Harris.'

3. Milward Rowe (ca 1716–92), chief clerk of the Treasury; commissioner in the Salt Office, 1772 (GM 1792, lxii pt i. 188; *Court and City Register,* 1773, pp. 102, 121).

4. See *ante* 24 March 1769, n. 1.

5. Brixton Causeway, in Surrey, continued to be the address of Charles Bedford after his father's death (H. B. Wheatley, *London Past and Present,* 1891, i. 276; *Isaac Reed Diaries 1762–1804,* ed. C. E. Jones, Berkeley and Los Angeles, 1946, p. 109).

I am sensible that you have done nothing but from zeal for me and regard to my interest—but my honour is infinitely more dear to me, and I most peremptorily charge you not to give into the least collusion with anybody of the Treasury, in order either to serve me by increasing my profits, or by gaining them to my interest. I will go shares with no man living in any dirt. I am aware that this may make those people my enemies, and may turn them to prejudice me by postponing my accounts, by delaying my payments, or, as your son said, by preventing their taking many articles from the office on which I should have a just profit. But I scorn such traffic, and had rather lose the office itself, than blush to hold it by such means. In short, I prefer being wronged to doing wrong.

In the present case, Mr Rowe is welcome to the cloth; but then I will pay for it myself, and do absolutely forbid you to charge it in any shape to the government. Should he ever make such another application to you, or should any other person, you must say that you dare not yield to it, and that I have positively forbidden it.

Mr Harris must be instructed thoroughly in all the duties of his place, but I do not desire he should know this transaction, for fear he should ever be tempted to imitate it. I am fully persuaded of your good intentions to me in it, and that your prudence and fear of making me an enemy induced you to comply. But I entreat you to remember, that as I have no worldly wisdom myself, I cannot let any man living use any for me contrary to right, justice, and the duty I owe to the public as a servant of the government. I have held the place now above thirty years through many storms, and sometimes under much oppression, but my conduct in it has been untainted; and as I have disdained to secure it by voting with ministers against my conscience,[6] you may depend upon it, I will not traffic for the favour of clerks by winking at their corruption.

I am, dear Sir,
Yours most sincerely,

Hor. Walpole

---

6. See *ante* 14 March 1763, n. 1.

From GROSVENOR BEDFORD, Friday 1 March 1771

Printed from *Works* ii. 382–3, where the letter was first printed. The history of the MS and its present whereabouts are not known.

Brixton Causeway, March 1, 1771.

Sir,

YOU may be assured of my perfect obedience to the commands I received yesterday.[1]

I am happy that you think I have served you with zeal—gratitude required and obliged me to it—affection is too familiar a word from me; and I do most solemnly assure you that my poor unfortunate son has not been less zealous, for he never thought your accounts high enough; and yet you may be quite easy and satisfied that nothing has been done that could bring the least reflection upon your honour. Our desires have been to oblige everybody, and we have done it honestly; and if I, knowing a gentleman to have an allowed right to a particular perquisite of office, which he did not always want in that shape, have gratified him with another thing in lieu of it *of equal value,* I did not perceive the injury to government, or think you would have any objection to it: but if you will not suffer such indulgence to be continued, and will be pleased to inform me so by my son, I will show the strictest regard to your commands.

There has never been anything charged in your accounts without a voucher of its delivery, which would always justify you; and the person who ordered it was to justify himself if called upon.

I am, Sir,
Your most obliged and obedient humble servant,

GROSVENOR BEDFORD

1. See previous letter.

TO GROSVENOR BEDFORD, Thursday 27 June 1771

Printed from Cunningham v. 311, where the letter was first printed. Reprinted, Toynbee viii. 53. The history of the MS and its present whereabouts are not known.

Arlington Street, June 27, 1771.

Dear Sir,

I AM very happy to be able to set your mind quite at ease about your place,[1] which was wanted for O'Brien,[2] of which I think you will hear no more. I would not enter into the method by which I got rid of the application, were it not to prove to you how sincerely I am your friend.[3] In two words then, when I found I could not beat them from the pursuit by any other means, I declared to Lord and Lady H[olland] that I would not request you to do a thing to which you had so great a repugnance; but if that would satisfy them, I would part with my own two little places in the Exchequer,[4] at what they should be reckoned worth fairly. They did not choose to pay the price for them, but the offer entirely put a stop to their insisting on your place,[5] which they could not in decency require, when they had the option of mine, and thus, in form, Lady H. told me she gave up the whole.

1. Deputy usher of the Exchequer.
2. William O'Brien (d. 1815), m. (1764) Lady Susan Fox Strangways, eldest dau. of the 1st E. of Ilchester and niece of Lord Holland; actor.
3. HW had previously interceded to save Bedford's sinecure office of collector of customs for Philadelphia; see ante 7, 8 September 1763.

4. 'Clerk of the estreats and comptroller of the pipe, which together produce about or near 300l. per annum' (HW's 'Account of My Conduct Relative to the Places I Hold under Government,' Works ii. 364; Royal Kalendar, 1771, pp. 110–11).
5. See ante 27 Feb. 1771, n. 1.

To Edward Louisa Mann,[1] Sunday 28 July 1771

Printed from N&Q 1850, 1st ser., i. 273–4, where the letter ('found among the papers of the late William Parsons'[2] by Spencer Hall, Esq.) was first printed. Reprinted, Cunningham v. 315–17; Toynbee viii. 58–61 (addressee unknown in N&Q and Cunningham). The letter is listed in HW's record of letters sent from Paris in 1771 (DU DEFFAND v. 393); the history of the MS after 1850 and its present whereabouts are not known.

Paris,[3] July 28, 1771.

Dear Sir,

I HAVE received no letter from my brother,[4] and consequently have no answer to make to him.[5] I shall only say that after entering into a solemn engagement with me, that we should dispose of the places alternately,[6] I can scarce think him serious, when he tells you he has made an *entirely* new arrangement for ALL the places, expects I should concur in it; and after that, is so good as to promise he will dispose of no more without consulting me. If he is so absolutely master of all, my concurrence is not necessary, *and I will give none.* If he chooses to dispose of the places without me, that matter with others *more important,* must be regulated in another manner,—and it is time they should, when no agreement is kept with me, and I find objections made which, upon the fullest discussion and after allowance of the force of my arguments and right, had been given up twenty years ago.

With regard to your letter,[7] Sir, some parts of it are, I protest, totally unintelligible to me. Others, which I think I do understand,

1. (1702–75), of Linton, Kent; army clothier; collector of customs London port inwards ca 1752–75; Sir Horace Mann's older brother (MANN i. 321 n. 22).

2. See *post* ?1790, n. 1.

3. In 1771 HW was in Paris from 10 July to 2 September ('Paris Journals,' DU DEFFAND v. 334, 342).

4. Sir Edward Walpole.

5. No letter from Sir Edward Walpole to HW around this date has been found, but HW wrote to him on 7 August and 22 August (both missing; see DU DEFFAND v. 393).

6. Mann, as collector of customs inwards, received an annual fixed income

by his patent; HW and his brother shared a larger income from fees paid into the office, as well as the power of appointing the deputies and clerks who actually transacted the business. The places consisted of a chief deputy, three clerks and three receivers by deputation, and nine minor clerks (see Appendix 16, MANN x. 52–4). After the death of his eldest brother Robert in 1751, HW made an agreement with Sir Edward to dispose of the places alternately as they became vacant.

7. Missing. HW noted in 'Paris Journals' *sub* 27 July: '*Letter from Mr Mann*' (DU DEFFAND v. 336).

require a much fuller answer than I have time to give now, as the post goes out tomorrow morning. That answer will contain matter not at all fit for the post, and which I am sure you would not wish should be handled there; for which reason I shall defer it, till I can give my answer at length into your own hands.[8] I will, I believe, surprise both you and my brother; and show how unkindly I have been treated after doing everything to accommodate both. As to the conditions which you say, Sir, you intend to exact from my brother, you will undoubtedly state them to him himself; and cannot expect I should meddle with them or be party to them. Neither you nor he can imagine that I am quite so tame an idiot as to enter into bonds for persons of *his* recommendation. If the office is *his,* he must be answerable for it, and for all the persons he employs in it. I protest against everything that is not my own act—a consequence he perhaps did not foresee, when he chose, contrary to his agreement with me, to engross the whole disposition. I have always known clearly what is my own right and on what founded; and have acted strictly according to my right, and am ready to justify every step of my conduct. I have sufficiently shown my disposition to peace, and appeal to you yourself, Sir, and to my brother, whether either can charge me with the least encroachment beyond my right; and whether I have not acquiesced in every single step that either has desired of me. Your letter, Sir, and that you quote of my brother,[9] have shown how necessary it is for me to take the measure I am determined to take. I would have done anything to oblige either you or my brother, but I am not to be threatened out of my right in any shape. I know when it is proper to yield and when to make my stand. I refused to accept the place for my own life when it was offered to me:[10] when I declined *that,* it is not probable that I would hold the place to the wrong of anybody else; it will and *must* be seen who claims any part or prerogatives of the place unjustly; my honour demands to have this ascertained, and I will add, that when I scorned a favour, I am not likely to be intimidated by a menace.

8. HW wrote Sir Horace Mann 22 Oct. 1771: 'Indeed I am as ill-circumstanced with your brother. . . . He has not only treated me with his usual peevishness, but with a good deal of insolence—I have not seen him since my return from Paris, and the subject is not proper for the post. I believe he is laid up with the gout at Richmond, which has prevented my answering a most provoking letter that I received from him while I was in France' (MANN vii. 340).

9. Missing.

10. By Henry Fox, in 1754; see *Mem. Geo. III* i. 166–7. See also MASON ii. 327 nn. 3, 4.

I say all this coolly and deliberately, and my actions will be conformable. I do not forget my obligations to you, dear Sir, or to your dead brother,[11] whose memory will ever be most dear to me. Unkind expressions shall not alter the affection I have for you or your family, nor am I so unreasonable, so unjust, or so absurd as not to approve your doing everything you think right for your own interest and security and for those of your family. What I have to say hereafter will prove that these not only are but *ever have been* my sentiments. I shall then appeal to your own truth whether it is just in you to have used some expressions in your letter, but as I mean to act with the utmost circumspection and without a grain of resentment to *anybody*, I shall say no more till I have had full time to weigh every word I shall use, and every step I mean to take. In the meantime I am,

Dear Sir,
Your obliged humble servant,

Hor. Walpole

PS. My refusal of the patent for my life has shown what value I set upon it; but *I will* have justice, especially for my character which no consideration upon earth shall prevent my seeking. It must and shall be known whether I enjoy the place to the wrong of any man living. You have my free consent, Sir, to show this letter to whom you please; I have nothing to conceal, and am ready to submit my conduct to the whole world.

---

11. Galfridus Mann (*ante* 2 April 1752, n. 3).

From the PRINCE DE MONACO,[1] Sunday 28 July 1771

Printed from the MS now WSL. First printed, Toynbee *Supp.* iii. 222–3. For the history of the MS see *ante* 21 Nov. 1765.

The year of the letter is established by HW's entry in 'Paris Journals' (see n. 3 below).

Ce dimanche 28 juillet.

LE Prince de Monaco recevrait comme une marque d'amitié de Monsieur Walpole qu'il se donnât la peine de venir avec M. Mariette[2] examiner ses tableaux, et qu'il voulût bien lui mander ce qu'ils jugent nécessaire de faire pour rétablir ceux qui en ont besoin, et entretenir les autres.[3]

L'homme dont il s'est servi s'appelle Donjeu,[4] et il demande deux cent cinquante louis pour ce qu'il a fait, et pour ce qu'il prétend avoir encore à faire. Le Prince de Monaco est très fâché d'être obligé de partir sans avoir l'honneur de revoir Monsieur Walpole auquel il fait mille compliments, et il le prie d'assurer Mme[5] et Mlle Churchill[6] de ses respects.

---

1. Honoré-Camille-Léonor Goyon-de-Matignon de Grimaldi (1720–95), Prince de Monaco 1732–92 (DU DEFFAND ii. 71 n. 5).

2. Pierre-Jean Mariette (*ante* 21 Nov. 1765, n. 1).

3. On 20 July 1771 HW went to 'see the Prince of Monaco's pictures' and made notes in 'Paris Journals' on the paintings (DU DEFFAND v. 335). On 2 Aug. he went with Mariette to inspect the pictures at the Hôtel de Monaco (ibid. v. 337). He reported to Lord Strafford 25 Aug. that 'the Prince of Monaco's [pictures] have been cleaned, and varnished so thick that you may see your face in them; and some of them have been transported from board to cloth, bit by

bit, and the seams filled up with colour; so that in ten years they will not be worth sixpence' (CHUTE 344–5).

4. Probably Rémy and Vincent Donjeux, painters and merchants in Paris (Thieme and Becker ix. 442–3).

5. Lady Mary Churchill, HW's half-sister. See *ante* 25 Feb. 1771, n. 6. The Churchills left Paris to return to England on 31 July ('Paris Journals,' DU DEFFAND v. 336).

6. Mary Churchill (b. 1750), eldest dau. of Charles and Lady Mary Churchill; m. (1777), as his second wife, Charles Sloane Cadogan (1728–1807), 3d Bn Cadogan, 1776, cr. (1800) E. Cadogan. She was divorced in 1796 (OSSORY i. 368 nn. 2, 3).

From the Duc de Nivernais,
Thursday 22 August 1771

Printed from the MS now wsl. First printed, Toynbee *Supp.* iii. 223–4. For the history of the MS see *ante* 11 May 1766. The letter is written in an unidentified hand, presumably that of Nivernais's secretary.

Le 22 août 1771.

LE Duc de Nivernois vient de communiquer à Mme de Rochefort le billet obligeant[1] dont Monsieur Walpole l'a honoré hier. L'un et l'autre sont infiniment sensibles à toutes ses politesses et ont bien du regret de jouir si peu de son petit séjour à Paris.[2] La partie de Ruel[3] leur serait très agréable, et ils seront toujours tout prêts à l'accepter le jour qui conviendra à Monsieur Walpole, mais, d'un autre côté, le Duc de Nivernois avait projetté de donner à dîner chez lui à Paris à Monsieur Walpole et à Mme la Duchesse d'Aiguillon parce qu'il désirerait faire voir sa maison, qu'il vient de faire rebâtir à Monsieur Walpole, et d'en soumettre les ornements à son jugement.[4] Il supplie Monsieur Walpole de vouloir bien lui accorder cette grâce, de la lui faire accorder aussi par Mme la Duchesse d'Aiguillon et de lui indiquer le jour qui leur conviendra le mieux à l'un et à l'autre, pourvu que ce ne soit ni un vendredi ni un samedi.

Le Duc de Nivernois a l'honneur de renouveler à Monsieur Walpole les assurances de son fidèle et inviolable attachement.

Le Duc de Nivernois croit devoir ajouter que Mme de Rochefort souhaiterait que le dîner que le Duc de Nivernois a l'honneur de proposer [soit] fait un mardi ou un jeudi[5] parce que les mercredis et dimanches elle est obligée de rester chez elle, et qu'elle serait bien affligée de manquer une occasion de passer quelques heures avec Monsieur Walpole, dont elle désire passionnément de conserver et cultiver l'amitié.

1. Missing.
2. See *ante* 28 July 1771, n. 3.
3. See *ante* mid-August 1768, n. 7. On 8 Aug. 1771 HW had 'Supped at Duchesse d'Aiguillon's at Rueil with Mmes du Deffand and Boufflers, Prince de Bauffremont and M. Bulkeley,' and also on 20 July he had supped there ('Paris Journals,' du Deffand v. 335, 337).

4. HW dined at the Duc de Nivernais's with the Duchesse d'Aiguillon, Mme de Rochefort, and twelve others on 29 Aug. He noted in 'Paris Journals': 'Fine salon. Vases of alabaster with dark bronze, serpents, and branches of *fleurs-de-lis* for candles' (ibid. v. 341).
5. 29 Aug. was a Thursday.

From Mrs Abington,[1] Saturday 31 August 1771

Printed from Toynbee *Supp.* ii. 141–2, where the letter was first printed. Damer-Waller; the MS was sold Sotheby's 5 Dec. 1921 (first Waller Sale), lot 84, to Quaritch; not further traced.
The year is established by HW's letter to Mrs Abington *post* 1 Sept. 1771.

Hôtel Turanne,[2] August 31st.

MRS Abington presents her compliments to Mr Walpole, and is very much mortified that she was not at home when he was pleased to call upon her yesterday[3]—she leaves Paris on Tuesday morning, and shall consider herself exceedingly flattered if he will permit her to thank him for the honour of his visit, in Southampton Street.[4]

To Mrs Abington, Sunday 1 September 1771

Printed from a photostat of the MS in the British Museum (Add. MS 9828, f. 145). First printed, Wright v. 427 (misdated 'September [1775]' and signature omitted). Reprinted, Cunningham v. 329; *The Life of Mrs Abington* ['By the Editor of the "Life of Quin" '], 1888, pp. 49–50; Toynbee viii. 77–8. The MS was acquired before 1836 by the British Museum in a volume of letters written to Mrs Abington.

Paris, 1 Sept. 1771.[1]

IF I had known, Madam, of your being at Paris, before I heard it from Colonel Blaquiere,[2] I should certainly have prevented your flattering invitation, and have offered you any services that could

---

1. Frances Barton (1737–1815), m. (1759) James Abington; actress (P. H. Highfill, Jr, K. A. Burnim, and E. A. Langhans, *A Biographical Dictionary of Actors, Actresses . . . in London, 1660–1800*, Carbondale, Illinois, 1973– , i. 12–20).
2. Hôtel Turenne, rue de Turenne, Paris. It was a convent of the Filles du Saint-Sacrement (Comte d'Aucourt, *Les Anciens hôtels de Paris*, 1890, p. 84).
3. In 'Paris Journals' HW records making 'visits of congé' on 30 Aug. He left Paris to return to England on 2 Sept. (DU DEFFAND V. 341–2).
4. Covent Garden. See following letter.

1. The date-line is not in HW's hand; it was presumably added by Mrs Abington.
2. John Blaquiere (1732–1812), Lt-Col. 17th Dragoons, 1763; K.B., 1774; cr. (1784) Bt and (1800) Bn de Blaquiere; M.P. (Ireland and U. K.) (OSSORY i. 161 n. 2). Blaquiere was at this time secretary of the British embassy at Paris (D. B. Horn, *British Diplomatic Representatives 1689–1789*, 1932, Camden Society, 3d ser., xlvi. 24). He visited HW on 30 Aug. and supped with him and other guests at the Marquis de Brancas's the following day ('Paris Journals,' DU DEFFAND V. 341–2).

depend on my acquaintance here. It is plain I am old, and live with very old folks, when I did not hear of your arrival. However, Madam, I have not that fault at least of a veteran, the thinking nothing equal to what they admired in their youth. I do impartial justice to your merit, and fairly allow it not only equal to that of any actress I have seen,[3] but believe the present age will not be in the wrong, if they hereafter prefer it to those they may live to see.

Your allowing me to wait on you in London, Madam, will make me some amends for the loss I have had here; and I shall take an early opportunity of assuring you how much

I am Madam

Your most obliged humble servant

HORACE WALPOLE

To RICHARD STONHEWER,[1]
Monday 16 September 1771

Printed from the MS now WSL. First printed in Paget Toynbee, 'Horace Walpole on Gray,' *The Times*, 30 July 1926, p. 15. Reprinted in *Correspondence of Thomas Gray*, ed. Paget Toynbee and Leonard Whibley, Oxford, 1935, iii. 1280–1. The MS was *penes* Sotheby's in Aug. 1847; sold Puttick and Simpson 2 Aug. 1856 (R. C. Lambe Sale), lot 292, to Holloway; *penes* A. Thomas Loyd, Lockinge House, Wantage, Berks, in 1926; resold Sotheby's 27 Nov. 1945 (property of the late A. T. Loyd), lot 526, to Maggs for WSL.

Strawberry Hill, Sept. 16, 1771.

I AM very sorry, Sir, for all the trouble you have had about sending me Mr Mason's kind letter,[2] and very sensible to any attention from two gentlemen who valued so much and were so much valued by Mr Gray. The loss of him[3] was a great blow to me,[4] and ought to

3. See HW to Robert Jephson *post* 13 July 1777, where he declares that 'Mrs Abington was equal to the first of her profession' in the rôle of Lady Teazle in Sheridan's *The School for Scandal*.

1. (ca 1728–1809), fellow of Peterhouse, Cambridge, 1751; under-secretary of state for the north 1765–6, and for the south, 1766; appointed private secretary to the Duke of Grafton, 1766; auditor of excise 1772–89; F.S.A., 1787 (MASON i. 11 n. 4). In a letter to Stonhewer 2 Nov. 1769, Thomas

Gray calls him 'my best friend' (*Corr. of Thomas Gray* iii. 1081).

2. Mason's letter to HW 28 Aug. 1771; in it Mason wrote: 'I hope this will find you in perfect health after your journey [from Paris], and I have sent it under Mr Stonhewer's cover that he may deliver it to you when he hears you are arrived in town' (MASON i. 18).

3. Gray died on 30 July 1771.

4. See HW to Chute 5 Aug. 1771, *sub* 'August 13' (CHUTE 127–8).

THOMAS GRAY, BY BENJAMIN WILSON

be to the world, as Mr Mason tells me he has left behind him nothing finished,[5] which might have compensated his death to them, though not to his friends. He was a genius of the first rank, and will always be allowed so by men of taste. You Sir will be honoured by them for having done justice to his merit; and as he was so averse to receiving favours, it will be a proof that he did justice to yours in consenting to be obliged to you.[6]

As I am not sure how long you stay at Middleton,[7] I direct this to your house in town,[8] whence, if absent, I conclude it will be sent to you; and I should be sorry to seem careless in answering the favour of yours,[9] as I am with great regard, Sir,

Your most obedient humble servant

Horace Walpole

From the Rev. James Granger,
Thursday 30 January 1772

Printed from the MS now wsl. First printed, Toynbee *Supp.* iii. 226–8; extract quoted in Hazen, *Bibl. of HW* 134. Damer-Waller; the MS was sold Sotheby's 5 Dec. 1921 (first Waller Sale), lot 134, bought in; resold Christie's 15 Dec. 1947 (second Waller Sale), lot 53 (with nine other letters to HW), to Maggs for wsl.

Shiplake, 30 Jan. 1772.

Honoured Sir,

As Mr Davies[1] is desirous of printing the *Supplement* to my book[2] *with all expedition*,[3] I am emboldened, in consequence of what

5. See Mason i. 18 n. 5.
6. See *ante* 20 Sept. 1768 and n. 9.
7. Presumably Middleton, Oxon, the seat of Lord Jersey.
8. Stonhewer lived at No. 14 Curzon Street (*Corr. of Thomas Gray* iii. 1177 n. 1).
9. Missing.

1. Thomas Davies (ca 1712–85), bookseller, who published Granger's *Biographical History of England* in 1769. See *ante* 3 April 1764, n. 2.
2. *A Supplement, Consisting of Corrections and Large Additions to A Biographical History of England . . . and a List of Curious Portraits of Eminent Persons*

not yet Engraved, Communicated, by the Honourable Horace Walpole, to the Author, published 17 Sept. 1774 (*Daily Adv.* 16 Sept.). 'Mr Granger, I see by the papers, has published his *Supplement.* . . . I am sorry his bookseller has quoted me for the list of unengraved portraits. It did not deserve such parade' (HW to John Fenn 17 Sept. 1774, Chatterton 234–5). See also Cole i. 348.
3. Davies had written to Granger 5 Nov. 1771: 'I begin to be impatient for your *Supplement:* I am afraid you are too solicitous to make improvements, and to collect additional matter.' He wrote again on 11 Jan. 1772: 'We [Thomas

you was pleased to signify to me about two years ago,[4] to beg the favour of you to cast an eye over the papers that accompany this letter, before they go to the press.[5] I have endeavoured to carry on the same thread, as evenly as I could, in this supplemental part. I have mentioned some prints of no authority, which all collectors give a place to in their collections, but have, at the same time, given sufficient intimation of their being unauthentic. I have great reason to believe, that if every king, founder, etc. were excluded, that is not authenticated, that it would greatly maim the first volume of my work[6] and perhaps sink it in the esteem of the generality of my readers. It is liable to censure for this licence; but I believe would not, upon the whole, be so well liked by collectors of prints, if it were absolutely without it. I have sent Sir, together with my papers, some few additions to the works of our noble authors, which though not mentioned in the second edition of your admired book,[7] have, perhaps, occurred to you since. They were written by a judicious and learned gentleman[8] in my neighbourhood, whose name I am not at liberty to mention. I have hinted at this worthy person in my preface.[9] I am promised from Dr Cooper,[10] who lately lived at Phillis

Cadell and Davies] are both highly pleased with the progress you have made in the *Supplement,* and heartily wish to have it published as soon as possible' (*Letters between the Rev. James Granger . . . and Many of the Most Eminent Literary Men of his Time,* ed. J. P. Malcolm, 1805, pp. 53–4).

4. Granger's letter to HW *ante* 19 May 1770 refers to HW's 'abundant candour in favour of my work.'

5. 'Mr Granger teases me to correct catalogues of prints' (HW to Mason 8 Dec. 1773, MASON i. 121).

6. The first volume includes engraved portraits of 'such persons as flourished before the end of the reign of Henry the Seventh.' In the Preface Granger writes: 'It will perhaps be objected, that I have given a place to mean engravings, and prints of obscure persons: but whoever studies for a useful collection should make it numerous. . . . Of many persons there are none but meanly engraved heads; but I can easily imagine that the meanest in this collection may preserve the likeness, which is the essence of a portrait, and might serve to ascertain a doubtful picture.'

7. *A Catalogue of the Royal and Noble Authors of England,* 2d edn, 2 vols, 1759.

8. John Loveday (1711–89), of Caversham, Berks; antiquary (BERRY i. 137). Loveday noted in his diary *sub* 12 May 1759: 'Sealed up the notes on Mr Walpole's book for him' (information kindly communicated by Mrs Sarah Markham, Loveday's great-great-great-granddaughter, owner of his MS diary). The 'notes' are missing.

9. 'I have received the greatest assistance from a truly worthy and judicious gentleman in the neighbourhood of Reading, though I am not at liberty to mention his name' (Preface in vol. I of the *Biographical History*). In the 'Advertisement' to the *Supplement,* Granger states that he is obliged *'principally* to John Loveday, Esq. of Caversham, in Oxfordshire, a gentleman, who, in conferring benefits, declines all thanks but those of his own conscience.'

10. Rev. Edward Cooper (1727–92), son of Gislingham Cooper, of Phillis Court, Henley-on-Thames, Oxon; prebendary of Bath and Wells, 1770; vicar of Sonning, Berks, and rector of Whaddon, Wilts

Court, near Henley, a few proofs from some small silver plates by Simon Pass,[11] two or three of which I have not seen before. These, Sir, shall very shortly be sent you.[12] I wish you may find them worth your acceptance, and that I had anything else which you want to send you at the same time. If you had been in England, Sir, when I did what I am afraid you will look upon as an ungrateful thing, I should by no means have done it, without asking your consent: I mean selling those heads out of my collection for 100 guineas, which Mr Gulston[13] wanted towards completing his series. Among those were some which you was so very generous as to give me, together with a great number more. The bulk of them were portraits of persons of whom I had several other prints. Mr Gulston made me a more considerable offer without seeing my collection; but I could not accept of it with a safe conscience, as I considered it as precipitate. He next fell to 100 guineas; but I refused this sum, till he saw my portfolios. After he had taken out what he wanted, he made me a present of the *Museum Florentinum*,[14] and has promised to do his utmost towards supplying the chasms in the series, which are in a great measure filled up already. My inducement to accept of this offer was to have a little reserve of money in case of sickness, and to enable myself to make a better collection than I had before. Gratitude had also its weight with me, as I had received many favours from this gentleman.

I am, honoured Sir,
Your ever obliged, and most grateful humble servant,

JAMES GRANGER

(J. S. Burn, *A History of Henley-on-Thames*, 1861, pp. 253–4; John Le Neve and T. D. Hardy, *Fasti Ecclesiæ Anglicanæ*, Oxford, 1854, i. 194; GM 1792, lxii pt ii. 867). On the death of his father in 1768, he joined with his mother in selling the manor of Phillis Court to Sambrook Freeman (Burn, loc. cit.). HW visited Phillis Court in 1763 (*Country Seats* 50).

11. Simon Passe (or de Passe) (?1595–1647), Dutch engraver born in Cologne who worked in England ?1613–?1624 (Thieme and Becker xxvi. 282; HW's *Catalogue of Engravers*, 2d edn, SH, 1765, pp. 28–31).

12. 'Seven silver plates engraved, by Pass, portraits of James I and his family' were sold SH xv. 72 to Miss Burdett

Coutts for £4.14.6 (now wsl). For an account of Passe's engraved portraits on silver see 'Miniatures in Silver by Simon de Passe,' *Connoisseur*, 1914, xl. 225–8.

13. Joseph Gulston (?1744–86), M.P.; collector of books and prints (COLE i. 287 n. 5).

14. *Museum Florentinum exhibens insigniora vetustatis monumenta quæ Florentiæ sunt*, edited and in part compiled by Antonio Francesco Gori, 12 vols, Florence, 1731–66. HW apparently owned only the three volumes on coins (vols IV–VI) entitled *Antiqua numismata . . . quæ in regio thesauro Magni Ducis Etruriæ adservantur*, Florence, 1740–2; his copy is Hazen, *Cat. of HW's Lib.*, No. 431. See MANN i. 49 n. 14.

I have, Sir, mentioned your name, where I speak of the antiquity of the portraits of Talbot Earl of Shrewsbury and his consort.[15] I received my authority from Mr Cole.[16] I should be very glad to receive the favour of any remarks that may occur to you, by the post,[17] and I will transmit them to the printer.

To Henry Sampson Woodfall,
Tuesday 24 March 1772

Printed from a photostat of the MS, in the hand of HW's deputy Charles Bedford, among the Woodfall papers in the British Museum (Add. MS 27,780, f. 16). First printed in Joseph Parkes and Herman Merivale, *Memoirs of Sir Philip Francis, K.C.B.*, 1867, i. 291 (misdated 'March 29, 1772'). The Woodfall papers were purchased by Joseph Parkes (d. 1865) from H. D. Woodfall, a grandson of Henry Sampson Woodfall; acquired by the British Museum in 1868.

Strawberry Hill, March 24, 1772.

Sir,

I AM much obliged to you for your kind attention, in sending me the note you enclosed,[1] as it certainly was not worth troubling the public with, yet very flattering to me. I am sorry to take up a corner of your paper,[2] but if you should have room at any time, it would be an additional favour, if you would be so good as to insert the advertisement below, from, though without the name, of, Sir

Your most obliged humble servant

HOR. WALPOLE

The author of a work[3] of which a new edition has been desired by a card sent to the printer of this paper, acquaints the persons who

---

15. Margaret Beauchamp (1404–67), m. (1425) John Talbot (ca 1384–1453), 7th Bn Talbot, 1421, cr. (1442) E. of Shrewsbury. 'Pictures of this Earl and his consort are in the gallery of Castle Ashby, in Northamptonshire, and judged by Mr Walpole to be the most ancient oil paintings in England' (Granger's *Supplement*, p. 14).
16. William Cole, HW's correspondent. HW had seen the portraits at Castle Ashby during a visit there with Cole in 1763; see

MONTAGU ii. 88, 336–7, and *Country Seats* 53–4.
17. No reply has been found.

———

1. Woodfall's letter and the note enclosed in it are missing.
2. Woodfall was the publisher of the *Public Advertiser* from 1760 to 1793.
3. Perhaps HW's *Catalogue of the Royal and Noble Authors of England*, SH, 1758; 2d edn, 1759. Several readers had sent HW corrections and additions

have done him the honour to make that request, that he has hitherto been prevented by various accidents, from giving another edition enlarged; but intends it as soon as he can offer it to the public, in as satisfactory a manner as he wishes to give anything of his writing, that they are pleased to regard favourably.

ERRAT.[4]

From Bishop Garnett,[1] ca March 1772

Printed for the first time from the MS now WSL. For the history of the MS see *ante* 25 July 1767.

Dated approximately by the endorsement.

Endorsed by HW: From Dr Garnet Bishop of Clogher. Received March 28, 1772. H. W.

IT is possible that Mr Walpole may not have forgotten an old university acquaintance[2] in the Bishop of Clogher, who sends him this abstract,[3] not to combat his opinion concerning King Richard III,[4] but to employ his curiosity about the *bolsters,*[5] if he thinks it deserves it after so manifest an anachronism in the gloss.[6]

for a revised edition of the *Catalogue;* he included some of the information in the 1787 quarto edition (*ante* 11 Feb. 1764, n. 2; see also *post* 5 Aug. 1789).

4. HW's 'advertisement' appeared (without the 'Errat') in the *Public Adv.* 26 March 1772.

———

1. Rev. John Garnett (1709–82), B.A. (Cantab.), 1729; fellow of Sidney Sussex College, Cambridge, 1730; D.D., 1752; Bp of Ferns, 1752–8, of Clogher 1758–82 (Venn, *Alumni Cantab.* ii. 196).

2. When HW was an undergraduate at King's College in 1735–8, Garnett was a fellow of Sidney Sussex College.

3. The 'abstract' is quoted from the Rev. John Johnson's *A Collection of all the Ecclesiastical Laws, Canons, Answers, or Rescripts . . . of the Church of England . . . and of all the Canons and Constitutions Ecclesiastical . . . that Have Hitherto Been Published in the Latin Tongue. Now First Translated into English with Explanatory Notes,* 1720,

vol. II ('Part the Second'), section 58. Johnson's source for the Latin text of Archbishop Bourchier's constitution (1463) outlawing 'the new ill-contrived fashions of apparel of the clergy' was Sir Henry Spelman's *Concilia* (n. 9 below).

4. 'With regard to the person of Richard, it appears to have been as much misrepresented as his actions. . . . The truth I take to have been this. Richard, who was slender and not tall, had one shoulder a little higher than the other: a defect, by the magnifying glasses of party, by distance of time, and by the amplification of tradition, easily swelled to shocking deformity' (*Historic Doubts on the Life and Reign of King Richard the Third,* 1768, pp. 102–3; *Works* ii. 166).

5. 'A padding in a garment used to fill up or round out some part' (OED *sub* 'bolster' 2d).

6. That is, the gloss 'on 'bolsters' provided by Johnson in his *Collection.* See following letter.

[Enclosure][7]

A.D. 1463

Archbishop Bourchier's[8] Constitutions
Sir H. Spelman Vol. 2, page 698.[9]

The Constitutions of Thomas Bourchier, Archbishop of Canterbury, primate of all England, legate of the Apostolical See, made in
the Cathedral Church of St Paul's London, the prelates and clergy
of the Province of Canterbury being then and there convocated, on
the sixth day of July 1463.

Par[agraph] 2.[10]

Although in this catholic and glorious kingdom of England, the
preachers of the word of God have sufficiently considered, and de-
claimed against the new ill-contrived fashions of apparel of the clergy
and people for several years, by reproof, reprehension, and entreaty,
according to the Apostle's doctrine; yet few or none desist from
these abuses, which is much to be lamented. It is fit then, that they,
who are not reclaimed by divine love, be restrained by fear of punishment. And if we, who by divine permission are set over others to
reform them, neglect to reform ourselves and clergy, we fear lest the
people subject to us, observing that our lives and manners differ from
our sermons, do thence take occasion to distrust our words, and so
be prompted (which God avert) to contemn the Church of Christ
and his ministers, and their sound doctrine and authority. Desiring
therefore to apply a remedy to this evil, so far as God enables us, that
we may not be to answer for it at the last day, we do by our metro-
political authority, with the unanimous assent and consent of our
venerable brethren, the Lords the Bishops, and of the whole clergy
of the Province of Canterbury, by a decree of this present Provincial
Council enact and ordain, that no priest, or clerk in holy orders, or
beneficed, do publicly wear any gown or upper garment, but what
is close before, and not wholly open, nor any bordering of skins, or
furs in the lower edges or circumference; and that no one who is

7. The 'abstract' is not in Garnett's
hand; it was presumably copied by his
secretary.

8. See *ante* 6 Feb. 1768, n. 2.

9. Sir Henry Spelman (?1564–1641), *Concilia, decreta, leges, constitutiones, in re*

ecclesiarum orbis Britannici, 1639–64, ii.
698–9. The second volume, which was
published posthumously, was edited by Sir
William Dugdale.

10. Marginal note in the MS.

not graduated in some university, or possessed of some ecclesiastical dignity, do wear a cap with a cape, nor a double cap, nor a single one with a cornet, or a short hood, after the manner of prelates and graduates (excepting only the priests and clerks in the service of Our Lord the King) or gold, or anything gilt on their girdle, sword, dagger, or purse. And let none of the abovesaid nor any domestics of an archbishop, bishop, abbot, prior, dean, archdeacon, or of any ecclesiastical man, who serves them for stipends or wages, and especially they who serve in a spiritual office, wear ill-contrived garments scandalous to the Church, nor **bolsters**[11] about their shoulders in their doublet, coat or gown, nor an upper garment so short as not to cover their middle parts, nor shoes monstrously long and turned up at the toes, nor any such sort of garments. If any transgressor of this statute and ordinance be discovered, after a month from the publication thereof, let him be wholly deprived of the perception of the profits of his ecclesiastical benefice, if he have any; if he have none, let him be wholly deprived of his office or service, whether he be clerk or laic, till he reform himself. And let the lord or master, who retains such an unreformed transgressor, or receives him again anew, take upon his own conscience the burden and peril before the supreme judge. And because we ourselves are disposed to use all diligence towards the observance of this Constitution in our own person, as God shall give us his grace, we do in the Lord exhort all our venerable the Lords the Bishops and other inferior ecclesiastical persons. We admonish all and singular persons subject to us, in virtue of strict obedience in the same Lord, that they so behave themselves in this respect, as may be to the praise of Almighty God, and for the avoiding scandal to his Church, that we may not hereafter be forced to aggravate the penalties of this Constitution.

Bolsters This word is expressed in English, and therefore there can be no mistake in it. It is commonly said, that in (King shall I call him?) Richard the Third's days, *bolsters* on the shoulders were in fashion, that men might seem to imitate that prince in his deformities, or lest it should seem a fault in subjects to appear straighter than their monarch. This, if true, was a fulsome flattery in all, especially in ecclesiastics. And it is probably true that this practice pre-

11. 'Vid. note' (marginal note in the MS).

vailed in Richard the Third's *usurpation;* for this Constitution was
made but about twenty years before he took possession of the throne.
But then it must not be said that it began in his reign, but might
then be continued in complaisance to the monstrous tyrant.[12]

Johnson's *Rights of the Clergy.*[13]

To Bishop Garnett, Sunday 29 March 1772

Printed for the first time from HW's MS copy, written on the blank conjugate leaf of Garnett's letter to HW *ante* ca March 1772, now WSL. The original letter sent to Garnett is missing.
Endorsed by HW: Answer [to Garnett's letter].

Strawberry Hill, March 29, 1772.

My Lord,

LORD HARDWICKE has given me the extract from Archbishop
Bourchier's Constitutions, which your Lordship was so good
as to send me.[1] I am not only much obliged to your Lordship for the
paper, but for the honour of your remembrance after so long an
interval. Though I have hazarded an opinion, my Lord, not agreeable to that generally received (and yet by no means peculiar to myself) still I should not adhere to it, had it received any solid answer.
Objections have been raised to some of my arguments; none to the
principal one; and nothing that pretends to coherence. Still less has
anything been said that corroborates the established story, or even
reconciles it to probability. These reflections have convinced me my
doubts were not ill-founded, and have more weight with me than my
own arguments. It is for this reason I have made no answer to sev-

12. A closely paraphrased version of
Johnson's gloss is printed in *A Supplement to Mr Chambers's Cyclopædia: or,
Universal Dictionary of Arts and Sciences,*
1753, vol. I, *sub* 'bolster.'

13. John Johnson, *The Clergyman's
Vade-Mecum: or, An Account of the Ancient and Present Church of England;
the Duties and Rights of the Clergy; and
of their Privileges and Hardships,* 1706–9,
published in two parts. Garnett apparently confused this work with Johnson's
Collection (n. 3 above) as the source of

the 'abstract'; the reference is in Garnett's hand.

1. See previous letter. Hardwicke's note
to HW 'forwarding him some antiquarian
remnants at the request of the Bishop
of Clogher,' dated 28 March 1772, was
offered in Thomas Thorpe's *Catalogue
of . . . Autograph Letters,* 1843, lot 1703;
not further traced. Garnett's letters to
Hardwicke are among the Hardwicke
papers in the British Museum (Add. MSS
35,597, 35,607–10, 35,612).

eral answerers.[2] I have waited to see if the story could be cleared from its difficulties. It was not worthwhile to trouble the public with controversy on immaterial parts. Will your Lordship forgive me if I think Richard's deformity of that number? Even granting it were important, I own I do not see how it can be proved or disproved by the Archbishop's reformation of dress. His Constitution mentions only the excess used by clergy and people; and intimates that that luxury was copied from the higher order of the clergy—not, as Johnson supposes, in compliment to the King's bad shape, which indeed it could not be, since, as Johnson himself observes, the ordinance was issued when Richard was not above fourteen.[3] It is therefore a very strained supposition in him to imagine that the people continued, in flattery to Richard's crookedness, a mode which they had notoriously practised in imitation of what they thought dignified the upper clergy. There would be equal reason for believing that all French officers wore full-bottomed wigs to the end of the reign of Louis XIV, because Marshal Luxembourg[4] was very ill made.[5] Men are more apt to copy what passes for an ornament to the person, than what is used to disguise its defects. If such strained conclusions are allowed, I do not know what may not be built on them.

I am at a loss, my Lord, to discover the anachronism on the gloss, at which your Lordship hints in the note endorsed on the paper you did me the honour to send me. There is no date on the gloss: and for the King's person it corresponds remarkably with another drawing of him made by his cotemporary Rous of Warwick in a very valuable roll in the possession of the Duke of Manchester, with the use of which I have been favoured, and a print of which I shall give some time or other in a future edition.[6] Your Lordship's candour, I am persuaded, will excuse my making this defence, which I thought a respect due to the notice with which you have honoured my work.

2. The 'answerers' included David Hume, William Guthrie, F. W. Guydickens, Jeremiah Milles, and Robert Masters; see *ante* 1 March 1768 *bis*, nn. 9–11, and Hazen, *Bibl. of HW* 72–3. HW replied to his critics in the 'Supplement to the Historic Doubts' (written in 1769), *A Reply to the Observations of the Rev. Dr Milles* (1770), *Short Observations on the Remarks of the Rev. Mr Masters* (1774), and the 'Postscript to my Historic Doubts' (1793); these pieces were pub-

lished together in *Works* (1798) ii. 185–252, although all but the last had been printed in 1774 or earlier.

3. Richard (b. 2 Oct. 1452) was ten years old when Archbishop Bourchier's constitution was enacted in July 1463.

4. François-Henri de Montmorency-Bouteville (1628–95), Duc de Luxembourg, 1661; Maréchal de France, 1675.

5. Luxembourg was a hunchback.

6. Of *Historic Doubts*. See *ante* 17 Feb. 1768, nn. 1–3.

As I have studied the subject much more perhaps than[7] it deserved, I am enabled possibly to answer weightier attacks than such as Johnson's.[8] What I have to say more in behalf of my opinion will be seen hereafter; but I am in no hurry: it has not been shaken hitherto by anything I have read in opposition to it. Nor can I think any opinion of mine of consequence enough to deserve a controversy. Even the matter itself is of little consequence: one of the reasons that renders it of most value to me, is, that it has procured me the honour of your Lordship's notice, and[9] in that light cannot be indifferent to

My Lord
Your Lordship's much obliged
and most obedient humble servant

HOR. WALPOLE

To Henry Sampson Woodfall,
Thursday 30 April 1772

Printed for the first time from a photostat of the MS in the British Museum (Add. MS 27,780, f. 19). For the history of the MS see *ante* 24 March 1772.

Endorsed in an unidentified hand: Horatio Walpole now Lord Orford.

Address: To Mr H. S. Woodfall in Paternoster Row. *Postmark:* PENNY POST PAID.

Arlington Street, April 30th 1772.

MR H. Walpole has received Mr Woodfall's letter,[1] and has written to his cousin accordingly, so that if Mr Woodfall calls on Mr *Thomas* Walpole[2] in Lincoln's Inn Fields,[3] he may make use of Mr Hor. Walpole's name, and will find that Mr T. W. is apprised of the request,[4] and Mr H. W. hopes it will be successful, of which he shall be very glad, as well as of his success upon the whole.

7. The MS reads 'that.'
8. Rev. John Johnson (1662–1725), vicar of Cranbrook, Kent, 1707; controversialist and divine. See previous letter, nn. 3, 6.
9. 'as such' crossed out in the MS.

1. Missing.
2. Hon. Thomas Walpole (1727–1803), 2d son of Horatio, 1st Bn Walpole of Wolterton; banker in London and Paris; M.P.; HW's first cousin and correspondent.
3. HW first wrote 'Great Broad Street in the City,' crossed it out in the MS, and added 'Lincoln's Inn Fields' as a footnote. Thomas Walpole was a partner in the merchant bank of Walpole and Ellison, 11 New Broad Street; he had a house in Lincoln's Inn Fields (*The New Complete Guide to all Persons who Have any Trade or Concern in the City of London*, 13th edn, [1772], p. 283; MANN ix. 55).
4. The nature of Woodfall's request is not known.

From SIR WILLIAM CHAMBERS,[1] Monday 8 June 1772

Printed from a photostat of Chambers's MS copy in his Letter Book in the British Museum (Add. MS 41,133, ff. 72–3). First printed in *Journal of the Royal Institute of British Architects*, 24 Aug. 1893, new ser., ix. 485–6. Chambers's Letter Book was in the collection of A. H. Heron in 1892; sold Sotheby's 23 June 1924 (J. Pearson and Co. Sale), lot 116, to the British Museum. The original letter is missing.

Endorsed by Chambers: To the Honourable Mr H. Walpole.

June 8th 1772.

Sir,

I SPENT a good part of the afternoon last Friday at the stone manufactory in examining Mrs Coade's[2] claim upon you[3] for the piers at Strawberry Hill.[4] I saw the model and she produced a letter from the maker,[5] who I know and believe to be a man of character, by which it appeared, as nearly as she could collect the time etc. from his books, it had cost £25, but as neither Mr Whatley,[6] her friend, nor I thought it worth any such sum, we put it down at £16, which we thought the full value of it and supposed that the remainder of the time etc. might have been employed on other things and charged by mistake to this article, or in making alterations of which we could take no account. We then saw the moulds, which are very formidable things, and we believed not overcharged in the

1. (1726–96), Knight of the Polar Star, 1771; R. A.; architect.

2. Mrs Eleanor Coade (ca 1732–1821), inventor of the artificial stone known as Coade stone, produced by her manufactory at King's Arms Stairs, Narrow Wall, Lambeth (GM 1821, xci pt ii. 572; Alison Kelly, 'Mrs Coade's Stone,' *Connoisseur*, 1978, cxcvii. 14–25). 'Coade's manufacture of artificial stone (now Messrs Coade and Sealy) was established at Lambeth in the year 1769. This composition, which is cast in moulds and burnt, is intended to answer the purpose of stone, for every species of ornamental architecture, at a much cheaper rate than carving' (Daniel Lysons, *The Environs of London*, 2d edn, 1811, i. 228).

3. Chambers had written Mrs Coade 26 May 1772: 'Mr Walpole insists upon your choosing a person to meet me in order to settle the dispute between you. Appoint therefore whoever you think proper and I will meet them at your

house any evening about five the beginning of next week' (MS copy in Chambers's Letter Book, BM Add. MS 41,133, f. 72).

4. 'The piers of the garden gates are of artificial stone, and taken from the tomb of William de Luda Bishop of Ely, in that cathedral' ('Des. of SH,' *Works* ii. 507). The design was prepared by James Essex through the good offices of William Cole; see HW's 'directions' for the garden gate in his letter to Cole 15 July 1769 (COLE i. 178–9 and illustration). The gate was apparently in place by 8 June 1771, when HW wrote to Mann: 'I have made a Gothic gateway to the garden, the piers of which are of artificial stone and very respectable' (MANN vii. 311).

5. Not identified.

6. Kemble Whately (d. 1780), of Lambeth (Lysons, *The Environs of London*, 1792–6, i. 534).

account any more than the quantity of the composition used; of the price we are no judges, but supposed from the nature of the materials of which it is composed and the method of preparing it that it must be worth as much as plaster; she has charged something less for it. We then saw an account of the expenses of burning a kiln of goods, as they call it, and it amounted to five guineas according to her book, but as there were some articles that we thought over-rated, we reduced it to four guineas, and upon inspection of the kiln, or rather oven, we believed that the piers could not be burnt in less than four times' firing.

The wages for modelling ornaments, moulding and repairing seemed to us both incredible, but she produced a book, wherein a regular account of time was kept which had all the marks of authenticity, from which we collected, I think, £52 of the sum charged. The remainder was for work done before the commencement of the book, for which there appeared no proofs, but we examined one[7] of the men who had been employed and he said he began to work at the piers as soon as he came into the manufactory, which was two months, we found, before the book was begun. We then examined some of the manufacture just taken out of the moulds and compared it with what was finished, and saw the method and difficulty of repairing it, which convinced us that the reparation was a very tedious and expensive work, much more so than could be imagined by any who have not seen it done. To conclude, we were mutually of opinion that the piers had cost Mrs Co[a]de upwards of £150 exclusive of profit etc.—as you will see by the enclosed state of the account, but as she had offered to accept of £100 rather than incur your displeasure, we both of us declined fixing any sum and advised her to leave it entirely to your goodness to settle it as you should judge reasonable.[8] With regard to the repair, she is willing to put up the one pinnacle that is wanting and the eight flowers without any expense to you, but if more should be wanting she hopes you will consider it.

I am, Sir, etc.,

[WM. CHAMBERS]

7. From this point the rest of the MS copy is in a different (unidentified) hand.

8. Chambers and Whately reckoned the sum of Mrs Coade's expenses to be £151.14.10. HW apparently accepted this figure; payment in exactly this amount for the 'Gothic gateway to the garden in

[Enclosure]

Mrs Co[a]de's charge

£				£	s.	d.
25	—	—	Model etc.	16	—	—
10	—	—	30 l[bs] plaster	10	—	—
5	5	—	Moulds, cases, oil and lard	5	5	—
21	—	—	3½ ton composition	21	—	—
21	—	—	4 kilns burning	16	16	—
64	6	4	Wages	64	6	4
5	15	6	Putting up the piers	5	15	6
23	6	—	Pincot's[9] attendance	12	12	—
175	12	10		151	14	10

Upon examination of the books, models, casts, moulds, etc., and upon questioning the men of the manufactory and inspecting into the nature of the work, we are of opinion that the piers made and erected at Twickenham for the Honourable Mr Walpole cost Mrs Co[a]de the sum of £151.14.10 exclusive of profit, house-hire, and some other trifling articles.

WM. CHAMBERS

KEMBLE WHATLEY

artificial stone' is recorded in his SH account book under the year 1773 (*Strawberry Hill Accounts . . . Kept by Mr Horace Walpole from 1747 to 1795*, ed. Paget Toynbee, Oxford, 1927, p. 13).

9. Daniel Pincot (d. 1797), surveyor at Lambeth; later a, glass and china merchant on Forty Hill, Enfield; author of *An Essay on the Origin, Nature, Uses, and Properties of Artificial Stone*, 1770 (GM 1789, lix pt ii. 1147; 1797, lxvii pt i. 262; Hazen, *Cat. of HW's Lib.*, No. 1609:26:4).

From the DUCHESSE DE MIREPOIX,[1]
Saturday 27 June 1772

Printed from the MS now WSL. First printed, Toynbee *Supp.* iii. 228–9. Damer-Waller; the MS was sold Sotheby's 5 Dec. 1921 (first Waller Sale), lot 160, passed; resold Christie's 15 Dec. 1947 (second Waller Sale), lot 55 (with other letters), to Maggs for WSL.

Address: À Monsieur Monsieur Horace Walpoll à Londres.

À Paris ce 27 juin 1772.

UNE si charmante lettre,[2] une si belle dame ne sauraient manquer d'inspirer le plus grand intérêt. Je témoignerai autant qu'il me sera possible à Madame Damer[3] la considération et l'amitié que j'aurai toujours pour Monsieur Walpole, mais la vie que je mène lui est connue, il sait que je ne dispose guère de mon temps.[4] Je ferai pourtant pour Madame Damer tout ce que la vieille Schirlei aurait fait pour Miss Biron.[5] Je l'admirerai tout autant, seulement je la prêcherai un peu moins. J'espère que j'aurai le plaisir de la voir danser.[6] Je la mènerai à la campagne aux spectacles;[7] enfin, je n'oublirai rien de tout ce qui pourra vous prouver, Monsieur, le cas infini que je fais de votre recommandation, et combien l'amitié dont vous m'honorez m'est précieuse.

BEAUVAU MIREPOIX

1. Anne-Marguerite-Gabrielle de Beauvau (1707–91), m. 1 (1721) Jacques-Henri de Lorraine, Prince de Lixin; m. 2 (1739) Gaston-Charles-Pierre Lévis de Lomagne, Marquis (Duc, 1751) de Mirepoix, Maréchal de France, 1757. See *ante* 19 Oct. 1765 and n. 26.

2. Missing; mentioned in Mme du Deffand to HW 23 June 1772: 'elle me dit avoir reçu une lettre de vous charmante' (DU DEFFAND iii. 259).

3. Anne Seymour Conway (1748–1828), only child of HW's cousin Henry Seymour Conway and Lady Ailesbury; m. (1767) Hon. John Damer; sculptress. She had recently arrived in Paris; Mme du Deffand reported 24 June: 'Mme de Mirepoix revint de Versailles hier pour souper avec moi; elle a vu madame votre cousine; elle la trouve belle et bien faite, bon air, bonne grâce; elle en est charmée' (ibid. iii. 260).

4. Writing to Lady Hervey 15 Sept. 1765, HW refers to 'my old friend Madame de Mirepoix . . . who is grown a most particular favourite of the King, and seldom from him' (MORE 47).

5. Harriet Byron, the heroine of Samuel Richardson's *The History of Sir Charles Grandison*, 1754. She was brought up by her grandmother, Henrietta Shirley, who took an active interest in the affairs of the young and did much to promote the marriage between Harriet and Sir Charles.

6. Mrs Damer was apparently an accomplished dancer. HW mentions her participation in a quadrille, dressed in the fashion of Queen Elizabeth, at a ball given by the French ambassador in 1773 (OSSORY i. 110).

7. At Versailles.

Pardonne mon griffonnage à deux petits chats qui écrivent avec moi.[8]

To JAMES WYATT,[1] Sunday 26 July 1772

Printed from a photostat of the MS in the British Museum (Egerton MS 3515, f. 1). First printed in Antony Dale, *James Wyatt*, Oxford, 1956, pp. 133–4. The MS is in a collection of Wyatt family papers acquired by the British Museum in July 1948; its previous history is not known.
Endorsed, possibly by Wyatt: Horace Walpole's letter.

Strawberry Hill, July 26, 1772.

Sir,

I BEG your pardon for asking you perhaps an impertinent question. It is whether you are descended from Sir Thomas Wyat,[2] who lived in the time of Henry VIII. I am employed in collecting materials for his life,[3] and very solicitous to find out some of his family. I know that some years ago there did live in Charterhouse Yard an old Mr Wyat,[4] who was the representative of the family and had portraits of his ancestors, which I should be very happy to discover. You have so much genius and merit yourself, Sir, that it can be of no consequence to you whether you are related to that family or not.[5] No man with such talents as yours[6] wants to be distinguished by the lustre of others. My curiosity you see is founded solely on my own business, and I trust you will excuse my making the application

8. 'Madame de Mirepoix, as I told her, is the most constant of women, for I found her *with a cat in her lap, drinking tea, and as obliging to me as formerly*' (HW to Anne Pitt 8 Oct. 1765, MORE 55).

1. (1746–1813), architect, whom HW commissioned to build the offices at SH in 1790 (MASON i. 31 n. 29).

2. Sir Thomas Wyatt (ca 1503–42), Kt, 1537; Henry VIII's ambassador to Charles V 1537–40; poet.

3. HW's 'Life of Sir Thomas Wyat, the Elder' was printed in *Miscellaneous Antiquities*, No. 2, SH, 1772, pp. 4–20. 'In July [1772] wrote the life of Sir Thomas Wyat, for No. II of my edition of *Miscellaneous Antiquities*' ('Short Notes,' (GRAY i. 47).

4. Not further identified. HW wrote in his 'Life of Sir Thomas Wyat,' p. 6: 'I find this notice in Vertue's MSS collections. He was acquainted with a Mr Wyat who lived in Charterhouse Yard, and was the representative descendant of that respectable family. In 1721 and at other times Vertue saw at that gentleman's house portraits of his ancestors for seven descents, and other pictures and ancient curiosities.' In a footnote HW added: 'It would be fortunate if mention of these pictures should lead to the knowledge of the person who now possesses them.'

5. See following letter.

6. HW called Wyatt's recently completed Pantheon 'the most beautiful edifice in England' (HW to Mason 29 July 1773, MASON i. 102).

to you—nor was I sorry to take an opportunity of telling you how extremely I admire your taste,[7] and how much I am

Sir

Your obedient humble servant

Hor. Walpole

From James Wyatt, Saturday 1 August 1772

Printed from a photostat of Wyatt's MS copy in the British Museum (Egerton MS 3515, f. 2). First printed in Antony Dale, *James Wyatt,* Oxford, 1956, p. 134. For the history of the MS copy see *ante* 26 July 1772. The original letter is missing. *Endorsed in an unidentified hand:* To Horace Walpole Esq. August 1st 1772.

Newport Street, August 1st 1772.

Sir,

THE loss of the best of fathers,[1] an account of whose death I received on Tuesday last, prevented my answering your very obliging and polite letter[2] so soon as I wished.

I cannot but regret the want of materials to furnish me with the means of giving you that intelligence you seek for—my pursuits having been of a different nature, the knowledge I have of my family is derived from oral traditions only, and goes no farther back than my great-grandfather,[3] who, as I have been told, was a farmer in Staffordshire, where I myself was born.[4] Whether therefore we are descendants of Sir Thomas Wyatt or not is a subject I am not in the least acquainted with or be assured, Sir, the ⟨honour⟩[5] of having contributed the least matter for the ⟨use of y⟩our pen, could have been exceeded by nothing ⟨but the app⟩robation of the works of,

Sir,

Your most obedient humble servant,

James Wyatt

7. 'Mr Wyat, the architect [of the Pantheon], has so much taste, that I think he must be descended from Sir Thomas' (HW to Mason 9 May 1772, ibid. i. 31).

1. Benjamin Wyatt (1709–72), of Weeford, Staffs; farmer and timber merchant, who also practised as a builder and architect. He died at Weeford in July 1772 (Dale, op. cit. 2–3).

2. *Ante* 26 July 1772.
3. Not further identified. His son, John Wyatt (1675–1742), lived and died at Weeford (ibid.).
4. James Wyatt, the sixth son of Benjamin Wyatt, was born at Blackbrook Farm, Weeford, on 3 August 1746 (ibid.).
5. Conjectural reading; the lower left-hand corner of the letter is missing.

From DR JAMES BROWN,[1] Tuesday 25 August 1772

Printed for the first time from a photostat of the MS in Pembroke College Library, Cambridge. The MS was sold Sotheby's 26 Oct. 1916 (Prideaux Sale), lot 115 (with MSS of Thomas Gray), to Dobell; *penes* Leonard Whibley in 1933, on whose death it passed to his widow; acquired by Pembroke College, 1949.

The year of the letter is established by HW to Mason 24 Aug. 1772 (see n. 7 below).

Aug. 25.

MR MASON[2] and Dr Brown present their compliments and desire the favour of Mr Walpole's acceptance of a Goa stone[3] and piece of bloodstone, which belonged to Mr Gray,[4] and which they thought Mr Walpole would value on that account.[5] The bloodstone with the seal engraved, Mr Gray used to say, belonged to his father.[6] Dr B. had intended to have done himself the honour of delivering them himself, had Mr Walpole been at home.[7]

1. (ca 1709–84), D.D. (Cantab.), 1771; fellow, 1735, and Master of Pembroke College, Cambridge, 1770–84; Vice-Chancellor 1771–2 (MASON i. 1 n. 7).

2. William Mason, HW's correspondent.

3. 'A fever medicine . . . consisting of various drugs made up in the form of a hard ball, from which a portion was scraped as required' (OED).

4. Thomas Gray, the poet, who was a fellow of Pembroke College, Cambridge. He died there 30 July 1771.

5. 'I shall lay them up in my cabinet at Strawberry Hill among my most valuables' (HW to Cole 25 Aug. 1772, COLE i. 275). The Goa stone and the seal are listed among the 'curiosities' kept in the Glass Closet: 'An agate puncheon with the arms of Mr Gray the poet, and a Goa stone; given to Mr Walpole by Doctor Browne and Mr W. Mason, Mr Gray's executors' ('Des. of SH,' *Works* ii. 499).

6. Philip Gray (1676–1741), 'an Exchange broker of reputation and fortune' (*Correspondence of Thomas Gray*, ed. Paget Toynbee and Leonard Whibley, Oxford, 1935, iii. 1306–7).

7. 'I happened to come hither [Arlington Street] today on business, and find Dr Brown has called twice, and left me in his own and your names a Goa stone and a bloodstone seal, which both belonged to Mr Gray. You know how really I shall value them' (HW to Mason 24 [25] Aug. 1772, MASON i. 43).

To Lord Hardwicke, November 1772

Printed from a photostat of the MS among the Hardwicke papers in the British Museum (Add. MS 35,610, f. 371). First printed, Toynbee viii. 213; extract quoted in G. E. Kendall, 'Notes on the Life of John Wootton with a List of Engravings after his Pictures,' *Walpole Society* 1932–3, xxi. 32. The Hardwicke papers were purchased by the British Museum from the 6th Earl of Hardwicke in 1899.

Dated approximately by the reference to HW's gout (see n. 9 below).

MR WALPOLE has received Lord Hardwicke's commands[1] and has in town what his mother always kept as the best picture of Sir R. Walpole, done when about forty.[2] It is painted by Richardson[3] in a green frock and hat, and the dogs and landscape by Wootton.[4] The most like print[5] which is in the Garter robes, was taken from this. At Rainham[6] is a very good one by Sir Godfrey Kneller.[7] If Lord Hardwicke chooses that in Arlington Street to be copied, it is very much at his Lordship's service.[8]

Mr W. begs pardon for writing so ill, but is in bed with the gout.[9]

1. Hardwicke's letter to HW is missing.

2. Probably the full-length portrait said to portray him as Ranger of Richmond Park, now at Houghton Hall, Norfolk. However, Sir Robert did not obtain the Rangership of Richmond Park until 1726, when he was about fifty (J. H. Plumb, *Sir Robert Walpole: The King's Minister*, 1960, p. 90; illustrated pl. VI, facing p. 149). Three other versions of this portrait are known; see John Kerslake, *Early Georgian Portraits*, National Portrait Gallery, 1977, i. 202, where the iconography of Sir Robert Walpole is fully discussed (i. 200–5).

3. Jonathan Richardson, the elder.

4. John Wootton (ca 1682–1764), landscape and sporting painter. Many of Wootton's pictures were painted in collaboration with other artists, including Richardson; see Kendall, op. cit. 28, 32.

5. Not identified.

6. Raynham Hall, Norfolk, the seat of George, 4th Vct Townshend, cr. (1787) M. Townshend.

7. Kneller's half-length portrait hung in the small dining-room at Raynham in 1829 ([John Chambers], *A General History of the County of Norfolk*, Norwich, 1829, i. 543). It is possibly the same portrait which was engraved in mezzotint by John Simon; see J. C. Smith, *British Mezzotinto Portraits*, 1878–84, iii. 1124, No. 160.

8. Sir William Musgrave, in a list of pictures at Wimpole Hall (Hardwicke's seat) compiled in 1798, mentions a copy after a portrait of Sir Robert Walpole by Jean-Baptiste Van Loo (BM Add. MS 6391, f. 20, cited in Kerslake, op. cit. i. 200).

9. 'Six weeks finish tomorrow, and I have not been yet out of my bedchamber, and little out of my bed, till lately, and in the middle of the day' (HW to Mason 10 Nov. 1772, Mason i. 53). See following letter.

To ?James Essex,[1] Friday 13 November 1772

Printed for the first time from the MS now WSL, removed from the first volume of Lord Cunliffe's copy of *Anecdotes of Painting in England,* ed. James Dallaway, 5 vols, 1826–8. This copy was sold Sotheby's 28 May 1946 (Lord Cunliffe Sale), lot 886, to Maggs for WSL; its earlier history is not known.

The addressee is conjecturally identified as James Essex. In early November, after coming from Cambridge to London for a stay of two or three weeks, Essex called at HW's house in Arlington Street and left a letter for him from William Cole (COLE i. 284–6). Essex wished to obtain HW's advice concerning his treatise on Gothic architecture (never published). HW was at SH, confined to his bed by the gout, and was unable to see anyone.

Strawberry Hill, Nov. 13, 1772.

Dear Sir,

AS I have had a return of pain, and have again been forced to keep in bed,[2] I did not send to claim your obliging offer of coming hither.[3] I am still confined to my room, and so faint as to be little capable of conversation. You shall not therefore throw yours away on one so little worthy of it. I am endeavouring by great quiet to collect strength enough to remove to town in a very few days,[4] and then I shall with a better conscience ask your charity, as it will be with much less trouble to yourself.

Yours most sincerely

H. WALPOLE

1. (1722–84), builder and architect, who designed the Gothic piers of the garden gate at SH (*ante* 8 June 1772, n. 4).

2. HW wrote Cole 7 Nov. 1772: 'I . . . am now confined to my bed with the gout in every limb, and in almost every joint. I have not been out of my bedchamber these five weeks today, and last night the pain returned violently into one of my feet' (COLE i. 285).

3. 'I am exceedingly sorry for his [Essex's] disappointment, and for his coming [to London] without writing first, in which case I might have prevented his journey. I do not know even whither to send to him, to tell him how impossible it is for me just now in my present painful and helpless situation to be of any use to him. . . . I cannot guess when it will be in my power to consider duly Mr Essex's plan with him' (ibid. i. 286). See headnote.

4. HW suffered another relapse of gout and apparently did not leave SH until shortly before Christmas; see ibid. i. 289 and MASON i. 58.

To Sir Thomas Cave,[1] ca 1773

Printed for the first time from the MS now WSL, removed from Sir Thomas Cave's copy of *Anecdotes of Painting in England,* 2d edn, SH, 1765. This copy descended to Cave's granddaughter, Sarah Otway-Cave, *suo jure* Baroness Braye; sold by the 7th Baron Braye to H. D. Lyons, the London bookseller, in 1970; acquired from Lyons by H. W. Liebert, of New Haven, Connecticut, who presented it to WSL, August 1970.

Dated approximately by the reference to the fourth volume of *Anecdotes* and to HW's publisher, John Bell (see nn. 2 and 6 below).

MR WALPOLE sends his respectful compliments to Sir Thomas Cave, and is extremely sorry he has had so much trouble about a trifling work, which Mr W. fears will not answer his expectations, and which is not yet published. There has been a little mistake, he apprehends, about the fourth volume of the *Anecdotes;*[2] the bookseller probably understood that Sir T. Cave meant the volume of *Engravers,*[3] which is sold with the three first volumes, and is often called the fourth,[4] which is indeed finished, but Mr Walpole being obliged to make some alterations,[5] cannot publish it yet and the bookseller Bell[6] has never seen it.

Mr W. is very much obliged to Sir Thomas for the honour he has done him in pointing out an error in the inscription, of which Mr W. had indeed been told by another gentleman,[7] but he is not the less obliged to Sir Thomas, and will wait on him to thank him for it and for the favour of his visit.

1. (1712–78), 5th Bt, 1734, of Stanford Hall, Leics; M.P.; antiquary and collector. His collections for a topographical history of Leicestershire were given by his grandson, Sir Thomas Cave, 7th Bt, to John Nichols, who used them in compiling *The History and Antiquities of the County of Leicestershire,* 4 vols, 1795–1815 (Nichols, *Lit. Anec.* i. 516).

2. *Anecdotes of Painting in England.* HW finished writing the fourth and final volume in 1770; the printing of it at the SH Press was completed on 13 April 1771, but it was not published until Oct. 1780 (Hazen, *SH Bibl.* 63).

3. *A Catalogue of Engravers Who Have Been Born or Resided in England,* SH, 1763; 2d edn, SH, 1765. Cave's copy of *Anecdotes* includes the *Catalogue* but lacks the fourth volume (see headnote).

4. The 'Direction to the Binder' in the *Catalogue of Engravers* reads: 'This volume should not be lettered as the fourth, but as a detached piece; another volume of the Painters being intended, which will complete the work.'

5. See *post* 21 Jan. 1773 and 4 Oct. 1780.

6. John Bell (1745–1831), bookseller 'near Exeter Change, in the Strand' (OSSORY ii. 247 n. 6; *Daily Adv.* 1 Jan. 1773). Bell sold the two numbers of *Miscellaneous Antiquities,* SH, 1772, as well as the fourth volume of *Anecdotes.*

7. Perhaps John Bromfield, who sent HW 'Notes, Strictures, and Corrections etc.' on *Anecdotes of Painting;* see *ante* 8 April 1764. The 'inscription' in question has not been identified.

To Lord Hardwicke, ?January 1773

Printed for the first time from the MS in Thomas Kirgate's hand, now WSL. The MS descended in the Yorke family to the 6th Earl of Hardwicke, who sold Wimpole Hall and its estates to the 2d Baron Robartes (6th Viscount Clifden, 1899) in 1891; sold by the 7th Viscount Clifden, through W. H. Robinson Ltd., to WSL, August 1954.

Dated conjecturally by HW's relapse of gout in Jan. 1773 (see n. 3 below).

YOUR Lordship's plan[1] is so curious and judicious, that I am sure I can add nothing but exhortation to pursue it; and may safely promise that it must be received with thanks by the public.[2] Not being able to write myself,[3] your Lordship will excuse my saying no more now than that

> I am, my Lord,
>> Your Lordship's most obliged
>>> and obedient humble servant,

>>>> H. Walpole

To Lord Sandwich, Saturday 9 January 1773

Printed from a copy collated with the MS then (1939) in the possession of the 9th Earl of Sandwich (d. 1962), Hinchingbrooke, Huntingdon. First printed, Toynbee *Supp.* iii. 328–9.

Arlington Street, Jan. 9, 1773.

My Lord,

AS YOUR Lordship has the double generosity of conferring favours, and of forgetting them, it is necessary perhaps to put you in mind how much I have been obliged to you.[1] But as it is only in

1. Presumably a plan for compiling *Miscellaneous State Papers, from 1501 to 1726*, 2 vols, 1778. HW's copiously annotated copy, now WSL, is Hazen, *Cat. of HW's Lib.*, No. 3236. See *post* 24 Jan. 1774.

2. HW wrote Cole 23 April 1778, shortly after Hardwicke's work was published: 'I have far advanced . . . in Lord Hardwicke's first volume of *State Papers*. I have yet found nothing that opens a new scene, or sets the old in a new light, yet they are rather amusing, though not in

proportion to the bulk of the volumes' (COLE ii. 75). He told Cole in 1781 that 'nothing upon earth was ever duller' (ibid. ii. 263).

3. The letter is in the hand of HW's printer and secretary, Thomas Kirgate. HW informed Mann 21 Jan. 1773: 'I have a little relapsed. . . . The gout is returned into both feet, and a little into one elbow' (MANN vii. 454).

———

1. See *ante* 17 Feb. 1768 and n. 4 below.

my power to give your Lordship testimonies of my gratitude, not real proofs, I flatter myself you will allow me to offer you a new edition of the *Mémoires de Grammont,²* of which I have printed but an hundred copies,³ and which therefore, besides the intrinsic merit of the book, have that of being rarities, though no other additional merit. Ninon Lenclos begs a place for her cotemporaries in your Lordship's library;⁴ and I am sure you will not refuse her request, my Lord, though you was Scipio enough to resign her to her admirer,⁵

Your Lordship's most obliged

and most obedient humble servant

Hor. Walpole.

From Madame Geoffrin,¹ Sunday 10 January 1773

Printed from Toynbee *Supp.* iii. 230–1, where the letter was first printed. Damer-Waller; the MS was sold Sotheby's 5 Dec. 1921 (first Waller Sale), lot 132 (with lot 133), to Maggs; not further traced.

À Paris ce 10 janvier 1773.

J'AI reçu, Monsieur, une marque de votre souvenir bien flatteuse et bien touchante.

Votre beau présent² va faire l'ornement de ma petite bibliothèque, et me procurer le nouveau plaisir de relire un livre délicieux et

2. *Mémoires du Comte de Grammont, par Monsieur le Comte Antoine Hamilton. Nouvelle edition, augmentée de notes et d'éclaircissemens nécessaires, par M. Horace Walpole,* SH, 1772 (Hazen, *SH Bibl.* 96–9).

3. 100 copies were printed at the SH Press 29 April 1771 – end of May 1772. HW sent 25 (or, possibly, 30) copies to France (ibid. 96).

4. In 1757 Sandwich gave HW a portrait of Ninon de Lenclos which had belonged to his grandmother; see *ante* 22 July 1757. HW had the portrait engraved by Thomas Worlidge (More 6 n. 2), and apparently gave an impression to Sandwich. The presentation copy of the *Mémoires,* in which a small print of

the portrait was inserted, was still in the library at Hinchingbrooke in 1925 (Toynbee *Supp.* iii. 329 n. 4).

5. HW frequently alludes to the 'continence of Scipio'; see Mason ii. 71, Ossory i. 265, and Conway i. 535.

1. Marie-Thérèse Rodet (1699–1777), m. (1713) François Geoffrin. Her salon, the rival of Mme du Deffand's, was frequented by the encyclopedists and other literary men. HW first met her at Paris in 1765 ('Paris Journals,' du Deffand v. 261); he describes her character in a letter to Gray 25 Jan. 1766 (Gray ii. 150).

2. Doubtless a copy of HW's edition of *Mémoires du Comte de Grammont,* SH, 1772. See previous letter, nn. 2, 3.

curieux, par les remarques dont vous l'avez enrichi. Cette lecture me rappellera vos bontés, dont je vous demande, Monsieur, la continuation.

Mes années qui s'accumulent m'ôtent l'espérance de pouvoir vous exprimer moi-même en vous embrassant ma sensibilité, ma reconnaissance, mon admiration, et mon attachement.[3] C'est avec ces sentiments que je conserverai dans mon cœur jusqu'à mon dernier moment que j'ai l'honneur d'être, Monsieur, votre très humble et très obéissante servante

GEOFFRIN

To LORD HARDWICKE, Thursday 21 January 1773

Printed from a photostat of the MS among the Hardwicke papers in the British Museum (Add. MS 35,611, f. 20). First printed, Toynbee viii. 227–8. For the history of the MS see *ante* Nov. 1772.

Arlington Street, Jan. 21, 1773.

My Lord,

I WAS in pain this morning[1] and could not have the honour of answering your Lordship's letter.[2] I am very sorry that it does not depend on me, without a breach of promise, to obey your Lordship's commands. You must allow me to explain the circumstances, which prevent my indulging myself in the flattering pleasure of obedience when it would do me so much honour. There is an unfortunate page or two in my book, which would hurt a person[3] now living, though I thought I had guarded with the utmost caution against any such case. My dread of offending even near relations of very indifferent artists has long obstructed my completion of the work,[4] and has kept it back, though printed off for some time. The

3. Mme Geoffrin saw HW several times when he was at Paris in 1775 ('Paris Journals,' DU DEFFAND v. 345–53).

1. See *ante* ?Jan. 1773, n. 3.
2. Missing; apparently requesting a copy of the fourth volume of *Anecdotes of Painting*.
3. Mrs Hogarth. HW delayed publication of the fourth volume of *Anecdotes* chiefly because of what he had written about Hogarth's 'Sigismunda.' See *ante* ca 1773, n. 2, and *post* 4 Oct. 1780.

4. 'This completion Mr Walpole told me, he had no design of publishing himself—perhaps he might leave it behind him. Truth, said he, which I am determined to adhere to, might offend the near relations and friends of some of the artists that are dead, and prejudice those that are living' (MS note, in Richard Bull's hand, in his copy of HW's *Catalogue of Engravers*, now WSL).

concern this accident has given me, not only made me determine to suppress my book till a fitter period, but made me give my honour to a friend[5] of the person interested, that I would not suffer a copy to go out of my hands, till that time. Indeed when I am well enough, I intend to alter the article in question,[6] and then your Lordship shall certainly command the first proof, which, you see, at present, I am not at liberty to send you, though I am,

My Lord
Your Lordship's most obedient humble servant

Hor. Walpole

To Lord Hardwicke, ?March 1773

Printed for the first time from a photostat of the MS in Thomas Kirgate's hand, furnished by the Public Record Office of Northern Ireland by permission of the owner, the Earl of Caledon, Caledon Castle, Co. Tyrone, Northern Ireland. The MS passed to the 3d Earl of Hardwicke, whose daughter and co-heir, Catharine Freeman Yorke, married the 2d Earl of Caledon in 1811, and from whom it descended to the 6th Earl of Caledon.

Dated conjecturally by the allusion to HW's long fit of gout and by the reference to *Mémoires du Comte de Grammont* (see nn. 3 and 6 below).

Address: To the Earl of Hardwicke St James's Square.

Endorsed in an unidentified hand: To the 2d Lord H. from Lord Orford. Mr W. Myst[erious] Mother.

MR WALPOLE is extremely obliged to Lord Hardwicke for the favour of seeing his drawings,[1] which are very beautiful, and in the purest taste, and which deserve to be executed[2] as well as they are designed.

As soon as ever he is able to go to Strawberry Hill,[3] Mr Walpole

5. Perhaps Adam Walker (1726–1821), author and inventor. He was a friend of Mrs Hogarth and later served as intermediary between her and John Nichols when Nichols was compiling his *Biographical Anecdotes of William Hogarth* (John Nichols and George Steevens, *The Genuine Works of William Hogarth,* 1808–17, iii. 315–17; Ronald Paulson, *Hogarth: His Life, Art, and Times,* New Haven, 1971, ii. 475–6).

6. HW later made some additions to his catalogue of Hogarth's works, but he does not appear to have altered the passage on 'Sigismunda.' In 1780 he substi-

tuted a new preface, explaining his reticence, in place of an apologetic preface that he wrote in 1773.

————

1. Possibly drawings by Hardwicke himself, although he is not known to have been an amateur artist. HW noted in his 'Book of Materials,' 1759, p. 152: 'Lady Anson, eldest daughter of Philip [1st] Earl of Hardwicke, painted remarkably well in crayons.' Perhaps HW refers to drawings by Hardwicke's younger sister.

2. That is, engraved.

3. 'After eleven weeks of suffering' from gout, HW came to town from SH in mid-

will have the honour of bringing his Lordship a *Mysterious Mother*,[4] though he fears it is not worth a second perusal. A *Grammont*,[5] it is totally out of his power to give his Lordship; nor had he one left after three months:[6] there were but one hundred copies printed, and of them, thirty were sent to France. His Lordship should certainly command one, if in Mr Walpole's power.[7]

To Lord Hardwicke, ?March 1773 *bis*

Printed for the first time from the MS in Thomas Kirgate's hand, now WSL. For the history of the MS see *ante* ?Jan. 1773.

Dated conjecturally by the previous letter.

Address: To the Earl of Hardwicke St James's Square.

My Lord,

MRS MIDDLETON[1] died at Isleworth in my memory. All I know more of her is, that she was sister of an old Mrs Bodens[2] that I remember at Somerset House, mother of the late Colonel Bodens,[3] and of the late Lord Conway's second wife.[4] The Duchess of Tirconnel,[5] and not the old Duchess of Marlborough,[6] who was

---

December 1772; he stayed in Arlington Street until 27 March 1773 (MANN vii. 450; OSSORY i. 113).

4. Hardwicke's presentation copy of HW's tragedy *The Mysterious Mother*, SH, 1768, has not been found.

5. See *ante* 9 Jan. 1773, nn. 2, 3.

6. HW began distributing copies of the book to friends in December 1772.

7. Hardwicke seems to have obtained a copy of the *Grammont;* see following letter.

———

1. Possibly Jane Myddelton (ca 1661–1740), who married —— May (G. S. Steinman, *Some Particulars Contributed towards a Memoir of Mrs Myddelton,* [Oxford], privately printed, 1864, pp. 55–8). Her mother, Jane Myddelton (or Middleton) (1645–92), the celebrated beauty of Charles II's court, is known to have resided at Isleworth (Daniel Lysons, *The Environs of London,* 1792–6, iii. 100).

2. Probably Althemea Boden, younger sister of Jane (Myddelton) May, in whose will (1739) she is named as executrix (Steinman, op. cit. 56).

3. Presumably Charles Bodens (d. 1762), Col. in the Foot Guards; gentleman usher to George II; author of *The Modish Couple,* a play acted at Drury Lane and published in 1732 (D. E. Baker, *Biographia Dramatica,* new edn, 1782, i. 30; GM 1762, xxxii. 600).

4. Jane Bowden (ca 1690–1716), dau. of 'Mr Bowden of Drogheda,' m. (1709), as his second wife, Francis Seymour Conway (1679–1732), cr. (1703) Bn Conway. It is possibly her daughter, Jane Conway (d. 1749, unmarried), who is mentioned in the will of Mrs Jane May (n. 2 above), her great-aunt (Collins, *Peerage,* 1812, ii. 561–2; Steinman, op. cit. 57).

5. Frances Jennings (ca 1649–1731), m. 1 (1665) George Hamilton (d. 1676), styled 'Sir George' and, in France, 'Comte' Hamilton; m. 2 (1681) Richard Talbot, cr. (1685) E. and (1689) titular Duke of Tyrconnell. She is referred to as 'la belle Jennings' in Anthony Hamilton's *Mémoires* (see n. 7 below).

6. Sarah Jennings (1660–1744), m. (1678) John Churchill, cr. (1682) Bn Churchill, (1689) E. and (1702) D. of Marlborough.

some years younger than her sister, was certainly the Fair Jennings, and as your Lordship sees by the conclusion of Grammont, married to her first husband George Hamilton.[7] I did know that Grammont told the two Hamiltons[8] that he had forgot to marry their sister;[9] but I know no more of Mrs Price[9a] and Mrs Wells[10] than is in the *Memoirs*.[11] I have the honour to be

> My Lord
> Your Lordship's most obedient humble servant,

> H. W.

To George Colman,[1] March 1773

Printed for the first time from the MS now wsl, acquired (with the original MS of *Nature Will Prevail*) from the estate of Richard Bentley the younger in 1937.

Dated approximately by the composition of *Nature Will Prevail* (see nn. 2 and 3 below).

Address: To George Colman Esq.

Sir,

A S THE enclosed piece[2] will admit a great deal of what the French call *le jeu de théâtre;* and has the merit or rarity of not being stolen from the French, it is offered to you, if you find it

7. 'Georges Hamilton, sous de meilleurs auspices, épousa la belle Jennings' (Anthony Hamilton, *Mémoires du Comte de Grammont*, SH, 1772, p. 290).

8. Anthony Hamilton (ca 1645–1719), the memoirist, and his older brother Sir George Hamilton (d. 1676). For the date of death of Anthony Hamilton, see Ruth Clark, *Anthony Hamilton, His Life and Works and his Family*, 1921, p. 165, n. 1, and Wilhelm Kissenberth, *Antoine d'Hamilton, Sein Leben und Seine Werke*, Berlin, 1907, p. 43, which gives a transcription of the parish record of his death.

9. Elizabeth Hamilton (1641–1708), eldest dau. of Sir George Hamilton (ca 1607–79), m. (1663) Philibert (1621–1707), Comte de Gramont. The events preceding her marriage are documented in *Memoirs of the Comte de Gramont*, trans. Peter Quennell, ed. C. H. Hartmann, New York, 1930, pp. 343–4).

9a. Goditha Price (d. 1678), dau. of Sir Herbert Price, Master of the Household to Charles II. She was a maid of honour to the Duchess of York and was for a time the Duke of York's mistress (ibid. 359).

10. Winifred Wells, youngest dau. of Gilbert Wells of Twyford, Hants, m. (1675) Thomas Wyndham. She was one of the original maids of honour to Queen Catherine (ibid. 369).

11. See *Mémoires . . . de Grammont*, pp. 187–8. Miss Price is frequently mentioned in the *Mémoires*.

———

1. George Colman, the elder (1732–94), manager of Covent Garden Theatre 1767–74, of the Little Theatre in the Haymarket 1777–89; dramatist. He owned a villa at Richmond (across the Thames from SH) which he built in 1766.

2. HW's *Nature Will Prevail: A Moral Entertainment, in One Act*, written 1–2 March 1773. The MS (with the original

worthy of being performed:[3] and I give you my honour it has not been offered to anybody else. As I never wrote for the theatre before,[4] I do not pretend to judge of what is fit for it, so well as one whose practice and interest must make him clearer-sighted than a novice author. You may be assured therefore, Sir, that you will not, for once at least, make an enemy by rejecting my essay. I am not influenced by interest or vanity to have it performed. If it is, I shall neither own it whether successful or otherwise; and it is offered you as a present, unless it should be acted six nights,[5] in which case I will only claim fifty pounds of you, which are designed as a gratification to some persons[5a] who are less at their ease than I am. The property of the copy I mean to reserve. You will be as little restricted in the disposition of the parts, the single one of *Current* being allotted to Mr Woodward[6] for whom it was written. The decorations will, I flatter myself cost you nothing, but a piece of rock to rise before and conceal the Fairy[7] when she vanishes. Except her dress, which may be supplied from your wardrobe, the three other characters[8] must be in modern English habits, *Current* being finer than the others. As much will depend on the actors and your servants, allow me to say the former should be very perfect, as the dialogue is rapid; and the others very attentive, especially in timing exactly the answers of Echo.

It is no commendation of a dramatic, or indeed of any work, that it was written in two days.[9] I mention it, Sir, to take off any repugnance you may have in rejecting it. An author cannot complain of loss of time, when he bestows no more on his labour.

title, 'The Contrast, a Comedy in two Acts,' crossed out by HW) is now WSL. The play was printed in 1773 or 1774 as part of HW's *Works*, 1770, ii. [*221] – *244; reprinted in *Works*, 1798, ii. [289]– 304 (Hazen, *SH Bibl.* 89, 91).

3. HW recorded in 'Short Notes' *sub* 1773: 'Wrote "Nature Will Prevail, a Moral Entertainment in one Act," which I sent (anonymously) to Mr Colman, manager of Covent Garden. He was much pleased with it, but thinking it too short for a farce, pressed to have it enlarged, which I would not take the trouble to do for so slight and extemporary a performance' (GRAY i. 48).

4. See *ante* 20 Oct. 1770, n. 11.

5. *Nature Will Prevail* had its first performance at the Little Theatre in the Haymarket on 10 June 1778 and was acted six other times the same year (*London*

Stage Pt V, i. 111, 180–2, 184, 188). It was performed several times in subsequent years through the 1786 season. See *post* 2 March 1778.

5a. Possibly imprisoned debtors.

6. Henry Woodward (1714–77), comic actor. At this time he was acting in Goldsmith's *She Stoops to Conquer;* according to HW, he spoke Garrick's prologue 'admirably' (HW to Lady Ossory 27 March 1773, OSSORY i. 109). He died on 17 April 1777, over a year before *Nature Will Prevail* was produced. The role of Current was first acted by Robert Palmer.

7. Almadine, a fairy (*Works* ii. [290]).

8. Current and Padlock, both men, and Finette, a country girl (ibid.).

9. HW noted at the end of the MS, 'begun March 1st and finished next day 1773.'

If you will be so good as to acquaint the bearer when he may wait on you for your answer, he shall attend you from

Sir

Your unknown humble servant

The Author

To George Colman, March 1773 *bis*

Printed from George Colman, the younger, *Posthumous Letters . . . Addressed to Francis Colman, and George Colman, the Elder,* 1820, p. 220, where the letter was first printed. Reprinted in R. B. Peake, *Memoirs of the Colman Family,* 1841, p. 22. The history of the MS and its present whereabouts are not known.

Dated approximately by the previous letter.

Address: To George Colman Esq.

THE author of *Nature Will Prevail* is extremely obliged to Mr Colman for his civility;[1] and sorry he cannot have the courage to be known for an author. He does not mean to give Mr Colman the trouble of correcting his farce, but, as he is very sensible of the little merit there is in it, Mr Colman is perfectly at liberty to make any alterations in it he pleases, as he must be a much better judge of what is proper for the stage than the writer can be. If Mr Colman has anything else he wishes to say, the bearer will attend him at any time he shall appoint to receive a note with his commands.

1. See previous letter, n. 3.

From Mrs Robert Wood,[1] Thursday 13 May 1773

Printed for the first time from a photostat of Mrs Wood's MS copy in the possession of Mr Robert W. Wood, Fields End, Roman Road, Lyme Regis, Dorset, kindly supplied by Mr Wood's father, the late Canon G. Robert Wood. For the history of the MS copy see *ante* 19 Nov. 1769. The original letter is missing.

Endorsed by Mrs Wood: Copy. To Mr Walpole 13 May 1773 when a copy of the enclosed[2] was also sent to him.

South Audley St, 13 May 1773.

MRS WOOD presents her compliments to Mr Walpole and begs leave to address herself to him for assistance on a melancholy subject of attention which she cannot turn her thoughts upon without feeling the keenest grief,[3] and also the greatest delicacy as to the mode of paying it; nobody can so well judge of what will be exactly right in all respects as Mr Walpole; therefore this application to him is natural, and his goodness has induced Mrs Wood to make it; but yet with perfect submission to his own inclination should he for any reason decline giving his directions, as she wishes he would, about the inscription, tombstone, etc., and desires he will employ whom he pleases, not sparing any expense he judges proper: it is in the open air.

1. Ann Skottowe (1732–1803), dau. of Thomas Skottowe, of Ayton, Yorks; m. Robert Wood (ca 1717–71) (Yorkshire Parish Register Society, *The Parish Register of Great Ayton*, 1931, xc. 45, 88; Surrey Parish Register Society, *The Parish Register of Putney*, Croydon, 1915, [xii]. 463; *ante* 19 Nov. 1769, n. 1).

2. Missing; the enclosure presumably supplied information about the birth and death of Mrs Wood's husband and son (see following note).

3. Robert Wood had died 9 Sept. 1771 and was buried in 'a new vault, in new bur[ial] ground' at Putney; a son, Thomas, had died in his ninth year on 25 Aug. 1772 and was buried in the vault with his father (*The Parish Register of Putney*, op. cit. [xii]. 409–10; *post* 16 May 1773). The memorial to her husband and son planned by Mrs Wood was to be placed in the Putney burial ground. See following letter.

To Mrs Robert Wood, Sunday 16 May 1773

Printed for the first time from a photostat of the MS in the possession of Robert W. Wood, Fields End, Roman Road, Lyme Regis, Dorset, kindly supplied by Mr Wood's father, the late Canon G. Robert Wood. For the history of the MS see *ante* 19 Nov. 1769.

Endorsed by Mrs Wood: Mr Walpole 16th May 1773.

Arlington Street,
May 16th 1773.

I THINK myself very much honoured and distinguished, Madam, by, I fear I must say, your partiality, in consulting me on an occasion so interesting both to you and to all who admired Mr Wood, that is, to all men of taste or genius. I dare not decline the task entirely, lest I should seem wanting in respect to his memory, or in gratitude to you, Madam: but I must only accept it on conditions, to which your regard for him, Madam, must make you subscribe. In one word, if I attempt to obey your commands, it can only be on condition that you will promise to reject my ideas either for the inscription or the tomb with the same kind frankness, with which you was so good as to allow me to waive obeying your orders, if I do not fully answer your expectation, or fail in the execution of what I should be very proud of performing in the manner the subject deserves; and which would demand the taste and pen of him, for whom you are pleased to ask my assistance.

I am no draughtsman, Madam, and therefore must not pretend to give a design for the tomb. All I can presume to do, is to hint to you the kind of monument I should think proper; or to choose a form agreeable to the turn of Mr Wood's pursuits. His affection for the pure antique arts seems to point out the proper kind; and I think some pattern taken from an ancient sarcophagus or urn would be the most suitable, on which there should be only so much richness employed as is consistent with simplicity. If you do not disapprove this idea, Madam, and will allow me a little time, I will look over my books, and submit some different designs to your option.[1] Either a

---

1. In 1775, at Mrs Wood's prompting, HW selected the design (a sarcophagus resting on a pedestal) for Wood's monu- ment. The design was executed by Joseph Wilton. See Mrs Wood to HW *post* 7 July and 17 Nov. 1775.

sarcophagus, or upright altar-tomb will be the more proper, as more durable, since it is to be placed in the open air; and will at the same time have a classic air, so characteristic of Mr Wood's talents.

As I never was a good poet, and have long disused metre, it is very natural for me not to adopt that kind of inscription. But I have a better reason: an epitaph in rhyme is a barbarous mode; and to make it excusable, ought to be much happier than it would be, if I composed it. Simplicity and brevity are the master beauties of Roman epitaphs. Some one great peculiarity stamps an inscription with dignity, and appropriates it to the person; and it effaces, or renders unnecessary a thousand little circumstances that might be related of many other men. For this reason I should choose to single out an illustrious point of Mr Wood's life, and which certainly distinguishes him from all other men. I mean his editions of *Palmyra* and *Balbec*.[2] Others have visited those renowned spots: Mr Dawkins[3] even partook of the journey: but nobody rivals Mr Wood in that part in which genius alone was concerned, the dissertations.[4] That part becomes by his art a sublime circumstance; though by my want of equal art I have not done justice to it. The fact however is true, and thence dignifies itself.

Let me again entreat, Madam, that you will freely make objections to any part or to the whole of my plan. You are the person to be satisfied; and I can only be so by succeeding. Let me beg you to consult others: let them point out any faults: I pretend to nothing but to please you; and I hope I have done that at least by trying to please, and by showing with what readiness I am

Madam
Your most obedient humble servant

HORACE WALPOLE

PS. I have inserted a Christian name at random,[5] not having the honour of knowing yours.

2. See *ante* 19 Nov. 1769, n. 1.

3. James Dawkins (1722–57), orientalist and traveller; M.P. He accompanied Wood on his archæological expedition to Asia Minor, Egypt, and the Levant in 1750–1.

4. The dissertation in *The Ruins of*

Palmyra, 1753. '*Palmyra* is come forth, and is a noble book; the prints finely engraved, and an admirable dissertation before it' (HW to Bentley 19 Dec. 1753, CHUTE 160).

5. See enclosure printed below.

[Enclosure][6]

To the beloved Memory
of
Robert Wood,
Who was born at the Castle of Riverstown
near Trim in the County of Meath,
and died September 9th 1771
in the fifty-fifth year of his Age;
and of
Thomas Wood
his Son,
who died August 25th 1772
in his ninth year;
Catherine[7]
their once happy Wife
and Mother
now dedicates this melancholy
and inadequate Memorial
of her Affection and Grief.
The beautiful Editions
of
Balbec and Palmyra,
illustrated by the classic Pen[8]
of Robert Wood
supplies a nobler
and more lasting Monument,
And will survive those august Remains.

6. The proposed inscription (in HW's hand) for Wood's monument. See Mrs Wood to HW *post* 27 May 1773, n. 3.
7. '*Catherine*' crossed out in the MS and '*Ann*' substituted in an unidentified hand.
HW placed a 'q.' (query) in the margin opposite '*Catherine*.'
8. The MS reads 'Men,' a slip which was later corrected.

From Mrs Robert Wood, Monday 17 May 1773

Printed for the first time from a photostat of Mrs Wood's MS copy in the possession of Mr Robert W. Wood, Fields End, Roman Road, Lyme Regis, Dorset, kindly supplied by Mr Wood's father, the late Canon G. Robert Wood. For the history of the MS copy see *ante* 19 Nov. 1769. The original letter is missing.

Endorsed by Mrs Wood: Copy to Mr Walpole 17 May 1773.

Audley Street, 17 May 1773.

ACCEPT, Sir, the warmest thanks of a grateful mind for the very handsome and most satisfactory manner in which you have, Sir, given me a proof of your regard to the memory of a friend, who had all the admiration and deference to Mr Walpole's judgment and taste which are so justly due; by your kind exertion of both, Sir, on this occasion he would have been pleased, and I believe in a parallel case would have highly approved. Having brought your design to this test, it is needless for me, Sir, to add that I am perfectly content, indeed very much flattered, to feel my own ideas so entirely correspond with yours, Sir. Yet one addition my heart tells me I should be happy to make if you permit it, and that is to mention in one line his leading virtue, *supreme benevolence;*[1] but I entreat that frankness and candour may govern you, Sir, with regard to me, for I shall be most thankful to be corrected by you, and beg you will consult your own understanding only, your convenience as to time, etc., and be assured of my considering it as increasing the favour conferred on,

> Sir,
> Your most respectful and obliged humble servant,

ANN WOOD

1. HW approved this addition; see *post* 27 May 1773.

To Thomas Pennant,[1] Monday 17 May 1773

Printed for the first time from the MS now wsl, purchased in May 1957 from Orion Booksellers Ltd., who previously acquired it from 'an English country library.'

Both the year and Walpole's signature have been cut out; '1773' and 'Hor. Walpole' are written underneath in an unidentified hand. The year is confirmed by Pennant's visit to 'the Castle' (Naworth Castle) in August 1773 (see n. 5 below).

Address: To Mr Pennant at Downing, Flintshire.

Arlington Street, May 17th ⟨1773.⟩[2]

Sir,

I HAVE seen Lord Carlisle,[3] who tells me he has written to his steward,[4] and given particular orders that you may see the Castle[5] and everything in it at your ease: so that if you go thither, and mention this, you will be properly received. Lord Carlisle says he fears you will be much disappointed, and that the library is very inconsiderable.[6]

I am Sir

Your most obedient humble servant

⟨Hor. Walpole⟩

PS. I beg pardon, Sir, for the impropriety of the direction, occasioned by my not knowing your Christian name.

1. (1726–98), traveller and naturalist.

2. The date has been cut out of the MS; see headnote.

3. Frederick Howard (1748–1825), 5th E. of Carlisle, 1758.

4. Not identified.

5. Naworth Castle, Lord Carlisle's seat near Brampton, Cumberland. In August 1773 Pennant visited Naworth Castle on a tour from Downing, Flintshire, to Har-rowgate, Durham. He describes Naworth in *A Tour from Downing to Alston-Moor*, 1801, pp. 172–7.

6. 'Lord William Howard's . . . library is a small room, in a very secret place high up in one of the towers, well secured by doors and narrow staircase. Not a book has been added since his days,' that is, since 1640 (ibid. 174).

To Thomas Pennant, Tuesday 25 May 1773

Printed for the first time from the MS now WSL. The MS was acquired from 'an English country library' by Orion Booksellers Ltd., who sold it to Henry Stevens, Son and Stiles in 1948; sold by them to WSL, April 1948.

Address: To Thomas Pennant Esq. at Downing Flintshire. *Postmark:* 25 MA.

Arlington Street, May 25, 1773.

Sir,

I AM very glad you have thoughts of taking copies of the Earl of Shrewsbury and his Countess[1] at Lord Northampton's,[2] for I see no progress made in the scheme of publishing more illustrious heads,[3] and I do not propose to do so myself.

Mr Mason,[4] I believe, has not more thoughts of reprinting Mr Gray's little book:[5] but it certainly would be worth while to draw up the Scotch and Welsh lists correctly; as they would contribute to a future enlarged and more perfect edition of that work.[6]

I am glad you have had so much pleasure in your journey, Sir, and am glad the public is to be the better for it.[7] You should not forget Drayton[8] on another opportunity.

1. See *ante* 30 Jan. 1772, nn. 15, 16.
2. Castle Ashby, Northants, the seat of Spencer Compton (1738–96), 8th E. of Northampton, 1763. In the spring of 1773 Pennant made his annual journey to London, stopping along the way to visit places of interest and keeping a regular journal of what he saw. In 1782 he published *The Journey from Chester to London*, 'formed from journals made at different times in my way to town.' He 'frequently made a considerable stay at several places, to give this book all the fullness and accuracy in [his] power' (*The Literary Life of the late Thomas Pennant, Esq. By Himself*, 1793, p. 28). Pennant writes in the *Journey*, p. 311: 'Mr Walpole had made me impatient for the sight of the picture of the hero John Talbot, first Earl of Shrewsbury, by informing me that such a portrait existed in this house [Castle Ashby].' The portraits of the Earl and Countess of Shrewsbury were engraved by James Basire for Pennant's *Journey*, pls XVIII and XIX, facing p. 312. See *post* 13 June 1782.
3. Doubtless an allusion to the *Supple-ment* to James Granger's *Biographical History of England*, which was in progress but did not appear until Sept. 1774 (*ante* 30 Jan. 1772). The Shrewsbury portraits are mentioned in Granger's *Supplement*, p. 14.
4. William Mason, HW's correspondent, who was then compiling his *Memoirs* of Thomas Gray's life and writings, published in 1775.
5. *A Catalogue of the Antiquities, Houses, Parks, Plantations, Scenes, and Situations in England and Wales*, printed by Mason in 1772 in an edition of 100 copies for private distribution. See MASON i. 56, 161 n. 2. HW's annotated copy (sent to Mason in 1774, not traced) is described in Hazen, *Cat. of HW's Lib.*, No. 3892.
6. The *Catalogue* is arranged in alphabetical order according to county. A *Supplement* was published anonymously in 1787.
7. See n. 2 above.
8. In Northants, the seat of Lord George Sackville, cr. (1782) Vct Sackville. HW visited it with William Cole in 1763;

The pictures at Woburn Abbey have been so much changed from the places they were in, when I made the list of them,[9] that I can not pretend to say whose the portrait is you mean.[10] I know there were two of Lucy Countess of Bedford,[11] one sitting, the other dancing in a fantastic habit.[12] There was a picture, which I rather take to be the one you mean, of Eliz. Bruges,[13] daughter of Lord Chandos; on it is written, Hieronymus Custodio[14] fecit 1589.[15] I have mentioned it in my *Anecdotes of Painting*.[16]

The five portraits you mention at Gothurst,[17] Sir, are of the Digbys;[18] and one of them I know is Sir Everard,[19] father of Sir Kenelm Digby,[20] which Everard was executed for the powder-conspiracy. With those at Tyringham[21] I am not acquainted.

It has been some disappointment to me, Sir, not to be permitted

---

see Montagu ii. 89–90, and *Country Seats* 55–8. Pennant saw Drayton in the spring of 1774, on the return from his annual trip to London (Pennant, *Literary Life*, p. 22).

9. HW visited Woburn Abbey, the seat of the Duke of Bedford, in Oct. 1751 (Montagu i. 123–4). His account of the house and its pictures is printed in *Country Seats* 17–20. In Sept. 1791, at Lady Ossory's request, HW revised his list of the pictures, and she sent it to the 5th Duke of Bedford (Ossory iii. 125–8, 130; *post* 8 Dec. 1791). The list was privately printed in 1800 as *Notes to the Portraits at Woburn Abbey* (Hazen, *Bibl. of HW* 85–7). See *post* 15 Oct. 1781.

10. For Pennant's account of Woburn Abbey see his *Journey*, pp. 346–75.

11. Hon. Lucy Harington (1581–1627), m. (1594) Edward Russell, 3d E. of Bedford, 1585.

12. 'In this room is a full-length of that fantastic lady, Lucy Countess of Bedford, in a dancing attitude, dressed in as fantastic a habit, with an immense transparent veil distended behind her.' 'Another portrait [in the Gallery] of Lucy Countess of Bedford, exactly resembling that at Alloa' (ibid. 353, 368).

13. Elizabeth Brydges (?1575–1617), dau. of Giles Brydges (ca 1548–94), 3d Bn Chandos, 1573, m. (1603) Sir John Kennedy, Kt (GEC iii. 127, n. *a*).

14. Hieronimo Custodis (d. 1593), Flemish painter working in England 1589–93

(R. C. Strong, 'Elizabethan Painting: An Approach through Inscriptions—II: Hieronimo Custodis,' *Burlington Magazine*, 1963, CV. 103–8).

15. 'Elizabeth Bruges, or Bridges, aged 14, 1589, painted in a flat style, by Hieronymo di Custodio, of Antwerp. She is represented in black, flowered with white, with full sleeves, a gold chain, a great pearl set in gold on one shoulder, and a gold ornament on the other' (Pennant, *Journey*, pp. 352–3).

16. 'At the Duke of Bedford's at Woburn is a portrait of Elizabeth Bruges, daughter of the Lord Chandois, with this inscription, Hieronymus Custodio, Antwerpiensis fecit 1589. The colouring is flat and chalky' (*Anecdotes of Painting*, SH, 1762–71, i. 157–8).

17. Gothurst, or Gayhurst, near Newport Pagnell, Bucks, the seat of the Wrighte family; formerly the seat of the Digby family. HW visited it with Cole in 1763; see Montagu ii. 332–3, and *Country Seats* 52. For Pennant's account of Gothurst see his *Journey*, pp. 325–38.

18. See Cole i. 26–7.

19. Sir Everard Digby (1578–1606), Kt, 1603; executed for conspiracy in the Gunpowder Plot.

20. (1603–65), Kt, 1623; diplomatist and author.

21. Tyringham House, Bucks, the seat of the Bakewell (or Backwell) family. See Pennant's *Journey*, pp. 339–41.

to see the remainder of miniatures of the Digbys, which were found along with those I purchased.²² You was so kind, Sir, as to say you would get me a sight of them. Miss Stapylton²³ proposed them to me of herself, and *promised* near a year ago I should see them as soon as they came to town. They are come, but I cannot obtain that favour. I told her I heard the Duchess of Portland²⁴ was in pursuit of them. Miss Stapylton answered with some confusion, that she was *ordered* to offer the refusal to another person²⁵ first, but *wished I* might have them that they might not be separated. I can scarce think the Duchess would have insisted on the refusal, as I have very often, always, and even this winter, forborne, at her Grace's request, and often have offered, not to bid against her Grace for any curiosities she wished to buy. The return would be the more unkind, as these miniatures are part of a set of which I have the rest. And I think the Duchess, who is always very good to me, the less likely to be so unkind, as she so justly complained this winter of Mrs West's²⁶ promising her the refusal of Mr West's MSS, and then selling them to Lord Shelburne.²⁷ The miniatures, I suppose, are sold to somebody or

22. In 1771 HW had bought nine miniatures of the Digby family from a collection of sixteen that was found at Penbedw, Flintshire,ʾ the seat of Watkin Williams (?1742–1808), M.P. Williams's father had married (as his second wife) Charlotta Mostyn (daughter of Richard Mostyn, of Penbedw), who was a great-granddaughter of Sir Kenelm Digby. After the miniatures were found, the collection was apparently divided between Williams (the owner of Penbedw) and his wife's family, who were also related by marriage to Sir Kenelm. Williams's wife, Elizabeth (1740–1825), was one of four surviving daughters of Col. James Russell Stapleton (d. 1743), of Bodrhyddan, Flintshire. Col. Stapleton's wife, Penelope, was the daughter (by his second wife) of Sir John Conway, 2d Bt, whose first wife was a granddaughter of Sir Kenelm Digby. The other three daughters were Penelope (b. 1732), Catherine (n. 23 below), and Frances (1741–1825); HW probably purchased the nine miniatures from these three daughters (J. B. Lewis, 'An Account of the Penbedw Papers in the Flintshire Record Office,' *Journal of the Flintshire Historical Society*, 1971–2, xxv. 127–130; Norman Tucker, 'Bodrhyddan and the

Families of Conwy, Shipley-Conwy and Rowley-Conwy,' pt II, ibid., 1962, xx. 3–9; Pennant's *Journey*, p. 337; COLE i. 358).

23. Catherine Stapleton (1734–1815), second dau. of Col. James Russell Stapleton; died unmarried (Tucker, op. cit. 8–9; MORE 170 n. 2). A close friend of Lady Blandford and the Dowager Lady Chatham, and possessing a very large income, she may have negotiated the sale of the nine Digby miniatures to HW in 1771. She seems to have acted as agent for Watkin Williams and his wife Elizabeth in selling the remaining seven Digby miniatures, which HW acquired after 'long haggling' in 1775 (MASON i. 180). These seven miniatures 'were the other division of that collection, and were purchased by Mr W[alpole] of the lady who shared them with the other heir' ('Des. of SH,' *Works* ii. 423).

24. See *ante* ca Nov. 1768, nn. 4, 5.

25. Not identified.

26. Sarah Steavens (d. 1799), m. (1738) James West (MANN iv. 371 n. 2). See *ante* 31 March 1764, n. 1.

27. West died 2 July 1772. His collection of manuscripts was sold privately to Lord Shelburne and formed a part of the Lansdowne MSS acquired by the British

other, though I dare to say not to the Duchess, since I am not even allowed to see them.[28]

I am Sir

Your obedient humble servant

Hor. Walpole

To Mrs Robert Wood, Thursday 27 May 1773

Printed for the first time from the MS now wsl. The MS is untraced until sold Christie's 19 Dec. 1963 (property of Mrs Boardman, deceased), lot 240, to Seven Gables for wsl.

Endorsed by Mrs Wood: Mr Walpole 27 May 1773.

Arlington Street, May 27, 1773.

I HAVE been so much taken up of late, Madam, by the unfortunate situation of Lord Orford's health,[1] that I have not had time to attend to the business with which you have honoured me[2] and I did not care to perform it in a negligent manner.

What you desire should be added to the inscription, Madam, will be very proper, and just. I have considered in what manner to introduce it best; and I can find in the epitaph you are pleased to approve, no place where it can be introduced without lameness or confusion but immediately after Mr Wood's name, and in your own words, which cannot be improved. They breathe that pathetic expression that surpasses eloquence, and is preferable. It will run thus,

To the Beloved Memory
of
Robert Wood,
a Man of Supreme Benevolence,
Who etc.[3]

Museum in 1807. See *A Catalogue of the Entire Collection of Manuscripts . . . of the late Most Noble William Marquis of Lansdowne . . . which will be sold by Auction by Leigh and S. Sotheby,* 1807, i. [i]–ii.

28. See *post* 20 Dec. 1773.

———

1. In late January HW's nephew, George, 3d Earl of Orford, had suffered his first attack of insanity, and he remained indisposed until the end of the year (Family 90). HW took charge of his affairs during the illness. See Appendix 6, 'Lord Orford's Illness,' ibid. 331–6.

2. See *ante* 17 May 1773.

3. The epitaph, with this addition, appears on Wood's monument in the cemetery at Putney. The inscription is printed in Daniel Lysons, *The Environs of Lon-*

I am extremely happy, Madam, to have in the least satisfied your intention: and yet I fear I must have fallen short of it. Your good nature, I fear, has a little accepted the inclination for the deed. I shall go to Strawberry Hill in a few days,[4] and then will submit different designs for the tomb to your consideration:[5] and am, Madam,

Your most obedient humble servant

HOR. WALPOLE

To DR JOHN BERKENHOUT,[1] Tuesday 6 July 1773

Printed from *Works* v. 645–6, where the letter was first printed. Reprinted, Wright v. 348–9; Cunningham v. 483–4 (closing and signature omitted in Wright and Cunningham); Toynbee viii. 303–4. The history of the MS and its present whereabouts are not known.

July 6, 1773.

Sir,

I AM so much engaged in private business at present,[2] that I have not had time to thank you for the favour of your letter:[3] nor can I now answer it to your satisfaction.

My life has been too insignificant to afford materials interesting to the public. In general, the lives of mere authors are dry and unentertaining; nor, though I have been one occasionally, are my writings of a class or merit to entitle me to any distinction. I can as little furnish you, Sir, with a list of them or their dates, which would give me more trouble to make out than is worth while. If I have any merit with the public, it is for printing and preserving some valuable works of others; and if ever you write the lives of printers,[4] I may be enrolled in the number.[5] My own works, I suppose, are dead and

don, 1792–6, i. 421; Owen Manning and William Bray, *The History and Antiquities of the County of Surrey*, 1804–14, iii. 289.

4. He went to SH on 11 June (OSSORY i. 120).

5. See *ante* 16 May 1773, n. 1.

---

1. (ca 1730–91), M.D. (Leyden), 1765; physician, naturalist, and writer (MASON i. 101 n. 18).

2. See previous letter, n. 1.

3. Missing. Berkenhout had asked HW for details of his life and writings, to be included in his *Biographia Literaria, or a Biographical History of Literature*, the first and only volume of which was published in 1777. HW's copy of this work is Hazen, *Cat. of HW's Lib.*, No. 3291.

4. Berkenhout never compiled such a work.

5. HW wrote Mason 29 July 1773: 'Has not a Dr Berkenhout sent to you for lists of your works and anecdotes of your life?'

buried; but as I am not impatient to be interred with them, I hope you will leave that office to the parson of the parish, and I shall be, as long as I live,

Your obliged humble servant,

Hor. Walpole

From David Garrick, Thursday 29 July 1773

Printed from a photostat of the MS in the Folger Shakespeare Library. First printed, Toynbee *Supp.* iii. 231. Reprinted in *The Letters of David Garrick*, ed. D. M. Little and G. M. Kahrl, Cambridge, Mass., 1963, ii. 888–9. Damer-Waller; the MS was sold Sotheby's 5 Dec. 1921 (first Waller Sale), lot 131, to Quaritch; subsequently acquired by Folger.

The year of the letter is established by the publication of *Miscellaneous Antiquities* 1 Jan. 1773 (see n. 2 below).

Address: To the Honourable Mr Walpole.

July 29.

MR GARRICK presents his respects to Mr Walpole and shall be much obliged to him if he would lend him the volumes of old tracts in which is Sir Thos. Wyatt's speech[1]—he sent to London for all the tracts,[2] and his bookseller[3] sends him word that Bell[4] (I suppose the publisher) has none left.[5] Mr Garrick's Theatre[6] prevents him from benefiting by these matters in the winter.

I am sure he ought, for he thought even of me. I sent him word that the only merit I was conscious of, was having saved and published some valuable works of others; and that whenever he should write the lives of printers, I should have no repugnance to appear in the catalogue' (Mason i. 101).

---

1. Sir Thomas Wyatt's 'Defence, after the Indictment and Evidence' at his trial in 1541, when accused by Bishop Bonner of high treason, printed in HW's *Miscellaneous Antiquities*, No. 2, SH, 1772, pp. 21–54. See Gray i. 47 n. 334, ii. 116 n. 62.

2. *Miscellaneous Antiquities,* Nos 1 and 2, were published simultaneously by John Bell 1 Jan. 1773 (*Daily Adv.* 1 Jan. 1773).

3. Probably James Dodsley, bookseller in Pall Mall; see Garrick's *Letters*, ed. Little and Kahrl, i. 370–1.

4. See *ante* ca 1773, n. 6.

5. HW discontinued the series because sales of the first two numbers were disappointing. 'The *Miscellaneous Antiquities* have not sold above a fifth of them, so there will be no more' (HW to Mason 2 March 1773, Mason i. 66).

6. Garrick was manager of Drury Lane Theatre.

To Lord Hardwicke, Tuesday 10 August 1773

Printed for the first time from a photostat of the MS, furnished by the Public Record Office of Northern Ireland by permission of the owner, the Earl of Caledon, Caledon Castle, Co. Tyrone, Northern Ireland. For the history of the MS see *ante* ?March 1773.

Endorsed in an unidentified hand: Mr Walp. M. Sévigné.

Strawberry Hill, Aug. 10, 1773.

I AM much obliged to your Lordship for your kind attention to my troublesome business.[1] I go to Houghton on Thursday se'n-night, the most unpleasant part of the whole.[2] After that I hope to have a little respite by having settled every thing on the best foot I can.

The family of Sévigné, which your Lordship inquires after, is literally extinct. The son[3] was married, but died without issue, having ended in deep devotion, converted from his agreeableness and pleasures by his wife. Madame de Grignan's[4] son,[5] of whom much is said in the letters, was stabbed in his bed by a friend with whom he had quarrelled; and left no children. Madame de Simiane,[6] Madame de Grignan's daughter Pauline, lived long and was much admired. She is a favourite of mine too by her veneration for her grandmother, which Madame de Grignan had not. I have even heard that on a silly pique between them, the latter used to pass by her mother's door, who died at Grignan,[7] without entering it to see her in her last illness. Madame de Simiane left two daughters;[8] I forget the name of one:[9] the other[10] who is dead too, was wife of a Monsieur de Castel-

1. See *ante* 27 May 1773, n. 1.
2. HW went to Houghton 19 Aug. 'to inform myself as well as I could of the state of my Lord's [Orford's] affairs, and to see what could be done to put them into any order' (HW to Thomas Walpole 4 Sept. 1773, FAMILY 94–5). He returned to Arlington Street 29 Aug.; see CONWAY iii. 172–3.
3. Charles (1648–1713), Marquis de Sévigné, son of Mme de Sévigné, m. (1684) Jeanne-Marguerite de Bréhan de Mauron.
4. Françoise-Marguerite de Sévigné (1646–1705), dau. of Mme de Sévigné, m. (1669) François de Castellane-Adhémar de Monteil, Comte de Grignan.
5. Louis-Provence de Castellane-Adhé-

mar de Monteil de Grignan (1671–1704), Marquis de Grignan, m. (1704) Anne-Marguerite de Saint-Amant.
6. Françoise-Pauline de Castellane-Adhémar de Monteil de Grignan (1674–1737), m. (1695) Louis de Simiane du Claret, Marquis de Truchenu et d'Esparron.
7. Mme de Grignan's seat in Provence.
8. A third daughter, Anne de Simiane, became a nun with the Filles du Calvaire (Mme de Sévigné, *Correspondance*, ed. Roger Duchêne, 1972–8, i. xxxviii).
9. Madelenie Sophie de Simiane, m. (1723) Alexandre-Gaspard de Villeneuve, Marquis de Vence.
10. See *ante* 19 Dec. 1767, n. 6.

lane, an intimate friend of the Duchess of Choiseul, and with whom
I have supped fifty times, and who is a very worthy man, but a hu-
mourist. Grignan is preserved in splendour; Lady Mary Coke[11] visited
it, and was extremely well received by the mistress of it, whose family
bought it,[12] and is considerable: I do not recollect their name. The
Rochers[13] in Bretagne was bought by a Jansenist lady[14] and is much
altered; Mr Selwyn[15] has a ground plan of it. Several portraits of
Mme de Sévigné are extant; I have copies of three at different ages;[16]
and a view of the Hôtel de Carnavelet in the rue Coulture-St-
Catherine which she hired.[17] It was built by Du Cerceau,[18] a very
good architect in the reign of Charles IX[19] whose works *complete* are
very rare; I have them in four volumes,[20] and value them much, as
many palaces now destroyed, are preserved in them. Apropos, did
your Lordship ever see a MS volume[21] of the like kind bought at

11. Lady Mary Campbell (1727–1811),
,m. (1747) Edward Coke (1719–53), styled
Vct Coke 1744–53; HW's friend and correspondent.

12. Grignan was purchased in 1732 by
Jean-Baptiste du Muy; it descended to
Louis-Nicolas-Victor de Félix (1711–75),
Comte du Muy, Maréchal de France, who
restored and refurbished the Château (Ossory iii. 86 n. 8). Lady Mary Coke visited
it 12 March 1770 and gives a full description of it in her Journal (*The Letters and
Journals of Lady Mary Coke*, ed. J. A.
Home, Edinburgh, 1889–96, iii. 224–6).
She was received by the Comte du Muy's
agent; there was no 'mistress' of Grignan
at that time, as the Comte did not marry
until 1774 (*Dict. de biographie française*
xii. 268).

13. Mme de Sévigné's château near Vitré
in Brittany. A view of Les Rochers drawn
by Hinchliffe was sold SH xi. 4.

14. Mme de Peyre (SELWYN 213).

15. George Augustus Selwyn (1719–91),
HW's friend and correspondent, who
shared HW's admiration for Mme de Sévigné.

16. A copy of the portrait that belonged
to Mme de Simiane, given to HW by Lady
Hervey in 1754 (CHUTE 198), and a miniature on the lid of a snuff-box sent to
him by Mme du Deffand in 1766 (DU DEF-
FAND i. 51). The third portrait has not
been identified. In 1766 HW saw an
enamel portrait of Mme de Sévigné by
Jean Petitot in a private collection in
Paris, and a medallion of her at Livry

(ibid. i. 73 n. 3; MONTAGU ii. 212). An
engraved portrait of her was sold SH
xxii. 15.

17. The Hôtel de Carnavelet, Mme de
Sévigné's residence in Paris after 1677,
was situated in the rue Culture-Ste-
Catherine (now the Musée Carnavelet,
rue de Sévigné). It was designed by Pierre
Lescot (d. 1578) and built by Jean Bul-
lant ca 1544 (Thieme and Becker xxiii.
120–1; Émile Gérard-Gailly, *Madame de
Sévigné*, 1971, pp. 172–3, 175). The view
of the Hôtel, by Raguenet, was commissioned by HW in 1766; see MASON i. 196
n. 13.

18. Jacques Androuet du Cerceau (ca
1510–85), architect and engraver.

19. Charles IX (1550–74), K. of France
1560–74.

20. HW presumably refers to *Le Premier [Second] volume des plus excellents
bastiments de France*, 2 vols, folio, 1576–9;
De architectura opus, 2 vols in 1, folio,
1559–61; and *Livre d'architecture*, folio,
1582. HW's copies of these works are, respectively, Hazen, *Cat. of HW's Lib.*, Nos
3671, 3672, 3673. HW also owned his
Livre des grotesques, folio, [?1566] (ibid.,
No. 3483).

21. 'It is a folio by one John Thorpe
[ca 1565–1655], in the reigns of Elizabeth
and James I, and contains many ground
plans and a few uprights of several goodly
mansions of those days' (HW to Lady Ossory 5 Dec. 1780, OSSORY ii. 248). See *post*
23 June 1782.

Warwick by the late Earl?[22] I know nothing so curious in its kind.

I must not omit to tell your Lordship that they are going to publish at Paris a dozen or twenty new letters of Madame de Sévigné,[23] which were treasured up by two very old ladies[24] lately dead; one of them, not curious, but in Mme de Sévigné's own writing, was procured for me three years ago by a French gentleman.[25] To this edition will be added her letters on M. de Fouquet's[26] trial, addressed to Monsieur de Pomponne:[27] I have had them [in] MSS some time, but believe they were printed formerly,[28] though I never could meet with them. My friend Mme du Deffand remembers to have been carried by her grandmother[29] to visit Madame de Coulanges.[30] These are trifling anecdotes, but as your Lordship is curious about that society, I would not omit them, and have the honour to be with great respect

Your Lordship's most obedient humble servant

HOR. WALPOLE

22. Francis Greville (1719–6 July 1773), 8th Bn Brooke, 1727, cr. (1746) E. Brooke and (1759) E. of Warwick.

23. *Lettres nouvelles ou nouvellement recouvrées de la marquise de Sévigné, et de la marquise de Simiane, sa petite-fille,* 1773. HW's copy (sent to him by Mme du Deffand 13 Nov. 1773) is Hazen, op. cit., No. 952. For his opinion of the volume see CHUTE 466, OSSORY i. 172.

24. The Mlles Girard (d. 1772) of Montpellier (*ante* 20 April 1768, n. 3).

25. The Comte de Grave, who sent HW the letter in 1768 (ibid.).

26. Nicolas Fouquet (1615–80), Louis XVI's superintendent of finances, who was convicted of embezzlement in 1664 and died in prison; see CHUTE 466 n. 11.

27. Simon Arnauld (1618–99), Marquis de Pomponne; French ambassador to Sweden 1665–8; minister of foreign affairs, 1671; friend of Fouquet (*Dict. de biographie française* iii. 890–5). Mme de Sévigné's fourteen letters to M. de Pom-

ponne 17 Nov. 1664–27 Jan. 1665 on Fouquet's trial were included in the *Lettres nouvelles,* 1773 (Duchêne, op. cit. i. 55–82).

28. MS copies of the letters were circulated early in the eighteenth century; they were first printed in *Lettres de Madame de S * * * à Monsieur de Pomponne,* Amsterdam [Paris], 1756. In Dec. 1766 Mme du Deffand had Jean-François Wiart make a copy of the volume and sent it to HW; the copy is now WSL (DU DEFFAND i. 193 and illustration).

29. Marie Bouthillier de Chavigny (1646–1728), m. 1 (1669) Nicolas Brulart, Marquis de la Borde; m. 2 (1699) César-Auguste, Duc de Choiseul.

30. Marie-Angélique du Gué Bagnolles (1641–1723), m. (1659) Philippe-Emmanuel, Marquis de Coulanges, Mme de Sévigné's first cousin. Mme du Deffand had entertained HW with her recollections of Mme de Coulanges; see ibid. ii. 62 n. 3.

To Lord Townshend,[1] Tuesday 24 August 1773

Printed for the first time from the MS now WSL, who acquired it from Francis Edwards Ltd. in Sept. 1932; its earlier history is not known.

Endorsed in an unidentified hand: From Mr Walpole, Houghton, August 24th 1773.

Houghton,[2] Aug. 24, 1773.

My Lord,

IT IS impossible to be more sensible than I am of your Lordship's goodness and countenance, and if I had a moment's interval from the variety of business I find here, and which is the heavier from my great ignorance and incapacity, I should still break my resolution and hasten to thank you. I should be as proud of receiving instruction and assistance, which your Lordship is so kind as to offer me,[3] and which I shall take leave to ask when I know a little better how and on what points to apply for it. At present I am merely learning the heads of my duty, and endeavouring to find out what I have to do, and what with the protection and advice of Lord Orford's friends I may be able to do for his service, and what the little power I have will warrant me to do. I flatter myself that I shall at least be capable of putting his affairs into so much method, that if he recovers, as I will still flatter myself he may do, he will find the first difficulties removed, and a groundwork laid for his retrieving his fortune. He is, thank God, better, and calm enough to take the air abroad. During the last sultry weather he was indeed exceedingly disordered, and alarmed me dreadfully for his life, which nothing but unrelaxed vigilance preserved, as he made every attempt in his power to destroy himself.[4] His health is very good, and the physicians are persuaded from the strength of his constitution and his temperate regimen, that

1. Hon. George Townshend (1724–1807), 4th Vct Townshend, 1764; cr. (1787) M. Townshend; Lord Lieutenant of Ireland 1767–72; Master of the Ordnance 1772–82, 1783; Gen., 1782; Field Marshal, 1796; M.P.

2. See *ante* 10 Aug. 1773, n. 2. Lady Gower wrote Mrs Delany from Holkham 27 Nov. 1773: 'I have nothing but Norfolk news, and that of the deplorable kind. Lord Orford carried to Stainsted under proper care. Houghton a ruin; Mr Horace Walpole has been there and ordered repairs. Lord Townshend having not paid the debts he contracted before he went to

Ireland, his creditors are so troublesome he could not stay long in the country . . . Houghton is a large field for contemplation, especially *to me* who remember it in *all its glory, almost the seat of empire!'* (*The Autobiography and Correspondence of Mary Granville, Mrs Delany,* ed. Lady Llanover, 1861–2, iv. 572). HW describes the 'destruction and desolation' at Houghton in his letter to Lady Ossory 1 Sept. 1773 (Ossory i. 140–3).

3. Perhaps in a missing letter.

4. 'He is forced to be confined in his bed at night, and pinioned in the day, as

he may live these forty years,[5] which it is so much the interest of his family as well as our earnest wish that he should do. His disorder increases generally once a month—the last fit was protracted by the heat. His physicians give us not much encouragement to expect his total recovery—yet he was once so much mended, that I cannot despair of his reestablishment. I will not make excuses to your Lordship for troubling you with so many circumstances; Dr Hammond[6] told me you wished for particulars, and I am too much convinced of your Lordship's friendship for my nephew to think they will be unwelcome.

I am informed that your Lordship would like to have a brace of Lord Orford's pointers to send into Ireland. I have taken the liberty to send two young ones, mottled, and so good, that they will yield to none after two or three days that they shall be entered. I am persuaded I do not exceed what my Lord himself would approve in offering your Lordship these dogs, though I had determined to part with nothing that could give Lord Orford pleasure, but on condition that every individual[6a] should be restored to him, if I am so happy as to see him recover. With this view I have reserved his five best pointers; and if your Lordship will please to accept one of those five on that condition, Flue, his mottled bitch shall be at your command.

I am going to sell all my Lord's horses,[7] and you will allow me to offer your Lordship the refusal of all or any of those that have been sent to Rainham[8] for your inspection. The chaise, if it is not impertinent in me to offer Lady Townshend[9] an old conveyance, I am sure my Lord would approve my saying is at her Ladyship's service, and I am only sorry it is not more fit for her.

I have the honour to be with great respect

       My Lord
          Your Lordship's most obedient humble servant

                            HOR. WALPOLE

he incessantly tries to escape, or to do himself mischief' (HW to Mann 15 Aug. 1773, MANN vii. 505).

5. He was to live another eighteen years.

6. Rev. Horace Hamond (1718–86), D.D. (Cantab.), 1755; rector of Harpley and Great Bircham, Norfolk, 1744–86; prebendary of Bristol 1754–6, of Norwich 1756–86; HW's first cousin (Venn, *Alumni Cantab.* ii. 294; John Le Neve and T. D. Hardy, *Fasti Ecclesiæ Anglicanæ*, Oxford,

1854, i. 230, ii. 502; FAMILY 14 n. 7).

6a. HW apparently means every individual object given away by him.

7. HW reported to the Hon. Thomas Walpole 4 Sept. 1773: 'I have got rid of his dogs and most of his horses; the rest will be sold in the beginning of October' (ibid. 95). See *post* mid-October 1773, n. 7.

8. Raynham Hall, Norfolk, Townshend's seat.

9. Anne Montgomery (d. 1819), m.

To Thomas Somersby,[1] Thursday 23 September 1773

Printed for the first time from the MS now WSL. The MS is untraced until it was offered by Dobell, Cat. No. 86 (1929), lot 802; offered by Radford and Co., *The Ingatherer*, No. 1 (Sept. 1929), lot 210; acquired by WSL, 1930.

Address: To Mr Somersby, Mayor Elect of Lynn, Norfolk. *Postmark:* 23 ⟨SE⟩. ISLEWORTH.

Strawberry Hill, Sept. 23d 1773.

MR H. WALPOLE has but this minute received the honour of a card[2] from Mr Somersby, and is extremely sorry that he cannot have the pleasure of waiting on Mr Mayor, as he is detained in and near London by Lord Orford's business.[3] Mr Walpole takes the invitation as a grateful honour to himself, and a very pleasing mark of regard to Lord Orford and his family; and though Mr Walpole's health and retirement forbid his ever thinking of engaging in public business, he shall always be happy to have an opportunity of showing his regard and gratitude to the gentlemen and town of Lynn,[4] and flatters himself they will be the more persuaded of his attachment, as he can have no personal interest in hoping to merit their good wishes. He begs Mr Mayor in particular to accept his respectful compliments.

(19 May 1773), as his second wife, George, 4th Vct Townshend.

1. Thomas Somersby, junior, Mayor of King's Lynn, Norfolk, 1773–4 (elected 29 Aug. 1773) (Hamon Le Strange, *Norfolk Official Lists,* Norwich, 1890, p. 196; information from the Town Clerk of King's Lynn).

2. Missing.
3. See *ante* 27 May 1773, n. 1.
4. HW represented King's Lynn in Parliament 1757–68 and was succeeded by his cousin, the Hon. Thomas Walpole. See *ante* 13 March 1767.

To Benjamin Ibbot,[1] Friday 24 September 1773

Printed from a photostat of the MS in the Pierpont Morgan Library. First printed, Toynbee *Supp.* i. 224–5. The MS, one of eleven letters from HW to Ibbot bound in a copy of the fourth volume of HW's *Anecdotes of Painting*, SH, 1762–71, was acquired by J. Pierpont Morgan before 1918; for the earlier history of the volume see Hazen, *SH Bibl.* 66, copy 1. The letters have now been removed from the volume.

Address: To Benjamin Ibbot Esq. in Dartmouth Street, Westminster. *Postmark:* 2⟨5⟩ SE. ISLEWORTH.

Strawberry Hill, Sept. 24, 1773.

Sir,

I AM much obliged to you for the favour of your letter,[2] and the trouble you have been so good as to give yourself about the pictures of the Cromwels.[3] I shall be glad to see them when I am in town in the winter, but I own, between you and me, I suspect that the Oliver is only a copy,[4] for I was positively told that the Duchess of Kingston[5] had bought the original.[6] If she has not, I should still be glad to know what is asked for it, for if the price is kept up to near what was asked of me formerly,[7] it would be to no purpose for me to see it, as I certainly would not think of it at so vast a rate. In short, Sir, it was valued at £400, and I will never give above a quarter of that sum, having bought things as fine cheaper, and nothing of

1. (1709–87), son of the Rev. Benjamin Ibbot (1680–1725), chaplain to George I and prebendary of Westminster 1724–5; collector (GM 1787, lvii pt ii. 1031; *European Mag.*, 1787, xii. 436; *BM Cat. of Engraved British Portraits* ii. 600). His collection of coins and medals was sold by Gerard on 16–17 April 1783 (Frits Lugt, *Répertoire des catalogues de ventes publiques*, The Hague, 1938– , vol. I, No. 3556).

2. Missing.

3. Three miniatures, in a single frame, of Oliver Cromwell, his wife, and one of his daughters, by Samuel Cooper, in the possession of Lady Frankland (nn. 6, 9 below).

4. It was the original. HW himself owned a copy in enamel by Charles Boit, given to him by his brother Robert, 2d Earl of Orford ('Des. of SH,' *Works* ii. 476).

5. Elizabeth Chudleigh (ca 1720–88), m. 1 (privately, 1744) Hon. Augustus John Hervey, 3d E. of Bristol, 1775; m. 2 (illegally, 1769) Evelyn Pierrepont, 2d D. of Kingston-upon-Hull, 1726.

6. Not so. After Lady Frankland's death in 1783, the Cromwell miniatures passed to Sir Thomas Frankland's grandnephew, Henry Cromwell Frankland; they were bought in at Christie's sale 2 May 1795, lot 95, and were acquired by the 5th Duke of Buccleuch in the nineteenth century. See *post* ca 1785; BERRY ii. 270; Daphne Foskett, *Samuel Cooper 1609–1672*, 1974, pp. 15, 18, 74–6).

7. HW wrote Mann 9 Feb. 1758: 'I know but one dear picture not sold, Cooper's head of Oliver Cromwell, an unfinished miniature; they asked me £400 for it!' (MANN v. 173).

the kind so high; though I certainly have the first miniature in the world.[8] It would be giving Lady Frankland[9] unnecessary trouble. I am not the less obliged to you for your goodness and am Sir

Your most obedient humble servant

Hor. Walpole

From Lady Fenouilhet,[1]
ca Wednesday 29 September 1773

HW wrote Lady Ossory 1 Oct. 1773: 'The next scene lies in Calais. You shall have the identic words of my Lady Fenouilhet's letter.' The letter is missing; for the extract quoted by HW see Ossory i. 150–1.

To Dr William Hunter,[1] Thursday 7 October 1773

Printed from a photostat of the MS in the Hunter-Baillie Collection, Royal College of Surgeons of England. First printed, Toynbee xv. 454. Reprinted in J. M. Oppenheimer, *New Aspects of John and William Hunter*, 1946, pp. 151–2; extract quoted in V. G. Plarr, 'Unpublished Letters to William Hunter,' *Chambers's Journal*, 1905–6, 6th Ser., ix. 35. The MS passed on Hunter's death (1783) to his nephew and executor, Matthew Baillie, whose granddaughter, Helen Hunter-Baillie, presented his collection of autographs to the Royal College of Surgeons of England.
Endorsed by Sophia Baillie (Mrs Matthew Baillie): Dr Hunter.

Strawberry Hill, Oct. 7th 1773.

Sir,

YOU shall certainly have all the satisfaction you can desire about Lord Orford's orignal.[2] Nay, if you or any friend of yours would be troubled with him, the animal himself shall be at your service:

8. In the 1774 edition of the *Description of SH* HW refers to his miniature of Lady Lucy Percy, the mother of Venetia Lady Digby, as 'perhaps the finest and most perfect miniature in the world' (*Works* ii. 422). This was one of nine miniatures of the Digby family that HW had purchased for 300 guineas in 1771 (ibid.).

9. Sarah Moseley (?1725–83), m. (1741) Sir Thomas Frankland (ca 1683–1747), 3d Bt, 1726.

1. Ann Franks (d. 1790), *alias* Nancy Day, mistress of Richard, Lord Edgcumbe, m. (1762) Sir Peter Fenouilhet (d. 1774), Kt, 1761 (Gray i. 36 n. 242).

1. (1718–83), brother of the eminent physician John Hunter; M.D. (Glasgow), 1750; physician to Queen Charlotte 1764–83; F.R.S., 1767; F.S.A., 1768; professor of anatomy at the Royal Academy, 1768; obstetrician and anatomist.

2. 'A Canadian name of the American

but pray do not think I pretend to be making you a present, for besides that I can only part with him on condition of his being restored to Lord Orford, if we should be so happy as to see his Lordship recover,[3] the poor creature is in a miserable condition, and when I saw him in August,[4] was almost the skeleton you ask for, having had a distemper and been neglected. As I have heard nothing of him since, he is probably recovered. Being young, and not arrived at his full growth, he had little appearance of horns. Such as he is, if you will send for him, and can have him kept in a paddock at New Park,[5] or any other place, you may command him.

I am Sir

Your most obedient humble servant

Hor. Walpole

PS. When I have the favour of your answer,[6] if you do not choose to have the animal, I will send your directions to Houghton.

To Lord Hardwicke, mid-October 1773

Printed from a photostat of the MS among the Hardwicke papers in the British Museum (Add. MS 35,611, f. 21). First printed, Toynbee viii. 349–50. For the history of the MS see *ante* Nov. 1772.

Dated approximately by the reference to the sale of Lord Orford's horses at Newmarket (see n. 7 below).

Address: To the Earl of Hardwicke at Richmond.

MR WALPOLE presents his compliments to Lord Hardwicke and should have had the honour of waiting on his Lordship before now, but has not been at Twickenham[1] for two days together,

---

moose' (OED). This male animal was first examined by Hunter in July 1772 at Bushey Park, where it had been sent as a present to Lady North. Lady North gave it to HW's nephew, Lord Orford. Hunter had previously studied the first male original to reach England, brought to London in Sept. 1770 by Col. (later Gen. Sir) Guy Carleton as a present to the Duke of Richmond; a painting of it by George Stubbs is in the Hunterian Collection at Glasgow (Sir Charles Illingworth, *The Story of William Hunter*, 1967, pp. 67–8; illustrated pl. IX, facing p. 64).

3. See *ante* 27 May 1773, n. 1. He recovered in late December and did not suffer a relapse until April 1777 (Family 333–5).

4. At Houghton, where HW went to oversee Lord Orford's affairs during his illness (*ante* 10 Aug. 1773, n. 2).

5. At Richmond, where there was a deer park.

6. Missing.

---

1. Across the Thames from Richmond, where Hardwicke lived.

being most unfortunately so involved in the care of Lord Orford's affairs[2] that he has not one minute of time to give even to his own. Lady Orford[3] has refused to meddle,[4] Sir Edward Walpole[5] has other business of consequence,[6] and the whole burthen lies on Mr Walpole, who is obliged to see the physicians, lawyers and stewards; and what he still less expected would ever happen to him, he is now perplexed with all Lord O.'s concerns at Newmarket, where the horses are to be sold next week.[7] Mr W. is therefore forced to entreat Lord Hardwicke will excuse him at present, but as soon as he has a minute's leisure, he will look out the papers[8] his Lordship wishes to see, and will beg the honour of his Lordship's company at Strawberry Hill, where he could amuse him with many things, which he is now obliged to abandon for objects he is little capable of executing as they ought to be; and which make him very unhappy, and will probably perplex the remainder of his life.

2. See *ante* 10 Aug. 1773.

3. Margaret Rolle (1709–81), m. 1 (1724) Robert Walpole, cr. (1723) Bn Walpole; 2d E. of Orford, 1745; m. 2 (1751) Hon. Sewallis Shirley; Bns Clinton (*s. j.*), 1760; mother of George, 3d E. of Orford.

4. HW wrote Mann 9 Sept. 1773: 'I have received a satisfactory, and even flattering, letter from Lady Orford this very day . . . . I shall do everything in my power to please her, and to do justice to her son and my family. I shall not often trouble her with letters, as she cares so little to be troubled, but you may assure her and she may depend upon it, that . . . I will do whatever she commands' (MANN vii. 514).

5. (1706–84), HW's older brother.

6. 'Sir Edward has been so good as to . . . say that he shall look on whatever I do as his own act' (HW to Thomas Walpole 1 July 1773, FAMILY 93).

7. 'To be sold by auction by Mr Bever, at Newmarket, on Wednesday the 20th, and Thursday the 21st instant, at eleven, The stud of brood mares, colts, fillies, hunters, hacks, etc., the property of a nobleman.

'To be viewed at Newmarket, and catalogues had there, and at Mr Bever's Repository [in London]' (*Daily Adv.* 9–18 and, with slight changes, 19–21 Oct.).

8. Perhaps materials to be used in compiling Hardwicke's *Miscellaneous State Papers, from 1501 to 1726* (ante ?Jan. 1773, n. 1).

To Benjamin Ibbot, Thursday 18 November 1773

Printed from a photostat of the MS in the Pierpont Morgan Library. First printed, Toynbee *Supp.* i. 228. For the history of the MS see *ante* 24 Sept. 1773. *Address:* To Benjamin Ibbot Esq. in Dartmouth Street, Westminster. *Postmark:* PENNY POST PAID.
Memorandum (in an unidentified hand, on the address leaf): Bishop.

Arlington Street, Nov. 18, 1773.

MR WALPOLE sends his compliments to Mr Ibbot, and will be much obliged to him if he will call, in his walks, in Arlington street any morning between eleven and one, after Monday next.[1]

To Richard Stonhewer, Saturday 27 November 1773

Printed from the MS now WSL. First printed, Toynbee xi. 64 (misdated 'Nov. 27, 1779'). The MS was *penes* Sotheby's in August 1847; sold Sotheby's 17 June 1875 (Euing Sale), lot 250, to Webster; resold Sotheby's 5 May 1892 (Webster Sale), lot 215, to Barker; resold Sotheby's 25 Feb. 1893 ('Other Properties'), lot 253, to Barker; resold Sotheby's 17 July 1894 ('Other Properties'), lot 370, to Power; resold Sotheby's 1 March 1896 ('Other Properties'), lot 473, to Maggs; offered (in a copy of the SH Sale Catalogue, 1842, formerly owned by J. H. Anderdon) by Davis and Orioli, Oct. 1941; acquired in a miscellaneous collection of autographs by Lew David Feldman (House of El Dieff, Inc.) ca 1963; resold Christie's 29 July 1971 ('Various Properties'), lot 538, to Maggs; offered by Maggs, Cat. 938 (1971), lot 93; sold by Maggs to WSL, Nov. 1971.
Endorsed by Stonhewer: Mr H. Walpole November 27th 1773.
Endorsed in an unidentified hand: On Mr Gray's *Memoirs* etc.

Nov. 27, 1773.

I AM extremely obliged to you, Sir, for the perusal of what you sent me.[1] It is so very interesting to *me,* that I am afraid to praise it as much as it deserves, lest that interest should have fascinated my

1. 22 November. We have found no record of any such visit.

1. The first part of William Mason's *Memoirs* of Thomas Gray, which was printed in June 1773; see MASON i. 90. HW wrote Mason the same day, 27 Nov.: 'Mr Stonhewer has sent me, and I have read, your first part of Gray's life, which I was very sorry to part with so soon. . . . I should say much more in praise, if, as I have told Mr Stonhewer, I was not aware that I myself must be far more interested in the whole of the narrative, than any other living mortal . . . . Of my two friends and me, I only make a most in-

eyes. And yet though it must touch me more than it will indifferent readers, the wit in Mr Gray's letters, and the tender friendship between him and our amiable West,[2] and the extraordinary abilities of both at so green an age, displayed to the fairest advantage by Mr Mason's singular address,[3] must I think charm everybody that has feeling or taste. I do not regret the insignificant figure I make myself. I never had any pretensions to parts like theirs, and I cheerfully consented to sacrifice myself to do honour to two dead friends that I valued so much.

Your obedient servant

HOR. WALPOLE

To LADY TEMPLE, Monday 20 December 1773

Printed from a photostat of the MS in the British Museum (Add. MS 42,087, f. 172). First printed in *The Grenville Papers*, ed. W. J. Smith, 1852–3, iv. 548–9. Reprinted, Cunningham vi. 32–3; Toynbee viii. 384–5. The MS was among the Temple papers preserved at Stowe; sold in a collection of papers from Stowe by the 2d Duke of Buckingham and Chandos to his attorney, Edwin James, who in turn sold this collection to John Murray in 1851; acquired by the British Museum in 1930.

Endorsed in an unidentified hand: XXII – 11.

Address: To the Countess Temple Pall Mall.

Dec. 20, 1773.

I HAD a person[1] with me that prevented my answering your Ladyship's kind letter[2] immediately, which I wished to do and to thank you for having relieved my mind from the greatest anxiety imagin-

different figure. I do not mean with regard to parts or talents. I never one instant of my life had the superlative vanity of ranking myself with them. They not only possessed genius, which I have not, great learning which is to be acquired, and which I never acquired; but both Gray and West had abilities marvellously premature' (ibid. i. 114). Mason's completed work, entitled *The Poems of Mr Gray, to which are Prefixed Memoirs of His Life and Writings*, was published 30 March 1775.

2. Richard West (1716–42), intimate friend and correspondent of Gray and

HW. Gray's correspondence with his mother and father, West, and HW occupies the first three sections of Mason's *Memoirs*.

3. 'You have with most singular art displayed the talents of my two departed friends to the fullest advantage; and yet there is a simplicity in your manner, which, like the frame of a fine picture, seems a frame only, and yet is gold' (HW to Mason 27 Nov. 1773, MASON i. 114).

————

1. Not identified.

2. Missing.

able. The enormous sum of £800 compared with £300, which I had thought a very great price, made me apprehensive that I should seem to have offered far below the value of the pictures,[3] the plain English of which could only be that I would have defrauded orphans for my own advantage, an idea that would make me shudder. If a lady[4] in the country is so amazingly deceived as to expect to get half the sum of £800, I doubt she will keep them till they are of no value at all, which must be the case of miniatures that must lose their beauty by time, and which makes them so greatly less valuable than enamels. My behaviour to Miss Stapleton[5] I hope has been perfectly respectful; and allow me to repeat, Madam, that my great esteem for her character, and gratitude for having made me the offer of purchasing the pictures, carried me beyond my judgment, and made me desirous of pleasing her by the handsomeness of the offer. I heartily beg her pardon if regard for my own honour has carried me too far in disculpating myself. The more esteem I had for her, the more shocked I was at seeming to have acted in an unworthy manner: and I own I should still wish that she would show the pictures to some good judge, and see what such a person would say of £800 for them. I shall always be Miss Stapleton's obliged humble servant if she justifies me,[6] and I shall be if possible more than ever Lady Temple's most devoted humble servant, who I am sure will forgive my not being able to bear the thought of being lowered in her esteem.

PS. I am prevented today, but will have the honour of calling on your Ladyship tomorrow.

---

3. The seven remaining miniatures of the Digby family from a collection of sixteen miniatures found at Penbedw, Flintshire; see *ante* 25 May 1773, n. 22. In 1771 HW had purchased the other nine Digby miniatures for 300 gns ('Des. of SH,' *Works* ii. 422). He had evidently offered to buy the second group for the same amount.

4. Presumably Elizabeth Stapleton (1740–1825), third surviving dau. of Col. James Russell Stapleton, of Bodrhyddan, Flintshire; m. (1767) Watkin Williams (?1742–1808), of Penbedw, Flintshire, M.P. She

apparently shared the ownership of the seven miniatures with her husband, and had asked £800 for them.

5. Catherine Stapleton (1734–1815), older sister of Elizabeth (Stapleton) Williams (*ante* 25 May 1773, n. 23). She was a first cousin once removed of Lord Temple, and seems to have acted as agent for Elizabeth and Watkin Williams in selling the seven miniatures.

6. After 'long haggling' HW acquired the seven miniatures in Feb. 1775 for an undisclosed price; see MASON i. 180.

To Lord Hardwicke, Monday 24 January 1774

Printed for the first time from the MS now wsl. For the history of the MS see
ante ?Jan. 1773.
Endorsed by Hardwicke: Mr Walpole.

Jan. 24, 1774.

I BEG your Lordship's pardon for so long detaining your valuable
volume of MSS.[1] The truth is, my Lord, that till yesterday I have
not had a minute's time to open and look into it. Indeed it deserves
more leisure than I have to peruse it. Lord Herbert's[2] petition and
the two subsequent papers are remarkable; and no doubt evince that
his dissatisfactions prevented his embarking in the King's[3] cause.
Lord Essex's[4] letter and verses are beautiful and touching. I have
some imperfect notion of having seen the letter, but none of the
poetry; I do not know whether they are in print. Lord Leicester's[5]
anecdotes are very curious; to me much, in one particular, relative to Rubens's father.[6] Your Lordship has done yourself great
honour by so noble and judicious a collection as yours. The world,
I hope, will one day or other be obliged to you for such rarities.[7]

Your Lordship has certainly detected the imposture of Anne
Boleyn's[8] letter, though not the forger. It is still however an admirable performance. I have not been able yet, my Lord, to look into
the Gazettes, but will take great care of them, and have the honour
to be your Lordship's

Most obliged humble servant

Hor. Walpole

1. Hardwicke had in his possession a
very large collection of original MSS and
transcripts of state papers which he did
not print in his *Miscellaneous State Papers, from 1501 to 1726,* 2 vols, 1778 (*ante*
?Jan. 1773, n. 1). Some of these documents
(now in BM Add. MS 35,837) were apparently to be included in an expanded
second edition of the work that was never
published. The entire collection is described in his *Catalogue of the Manuscripts in the Possession of the Earl of
Hardwicke,* privately printed, 1794.
2. See *ante* 7 June 1758 and n. 9. 'Lord
Herbert's Petition to the King, and the
Answer' are listed in Hardwicke's *Catalogue,* p. 33 (vol. 108).

3. Charles I.
4. Doubtless Robert Devereux (1566–
1601), 2d E. of Essex, 1576. HW perhaps
refers to a letter of 1586 from Essex to
William Davison, Queen Elizabeth's secretary of state, that is listed in Hardwicke's
Catalogue, p. 34 (vol. 109).
5. Robert Sydney (1595–1677), 2d E. of
Leicester, 1626. 'Anecdotes of Robert, second Earl of Leicester' (1621) are listed in
Hardwicke's *Catalogue,* p. 33 (vol. 108).
6. Jan Rubens (d. 1587), father of the
painter Peter Paul Rubens.
7. See n. 1 above.
8. (1507–36), Henry VIII's second wife.
HW possibly refers to a letter of 1533
from Anne Boleyn to Thomas Josselyn

To Lord Hardwicke, Tuesday 1 February 1774

Printed for the first time from the MS now WSL. For the history of the MS see *ante* ?Jan. 1773.
Address: To the Earl of Hardwicke, St James's Square.

Feb. 1, 1774.

My Lord,

I HAD Lord Orford's lawyer[1] with me when I received the honour of your Lordship's note,[2] and could not possibly answer it then. I am extremely sorry to hear your Lordship is troubled with the gout, of which I cannot wish you joy, knowing how dreadful an affliction it is. I am almost as sorry not to be able to contribute anything to your Lordship's amusement. I have not a MS in town, nor a book but a very few common ones. I send the only thing[3] I can recollect that will be new to your Lordship, and that but for a moment: nor shall I be able I fear to pay my duty to you for two or three days, which will be extremely occupied, as I saw Lord Orford yesterday, who is perfectly well, and to whom I am to give an account on Friday of all that has been done in his illness.[4] After this I hope to be again a very idle man,[5] and consequently entirely at your Lordship's commands.

I have indeed let Shropshire[6] impose upon me abominably, more to my own reproach than his: and I doubt I am going to play the fool again, with my eyes open, which shows the folly of collections, as there is no resisting the silly vanity of making them perfect. I am ashamed to own, too, that I have always repented more of resisting such temptations, than the expense I have been at in indulging them,

('on the birth of Queen Elizabeth') that is listed in Hardwicke's *Catalogue*, p. 33 (vol. 109).

———

1. Presumably Charles Lucas (living in 1797), who is known to have been Lord Orford's lawyer from 1781 until Orford's death in 1791 (MANN ix. 123). See *ante* 27 May 1773, n. 1.
2. Missing.
3. Not identified.
4. Lord Hertford wrote to the King on Friday, 4 Feb.: 'Mr Walpole who has seen him [Lord Orford] this morning says he never saw him more in his senses. . . . I

propose to call at his door tomorrow as he is coming to Court' (*The Correspondence of King George the Third from 1760 to December 1783*, ed. Sir John Fortescue, 1927–8, iii. 60). HW reported to Mann 2 Feb. that Lord Orford had 're-covered entirely' (MANN vii. 548).
5. 'I am now at liberty again' (HW to Cole 4 May 1774, COLE i. 324).
6. Walter Shropshire (d. 1785), bookseller in New Bond Street 1767–79 (Ian Maxted, *The London Book Trades 1775–1800*, 1977, p. 204). He was also a dealer in prints, known for his high prices.

which at least proves I continue to be pleased with what I have bought long after the purchase. I have the honour to be

My Lord,
                    Your Lordship's most obedient humble servant

                                                        Hor. Walpole

To Lady Holland,[1] Saturday 19 February 1774

Printed for the first time from a photostat of the MS among the Holland House papers in the British Museum (Add. MS 51,404, f. 233). For the history of the MS see *ante* 20 Aug. 1753.

Arlington Street, Feb. 19th 1774.

I AM very sorry, dear Madam, that your Ladyship should give yourself the trouble of writing with your own hand, as a line from anybody else would have been fully sufficient. I am much more unhappy at your illness,[2] as it is impossible for any man to have more esteem, or more regard for your welfare than I have, who have so long known your worth and experienced your unalterable goodness to me. My only satisfaction is hearing from Lady Mary[3] that the doctors are convinced they see an amendment.

Your Ladyship may be perfectly assured that the Duke and Duchess of Gloucester[4] will approve extremely the very prudent reasons you give, Madam, for declining their offer. As his Royal Highness has few opportunities of giving proofs of his sensibility to the few persons who have shown their respect and good wishes,[5] and as there is no-

1. Lady Georgiana Caroline Lennox (1723–74), m. (1744) Henry Fox, cr. (1763) Bn Holland; cr. (1762) Bns Holland, s.j.

2. Lady Holland had 'an internal cancer' from which she died 24 July 1774 'after many months of dreadful sufferings. For some weeks she had taken 500 and 600 drops of laudanum every day' (*Last Journals* i. 363). 'The accounts of Lady Holland are most cruel and melancholy. I have not yet been able to go to Holland House; partly from my disorder and business; still more from not having spirits to bear the sight. But I will gather resolution—and perhaps she will not see me' (HW to Lady Ossory 12 Feb. 1774, Ossory i. 188).

3. Lady Mary Fitzpatrick (ca 1746–78), m. (1766) Hon. Stephen Fox, 2d Bn Holland, 1774; Lady Holland's daughter-in-law.

4. Maria Walpole (1736–1807), dau. of HW's brother Sir Edward Walpole, m. 1 (1759) James Waldegrave (1715–63), 2d E. Waldegrave, 1741; m. 2 (1766) William Henry (1743–1805), cr. (1764) D. of Gloucester, George III's younger brother.

5. An allusion to the King's disapproval of the Duke's having secretly married the widowed Lady Waldegrave in 1766. After their marriage was publicly acknowledged in 1772, the King forbade their coming to Court.

body for whom he has more esteem than for your Ladyship and Lord Holland, he was impatient to make the first offer in his power to your son;[6] but as I told the Duchess of Richmond[7] and Lady Mary Fox, his Royal Highness desired that offer might not lay your Ladyship and Lord Holland under the least difficulty, much less contribute any prejudice to Mr Fox's preferment, for which the Duke and Duchess must be and are equally solicitous. The Duke would have been happy to have so amiable a young man attached to him, but is too noble-minded to wish his friends should suffer for their regard to him; and therefore I may venture to say, that as the offer was most sincerely made, the declension will be as graciously accepted;[8] and should his Royal Highness ever have it in his power to be serviceable to your Ladyship's family, I am persuaded, his R. H. will be as glad as he was now, to give proofs to them of his good will.

I will immediately acquaint the Duchess, Madam, with your Ladyship's reasons and answer; I know her infinite regard and concern for your Ladyship, and she is too tender a mother herself not to enter warmly into such sensible interests; at the same time I know that nothing can make her happier than a good account of your Ladyship.

For myself, Madam, I most anxiously pray for the alleviation of all your sufferings. All I flatter myself will be lightened and vanish, and I trust such unerring goodness as yours will be rewarded even in this life with every comfort you have reason to expect, and so well deserve.

I have the honour to be with the highest esteem

    Madam
       Your Ladyship's most faithful humble servant

            HOR. WALPOLE

---

6. Hon. Henry Fox (1755–1811), the Hollands' youngest son. The Duke of Gloucester had probably offered Fox a place in his regiment, the 1st Foot Guards. But Fox had recently (14 Feb.) been promoted from Cornet in the 1st Dragoon Guards to Captain in the 38th Foot, then stationed at Boston (*Army Lists*, 1773, p. 26; 1775, p. 92). Fox served in America throughout the war for independence; he became Col. and aide-de-camp to George III in 1783, and General in 1808 (MANN viii. 5 n. 29; OSSORY i. 198 n. 2).

7. See HW to Mme de Forcalquier *ante* 27 Oct. 1766, n. 9. The Duchess was Lady Holland's sister-in-law.

8. See following letter.

To Lady Holland, Saturday 26 February 1774

Printed for the first time from a photostat of the MS among the Holland House papers in the British Museum (Add. MS 51,404, f. 234). For the history of the MS see *ante* 20 Aug. 1753.

Arlington Street, Feb. 26, 1774.

Madam,

THE Duchess of Gloucester has ordered me to say to your Ladyship that she would have written to you herself, if she had not feared it would have engaged your Ladyship to take the trouble of writing an answer, which she should be extremely sorry to have you do till you are better, which she most sincerely wishes to hear you are. His Royal Highness the Duke is most perfectly satisfied with the prudent reasons your Ladyship gives for declining his offer,[1] and approves them; and I am commanded to say, Madam, that whenever your son shall live in town, he will always find a protector in his Royal Highness, though not of his own family, both from Mr Fox's own merit, and from the great regard his Royal Highness has for your Ladyship and Lord Holland.

I entreat your Ladyship not to think of answering this; it would be unkind to me not to be sure that it would concern me greatly to give you the least pain. I will wait on Lord Holland very soon, and shall exceedingly rejoice, Madam, whenever you are well enough[2] to admit your Ladyship's

Most faithful humble servant

Hor. Walpole

1. See previous letter, n. 6.
2. 'Lord Holland drags on a wretched life, and Lady Holland is dying of a can-

cer' (HW to Mann 15 May 1774, Mann viii. 5). Holland died 1 July 1774; his wife died twenty-three days later.

To Mrs Delany,[1] after Thursday 7 April 1774

Printed from the MS now WSL. First printed in *The Tenbury Letters,* ed. E. H. Fellowes and Edward Pine, 1942, p. 90 (facsimile of the MS, p. 230). The MS was formerly part of the autograph collection formed by Mary Jane Ouseley (1807–61), a sister of Sir Frederick Arthur Gore Ouseley, 2d Bt, who was the founder of St Michael's College, Tenbury Wells, Worcs; after her death the collection passed into the possession of the College; the MS was sold Sotheby's 23 October 1956 (property of St Michael's College), lot 436, to Maggs for WSL.

Lord Chesterfield's *Letters . . . to His Son* was published 7 April 1774; the letter was doubtless written during the next few months.

Endorsed in an unidentified hand: From Horace Walpole afterwards Lord Orford.

MR WALPOLE returns Mrs Delane Lord Chesterfield's *Letters*[2] with many thanks, and has read them with more curiosity than satisfaction.[3] They seem to be an intended portrait of himself, or of what he flattered himself he had arrived, by great art, at being; and which without being much more, I should think would not flatter one much to be. With so much marked contempt for fools, what martyrdom to have aimed at their affections! and who will believe that mere dread of their hatred prescribed such rigorous attention! My Lord's definition of *good company* makes it what I believe it is, very contemptible, and what habit makes one suffer, rather than choice prefer. He has indeed fitted his pupil[4] for it, for good humour seems to be the best ingredient of good company, and good breeding of the candidate. *Their* vices and faults are tuned not to shock; and *his* merit is to consist in not shocking the polish with which they have smoothed over their passions. How little this tract of education

1. Mary Granville (1700–88), m. 1 (1718) Alexander Pendarves (d. 1725); m. 2 (1743) Patrick Delany (ca 1685–1768), Dean of Down, 1744.

2. *Letters Written by the Late Right Honourable Philip Dormer Stanhope, Earl of Chesterfield, to His Son, Philip Stanhope, Esq.,* 2 vols, published 7 April 1774 (MASON i. 146 n. 25). HW obtained a copy on 8 April and commented on the letters the next day in a letter to Mason (ibid. i. 146–7). His profusely annotated copy, now WSL, is Hazen, *Cat. of HW's Lib.,* No. 436.

3. Mrs Delany wrote to her brother Ber- nard Granville 4 Sept. 1774: 'The general opinion of these letters among the better sort of men is, that they are ingenious, useful as to polish of manners, but *very hurtful* in a *moral sense.* He mentions a decent regard to religion, at the same time recommends falsehood even to your most intimate acquaintance—and adultery as an accomplishment. *Les graces* are the sum total of his religion' (*The Autobiography and Correspondence of Mary Granville, Mrs Delany,* ed. Lady Llanover, 1861–2, v. 27–8).

4. Philip Stanhope (1732–68), Chester- field's illegitimate son; diplomatist.

is suited to that of an Englishman, appears from his Lordship being reduced to borrow French terms for all the duties of life that he enjoins. It is just to say that he calls these letters only *the art of pleasing*. I hope it was not *all* he taught his scholar.

To John Cowslade,[1] ?Friday 16 September ?1774

Printed from a photostat of the MS in the Hyde Collection, Sommerville, New Jersey. First printed, Toynbee xv. 442–3. The MS is untraced until it was acquired by R. B. Adam before 1905; sold with the Adam collection to Donald F. Hyde, 1948.

Dated conjecturally by the 'ticket' to view SH in which HW did not 'fill up the blank.' HW presumably refers to the printed ticket which HW had prepared in 1774 only; see Hazen, *SH Bibl.* 210.

Address: To John Cowslade Esq. in Berkeley Square, London. *Postmark:* 16 SE. ISLEWORTH.

Strawberry Hill, Sept. 16th.

Dear Sir,

I ENCLOSE the ticket[2] with pleasure because I love to obey you; and I do not fill up the blank, that you may fix what day you please. I must only beg it may not be next Monday, when I am to have a good deal of company, nor on the 24th when I am to have people on business.[3]

Can you tell me anything of Mr Chute,[4] I mean that he is well? He promised to come hither this month, and though it is not elapsed, I am a little afraid of his having the gout,[5] as he sent me some game without a line, and I have not heard a word of him for above a fortnight, which would not surprise me at any other time. If I knew when he would be here, I know what I should ask. If you know, cannot you ask the favour I should ask? in short, with him or without him your company will be always most acceptable to

Dear Sir

Your obedient humble servant

Hor. Walpole

1. (d. 1795), of Donnington, Berks; commissioner for appeals and regulating duties in the Excise Office 1763–95; gentleman usher to the Queen 1761–95; friend of John Chute (Ossory ii. 170 n. 1).

2. Missing; see headnote.

3. HW's engagements on 19 and 24 Sept. are not mentioned in his other letters that have survived.

4. John Chute (1701–76), of the Vyne, Hants; HW's correspondent.

5. 'Mr Chute for these last two or three

To John Craufurd, Monday 26 September 1774

Printed from the MS now WSL. First printed, Cunningham vi. 121–2. Reprinted, Toynbee ix. 52–4; *A Selection of the Letters of Horace Walpole,* ed. W. S. Lewis, 1926, ii. 264–7; *Letters of Horace Walpole,* ed. W. S. Lewis, 1951, pp. 163–5; *Selected Letters of Horace Walpole,* ed. W. S. Lewis, New Haven, 1973, pp. 188–9 (both postscripts omitted). For the history of the MS see *ante* 6 March 1766.

Address: To John Craufurd Esq. at Mr John Tait's,[1] Writer to the Signet, Edinburgh.[2] *Postmark:* 29 E. E⟨K⟩.

Strawberry Hill, Sept. 26, 1774.

YOU tell me to write to you, and I am certainly disposed to do anything I can to amuse you; but that is not so easy a matter, for two very good reasons: you are not the most amusable of men, and I have nothing to amuse you with; for you are like electricity, you attract and repel at once; and though you have at first a mind to know anything, you are tired of it before it can be told. I don't go to Almack's[3] nor amongst your acquaintance;[4] would you bear to hear of mine? of Lady Blandford,[5] Lady Anne Conolly[6] and the Duchess of Newcastle? for by age and situation I live at this time of year with nothing but old women. They do very well for me, who have little choice left, and who rather prefer common nonsense to wise nonsense, the only difference I know between old women and old men. I am out of all politics, and never think of elections, which I think I should hate even if I loved politics,[7] just as if I loved tap-

years was much broken by his long and repeated shocks of gout, yet was amazingly well, considering he had suffered by it from twenty to seventy-three' (HW to Mann 27 May 1776, MANN viii. 210).

———

1. John Tait (d. 1800), of Harvieston, Midlothian; Writer to the Signet, 1763 (*A History of the Society of Writers to Her Majesty's Signet,* Edinburgh, 1890, p. 199; *Scots Magazine,* 1800, lxii. 215).

2. Address crossed out in the MS; 'at John Ross Mackie's Esq. By Paisley' substituted in a different hand. John Mackye (after 1755, Ross Mackye) (1707–97), of Palgowan, Kirkcudbright Stewartry; admitted as advocate, 1731; M.P.

3. The gaming club in Pall Mall founded in 1764; Craufurd was one of the original members.

4. Notably George Selwyn and Stephen Fox, later 2d Bn Holland.

5. Maria Catharina Haeck de Jong (1695–1779), m. 1 (1729) William Godolphin, styled M. of Blandford; m. 2 (1734) Sir William Wyndham, 3d Bt, 1695 (baptismal record kindly communicated by Dr J.E.A.L. Struick, Town Archivist, Gemeentelijke Archiefdienst Utrecht).

6. Lady Anne Wentworth (1713–97), sister and heir of HW's friend and correspondent, 2d E. of Strafford; m. (1733) William Conolly, of Castletown, co. Kildare (BERRY i. 56 n. 8). She lived at Twickenham.

7. In 1768 HW had given up his seat as M.P. for King's Lynn. He remained a close observer of the political scene, particularly during the war in America.

estry, I do not think I could talk over the manufacture of worsteds. Books I have almost done with too; at least read only such as nobody else would read—in short, my way of life is too insipid to entertain anybody but myself, and though I am always employed, I must say I think I have given up everything in the world, only to be at liberty to be very busy about the most errant trifles.

Well! I have made out half a letter with a history very like the journal in the *Spectator* of the man, the chief incidents of whose life were stroking his cat and walking to Hampstead.[8] Last night indeed I had an adventure that would make a great figure in such a narrative. *You* may be enjoying bright suns and serene horizons under the Pole,[9] but in this dismal southern region it has rained for this month without interruption. Lady Browne[10] and I dined as usually on Sundays with Lady Blandford.[11] Our gentle Thames was swelled in the morning to a very respectable magnitude, and we had thought of returning by Kew Bridge—however I persuaded her to try if we could not ferry,[12] and when we came to the foot of the hill, the bargemen told us the water was sunk. We embarked, and had four men to push the ferry. The night was very dark, for though the moon was up, we could neither see her nor she us. The bargemen were drunk, the poles would scarce reach the bottom, and in five minutes, the rapidity of the current turned the barge round, and in an instant we were at Isleworth. The drunkenest of the men cried out, 'She is gone! she is lost!' meaning they had lost the management. Lady Browne fell into an agony, began screaming and praying to Jesus and every land and water god and goddess, and I who expected not to stop till we should run against Kew Bridge, was contriving how I should get home, or what was worse, whether I must not step into some mud up to my middle, be wet through, and get the gout. With much ado they recovered the barge and turned it—but then we ran against the piles of the new bridge,[13] which startled the horses who began kicking. My Phillis's terrors increased, and I thought every minute she would have

8. *Spectator* No. 317; no cat is mentioned. See Ossory ii. 464.

9. That is, in Scotland.

10. Frances Sheldon (1714–90), m. 1 (1736) Henry Fermor; m. 2 Sir George Browne, 3d Bt, 1751. She lived at Twickenham (More 287 n. 7).

11. At her country house at East Sheen, Surrey, in the vicinity of Richmond Park (Daniel Lysons, *The Environs of London,*

1792–6, i. 388; More 189). The company at Lady Blandford's included Lady Mary Coke, Lady Howe, and Mrs Howe; for Lady Mary's account of the party, see her journal quoted ibid. 180.

12. From Richmond to Twickenham.

13. Then under construction to take the place of the ferry; see Conway iii. 176 n. 12.

begun confession—Thank you, you need not be uneasy; in ten minutes we landed very safely,[14] and if we had been drowned, I am too exact not to have dated my letter from the bottom of the Thames—There! there's a letter, I think you would not want to read such another, even if written to somebody else.

Yours ever

H. W.

PS. Pontdeyvelde[15] is dead, and our friend[16] fancies she is more sorry, than she fancied she should be: but it will make a vacuum in her room rather than in her entertainment.

Arlington Street, Sept. 29.

This letter, which should have gone two days ago, but I had no direction, will come untimely, for you will be up to the ears in your canvass,[17] as the Parliament is to be dissolved the day after tomorrow.[18]

14. HW also describes this episode in his letter to Conway 27 Sept. (ibid. iii. 187).

15. See *ante* 26 Dec. 1770, n. 42. Pont-de-Veyle died at Paris 3 Sept. 1774.

16. Mme du Deffand. See her letter to HW 4 Sept. 1774 (DU DEFFAND iv. 91).

17. According to a previous agreement with Craufurd's father, William McDowall (M.P. for Renfrewshire 1768–74) supported Craufurd in the 1774 general election; the opposing candidate, John Shaw Stewart, withdrew before polling day (Namier and Brooke i. 494). See following note.

18. Parliament was dissolved 30 Sept. (*Journals of the House of Commons* xxxv. 3). Craufurd was elected M.P. for Renfrewshire on 24 Oct. without opposition.

To Isaac Reed,[1] Friday 11 November 1774

Printed from the MS now WSL. First printed, Cunningham ix. 491–2. Reprinted, Toynbee ix. 88–9. The MS was formerly in the possession of Mrs Erskine (a great-niece of HW's deputy, Grosvenor Bedford), of Milton Lodge, Gillingham, Dorset; sold Sotheby's 15 Nov. 1932 (property of Mrs Erskine), lot 494, to Maggs for WSL.

Endorsed by Reed: 11 November 1774 Mr Walpole.

Address: To Mr I. R. to be left at the Chapter Coffee House,[2] London. *Postmark:* 12 NO.

Strawberry Hill, Nov. 11, 1774.

Sir,

THOUGH you have not been so good as to let me know to whom I am so much obliged,[3] yet I am very glad you have given me an opportunity at least of thanking you. Had I sooner known how, I should have saved you some trouble, as several of the notices you have sent me, had already come to my knowledge, and are actually inserted in a new edition of my *Catalogue*,[4] which has been long printed,[5] though from some other reasons not yet published.[6] Indeed, Sir, I am ashamed that you should have thrown away so much time upon a work that deserved it so little, and which I am sorry I cannot now make more perfect by your assistance, it being printed with other trifles of my own,[7] and consequently I should be obliged to throw away the whole edition, if I altered it; and that is too late to do at my time of life, subject as I am to long confinements from the gout: a reflection that has made me give over all thoughts of troubling the public any more, which has been too indulgent to me already.

If you were inclined to be still more kind to me, it would be by letting me have the pleasure of knowing to whom I am so much in-

---

1. (1742–1807), scholar and antiquary.

2. On the west corner of Paul's Alley, Paternoster Row. It was known particularly as a meeting place of the London booksellers (H. B. Wheatley, *London Past and Present*, 1891, i. 350).

3. Reed's letter to HW, presumably signed only with his initials, is missing (see address in headnote).

4. *A Catalogue of the Royal and Noble Authors of England*, originally printed in 2 vols, SH, 1758, and included in the first volume of HW's *Works* in quarto, SH, 1770 (Hazen, *SH Bibl.* 33–7, 87–95).

5. The printing of the first volume of the quarto *Works* was probably completed early in 1770 (ibid. 89).

6. HW did not continue the quarto edition beyond vol. II, which was left incomplete. See *post* 30 Aug. 1792.

7. For the contents of the first volume see Hazen, op. cit. 91.

debted. I shall not be in town to stay probably till after Christmas,[8] and then should be very glad to wait on you, or to see you in Arlington Street, to assure you [how] much I am Sir

Your obliged and obedient humble servant

Hor. Walpole

To John Craufurd, Monday 2 January 1775

Printed from the MS now wsl. First printed, Cunningham vi. 165–6. Reprinted, Toynbee ix. 120–1. For the history of the MS see *ante* 6 March 1766.

Address: To John Craufurd, Esq. at Earl Spencer's at Althorp, Northamptonsh[ire]. *Postmark:* 3 IA. EK.

Arlington Street, Jan. 2, 1775.

I WAS not surprised, but rather the more grateful because I was not surprised, at your kind letter.[1] I am totally recovered excepting my right hand;[2] I walk without a stick; nay am told look as well as ever I did, which never could be a compliment to me in any part of my life. However, as I advance with dignity, I shall descend to the first floor but tomorrow, finding it in vain to wait till I am *sent for;* a mishap that has befallen greater folk than me. Still I am content with being confined but five weeks instead of five months; and though it will make the faculty more violent than ever against the bootikins, me at least they shall not persuade out of them;[3] and though they will be ready to poison me for speaking the truth, it shall not be by any of their own potions.

---

8. HW went to town on the death (20 Nov.) of Joseph Tullie, his deputy in the Exchequer (Ossory i. 217). He was again in Arlington Street on 26 Nov. (Conway iii. 220) and apparently remained there for the rest of the year, following an attack of gout.

---

1. Missing.

2. HW wrote Mann 9 Jan. 1775: 'I am quite recovered of the gout, except in the hand I write with. . . . The bootikins have proved themselves to demonstration. I had the gout in both hands, both feet, both elbows, and one wrist, and yet could walk without a stick in less than a month, and have been abroad twice in less than five weeks. It came in each part as rapidly as it could, and went away so too; and though I had some acute pain, much less in quantity than in any fit these ten years' (Mann viii. 70).

3. 'The bootikins do not cure the gout, but if they defer it, lessen it, shorten it, who would not wear them? . . . the physicians and apothecaries, who began by recommending them, now, finding they are a specific, cry them down' (ibid. viii. 70–1).

I hope you have been diverted with your tour,[4] and I am sure you are always the better for being diverted. I have received a charming present, and more charming verses, from Ampthill.[5] You shall see both at your return, if you have not already seen them.

Tuesday 3d.

Cybèle va descendre[6]—that is, an old woman—or an old man, which is the same thing—is come downstairs, and writes to you with her own hand,[7] which goddesses never do, but when they assume a mortal shape; and then billets-doux and all the rest follow of course. Indeed there is more of the goddess than the woman in my partiality for you. I doubt your *petite santé* would tempt no ancient dame to choose you for her Atys,[8] though a divinity who would know the goodness of your heart, would prefer you to Hercules. All this rigmarole only to tell you I am much better and

Very sincerely yours

H. WALPOLE

4. Craufurd was visiting Lord and Lady Spencer at Althorp (see address in headnote). HW learned on 12 Jan. that Craufurd had gout while at Althorp; see DU DEFFAND iv. 137.

5. Ampthill Park, Beds, the seat of Lord and Lady Ossory. Lady Ossory had sent HW a waistcoat embroidered by herself; the accompanying verses were apparently an ode to 'Friendship.' HW offers effusive thanks for 'a shining vest, and . . . a fair epistle, written in celestial characters' in his letter to her 1 Jan. (OSSORY i. 219–20).

6. 'Allons, allons, accourez tous,
    Cybèle va descendre.'
These are the opening lines (Act I, Scenes

i, ii, iii) of *Atys,* a tragic opera with words by Philippe Quinault and music by Jean-Baptiste de Lulli, first performed in 1676. *Atys* was one of Mme du Deffand's favourite operas (DU DEFFAND i. 119), but HW may have known these lines from Mme de Sévigné's letter to Mme de Grignan 6 Aug. 1677, in which they are quoted.

7. The portion of the letter dated 'Tuesday 3d' is in HW's hand; the earlier portion is in the hand of HW's secretary, Thomas Kirgate. See *post* 12 Jan. 1775.

8. In Greek legend, Atys was a handsome shepherd with whom the Phrygian goddess Cybele fell in love.

THOMAS KIRGATE,

Printer at Strawberry-Hill.

With a View of the Printing House.

Published in 1798.

THOMAS KIRGATE, AFTER SILVESTER HARDING

To Lord Hardwicke, Thursday 12 January 1775

Printed from a copy (now WSL) sent in 1900 to Paget Toynbee by George Pritchard, of Poole, Dorset, who then owned the MS. First printed, Toynbee ix. 128–30. The MS was sold Sotheby's 25 March 1904 (Autograph Letters and Historical Documents Sale), lot 118 (with another letter), to Maggs; offered by them, Cat. No. 203 (1904), lot 844; later acquired by Alvin J. Scheuer, of New York City; not further traced.

Arlington Street, Jan. 12th 1775.

My Lord,

THOUGH I was so unfortunate as to be able to send your Lordship an immediate answer[1] to the honour you offered me,[2] yet, having company[3] with me, I could not do it in a manner satisfactory to myself, as I had not time to state to your Lordship the particular reasons I have for declining what would do so much credit to my press and me, as printing anything furnished by your Lordship.[4]

I will not trouble you, my Lord, with recapitulating many private reasons that have induced me to put a stop to my press, which has not worked in a manner for these two years.[5] I even two months ago gave my printer[6] warning to provide for himself, having no farther use for him: and though it is true that I have retained him since, by the occasion I had for him as a secretary to write my letters during the incapacity of my hand in the gout,[7] yet it is with no present

1. Missing.
2. Hardwicke had asked HW to reprint at the SH Press the *Letters from and to Sir Dudley Carleton, Knight, during his Embassy in Holland*, first issued by Hardwicke in a privately printed edition in 1757. HW commented on the request in his letter to Cole 22 Aug. 1778: 'He solicited me to reprint his Boeotian volume of Sir Dudley Carleton's papers, for which he had two motives. The first he inherited from his father, the desire of saving money. . . . The second inducement was, that the rarity of my editions makes them valuable, and though I cannot make men read dull books, I can make them purchase them' (COLE ii. 109). See MASON ii. 183.
3. Not identified.
4. Despite HW's refusal, Hardwicke issued a second edition of the Carleton let-

ters which appeared towards the end of 1775. Only fifty copies were printed; HW's copy is Hazen, *Cat. of HW's Lib.*, No. 3166. In this edition Hardwicke answered HW's criticism of the letters in *Royal and Noble Authors*; see COLE i. 379–80. HW wrote Mason 18 Feb. 1776: 'I have received many indirect little mischiefs from the Earl [of Hardwicke], who has of late courted me as much, and I have been civil to him' (MASON i. 246).
5. HW deliberately makes no mention of the *Description of SH*, which was printed (100 copies) intermittently in 1773–4 (see following letter). *Miscellaneous Antiquities*, Nos 1 and 2, were completed in Dec. 1772 (Hazen, *SH Bibl.* 103). See *ante* 29 July 1773, n. 5.
6. Thomas Kirgate (1734–1810).
7. See previous letter.

thoughts of employing him again in his profession.[8] But indeed the insurmountable difficulty I have in gratifying myself with the flattering employment of printing for your Lordship, is this (and one material cause of my suspending my press). I have been earnestly requested by a near relation to print a work,[9] which was not agreeable to me to print, though offensive to nobody; and the chief argument I urged was the bulk of it. Now your Lordship's candour I am sure will do me the justice to allow, that I deprive myself of one of my chief pleasures, that of contributing to the publication of historic pieces, when I deny myself the satisfaction of serving you in that light. I could not print them without exposing myself to a rupture with one of my own family. I trust your Lordship will not mention this, as I should not have uttered it, but to prove my inability of obeying you; for I could not content myself with pleading to you, my Lord, what has been another cause of my interrupting my press, the laziness and indifference to even literary amusements, which age and the gout have brought upon me. You would have tempted me, my Lord, to renew them, if such strong motives did not restrain me.

I beg to know what the *Catalogue*[10] is your Lordship means. I conclude the *Anecdotes of Painting;* but I would not send them till I was sure.

The print of Monsieur de Choiseul[11] is a general, but very imperfect likeness; with nothing of the countenance, and as little of his vivacity; the person is very much his. The present King of France is exceedingly like, my Lord; and like the Duke of Grafton too, as you have heard. I can scarce discover the least distant resemblance to the Queen,[12] who is as strangely like the present Duchess of Grafton[13] though infinitely better.[14]

8. HW continued to employ Kirgate as his printer and secretary until his death in 1797.

9. The 'near relation' was probably Lord Hertford and the 'work' the 'vast quantities of letters and state papers of the two Lords Conway, Secretaries of State,' that HW discovered in 1758 at Ragley Hall, the seat of his cousin, Lord Hertford (Chute 104). HW planned to print 'some volumes of what is very curious and valuable' but never did (ibid.).

10. See following letter, n. 1.

11. The Duc de Choiseul. There are numerous engraved portraits of Choiseul; it is not clear which one HW refers to.

12. Marie-Antoinette (1755–93), m. (1770) Louis (XVI), Dauphin, K. of France, 1774.

13. Elizabeth Wrottesley (1745–1822), m. (1769), as his second wife, Augustus Henry Fitzroy (1735–1811), 3d D. of Grafton, 1757.

14. HW first saw Marie-Antoinette in Paris in July 1771. When he saw her again in Aug. 1775, he decided that she no longer bore a resemblance to the Duchess of Grafton. See Ossory i. 254, where the 'English Duchess' is erroneously identified as Lady Ossory, who was formerly married to the Duke of Grafton.

I cannot at present, my Lord, recollect where there is any miniature or wax cast of my father, that is to be parted with;[15] if I can
hear of any such thing your Lordship shall know.

I have the honour to be

> With great respect
>> My Lord
>>> Your Lordship's most obedient humble servant
>>>> Hor. Walpole

To Lord Hardwicke, mid-January 1775

Printed for the first time from the MS now WSL, acquired in June 1941 from
a Buckinghamshire family, through the good offices of John E. Hodgson; its
earlier history is not known.

Dated approximately by the reference to 'my catalogue,' which is mentioned
ante 12 Jan. 1775.

Address: To the Earl of Hardwicke in St James's Square.

YOUR Lordship shall certainly command my catalogue,[1] though
indeed I neither thought it was known of, nor intended it
should be yet, for it is both very imperfect and very faulty. I printed
a very few as a sample,[2] intending to have prints to it.[3] Mr Lort[4] saw
the specimen and begged one,[5] but I desired it might be a secret, as
I never design it should be published, but meant it for presents. Your
Lordship should see it now, but I have not one in town; and I hope
soon to show it you myself.

I have the book[6] your Lordship mentions, but indeed had not pa-

---

15. HW's older brother, Sir Edward
Walpole, owned a wax portrait medallion
of Sir Robert Walpole; it is now WSL (illustrated in W. S. Lewis, *Horace Walpole*,
New York, 1961, pl. 68, facing p. 188).

1. *A Description of the Villa of Horace
Walpole . . . at Strawberry Hill*, SH, 1774
(Hazen, *SH Bibl.* 107–10). 'I have finished
the catalogue of my collection. . . . I propose in time to have plates of my house
added to the catalogue, yet I cannot afford them unless by degrees' (HW to Cole
21 July 1774, COLE i. 338).

2. Six copies on large paper, 100 copies
in the whole edition (Hazen, loc. cit.).

3. The plates, 27 in all, were prepared
at intervals during the next few years
(ibid.).

4. Rev. Michael Lort, HW's correspondent (*ante* 24 Jan. 1760, n. 1).

5. Presumably on 30 Oct. 1774, when
William Cole was visiting HW at SH.
Cole's account of his visit records that 'On
Sunday, Mr Lort, Fellow of Trinity Col-
lege, came over, as we had agreed, to din-
ner, and stayed the evening' (COLE ii. 375).
On the previous day, the 29th, HW gave
Cole one of the six large-paper copies
(*Journal of the Printing-Office* 60).

6. Not identified.

tience to read it. One must be younger than I am I doubt to have pleasure in foreign politics—I am so tired of them at home that I scarce ever read anything of the sort.

I am your Lordship's
Most obedient etc.

H. Walpole

To Robert Jephson,[1] Friday 24 February 1775

Printed from the MS copy in Thomas Kirgate's hand, now wsl. First printed, *Works* ii. 305–7. Reprinted, Toynbee *Supp.* i. 245–7. The MS copy (along with two others to Jephson in Feb. 1775, comprising HW's 'Thoughts on Tragedy') descended in the Waldegrave family to the 12th Earl Waldegrave, from whom wsl acquired it in 1948. The original letters are missing.

Endorsed by HW: Thoughts on Tragedy: in three letters to Rob. Jephson Esq. (to precede the Thoughts on Comedy).[2]

Arlington Street, Feb. 24, 1775.[3]

AFTER the very great and general applause given to *Braganza*,[4] my admiration of it, Sir, can be of little value, though very precious to me, as it has procured me so very obliging, and forgive my saying, far too flattering, a mark of attention from you.[5] The pleasure I once had of being acquainted with you,[6] naturally attracted my expectation from your play. It is but true to say, that it far exceeded it.[7] I did not expect that a first production in a way in which I did not know you, would prove the work of a master poet. Even on hearing the three first acts,[8] I was struck, not only with the

---

1. (1736–1803), Irish poet and dramatist.

2. HW's 'Thoughts on Tragedy: in three letters to Robert Jephson, Esq.' is printed in *Works* ii. 305–14; it precedes his 'Thoughts on Comedy; Written in 1775 and 1776' (ibid. ii. 315–22).

3. The date appears in Kirgate's hand at the end of the letter; HW also added the date at the beginning.

4. Jephson's tragedy, first performed at Drury Lane 17 Feb. 1775 (*London Stage* Pt IV, iii. 1869–70). For HW's account of the first-night audience's tumultuous reception, and his opinion of the play's merits and defects, see Mason i. 176–8.

5. Presumably a (missing) letter, thanking HW for 'having facilitated and has-

tened *Braganza*'s appearance on the stage' and for contributing the epilogue (see below).

6. In her letter to HW 20 Jan. 1766, Lady Hertford refers to Jephson as 'a person I believe you know, at least from character' (Conway iii. 49).

7. 'Mr Jepson's tragedy, which I concluded would not answer all I had heard of it, exceeded my expectations infinitely' (HW to Lady Ossory 1 Feb. 1775, Ossory i. 232–3).

8. At Mrs Vesey's on 29 Jan. HW attended her party 'to hear a Mr Tig-he, repeat parts of Mr Jepson's tragedy' (HW to Lady Ossory 19 Jan. 1775, ibid. i. 229).

language, metaphors and similes, which are as new, as noble and beautiful, but with the modulation of the numbers. Your ear, Sir, is as perfect as your images, and no poet we have, excels you in harmony. It enchanted me so much, that it had just the contrary effect from what it ought to have had; for, forgetting how bad a figure I should make by appearing in company with such verses, I could not refuse Mr Tighe's[9] request of writing an epilogue,[10] though I never was a poet, and have done writing—but in excuse, I must say, I complied, only because an epilogue was immediately wanted. You have by this time, I fear, Sir, seen it in the newspapers:[11] it was written in one evening; I knew it was not only bad, but most unworthy of such a play; and when I heard it spoken,[12] though pronounced better than it deserved, I thought I never heard, to any play, a flatter epilogue. I beg your pardon, Sir; I am ashamed of it—the prologue[13] is really a very fine one—but you wanted no assistance, no props; the immense applause which you drew from the audience, was owing to yourself alone. Mrs Yates[14] and Mr Smith[15] played well, not quite equally to their parts—Two other principal parts[16] were so indifferently performed, that your own merit appeared the greater; and I will venture to say, that Braganza will always charm more when read,[17] than when seen; for I doubt there never will be found a whole set of actors together, who can do it full justice. For my own part, though so discontent with my epilogue, I shall always be proud of having facilitated and hastened Braganza's appearance on the stage, by the zeal with which I solicited the licence,[18] and which I hope atones

9. Edward Tighe (fl. 1759–97), lawyer; M.P. (Ireland); friend of Jephson (ibid. i. 229 n. 36).

10. HW composed the epilogue before 29 Jan. (MASON i. 175–6). He wrote Lady Ossory 1 Feb. that his Irish friends, Sir Charles and Lady Bingham, had 'overpersuaded' him to write the epilogue: 'They gave me the subject, which I have executed miserably' (OSSORY i. 233). The epilogue is printed in Works iv. 400–1.

11. It appeared (without HW's name) in the London Chronicle 21–23 Feb., xxxvii. 180.

12. By Mrs Yates, who had the leading rôle of Louisa, Duchess of Braganza, in the play. The London Chronicle 16–18 Feb., xxxvii. 167, called HW's lines 'a singsong kind of epilogue.'

13. By Arthur Murphy (1727–1805).

14. Mary Ann Graham (1728–87), m. (ca 1756) Richard Yates.

15. William Smith (ca 1739–1819), called 'Gentleman' Smith. He played the rôle of Velasquez, minister of Spain.

16. The Duke of Braganza, played by Samuel Reddish (1735–85); and Almada, played by James Aickin (or Aikin) (ca 1735–1803). 'Reddish was pitiful and whining in the Duke; Aikin ridiculous in the first old conspirator' (HW to Mason 18 Feb. 1775, MASON i. 177).

17. The play was published 27 Feb. (Public Adv. 23, 27 Feb.). HW's copy, now wsl, is Hazen, Cat. of HW's Lib., No. 1810:23:9.

18. The lord chamberlain, who had responsibility for licensing all new plays, was HW's cousin, Lord Hertford.

for my miscarriage in the other. I am indifferent to fame on my own account, but glory in having served yours.

My self-condemnation ought to deter me, from obeying your further commands, however graciously laid on me. Can you want counsel, Sir, who have produced *Braganza?* Or am I fit to give counsel, who have written a tragedy[19] that never can appear on any stage?[20] and who am not only sensible of the intrinsic fault in the choice of the subject, but of many others, that happily will not come into question?

It is true, I have thought often on the subject, though not of late till I saw your tragedy. I was very attentive to that, and observed what parts made impression on the audience,[21] and which did not; for every part even of so beautiful a composition, and so faultless in the poetry, could not have equal effect on a vast audience, where the greater part could not be judges, but from the operation on their passions. My letter, Sir, is already too long, nor can I delay thanking you, till I have time to recollect my thoughts. I shall certainly never pretend to give you instruction; but if either in the future choice of a subject, or in any observations which I have made on the construction of tragedies, I can furnish you with any hints, (for I certainly do not mean to write a treatise, or even methodize my thoughts) I will so far obey you, as to lay them before you[22]—though I own I wish rather to see you perform, what I am sure I can give no advice upon, as I hold a good comedy the chef [d']œuvre of human genius, I wish, I say, you would try comedy[23]—though you will be unpardonable too if you neglect tragedy, for which you have so marked a vocation.

I have the honour to be, Sir, with the greatest respect, esteem and admiration,

Your most obedient humble servant,

Hor. Walpole[24]

---

19. *The Mysterious Mother.*
20. Because of the play's theme of incest.
21. See n. 4 above.

22. See the following two letters.
23. In his letter to Jephson *post* 13 July 1777, HW again urges him to 'try comedy.'
24. The signature is in HW's hand.

To Robert Jephson, late February 1775

Printed from the MS copy in Thomas Kirgate's hand, now WSL. First printed, *Works* ii. 307–10. Reprinted, Toynbee *Supp.* i. 248–52. For the history of the MS copy see *ante* 24 Feb. 1775. The original letter is missing.

Dated approximately by the previous letter and HW's 'Short Notes' *sub* Feb. 1775 (GRAY i. 49).

Endorsed by HW: 2.

Sir,

IN consequence of your orders and of my own promise,[1] I will venture to lay before you, not advice, but some indigested thoughts on subjects for tragedy, and on the composition of one, rather for the sake of talking with you on a matter agreeable to us both, than to dictate on what I have but once attempted, and never sufficiently studied; indeed not at all till I had executed some part of my piece.

I am ill-qualified, Sir, to recommend a subject to you; since, though I confess I thought I had found some talent in myself for tragedy (after having vainly tried at comedy to which I was more inclined) I have never been able to find a second story,[2] that pleased me, at least, that touched me enough to pursue it. My wish was to work on that of Sir Thomas More—but the difficulties were various and too great. In the first place, it would not be painting him, to omit his characteristic pleasantry. Yet who but Shakespeare could render mirth pathetic? His exquisite scene of the gravediggers[3] is an instance of that magic and creative power—now so overwhelmed by the ignorance of French criticism,[4] that it is acted no more![5]—and

1. See previous letter.

2. Concerning the sources for the story used by HW in *The Mysterious Mother* see the 'Postscript,' *Works* i. 125–6; CHATTERTON 165; CONWAY iii. 102–3.

3. *Hamlet* V. i. HW greatly admired this scene; see his Preface to the second edition of *The Castle of Otranto, Works* ii. 8.

4. That is, the criticism of Voltaire. He had first expressed his scorn of the gravediggers' scene in Letter XVIII ('Sur la tragédie') of the *Lettres philosophiques*, 1734 (*Œuvres complètes de Voltaire*, ed. L.-E.-D. Moland, 1877–85, xxii. 149); he returned to it in his *Dissertation sur la tragédie ancienne et moderne*, 1748 (ibid.

iv. 502), and mentioned it again in the *Appel à toutes les nations de l'Europe*, 1761 (ibid. xxiv. 199).

5. In David Garrick's altered version of *Hamlet*, first performed at Drury Lane 18 Dec. 1772, the gravediggers' scene was entirely omitted; the alteration was a popular success and held the stage for eight years (*London Stage* Pt IV, iii. 1680; G. W. Stone, Jr, 'Garrick's Long Lost Alteration of *Hamlet*,' *Publications of the Modern Language Assoc.*, 1934, xlix. 890–921). Garrick wrote Pierre-Antoine de Laplace 3 Jan. 1773: 'I have ventured to alter *Hamlet*, and have greatly succeeded; I have destroyed the grave diggers, (those favourites of the people) and almost all of

would not such barbarous blunders stifle genius itself? Not to miscarry in an imitation of Shakespeare, would be to be Shakespeare—It would be still meritorious to aim at it. But there are other difficulties: one must pass censure on Sir Thomas's bigotry, or draw him as a martyr to a ridiculous worship without censuring that worship, for even an oblique censure on it out of the mouth of one of his *reformed* persecutors would flatten the glory of his martyrdom.—These two difficulties combined, made me drop all thoughts of that story, though so fertile of great and bold situations. Anne Boleyn[6] would please me, but Henry VIII is too perfectly drawn by Shakespeare to admit a second and much weaker edition.

There is one subject, a very favourite one with me, and yet which I alone was accidentally prevented from meddling with, Don Carlos. Otway, the next to Shakespeare in boldness, though only next but one in strokes of nature in my opinion, as I prefer the tragic scenes in *The Fatal Marriage*[7] and *Oroonoko*[8] to *Venice Preserved*[9] and *The Orphan*,[10] has miscarried woefully in *Don Carlos*.[11] Sir Charles Williams,[12] who had long intended to write a tragedy on that subject, and who I believe had no tragic powers, never set about it till he was mad[13]—and madness did not assist him as it did Lee;[14] nor allowed him to finish it. Yet how many capital ingredients in that story! Tenderness, cruelty, heroism, policy, pity, terror! The impetuous passions of the Prince, the corrected and cooler fondness and virtue of

the 5th Act—it was a bold deed, but the event has answered my most sanguine expectation' (*The Letters of David Garrick*, ed. D. M. Little and G. M. Kahrl, Cambridge, Mass., 1963, ii. 840). See Appendix 3, Mason ii. 368–70.

6. (1507–36), Henry VIII's second wife.

7. By Thomas Southerne (1660–1746), first performed at Drury Lane in 1694. It was based on Aphra Behn's novel *The Nun*.

8. By Southerne, first performed at Drury Lane in 1695; based on Mrs Behn's tale of the same name. 'There are parts of *Oroonoko* and *The Fatal Marriage* worthy a disciple of Shakespeare' (HW to Jephson *post* 8 Nov. 1777).

9. By Thomas Otway (1652–85), first performed at the Dorset Garden Theatre in 1682.

10. By Otway, first performed at the Dorset Garden Theatre in 1680.

11. By Otway, first performed at the Dorset Garden Theatre in 1676.

12. Sir Charles Hanbury Williams (*ante* 2 Sept. 1755, n. 2).

13. On his return from Russia in Feb. 1758, Williams appeared to be 'disordered in his senses' and was put under the care of Dr Battie. He recovered in a few weeks, but relapsed in December and was confined until his death 2 Nov. 1759 (Selwyn 322; Ossory ii. 78 n. 12).

14. Nathaniel Lee (ca 1648–92), dramatist. Lee became insane and was confined in Bethlehem Hospital, London, 1684–9. According to Tom Brown, he composed a play of twenty-five acts during his confinement (R. G. Ham, *Otway and Lee*, New Haven, 1931, pp. 209–12, 218). His two plays that were performed on the stage after his release from Bedlam were works that he had written before his insanity.

the Queen, the King's dark and cruel vengeance, different shades of policy in Rui Gomez, policy and art with franker passions in the Duchess of Eboli, how many contrasts—and what helps from the religion and history of the times or even of the preceding reign!—In short, Sir, I see nothing against it but the notoriety of the story, which I think always disadvantageous as it prevents surprise, though a known story saves the author some details—which if exhibited, as the French practice, by telling you all the preceding circumstances in the first scene, appear to me a greater crime than any of the improprieties that Shakespeare has crowded into *The Winter Evening's Tale;* for novelty, however badly introduced, can never be so insipid, or more improbable, than two courtiers telling one another, what each must know more or less, though one of them may have been absent two or three years. Shakespeare's prologues are far more endurable.

Why I gave up this fruitful canvas, was merely because the passion is incestuous as is most unfortunately that of my *Mysterious Mother,* though at different points of time, and that of Carlos a pardonable and not disgusting one. I shall rejoice at having left it, if you will adopt it.

For all other subjects, I have said not one pleased me exactly. I think it would not be unadvisable to take any you like, changing the names and the country of the persons; which would prevent the audience being forestalled—though this is less an inducement to you, Sir, who have rendered the last act of *Braganza* the most interesting, though half the audience expected the catastrophe—not indeed so strikingly as you have made it touch them. Still as the *dénouement* is your own, and one of the finest *coups de théâtre* I ever met with, it proves that a known story wants some novelty; and I confess that in your most tender scenes, I felt less than I should have done, had I not foreknown the prosperous event.

Changing the persons and country is just the reverse of the bungling contrivance in *Le Comte de Warvic,*[15] where the author has grossly perverted a known story without amending it.

One art I think might be used, though a very difficult one, and yet I would not recommend it to you, Sir, if I did not think you

15. *Le Comte de Warwick,* a tragedy by Jean-François de la Harpe (1739–1803), first performed at Paris in 1763 (CONWAY ii. 276 n. 34). In his letter to Lord Hert- ford 29 Dec. 1763, HW comments on 'the preposterous perversion of history in so known a story' (ibid. ii. 277 and n. 36).

capable of employing it; and that is, *a very new and peculiar style.*
By fixing on some region of whose language we have little or no
idea, as of the Peruvians in the story of Atabalipa,[16] you might frame
a new diction, even out of English, that would have amazing effect,
and seem the only one the actors could properly use. It is much easier
to conceive this, than to give rules for it—but Milton certainly made
a new English language, and Shakespeare, always greater than any
man, has actually formed a style for Caliban, that could suit no
other kind of being. Dryden, vast as his genius was, tried the same
thing more than once, but failed. He wanted to conceive how the
Mexicans must have felt the miracles of ships, and gunpowder, etc.
imported by the Europeans[17]—he wrote most harmoniously for
them; and it might be poetry, but was not nature. He miscarried
still more, when he wanted to forget all he had learned by eyesight,
and to think for blind Emmeline[18]—he makes her talk nonsense—
when she supposes her lover's[19] face is of *soft black gold,*[20] it conveys
no idea at all. When blind Professor Sanderson[21] said, he supposed
scarlet was like the sound of a trumpet, it proved he had been told
that scarlet was the most vivid of colours, but showed he had no[t]
otherwise an idea of it.

The religion of the Peruvians, their demons, which I would allow
to be real existencies, oracles and prophecies foretelling their ruin
and the arrival of strangers, would add great decoration. I love decorations whenever they produce unexpected *coups de théâtre*—In
short, we want new channels for tragedy, and still more for poetry.
You have the seeds, Sir; sow them where you will, they will grow.
Had I your genius, I would hazard a *future* American story—Suppose
empires to be founded there—give them new customs, new manners
—but I grow visionary[22]—and this letter is too long—I will try to

16. (Atahuallpa) (ca 1502–33), the last
ruler of the Incas of Peru, executed by
Francisco Pizarro. See MASON ii. 102 n. 19.

17. HW refers to *The Indian Emperour;
or, The Conquest of Mexico by the Span-
iards,* first performed in 1665.

18. The daughter of Conon, Duke of
Cornwall, in *King Arthur; or, The British
Worthy,* first performed in 1691.

19. King Arthur.

20. *King Arthur* II. ii:
   Why then, since gold is hard, and yet
   is precious,
   His face must all be made of soft,
   black gold.

21. Nicholas Sanderson (or Saunderson)
(1683–1739), LL.D., Lucasian Professor of
Mathematics at Cambridge 1711–39; blind
from infancy (GRAY i. 6 n. 22). As an undergraduate, HW attended his lectures for
a brief period.

22. 'I have many visions about that
country, and fancy I see twenty empires
and republics forming upon vast scales
over all that continent, which is growing
too mighty to be kept in subjection to
half a dozen exhausted nations in Europe'
(HW to Mann 6 May 1770, MANN vii. 209–
10).

have more common sense in the next,²³ not having left enough room
in this to tell you how much I am

Your obedient servant

H[or.] W[alpole]²⁴

To Robert Jephson, late February 1775 *bis*

Printed from the MS copy in Thomas Kirgate's hand, now wsl. First printed,
Works ii. 310–14. Reprinted, Toynbee *Supp.* i. 252–7; *A Selection of the Let-
ters of Horace Walpole*, ed. W. S. Lewis, 1926, ii. 270–6; *Letters of Horace
Walpole*, ed. W. S. Lewis, introd. R. W. Ketton-Cremer, 1951, pp. 170–4; *Se-
lected Letters of Horace Walpole*, ed. W. S. Lewis, New Haven, 1973. pp. 191–5.
For the history of the MS copy see *ante* 24 Feb. 1775. The original letter is
missing.
Dated approximately by the previous letter.
Endorsed by HW: 3.

YOU have drawn more trouble on yourself, Sir, than you expected;
and would probably excuse my not performing the rest of my
promise: but though I look upon myself as engaged to send you my
thoughts, you are neither bound to answer them, nor regard them.
They very likely are not new, and it is presumption in me to send
hints to a much abler writer than myself. I can only plead in apology,
that I interest myself in your fame; and as you are the only man
capable of restoring and improving our stage, I really mean no more
than to exhort and lead you on to make use of your great talents.

I have told you, as is true, that I am no poet. It is as true, that
you are a genuine one, and therefore I shall not say one word on
that head. For the construction of a drama, it is mechanic, though
much depends on it. A bystander may be a good director at least,
for mechanism certainly is independent of, though easily possessed
by, a genius. Banks¹ never wrote six tolerable lines, yet disposed his
fable with so much address, that I think three plays have been constructed on his plot of *The Earl of Essex*,² not one of which is much

---

23. See following letter.
24. The initials are in HW's hand.

---

1. John Banks (ca 1653–1706), dramatist
(Banks, *The Unhappy Favourite or The
Earl of Essex*, ed. T. M. H. Blair, New
York, 1939, pp. 5–6).
2. *The Unhappy Favourite; or, The*

Earl of Essex, first performed at Drury
Lane, probably in 1681. The three plays
that were based on Banks's tragedy were
James Ralph's *The Fall of the Earl of
Essex* (first performed in Goodman's
Fields in 1731), Henry Brooke's *The Earl
of Essex* (Smock Alley Theatre, Dublin,
1750; Drury Lane, 1761), and Henry

better than the original. The disposition is the next step to the choice of a subject, on which I have said enough in a former letter.[3] A genius can surmount defects in both: if there is art in *Othello,* and *Macbeth,* it seems to have been by chance, for Shakespeare certainly took no pains to adjust a plan, and in his historic plays, seems to have turned Hollinshed[4] and Stowe[5] into verse and scenes as fast as he could write, though every now and then his divine genius flashed upon particular scenes and made them immortal, as in his *King John,* where nature itself has stamped the scenes of Constance, Arthur, and Hubert, with her own impression, though the rest is as defective as possible. He seems to recall the Mahometan idea of lunatics, who are sometimes inspired, oftener changelings. Yet what signifies all his rubbish? He has scenes and even speeches, that are infinitely superior to all the correct elegance of Racine. I had rather have written the two speeches of Lady Percy, in the second part of *Henry IV*[6] than all Voltaire, though I admire the latter infinitely, especially in *Alzire, Mahomet,* and *Sémiramis.* Indeed when I think over all the great authors of the Greeks, Romans, Italians, French, and English, and I know no other languages, I set Shakespeare first and alone, and then begin anew.

Well, Sir, I give up Shakespeare's dramas, and yet prefer him to every man. Why? For his exquisite knowledge of the passions and nature. For his simplicity too, which he possesses too when most natural. Dr Johnson says he is bombast, whenever he attempts to be sublime;[7] but this is never true but when he aims at sublimity in the expression; the glaring fault of Johnson himself—but as simplicity is the grace of sublime, who possesses it like Shakespeare? Is not the

Him, wondrous him!

Jones's *The Earl of Essex* (Covent Garden, 1753) (ibid. [123]–7; *London Stage* Pt III, i. 113; Pt IV, i. 353, ii. 835).

3. *Ante* late Feb. 1775.

4. Raphael Holinshed (d. ?1580), whose *Chronicles* (1587 edn) provided Shakespeare with the basic source material for his ten English history plays and for *King Lear, Macbeth,* and *Cymbeline.*

5. John Stow (ca 1525–1605), whose *Chronicles of England,* 1580, was used by Shakespeare in writing the first and second parts of *Henry IV.*

6. II. iii. 9–45, 53–61.

7. HW perhaps has in mind a passage from Johnson's *Preface to Shakespeare,* 1765: 'He knew how he should most please; and whether his practice is more agreeable to nature, or whether his example has prejudiced the nation, we still find that on our stage something must be done as well as said, and inactive declamation is very coldly heard, however musical or elegant, passionate or sublime' (*The Yale Edition of the Works of Samuel Johnson,* New Haven, 1958– , vii. ed. Arthur Sherbo, 84). See MASON ii. 370.

in Lady Percy's speech,[8] exquisitely sublime and pathetic too? He has another kind of sublime which no man ever possessed but he; and this is, his art in dignifying a vulgar or trivial expression. Voltaire is so grossly ignorant, and tasteless, as to condemn this,[9] as to condemn *the bare bodkin*[10]—but my enthusiasm for Shakespeare runs away with me.

I was speaking of the negligence of his construction. You have not that fault. I own I do not admire your choice of Braganza,[11] because in reality it admits of but two acts, the conspiracy and the revolution.[12] You have not only filled it out with the most beautiful dialogue, but made the interest rise, though the revolution has succeeded. I can never too much admire the appearance of the Friar,[13] which disarms Velasquez;[14] and yet you will be shocked to hear, that notwithstanding all I could say at the rehearsal,[15] I could not prevail to have Velasquez drop the dagger instantly, the only artful way of getting it out of his hand; for, as Lady Pembroke[16] observed, if he kept it two moments, he would recollect that it was the only way of preserving himself. But actors are not always judges. They persisted, for show sake, against my remonstrances, to exhibit the Duke and Duchess on a throne in the second act, which could not but make

8. 'And him—O wondrous him! / O miracle of men!' (*2 Henry IV* II. iii. 32–3).

9. HW possibly refers to Voltaire's scorn for the language of the gravediggers' scene in *Hamlet* (V. i); in his *Dissertation sur la tragédie ancienne et moderne*, 1748, Voltaire wrote that 'des fossoyeurs disent des quolibets dignes d'eux, en tenant dans leurs mains des têtes de morts; le prince Hamlet répond à leurs grossièretés abominables par des folies non moins dégoûtantes' (*Œuvres complètes de Voltaire*, ed. L.-E.-D. Moland, 1877–85, iv. 502). See previous letter, n. 4.

10. 'When he himself might his quietus make / With a bare bodkin' (*Hamlet* III. i. 75–6).

11. João (1604–56), son of Teodósio II, 7th D. of Bragança; King of Portugal 1640–56 as João IV. Jephson's play was largely based on historical events; see Ossory i. 233 n. 7.

12. 'From the defect in the subject, which calls for but two acts, several scenes languished' (HW to Mason 18 Feb. 1775, Mason i. 177–8).

13. Ramirez, played by John Hayman Packer (1730–1806).

14. See *ante* 24 Feb. 1775, n. 15. In the climax of the final scene (V. ii), the wounded Ramirez, whom Velasquez thinks he has killed, enters just as Velasquez is preparing to stab the Duchess of Braganza; the startled Velasquez is quickly seized.

15. HW wrote Mason 18 Feb.: 'I went to the rehearsal with all the eagerness of eighteen, and was delighted to feel myself so young again. The actors diverted me with their dissatisfactions and complaints, and, though I said all I could, committed some of what they called proprieties, that were very improper, as seating the Duke and Duchess on a high throne, in the second act, which made the spectators conclude that the revolution . . . had happened' (Mason i. 177).

16. Lady Elizabeth Spencer (1737–1831), m. (1756) Henry Herbert, 10th E. of Pembroke, 1750.

the audience conclude that the revolution had even then taken place.

If I could find a fault in your tragedy, Sir, it would be a want of more short speeches, of a sort of serious repartee, which gives great spirit.[17] But I think the most of what I have to say may be comprised in a recommendation of keeping the audience in suspense, and of touching the passions by the pathetic familiar. By the latter, I mean the study of Shakespeare's strokes of nature, which, soberly used, are alone superior to poetry, and with your ear may easily be made harmonious.

If there is any merit in *my* play,[18] I think it is in interrupting the spectator's fathoming the *whole* story till the last, and in making every scene tend to advance the catastrophe. These arts are mechanic, I confess; but at least they are as meritorious as the scrupulous delicacy of the French in observing, not only the unities, but a fantastic decorum,[19] that does not exist in nature, and which consequently reduce all their tragedies, wherever the scene may lie, to the manners of modern Paris. Corneille could be Roman, Racine never but French; and consequently, though a better poet, less natural and less various. Both indeed have prodigious merit. *Phèdre* is exquisite, *Britannicus*[20] admirable; and both excite pity and terror. Corneille is scarce ever tender, but always grand: yet never equal in a whole play to Racine. *Rodogune*,[21] which I greatly admire, is very defective, for the two princes are so equally good, and the two women so very bad, that they divide both our esteem and indignation. Yet I own, Racine, Corneille, and Voltaire, ought to rank before all our tragedians, but Shakespeare. *Jane Shore*[22] is perhaps our best play after his. I admire *All for Love*[23] very much; and some scenes in *Don Sebastian*,[24] and Young's *Revenge*.[25] *The Siege of Damascus*[26] is very pure—and *Phædra and Hippolitus*[27] fine poetry, though wanting all

17. 'He [Jephson] has another fault, which is a want of quick dialogue; there is scarce ever a short speech, so that it will please more on reading, than in representation' (HW to Mason 18 Feb., ibid. i. 178).

18. *The Mysterious Mother.*

19. HW makes similar comments on his play and on French tragedy in the 'Postscript' to *The Mysterious Mother*, *Works* i. 128–9.

20. Both plays by Racine.

21. By Corneille.

22. By Nicholas Rowe, first performed at Drury Lane in 1714.

23. By Dryden, first performed in 1677.

24. Also by Dryden, probably first performed in 1689.

25. *The Revenge*, by Edward Young (1683–1765), first performed at Drury Lane in 1721.

26. By John Hughes (1677–1720), first performed at Drury Lane in 1720.

27. By Edmund Smith (1672–1710), first performed at the Queen's Theatre, Haymarket, in 1707. It was modelled on Racine's *Phèdre*.

the nature of the original. We have few other tragedies of signal merit, though the four first acts of *The Fair Penitent*[28] are very good. It is strange that Dryden, who showed such a knowledge of nature in *The Cock and Fox,*[29] should have so very little in his plays—he could rather describe it than put it into action—I have said all this, Sir, only to point out to you what a field is open for you—and though so many subjects, almost all the known, are exhausted, nature is inexhaustible, and genius can achieve anything. We have a language far more energic, and more sonorous too than the French. Shakespeare could do what he would with it in its unpolished state. Milton gave it pomp from the Greek, and softness from the Italian; Waller now and then, here and there, gave it the elegance of the French. Dryden poured music into it; Prior gave it ease, and Gray used it masterly for either elegy or terror. Examine, Sir, the powers of a language you command, and let me again recommend to you a diction of your own,[30] at least in some one play. The majesty of *Paradise Lost* would have been less imposing, if it had been written in the style of the *Essay on Man*. Pope pleases, but never surprises; and astonishment is one of the springs of tragedy. *Coups de théâtre,* like the sublime one in *Mahomet,*[31] have infinite effect. The incantations[32] in *Macbeth,* that almost border on the burlesque, are still terrible. What French criticism can wound the ghosts of Hamlet[33] or Banquo?[34] Scorn rules, Sir, that cramp genius, and substitute delicacy to imagination in a barren language. Shall not we soar, because the French dare not rise from the ground?

You seem to possess the tender. The terrible is still more easy, at least I know to me. In all my tragedy, Adeliza[35] contents me the least. Contrasts, though mechanic too, are very striking; and though Molière was a comic writer, he might give lessons to a tragic—but

28. By Nicholas Rowe, probably first performed in 1703.

29. *The Cock and the Fox: or, The Tale of the Nun's Priest, from Chaucer,* in Dryden's *Fables Ancient and Modern,* 1700.

30. Mr Jephson followed this advice in his *Law of Lombardy*—but was not happy in his attempt (HW). See HW to Jephson *post* 17 Oct., 8 Nov. 1777.

31. In Act IV, Scene v, of Voltaire's *Mahomet,* Séide learns that Zopire, whom he has mortally wounded, is his father, and that Palmire, with whom he is in love, is his sister.

32. Of the three witches, the Weird Sisters (*Macbeth* IV. i).

33. In his *Dissertation sur la tragédie ancienne et moderne,* Voltaire admitted: 'Il faut avouer que, parmi les beautés qui étincellent au milieu de ces terribles extravagances, l'ombre du père d'Hamlet est un des coups de théâtre les plus frappants' (Moland, op. cit. iv. 502).

34. *Macbeth* III. iv.

35. The daughter of the Countess of Narbonne, the 'mysterious mother.' Adeliza was the incestuous offspring of the Countess and her son, Edmund.

I have passed all bounds; and yet shall be glad if you can cull one useful hint out of my rhapsodies. I here put an end to them; and wish out of all I have said, that you may remember nothing, Sir, but my motives in writing, obedience to your commands, and a hearty eagerness for fixing on our stage so superior a writer.

I am, Sir,

With great esteem and truth,

Your most obedient humble servant

H[OR.] W[ALPOLE]36

PS. I must beg you, Sir, not to let these letters go out of your hands, for they are full of indigested thoughts, some perhaps capricious; as those on novel diction—but I wish to tempt genius out of the beaten road, and originality is the most captivating evidence of it.

From Lord Falkland,1 Tuesday 14 March 1775

Printed from Toynbee *Supp*. iii. 241, where the letter was first printed. Damer-Waller; the MS was sold Sotheby's 5 Dec. 1921 (first Waller Sale), lot 122, to Field; not further traced.

Black Heath,2 March 14th 1775.

Sir,

YESTERDAY favoured me with your letter.3 I can give you a very particular account of the picture4 you mention; I hope you can recollect when and where that picture was put up to sale.

I shall be in town next Friday, and will, with your leave, call upon you about one o'clock.

I am,

Sir,

Your obedient humble servant,

FALKLAND

36. The initials are in HW's hand.

———

1. Lucius Charles Cary (ca 1707–85), 7th Vct Falkland, 1730.
2. Falkland lived at Billingham Manor, Southend, Blackheath.

3. Missing.
4. This was a picture of Lord Burleigh and three other lords of Queen Elizabeth's court playing at cards, and it is now at Lord Falkland's at Blackheath (HW). The picture is mentioned in James Granger's

From the DUKE OF RICHMOND, Tuesday 9 May 1775

Printed from the MS now WSL. First printed, Cunningham vi. 275–7. For the history of the MS see *ante* 15 March 1763.

Endorsed by HW: To H. W.

Goodwood,[1] May the 9th 1775.

My dear Sir,

MANY thanks to you for the Duc d'Aiguillon's correspondence,[2] which is enough to convince you and I and every impartial man that Lord Rochford[3] in the H[ouse] of Lords and Lord North[4] in the House of Commons were not very correct in the account they gave of the disarming[5]—but yet it is not sufficient to convict them legally of giving a false account, for all this is upon the word of two Frenchmen[6] and our ministers will say they are not to be credited. Perhaps some day or other we may come at more complete evidence. I shall be in London the 16th instant to attend a motion of Lord

Supplement . . . . to A Biographical History of England, 1774, p. 536: 'Mr Walpole has seen a picture of Lord Treasurer BURLEIGH, and three other Lords, playing at cards, which would make a large print; but does not recollect where he saw it.' In his copy of the *Supplement* (now WSL; Hazen, *Cat. of HW's Lib.,* No. 541), HW noted: 'It is at Lord Falkland's at Blackheath. Since sold.' The picture has not been further traced.

1. The Duke of Richmond's seat, near Chichester, Sussex.

2. *Correspondance de Monsieur le Duc d'Aiguillon, au sujet de l'affaire de Monsieur le Comte de Guines et du Sieur Tort, et autres intéressés, pendant les années 1771, 1772, 1773, 1774, et 1775,* published 3 April 1775 (DU DEFFAND iv. 175). Mme du Deffand had sent HW a copy ca 9 April (ibid. iv. 176, 179). See MANN viii. 90.

3. William Henry Nassau de Zuylestein (1717–81), 4th E. of Rochford, 1738; ambassador to France 1766–8; secretary of state for the north 1766–70, for the south 1770–5.

4. Hon. Frederick North (1732–92), styled Lord North 1752–90; 2nd E. of

Guilford, 1790; first lord of the Treasury 1770–82.

5. In the debate in the House of Lords 20 Jan. 1775, 'the Duke [of Richmond] . . . attacked the ministers on the base and timid conduct of the Court on the affair of Falkland's Island, it having just appeared in the defence of M. de Guines *that we had offered to disarm first.* Lord Rochford intrepidly denied it, said both Courts had agreed to disarm on the same day, and France and Spain had begun to disarm first' (*Last Journals* i. 422). To this account HW added the following note: 'Though Lord Rochford had the confidence to deny this, solemnly, it was *proved* in the month of April following, by the publication of the correspondence between the Duc d'Aiguillon and M. de Guines, on the latter's cause. It appeared there that Lord Stormont had desired to have some expressions in those letters *altered;* and from two of the letters that we had absolutely offered to disarm first' (ibid.). See Cobbett, *Parl. Hist.* xviii. 167–8. North's account in the Commons concerning the disarming is apparently unrecorded.

6. The Duc d'Aiguillon and the Comte de Guines.

Camden's about the Quebec Bill,[7] and will then return you your pamphlet with many thanks.

You abuse me for leaving town, for preferring the enjoyment of the country,[8] to the care of the nation. All amusements ought certainly to give way to duties, and though I prefer living in this place to any other, though I am never well in London, I would readily sacrifice both health and amusement, if I found that after all I did any good by attending to politics. But if I do none, surely 'tis pardonable to follow my inclinations, and where I hope I do some good too. The East India Company's affairs have given me a strong proof that one often does real harm with the best intentions.[9] I found it in a wavering state, roguery and private jobs pulling hard against their own general interest. I thought that my taking a part might do some good, unite some straggling parties and make a head against their directors, who were selling them. All my plan succeeded as I could wish, I had not hoped too much; many different sets united with me, and we convinced the proprietors that they should be firm and resist.[10] They did so, but our victories in Leadenhall Street[11] have forever lost the independency of the Company. The very thing I stirred to prevent has happened. The ministry, finding they were detected

7. The bill passed by Parliament in 1774 'for making more effectual provision for the government of the province of Quebec,' enacted as 14 Geo. III, c. 83; see CONWAY iii 175 n. 4. In the House of Lords 17 May, Lord Camden presented a bill for the repeal of the Quebec Act. Richmond spoke in the long debate on the bill, which was rejected by a vote of 88 to 28 (*Journals of the House of Lords* xxxiv. 458; *Last Journals* i. 462–3).

8. 'There is no drawing him [Richmond] out of the country' (HW to Lord Camden *post* ca 12 June 1775).

9. In 1772 reports of the East India Company's abuses and misrule in India, and of its serious financial difficulties, led to a Parliamentary inquiry into the Company's management and finances. The inquiry was viewed by the Company's directors as a first step by the government to destroy its independence and to assume its patronage. Early in 1773 the Duke of Richmond, a Company stockholder, determined to lead the opposition in the Court of Proprietors against government intervention, and for more than a year he

devoted himself to annoying and embarrassing Lord North's ministry in its attempts to regulate the Company's affairs. HW chronicles Richmond's involvement in *Last Journals* i. 173, 203, 229, 234–5, 237–9, 282, 286–7, 315. See also L. S. Sutherland, *The East India Company in Eighteenth-Century Politics*, Oxford, 1952, pp. 213–68.

10. On 14 May 1773 'The Court of East India Proprietors voted, 319 to 149, not to agree with the government's plan. They were chiefly led by the Duke of Richmond and Governor Johnston[e]' (*Last Journals* i. 203). 'It was rather an essay than a plan of government. He [Lord North] endeavoured to awe the Company into submission by forcing them to pay their debts, which they were unable to do; but the Duke of Richmond wrought the Company up to enthusiasm of resistance, and threw every possible difficulty into the way of government, whose measures created many real enemies' (ibid. i. 235).

11. East India House, built in 1726, stood on the south side of Leadenhall Street (BERRY i. 124 n. 22).

and foiled upon the old constitution of the Company, were drove to alter that constitution by force and arbitrary acts of Parliament.[12] This I could not foresee or help, I had not the Parliament as I had the proprietors, and now 'tis irretrievably gone. If I had not united the Company against the ministers, they would have been content to thieve a little by connivance, and the resources of the constitution might have been left to have been more fortunately exercised—so it might be with the state if I, or any man, had it in his power to unite the country against the ministry. They would overturn the constitution and the army would be to the nation what Parliament has been to the India Company, an engine of violence and oppression—I don't say, that could I hope to be as lucky in uniting the nation as I was the proprietors, I would not try. I certainly should, and should think the nation a better match for the army than the proprietors were for the Parliament, but alas, my dear Sir, what prospect is there (I will not say that I) but that any man can bring this country to its senses? Indeed I fear it is quite labour in vain to attempt it, and particularly for me who lie under so many disadvantages. All I can do is now and then to join with a few to show the nation that although but a few, yet all are not sold.[13] I know what you will say to all this, that activity and perseverance will do a great deal and that one must not give things up, for that if everybody does, there is no hopes left. But, my dear Sir, recollect that to be very active in any business one must be very healthy. I am not often so here, but never in London, and to attempt politics without health is sailing in a very leaky boat. Indeed these considerations strongly induce me to think it better and more prudent to be satisfied with doing some little good here, and to enjoy more health and satisfaction than London can afford. Forgive this long detail, but your partiality and kindness make me wish to satisfy you that I am acting reasonably, and not from in-

12. Parliament passed three acts in 1773 relating to the East India Company: 13 Geo. III, c. 44, which gave the Company certain concessions in the export of tea; 13 Geo. III, c. 63, the 'Regulating Act,' which instituted reforms in the Company's organization and gave the government partial responsibility for its management and for the administration of India; and 13 Geo. III, c. 64, which provided, under strict financial conditions, the loan needed by the Company to carry on its business (*Statutes at Large*, ed. Owen Ruffhead, 1763–1800, xi. 723–5, 814–29).

13. HW wrote of Richmond's 'Indian campaign': 'his spirit, address, insinuation, and application had greatly distinguished him, and acquired a large number of adherents, by whom he had so long balanced the power of government, at a moment when Opposition had in a manner given up the contest in Parliament' (*Last Journals* i. 287).

dolence or disgust. Adieu, love me a little and be assured that I am ever

Your very faithful humble servant,

RICHMOND etc.

To LORD CAMDEN, ca Monday 12 June 1775

Printed for the first time from a photostat of the MS deposited in the Kent Archives Office, County Hall, Maidstone, by kind permission of the owner, the Marquess Camden, Bayham Abbey, Lamberhurst, Kent. The Camden MSS were deposited in the Kent Archives Office by the 5th Marquess Camden before 1969.

Dated approximately by the reference to the seizure of two ships at New York on 23 April 1775, mentioned in HW's letter to Mason 12 June 1775, and by the allusion to rumours of a change in administration, hinted at in the letter to Mason (see nn. 2 and 5 below).

My Lord,

THE distinguished honour you have done me in speaking to me with confidence on the most unhappy situation of this country, has not only been received by me with the utmost gratitude, but perhaps has intoxicated my vanity so much, that it makes me flatter myself you will hear without disdain my sentiments on the present moment. Your Lordship's wisdom in vain foretold, on every step taken by the administration for the two last winters, all the fatal consequences that would ensue. It prevented nothing—because the object was too dear for the consequences to be attended to! National blindness (which might be accounted for too) encouraged the ministers to precipitate everything—and the moment has advanced faster than they, or perhaps even your Lordship foresaw. The war is begun, and whether the event is considerable or trifling in itself, the consequences are vast. The Americans are both enraged and encouraged, and the first success[1] will compensate many checks, if they should receive them. I need not to so penetrating an eye suggest the prospect that arises. The purpose of my letter is not to speculate on the war itself. There is a nearer consideration that calls for reflection,

---

1. On 19 April the provincial militia at Concord drove back British troops sent out by Gen. Gage to seize an arms magazine there; see n. 4 below. 'The action at Concord flew like wildfire, and threw the whole continent into a flame' (*Last Journals* i. 465).

and which I do not doubt has already presented itself to your Lordship's prudence.

The administration is thunderstruck, more even at what has happened at New York, where on the news of the success the mob seized, unloaded and destroyed the cargoes of two ships bound with provisions for Boston,[2] than at Gage's[3] miscarriage.[4] The town imputes to them thoughts of making some changes:[5] I do not believe they have any such thoughts *yet*—but they will have, my Lord, if misfortunes come thick—and if they do, the several factions in the ministry will certainly look then, as they already have begun to do, for various protection. The *Cabal's*[6] first thought will be double; to get assistance, and to disunite those who would give it: in the first place, not to leave the Opposition strong; and in the second, that the parts that are meant to be *always* constituent, may have farther resources to try. This game has been played so often, it can dupe nobody. Indeed it has rendered opposition so small, that very small bodies must be called in, if subdivisions are again to be tried. The trial would in truth answer ill: a civil war, so extensive in its consequences, cannot be supported, palliated, indemnified, if the present administration cannot support it itself, by a trifling accession of strength. The acceders might lessen the odium of the ministers, but only by incurring it themselves, and then be swept away with the guilty mass.

In my own opinion, my Lord, I speak it with great submission,

2. 'The news of the attack at Boston reached New York on Sunday the 23d [of April], and that very day the populace seized the city arms, and unloaded two provision vessels bound for the troops at Boston' (*Daily Adv.* 17 June, *sub* New York, 1 May). 'Two ships laden with provisions for him [Gage] have been destroyed at New York' (HW to Mason 12 June 1775, MASON i. 206). See also MANN viii. 111 and n. 13; *Last Journals* i. 465.

3. Hon. Thomas Gage (1719 or 1720–87), Lt.-Gen., 1770; acting commander-in-chief in North America Nov. 1763–June 1773, May 1774–Oct. 1775; governor of Massachusetts Bay 1774–5 (J. R. Alden, *General Gage in America*, Baton Rouge, Louisiana, 1948, pp. 61, 192–3, 202–4, 283).

4. At Concord and in the ensuing battle at Lexington. 'General Gage had sent a party to seize a magazine belonging to the provincials at Concord, which was guarded by militia of the province in arms. The regulars, about 1000, attacked the pro-

vincials, not half so many, who repulsed them, and the latter retired to Lexington. Gage sent another party under Lord Percy to support the former; he, finding himself likely to be attacked, sent for fresh orders, which were to retreat to Boston. The country came in to support the provincials, who lost about 50 men, and the regulars 150. . . .Thus was the civil war begun, and a victory the first fruits of it on the side of the Americans' (*Last Journals* i. 463–4).

5. HW wrote Mason 12 June: 'The City says there must be a pacification [in America] and a change of actors. Much good may it do those who will read their parts! Old *Garrick* [Lord Chatham] perhaps will return to the stage' (MASON i. 206). 'It was yesterday reported, that a change in the administration will soon take place' (*Daily Adv.* 20 June).

6. 'The secret cabal at Court' (*Mem. Geo. III* iii. 24 n. 1).

the guilt incurred is too enormous, for partial changes to atone. Unless there is total confession of the erroneousness of the system, no shifting of the decorations can avail. It is not the sacrifice of a Lord North that can excuse the fabricator of the Boston,[7] Quebec[8] and restraining[9] bills. The real authors of the measures[10] must be given up, or the measures will never be changed. It is not sending for this man and that; it must be the dismissing and stigmatizing this man and that, that will compensate to the nation in part for evils, for which, I fear, nothing can compensate.

I will now explain, my Lord, my true motive for troubling your Lordship with this letter. I have no doubt, but on the first material distress, some tub will be thrown out to the public, some such ridiculous and pretended alteration attempted, as we have often seen. As Lord Rockingham's weakness and impatience makes him the most obvious dupe, he will probably be the first applied to. I have already written my thoughts to the Duke of Richmond,[11] but as there is no drawing him out of the country,[12] I would, if I dared advise your Lordship, presume to beg you would fortify Lord Rockingham against their delusions.[13] If we are so happy as to see a change, it

7. The Boston Port Bill 'to discontinue . . . the landing and discharging, lading or shipping, of goods, wares, and merchandise, at the town, and within the harbour, of Boston,' enacted in 1774 as 14 Geo. III, c. 19 (*Statutes at Large*, ed. Owen Ruffhead, 1763–1800, xii. 47–9). See Mann vii. 561 n. 5.

8. See previous letter, n. 7.

9. Parliament passed two bills in 1775 'to restrain the trade and commerce' of the American colonies 'to Great Britain, Ireland, and the British islands in the West Indies.' The first, enacted as 15 Geo. III, c. 10, applied to the colonies in New England, and also prohibited them 'from carrying on any fishery on the Banks of Newfoundland, or other places therein mentioned'; the second bill (15 Geo. III, c. 18) related to the colonies to the south (Ruffhead, op. cit. xii. 227–31, 257–60; see also Mason i. 179 n. 4). Both the Boston Port Act and the 'Restraining' Acts were repealed by the act of 16 Geo. III. c. 5, in Dec. 1775 (Mann viii. 158 n. 43).

10. HW probably has Lord Mansfield chiefly in mind. In his account of the debate on the Boston Port Bill in the House of Lords 11 May 1774, he noted: 'Lord Camden spoke out too . . . saying he loved this country so well that, though in the wrong, he should wish it success. He then more warmly attacked Lord Mansfield, *whom he treated as author of the bills and of all the present measures*' (*Last Journals* i. 344–5).

11. HW's letter is missing.

12. See previous letter.

13. 'In the meantime the Duke of Richmond, thinking the ministers could not stand it, had gone to Lord Chatham, and told him that, as it was likely they should be sent for, it would be necessary to settle some plan of administration. Lord Chatham allowed it, and said his Grace and Lord Shelburne must be secretaries of state, and greatly commended the Duke's zeal and activity. "Ay, my Lord," said the Duke, "but who is to be at the head of the Treasury?" Lord Chatham would not name anybody, but described the Duke of Northumberland—on this the Duke of Richmond left him abruptly, as he had not agreed to Lord Rockingham having the Treasury' (*Last Journals* i. 467–8, *sub* June 1775). See n. 15 below.

must be a total one, and the Court has taken care that it should not be easy to fill up their places, though the whole Opposition should be taken in. In truth, my good Lord, I lament that the nation has so little choice—but should we be where we are, if the choice was not so limited? The most that can be said for most of the Opposition, is, that they are dear to the Americans, who will not trust us, unless they see all their friends in power. This is so very cogent an argument, that no means should be left untried of cementing the Opposition together as much as possible. Should a man of the *Cabal* remain, America will never believe us in earnest.

In fact, my Lord, I am convinced, that *being sent for*, is itself a delusion. To send for others, is, but saying, those I have dismissed were incapable; I will try if others cannot execute my measures more ably. I would say, if I could dictate, none must go for being sent for. They must not go till they are called for, called for by the nation, or they can do no good. The nation has been so intoxicated, so artfully imposed upon, that it must be roused by its own distress. Then it will swallow the remedy. When a regular physician advises sending for Dr James,[14] I know that patient is given over—and I know too, that Dr James is often turned off, if his medicines begin to take place.

Pray forgive me, my Lord, for troubling you so long, and I fear impertinently, but are not these times that agitate one's thoughts, and force one to communicate them? Cæsar certainly was plagued with many that he thought impertinent letters, but Brutus who received much fewer, I dare say held no honest Roman troublesome, even if the poor man was silly enough to tell him how he might redeem Rome. I have the honour to be, my Lord, with the greatest esteem

Your Lordship's most faithful humble servant

Hor. Walpole

PS. This letter, as your Lordship will see, was written some days ago, but I had no opportunity of conveying it; and I must beg no answer by the post.[15]

14. Dr Robert James (1705–76), whose powders ('James's Powders') were HW's favourite nostrum. Although he was created M.D. at Cambridge in 1728 by royal mandate and was later admitted a licentiate of the College of Physicians, Dr James was generally regarded as a quack.

15. 'I had written a strong letter in the

From PETER ELMSLY,[1] Friday 7 July 1775

Printed from a photostat of the MS inserted in HW's presentation copy of Robert Wood's *Essay on the Original Genius and Writings of Homer*, 1775, in the Henry E. Huntington Library. First printed in H. M. Nixon, 'Baumgarten's Will,' *Festschrift Ernst Kyriss*, Stuttgart, 1961, p. 400. For the history of the copy of Wood's *Homer* see Hazen, *Cat. of HW's Lib.*, No. 37.

July 7th 1775.

P. Elmsly presents his respects to Mr Walpole and, by order of Mrs Wood,[2] sends him a copy of the late Mr Wood's *Essay on Homer;*[3] he had orders to bind the copy in the most elegant manner[4] and hopes it pleases.[5]

summer to Lord Camden, begging him, if sent for, not to accept till the King was so reduced, and the nation so provoked, that the authors of the late measures might be punished, and a total end put to the plan of despotism. I sent the letter by a messenger, but Lord Camden pretended to be afraid of answering it even that way. But as he even did not come to me on my return from France [17 Oct. 1775], I saw he was displeased at my advising him to hesitate a moment about accepting the seals' (*Last Journals* i. 494).

1. (1736–1802), bookseller in the Strand. He was one of the most prominent booksellers in London, and his customers included the Duke of Grafton, Lord Spencer, Topham Beauclerk, John Wilkes, Sir Joseph Banks, and Gibbon (whose *Decline and Fall* he declined to publish) (Nichols, *Lit. Anec.* vi. 440–1; OSSORY ii. 90 and n. 7).

2. See *ante* 13 May 1773, n. 1.

3. *An Essay on the Original Genius and Writings of Homer: With a Comparative View of the Ancient and Present State of the Troade*, 1775, by Robert Wood (ca 1717–71), the traveller and antiquary. This posthumous work, which was published jointly by Elmsly and Thomas Payne on 7 July, was prepared for the press by Jacob Bryant (MASON i. 212 n. 12). Wood had sent HW a copy of the 1769 edition of his *Essay*, and HW offered detailed comments on it; see *ante* 19, 23 Nov. 1769. HW wrote Mason 10 July 1775: 'Mrs Wood publishes an essay, which her husband showed me and I liked, on Homer's country' (MASON i. 212).

4. HW's copy, now in the Huntington Library, is handsomely bound in gold-tooled green morocco with HW's arms on the sides. Mr H. M. Nixon, Librarian of Westminster Abbey, believes this binding to be the work of the man who bound the special copy of the *Mysterious Mother* that was kept in the Beauclerk Closet at SH. The binder was probably John Baumgarten (Hazen, *op. cit.*, No. 37; Nixon, *op. cit.* 400, illustrated p. 399).

5. See following letter.

To Mrs Robert Wood, Friday 7 July 1775

Printed for the first time from a photostat of the MS in the possession of Mr Robert W. Wood, Fields End, Roman Road, Lyme Regis, Dorset, kindly supplied by Mr Wood's father, the late Canon G. Robert Wood. For the history of the MS see *ante* 19 Nov. 1769.

Endorsed by Mrs Wood: Mr Walpole 7th July 1775. Answered the same day.

July 7th 1775.

IF anything could add value to a work of Mr Wood in Mr Walpole's eyes, it would be the very kind and obliging manner in which he has received the *Essay on Homer* from Mrs Wood;[1] he begs her to accept his most grateful acknowledgments, and assures her that nobody but she herself will receive more pleasure than Mr Walpole from the justice which he is persuaded the public will pay by its praises to the present she makes it in so excellent a book.

From Mrs Robert Wood, Friday 7 July 1775

Printed for the first time from a photostat of Mrs Wood's MS copy in the possession of Mr Robert W. Wood, Fields End, Roman Road, Lyme Regis, Dorset, kindly supplied by Mr Wood's father, the late Canon G. Robert Wood. For the history of the MS copy see *ante* 19 Nov. 1769. The original letter is missing.

Endorsed by Mrs Wood: Copy to Mr Walpole 7th July 1775.

South Street,[1] 7th July 1775.

Sir,

I BEG leave to return my best thanks for the very acceptable pleasing manner in which you have received the *Essay,* and express your approbation of it,[2] and thereby give me the highest satisfaction.

I am unhappy that I cannot address myself to you, Sir, without renewing the subject of a melancholy debt yet unpaid,[3] which is

1. See previous letter.

---

1. Grosvenor Square.
2. See previous letter.
3. In her letter *ante* 13 May 1773, Mrs Wood asked HW to suggest the design for a monument to her husband, to be placed in the cemetery at Putney. HW promised to 'look over my books, and submit some different designs to your option' (HW to Mrs Wood *ante* 16 May 1773).

heavy upon my mind, and the more so, as my great delicacy in every circumstance that concerns it, will not permit me to decide without troubling you, as I think your direction about the form, whether a sarcophagus, or an urn, absolutely necessary in order to its being perfect; I entreat then, Sir, that you will determine this point also, which will complete your kindness; when you have fixed,⁴ it shall be ordered directly, that it may be done while the days are long. I must observe at the same time that you have conferred on me a most sensible obligation by the honour of your kind attention and assistance in this interesting object of my anxious care. You have done it in such a way as to make it a most pleasing reflection to me, Sir, that it is to you I owe every comfort that can result from doing all the justice in our power to it. I am,

>Sir,
>>With great respect and truth,
>>>Your most obliged and obedient

>>>>>ANN WOOD

From TOPHAM BEAUCLERK,¹ Saturday 19 August 1775

Printed from the MS now WSL. First printed, Toynbee *Supp.* iii. 242–3. Damer-Waller; the MS was sold Sotheby's 5 Dec. 1921 (first Waller Sale), lot 89, to Maggs; offered by them, Cat. No. 433 (Christmas 1922), lot 2963; later acquired from Maggs by Capt. Frank L. Pleadwell, M.D., USN, of Honolulu; resold Parke-Bernet Galleries 7 Oct. 1958 (Pleadwell Sale), possibly in lot 158, to Walter R. Benjamin, who sold it to WSL, Oct. 1958.

The year is established by the reference to 'the paper war . . . between the Duchess K[ingston] and Foote' (see n. 9 below).

>>>>Muswell Hill,² Aug. 19.

AT Alincourt is an enigmatical epitaph which in English runs thus:

>Here lies the son, here lies the mother,
>Here lies the daughter with the father,
>Here lies the sister, and the brother;
>The husband and the wife lie here,
>And yet here but three bodies are.

4. See *post* 17 Nov. 1775.

1. (1739–80), wit; friend of Dr Johnson.

2. Beauclerk's villa in Middlesex, near Highgate (OSSORY i. 122 n. 11).

The subject of this epitaph is as strange as true, being occasioned by a young man of this place who got the maid's consent to come to bed to her at night; but his mother being a widow, and advertised of the assignation, put herself in the maid's place, and was got with child by her own son. The wicked woman concealed the matter so well that she was privately brought to bed of a daughter, who was brought up at Paris and at fifteen years of age taken home and educated by the mother, who gave her out for a poor orphan left by a friend of hers. The son, perceiving a more than ordinary share of wit and beauty in this young girl, married her privately, making her his wife, who was before his daughter and his sister.[3] The old woman, outliving them both, discovered the whole fact upon her death bed and was buried in the same grave.

p. 70, *Travels through France* etc. by E. Veryard, M.D.
Fol[io], Lond[on], 1701.[4]

I have just found this passage, which I mentioned to you, when I saw you last,[5] but could not recollect where it was; I thought perhaps you would choose to have the French epitaph, which is the reason of my troubling you with this. Alincourt is in the road from Paris to Rouen.[6]

I hope you have got safe and well to Paris,[7] but you have left England at an unlucky time, now the paper war is broke out between the Duchess K[ingston][8] and Foote.[9] Lady D.[10] tells me she sent you

3. Beauclerk communicated this story of double incest no doubt because of its similarity to the plot of HW's tragedy *The Mysterious Mother;* see MASON i. 10 n. 1. HW gave Lady Diana Beauclerk a copy of the play (now at Princeton; Hazen, *SH Bibl.* 84, copy 5); six of her seven drawings in bistre illustrating scenes from the play are now WSL (*post* ?16 Dec. 1775).

4. E[llis] Veryard, *An Account of Divers Choice Remarks . . . Taken in a Journey through the Low-Countries, France, Italy, and Part of Spain,* 1701, folio. The paragraph quoted (with several variations) by Beauclerk appears on pp. 70–1.

5. Possibly in mid-July, when the Beauclerks spent two days at SH (OSSORY i. 242).

6. HW's 'Paris Journals' for 1775 make no reference to a trip to Alincourt.

7. HW left London 16 Aug., arriving at

Paris on the 19th for an eight-week visit ('Paris Journals,' DU DEFFAND v. 342–3, 353).

8. See *ante* 24 Sept. 1773, n. 5.

9. Samuel Foote, the actor and playwright. In the spring of 1775 Foote wrote a comedy entitled *A Trip to Calais,* satirizing the scandalous amours of the Duchess of Kingston in the character of 'Lady Kitty Crocodile.' The Duchess appealed to Lord Hertford, the lord chamberlain, who refused to license the play. After Foote threatened to publish the play with a dedication to her, the Duchess, in a private interview, offered to buy the play, but he refused her bribe. Foote himself was vigorously attacked in the newspapers, and on 13 Aug. 1775 he wrote to the Duchess that he would abandon the play if she stopped her public attacks on him. She scornfully declined his offer in a letter written to him the same day,

the letters.[11] I shall be much obliged to you if you will inform me if the Chev[alier] Lorency[12] is living and, if you see him,[13] to make my compliments to him.

Believe me to be, dear Sir, with great regard,

Your most obedient and most humble servant,

T. BEAUCLERK

To the DUKE OF RICHMOND, Friday 27 October 1775

Printed from the MS now WSL. First printed, Cunningham vi. 274–5. Reprinted, Toynbee ix. 274–6. For the history of the MS see *ante* 15 March 1763.
Endorsed by HW: To the Duke of Richmond.
Endorsed by Richmond: Mr Walpole Oct. 27th 1775. Ans[were]d.[1]

Oct. 27, 1775.

My dear Lord,

YOU have not been a very active Opposition, but may plead in excuse that you could do no good.[2] *Now* you can—or never.[3] Give the ministers no respite. Press them with questions and mo-

and 'Foote, with all the delicacy she ought to have used, replied only with wit, irony, and confounded satire' (HW to Mann 7 Sept. 1775, MANN viii. 126). The letters were printed in several newspapers; see MASON i. 222 n. 16; OSSORY i. 297 n. 16. An affidavit by the Duchess's chaplain, the Rev. John Forster, swearing that Foote had tried to blackmail the Duchess, was printed in the *London Chronicle* 17–19 Aug., xxxviii. 176. The documents are printed in full in Simon Trefman, *Sam. Foote, Comedian, 1720–1777* (New York, 1971), pp. 240–5. Foote later removed the offending scenes and the altered version was produced in 1776 at the Haymarket as *The Capuchin. A Trip to Calais* was not printed in its original form until 1778, the year after Foote's death.

10. Lady Diana Spencer (1734–1808), eldest dau. of the 3d D. of Marlborough, m. 1 (1757) Frederick St John, 2d Vct Bolingbroke (divorced, 1768); m. 2 (1768) Topham Beauclerk. The MS reads 'L.ᵈ D:', apparently a slip of the pen.

11. HW may have seen the initial exchange between Foote and the Duchess that appeared in the *London Chronicle*

the day before he set out for Paris. His letters to Mason 6 Sept. and to Mann 7 Sept. show that he had by then also read Foote's second letter (MASON i. 222; MANN viii. 126). He wrote to Lady Diana from Paris on 23 Aug. and 10 Sept. (both missing), presumably to thank her for sending him the correspondence in the newspapers ('Paris Journals,' DU DEFFAND v. 395–6). His letter to Beauclerk 29 Aug. sent 'by Mr Edmondson' is also missing (ibid.).

12. Jacques Roland (d. 1784), Chevalier de Lorenzi. HW had met him at Florence, while he was on the Grand Tour, and saw him again at Paris in 1765–6 (*ante* 6 March 1766 and n. 32). His brother, the Conte Lorenzi (d. 1766), had been the French minister at Florence.

13. HW saw Lorenzi at Mme du Deffand's on 23 Aug. ('Paris Journals,' DU DEFFAND v. 344).

———

1. Richmond's reply is missing.

2. See *ante* 9 May 1775.

3. Edmund Burke also wrote to Richmond 26 Sept. 1775 urging him to action: 'I should hardly take the liberty of trou-

tions; leave their poor heads no time to think of what they ought to think of, the next campaign. Call for papers. Don't mind being refused. Talk of their waste, ask for pension lists, inquire after those scandalous ones to the widows or wives of Bradshaw,[4] Nuthall,[5] Fordyce.[6] Lament the hard fate of the *poor country gentlemen* who must pay for all this waste, and the enormous expenses of the war, too. Inquire how much of the national debt has been paid in twelve years[7]—and how much the late addresses[8] have cost. Ask if £5000 has not been sent this year to bribe the Indians,[9] who yet have not

bling your Grace at this time, if I were not most thoroughly persuaded, that there is a very particular call of honour and conscience, on all those of your Grace's situation and of your sentiments, to do something towards preventing the ruin of your country; which if I am not quite visionary, is approaching with the greatest rapidity. . . . [Y]our Grace can do more than anybody else, at all times; at this time nobody but your Grace, can do, what I apprehend to be for the most essential service to the public' (*The Correspondence of Edmund Burke*, ed. T. W. Copeland, Chicago, 1958–   , iii. 217–18).

4. Elizabeth Wilson, m. (1757) Thomas Bradshaw (1733–74), M.P., secretary of the Treasury 1767–70 and a lord of the Admiralty 1772–4. Overwhelmed with debts, Bradshaw is said to have committed suicide; shortly after his death his widow received a secret service pension of £500 a year and £300 a year for his children (Ossory i. 214 n. 2; Conway iii. 210 n. 4; *Last Journals* i. 407; Namier and Brooke ii. 110–11).

5. ——, m. 1 Hambleton Costance; m. 2 (1757) Thomas Nuthall (d. 7 March 1775), solicitor to the Treasury. 'The widow of Nuttal, . . . who had embezzled £19,000, had a pension of £300 a year to induce her to give up her husband's papers, who had been engaged in many election matters' (*Last Journals* i. 469–70).

6. Lady Margaret Lindsay (1753–1814), 2d dau. of the 5th E. of Balcarres, m. 1 (1770) Alexander Fordyce (d. 1789); m. 2 (1812) Sir James Bland Burges (after 1821, Lamb), 1st Bt. 'Lady Margaret Fordyce, wife of that infamous banker who had ruined so many, and driven two or three persons to make away with their own lives, had a pension' (ibid. i. 469).

7. The total national debt in 1763, at the end of the financial year, was £132.6 million; in 1775 it was £127.3 million, a reduction of £5.3 million from twelve years earlier (B. R. Mitchell, *Abstract of British Historical Statistics*, Cambridge, 1962, p. 402). 'It [the American war] had already cost three millions, as much as had been pretended, and but pretended, to be paid of the national debt after twelve years of peace' (*Last Journals* i. 478, *sub* Oct. 1775).

8. '6th [September 1775]. The Court procured by money an address to the King from the Jacobites of Manchester, advising him to prosecute the war. This was immediately followed by Liverpool, and Lancaster, and Leicester; which being trading towns, the addresses must have been dearly bought. They were followed by Poole, Coventry, Warwick, Exeter, Beverley, Gloucester, Suffolk, Taunton, Dover, and Devonshire, and with a very ill-attended one from Yarmouth. [King's] Lynn was said to have addressed. . . . Leith and Montrose, in Scotland, addressed, but Edinburgh and Glasgow refused. . . . The Mayor and Aldermen of Bristol addressed, but near a thousand of the merchants there soon presented a counter-address' (ibid. i. 474–5). The addresses were printed or mentioned in several newspapers during September and October 1775; see Mann viii. 132 n. 2; Conway iii. 270 n. 8; Copeland, op. cit. iii. 223 n. 2.

9. Perhaps an allusion to funds allocated to buy presents for the Indians, with the aim of securing their assistance against the American colonists. Lord Dartmouth, the secretary of state for the American department, wrote to the commander-in-chief, Gen. Thomas Gage, 2 Aug. 1775: 'The steps which you say the [American] rebels have taken for calling

joined *them*.[10] Ask what *douceurs* have been given to Scotch con-
tractors.[11] Ask what the Catholics in Canada have done in return for
the restoration of their religion and the abolition of juries[12]—and
will you not ask who was the author of that code?[13] Is abolition of
juries part of the spirit of toleration? Will you not inquire whether
Lord Dunmore[14] has not for these two years (before the Virginians
took any part) endeavoured to involve them in a war with the Indians[?][15] Will you not ask whether they have not tried to raise

in the assistance of the Indians, leave no
room to hesitate upon the propriety of
our pursuing the same measure; for that
purpose I enclose to you a letter to
Colonel [Guy] Johnson [the superintendent of the Indian department, northern
district], containing his Majesty's commands for engaging a body of Indians,
and shall by the first ship of war that
sails after the Cerberus send you a large
assortment of goods for presents, which
you will contrive the means of safely conveying to the Colonel' (*The Correspondence of General Thomas Gage*, ed. C. E.
Carter, New Haven, 1931–3, ii. 204).

10. An American letter written from
Ticonderoga 4 August 1775 reported that
Col. Johnson had just arrived at Montreal
with five hundred Indians, who were 'going to join the English rebels against us.
. . . The Canadians are determined not
to fight against us unless forced by a
formidable army' (*American Archives*, ed.
Peter Force, 4th ser. iii [Washington, 1840].
26).

11. It was frequently alleged, particularly during the early years of the war,
that government contract business was
being dominated by Scots or by men with
Scottish connections. In 1776 the *London
Evening Post* vigorously supported this
view and printed letters in which it was
claimed that Scottish firms were given
preference in the awarding of contracts
and were paid exorbitant prices to supply
articles and provisions to the military.
The Scots were said to be 'eagerly promoting this most expensive war, because they
are the chief gainers by it. Are not all the
contracts, jobs and douceurs given to
them?' (*London Evening Post* 3 Sept.
1776). For example, during the summer of
1775, when it became necessary to supply
the British troops at Boston, the Treasury
contracted with the firm of Mure, Son,
and Atkinson to transport provisions there

at the freight rate current in peacetime.
But of the forty-six men who held contracts, either individually or in partnership, for the supply of provisions, rum,
coal, and specie during the war, only six
were Scots or had Scottish connections
(Norman Baker, *Government and Con-
tractors: The British Treasury and War
Supplies 1775–1783*, 1971, pp. 166–7, 216,
221–3; David Syrett, *Shipping and the
American War 1775–83*, 1970, p. 129). See
n. 20 below.

12. Under the provisions of the Quebec
Act (14 Geo. III, c. 83) passed by Parliament in 1774, Roman Catholics in Canada
were granted freedom to practise their religion, subject to the supremacy of the
Crown, and their clergy could receive
their accustomed 'dues and rights' from
members of the faith; trial without jury
in civil cases was restored, in accordance
with the old French regime, although the
jury trial was retained in criminal cases
arising under British rule (*Statutes at
Large*, ed. Owen Ruffhead, 1763–1800, xii.
184–7, esp. sections V, VIII, XI).

13. HW probably refers to Lord Mansfield; see *ante* ca 12 June 1775, n. 10.

14. John Murray (1730–1809), styled Vct
Fincastle 1752–6; 4th E. of Dunmore,
1756; Scottish representative peer 1761–74,
1776–90; governor of New York 1769–70,
of Virginia 1770–6, of the Bahama Islands
1787–96.

15. In the summer and fall of 1774,
militia from the frontier counties of
Virginia, under orders from Governor
Dunmore, engaged the Shawnee Indians
in a struggle for possession of land in the
upper Ohio valley. For the background of
the conflict, known as Dunmore's War, see
J. M. Sosin, 'The British Indian Department and Dunmore's War,' *Virginia Magazine of History and Biography*, 1966,
lxxiv. 34–50.

Roman Catholics in Ireland?[16] Suppose you inquired what the prosecutions of Wilkes[17] cost (above £100,000) and whether they intend (for the ease of country gentlemen) to lay out as much on Sayer?[18] Will you not complain how long the half-pay was delayed?[19] nor inquire into the expenses of the transports to Boston?[20] Will you not lament the hard fate of the soldiers forced to go against their countrymen, and then left without bark or bandages for their wounds, and with nothing but salt provisions?[21] Will you not smile at Gage[22] being recalled and made Generalissimo?[23] in short, will you neither

16. 'The government declined offers made to them of raising Highland regiments, but attempted to raise a regiment of Irish Catholics, but these would not [en]list, nor could they in the whole summer [of 1775] get above 400 recruits in England' (*Last Journals* i. 473). In 1776, however, 'Recruiting agents traversed . . . the most remote districts of Ireland, and the poor Catholics of Munster and Connaught, who had been so long excluded from the English army, were gladly welcomed' (W. E. H. Lecky, *A History of England in the Eighteenth Century*, New York, 1878–91, iii. 495). In the debate in the House of Lords at the opening of Parliament 26 Oct. 1775, Lord Townshend expressed his approval of taking 'foreigners into our pay, and Irish papists into our service' (Cobbett, *Parl. Hist.* xviii. 705). See *Last Journals* i. 532.

17. In 1763–4 John Wilkes was prosecuted on two charges of libel for the printing and publication of the *North Briton*, No. 45, and of the scandalous *Essay on Woman*. He was convicted on both charges, but he failed to appear for sentencing and was outlawed. After four years in exile on the Continent, he returned to England in 1768. His outlawry was reversed, but the prior convictions were upheld and he was fined and sentenced to twenty-two months in the King's Bench prison. His legal entanglements were protracted by various countersuits and appeals.

18. Stephen Sayre (1736–1818), merchant and banker, who had been sheriff of London in 1773. He was arrested 23 Oct. 1775 and committed to the Tower on a charge of high treason; four days later he was released by a writ of *habeas corpus*. In 1776 he brought a successful suit for false arrest against Lord Rochford, at whose

instance he had been committed (MANN viii. 138 and n. 3; MASON i. 227 and n. 10, 229, 246; *Last Journals* i. 481–2).

19. 'The officers in half-pay were not paid, which has never happened even in time of war—but all the money went in corruption, or to the American war' (ibid. i. 469).

20. 'Towards the latter part of the season, government went to a vast expense, in sending out provisions and necessaries of all sorts, for the supply and relief of the army in Boston. . . . The immense charge of supplying an army at such a distance, was now for the first time experimentally felt. . . . From the multitude of transports employed in the different parts of the service, the price of tonnage was raised one-fourth above its usual rate. . . . the contracts were very lucrative' (*The Annual Register . . . for the Year 1776*, 1777, p. 51). 'In the meantime ships and stores were sent without end to Boston, but with so much negligence and ignorance that at the end of October many of the transports were not sailed' (*Last Journals* i. 473, *sub* Aug. 1775).

21. 'Boston was turned into an hospital, where more died of famine and want of care, than by the sword' (Lord Lyttelton's speech in the House of Lords 26 Oct., reported in Cobbett, *Parl. Hist.* xviii. 714; see n. 25 below). The immediate problems of food shortages and supply of provisions are discussed in R. A. Bowler, *Logistics and the Failure of the British Army in America 1775–1783* (Princeton, 1975), pp. 52–4, 93–5.

22. See *ante* ca 12 June 1775, n. 3.

23. Lord Dartmouth's letter to General Gage 2 Aug. 1775 recalling him to England 'in order to give his Majesty exact information of every thing that it

laugh nor cry, and will you leave them to laugh if you do not make them cry?—The Duke of Grafton and Lord Lyttelton[24] see their difficulties;[25] will you not make them feel them? Why did General Burgoyne[26] desire to be recalled? and why is he still employed?[27] Since the Prerogative Proclamation[28] cuts off all intercourse, is Parliament to vote money in the dark? Will you not move to know whether Halifax and Nova Scotia and Quebec are gone?[29] Will you

may be necessary to prepare as early as possible for the operations of the next year' is printed in Carter, op. cit. ii. 203. Gage sailed for England from Boston 11 Oct. and arrived in London 14 Nov. (J. R. Alden, General Gage in America, Baton Rouge, Louisiana, 1948, p. 283). He received a new commission as commander-in-chief when he was recalled. In the debate in the House of Lords 5 March 1776, Richmond 'made some observations on the supersession of the several officers in the naval and military departments, in which he maintained, that nothing like it had ever happened in the British service, without complaint or inquiry. Great faults had been found with General Gage and Admiral Graves; . . . yet no charge is made against them, but they are recalled. To keep up the farce, the former is received coolly, but in a few days after a new commission is made out, appointing him commander-in-chief; and in a few days again, without any cause even pretended, he is superseded, and General Howe appointed in his room' (Cobbett, Parl. Hist. xviii. 1194–5). See Alden, op. cit. 285 and n. 22.

24. Thomas Lyttelton (1744–79), 2d Bn Lyttelton, 1773; M.P.

25. In the debate in the House of Lords 26 Oct. on the address of thanks to the King, Grafton and Lyttelton opposed the administration and condemned its American policy; for their speeches see Cobbett, Parl. Hist. xviii. 710–11, 713–14. Lyttelton declared 'he could no longer lend his support to such measures . . . and consequently must unite in opinion with the noble duke, in wishing that all the Acts [of Parliament] respecting America, passed since the year 1763, might be repealed, as a ground for conciliation, a full restoration of the public tranquillity, and return of America to her wonted obedience, and

subordinate dependence on the mother country' (ibid. xviii. 714). See also Last Journals i. 483–4; Ossory i. 273 nn. 4, 8; Mann viii. 139 and nn. 7, 8.

26. John Burgoyne (1723–92), Maj.-Gen., 1772; M.P. He had sailed for America with Generals Howe and Clinton in April 1775.

27. In a letter to Lord North, written from Boston 14 June 1775, Burgoyne mentions 'private exigencies that demand my presence' at home (chiefly his wife's precarious health) and his being 'in too humble a situation to promise myself any hope of contributing essentially to his Majesty's service in the military line in America' as reasons for wanting 'to return to England during the ensuing winter' (E. B. de Fonblanque, Political and Military Episodes . . . from the Life and Correspondence of the Right Hon. John Burgoyne, 1876, p. 137; see also ibid. 121–3, 205–6). Burgoyne left America in Nov. 1775 and arrived in London 27 Dec. (Ossory i. 286 n. 3). 'Burgoyne, disgusted, or not liking the service, had desired to be recalled' (Last Journals i. 472).

28. On 23 August 1775 George III issued 'A Proclamation, for Suppressing Rebellion and Sedition,' ordering all civil and military officers of the Crown, as well as loyal subjects, to 'disclose and make known all treasons and traitorous conspiracies which they shall know to be against us,' and also to report 'due and full information of all persons who shall be found carrying on correspondence with . . . persons now in open arms and rebellion against our government within any of our colonies and plantations in North America' (London Gazette, No. 11590, 22–26 Aug. 1775). 'The King issued a proclamation declaring the Americans rebels, and forbidding to assist them' (Last Journals i. 473).

29. '22nd [Oct. 1775], intelligence came

not complain of all intelligence being stifled, and the nation being kept in profound ignorance, and delusion? Are there no petitions from the West Indian islands?[30] Shall not the good country gentlemen be let into their situation? In short, my dear Lord, if you please, you may pelt and harass them with questions and delays, which they will attend more to than to America. Frighten them, or at least other people, with the French preparing to attack us in the East Indies— and pray ask whether the stocks have not been kept up by the trust-money in Chancery.[31] I will engage to furnish you with motions and grievances to midsummer—and if you keep this and turn to it, you will not want subjects. Tell them of all their false promises and prophecies, not one of which has been fulfilled—and do not forget Lord Hilsborough's[32] breach of the King's faith.[33] You have spirit

that the Provincials had seized Nova Scotia and Halifax, and made themselves masters of 7000 stand of arms, a train of artillery, stores, and provisions, all which by marvellous negligence had been guarded but by 50 men. The ministers denied having any information of it' (ibid. i. 480). This report proved to be false; see MANN viii. 138 and n. 1. 'Just as the Parliament was ready to open, new difficulties fell on the ministers. They learnt that two separate bodies of Provincials were marched to attack Quebec' (Last Journals i. 480). See MANN viii. 132 and n. 4. The attack on Quebec was defeated by the British in December, ending the American campaign for the conquest of Canada (ibid. viii. 185 and n. 1).

30. On 2 February 1775 a 'Petition of the planters of his Majesty's sugar colonies residing in Great Britain, and of the merchants of London trading to the said colonies,' was presented to the House of Commons, urging the House to consider the serious consequences of the non-importation agreement adopted by the American Congress in Philadelphia on 5 Sept. 1774 and to take the necessary measures 'to preserve the intercourse between the West India islands and the northern colonies' (Journals of the House of Commons xxxv. 91–2).

31. 'The keeping up of the stocks was the inexplicable phenomenon of the year, and which, it is just to say, the government managed with great address. In the first place, they applied the large sums of

trust money in Chancery to buy into stock, which they sold out again, and repeated this manœuvre. In the next the stagnation of the American trade induced people that had money to buy into the stocks rather than let it lie dead' (Last Journals i. 477).

32. Wills Hill (1718–93), 2d Vct Hillsborough, 1742; cr. (1751) E. of Hillsborough and (1789) M. of Downshire; M.P.; secretary of state for the American department 1768–72.

33. Apparently a reference to the circular letter, dated 13 May 1769, sent by Lord Hillsborough to the royal governors of the American colonies, in which it was stated that 'his Majesty's present administration have at no time entertained a design to propose to Parliament to lay any further taxes upon America for the purpose of raising a revenue' (Copy of the circular, quoted in Autobiography and Political Correspondence of Augustus Henry Third Duke of Grafton, ed. Sir W. R. Anson, 1898, p. 233). After the letter had been sent off, Lord Camden complained to Hillsborough that it did not accurately express the opinion of the Cabinet, as agreed upon in a meeting held on 1 May 1769 and recorded in a Cabinet minute; 'parts of the minute, which might be soothing to the colonies were wholly omitted' (ibid. 230; see also ibid. 231–2). In HW's view, Hillsborough's letter represented a breach of the King's faith because it implied that the King, as well as his ministers, disapproved of taxing the

and activity enough yourself, my Lord—breathe it into your friends; and make them inquire whether the conciliatory commissioners are gone, and what their commissions are;[34] and whether they expect the Americans will trust them, *when the vile equivocatory bill of conciliation*[35] *last year Lord North himself could not carry, till Wedderburn*[36] *declared it was not meant in earnest?*[37]—but is it not plain, by their having recourse to it in the speech,[38] that they are already treating? Nor is this the only falsehood in the speech: they talk of foreign powers offering them troops:[39] is *begging* being *offered?* and if those foreign powers are not Russia, but little Hesse etc., are those foreign *powers?*[40] I would even move to address, that if Russians are

colonies and intended to pursue a more lenient policy in the future, whereas in fact Parliament subsequently passed a series of 'coercive' acts to regulate the colonies. HW refers to 'the treachery to the Americans after the promises made to them by Lord Hillsborough's letter' (*Last Journals* i. 532). See ibid. i. 343, 410–11, 454; Cobbett, *Parl. Hist.* xvii. 1314, xviii. 33–6.

34. In his speech at the opening of Parliament 26 Oct., the King announced that he would 'give authority to certain persons upon the spot [in America] to grant general or particular pardons and indemnities, in such manner, and to such persons, as they shall think fit, and to receive the submission of any province or colony which shall be disposed to return to its allegiance: it may be also proper to authorize the persons so commissioned to restore such province or colony, so returning to its allegiance, to the free exercise of its trade and commerce, and to the same protection and security as if such province or colony had never revolted' (*Journals of the House of Commons* xxxv. 398). See *Last Journals* i. 483. In the House of Commons 7 Nov., Temple Luttrell moved that the commissioners to be sent to America 'be empowered . . . to receive proposals for reconciliation from any general convention, congress, or other collective body'; the motion was defeated (*Journals of the House of Commons* xxxv. 428; see Mann viii. 141 and n. 4).

35. On 20 Feb. 1775 Lord North carried a resolution to permit the American colonies to tax themselves, though the tax would be subject to approval by Parliament (Cobbett, *Parl. Hist.* xviii. 319–38; *Last Journals* i. 436–7).

36. Alexander Wedderburn (1733–1805), cr. (1780) Bn Loughborough, (1801) E. of Rosslyn; solicitor-general 1771–8; attorney-general 1778–80; lord chief justice of the Common Pleas 1780–93; lord chancellor 1793–1801; M.P.

37. 'Wedderburn . . . broke forth from all candour, and crammed the motion down, by protesting no lenity, no relaxation of severity was in reality intended—a conduct . . . so ill calculated to have any effect on the colonies, that . . . they could conceive nothing but contempt and distrust of measures in which appeared as little sincerity as stability' (ibid.). Wedderburn's speech in the debate on North's proposal for conciliation is not reported in Cobbett, *Parl. Hist.*

38. The King's speech at the opening of Parliament 26 Oct. (*Journals of the House of Commons* xxxv. 397–8).

39. 'I have also the satisfaction to inform you, that I have received the most friendly offers of foreign assistance; and if I shall make any treaties in consequence thereof, they shall be laid before you' (ibid. xxxv. 398).

40. 'The King opened the session with a very extraordinary speech, in which were three or four gross falsehoods: . . . that foreign powers had offered us assistance; if this meant Russia, it was false, for they had been begged, not offered; and if it alluded to little Princes in Germany, they could not with propriety be called foreign *powers*' (*Last Journals* i. 482–3). In response to George

sent, no port may be put into their hands—no matter for a negative being put; it would get into the votes and spread jealousy.

There, my Lord, is a plan for your campaign. I am very presumptuous—but I will ask an account of it at the end of the session. I hope you are content with Mr C[onway].[41]

From Mrs ROBERT WOOD, Friday 17 November 1775

Printed for the first time from a photostat of Mrs Wood's MS copy in the possession of Mr Robert W. Wood, Fields End, Roman Road, Lyme Regis, Dorset, kindly supplied by Mr Wood's father, the late Canon G. Robert Wood. For the history of the MS copy see *ante* 19 Nov. 1769. The original letter is missing.

Endorsed by Mrs Wood: Copy to Mr Walpole 17th November 1775.

South Street, 17th November 1775.

Sir,

HAVING seen the design for the tomb which you have kindly chosen,[1] I cannot suppress the desire I feel to return you my sincere thanks for this last proof of your extreme goodness, which completes the honour and satisfaction you have been pleased to confer on me in every circumstance of delicate attention respecting an arduous object of my melancholy and affectionate regard. Upon this subject, Sir, you will believe, I hope, that I cannot dissemble, and I trust will for that reason be glad to know that you have on this

III's request for Russian infantry to be used in America, Catherine II of Russia initially gave assurances of her willingness to help; she later refused the King's specific request for 20,000 disciplined troops (MANN viii. 127 n. 15, 138 n. 2). The treaties for Hessian troops were not signed until January and February 1776 (Cobbett, *Parl. Hist.* xviii. 1156–67; MANN viii. 175 n. 11).

41. In the debate in the House of Commons 26 Oct. on the address of thanks to the King, 'General Conway spoke with the highest spirit and universal applause, even from the courtiers and his rival Lord George [Germain]' (*Last Journals* i. 485). Conway's speech opposing the address is summarized in Cobbett, *Parl. Hist.* xviii.

761; see also MANN viii. 139 and n. 10. Except as indicated in n. 23 above, none of the topics mentioned by HW appear to have been raised by the Opposition during the 1775–6 session.

———

1. See Mrs Wood to HW *ante* 7 July 1775 and n. 3. A detailed pen-and-ink drawing, endorsed in an unidentified hand 'Mr Wilton's design for the monument and the epitaph [to Robert Wood] by Mr Walpole,' is preserved with the MS; a side view and an end view of the monument are depicted. For Joseph Wilton's execution of the design see the following letter.

occasion given me in every particular the utmost gratification, and made me ever with the greatest truth and respect,

Sir,

Your most obliged and obedient

ANN WOOD

To MRS ROBERT WOOD, Saturday 18 November 1775

Printed from Toynbee *Supp.* iii. 21–2, where the letter was first printed. The MS is untraced until sold Sotheby's 12 April 1921 (Autograph Letters and Historical Documents Sale), lot 397, to Dobell; *penes* Dobell in 1925; not further traced.

Address: To Mrs Wood, in South Street.

Arlington Street, Nov. 18, 1775.

I AM extremely happy, Madam, that you are contented;[1] but I must take very little merit to myself beyond that of zeal for your satisfaction. I merely chose what Mr Wilton's[2] taste designed. The monument, I think, will be simple, graceful and new;[3] but it is Mr Wood's name that will make it respectable. I have the honour to be

Madam

With the greatest regard

Your most obedient humble servant

HOR. WALPOLE

1. See previous letter.

2. Joseph Wilton (1722–1803), sculptor. See *ante* 10 July 1761 n. 4.

3. 'Another and more extensive cemetery [at Putney], which occupies about four acres on the upper road to Richmond, was consecrated in the year 1763. . . . It contains a number of handsomely-decorated monuments; that attracting most notice being a sarcophagus of white marble, in memory of Robert Wood, Esq., the celebrated eastern traveller. It stands upon a massive pedestal richly-ornamented with emblems, and the armorial bearings of the deceased' (E. W. Brayley, *A Topographical History of Surrey,* 1841, iii. 479). HW's epitaph to Wood is carved on the side of the pedestal. See illustration.

ROBERT WOOD'S MONUMENT AT PUTNEY

To the Hon. Mrs John Grey,[1]
Saturday 9 December 1775

Printed from Wright v. 356, where the letter was first printed. Reprinted, Cunningham vi. 27; Toynbee viii. 378 (misdated 'Dec. 9, 1773' in Wright, Cunningham, and Toynbee). The whereabouts of the MS is not known. A MS copy in two hands (both unidentified) is now WSL, acquired from the estate of Richard Bentley the younger in 1937; the text consists of one paragraph and omits the closing.

Dated 1775 in the MS copy; the year is confirmed by the references to Lady Blandford's gout and to HW's 'going out of town till Monday' (see nn. 4, 6 below).

Address (on the MS copy): To the Honourable Mrs Grey.

Dec. 9, 177[5].[2]

Dear Madam,

AS I hear Lady Blandford[3] has a return of the gout,[4] as I foretold last night from the red spot being not gone, I beg you will be so good as to tell her, that if she does not encourage the swelling by keeping her foot wrapped up as hot as possible in flannel, she will torment herself and bring more pain. I will answer that if she will let it swell, and suffer the swelling to go off of itself, she will have no more pain; and she must remember, that the gout will bear contradiction no more than she herself. Pray read this to her, and what I say farther—that though I know she will not bear pain for herself, I am sure she will for her friends. Her misfortune has produced the greatest satisfaction that a good mind can receive, the experience that that goodness has given her a great many sincere friends, who have shown as much concern as ever was known, and the most disinterested; as we know her generosity has left her nothing to give. We wish

1. Lucy Danvers (d. 1799), dau. of Sir Joseph Danvers, 1st Bt, m. (1748) Hon. John Grey (ca 1724–77), M.P.; friend of Lady Blandford (Namier and Brooke ii. 553).

2. See headnote.

3. See *ante* 26 Sept. 1774, n. 5.

4. Lady Blandford's close friend, Lady Mary Coke, noted in her unpublished journals (in the possession of the Earl of Home) *sub* Wednesday, 6 Dec. 1775: 'I called at Lady Blandford's, and had the pleasure of hearing she had had a very good night and was quite easy and cheerful. She sent for her bullfinch and said she began to think she should see her friends again; the gout has certainly done her good, but I fear there is little hopes of the bone knitting; however, if she can live with ease to herself, one must wish to keep her as long as one can.' On 20 Nov. Lady Blandford had fallen and broken her thigh (OSSORY i. 278). During her convalescence at her house in Grosvenor Square, Mrs Grey was in almost constant attendance.

to preserve her for her own sake and ours, and the poor beseech her to bear a little pain for them.[5]

I am going out of town till Monday,[6] or would bring my prescription myself. She wants no virtue but patience; and patience takes it very ill to be left out of such good company. I am, dear Madam,

Your obedient servant,

DR WALPOLE

To the REV. THOMAS PERCY, Thursday 14 December 1775

Printed from a photostat of the MS in the British Museum (Add. MS 32,329, f. 81). First printed, Toynbee ix. 296. For the history of the MS see *ante* 5 Feb. 1765.

Address: To the Reverend Dr Percy at Northumberland House.

Dec. 14, 1775.

MR Walpole is extremely sorry he was out twice when Dr Percy gave himself the trouble of calling, and will have the honour of waiting on Dr Percy next Tuesday at one o'clock if he will give leave. In the meantime Mr Walpole (who is going out of town for two days[1]) is very happy to oblige the Doctor and consequently the public, with the use of Sir T. Wyat's speeches:[2] and will be as ready to lend the drawings of Lord Surrey[3] and Sir Thomas,[4] if the Doctor intends to give prints of them.[5]

5. 'I went to town this morning to inquire after Lady Blandford. She had just been taken up and placed in a chair, with which she seemed quite happy. 'Tis surprising how little she has lost her strength, for though no doubt it must have been a fatiguing operation, Mrs Grey said she did not appear in the least faint' (Coke, 'MS Journals' 9 Dec.).

6. HW was at SH on Sunday, 10 Dec., and returned to Arlington Street by the 12th (COLE i. 378; CONWAY iii. 272).

1. HW went to SH, returning to Arlington Street on Monday, 18 Dec. (MANN viii. 149, 154).

2. See *ante* 29 July 1773, n. 1.

3. Henry Howard (ca 1517–47), styled E. of Surrey; poet. The drawing of Surrey was probably one of the 'tracings on oil paper by Vertue and Müntz from the original drawings by Holbein in the royal collection at Buckingham House,' sold SH xx. 32 to Luxmoore for £36.15.0.

4. A drawing of Sir Thomas Wyatt by George Vertue (probably after the portrait by Holbein then at Kensington Palace) was sold SH xx. 70 to Strong of Bristol for £2.10.0. See *Anecdotes of Painting*, SH, 1762–71, i. 80.

5. In 1763, at the instance of the bookseller Jacob Tonson, Percy had undertaken to edit the works of Surrey and Wyatt. The edition was partially com-

From LADY DIANA BEAUCLERK,[1]
Saturday ?16 December 1775

Printed for the first time from the MS now WSL. For the history of the MS see *ante* 15 March 1763.

Dated conjecturally by the reference to Lady Diana Beauclerk's drawings for *The Mysterious Mother*, which were 'conceived and executed in a fortnight' ('Des. of SH,' *Works* ii. 504); the first three drawings were sent to HW before 27 Dec. 1775 (Ossory i. 289). Since Lady Di says she is 'going to town' and asks if he has 'any commands,' HW was clearly at SH. The only time that HW went to SH in Dec. 1775 was the weekend of the 16th (see previous letter, n. 1). Lady Di was doubtless writing from Muswell Hill, the Beauclerks' villa not far from Twickenham.

Endorsed, on the verso, in an unidentified hand: Walpole

Mr

Verses by HW, on the verso:[2]

> Pray good House of Commons, help Mr Dundas[3]
> To three or four places again,[4] Sirs,
> For patriots will be in a pitiful case
> If you do not promote all Drawcansirs.[5]

> Besides if you let this true weathercock rust,
> Who has chang'd with each wind in the nation,
> The mild Christian term of his own coinage must
> Be applied to his own case, starvation.[6]

pleted and printed off when Tonson died in 1767, after which it was discontinued. At this time Percy apparently asked to see materials in HW's possession that might be useful in completing his edition. With the help of his nephew, Percy resumed work on it in 1792; it was still unfinished in 1808, when a fire in John Nichols's warehouse destroyed the printed sheets and Percy had to abandon it, along with his uncompleted edition of the Duke of Buckingham's works (Nichols, *Lit. Illus.* vi. 560, 571, 588; viii. 89; *post* 11 and 20 Aug., 18 Sept. 1792).

---

1. Lady Diana Spencer (1734–1808), eldest dau. of the 3d D. of Marlborough, m. 1 (1757) Frederick St John, 2d Vct Bolingbroke (divorced, 1768); m. 2 (1768) Topham Beauclerk.

2. Probably written in 1782, when Henry Dundas was about to obtain the treasurership of the Navy (see n. 4 below).

3. Henry Dundas (1742–1811), cr. (1802) Vct Melville; M.P.

4. Within three months of making his first speech in the House of Commons (20 Feb. 1775), Dundas was appointed lord advocate of Scotland, an office he held until 1783 concurrently with those of joint keeper of the Signet (1777–9) and sole keeper (1779–1800). HW wrote Mason 7 Feb. 1782: '*Starvation* [Dundas] himself is rewarded . . . with the place of treasurer of the Navy (£6000 per year)' (Mason ii. 177). In July 1782 Dundas accepted the treasurership on condition that he also retain the sinecure office of keeper of the Signet, which he had been holding only at the King's pleasure (ibid. n. 15).

5. Drawcansir is a bellicose character in Buckingham's *The Rehearsal*. 'Drawcansir in *The Rehearsal* pulls kings of all sides by the nose' (HW to Lady George Lennox 20 April 1766, More 117).

6. In his speech in the House of Com-

Saturday.

I SEND you the drawings,[7] but I find the bistre[8] will not take well
on the old cards. The bistre I have now seems of a browner tint
also.

I am going to town for the night. Have you any commands?

Yours,

D. B.

To THOMAS ASTLE, Tuesday 19 December 1775

Printed from a photostat of the MS copy in Thomas Kirgate's hand (enclosed
in HW's letter to William Cole 26 Jan. 1776) in the British Museum (Add. MS
5952, ff. 148–9). First printed, *Letters from the Hon. Horace Walpole, to the
Rev. William Cole, and Others*, 1818, pp. 119–20 (signature omitted). Reprinted,
Wright v. 437–8 (signature omitted); *The Correspondence of Horace Wal-
pole . . . and the Rev. William Mason*, ed. John Mitford, 1851, i. 224–6; Cun-
ningham vi. 294–5; Toynbee ix. 300–302 (signature omitted in Cunningham and
Toynbee). The original letter is missing. Cole made a copy of it for himself (Add.
MS 5824, f. 92); this copy and the copy sent to him by HW are part of Cole's
bequest of MSS to the British Museum. HW sent a copy of the letter to William
Mason 21 Dec. 1775 as well as to Cole (see n. 1 below).
Endorsed by Kirgate: To Thomas Astle, Esq.

Dec. 19, 1775.

Sir,

I AM much obliged to you and return you my thanks for the paper
you have sent me.[1] You have added a question to it, which, if I
understand it, you yourself, Sir, are more capable than anybody of

mons 6 March 1775 supporting the Massachusetts Bay Restraining Bill, Dundas
avowed that he 'wished the bill might
starve the inhabitants of that province'
(*Last Journals* i. 441). 'I believe it was on
this occasion that Dundas coined the word
starvation, which became a nickname for
him' (ibid. n. 1). See MASON ii. 135 and
n. 11.

7. See headnote. HW wrote Mason
18 Feb. 1776: 'Lady Di Beauclerc has
made seven large drawings in soot-water
(her first attempt of the kind) for scenes
of my *Mysterious Mother*. Oh! such drawings! Guido's grace, Albano's children,
Poussin's expression, Salvator's boldness in

landscape and Andrea Sacchi's simplicity
of composition might perhaps have
equalled them had they wrought all together very fine' (ibid. i. 244). In 1776
HW built the Beauclerk Closet at SH to
exhibit them. Six of the seven drawings
are now WSL; see OSSORY i. 289 n. 18 and
illustration.

8. 'A brown pigment prepared from
common soot' (OED).

———

1. Astle's letter to HW 18 Dec. 1775 is
missing. HW wrote Mason 21 Dec.: 'On
Monday he [Astle] sent me a printed copy
of the act of attainder of George, Duke
of Clarence (which corroborates remark-

'THE MYSTERIOUS MOTHER ACT 3D. SCENE 3D.
BY LADY DIANA BEAUCLERC 1776'

answering. You say, 'Is it probable that this instrument was framed by Richard Duke of Gloucester?' If by *framed* you mean drawn up, I should think princes of the blood, in that barbarous age, were not very expert in drawing acts of attainder, though a branch of the law more in use then than since. But as I suppose you mean *forged*, you, Sir, so conversant in writings of that age, can judge better than any man—you may only mean *forged by his order*. Your reading, much deeper than mine, may furnish you with precedents of *forged acts of attainder;* I never heard of one; nor does my simple understanding suggest the use of such a forgery, on cases immediately pressing; because an act of attainder being a matter of public notoriety, it would be revolting the common sense of all mankind to plead such an one, if it had not really existed. If it could be carried into execution by force, the force would avail without the forgery, and would be at once exaggerated and weakened by it. I cannot therefore conceive why Richard should make use of so absurd a trick, unless that having so little to do in so short and turbulent a reign, he amused himself with treasuring up in the Tower a forged act for the satisfaction of those who three hundred years afterwards should be glad of discovering new flaws in his character. As there are men so bigoted to old legends,[2] I am persuaded, Sir, that you would please them by communicating your question to them. They would rejoice to suppose that Richard was more criminal than even the Lancastrian historians represent him; and just at this moment I don't know whether they would not believe that Mrs Rudd[3] assisted him. I, who

ably one of my arguments), but which he not perceiving, very impertinently added a *quære*, which implied I had been in the wrong. The *quære* itself was so absurd that I could not deny myself the pleasure of laughing at him and his council. I send you a copy of my letter as the shortest way of explaining what I have told you' (Mason i. 238–9; see also Cole ii. 2; Dalrymple 176; *post* 4 March 1777). 'The Attainder of George, Duke of Clarence' was printed in *Rotuli parliamentorum,* 1767–77, vi. 193–5. Astle, one of the editors of the *Rotuli,* probably sent HW only the sheets containing the copy of the attainder, as the sixth volume of the *Rotuli* was not published until 1777.

2. HW doubtless has in mind Jeremiah Milles and Robert Masters, both members of the Society of Antiquaries, who had

published answers to HW's *Historic Doubts* in *Archæologia* (ante 29 March 1772, n. 2). 'I conclude the foolish Society of Antiquaries will be convinced he [Astle] has guessed happily, and that we shall have a new dissertation against me in the next volume of . . . the *Archæologia*' (HW to Mason 21 Dec. 1775, Mason i. 239).

3. Margaret Caroline Young (or Youngson) (ca 1745–97), m. (ca 1762) Valentine Rudd. She left her husband soon after their marriage, and in 1770 became the mistress of Daniel Perreau. She was involved, along with Perreau and his brother Robert, in a series of forgeries for which the brothers were ultimately hanged; in a separate trial, concluded 8 Dec. 1775, Mrs Rudd was acquitted (Mann viii. 152 n. 15; Mason i. 192 n. 13; Berry i. 208

am probably as absurd a bigot on the other side, see nothing in the paper you have sent me, but a confirmation of Richard's innocence of the death of Clarence.[4] As the Duke of Buckingham[5] was appointed to superintend the execution,[6] it is incredible that he should have been drowned in a butt of malmsey,[7] and that Richard should have been the executioner. When a seneschal of England, or as we call it, a Lord High Steward, is appointed for a trial, at least for execution, with all his officers, it looks very much as if even in that age proceedings were carried on with a little more formality than the careless writers of that time let us think. The appointment too of the Duke of Buckingham for that office, seems to add another improbability (and a work of supererogation) to Richard's forging the instrument. Did Richard really do nothing but what tended to increase his unpopularity by glutting mankind with lies, forgeries, and absurdities, which every man living could detect?

I take this opportunity, Sir, of telling you how sorry I am not to have seen you so long,[8] and how glad I shall be to renew our acquaintance,[9] especially if you like to talk over this old story with me, though I own it is of little importance, and pretty well exhausted.[10]

I am, Sir, with great regard,

Your obliged humble servant,

H[or.] W[alpole]

n. 22). 'A fair one . . . has just foiled the law, though nobody questions her guilt' (HW to Mann 17 Dec. 1775, MANN viii. 152).

4. See *ante* 29 Dec. 1767, n. 16.

5. Henry Stafford (1455–83), 2d D. of Buckingham, 1460; lord high steward, 1478; lord high constable, 1483.

6. Buckingham was appointed lord high steward by Edward IV in order to pronounce the sentence of death upon Clarence 7 Feb. 1478 (*Rotuli parliamentorum* vi. 195). The appointment is printed immediately after the act of attainder, and was probably on the sheets sent by Astle to HW.

7. Clarence was privately executed in the Tower 18 Feb. 1478. 'The story of Clarence's demise in malmsey wine is so widespread and persistent that it cannot

be discounted. . . . Despite its inherent improbability, the tale is very likely true' (P. M. Kendall, *Richard the Third*, New York, 1956, p. 533, n. 12).

8. HW had not seen Astle since the controversy over the alleged 'coronation roll' of Richard III, of which Astle had lent him an extract in 1768 (MASON i. 238; *ante* 6 Feb. 1768, n. 1).

9. HW wrote Cole 1 March 1776: 'Mr Astle has at last called on me, but I was not well enough to see him. I shall return his visit, when I can go out' (COLE ii. 7).

10. In the copy of this letter sent to Cole 26 Jan. 1776, HW's 'Queries to be added' to it follow the text; they are printed in COLE ii. 3 n. 13. Cole's comments appear in his letter to HW 30 Jan. 1776 (ibid. ii. 5–6).

From JOHN ROBINSON,[1] Saturday 23 December 1775

Printed from *Works* ii. 383–4, where the letter was first printed. The history of the MS and its present whereabouts are not known.

Treasury Chambers, December 23, 1775.

Sir,

I AM directed by Lord North to send you a copy of the representation[2] which the Commissioners of the Customs have made to the Board of Treasury relative to the difficulty which hath arose in the management of the office,[3] in which you are so much interested,[4] by the death of Mr Mann.[5] His Lordship orders me to say that he is desirous of arranging this business in any way that is practicable and most agreeable to you, and to appoint (if it can be) Mr Suckling,[6] or who you choose, as temporary collector.[7]

I shall be at my house at Sion Hill[8] tomorrow morning, and shall be glad to receive your answer[9] to that place; or, if it is agreeable to

1. (1727–1802), M.P.; joint secretary to the Treasury 1770–82; surveyor-general of woods and forests 1787–1802.

2. See enclosure printed below. According to E. E. Hoon, *The Organization of the English Customs System 1696–1786*, New York, 1938, p. 14, n. 7, the original memorial is in the Public Record Office, Treasury Papers, Bundle 516, No. 248.

3. Collector of customs London port inwards.

4. See HW to Edward Louisa Mann *ante* 28 July 1771, n. 6.

5. Edward Louisa Mann (1702–16 Dec. 1775), elder brother of Sir Horace Mann; army clothier; collector of customs London port inwards ca 1752–75 (GM 1775, xlv. 607; MANN i. 321 n. 22). On his death the patent place of collector of customs inwards devolved to Sir Horace Mann, HW's correspondent (OSSORY i. 283 n. 23).

6. William Suckling (1730–98), deputy collector of customs 1772–98; HW's cousin (MANN viii. 178 n. 7).

7. HW wrote Sir Horace Mann 15 Feb. 1776: 'Your late brother held for me and my brother our place in the Custom-House; as you succeed to all his rights, the patent falls to you and is held in your

name. The Commissioners of the Customs represented against your absence, and I was desired to give you notice. I peremptorily refused. I said I had acquainted you with your brother's death, and had pressed you to come over [from Italy]; but . . . nothing should induce me to urge you to come, if you did not think it safe for your health. In the meantime, as the office could not stand still, Lord North very obligingly offered me to settle a deputation in any manner I should propose. That too I declined, and submitted the whole disposition to his Lordship's discretion. In one word, the Treasury have appointed Mr Suckling, our cousin and deputy, to act for you till you come; which will be as long as you live, unless Sir Edward [Walpole] dies first, when the patent expires' (ibid. viii. 177–8). Mann continued to live in Italy; Sir Edward Walpole died in 1784, predeceasing Mann by almost three years.

8. Syon Hill, Isleworth. In 1778 Robinson purchased the manor of Wyke, near Syon Hill (Daniel Lysons, *The Environs of London*, 1792–6, iii. 98).

9. *Post* 25 Dec. 1775.

you, I will wait on you at Strawberry Hill to receive your commands.
I have the honour to be with great respect,

Sir,

Your most obedient servant,

JOHN ROBINSON

[Enclosure]

To the Right Hon. the Lords Commissioners of his Majesty's
Treasury.

Custom House, London, December 22, 1775.

Memorial of the Commissioners for managing and causing
to be levied and collected his Majesty's Customs, etc.

SHEWETH,

That his late Majesty King George I by his letters patent bearing
date 28th of June 1716, did grant unto [Henry] Hare,[10] Esq. and
Robert Mann,[11] Gentleman, the office of Collector Inwards of the
Customs in the Port of London, and the members and creeks thereof,
for and during the natural lives of Robert Walpole, jun. Esq. and
Edward Walpole, Esq. sons of the Right Honourable Robert Walpole, Esq. and during the life of the longest liver of them, with full
powers to execute the said office by themselves, or their sufficient
deputy or deputies.

That Mr Suckling, the present deputy to the Collector Inwards,
acquainted us, that Edward Louisa Mann, Esq. the last person admitted to that office, is now dead, and that the same devolves to Sir
Horace Mann, Bart. his Majesty's minister at Florence, who not being in England cannot immediately attend to take the oath of office.

We beg leave to represent the same to your Lordships; and as the
case is unprecedented, we are at a loss to know how and by whom

---

10. (d. 1733), of King's Lynn, Norfolk;
collector of customs inwards 1721–33 (GM
1733, iii. 550; MANN x. 52). The name
'Robert Hare, Esq.' appears in *Works;*
that this is an error for Henry Hare is
shown by the royal warrant for a great
seal, 22 June 1716 (ibid.).

11. (d. 1752), of Linton, Kent; deputy
treasurer of Chelsea Hospital 1720–43;
collector of customs inwards 1721–52;
father of Edward Louisa Mann and
Horace Mann (ibid. i. 27 n. 9).

the collection is to be carried on during this interval, and in what manner and in whose name the money so collected is to be paid into the hands of the Receiver-General, in order to its being paid into the Exchequer.

This being a matter of very great importance, as well as peculiar nicety and difficulty in point of law and prudence, we think it necessary to give your Lordships this early intimation of it, and pray to receive your Lordships' directions herein.

H. BANKES[12]

W. MUSGRAVE[13]

CN. MORRIS[14]

JS. JEFFERYS[15]

To JOHN ROBINSON, Monday 25 December 1775

Printed from *Works* ii. 384–6, where the letter was first printed. Reprinted, Toynbee ix. 308–10. The history of the MS and its present whereabouts are not known.

Arlington Street, December 25, 1775.

Sir,

I HAVE but this minute received the honour of your most obliging letter,[1] and do not lose a minute in answering it.

It is impossible to be more sensible than I am of Lord North's goodness, and I must beg you, Sir, to express my gratitude to his Lordship, as I shall have the honour of doing in person. His Lordship's condescension to me is as flattering as unmerited; and the only way I can at all pretend to deserve it is by doing what I ought; that is, as far as the case regards myself, prefer the public service to myself, and submit myself in the care of that interest to his Lordship's wisdom: at the same time having so just a sense of the duty of grati-

---

12. Henry Bankes (1700–76), M.P.; commissioner of customs 1762–76.

13. Sir William Musgrave (1735–1800), 6th Bt, 1755; barrister and antiquary; commissioner of customs 1763–85 (GEC ii. 436; *Court and City Register*).

14. Corbyn Morris (d. 1779), F.R.S.,

1757; economist; commissioner of customs 1763–79 (DNB; *Court and City Register*).

15. James Jeffreys (d. 1786), commissioner of customs 1766–86 (GM 1786, lvi pt ii. 908; *Court and City Register*).

1. *Ante* 23 Dec. 1775.

tude, that I think myself equally obliged by a kind offer, whether accepted or declined.

The Collectorship of the Customs is an office of such importance, that my family or I, who have received such favours from the government,[2] ought to be the first to take care that the public suffers no detriment in an office in which we are concerned. I, it is true, have a great, though a temporary, interest in that office, but it is my brother, Sir Edward, in whom it is vested for his life;[3] and therefore I flatter myself that both Lord North and you, Sir, will consider my answer as only regarding myself; for though I am persuaded that my brother has the public service full as much at heart as I have, I must not take upon me to answer for him about an office that virtually and ultimately rests in him. For myself, I am persuaded that I cannot serve the public more essentially than by waiving my own interest entirely, and referring the whole disposition of the present difficulty to Lord North's discretion, and submitting myself entirely to what he shall direct. The situation of the office by the absence of Sir Horace Mann is certainly extremely momentous, and ought not to remain precarious; therefore, I beg very respectfully and gratefully too, that I may not be considered for an instant, but that his Lordship will give orders for the security of the office in whatever manner he thinks fit, till Sir Horace can come over and accept it; and whatever his Lordship shall determine[4] will be cheerfully acquiesced in by,

Sir,

His Lordship's and your most grateful
and most obedient humble servant,

HORACE WALPOLE

Postscript.

Sir,

I was so convinced that my brother Sir Edward prefers the service of the public to his own interest, at least as much as I do, that I de-

---

2. For HW's 'Account of My Conduct relative to the Places I Hold under Government, and towards Ministers' see *Works* ii. 364–70.

3. 'As the patent now stands, it is for my brother's life, but far the greater

profits are given to me. If he dies, the whole drops: if I die first, the whole falls to him' (HW to Henry Pelham *ante* 25 Nov. 1752).

4. HW's letter to Mann 15 Feb. 1776 describing the outcome (see previous let-

ferred sending my immediate answer till I had communicated it to my brother;[5] and he authorizes me to say that he submits himself entirely to Lord North's arbitration for the safety of the office till Sir Horace Mann can be admitted to it according to the intention of the patent.

To Elizabeth Ryves,[1] ?1776

Printed from the MS now WSL. First printed, Toynbee *Supp.* iii. 340. The MS is untraced until offered by Maggs, Cat. Nos 433 (Christmas 1922), lot 3810; 486 (Christmas 1926), lot 2438; 516 (spring 1929), lot 592; 551 (Christmas 1930), lot 2308; sold by them to WSL, June 1932.

Dated ca 1785 by Dr Toynbee, but the 'poems' mentioned in the letter were probably her *Poems*, 1777, still in MS (see n. 2 below); HW's hand is certainly of the earlier period.

MR Walpole is sorry he was obliged to go to London on business, and could not stay to receive Mrs Ryves; but as he has no credit or interest, it would be deceiving her to flatter her with hopes of his being of use to her, which he cannot be; and therefore he takes the liberty of returning her poems;[2] but he assures her without meaning the least disrespect.

ter, n. 7) implies that there was further correspondence on the subject between HW and Robinson, but no other letters have turned up.

5. This communication, if contained in a letter to Sir Edward, is missing.

———

1. (1750–97), poet, playwright, and translator; author of *Ode to the Rev. Mr Mason*, 1780 (MASON ii. 40 n. 7).

2. Probably the manuscript of her *Poems on Several Occasions*, published in 1777. Miss Ryves may have asked permission to dedicate her work to HW. His copy of her *Poems* is Hazen, *Cat. of HW's Lib.*, No. 2465.

From the PRINCE DE BEAUVAU,
Saturday 27 January 1776

Printed for the first time from the MS now WSL. The MS was among the Du Deffand letters sold SH vi. 107 to Dyce-Sombre, whose widow (later Lady Forester) died in 1893 leaving them to her nephew, W. R. Parker-Jervis; resold Sotheby's 12 March 1920 (Parker-Jervis Sale), lot 394 (with other Du Deffand MSS), to Maggs; acquired from them by WSL, May 1934.

Endorsed by Beauvau: Mr Walpole.

Paris ce 27 janvier 1776.

JE comptais, Monsieur, vous marquer seulement ma très sincère reconnaissance du souvenir très flatteur que vous avez bien voulu me témoigner en m'envoyant des pâtés d'ananas excellentes.[1] Il se trouve qu'après avoir reçu ce présent de vous, j'ai encore un service à vous demander; vous trouverez ci-joint le détail de ce que j'ai intérêt de savoir et que je prends la liberté de vous prier de faire éclaircir avec tout le soin et la discrétion dont vous êtes capable.[2] En même temps que j'en use avec vous avec cette confiance, je dois vous assurer qu'il ne peut rien résulter de ces éclaircissements qui puisse déplaire aux personnes qui en sont l'objet.

Je ne puis assez vous dire, Monsieur, combien j'ai été sensible à une attention de votre part qu'il me serait bien doux de reconnaître en m'employant dans ce pays-ci à ce que vous voudriez y faire faire; vous ne pourriez obliger davantage celui qui depuis qu'il a le bonheur de vous connaître,[3] n'a cessé de désirer que vous lui fissiez l'honneur de le croire plus véritablement que personne, Monsieur, votre très humble et très obéissant serviteur,

LE PRINCE DE BEAUVAU

1. HW noted in his list of commissions and presents for French people in 1775: 'Princesse Beauvau, ananas confit and receipt' (DU DEFFAND v. 417). 'Les confitures sont trouvées excellentes par M. de Beauvau. . . . M. de Beauvau est très reconnaissant, il voudrait imaginer ce qui pourrait vous faire plaisir, il dit que vous le comblez d'attentions' (Mme du Deffand to HW 16 Jan. 1776, ibid. iv. 259).

2. See enclosure (in a different hand) printed below. The Prince's inquiry concerning the Smyth family was apparently made at the instance of Mme de Beauvau, whose brother, the Comte de Jarnac, married Elizabeth Smyth in Sept. 1776 (n. 6 below): see DU DEFFAND iv. 452.

3. See *ante* 19 Oct. 1740 NS, n. 3.

La santé de notre amie commune (Mme du Deffand) a encore été bien chancelante depuis votre départ,[4] mais je la trouve à présent bien raffermie; son esprit est toujours aussi agréable et son cœur bien rempli de vous.

Mme Matheus[5] et Mlle Smith[6] dont il est question dans le papier ci-joint, ont été souvent à Paris; permettez-moi de vous recommander encore le secret.

Mme de Beauvau qui partage avec moi le plaisir de manger vos ananas, veut absolument, Monsieur, que je la rappelle l'honneur de votre souvenir.

[Enclosure]

Milord Clanricarde[7] n'est-il pas le premier comte au Parlement d'Irlande?[8]

Son nom de famille n'est-il pas Smith?[9]

Milady Brandon,[10] tante de Mme Matheus et de Mlle Smith, l'est-elle par elle-même ou par Monsieur son mari?

M. Smith,[11] frère de Mme Matheus et de Mlle Smith, n'est-il pas fort riche?

Est-il appellé à succéder au titre de Milord Clanricarde si les enfants manquaient à celui-ci?[12]

4. HW left Paris for England 12 Oct. 1775 after an eight-week visit ('Paris Journals,' DU DEFFAND v. 353).

5. Ellis (or Elisha) Smyth (ca 1743–81), dau. of James Smyth (d. 1771), of Tinney Park, co. Wicklow, m. (1764) Francis Mathew (d. 1806), cr. (1783) Bn, (1793) Vct, and (1797) E. of Landaff. See DU DEFFAND ii. 258 n. 15.

6. Elizabeth Smyth (d. 1843), sister of Mrs Mathew, m. (29 Sept. 1776) Marie-Charles-Rosalie de Rohan-Chabot (1740–1813), Vicomte de Chabot, later Comte de Jarnac (OSSORY i. 357 n. 14).

7. John Smith Bourke (after 1752, de Burgh) (1720–82), 11th E. of Clanricarde, 1726.

8. When Clanricarde took his seat in the Irish House of Lords 12 Jan. 1743, he was the second earl in order of precedence in the Irish Parliament, after the Earl of Kildare (Journals of the House of Lords, Dublin, 1779–1800, iii. 559). On the Earl of Kildare's creation as Marquess of Kil-

dare in 1761, Clanricarde became the first earl in the Parliament.

9. See n. 7 above. His mother was Anne, dau. of John Smith, of Beaufort Buildings, London (GEC iii. 235). He is referred to as 'the Right Hon. Smith Earl of Clanrickard' in the Journals of the House of Lords for 12 Jan. 1743 (see previous note).

10. Ellis Agar (ca 1708–89), m. 1 (1726) Theobald Bourke, 7th Vct Mayo, 1741; m. 2 (1745) Francis Bermingham, 14th Bn Athenry; cr. (1758) Cts of Brandon (s.j.). See n. 14 below.

11. Edward Skeffington Smyth (1745–97), son of James Smyth (d. 1771), of Tinney Park, cr. (5 Aug. 1776) Bt.

12. Edward Skeffington Smyth was not related to Lord Clanricarde, whose son, Henry de Burgh (1743–97), succeeded him as 12th Earl of Clanricarde in 1782 and was created Marquess of Clanricarde in 1789.

Que leur est Milord Courtown?[13]
Qu'est Mme Smith[14] la mère en son nom?
À quel degré de parenté est avec eux le Duc de Leinster?[15]

From LADY ALBEMARLE,[1] Sunday 28 January 1776

Printed from a transcript, now WSL, of Thomas Kirgate's note that he wrote in his copy of the *Description of SH*, which in 1821 was in the possession of 'Mr Hodges.' At that time Kirgate's note was transcribed by an unidentified person into another copy of the *Description* that was part of vol. II of HW's *Works* (1798); this copy, containing the transcript from Kirgate's copy, is now WSL. First printed in MASON i. 313 n. 2.

The transcript is misdated 'Sunday, Nov[embe]r 28, 1776,' doubtless a copying error. HW wrote Mann Sunday, 28 Jan. 1776: 'I have had a red hat given to me today—it was Cardinal Wolsey's' (MANN viii. 174). 28 Nov. 1776 was a Thursday.

Sunday, [Jan.][2] 28, 1776.

THIS hat was Cardinal Wolsey's,[3] and when Bishop Burnet[4] was Clerk of the Closet to Queen Anne, he took it *or stole it* out of

13. James Stopford (1731–1810), 2d E. of Courtown, 1770. His mother, née Elizabeth Smyth (1705–88), was the daughter of Edward Smyth (1662–1720), Bishop of Down, by his first wife and cousin, Elizabeth Smyth; James Smyth (d. 1771), the father of Mrs Mathew, Miss Elizabeth Smyth (later Comtesse de Jarnac), and Edward Skeffington Smyth, was the son of the Bishop of Down by his second wife, the Hon. Mary Skeffington. Lord Courtown and the children of James Smyth were therefore first cousins (GEC; Burke, *Landed Gentry of Ireland*, 10th edn, 1904, p. 554).

14. Mary Agar, dau. of James Agar, m. (1742) James Smyth (d. 1771), of Tinney Park. She was the younger sister of the Countess of Brandon (Collins, *Peerage*, 1812, viii. 364).

15. William Robert Fitzgerald (1749–1804), 2d D. of Leinster, 1773. He was probably a distant relation of the Smyth family by his Clotworthy ancestors: his grandfather, the 19th Earl of Kildare, was the son of the Hon. Robert Fitzgerald by his marriage to Mary Clotworthy, daughter of Col. James Clotworthy, of Monni-

more, co. Londonderry; Mary Skeffington (n. 13 above) was the granddaughter of Mary Clotworthy (d. 1686), who married in 1654 John Skeffington (d. 1695), 2d Vct Massereene (GEC vii. 244, viii. 544–5).

1. Lady Anne Lennox (1703–89), 2d dau. of the 1st D. of Richmond, m. (1723) William Anne van Keppel (1702–54), 2d E. of Albemarle, 1718.

2. See headnote.

3. 'The red hat of Cardinal Wolsey; it was found in the Great Wardrobe by Bishop Burnet when Clerk of the Closet; his son Judge Burnet left it to his housekeeper, who gave it to the butler of Lady Anne Lenox, first Countess Dowager of Albemarle; he gave it to his Lady, and she to Mr Walpole in 1776' (HW's MS note in his extra-illustrated copy, now WSL, of the *Description of SH*, 1774, p. 59). The hat, which was kept in the Holbein Chamber at SH ('Des. of SH,' *Works* ii. 455), was sold SH xvii. 73 to Charles Kean for £21, and is now in the library of Christ Church, Oxford.

4. Gilbert Burnet (1643–1715), Bp of Salisbury 1689–1715.

the Wardrobe, and left it to his son Judge Burnet.⁵ He gave it to his housekeeper, and she gave it to Gerrard, my butler, who gave it to me, who beg Mr Walpole's acceptance of it.

To EDWARD GIBBON,¹ ca Monday 12 February 1776

Printed from a photostat of the MS in Thomas Kirgate's hand among the Gibbon papers in the British Museum (Add. MS 34,886, f. 53). First printed in *Miscellaneous Works of Edward Gibbon, Esq.*, ed. Lord Sheffield, [2d edn,] 1814, ii. 153–4. Reprinted in *Miscellaneous Works*, ed. Sheffield, 1796–1815, iii. 602; Wright v. 441; Cunningham vi. 306–7; Toynbee ix. 322–3. Gibbon bequeathed his papers to his executor, the first Earl of Sheffield, whose grandson, the third Earl, sold them to the British Museum in 1895–6. A MS copy of the letter, in the hand of an amanuensis, is bound in Lord Sheffield's interleaved copy of the *Miscellaneous Works*, 2 vols, 1796, now in the Yale University Library (vol. I, pt 2, following p. 498).

Dated approximately by Gibbon's letter to his friend J. B. Holroyd (later Lord Sheffield) 9 Feb. 1776, in which he writes: 'I think you will have your book [i.e., Holroyd's presentation copy of the *Decline and Fall of the Roman Empire*] Monday [12 Feb.]' (*The Letters of Edward Gibbon*, ed. J. E. Norton, 1956, ii. 98). HW received a presentation copy from Gibbon before 14 Feb. (*post* 14 Feb. 1776) and probably about the same time Holroyd received his copy.

M R Walpole cannot express how much he is obliged to Mr Gibbon for the valuable present² he has received; nor how great a comfort it is to him in his present situation,³ in which he little expected to receive singular pleasure. Mr W. does not say this at random, nor from mere confidence in the author's abilities, for he has already (all his weakness would permit) read the first chapter, and is in the greatest admiration of the style, manner, method, clearness, and intelligence. Mr Walpole's impatience to proceed will struggle with his disorder, and give him such spirits, that he flatters

5. Sir Thomas Burnet (1694–1753), third and youngest son of Bp Burnet; Kt, 1745; justice of the Court of Common Pleas, 1741.

1. (1737–94), M.P.; historian.
2. The first volume of Gibbon's *The History of the Decline and Fall of the Roman Empire*, published 17 Feb. (MASON i. 243 n. 15). HW's copy of the entire work, 6 vols, 1776–88 (now in the Rothschild Library at Trinity College, Cambridge), is Hazen, *Cat. of HW's Lib.*, No. 3188; the first volume is inscribed (in the hand of an amanuensis) 'From the Author' and contains many MS notes by HW.

3. HW wrote Mason 6 Feb. 1776: 'I . . . have been this week confined to my bed with the gout in six or seven different places' (MASON i. 240). He was still confined, though recovering, when he wrote to Mann 22 March (MANN viii. 184). The present letter is in Kirgate's hand.

himself he shall owe part of his recovery to Mr Gibbon, whom, as soon as that is a little effected, he shall beg the honour of seeing.[4]

To Edward Gibbon, Wednesday 14 February 1776

Printed from a photostat of the MS (lacking the last page) among the Gibbon papers in the British Museum (Add. MS 34,886, f. 54) and from the MS fragment of the last paragraph, which is now wsl. First printed in *Miscellaneous Works of Edward Gibbon, Esq.,* ed. Lord Sheffield, [2d edn,] 1814, ii. 154–6. Reprinted in *Miscellaneous Works,* ed. Sheffield, 1796–1815, iii. 602–3; Wright v. 441–3; Cunningham vi. 307–8; Toynbee ix. 323–5 (signature omitted in Wright, Cunningham, and Toynbee). For the history of the Gibbon papers in the BM see *ante* ca 12 Feb. 1776. The MS was presumably intact when Lord Sheffield printed the letter in 1814; probably after his death (1821) but before the sale of Gibbon's papers to the BM in 1895–6, the last page of the letter became separated; this fragment was sold Anderson Auction Co. 21 April 1908 (Preston A. Perry Sale), lot 418, to unknown; resold American Art Association 6 Nov. 1923 (William F. Gable Sale, Part I), lot 716 (laid in a copy of HW's *Essay on Modern Gardening,* SH, 1785, with the bookplate of George Soaper), to unknown; acquired from Alston Deas, of Mount Pleasant, South Carolina, by wsl, Dec. 1957. A MS copy of the letter, in the hand of an amanuensis, is bound in Lord Sheffield's interleaved copy of the *Miscellaneous Works,* 2 vols, 1796, now in the Yale University Library (vol. I, pt 2, following p. 498).

'1776' has been added to the date in an unidentified hand; the year is confirmed by the reference to the first volume of Gibbon's *Decline and Fall.*

Endorsed by Gibbon on the verso of the fragment: Mr Horace Walpole February the 14th 1776.

Endorsed, in an unidentified hand, on the recto of the fragment: Horace Walpole Feb. 14— 1776.

Wednesday, Feb. 14th.

AFTER the singular pleasure of reading you, Sir, the next satisfaction is to declare my admiration. I have read great part of your volume,[1] and cannot decide to which of its various merits I give the preference, though I have no doubt of assigning my partiality to one virtue in the author, which, seldom as I meet with it, always strikes me superiorly. Its quality will naturally prevent your guessing which I mean. It is your amiable modesty. How can you know so much, judge so well, possess your subject and your knowledge and your power of judicious reflection so thoroughly, and yet command

4. See following letter.   1. See previous letter, n. 2.

yourself and betray no dictatorial arrogance of decision? How unlike very ancient and very modern authors! You have unexpectedly given the world a classic history.[2] The fame it must acquire will tend every day to acquit this panegyric of flattery. The impressions it has made on me are very numerous. The strongest is the thirst of being better acquainted with you—but I reflect that I have been a trifling author, and am in no light profound enough to deserve your intimacy, except by confessing your superiority so frankly, that I assure you honestly I already feel no envy, though I did for a moment. The best proof I can give you of my sincerity, is to exhort you warmly and earnestly to go on with your noble work—the strongest, though a presumptuous, mark of my friendship, is to warn you never to let your charming modesty be corrupted by the acclamations your talents will receive. The native qualities of the man should never be sacrificed to those of the author, however shining. I take this liberty as an older man,[3] which reminds me how little I dare promise myself that I shall see your work completed![4] But I love posterity enough to contribute, if I can, to give them pleasure through you.

I am too weak to say more, though I could talk for hours on your *History*. But one feeling I cannot suppress, though it is a sensation of vanity. I think, nay I am sure I perceive, that your sentiments on government agree with my own. It is the only point on which I suspect myself of any partiality in my admiration. It is a reflection of a far inferior vanity that pleases me in your speaking with so much distinction of that alas! wonderful period in which the world saw five good monarchs succeed each other.[5] I have often thought of

2. 'Lo, there is just appeared a truly classic work: a history, not majestic like Livy, nor compressed like Tacitus; not stamped with character like Clarendon; perhaps not so deep as Robertson's *Scotland*, but a thousand degrees above his *Charles*; not pointed like Voltaire, but as accurate as he is inexact; modest as he is *tranchant* and sly as Montesquieu without being so *recherché*. The style is as smooth as a Flemish picture, and the muscles are concealed and only for natural uses, not exaggerated like Michael Angelo's to show the painter's skill in anatomy; nor composed of the limbs of clowns of different nations, like Dr Johnson's heterogeneous monsters. This book is Mr Gibbon's *History of the Decline and Fall of the Roman Empire*. . . . I know him a little, never suspected the extent of his talents, for he is perfectly modest, or I want penetration, which I know too, but I intend to know him a great deal more' (HW to Mason 18 Feb. 1776, MASON i. 243–4).

3. HW was fifty-eight, Gibbon thirty-eight.

4. The last three volumes of the *Decline and Fall* were published in 1788, nine years before HW's death.

5. 'The world will no more see Athens, Rome, and the Medici again, than a succession of five good emperors, like Nerva, Trajan, Adrian, and the two Antonines' (HW to Chute 5 Aug. 1771, CHUTE 127).

treating that Elysian era. Happily it has fallen into better hands![6]

I have been able to rise today for the first time, and flatter myself that if I have no relapse, you will in two or three days more give me leave, Sir, to ask the honour of seeing you. In the meantime be just, and do not suspect me of flattering you. You will always hear that I say the same of you to everybody. I am with the greatest regard, Sir,

Your most obedient humble servant

Hor. Walpole

From Lady Craven,[1] Saturday 17 February 1776

Printed from the MS now wsl. First printed, Toynbee *Supp.* ii. 148–50. Damer-Waller; the MS was sold Sotheby's 5 Dec. 1921 (first Waller Sale), lot 114, bought in; resold Christie's 15 Dec. 1947 (second Waller Sale), lot 9, to Maggs for wsl.

Dated by HW's reply written the same day (see n. 5 below).

Endorsed in an unidentified hand: Verses from Lady [Craven] and an answer by Lord Orford.

Address: To the Honourable Horace Walpole Esq.

Saturday.

LADY Craven hopes Mr Walpole is better,[2] and encloses him her country eclogue—which she begs he will not criticize, as it is a young and careless *Dorinda*[3] as full of faults as possible.

[Enclosure]

Dorinda on her couch reclined,
Of country sports grown weary—
Hails in her youthful joyous mind
The month of January.

6. The rest of the text is contained in the MS fragment (see headnote).

———

1. Lady Elizabeth Berkeley (1750–1828), 2d dau. of the 4th E. of Berkeley, m. 1 (1767) William Craven, 6th Bn Craven, 1769 (from whom she separated ca 1783); m. 2 (1791) Christian Friedrich Karl Alex-ander, Margrave of Brandenburg-Ansbach and Bayreuth. See Mason i. 247 n. 50.

2. See *ante* ca 12 Feb. 1776, n. 3.

3. *Dorinda, a Town Eclogue*, written by the Hon. Richard Fitzpatrick (Lord Ossory's younger brother) and printed by HW at the SH Press in June 1775 (Hazen, *SH Bibl.* 112; Mason i. 202 n. 2).

Adieu, she cries, ye leafless trees,
   Ye downs and woods so dreary;
I gladly quit such scenes as these
   For town in January.

Hear me, each married dame, O hear,
   And blooming virgins hear me:
No month for us in all the year
   Is like dear January.

The birthday fine, the sportive ball,
   And beaux whose merits vary:
If these are joys, we find them all
   In charming January.

In beauteous groups each day we meet,
   See objects gay and airy,
Who pay their homage at our feet
   To welcome January.

May wit and mirth each hour employ
   No fools or fogrums⁴ near ye
To chill with frowns our rising joy,
   Like frost in January.

Alike the fogrum and the fool
   In converse ne'er can spare ye,
Of scandal each the willing tool
   In busy January.

Avoid them all like some disease,
   Through envy they would mar ye—
Their very looks, their thoughts must freeze
   Like winds in January.

Celia, so oft in pettish mood,
   You cry, 'Why did I marry?

4. Fogram or fogrum, 'an antiquated or
old-fashioned person, a fogy' (OED).

A country life does me no good
   From June to January.'

My dear, thy spouse, of hunting fond,
   May o'er a gate miscarry;
A frost may spoil the plainest ground
   In charming January.

By yon pale moon, my lovely friend,
   By that bright heaven so starry,
I swear I mean not to offend,
   But plead for January.

You then might choose a Valentine,
   Of false ones pray beware ye;
Now think of yours, I'll think of mine,
   To grace this January.

Up with thought she starts to call
   John, Thomas, William, Harry.
My feathers, hey! Where are you all?
   I fly in January.[5]

5. 'Lady Craven sent these lines to Mr Walpole in a fit of the gout, desiring he would not criticize them: he immediately returned the following answer; . . . Feb. 17, 1776' (HW's MS note; for the verses in answer see the following letter).

To Lady Craven, Saturday 17 February 1776

Printed from HW's MS copy written on the last page of Lady Craven's letter to him 17 Feb. 1776 (see previous letter, n. 5). HW wrote Mason 18 Feb.: 'I shall take the liberty . . . to trespass on your decorum by sending you an impromptu I wrote yesterday, to pretty Lady Craven, who sent me an eclogue of her own, every stanza of which ended with *January*, and which she desired me not to criticize, as some of the rhymes were incorrect, a licence I adopted in my second line' (Mason i. 247). Previously printed in *Horace Walpole's Fugitive Verses*, ed. W. S. Lewis, 1931, p. 168. The original letter is missing.

Feb. 17, 1776.

Tho' lame and old, I do not burn
With fretfulness to scare ye;
And charms and wit like yours would turn
To May my January.

The God, that can inspire and heal,
Sure breath'd your lines, sweet Fairy;
For as I read, I feel, I feel—
I'm[1] not quite January.

To the Comte de Guines,[1] Sunday 18 February 1776

Printed for the first time from a photostat of the MS in the Bibliothèque Municipale de Nantes (Collection Labouchère, MS français 674,250). The collection of autographs formed by Pierre-Antoine Labouchère was bequeathed by him to the city of Nantes in 1873.

Ce 18 févr[ier] 1776.

UNE maladie longue et douleureuse,[2] qui m'ôta l'usage des mains, a été l'unique cause, Monsieur l'Ambassadeur, que je n'ai pas pu vous marquer ni en personne ni par écrit l'intérêt extrême que je prends à tout ce qui vous regarde, et la sensibilité dont me pénètre votre rappel.[3] Vous n'en doutez pas, je me flatte: vous

1. 'I am' in the copy sent to Mason (see headnote).

1. Adrien-Louis de Bonnières (1735–1806), Comte and (10 May 1776) Duc de Guines; French ambassador to England 1770–6.
2. See *ante* ca 12 Feb. 1776, n. 3.
3. In late January Guines was recalled from his embassy at London; his letter to

ne me soupçonnerez pas, Monsieur le Comte, d'être le seul anglais de tous ceux qui ont eu l'honneur de vous connaître, qui ne partage pas les sentiments de mes compatriotes. L'honneur que Votre Excellence m'a faite de passer à ma porte, et que je n'étais pas en état de recevoir, me comble de reconnaissance, et m'arrache des lignes que je n'écris pas sans peine. Puissiez-vous surmonter les cabales de tous vos ennemis!4 Puisse le triomphe de la vertu être aussi éclatant que le calme de votre belle âme! La fortune vous aura éprouvé; si elle vous abandonne, elle n'aura fait qu'embellir votre mérite. J'ai l'honneur d'être avec le plus grand respect, Monsieur l'Ambassadeur

Votre très humble et très obéissant serviteur

Horace Walpole

From the Comte de Creutz,[1] Wednesday 6 March 1776

Printed from a photostat of the MS in the Bodleian Library (MS Toynbee d.11, pp. 73–5). First printed in *Lettres de la Marquise du Deffand à Horace Walpole (1776–1780)*, ed. Mrs Paget Toynbee, 1912, iii. 183. For the history of the MS see *ante* 20 April 1768.

Paris, ce 6 mars 1776.

C'EST avec un plaisir infini, Monsieur, que j'ai reçu les jolis présents que Madame du Deffand m'a remis de votre part,[2] et je vous en offre ici l'hommage de ma vive reconnaissance. Je n'ai

---

Lord Weymouth, transmitting his 'lettre de rappel,' is dated 2 Feb. 1776. His recall was said to be the result of 'a successful cabal of his enemies' (HW to Mann 15 Feb. 1776, Mann viii. 178; see ibid. n. 11 and *Last Journals* i. 517–21, where his career as ambassador is discussed). He left England 26 Feb. (*Recueil des instructions données aux ambassadeurs et ministres de France*, 1884–   , xxv pt ii, ed. Paul Vaucher, 477).

4. 'C'est un homme bien malheureux, mais comme je crois qu'il n'a point de tort, mais seulement des ennemis, et qu'il a un courage étonnant, il ne se laissera point accabler, et parviendra à prendre le dessus. Il n'y a que les gens faibles qui

succombent et qu'on écrase impunément. Depuis son retour il n'a point quitté Versailles' (Mme du Deffand to HW 27 March 1776, du Deffand iv. 290).

———

1. Gustaf Philip Creutz (1731–85), greve, Swedish ambassador at Paris 1766–83. HW met him at Paris in 1765 (du Deffand i. 182 n. 13, v. 283).

2. Mme du Deffand wrote HW 24 Jan. 1776: 'Je crois vous avoir rendu comte de toutes vos commissions. Je vis hier M. de Creutz pour la première fois parce qu'il a eu la goutte; il est charmé de ses médaillons; il m'en demanda le prix' (ibid. iv. 261). The portrait medallions have not been further identified.

jamais rien vu de mieux fini, ni de mieux senti pour l'expression, ni de plus heureux pour le choix. Je les conserverai comme une marque d'amitié infiniment chère de l'homme que j'honore le plus pour ses lumières et pour son caractère aimable.

Vous avez été tourmenté de la goutte, Monsieur; je l'ai été de même pour la première fois.[3] Il faut tôt ou tard se familiariser avec la douleur. Je me sers d'un remède très innocent et dont je me trouve parfaitement bien. C'est de prendre le soir en me couchant une seule tasse de thé de fleur de sureau,[4] qui fait transpirer doucement, et de mettre tous les matins les pieds dans l'eau. Le Comte d'Affry[5] a été tourmenté de la goutte, il avait jusqu'à quatre accès par an, et voilà onze ans qu'il en est quitte depuis qu'il se sert de ce remède. Il doit être innocent, car les bains de pieds ne font que favoriser la transpiration.

Quand est-ce vous nous reviendrez, Monsieur?[6] Vous savez combien vous êtes cher à vos amis et combien vous êtes nécessaire à leur bonheur. J'espère avec le temps obtenir leurs droits puisque j'ai déja leurs sentiments. On ne vous connaît pas sans avoir le désir de vivre avec vous et de conserver une place dans votre souvenir.

Je vous prie d'agréer les assurances de l'attachement sincère et inviolable avec lequel j'ai l'honneur d'être,

> Monsieur,
> Votre très humble et très obéissant serviteur,
>
> Le Comte de Creutz

---

3. Creutz is said to have died from a violent attack of gout, from which he suffered for many years (*Biographie universelle*, ed. Michaud, 1811–28, x. 249).

4. 'The flowers [of the elder tree] are very salutary, and being infused in the manner of tea, are very proper in all hot, feverish, variolous and morbillous distempers' (Robert James, *A Medicinal Dictionary*, 1743–5, iii. *sub* Sambucus). 'The stones of the berries, by expression, yield an oil which eases the pain of the gout. An oil is, also, made for this distemper by dissolution of its leaves' (ibid.). HW used a solution of rum and elder-flower water to relieve his eyes (Mann v. 167–8).

5. Louis-Auguste-Augustin (1713–93), Comte d'Affry; Col. of the Swiss Guards; Lt-Gen.; minister (1755–6, 1756–8) and ambassador (1758–62) to Holland (Mann v. 298 n. 5).

6. HW's last visit to Paris was in 1775.

To the Contessa di Viry, ca Tuesday 2 April 1776

Printed from the MS copy, in Jean-François Wiart's hand, of a French translation of HW's letter by Vincent-Louis Dutens (*ante* 17 Nov. 1766, n. 3), in Mme du Deffand's *Recueil de lettres choisies de différentes personnes*, pp. 387–8, now WSL. The MS copy contains HW's 'Notes' (written after 1780) at the end of the letter. First printed, Toynbee ix. 452–4. The *Recueil de lettres* was among the MSS bequeathed by Mme du Deffand to HW and sold SH vi. 107 to D. O. Dyce-Sombre, whose widow (later Lady Forester) died in 1893 leaving them to her nephew, W. R. Parker-Jervis; resold Sotheby's 12 March 1920 (Parker-Jervis Sale), lot 390, to Maggs; acquired from them by WSL (see DU DEFFAND i. xlvi, xlviii). The original letter is missing.

Dated approximately by Mme du Deffand's references to the letter in her letters to HW 27 April and 5 May 1776 (see n. 2 below), and by the likelihood that it was sent to Paris via Col. Horace St Paul with HW's letter to Mme du Deffand ca 2 April (DU DEFFAND iv. 294).

Endorsed by Wiart: De Monsieur Horace Walpole à Mme de Viry[1]— ambassadrice de Sardaigne en France 1776.[2]

LADY[3] Weymouth[4] m'a dit, Madame, que vous me reprochiez de ne vous avoir pas envoyé la Vie de Mr Gray[5] comme je vous l'avais promis. J'avoue à ma honte que vous avez raison, et que vous me rendriez justice si vous me grondiez sans pitié. Cependant comme il n'y a si mauvaise cause qui ne puisse se défendre, il me semble que si j'avais un peu d'éloquence, je désarmerais non seulement votre colère, mais je craindrais de vous voir comme Niobé convertie en

1. Miss Speed was brought up by the Lady Viscountess Cobham, who left her about £40,000. She married le Baron de Perrier, only son of the Comte de Virri, ambassador to England from Sardinia, whom he succeeded in the title of Virri, and was himself ambassador in Spain and France. Madame de Virri had a great deal of wit (HW). See *ante* 25 Feb. 1771, n. 1.

2. This letter was certainly written in English. I do not know by whom it was translated. Madame du Deffand did not understand a word of English (HW). Mme du Deffand wrote HW 27 [28] April 1776: 'J'ai la traduction de votre lettre à l'ambassadrice de Sardaigne. C'est une galanterie que m'a faite M. Dutens'; and again on 5 May: 'Le bon M. Dutens a traduit votre lettre à l'ambassadrice de Sardaigne pour me la faire voir, elle est très jolie' (DU DEFFAND iv. 308, 310).

3. 'Lord' crossed out by HW in the MS copy and 'Lady' written above.

4. Lady Weymouth was daughter of the Duke of Portland, and Lady of the Bedchamber to Queen Charlotte (HW). Lady Elizabeth Cavendish Bentinck (1735–1825), eldest dau. of the 2d D. of Portland, m. (1759) Thomas Thynne, 3d Vct Weymouth, 1751, cr. (1789) M. of Bath; lady of the Bedchamber to Queen Charlotte 1761–93; mistress of the robes 1793–1818 (MANN v. 518 n. 23).

5. The *Life* of Mr Gray by Mr Mason. Miss Speed was one of the heroines of Mr Gray's *Long Story* (HW). See *ante* 27 Nov. 1773, n. 1. Miss Speed (later Contessa di Viry) and Lady Schaub are the heroines of Gray's poem 'A Long Story'; see *Correspondence of Thomas Gray*, ed. Paget Toynbee and Leonard Whibley, Oxford, 1935, i. 333 n. 2.

pierre à force de pleurer. En un mot, la goutte m'a mis à la torture depuis quatre mois;[6] or, je ne sais comment cela se fait, mais les douleurs excessives ne me rappellent jamais rien d'agréable. Comment s'attendre donc que les angoisses, l'apothicaire Graham,[7] les flanelles,[8] et une chaise longue pussent rappeler à ma mémoire, l'esprit, la vivacité, la bonne humeur et la gaîté? Bien loin de cela, Madame, je vous proteste que quand Lady Weymouth prononça votre nom, je me reveillai comme sortant d'un rêve. Il m'est arrivé comme au sultan des *Mille et une nuits,* qui ayant plongé sa tête dans une cuve d'eau, s'imagina avoir passé vingt ans dans la pauvreté et dans la misère, et quant il sortît sa tête hors de l'eau, se trouva au milieu de sa cour, et aussi sultan que jamais. Je me ressouviens à présent qu'au mois d'août et de septembre dernier, j'ai vu Mme de Viry fêter toute la France,[9] répandant la gaîté au milieu des cérémonies, mettant la foule à son aise et paraissant elle-même aussi gaie, aussi amusante et amusée, que si (au lieu d'avoir imaginé des projets de pompe et de plaisirs pour tout Versailles et Paris) il y avait eu des légions de fées et de grâces occupées à l'amuser. Vous voyez, Madame, par la vérité de ce portrait que j'ai certainement recouvré mes sens et ma mémoire, qu'il fallait que j'eusse perdus quand je vous oubliai. À l'avenir je craindrai plus que jamais la goutte, n'ayant pas su jusqu'à présent qu'elle attaquait ma tête.

Lady Temple, Lord et Lady Edgcumbe[10] et Lord Nuneham,[11] qui

6. See *ante* ca 12 Feb. 1776, n. 3.

7. James Graham (1745–94), quack doctor, who was at this time established in practice in Pall Mall.

8. See *ante* 9 Dec. 1775.

9. Mr Walpole was at Paris in 1775 when Madame [Clotilde], eldest sister of Louis XVI was married to the Prince of Pie[d]mont. Monsieur and Madame de Virri made great entertainments on that occasion, and all that is said here of her address was strictly true. They were soon after disgraced, recalled, and banished to their estate on the King of Sardinia's discovering a secret correspondence between the Count and a clerk in the Secretary's office, the true history of which is not known (HW). Marie-Adélaïde-Clotilde-Xavière (1759–1802), m. (21 Aug. 1775) Charles Emmanuel, P. of Piedmont, later (1796) Charles Emmanuel IV of Sardinia. See Ossory i. 246 and n. 26. 'The Sardinian ambassador, charged to demand the Princess Clotilda of France in marriage for the Prince of Piedmont, made his public entry in a most magnificent manner at Paris. A dinner of fifty covers was afterwards given by the King, to which the great officers of state and all the foreign ambassadors were invited. Prince Narsan of Lorraine did the honours of the table' (GM 1775, xlv. 403, 'Historical Chronicle' *sub* 9 Aug. 1775).

10. Emma Gilbert (1729–1807), only dau. of John Gilbert (1693–1761), Abp of York, m. (1761) George Edgcumbe (1721–95), 3d Bn Edgcumbe, 1761, cr. (1781) Vct Mount Edgcumbe and (1789) E. of Mount Edgcumbe.

11. These were particular friends of Miss Speed, before her leaving England. Anna Chamber Countess Temple was niece by marriage of Lady Cobham. George Lord Edgcumbe was the third

m'ont consolé dans mon *béquillage*[12] et en ont été témoins, m'ont caché avec soin cette fâcheuse partie de ma situation, mais je suis désolé de cette découverte, et à moins qu'au lieu de me blâmer, vous ne me disiez que vous avez pitié de moi, je suis menacé d'une rechute, mais je me flatte que Mr Gray fera ma paix; ses lettres vous mettront ou plutôt vous entretiendront tellement en bonne humeur que vous oublierez mon oubli et me croirez encore, Madame,

Votre etc.

To Dr Richard Gem,[1] Thursday 4 April 1776

Printed from *Works* v. 649–51, where the letter was first printed. Reprinted in *Elegant Extracts . . . Originally Compiled by the Rev. Vicesimus Knox, D.D.*, ed. J. G. Percival, Boston, [? 1826], iv. 289–90; Wright v. 443–6; Cunningham vi. 320–2 (signature omitted in Percival, Wright, and Cunningham); Toynbee ix. 340–2. The history of the MS and its present whereabouts are not known.

The letter as it appears in *Works* includes four identifying footnotes (here omitted) by Mary Berry; later editors have mistakenly assumed that the notes were HW's and have printed them as such.

Arlington Street, April 4, 1776.

IT IS but fair, when one quits one's party, to give notice to those one abandons—at least, modern patriots, who often imbibe their principles of honour at Newmarket, use that civility. You and I, dear Sir, have often agreed in our political notions; and you, I fear, will die without changing your opinion. For my part, I must confess I am totally altered; and, instead of being a warm partisan of liberty, now admire nothing but despotism. You will naturally ask what

Baron, and first Viscount of that family: his wife was daughter and heiress of Dr Gilbert Archbishop of York. George Simon Lord Nuneham was the second Earl of Harcourt (HW).

12. I do not recollect what the word was in the original (HW).

1. (ca 1717–1800), English physician resident in Paris; educated at Cambridge; appointed physician to the British embassy at Paris, 1762 (N&Q 1910, 11th Ser., ii. 121–3). HW met him at Paris in 1765

(Selwyn 208) and saw him there several times during his visit in 1775 ('Paris Journals,' du Deffand v. 345–6, 350–1, 353). William Cole, who also visited Paris in 1765, described him as 'a very tall awkward kind of man, of a solemn figure, and no great conversation' (Cole, *A Journal of My Journey to Paris in the Year 1765*, ed. F. G. Stokes, 1931, p. 63). A staunch republican in politics, Dr Gem sympathized with the French Revolution and continued to live in France until his death.

place I have gotten, or what bribe I have taken? Those are the criterions of political changes in England—but as my conversion is of foreign extraction, I shall not be the richer for it. In one word, it is the *Relation du lit de justice*[2] that has operated the miracle. When two ministers[3] are found so humane, so virtuous, so excellent, as to study nothing but the welfare and deliverance of the people; when a king listens to such excellent men; and when a parliament, from the basest, most interested motives, interposes to intercept the blessing,[4] must I not change my opinions, and admire arbitrary power? or can I retain my sentiments, without varying the objects?

Yes, Sir, I am shocked at the conduct of the Parliament—one would think it was an English one! I am scandalized at the speeches of the *Avocat Général*,[5] who sets up the odious interests of the nobility and clergy against the cries and groans of the poor, and who employs his wicked eloquence to tempt the good young monarch, by personal views, to sacrifice the mass of his subjects to the privileges of the few—but why do I call it eloquence? The fumes of interest had so clouded his rhetoric, that he falls into a downright Iricism.[6]—

2. The *lit de justice* held on 12 March 1776, reported in *Mercure historique et politique* clxxx. 469–84, 554–85, April and May 1776. A copy of the *procès-verbal* was apparently sent to HW by Mme du Deffand (DU DEFFAND iv. 284, 291, 296).

3. Chrétien-Guillaume de Lamoignon de Malesherbes (1721–94), first president of the Cour des Aides until 12 July 1775; minister of the King's Household 1775–6, 1787–8. Anne-Robert-Jacques Turgot (1727–81), Baron de l'Aulne; controller-general of finances 1774–6. 'Messieurs de Turgot and Malesherbes are philosophers in the true sense, that is, legislators—but as their plans tend to serve the public, you may be sure they do not please interested individuals' (HW to Mann 10 Oct. 1775, MANN viii. 133).

4. 'The virtuous President de Malesherbes . . . showered down blessings, and in vain attempted to extend his benevolence by reforming all crying abuses, in concurrence with Turgot, who resolved to brave every danger and difficulty in correcting an oppressive constitution. When Intendant of a province, Turgot had raised the Corvées within his jurisdiction, and now set about abolishing them, and other crying grievances, obtaining the King's consent and support. The clergy and gentry, whose estates would have suffered by this relief of the woes of the poor, united against salutary reform: and the restored Parliament in the same cause, and for the same interests, remonstrated against the King's arrêts. . . . Their opposition was so stout that most of the Council advised the King to recede. . . . The intrepid Turgot persisted, carried the King to a Lit de Justice, and forced obedience to all the godlike acts' (*Last Journals* i. 547–8). In January 1776 Turgot had submitted to the Council a series of reforms known as the Six Edicts. When the edicts were submitted to the Parliament on 7 Feb., the magistrates (many of whom were members of the nobility) protested against them. In spite of the opposition, Louis held a *lit de justice* on 12 March to enforce the registration of the edicts.

5. Antoine-Louis Séguier (1726–92), advocate-general of the Parliament of Paris.

6. 'An Irish trait of character, expression, etc.; an Irishism, Hibernicism' (OED).

He tells the King, that the intended tax on the proprietors of land will affect the property not only of the rich, but of the poor. I should be glad to know what is the property of the poor? Have the poor landed estates? Are those who have landed estates the poor? Are the poor that will suffer by the tax, the wretched labourers who are dragged from their famishing families to work on the roads?[7]—But *it is* wicked eloquence when it finds a reason, or gives a reason, for continuing the abuse.—The Advocate tells the King, those abuses are *presque consacrés par l'ancienneté.*[8]—Indeed he says all that can be said for nobility, it is *consacrée par l'ancienneté*—and thus the length of the pedigree of abuses renders them respectable!

His arguments are as contemptible when he tries to dazzle the King by the great names of Henri Quatre and Sully,[9] of Louis XIV and Colbert,[10] two couple whom nothing but a mercenary orator would have classed together.[11] Nor, were all four equally venerable, would it prove anything. Even good kings and good ministers, if such have been, may have erred; nay, may have done the best they could. They would not have been good, if they wished their errors should be preserved, the longer they had lasted.

In short, Sir, I think this resistance of the Parliament to the adorable reformation planned by Messrs de Turgot and Malesherbes, is more phlegmatically scandalous than the wildest tyranny of despotism. I forget what the nation was that refused liberty when it was offered. This opposition to so noble a work is worse. A whole people may refuse its own happiness; but these profligate magistrates resist happiness for others, for millions, for posterity!—Nay, do they not

---

7. One of the Six Edicts (n. 4 above) abolished the *corvée*, the unpaid work on roads performed by the peasantry for the state. To replace the *corvée*, there was to be a tax levied on all landowners in order to provide funds to pay labourers who worked on the roads. The peasants had formerly been required to work on the roads fifteen days every year.

8. These words do not appear in Séguier's speech as reported in *Mercure historique et politique* clxxx. 555–85, but he is quoted as saying that the proposed tax on property owners would in principle destroy 'les franchises de la noblesse, aussi ancienne que la monarchie' (ibid. clxxx. 557).

9. Maximilien de Béthune (1559 *or*

1560–1641), Duc de Sully; Henri IV's chief minister (David Buisseret, *Sully and the Growth of Centralized Government in France, 1598–1610*, 1968, p. 38, n. 1).

10. Jean-Baptiste Colbert (1619–83), Marquis de Seignelay; minister under Louix XIV. HW contrasts Sully and Colbert in his letter to Mme du Deffand ca 5 Oct. 1773 (DU DEFFAND iii. 407).

11. 'Jamais Prince n'a été plus chéri que Henri IV; jamais la France n'a été plus florissante que sous Louis XIV; jamais le commerce n'a été plus étendu, plus profitable que sous l'administration de Colbert; c'est néanmoins l'ouvrage de Henri IV et de Louis XIV, de Sully et de Colbert qu'on vous propose d'anéantir' (*Mercure historique et politique* clxxx. 583–4).

half vindicate Maupeou,[12] who crushed them?—And you, dear Sir, will you now chide my apostasy? Have I not cleared myself to your eyes? I do not see a shadow of sound logic in all Monsieur Séguier's speeches, but in his proposing that the soldiers should work on the roads, and that passengers should contribute to their fabric;[13] though, as France is not so luxuriously mad as England, I do not believe passengers could support the expense of the roads. That argument, therefore, is like another that the *Avocat* proposes to the King, and which, he modestly owns, he believes would be impracticable.

I beg your pardon, Sir, for giving you this long trouble; but I could not help venting myself, when shocked to find such renegade conduct in a Parliament that I was rejoiced had been restored. Poor human kind! is it always to breed serpents from its own bowels? In one country it chooses its representatives, and they sell it and themselves—in others it exalts despots—in another it resists the despot when he consults the good of his people!—Can we wonder mankind is wretched, when men are such beings? Parliaments run wild with loyalty, when America is to be enslaved or butchered. They rebel, when their country is to be set free!—I am not surprised at the idea of the devil being always at our elbows. They who invented him, no doubt could not conceive how men could be so atrocious to one another, without the intervention of a fiend. Don't you think, if he had never been heard of before, that he would have been invented on the late partition of Poland?[14] Adieu, dear Sir!

Yours most sincerely,

Hor. Walpole

12. René-Nicolas-Charles-Augustin de Maupeou (1714–92), Chancellor of France, 1768 (Berry i. 28 n. 28). Maupeou was the leading supporter of the absolutist policies of Louis XV.

13. *Mercure historique et politique* clxxx. 558–60.

14. The first partition of Poland in 1772; see Mann vii. 419 and nn. 8, 9; vii. 436–7.

To Count Shuvalov,[1] Sunday 23 June 1776

Printed from a photostat of the MS in the Dumbarton Oaks Research Library and Collection, Washington, D.C. First printed (in facsimile) in *Correspondance complète de la Marquise du Deffand avec ses amis le Président Hénault—Montesquieu—d'Alembert—Voltaire[—]Horace Walpole,* ed. M.-F.-A. de Lescure, 1865, ii. between 560 and 561. Reprinted, Toynbee ix. 378–9. The MS is untraced until sold Sotheby's 17 March 1875 (Most Important and Valuable Series of Autograph Letters and Historical Documents Sale), lot 180, to Naylor; offered by Dodd, Mead and Co., Catalogue of Autographs and Manuscripts, March 1901, lot 345; later acquired by Mrs Robert Woods Bliss, who, with her husband, donated the Dumbarton Oaks collection to Harvard University in 1940.

Address: À Monsieur M. le Comte de Schouallow à Paris.

De Strawberry Hill ce 23 juin 1776.[2]

JE ME flatte, M. le Comte, que vous aurez reçu avant cette lettre une petite caisse de médaillons,[3] que j'ai adressée à notre bonne amie de St-Joseph.[4] J'ai dépensé tout votre argent, mais la quantité n'est pas inconsidérable, et cependant il m'en reste encore deux à vous envoyer, que le marchand avait oubliées, et qu'il ne m'a remis, qu'après la caisse partie. Parmi celles que vous avez, il y a une tête en profile de My Lord Chatham,[5] que vous reconnaîtrez très facilement. Si vous êtes content de mes soins, n'oserai[-je] pas me flatter que vous voulez bien me faire l'honneur d'être votre commissionaire? Il me sera bien sensible d'avoir occasion de vous faire souvenir de moi. Ce n'est point assurément que vous ne m'ayez bien trop distingué par la place que vous m'avez destiné dans certain portrait

1. Ivan Ivanovich Shuvalov (1727–97), courtier, founder of the University of Moscow, 1755; favourite of the Empress Elizabeth (DU DEFFAND i. 4 n. 11; MANN vi. 59 n. 56, 289 n. 9; *Mem. Geo. III* i. 119). An ardent patron of the arts, Shuvalov made many contributions to cultural life in Russia. He left Russia in 1763 and lived abroad until 1777 (CONWAY ii. 516 n. 5). He was a friend of Mme du Deffand, and HW often saw him during his visits to Paris. HW entertained him at SH in June 1765 (MONTAGU ii. 156–7).

2. HW also wrote the place and date at the end of the letter.

3. It is not clear whether these medallions were painted, ceramic, or metallic. See n. 5 below.

4. Mme du Deffand, who had an apartment in the convent of St-Joseph. She wrote HW 30 June 1776: 'Tout ce que vous me dites à l'occasion du Schuwalof est excellentissime. Il revient aujourd'hui de la campagne, je crois que je le verrai. Je lui remettrai vos paquets, sinon je les lui enverrai demain matin' (DU DEFFAND iv. 335).

5. William Pitt, cr. (1766) E. of Chatham. According to M. H. Grant, 'British Medals since 1760,' *British Numismatic Journal,* 1934–7, xxii, 3d Ser., ii. 273, there were seven different medals of Chatham issued in 1766.

précieux que je n'ai pas la hardiesse de montrer. Mon estampe sera encore trop glorieuse si vous lui faites l'honneur de la garder dans votre chambre;[6] mais jamais je n'aurai le front de me faire encadrer avec vous. Vous me privez de l'honneur de me vanter d'avoir votre portrait,[7] et je vous supplie de ne pas attribuer à la fausse modestie ma répugnance à occuper une place aussi honorable, et qui n'est pas faite pour un petit homme comme moi, qui n'ai jamais rien fait de méritoire. Votre portrait serait déprécié à cause de l'accessoire. Si vous me fâchez, je vous ferai tenir à la main le Cardinal de Richelieu, aussi indigne d'être votre associé que ne l'est

Monsieur le Comte
Votre très dévoué serviteur

HORACE WALPOLE

To ? JAMES BINDLEY,[1] Friday 5 July 1776

Printed from an extract quoted in Puttick and Simpson's auction catalogue of the S. George Christison Sale 14–16 Dec. 1850, lot 675. The MS is described as an autograph letter signed by HW, one page, quarto, 'conveying an invitation.' It was sold to Captain Montagu Montagu, R.N., but was apparently not included in the Montagu bequest of MSS to the Bodleian Library in 1863; not further traced.

The addressee is conjecturally identified as James Bindley. HW's presentation copy to him of Hentzner's *Journey into England*, SH, 1757, is inscribed by Bindley: 'The gift of the Honourable Mr Horace Walpole at Strawberry Hill. July 10, 1776. J. B.' (now in the Rothschild collection at Trinity College, Cambridge; see *The Rothschild Library*, Cambridge, privately printed, 1954, i. 67, No. 370).

[Strawberry Hill, July 5, 1776.]

. . . I have more to show you than can be dispatched in two or three hours.

---

6. Mme du Deffand wrote HW 28 April: 'Je voudrais avoir [la lettre] que vous avez écrite à M. Schuwalof. Je trouve l'idée charmante de s'être fait peindre votre estampe à la main' (DU DEFFAND iv. 308). The letter referred to is missing.

7. HW's portrait of 'Count Schouallow, favourite of the Czarina Elizabeth, whose image he holds. . . . Painted at Paris in

1775,' was hung in the Beauclerk Closet at SH ('Des. of SH,' *Works* ii. 504); it was sold SH xvii. 37.

---

1. (1737–1818), commissioner of stamp duties 1765–1818; F.S.A., 1765; collector of books, prints, and medals (CHATTERTON 301 n. 15).

TO JAMES BINDLEY, Saturday 9 November 1776

Printed from an extract quoted in Sotheby's auction catalogue of 17 Dec.
1973 (property of a Gentleman), lot 252. The MS is described as an autograph
letter signed by HW, one page, quarto, with address and postmark, 'promising
to let him have the second part of *The Wits' Commonwealth* [Francis Meres,
Palladis Tamia; Wits Treasury Being the Second Part of Wits Commonwealth,
1598] on the following Tuesday, thanking him for the offer of a print of Madame de Bury, asking him to bring a medal of the late Czarina Elizabeth, if he
has one, as he needs a drawing of her head, and telling him that the ticket for
the parks has not been struck off.' The MS was sold to Walter T. Spencer, who
has informed us that the present owner will not permit a copy of the letter to
be made.

[Strawberry Hill, Nov. 9, 1776.]

. . . my nephew[1] does not always execute all he intends; and none
are to be given till the King has one[2] . . .

TO GEORGE ALLAN,[1] Monday 9 December 1776

Printed from the MS now WSL. First printed, Nichols, *Lit. Anec.* viii. 509. Reprinted, Toynbee ix. 447. The MS is untraced until sold by Stanislaus Vincent
Henkels of Philadelphia 8 May 1895 (J. Henry Rogers Sale), lot 713, to
unknown; resold C. F. Libbie and Co. 3 May 1901 (Frederick W. French Sale),
lot 1330, to unknown; acquired from the Brick Row Bookshop by WSL, May 1933.
    Address: To George Allan Esq. at Darlington in the County of Durham.
Postmark: 9 DE. ISLEWORTH.

Strawberry Hill, Dec. 9, 1776.

Sir,

AS I have not the satisfaction of being acquainted with you, I
must think myself very particularly obliged by your present of
the two fine and very like prints of Bishop Trevor,[2] and beg you will

---

1. George Walpole, 3d Earl of Orford.
2. As Ranger of St James's and Hyde
Parks, Lord Orford was doubtless responsible for issuing tickets for the two parks.
See headnote; FAMILY 37 and n. 6; MANN
ix. 266 n. 11.

1. (1736–1800), topographer and antiquary.

2. Richard Trevor (1707–71), Bp of St
David's 1744–52, of Durham 1752–71. The
portrait of Bishop Trevor was engraved
by Joseph Collyer after a drawing by
Robert Hutchinson; it is the frontispiece
to Allan's *A Sketch of the Life and Character of the Right Honorable and Rev-*

be pleased to accept my sincere thanks. If you ever happen to pass this way, I shall be extremely glad to show you the collection[3] you have so handsomely adorned, and to have an opportunity in person of assuring you how gratefully

> I am Sir
> Your most obliged and obedient humble servant

HOR. WALPOLE

To George Colman, Saturday 28 December 1776

Printed for the first time from the MS in Thomas Kirgate's hand, bound in Kirgate's copy of *Designs by Mr R. Bentley, for Six Poems by Mr T. Gray,* containing mixed sheets of the 1775 and 1789 editions, now WSL. An extract of the letter is printed in Hazen, *Cat. of HW's Lib.,* No. 1811. For the history of Kirgate's copy of Bentley's *Designs* see Hazen, *Bibl. of HW* 120, copy 6.

Endorsed in an unidentified hand: Mr G.

Address: To George Colman Esq.

Arlington Street, December 28, 1776.

MR Walpole is so extremely out of order with the gout,[1] that his servants could not tell him till just now that Mr Colman had done him the honour of sending him his *Works.*[2] Mr Walpole is extremely grateful for so valuable a present, and will certainly wait on Mr Colman and thank him in person as soon as he is able, which indeed he fears will not be for a great while.[3]

---

erend Richard Trevor Lord Bishop of Durham, printed at Allan's private press at Blackwell Grange, near Darlington, Durham, 1776 (reprinted in Nichols, *Lit. Anec.* ix. 241–50; the engraved portrait, taken from the original plate, is opp. p. 241). HW gave one of the two impressions of the print to William Cole, enclosing it with his letter to Cole written the same day (COLE ii. 27–8).

3. Of engraved English portraits. See *ante* 3 April 1764, n. 3.

---

1. On 13 Dec. HW suffered an attack of gout (OSSORY i. 336). It was 'gone' by 24 Jan. 1777, when HW wrote Mann: 'I

call this a short and favourable fit, having, from its first moment to my airing, lasted *but* six weeks; and though I had it in both hands, wrists and elbows, there was not much pain for above 30 hours; and my feet escaped' (MANN viii. 272).

2. *The Dramatic Works of George Colman,* 4 vols, 1777. HW's presentation copy from Colman (not traced) is Hazen, *Cat. of HW's Lib.,* No. 1811.

3. In his letter to Colman *post* 2 March 1778, HW says that he 'waited on you at Richmond in the summer [of 1777] to thank you (though I believe you did not hear it).'

To Lord Hardwicke, Wednesday 29 January 1777

Printed for the first time from the MS now WSL. For the history of the MS see *ante* ? Jan. 1773.

Endorsed by Hardwicke: Mr W.

Jan. 29, 1777.

I DO not know, my Lord, nor ever heard of any portrait of Lady Douglas Sheffield.[1] I have a picture of her first husband, Lord Sheffield,[2] whom Lord Leicester was supposed to poison,[3] by Antonio More:[4] I bought it at the sale of the pictures in Buckingham House.[5]

I have the honour of sending your Lordship the play[6] you was pleased to order, and the little volume of poems,[7] and am with great respect

Your Lordship's most obedient humble servant

Hor. Walpole

1. Douglas Howard (ca 1545–1608), m. 1 (ca 1562) John Sheffield (ca 1538–68), 2d Bn Sheffield, 1549; m. 2 (1573) Robert Dudley (1532 *or* 1533–88), cr. (1564) E. of Leicester; m. 3 (1579) Sir Edward Stafford (d. 1605).

2. 'John Lord Sheffield, husband of Lady Douglas Sheffield, on whose account it was surmised that he was poisoned by R[obert] Earl of Leicester; by Ant. More: from Buckingham House' ('Des. of SH,' *Works* ii. 464). The portrait, which hung in the Gallery at SH, was sold SH xxi. 63 to Richard R. Preston for £14.14.0.

3. The story that Leicester was suspected of having Sheffield poisoned comes from the scurrilous work usually known as *Leicester's Commonwealth,* first printed (possibly at Antwerp) in 1584 and reprinted at London in 1641.

4. Anthonis Mor (1519–1575), Flemish painter.

5. The Buckingham House sale, at which HW made other purchases, took place on 25 Feb. 1763; see Dalrymple 95 n. 10. Buckingham House had been sold by Sir Charles Sheffield, the natural son of the Duke of Buckingham, to George III in 1762.

6. Probably the Président Hénault's tragedy *Cornélie Vestale,* which HW printed at the SH Press in 1768 (*ante* 27 Nov. 1767, nn. 1, 3).

7. Probably *Poems by the Reverend Mr Hoyland,* SH, 1769, or perhaps *Poems by Anna Chamber Countess Temple,* SH, 1764 (Hazen, *SH Bibl.* 85–7; *ante* 28 Jan. 1764, n. 3).

To Johannes von Müller,[1]
Thursday 30 January 1777

Printed from a photostat of the MS in the Stadtbibliothek Schaffhausen, Schaff-hausen, Switzerland, kindly furnished by Dr Barbara Schnetzler (Müller-Briefsammlung, Fasz. 86/3). First printed in Edgar Bonjour, *Studien zu Johannes von Müller*, Basle and Stuttgart, 1957, pp. 83–4. The MS is among the collection of Müller's papers that passed on his death in 1809 to his younger brother, Johann Georg Müller (1759–1819), a theologian at Schaffhausen, and from him to their nephew, Johann Jakob Meyer (d. 1823), who bequeathed the collection to the Stadtbibliothek Schaffhausen.

Arlington Street, London, Jan. 30, 1777.

I ought to be greatly flattered, Sir, at receiving encomiums from another country, from a person to whom I have not the honour of being known, and from a gentleman of such estimable principles.[2] But I should deserve your praise, Sir, still less than I do, if I did not feel that I am not entitled to the rank you are pleased to allot to me in the List of Authors.[3] My book[4] certainly owes its celebrity (and I doubt, your partiality) to its having been mentioned by Monsieur

1. (1752–1809), Swiss historian, diplo-matist, and political writer, called the 'Swiss Tacitus' (*Dictionnaire historique et biographique de la Suisse*, Neuchâtel, 1921–33, v. 40; Karl Schib, *Johannes von Müller 1752–1809*, Schaffhausen and Kon-stanz, 1967).

2. Müller had written to HW 14 Jan. 1777, enclosing his letter in another to his friend Thomas Boone. Boone wrote Mül-ler 30 Jan.: 'I received . . . the favour of your letter . . . enclosing one for Mr Walpole, which I sent to his house, the morning after it came to my hands; he is known to everybody, formerly I had the honour of being acquainted with him; at present I see him only in his compositions, which are clever, lively and full of imagi-nation' (MS in the Stadtbibliothek Schaff-hausen, Müller-Briefsammlung, Fasz. 81). Müller's letter to HW is missing. His friend Francis Kinloch wrote to him from England 16 May 1777: 'Horace Walpole has spoken with great praise of your letter to an acquaintance of mine, and told him he expected he should hear from you again' (ibid. Fasz. 85/122). No other letters

between HW and Müller are known to have survived.

3. Perhaps a list of writers who had published works concerning the history of England.

4. *Historic Doubts on the Life and Reign of King Richard the Third*, 1768. The Rev. Norton Nicholls, Gray's friend, had previously written to Müller: 'I have the honour of knowing Mr Horace Wal-pole very well and will take some oppor-tunity of communicating to him your favourable opinion of the little work you mention as well as your criticisms. He is not a Lord but son of the famous Sir Robert Walpole, who was afterwards created Earl of Orford, and author of the *Lives of Royal and Noble Authors in En-gland*, of *Anecdotes of Painting in En-gland* and other pieces both in verse and prose which have all some marks in them of his brilliant wit, vivacity, acuteness and great reading' (MS in the Stadtbibliothek Schaffhausen, Müller-Briefsammlung, Fasz. 75). The book had been brought to Müller's attention by John North (Edgar Bonjour, *Studien zu Johannes von Müller*, Basle

de Voltaire in a favourable manner.[5] Our language not being universal has kept much better authors of our country from being known in Europe. Forgive me, Sir, if I say, that I am much more flattered with my devotion to liberty having attracted your notice, than with any glory I could attain by my writings. A critical disquisition into a morsel of obscure history, is no great merit; nor have I been so successful as to convince several.[6] In truth, I could not expect it; for though I am clear that Richard III did not commit many crimes charged on him, I neither acquit him of all nor pretend to say what did happen —but I shall not trouble you, Sir, with more of that controversy. Allow me to return to Monsieur de Voltaire, to whom I acknowledge my obligations; and yet he has wounded me in a point, to which I am far more sensible than to my own fame. In his letter to me on the French stage,[7] he has paid me a compliment at the expense of my father, who was one of the wisest and best of men. Nothing can be more inferior to another than I to him both in virtues and abilities, nor can any Englishman read the comparison without a smile. I wish all Europe felt the injustice as strongly!

There is but the single point of unalterable attachment to liberty on which I can flatter myself, Sir, with deserving your regard. Would to God, Sir, more Englishmen, more Europeans, more inhabitants of the whole earth were inflamed with your sentiments! May your happy rocks forever value and retain the blessing! You have no reason to envy more fertile or more wealthy countries. From us, I fear, *that* blessing is vanishing! Riches, extravagance, corruption, and infatuation are hurrying us fast to the period of happiness, and glory![8]— but perhaps, when one considers the passions and folly of mankind, it is much more extraordinary that we should have preserved our freedom so long, than it will be if we lose it.

I am exceedingly obliged to you for the account you give me of your intended work,[9] Sir: I shall not only claim your promise of

and Stuttgart, 1957, p. 115; see also Thomas Grütter, *Johannes von Müllers Begegnung mit England,* Basle and Stuttgart, 1967, pp. 49, 96).

5. See Voltaire to HW *ante* 15 July 1768. That letter, in which Voltaire praises *Historic Doubts,* was printed in Voltaire's *Commentaire historique sur les œuvres de l'auteur de la Henriade,* Basle, 1776, pp. 199–209. Müller had very likely seen the letter there.

6. HW doubtless alludes to the various

answers attacking *Historic Doubts.* See *ante* 29 March 1772, n. 2.

7. The letter cited in n. 5 above.

8. HW expresses a similar concern in *Last Journals* ii. 284 (*sub* March 1780), where he speaks of 'the corruption of the whole nation, the servility of the nobility and gentry, the consequences of their extravagance.'

9. *Die Geschichten der Schweitzer,* Boston, 1780.

being favoured with the sight of it,[10] but shall be most happy if I can contribute the least trifle in my power towards clearing any point on which you are in doubt, though I assure you my knowledge in our own story is far more scanty and superficial than you imagine. Just at present I am in town and my books are in my library in the country; but I can promise you better assistance than my own; I have some antiquarian friends,[11] whom I will consult about your queries, and will take the liberty of sending you all I learn. I would engage immediately in your service myself, but am confined with the gout,[12] which is my annual companion, and which with fifty-nine years that I have lived, have made me little fit for anything but indifference and repose. You, Sir, who, I hope, have more youth[13] and better health, should inculcate the noble sentiments you feel. Make your honest countrymen sensible of their felicity—and be assured that your book will always be precious to the few patriots and virtuous men of future ages. The applause of a million slaves is not worth a wish.

The Princess Isabella,[14] one of the daughters of Edward III was married to Ingelram de Coucy. This is the only solution, Sir, I can give at present in my situation to any of your queries. Your correction of my negligence on Joan I[15] I receive with great gratitude,[16] and if my book should be reprinted,[17] which is not probable, I will take care to acknowledge to whom I am obliged. I have another debt to

10. No work by Müller appears in the SH records.

11. Chiefly William Cole, along with Michael Lort, Andrew Coltee Ducarel, and others.

12. Strictly speaking, this was not true, but HW had only very recently recovered from an attack of gout; see *ante* 28 Dec. 1776, n. 1. HW wrote Mason 17 Feb. 1777: 'I have gone about these three weeks and had no return of my disorder' (MASON i. 284).

13. Müller was then twenty-five years old.

14. Isabella (1332–79), eldest dau. of Edward III, m. (1365) Enguerrand (or Ingelram) VII (ca 1340–97), Lord of Coucy.

15. Giovanna I (1326–82), Q. of Naples 1343–82; m. 1 (1333) Andreas of Hungary; m. 2 (1346) Louis of Taranto; m. 3 (1363) James III, K. of Mallorca; m. 4 (1376) Otto, Duke of Brunswick-Grubenhagen.

16. HW had written in *Historic Doubts*, 1768, pp. 68–9: 'It is well known that the famous Joan of Naples was dethroned and murdered by the man she had chosen for her heir, Charles Durazzo. Ingratitude and cruelty were the characteristics of that wretch.' Müller had probably pointed out to HW that after adopting Charles of Durazzo as her heir, she later repudiated him and declared Louis of Anjou her successor. In 1381, supported by Pope Urban VI, Charles invaded Naples and imprisoned Giovanna; the following year she was put to death at his order (Émile G. Léonard, *Les Angevins de Naples*, 1954, pp. 462–9).

17. No later edition of *Historic Doubts* appeared during HW's lifetime. The passage concerning 'Joan of Naples' is unchanged in *Works*, 1798, which apparently follows the text of the first edition throughout (Hazen, *Bibl. of HW* 72).

you, Sir, for which I am not less thankful, your permission of writing
to you in my own language; not from any vanity of thinking I write
it well, but because I am sure I write French very ill—and I should
be very sorry to express my gratitude to you, Sir, in weaker terms
than my heart naturally suggests to me. I have the honour to be, Sir,
with great regard

Your most obliged and most obedient humble servant

Horace Walpole

To Lord Dacre, Tuesday 4 March 1777

Printed from a photostat of the MS in the Fitzwilliam Museum, Cambridge.
First printed, Toynbee *Supp.* iii. 25–6. The MS is untraced until acquired by
the Fitzwilliam Museum in Nov. 1917 as part of a miscellaneous collection of
manuscripts, the gift of Charles Fairfax Murray.

The identity of HW's correspondent, unknown to Dr Toynbee, is established
by the endorsement in Dacre's hand.

Endorsed by Dacre: A note from Mr Horace Walpole March 1777.

March 4th 1777.

My dear Lord,

I HAVE not had time till this minute to thank your Lordship for
the honour of your letter[1] and for the communication of the other
paper,[2] which Mr Astle showed me some time ago.[3] It certainly shows
very clearly how much more deliberate proceedings were even in that
barbarous age than was supposed: and it contains many other con-
futations of the popular story,[4] that are too long for a letter. I have
a quantity of other answers to Dr Milles's[5] and the rest of the childish
or rather old womanish replies to my book;[6] but I have no thoughts

1. Missing.
2. 'The Attainder of George, Duke of
Clarence,' printed in *Rotuli parliamentorum, 1767–77,* vi. 193–5. The sixth
volume of the *Rotuli* had just been published.
3. In Dec. 1775. See HW to Astle *ante*
19 Dec. 1775.
4. The story that Clarence was drowned
in a butt of malmsey (see ibid. n. 7).
5. Jeremiah Milles (1714–84), D.D., Dean

of Exeter and president of the Society of
Antiquaries, had replied to HW's *Historic
Doubts* (1768) in 'Observations on the
Wardrobe Account for the Year 1483,'
published in *Archæologia,* 1770, i. 361–83.
HW's *Reply to the Observations of the
Rev. Dr Milles* was printed at SH ca 1770–
4 but not published until after HW's
death (*Works* ii. *221–*44; Hazen, *SH
Bibl.* 95).
6. See *ante* 29 March 1772, n. 2.

of publishing them yet, nor care how much longer anybody chooses to believe a silly story. They like that tale, because it is old, and believe in Chatterton's poems,[7] because they are told they are old, though they are ten thousand times more curious for not being so. I am with great regard

My dear Lord

Your Lordship's most obedient humble servant

HOR. WALPOLE

From the PRINCE DE BEAUVAU, Saturday 29 March 1777

Printed for the first time from the MS now WSL. For the history of the MS see *ante* 27 Jan. 1776.

Endorsed by Beauvau: M. Horace Walpole.

Paris, ce 29 mars 1777.

MONSIEUR de Poix[1] m'a rendu, Monsieur, son voyage en Angleterre[2] bien agréable, en me rapportant un témoignage aussi flatteur de votre souvenir que l'est la lettre[3] dont vous avez bien

---

7. *Poems, Supposed to Have Been Written at Bristol, by Thomas Rowley, and Others, in the Fifteenth Century . . . to which Are Added, a Preface. . . . and a Glossary,* edited by Thomas Tyrwhitt (1730–86), had been published 8 Feb. 1777 (MASON i. 281 n. 4). 'Mr Tyrrwhitt has at last published the Bristol poems. He does not give up the antiquity, yet fairly leaves everybody to ascribe them to Chatterton if they please, which I think the internal evidence must force every one to do, unless the amazing prodigy of Chatterton's producing them should not seem a larger miracle than Rowley's and Canning's anticipation of the style of very modern poetry. . . . Mr Tyrrwhitt seems to have dreaded drawing himself into a controversy, which joys me, who dreaded being drawn into one too' (HW to Mason 17 Feb. 1777, ibid. i. 281–2). For HW's involvement in the Chatterton controversy see CHATTERTON *passim;* HW to Malone *post* 4 Feb. 1782; HW to Buchan *post*

2 June 1782. Milles believed in the authenticity of the Rowley poems and in 1781 published *Poems, Supposed to Have Been Written . . . by Thomas Rowley . . . with a Commentary, in which the Antiquity of them is Considered, and Defended.*

---

1. Philippe-Louis-Marc-Antoine de Noailles (1752–1819), Prince de Poix; Beauvau's son-in-law.

2. Poix, accompanied by the young Marquis de la Fayette, left Paris 16 Feb. 1777 and arrived in England on the 24th. HW met them at a dinner given by the Marquis de Noailles, the French ambassador to England (Poix's first cousin and the uncle of La Fayette's wife), and was apparently much impressed with Poix. La Fayette returned to France shortly after 9 March, just before embarking for America (André Maurois, *Adrienne: The Life of the Marquise de la Fayette,* trans. Gerard Hopkins, New York, 1961, pp. 45–8;

voulu le charger pour moi: les éloges qu'elle contient de lui me causaient aussi beaucoup de joie, parce que je juge qu'il en a mérité une partie en s'occupant de plaire et surtout en s'acquittant fidèlement de ce que je lui avais très fort recommandé, qui était d'avoir l'honneur de vous voir le plus qu'il pourrait; il a sûrement beaucoup perdu à ce que ce ne fut pas à votre maison de campagne.

Recevez encore tous mes remerciements de vos bontés pour mon gendre et pour moi et les assurances de l'ancien et inviolable attachement avec lequel j'ai l'honneur d'être, Monsieur, votre très humble et très obéissant serviteur

LE PRINCE DE BEAUVAU

To John Robinson, Monday 9 June 1777

Printed from *Works* ii. 386, where the letter was first printed. Reprinted, Toynbee x. 55–6. The history of the MS and its present whereabouts are not known.

Arlington Street, June 9, 1777.

Sir,

MY deputy, Mr Bedford,[1] has acquainted me that you are desirous of knowing the prices I pay for the several articles with which, as Usher of the Exchequer, I supply the Treasury;[2] and he told me that you added, that Lord North has a mind to make new regulations that may be economic for the public. I have accordingly, Sir, ordered Mr Bedford to give you the most exact information on every particular.[3] He told me too that Lord North would be so just

Louis Gottschalk, *Lafayette Comes to America*, Chicago, 1935, pp. 89–92; DU DEFFAND iv. 424, 427).

3. Missing; mentioned in Mme du Deffand to HW 27 March 1777: 'celle que M. de Beauvau a reçu de vous, et qu'il me lut hier, me fait sauter sur toutes considérations. . . . rien n'est si charmant que cette petite lettre; elle a toute la politesse, l'élégance, la grâce possibles. M. de Beauvau en est charmé, je lui demanderai à voir la réponse' (ibid. iv. 425).

1. Charles Bedford, HW's deputy in the Exchequer 1774–97.

2. HW discusses the duties and benefits of this sinecure office in his 'Account of My Conduct Relative to the Places I Hold under Government, and towards Ministers,' *Works* ii. 367–70.

3. In Aug. 1782, when HW was required to furnish a similar account in connection with the government's plan for economic reform, HW pointed out to George Rose, the Treasury secretary, that 'I once received an inquiry from Mr Robinson something parallel, Sir, to yours, and, as Mr Bedford can tell you, immediately complied with his request' (*post* 18 Aug. 1782).

as, I do not doubt, to make compensations to anybody that should suffer by such alterations. Give me leave, Sir, to say that it is not on that ground that I now trouble you. On the contrary, it is to beg you will be so good as to acquaint Lord North, that he may not only command any information from me on that subject, as far as I myself am concerned, and which it is my duty to give, but that I shall cheerfully acquiesce in whatever new regulations he shall be pleased to make for the benefit of the public. No rights or interest of mine shall stand in the way of so good a purpose; and when I use the word *rights,* it is not to support, but to waive them for any national benefit. I have received too great benefits and too long from the Crown and the public, not to owe any facility in my power, as far as so inconsiderable a person can do it, to ease the burthens of both, and I shall with great willingness accept whatever shall be thought proper for me on any new plan of public economy. I should think myself of too little consequence to say this, were it not that the example of the most private man may be of use on such an occasion. I am, Sir, with great regard,

Your obedient humble servant,

Horace Walpole

To Lord Dacre, Friday 11 July 1777

Printed for the first time from a photostat of the MS in the Essex Record Office, County Hall, Chelmsford, Essex, kindly furnished by Mr K. C. Newton. The MS descended in the Barrett-Lennard family to Sir Richard Barrett-Lennard, 5th Bt, who deposited the family archives in the Essex Record Office in November 1945; the archives were formally presented to the Record Office in March 1974.

Strawberry Hill, July 11th 1777.

I CANNOT receive joy from Bellhouse,[1] my dear Lord, without giving it, and without telling your Lordship how particularly kind I took it from Mr Hardinge[2] in acquainting me with his intended marriage.[3] I had no right to expect such attention but by my

---

1. Belhus, Dacre's seat, near Aveley, Essex.
2. George Hardinge (1743–1816), lawyer and author; HW's correspondent.

3. Hardinge wrote to HW 6 July 1777 announcing his intended marriage to Lucy Long (d. 1820), daughter and heiress of Richard Long, of Hinxton, Cambs; HW

zealous wishes for his happiness. When anybody that is perfectly content, as he seems to be, thinks of making others happy, it is the best proof of a good heart. When misery is communicative, it may flow from want of pity, comfort, advice or assistance: but when happiness is neither insolent nor selfish, the monitor must be benevolence. Without including myself in this description, I enjoy the satisfaction your Lordship, Lady Dacre,[4] Mrs Hardinge[5] and Lord Camden[6] must have in the felicity and merit of so deserving a young man—it is talking too like an old one, but surely all the rising young men of the age have not Mr Hardinge's good qualities.

Your Lordship did me the honour of inviting me to Bellhouse; it seemed ungrateful not to thank you, and yet gratitude was the true motive of my silence. I waited till I could tell you that I could accept the honour of your offer. I have had company and various engagements[7] that prevented me, and am not yet at liberty from the precarious state of his R[oyal] H[ighness] the Duke of Gloucester's health, and from expecting him and the Duchess in England.[8]

I was still more flattered, though very unworthy, by your Lordship's thinking of consulting me on your improvements at Bellhouse. Nobody is more attached to the beauty of your seat, nor shall see your additions with more pleasure; but I have not the vanity to presume to direct them. You have not only done everything there with taste, my Lord, but to my taste.[9] You know I love the spirit of

offered Hardinge his 'warm good wishes' in his reply 9 July (CHUTE 590–2; BERRY ii. 198 n. 4). The marriage took place 20 Oct. 1777.

4. See *ante* 9 June 1761, n. 2. Lady Dacre was Hardinge's aunt. 'The *Dacres* are, you may suppose, not indifferent to this good fortune of mine' (Hardinge to HW 6 July 1777, CHUTE 591).

5. Jane Pratt (d. 1807), sister of HW's friend and occasional correspondent Lord Camden, m. (1738) Nicholas Hardinge; George Hardinge's mother (CONWAY i. 418 n. 2).

6. Hardinge's uncle.

7. Doubtless business engagements having to do with the management of Lord Orford's affairs during his second attack of insanity. HW wrote Robert Jephson two days later: 'The melancholy situation of my nephew Lord Orford engages me particularly' (*post* 13 July 1777).

8. The Duke had fallen 'dangerously ill at Verona' in mid-June; 'Bryant, his sur-

geon, advised his returning to England; and his danger increased so fast, that he was taken out of his bed and put into his post-chaise. He got to Trent, seemed to mend by the journey and by the coolness of the air from the mountains; but his flux returned, and he was again confined to his bed for some days' (*Last Journals* ii. 38–9). See OSSORY i. 362–3, 365; FAMILY 125; CHUTE 472–3.

9. See *ante* 9 June 1761, n. 3. A new wing to the east side of the south front of Belhus was apparently completed in 1778, when a man named Watson was paid for its construction (information kindly communicated by Dr Michael McCarthy, citing documents in the Essex Record Office). For Dacre's earlier alterations in the Gothic style see the two articles by H. A. Tipping in *Country Life*, 1920, xlvii. 656–62, 690–6; *An Eighteenth-Century Correspondence*, ed. Lilian Dickins and Mary Stanton, 1910, *passim*.

ancienne noblesse; and since cheesemongers can be peers, I would have the mansions of old barons[10] powdered with quarterings, for distinction; and since Mr Adam[11] builds for so many of them, I wish he would deviate from his style of filigraine, and load them with the Tuscan order, which admits very speaking columns.

When I have a day at command, will Lady Dacre and your Lordship allow me to make use of your permission and wait on you? I will not take that liberty however, without asking if my visit will be seasonable. I am, my dear Lord, with the truest regard

Your Lordship's most obedient humble servant

Hor. Walpole

To Robert Jephson, Sunday 13 July 1777

Printed from the MS now wsl. First printed, Wright v. 467–70. Reprinted, Cunningham vi. 457–9; Toynbee x. 80–3 (closing and signature omitted in Wright, Cunningham, and Toynbee); extracts quoted in *London Stage* Pt V, i. 43, 81. For the history of the MS see *ante* 15 March 1763.

Strawberry Hill, July 13, 1777.

YOU have perhaps, Sir, paid too much regard to the observations I took the liberty to make by your order to a few passages in *Vitellia,*[1] and I must hope they were in consequence of your own judgment too. I do not doubt of its success on the stage, if well acted—but I confess I would answer for nothing with the present set of actors, who are not capable in tragedy of doing any justice to it. Mrs Barry[2] seems to me very unequal to the principal part,[3] to which

10. The Dacre barony extended back to 1321. In that year Sir Randolf de Dacre was summoned to Parliament by writ, and is thereby considered to have become Lord Dacre. HW's friend was the 17th Baron Dacre.

11. Robert Adam, the architect.

1. HW wrote Mason 28 March 1777: 'Mr Jephson has sent me his *Vitellia,* which Garrick rejected last year [in Dec. 1775] with as much judgment as he acted all the wretched pieces that appeared at Drury Lane for so many years; it has beautiful poetry as *Braganza* had, and more action and more opportunities for good actors, if there were any' (Mason i.

294). HW's letter to Jephson containing his 'observations' on the play is missing. *Vitellia* was eventually produced, under the title of *The Conspiracy,* at Drury Lane in 1796 (*London Stage* Pt V, iii. 1914–15).

2. Ann Street (1734–1801), m. 1 (1754) William Dancer (d. 1759); m. 2 (1767 or 1768) Spranger Barry (?1717–10 Jan. 1777); m. 3 (1778) Thomas Crawford (1750–94) (P. H. Highfill, Jr, K. A. Burnim, and E. A. Langhans, *A Biographical Dictionary of Actors . . . in London, 1600–1800,* Carbondale, Illinois, 1973–   , i. 339–51).

3. The rôle of Vitellia was played by Sarah Siddons in 1796 (see n. 1 above).

Mrs Yates[4] alone is suited: and were I the author, I should be very sorry to have my tragedy murdered, perhaps miscarry. Your reputation is established; you will never forfeit it yourself—and to give your works to unworthy performers, is like sacrificing a daughter to a husband of bad character. As to my offering it to Mr Colman,[5] I could merely be the messenger. I am scarce known to him, have no right to ask a favour of him, and I hope you know me enough to think that I am too conscious of my own insignificance and private situation to give myself an air of protection, and more particularly to a work of yours, Sir. What could I say, that would carry greater weight, than *This piece is by the author of Braganza?*[6]

A tragedy can never suffer by delay. A comedy may, because the allusions or the manners represented in it may be temporary. I urge this, not to dissuade your presenting *Vitellia* to the stage, but to console you if both theatres should be engaged next winter. My own interest from my time of life would make me with reason more impatient than you to see it represented, but I am jealous of the honour of your poetry, and should grieve to see *Vitellia* at Covent Garden—not, that except Mrs Yates, I have any partiality to the tragic actors at Drury Lane, though Smith[7] did not miscarry in *Braganza*—but I speak from experience. I attended *Caractacus*[8] last winter, and was greatly interested, both from my friendship for Mr Mason and from the excellence of the poetry. I was out of all patience, for though a young Lewis[9] played a subordinate part very well, and Mrs Hartley[10] looked her part charmingly, the Druids were so massacred and Caractacus[11] so much worse, that I never saw a more barbarous exhibition. Instead of hurrying *The Law of Lombardy,*[12]

4. See *ante* 24 Feb. 1775, n. 14.

5. George Colman, the elder, the manager of the Little Theatre in the Haymarket, with whom HW was on cordial terms (see *ante* 28 Dec. 1776). Colman produced HW's 'moral entertainment' *Nature Will Prevail* at the Haymarket in 1778 (*post* 2 March 1778).

6. Jephson's tragedy, produced with great success in 1775 (*ante* 24 Feb. 1775 and n. 4).

7. See ibid. n. 15.

8. A dramatic poem by HW's friend William Mason, first published in 1759 and 'altered for theatrical representation' in 1776. HW attended the first performance at Covent Garden 6 Dec. 1776; see Ossory i. 335 and nn. 17, 18.

9. William Thomas Lewis (1749–1811), called 'Gentleman' Lewis; actor; deputy manager of Covent Garden Theatre 1782–1803 (GM 1811, lxxxi pt i. 90–1; DNB). He played the rôle of Arviragus in *Caractacus* (*London Stage* Pt V, i. 42).

10. Elizabeth White (1751–1824), married or assumed the name of her lover (1772 or earlier) —— Hartley; actress (Ossory i. 106 n. 17). She played the rôle of Evelina in *Caractacus* (*London Stage* Pt V, i. 42).

11. Played by Matthew Clarke (d. 1786) (ibid.).

12. Jephson's tragedy, first performed at Drury Lane in 1779 (ibid. Pt V, i. 233). See *post* 17 Oct., 8 Nov. 1777.

which however I shall delight to see finished, I again wish you to try comedy. To my great astonishment there were more parts performed admirably in *The School for Scandal*[13] than I almost ever saw in any play. Mrs Abington[14] was equal to the first of her profession; Yates[15] the husband, Parsons,[16] Miss Pope[17] and Palmer[18] all shone. It seemed a marvellous resurrection of the stage. Indeed the play had as much merit as the actors. I have seen no comedy that comes near it since *The Provoked Husband*.[19]

I said I was jealous of your fame as a poet, and I truly am. The more rapid your genius is, labour will but the more improve it. I am very frank, but I am sure that my attention to your reputation will excuse it. Your facility in writing exquisite poetry may be a disadvantage, as it may not leave you time to study the other requisites of tragedy so much as is necessary. Your writings deserve to last for ages, but to make any work last, it must be finished in all parts to perfection. You have the first requisite to that perfection, for you can sacrifice charming lines, when they do not tend to improve the whole. I admire this resignation so much that I wish to turn it to your advantage. Strike out your sketches as suddenly as you please, but retouch and retouch them, that the best judges may forever admire them. The works that have stood the test of ages and been slowly approved at first, are not those that have dazzled cotemporaries and bore away their applause, but those whose intrinsic and laboured merit have shone the brighter on examination—I would not curb your genius, Sir, if I did not trust it would recoil with greater force for having obstacles presented to it.

You will forgive my not having sent you the *Thoughts on Comedy*[20] as I promised. I have had no time to look them over and put them into shape. I have been and am involved in most unpleasant affairs of family,[21] that take up my whole thoughts and

---

13. Sheridan's comedy had its first performance at Drury Lane on 8 May 1777 (ibid. Pt V, i. 81).

14. Who played Lady Teazle (ibid.).

15. Richard Yates (ca 1706–96), who played Sir Oliver Surface (ibid.).

16. William Parsons (1736–95), who played Crabtree (ibid.).

17. Jane Pope (1742–1818), who played Mrs Candour (ibid.).

18. John Palmer (ca 1742–98), who played Joseph Surface (ibid.).

19. Colley Cibber's completion (first

acted at Drury Lane in 1728) of Vanbrugh's fragment, *A Journey to London*. HW wrote Mason 16 May 1777: 'I have seen Sheridan's new comedy, and liked it much better than any I have seen since *The Provoked Husband*. There is a great deal of wit and good situations. . . . It is admirably acted' (MASON i. 309).

20. 'Thoughts on Comedy; Written in 1775 and 1776,' published posthumously in *Works* ii. 315–22. See *ante* 24 Feb. 1775, n. 2.

21. See previous letter, nn. 7, 8.

attention. The melancholy situation of my nephew Lord Orford engages me particularly, and I am not young enough to excuse postponing business and duties for amusement. In truth I am really too old not to have given up literary pleasures. Nobody will tell one when one grows dull, but one's time of life ought to tell it one. I long ago determined to keep the Archbishop in *Gil Blas* in my eye when I should advance to his caducity[22]—but as dotage steals in at more doors than one, perhaps the sermon I have been preaching to you is a symptom of it. You must judge of that, Sir. If I fancy I have been wise, and have only been peevish, throw my lecture into the fire. I am sure the liberties I have taken with you deserve no indulgence, if you do not discern true friendship at bottom of them. I am very sincerely dear Sir

Your obedient humble servant

Hor. Walpole

To Lord Hardwicke, Wednesday 16 July 1777

Printed for the first time from the MS now WSL. For the history of the MS see *ante* ? Jan. 1773.

Strawberry Hill, July 16, 1777.

MR Walpole returns Lord Hardwicke the volume of letters[1] with many thanks, and as many for the print, which he admires extremely, and the design.[2] He does not like the verses[3] less, which are very just.

The Countess of Westmorland[4] who wrote the letter his Lordship spoke of to Mr W. in the volume,[5] was past all doubt, Mary, sole daughter and heiress of Sir Antony Mildmay[6] of Apethorpe in North-

22. See *ante* 14 April 1764, n. 2.

1. See *ante* 24 Jan. 1774, n. 1.
2. Neither the print nor the design has been identified.
3. Possibly MS verses contained in the volume of letters, but not otherwise identified.
4. Mary Mildmay (ca 1582–1640), m. (1599) Sir Francis Fane (1580–1629), K. B., 1603; cr. (1624) Bn of Burghersh and E. of

Westmorland; Bn Le Despenser, 1626. According to GEC xii pt ii. 567, she was the 'daughter and eventually sole heir' of Sir Anthony Mildmay (n. 6 below).
5. The letter is not listed in the *Catalogue of the Manuscripts in the Possession of the Earl of Hardwicke*, privately printed, 1794.
6. Sir Anthony Mildmay (d. 1617), of Apethorpe, Northants; Kt, 1596 (GRAY ii. 113 n. 45).

amptonshire, whence she dates her letter, and which she carried to the family of Fane. She was wife of Francis Fane Knight of the Bath, and Lord Despencer in right of his mother Mary Neville[7] sole daughter and heiress of Henry Neville Lord Abergavenny.[8] Sir Francis Fane Lord Despencer was created Baron Burgersh and Earl of Westmorland 22d of James I. It was Mildmay Fane[9] his eldest son by Mary Mildmay, who wrote a small book of poems mentioned in vol. 1 of R[oyal] and Noble Authors.[10]

To Lady Cecilia Johnston, Tuesday 19 August 1777

Printed from a photostat of the MS in the Halsey Collection, Hertfordshire County Record Office, Hertford, through the kind offices of Col. W. Le Hardy. First printed, Cunningham vi. 467. Reprinted, Toynbee x. 96; *Horace Walpole's Fugitive Verses*, ed. W. S. Lewis, 1931, p. 169. For the history of the MS see HW to Lady Henrietta Cecilia West *ante* before 4 May 1762.

Endorsed (probably by Lady Cecilia Johnston): Mr Walpole 1777. Strawberry Hill.

Address: To the Right Honourable Lady Cecilia Johnstone.

Aug. 19, 1777.

> Our abdicated monarch Lear,[1]
> And bonny Dame Cadwallader,[2]
> With a whole theatre in one[3] from France,

7. Mary Neville (1554–1626), m. (1574), as his second wife, Sir Thomas Fane (d. 1589), Kt, 1573; Bns Le Despenser (*s.j.*), 1604.

8. Henry Nevill (or Neville) (after 1527–1587), 6th Bn Bergavenny (or Abergavenny), 1535.

9. Mildmay Fane (1602–66), styled Lord Burghersh 1624–6 and Lord Le Despenser 1626–9; 2d E. of Westmorland, 1629.

10. 'All I can say of this Lord, is, that he wrote "A very small book of poems," which he gave to, and is still preserved in the library of Emanuel College, Cambridge' (HW's *Catalogue of the Royal and Noble Authors of England*, 2d edn, 1759, i. 231). The book is *Otia sacra*, privately printed (by Richard Cotes), 1648, 4to.

———

1. David Garrick, who had retired from the stage on 10 June 1776. King Lear was among his greatest tragic rôles; see K. A.

Burnim, *David Garrick, Director*, Pittsburgh, 1961, pp. 141–51. He played Lear in his penultimate performance at Drury Lane 8 June 1776 (*London Stage* Pt IV, iii. 1985). Benjamin Wilson's painting of Garrick as Lear was engraved by James McArdell and published in 1761 (*BM Cat. of Engraved British Portraits* ii. 283, No. 126).

2. Kitty Clive, the actress, who lived at Little Strawberry Hill ('Cliveden') in her retirement. She created the rôle of Mrs Cadwallader in Samuel Foote's farce *The Author*, first performed at Drury Lane 5 Feb. 1757 (*London Stage* Pt IV, ii. 580).

3. Le Texier (HW's marginal note in the MS). Antoine-A. Le Texier (ca 1737–1814), French actor (CONWAY iii. 273 n. 7). He came to England in Sept. 1775; at a supper party given by the Duc de Guines two months later, HW was 'singularly entertained' by Le Texier, who 'acted an en-

And Raftor,[4] wont th'eclipse in hays to dance,[5]
Next Saturn's day,[6] if fair or foul,
On bacon-ham and chicken-fowl,
Intend with Horace—no great bard,
Nor one of Epicurus' herd,
To dine—Oh! would divine Cecilia deign
With her brave warrior[7] to augment the train;
From every castle fam'd in days of yore,
Of which or poets or romancers tell,
For wit and cheerfulness and humour store
My Strawberry, my Strawberry shall bear away the bell.[8]

On 19 Sept. 1777 HW sent William Storer (fl. 1777–85), optician, of Saham Toney, near Swaffham, Norfolk, a letter containing a description of the 'Delineator,' an optical instrument invented by Storer to facilitate the exact drawing or copying of views and pictures. This description was apparently furnished to Storer at his request, and was later printed (possibly with alterations by Storer) in his *Syllabus to a Course of Optical Experiments, on the Syllepsis Optica; or the New Optical Principles of the Royal Delineator Analysed*, [1782], pp. 18–21. HW's original letter is missing; his description is reprinted in Appendix 4, MASON ii. 371–2.

---

tire play of ten characters, and varied his voice and countenance and manner for each so perfectly, that he did not name the persons that spoke, nor was it necessary' (HW to Lady Ossory 23 Nov. 1775, OSSORY i. 277). HW called him a 'real prodigy, who acts whole plays, in which every character is perfect' (HW to Mason 18 Feb. 1776, MASON i. 245).

4. James Raftor (d. 1790), actor; Mrs Clive's brother or half-brother, with whom she lived at Little Strawberry Hill (CHUTE 244 n. 17).

5. 'Mr Raftor told me that formerly when he played Luna in *The Rehearsal*, he never could learn to dance the hays, and at last he went to the man that teaches grown gentlemen' (HW to Lord Nuneham 6 Dec. 1773, CHUTE 468). The 'hay' or 'hays' was a serpentine figure in country dancing. In Buckingham's *The Rehearsal* V. i, Bayes explains how he represents an eclipse on the stage: 'Well, Sir; what do me I, but make the Earth,

Sun, and Moon, come out upon the stage, and dance the hey: hum? And, of necessity, by the very nature of this dance, the Earth must be sometimes between the Sun and the Moon, and the Moon between the Earth and Sun; and there you have both your eclipses.' Raftor's first recorded performance in *The Rehearsal* is apparently that of 4 Jan. 1750 at Drury Lane (*London Stage* Pt IV, i. 165).

6. 23 August. There is no other mention of this dinner party in HW's surviving correspondence. HW dined at Lady Cecilia's on Sunday, the 24th (CHUTE 475).

7. General Johnston, her husband.

8. This line was the refrain of a song written by George Bubb Dodington (later Lord Melcombe) 'in praise of Mrs Strawbridge, a lady with whom Mr Doddington was in love' ('Des. of SH,' *Works* ii. 513n). In 1755 Lord Bath composed a ballad celebrating Strawberry Hill that borrowed (with slight modifications) the earlier refrain (ibid. ii. 513–14; MONTAGU i. 168–9).

To Robert Jephson, Wednesday 1 October 1777

Printed from the MS now wsl. First printed, Wright v. 476–7. Reprinted, Cunningham vi. 490–1; Toynbee x. 123–4 (closing and signature omitted in Wright, Cunningham, and Toynbee). For the history of the MS see *ante* 15 March 1763.

Address: To Robert Jephson Esq. at the Castle, Dublin. *Postmark:* 1 OC. ISLEWORTH. OC 6.

Strawberry Hill, Oct. 1, 1777.

TO confer favours, Sir, is certainly not giving trouble: and had I the most constant occupation, I should contrive to find moments for reading your works. I have passed a most melancholy summer from the different distresses in my family;[1] and though my nephew's situation and other avocations prevent my having but very little time for literary amusements, I did not mean to debar myself of the pleasure of hearing from my friends.

Unfortunately at present it is impossible for me to profit of your kindness, not from my own business, but from the absence of Mr Garrick.[2] He is gone into Staffordshire to marry a nephew,[3] and thence will pass into Wales to superintend a play that is to be acted at Sir Watkin Williams's.[4] I am even afraid I shall not be the first

1. HW's nephew Lord Orford suffered a second attack of insanity in April from which he had not yet recovered; see Family 335–6. In June the Duke of Gloucester, travelling in Italy, became seriously ill (*ante* 11 July 1777, n. 8); his improvement was gradual, but on his return to England in late October (n. 5 below) he was 'much recovered, and had only a swelled leg and lameness remaining' (*Last Journals* ii. 59).

2. Jephson had apparently given Garrick the manuscript of his tragedy *The Law of Lombardy* to get his opinion of it. (Garrick had successfully produced Jephson's *Braganza* at Drury Lane in 1775.) It is evident from HW's letter *post* 17 Oct. 1777 that Jephson also wished to have HW's criticisms of the play, which was first performed at Drury Lane 8 Feb. 1779 (*London Stage* Pt V, i. 233).

3. In a letter to Lord Camden written from Hampton 16 Sept. 1777, Garrick says that he and his wife must 'go immediately to Litchfield, where my family

expects me and a marriage to be soon completed between a niece of mine and a gentleman in the neighbourhood' (*The Letters of David Garrick*, ed. D. M. Little and G. M. Kahrl, Cambridge, Mass., 1963, iii. 1191). None of Garrick's three nieces, however, married at this time. There seems to have been a change of plans; writing to his brother Peter from Wales 30 Sept., Garrick speaks of meeting him in Birmingham and then returning with him to Lichfield for a short visit (ibid. iii. 1193–4).

4. Sir Watkin Williams Wynn (1748–89), 4th Bt, 1749; M.P. His private playhouse at Wynnstay, his seat near Wrexham, Denbighshire, was the scene of amateur theatricals each year from 1770 until his death (Ossory iii. 4 n. 33; Cecil Price, *The English Theatre in Wales in the Eighteenth and Early Nineteenth Centuries*, Cardiff, 1948, pp. 61–7). Garrick arrived at Wynnstay before 26 Sept. and apparently stayed there until 4 Oct. (Little and Kahrl, op. cit. iii. 1192–3). He at-

apprised of his return, as I possibly may remove to town in expectation of the Duchess of Gloucester, before he is at home again.[5] I shall not neglect my own satisfaction, but mention this circumstance, that you may not suspect me of inattention, if I should not get sight of your tragedy so soon as I wish. I am, Sir, with great regard

Your most obliged humble servant

HOR. WALPOLE

To ROBERT JEPHSON, Friday 17 October 1777

Printed from the MS now WSL. First printed, Wright v. 479–82. Reprinted, Cunningham vi. 499–501; Toynbee x. 137–40 (closing and signature omitted in Wright, Cunningham, and Toynbee). For the history of the MS see *ante* 15 March 1763.

Strawberry Hill, Oct. 17, 1777.

MR Garrick returned but two days ago,[1] Sir, and I did not receive your tragedy till this morning, so I could only read it once very rapidly, and without any proper attention to particular passages, though even so, some struck me as very fine.

You have encouraged me rather to criticize than flatter you; and you are in the right, for you have even profited of so weak a judgment as mine, and always improved the passages I objected to. Indeed this was not quite a fair return, as it was inverting my method, by flattering, instead of finding fault with me; and a critic that meets with submission, is apt to grow vain and insolent and capricious. Still, as I am persuaded that all criticisms, though erroneous, *before*

tended (but did not superintend) a special performance of Henry Carey's *Chrononhotonthologos* and Arthur Murphy's *The Upholsterer* at the Wynnstay theatre on 2 Oct.; 'the theatre and design of the performance were kept an entire secret from Mr Garrick till the moment of the company's being conducted there' (Price, op. cit. 62–3, quoting a report in *Adams's Weekly Courant* 7 Oct. 1777; see also George Colman, the younger, *Random Records*, 1830, ii. 55–6).

5. HW wrote Jephson *post* 17 Oct. 1777;

'Mr Garrick returned but two days ago, Sir, and I did not receive your tragedy till this morning.' However, in a letter to Mme Riccoboni written from Hampton also on the 17th, Garrick says that he 'returned last night from a long journey into Wales' (Little and Kahrl, op. cit. iii. 1195). HW remained at SH until 24 Oct., when he went to town to greet the Duke and Duchess of Gloucester on their return from the Continent (FAMILY 155).

1. See previous letter, n. 5.

an author appeals to the public, are friendly, I will fairly tell you what parts of your tragedy have struck me as objectionable on so superficial a perusal.

In general, the language appears to me too metaphoric, especially as used by all the characters. You seem to me to have imitated Beaumont and Fletcher, though your play is superior to all theirs. In truth I think the diction is sometimes obscure from being so figurative, especially in the first act. Will you allow me to mention two instances?

> And craven Sloth moulting his sleekless plumes,
> Nods drowsy wonder at th'advent'rous wing
> That soars the shining azure o'er his head.[2]

I own I do not understand why Sloth's plumes are *sleekless;* and I think that *nodding wonder,* and *soaring the azure* are expressions too Greek to be so close together, and too poetic for dialogue. The other passage is

> The wise should watch th'event on fortune's wheel,

and the seven following lines.[3] The images are very fine, but demand more attention than common audiences are capable of. In *Braganza*[4] every image is strikingly clear.

I am afraid I am not quite satisfied with the conduct of your piece. Bireno's conduct in the attack on the Princess seems too precipitate, and not managed. It is still more incredible that Paladore should confess his passion to his rival; and not less so, that a private man and a stranger should doubt the Princess's faith, when she had preferred

2. In the printed version of *The Law of Lombardy*, 1779, these lines read (I. v):

And craven Sloth molting his sleekless plumes
With drowsy wonder views the adven-
    t'rous wing
That soars the shining azure o'er his head.

3. In the printed play these lines run (I. vi, Bireno's soliloquy, the final speech of Act I):

The wise should watch the event on fortune's wheel,
That for a moment circles at the top,

And seiz'd not, vanishes—I must about it,
My all's at stake—Ye ministers of ven-
    geance!
That hide your gory locks in mist-
    hung caves,
And roll your deadly eyeballs o'er the edge
Of your insatiate daggers, shaking ever
Dews of oblivious sleep from your
    stung brows,
Receive me of your band! . . . .

4. Jephson's tragedy, successfully produced at Drury Lane in 1775 (*ante* 24 Feb.
1775 and n. 4).

him to his rival, a prince of the blood and her destined husband;[5] and that without the smallest inquiry he should believe Bireno was admitted privately to her apartment, when on her not rejecting him, he might have access to her openly. One cannot conceive her meaning in offending her father by refusing so proper a match, and intriguing with the very man she was to marry, and whom she had refused. Paladore's credulity is not of a piece with the account given of his wisdom which had made him admitted to the King's councils.

I think when you bestow Sophia[6] on Paladore, you forget that the King had declared he was obliged to give his daughter to a prince of his own blood; nor do I see any reason for Bireno's stabbing Ascanio, who was sure of being put to death when their treachery was discovered.

The character of the Princess is very noble and well sustained. When I said I did not conceive her meaning, I expressed myself ill. I did not suppose she did intrigue with Bireno; but I meant that it was not natural Paladore should suspect she did, since it is inconceivable that a princess should refuse her cousin in marriage for the mere caprice of intriguing with him. Had she managed her father, and from dread of his anger, temporized about Bireno, Paladore would have had more reason to doubt her. Would it not too be more natural for Bireno to incense the King against Paladore, than to endeavour to make the latter jealous of Sophia? At least I think Bireno would have more chance of poisoning Paladore's mind, if he did not discover to him that he knew of his passion. Forgive me, Sir, but I cannot reconcile to probability Paladore's believing that Sophia had rejected Bireno for a husband, though it would please her father, and yet chose to intrigue with him in defiance of so serious and extraordinary a law.[7] Either his credulity or his jealousy reduce Paladore to a lover very unworthy of such a woman as Sophia. For her sake I wish to see him more deserving of her.

You are so great a poet, Sir, that you have no occasion to labour anything but your plots. You can express anything you please. If the conduct is natural, you will not want words. Nay, I rather fear your

5. See Act I, Scene v. Following HW's advice, Jephson apparently made alterations to this and other scenes in the play.
6. That is, the Princess.
7. The law of Lombardy provided that a woman proved to be unchaste should be sentenced to death. She was allowed a champion to defend her honour in the lists. If her champion defeated her accuser, she was set free; if her accuser triumphed, his victory confirmed her guilt and she was executed. See Act III, Scene vi.

indulging your poetic vein too far, for your language is sometimes sublime enough for odes, which admit the heighth of enthusiasm, which Horace will not allow to tragic writers.[8] You could set up twenty of our tragic authors with lines that you could afford to reject, though for no reason but their being too fine, as in landscape painting some parts must be under-coloured to give the higher relief to the rest. Will not you think me too difficult and squeamish, when I find the language of *The Law of Lombardy* too rich?

I beg your pardon, but it is more difficult for you to please me, than anybody. I interest myself in your success and your glory. You must be perfect in all parts, in nature, simplicity and character, as well as in the most charming poetry, or I shall not be content. If I dared, I would beg you to trust me with your plots, before you write a line. When a subject seizes you, your impetuosity cannot breathe till you have executed your plan. You must be curbed, as other poets want to be spurred. When your sketch is made, you must study the characters and the audience. It is not flattering *you* to say, that the least you have to do, is to write your play. I am with great regard, Sir,

Your obedient humble servant

Hor. Walpole

To Robert Jephson, Saturday 8 November 1777

Printed from the MS now wsl. First printed in N & Q 1870, 4th ser., vi. 107–8. Reprinted, Toynbee x. 153–7. The MS passed to Jephson's nephew and heir, the Rev. John Jephson; he gave it 'as a contribution to a book of autographs' to 'an old Irish lady,' who owned it in 1870; not further traced until sold Sotheby's 19 Feb. 1947 (property of Miss Zoe Stronge), lot 641, to Maggs for wsl.

Arlington Street, Nov. 8, 1777.

THE justice you do me, Sir, in forgiving the liberty I have taken with you from sincere zeal for your glory, is still an uncommon instance of a great poet's bearing to have his works criticized:[1] and though true poets are not frequent, one that can endure the objec-

---

8. See *Ars poetica*, ll. 220–50.

1. Jephson's reply to HW's letter *ante*

17 Oct. 1777, criticizing his tragedy *The Law of Lombardy,* is missing.

tions of a friend is a greater rarity, and displays as much the coolness of good sense, as his writings the warmth of imagination. It was conviction of the torrent of the latter, though ignorant of the extent of the former, that made me presume to offer my opinion on your plans, before you should let loose your poetry on the execution; thinking you could not be offended at objections to the design, though you might be displeased at disapprobation of any of your verses; and indeed liking them too much to be ready to wish them effaced myself. You have convinced me, Sir, that I neither understand the latitude of your patience, nor your good nature; and yet I have put both to the proof; I have ventured to try both to the utmost, nor reserved any criticisms in store.

You will be so good as to observe that there were but two faults I found, improbability in the conduct, and too figurative expression in the dialogue. You have obviated part of the former by the corrections you have condescended to make, and perhaps have condescended too much; for if I alone have made the observations, I am so far from attributing it, as you are so obliging to do, to more penetration, that I doubt it is rather owing to singularity or to the peevishness of age—and perhaps men who have a little reading and some experience, are worse judges of a drama that is calculated for everybody, than a more informed auditor. An infinitely greater man, Molière, trusted the feelings of his old housekeeper more than those of Boileau,[2] another man, much greater—I can scarce venture to say than I—for what am I? to name myself at all looks as if I had some pretensions to something. I assure you I only meant to prefer the housekeeper to myself, but arranged my words so awkwardly, that to my great astonishment I found myself à côté de Boileau.

Yet I am not quite modest, nor possess your modesty, Sir. I am still a little obstinate on one point, I mean, in general; and that is, metaphoric diction in tragedy; and forgive me once more, if I do not submit to your argument in its defence, that Shakespeare's, Beaumont's, Fletcher's, and Massinger's pieces, though crowded with figures, are still tasted. I believe the most figurative passages in Shakespeare, are not the most admired. Dr Johnson goes much farther, far beyond truth, and says that that most sublime genius

2. The source of this story has not been found.

never attempted to be sublime without being bombast[3]—but indubitably Shakespeare is never so superior to all mankind as where he is most simple and natural. Recollect Constance, Arthur,[4] Juliet, Desdemona, or Hotspur's mockeries of Glendower.[5] What strikes one's soul with horror like Macbeth's account of the two grooms when he had murdered Duncan?[6] The passage so foolishly ridiculed by Voltaire,[7] because he is incapable of feeling that simplicity is the heighth of the sublime,

> When he himself can his quietus make
> With a bare bodkin,[8]

and Henry IV's image of the cabin-boy *in a night so rude,*[9] and Richard II's sensibility to his favourite horse being pleased with the load of Bolinbroke,[10] are texts out of the book of nature, in comparison of which the works of all other writers in every language that I understand, are to me apocryphal.

But to descend from enthusiasm, which seizes me whenever I name our first of men, I think there is a plain reason why the metaphoric style of that age is not to be imitated now. In the first place, allow me (and it is a question I must beg) that chastity of criticism was not known in that age. Theatric representations were new; whatever the authors pleased to produce was thankfully accepted—and even the most turgid and unintelligible passages of those writers, mouthed out emphatically by popular actors, are still received with applause by the multitude. Perhaps I suspect that the natural parts of their plays were what ensured to them permanent approbation. Be that as it may, the tragedies of the four[11] you cite, Sir, were received with admiration, and have been handed down to us with that imprimatur. You will grant me that our language is altered since 1625; and many passages in the four were understood then, which are total darkness now—yet are repeated, because they are familiar

3. See HW to Jephson *ante* late Feb. 1775 *bis* and n. 7.

4. See ibid. and Mason ii. 370 and n. 3.

5. *1 Henry IV* III. i.

6. *Macbeth* II. ii. 23–43.

7. In his *Lettre . . . à l'Academie française,* 1776, Voltaire specifically criticizes the language of the Porter in *Macbeth* II. iii, but gives only the briefest summary of the preceding scene in which Macbeth is horrified by the thought of Duncan's murder (*Œuvres complètes de Voltaire,* ed. L.-E.-D. Moland, 1877–85, xxx. 354).

8. See *ante* late Feb. 1775 *bis,* n. 10.

9. *2 Henry IV* III. i. 18–30; HW misquotes line 27: '. . . the wet seaboy in an hour so rude.'

10. *Richard II* V. v. 84–94.

11. Shakespeare, Beaumont, Fletcher, and Massinger (see above).

to our ears, though lost on our understanding. You will say I make no distinction between obsolete diction and metaphor; but all I mean is, that obscurity being accepted by prescription cannot be cited as a precedent for any kind of obscurity that is new: nor if fashion tolerated metaphoric language in that age, can it prove that it is the true taste. It is a general objection to tragedy that it is an unnatural elevation of nature. Its sentiments are exaggerated; surely if those deviations from nature are amplified by the expression, tragedy wanders still farther from its aim, the representation of the passions and conduct of mankind. Of late the world has been forced to accept a mezzo-termine, the *tragédie bourgeoise*.[12] Kings, heroes and heroines could not be persuaded to lower their style. Their etiquette would not allow them to be natural. We were forced to descend amongst ourselves, and seek nature where it grovelled yet.

I am sensible that our language has not the charming and facile grace of the French for conversation. In dialogue (I do not mean theatric) we have never succeeded. Lord Shaftsbury[13] meant to attain the majesty of Plato,[14] missed his way, and found himself in the clouds. Yet what is impossible to genius? *The Man of Mode*,[15] *The Careless Husband*[16] and Vanbrugh[17] have shown that our tongue can utter the genteelest language. *Jane Shore*[18] is a perfect tragedy both in conduct and language, though not a capital one. There are parts of *Oroonoko* and *The Fatal Marriage*[19] worthy a disciple of Shakespeare. It would look like flattery to name *Braganza;* which, I own, though I have again examined it very carefully, I prefer to *The Law of Lombardy.*

Yet, if not quite content with the latter, you may depend upon it I shall not let my objections be known. Mr Garrick does not know

12. *Tragédie bourgeoise*, or, more properly, *le drame bourgeois*, refers to plays of social realism during the second half of the eighteenth century in France, constructed according to principles outlined by Diderot in his *Entretiens sur Le Fils naturel*, 1757. See F. Gaiffe, *Le Drame en France au XVIIIe siècle*, 1910.

13. Anthony Ashley Cooper (1671–1713), 3d E. of Shaftesbury, 1699; author of *Characteristics of Men, Manners, Opinions, Times*, 3 vols, 1711.

14. HW doubtless has in mind the fifth treatise of the *Characteristics*, entitled 'The Moralists, A Philosophical Rhapsody,' which consists primarily of dialogues of the Socratic type between 'Philocles' and 'Theocles.'

15. By Sir George Etherege (?1636–?1692), first performed at the Dorset Garden Theatre in 1676.

16. By Colley Cibber, first performed at Drury Lane in 1704.

17. For HW's high opinion of Vanbrugh and Cibber's *The Provoked Husband* see *ante* 13 July 1777 and n. 19.

18. See *ante* late Feb. 1775 *bis* and n. 22.

19. See *ante* late Feb. 1775 and nn. 7, 8.

them, to whom I have returned your play.[20] My observations were those of a sincere friend. Were I insolent enough to think my sentiments a standard, I hope I am honest enough to conceal them but the more carefully. I have ever to my little power made the interests of your fame my own. I ventured my credit with you rather than act a base part and applaud when I was not satisfied. You have accepted my duty like a man, and I shall willingly give up my judgment as a critic, if you are convinced that I am Sir

Your sincere friend

Hor. Walpole

To Edmund Burke,[1] Wednesday 3 December 1777

Printed from a photostat of the MS among the Wentworth Woodhouse papers in the Sheffield Central Library, by kind permission of the Earl Fitzwilliam and the Trustees of the Wentworth Woodhouse Estates. First printed in Dixon Wecter, 'Horace Walpole and Edmund Burke,' *Modern Language Notes*, 1939, liv. 124. The MS was among Burke's papers left to his literary executors, Dr French Laurence and Dr Walker King; on King's death in 1827, the papers passed to the 4th Earl Fitzwilliam, whom Mrs Burke had named as an additional literary executor after Burke's death. In 1948 the 9th Earl Fitzwilliam deposited the papers previously kept at Wentworth Woodhouse, his seat in Yorkshire, in the Sheffield Central Library.

Endorsed by Burke: Horace Walpole   December 3d 1777.

Arlington Street, Dec. 3, 1777.

I WAS extremely sorry, Sir, to be obliged to deny myself the pleasure of seeing you when you did me the honour of calling on me this morning. I had just heard that Mr Acland[2] was killed;[3] and as

---

20. *The Law of Lombardy* had a successful run of ten nights when it was produced at Drury Lane in 1779 (*London Stage* Pt V, i. 233–6, 249). The critical reception of the play was mixed; see M. S. Peterson, *Robert Jephson (1736–1803): A Study of his Life and Works*, Lincoln, Nebraska, 1930, pp. 33–4.

1. (1729–97), statesman; M.P.
2. John Dyke Acland (1746–78), Maj. 20th Foot, 1775;. Col. of the 1st Battalion, Devonshire militia; M.P. Callington 1774–8 (*Devon and Cornwall Notes and Queries,*

1932–3, xvii. 13; Namier and Brooke). He served with his regiment in America 1776–8.

3. Acland was reported killed in the second battle of Saratoga 7 Oct. 1777. 'In the action that happened on the 7th of October, Col. Frazer and Col. Ackland, two very gallant officers, were killed on the spot' (*London Chronicle* 2–4 Dec. 1777, xlii. 544). The report was called 'not true' a few days later, but Acland had in fact been badly wounded and was captured (Ossory i. 402 n. 18).

he came in for Callington, where Lord and Lady Orford[4] have the principal interest,[5] I had my Lord's steward[6] and lawyer[7] with me consulting on the necessary measures to be taken for keeping up my unfortunate nephew's[8] interest. I flatter myself this will plead my excuse to you,[9] Sir, since I was the only loser. I should have had the honour of waiting on you myself before this time, but knew you was much better employed; and intended to defer my visit to the recess, when you might have leisure to receive so insignificant an old man as

Your most obedient humble servant

Hor. Walpole

To Sir William Musgrave, 1778

Printed for the first time from the MS fragment in Sir William Musgrave's collection of autographs in the British Museum (Add. MS 5726A, f. 175).
Dated by the endorsement.
Endorsed by Musgrave: Horace Walpole afterwards 4th E. of Orford. 1778.

Mr Walpole was out of town when Sir William Musgrave . . .

4. See *ante* mid-Oct. 1773, n. 3.
5. Acland was returned to Parliament for Callington on the Orford interest in 1774; see Conway iii. 192.
6. William Moone (ca 1725–97), a clerk in the Exchequer ca 1770–97 and Lord Orford's steward (Ossory i. 135 n. 8).
7. Charles Lucas (*ante* 1 Feb. 1774, n. 1).

8. In April 1777 Lord Orford had suffered a second attack of insanity from which he had not yet recovered (Family 335–6).
9. HW may have suspected that Burke's call had to do with Acland's seat in Parliament, and wanted to avoid any possible interference in the matter.

To Charles Rogers,[1] Tuesday 27 January 1778

Printed from a photostat of the MS in the Cottonian Collection, Plymouth Museum and Art Gallery, Devon. First printed in *A Descriptive Catalogue of Some Pictures, Books and Prints, Medals, Bronzes and Other Curiosities Collected by Charles Rogers Esq. and now in the Possession of William Cotton, of the Priory, Leatherhead, Surrey*, 1836, p. x. Reprinted, Toynbee *Supp.* iii. 31–2. The MS passed with Rogers's collection of prints, medals, and art objects to his brother-in-law William Cotton (d. 1791), from whom it descended to his son William Cotton (d. 1816); a large portion of the collection was sold at auction, the remainder passing in 1816 to his son William Cotton (d. 1863), who turned over the remaining collection to the Plymouth Public Library in two instalments, in 1852 and 1862.

Address: To Charles Rogers Esq. in Lawrence Pountney Lane, London.

Arlington Street, Jan. 27, 1778.

MR Walpole was surprised and confounded, when he came home last night, at finding Mr Rogers's magnificent present,[2] which he is ashamed to accept from its value, but afraid to refuse, lest Mr Rogers should think it disrespect to so very fine and beautiful a work, or want of proper esteem (which he is still less capable of wanting) for the generous, friendly and excellent editor. Mr Walpole would have waited on Mr Rogers to thank him in person, but came home last night with a great cold.[3] But shall be very happy to know when to find Mr Rogers at home, or to see him in Arlington Street any morning but Saturdays, Sundays and Mondays, between eleven and one: as he is very impatient to express his gratitude for the gift, and his admiration of the work, which he shall study with infinite pleasure.

1. (1711–84), clerk of the certificates in the Custom House 1747–84; F.S.A., 1752; F.R.S., 1757; art collector.

2. A copy of *A Collection of Prints in Imitation of Drawings. To which Are Annexed Lives of their Authors with Explanatory and Critical Notes by Charles Rogers Esq. F.R.S. and S.A.L.*, 2 vols, folio, 1778. HW's copy (untraced since 1928) is Hazen, *Cat. of HW's Lib.*, No. 3627.

3. 'All last week I was confined with a great cold . . . I was blooded in spite of the gout's teeth, and yet am well again' (HW to Mason 4 Feb. 1778, Mason i. 348).

From LORD NORTH,[1] Monday 9 February 1778

Printed from the MS copy in Thomas Kirgate's hand (sent by HW to Sir Edward Walpole, along with a copy of his reply to North *post* 11 Feb. 1778), now WSL. First printed, Toynbee *Supp.* i. 270 n. 2. For the history of the MS copy see HW to Sir Edward Walpole 28 April 1769 (FAMILY 51). The original letter is missing.

Endorsed by Sir Edward Walpole: Lord North's letter to my brother and my brother's answer upon the King's appointment of a deputy ranger to the Parks—Feb. 11, 1778.

Downing Street, Feb. 9, 1778.

Sir,

MR Shirley[2] having signified his desire to resign the Deputy Rangership of St James's and Hyde Parks to Lord William Gordon,[3] I was desired by the latter to mention this arrangement to the King, and to entreat his Majesty's consent and approbation. My application was successful,[4] and I trouble you, in consequence, with this letter and the enclosure to Lord Orford,[5] which, as Lord William informs me, is necessary to authorize you to put him in possession.[6] You have, I understand, been already made acquainted with this agreement, and have given your consent thereto, so that nothing is now wanting, but the enclosed notification of his Majesty's pleasure.[7]

1. Hon. Frederick North (1732–92), styled Lord North 1752–90; 2d E. of Guilford, 1790; first lord of the Treasury 1770–82.

2. Hon. Thomas Shirley (1733–1814), Capt. R.N., 1759; Deputy Ranger of St James's and Hyde Parks ca 1769–78 (Burke, *Peerage*, 1928, p. 926; Collins, *Peerage*, 1812, iv. 102; John Charnock, *Biographia Navalis*, 1794–8, vi. 378–9; *Court and City Register*, 1770, p. 75; 1778, p. 76). He was a nephew of the Hon. Sewallis Shirley (1709–65), Lord Orford's stepfather.

3. (1744–1823), second son of the 3d D. of Gordon; M.P.

4. 'Lord Orford being mad, Mr Shirley, Deputy Ranger of the Parks, made an agreement with Lord William Gordon to cede it to him, and the latter proposed it to Lord North, who spoke to the King, though the King had nothing to do with

it, for the Ranger not only appoints his Deputy, but pays him his salary. The King ordered Lord William should have it' (*Last Journals* ii. 113).

5. Missing; it was a 'notification of his Majesty's pleasure' (see below). Orford was Ranger of St James's and Hyde Parks 1763–83, 1784–91.

6. North apparently assumed that HW was in charge of Orford's affairs during his second attack of insanity, but (as HW pointed out in his reply *post* 11 Feb.) they were in fact being managed by 'Lord Orford's servants,' i.e., his steward and his lawyer.

7. HW wrote Sir Edward Walpole 11 Feb. 1778: 'Lord William Gordon was with me this morning, and brought me Lord North's letter, which being something different from what I expected, I have sent a different answer from that

I have the honour to be with great respect,

Sir,

Your very faithful humble servant,

NORTH

To LORD NORTH, Wednesday 11 February 1778

Printed from the MS copy in Thomas Kirgate's hand (sent by HW to Sir Edward Walpole, along with a copy of North's letter to him *ante* 9 Feb. 1778), now WSL. First printed, Toynbee *Supp.* i. 270–2. For the history of the MS copy see HW to Sir Edward Walpole 28 April 1769 (FAMILY 51). The original letter is missing.

Arlington Street, Feb. 11, 1778.

My Lord,

I RECEIVED the honour of your Lordship's letter,[1] with the notification of his Majesty's pleasure about the Deputy Rangership of the two Parks, and immediately paid all the profound respect and submission to his Majesty's commands, that I ought and wish to show, as far as it depended on me, by troubling Lord William Gordon with a letter[2] to Lord Orford's servants, acquainting them with his Majesty's nomination of Lord William to be Deputy Ranger, and that I was persuaded my nephew, if in health, would expect them to show all proper obedience to Lord William.[3]

I must entreat your Lordship to favour me with a moment's patience, while I explain the reasons of the limitation of my expressions, reasons that indeed are very unimportant to your Lordship, but which my unfortunate situation obliges me to weigh and state with precision as a future vindication of my brother and myself, and which if I did not specify, I might appear to be wanting in the duty and reverence I have for his Majesty's commands.

Many unhappy circumstances, too tedious to trouble your Lord-

I showed you last night, almost as *civil* in expression, but more intimating my sense of the affront we have received, as his Lordship asserts his being told I had *assented*' (FAMILY 157).

1. *Ante* 9 Feb. 1778.
2. Missing; it was addressed to William

Moone, Lord Orford's steward. See following note.

3. 'At Lord William's desire, I gave him a letter to Moone, in which I was as cautious to give *no* orders, but only said I concluded Lord Orford's servants *would* obey Lord William' (HW to Sir Edward Walpole 11 Feb. 1778, FAMILY 158).

ship with, have obliged Sir Edward and me to decline the management of Lord Orford's affairs, or even in the interfering in them at all. They,[4] who have taken possession of them, have reduced us to declare on every application *that we neither assent nor dissent,* and as any act of concurrence on our part might preclude us from applying to the law, if necessary, for a remedy of the violent exclusion of us from the care of our nephew's affairs, when Mr Shirley first acquainted me yesterday with the new arrangement, I expressed in the fullest manner I was able my dutiful submission to his Majesty's commands, but begged to be excused from saying anything that might imply Sir Edward's or my having anything to do with the management of the Parks; and therefore your Lordship will be so good as to understand, that though I had no dislike or disapprobation of the new arrangement, much less any thought of objecting to his Majesty's commands, it was not in my power to give any consent to what in no shape depended on my consent[5]—and this I did very particularly state to Mr Shirley, who acknowledged the necessity of the distinction.

I beg your Lordship a thousand pardons for troubling you with this impertinent detail, much more necessary for me to write than for your Lordship to read. The use of it is, that should I ever be so happy as to see my nephew's recovery,[6] and should be misrepresented to him by the bad people about him, as having taken on me to consent for him [to] a new arrangement of places under him, I flatter myself that your Lordship's good nature will permit me to appeal to you for my innocence, and will bear me testimony, that I did nothing more than receive the notification of his Majesty's commands with the utmost reverence, and your Lordship's communication of his will with respect and gratitude.[7]

I have the honour to be, with great regard,

> My Lord,
> Your Lordship's most obedient humble servant

> Hor. Walpole

4. William Moone, Lord Orford's steward, and Charles Lucas, his lawyer (*ante* 8 Dec. 1777, nn. 6, 7).

5. 'Shirley told me the letter [from Lord North to HW] was actually written; so they depended on my consent, which I took care not to give' (HW to Sir Edward Walpole 11 Feb. 1778, FAMILY 157–8).

6. He regained his sanity in late March of this year (ibid. 336).

7. Lord William Gordon succeeded Shirley as Deputy Ranger of the Parks and retained the post until his death in 1823. 'Lord W. Gordon was made Deputy Ranger of the Parks, by a bargain with Captain Shirley, so very advantageous to

TO EDWARD JERNINGHAM,[1] Friday 13 February 1778

Printed from a photostat of the MS in the Henry E. Huntington Library. First printed in Lewis Bettany, *Edward Jerningham and his Friends*, 1919, pp. 44–5. Reprinted, Toynbee *Supp.* iii. 32–4. The MS descended in the Jerningham family to Sir Henry Stafford Jerningham, 11th Bt, who owned it in 1919; offered by Charles J. Sawyer Ltd., Cat. No. 81 (1925), p. 76; sold by them to Huntington, 1925.

Address: To Edward Jerningham Esq. in Conduit Street.

Arlington Street, Feb. 13, 1778.

Dear Sir,

IF I was speaker of both Houses and of all houses, I would return you the thanks of the public for the new volume of your poems.[2] To thank you for your present to myself, is too cold and too selfish. Gratitude is a return to a mark of friendship; but a private individual can no more pay the debts of the public, than the public can pay—any of its own. Nay, I cannot, like the nation, pay you interest by a poetic annuity; so I must call your gift by that long obsolete, but now revived term, a *Benevolence.*[3] *Yours,* I hope, will grow an established duty; as if you presented a brace of carp to a judge on the circuit, all the twelve judges would claim them forever, as often as they go their rounds of *justice* near your fish pond.

I have not time to tell you all I like in your small volume; but must mention one passage that struck me particularly, as touches of nature and tenderness always do. Margaret's[4] answer to the robber, when he says

——— if thou hast ought concealed[5]

the latter that it was supposed the Government really paid the charge, to soothe Lord William and the Duke [of Gordon] his brother for the refusal of the command of their new regiment to the younger' (*Last Journals* ii. 105, *sub* Feb. 1778).

———

1. (1737–1812), poet and dramatist.

2. *Fugitive Poetical Pieces*, 1778. In 1794 HW seems to have extracted *Margaret of Anjou, An Historical Interlude* from his copy of *Fugitive Poetical Pieces* and included it in a volume of his 'Theatre of Geo. 3.' The piece was later disbound from the volume and is now WSL; see Hazen, *Cat. of HW's Lib.*, No. 1810 : 54 : 2.

3. 'A forced loan or contribution levied,

without legal authority, by the kings of England on their subjects. First so called in 1473 when astutely asked by Edward IV, as a token of goodwill towards his rule' (OED 4).

4. Margaret (ca 1430–82) of Anjou, m. (1445) Henry VI of England. She is the subject of Jerningham's 'historical interlude' *Margaret of Anjou*, performed at Drury Lane 11 March 1777 as part of a benefit for Elizabeth Younge, who played the title-rôle (*London Stage* Pt V, i. 64). The work was first published in Jerningham's *Fugitive Poetical Pieces*.

5. '. . . if ought thou hast conceal'd' (*Fugitive Poetical Pieces*, p. 9).

Within this wood, give me the hoarded treasure.

and she replies

Ah! here is all my treasure (pointing to her child).

This is sweetly pathetic, and preferable to all the poetry of Pindar, that soars out of sight, and beyond comprehension. I love poets that speak to the heart's ears—for those that grow on the head, and whose veins only go to the brain, and not to the palpitation of the heart, I do not value them of a rush. I own that when the brain on revision confirms the heart's tears, the bard has double merit—treble, if the brain discovers more than the heart conceived—and your hemistich has that triple portion. The sentence would penetrate in the mouth of any mother—when it is a queen that has lost husband, crown, power, court, everything but her child, the thought improves on reflection, and deepens all the accents on hère, àll, my trèasure. An actress would perhaps be to blame to pronounce all those four syllables with the full emphasis that belongs to them; for *here* is opposed to England, *all* to the Exchequer, *my* to the regal style *our*, and *treasure* transfers the idea of riches to that of an only child.

I beg your pardon, and may have refined too much. We commentators do sometimes discover more than our author intended; but when nature speaks, it is prodigious how far the justness of her thoughts will vibrate. Shakespeare who wrote down what she dictated, must often have perceived more beauties than he was aware of at first, in committing her words to paper. I have taken up too much of your time, and am dear Sir

Your obliged humble servant

Hor. Walpole

To George Colman, Monday 2 March 1778

Printed from the MS now wsl. First printed, Toynbee *Supp.* i. 273–4. The MS is untraced until 1918, when it was *penes* F. T. Sabin, 172 New Bond Street, London; later acquired by Walter T. Spencer, who sold it in a collection to wsl, Sept. 1932.

Endorsed in an unidentified hand: 20.

Arlington Street, March 2d 1778.

I AM much ashamed, Sir, that you should think it necessary to make so much apology for doing me an honour, as your approbation certainly is.[1] I do not guess how you discovered the author, but own I shall be glad to know. The thing was a hasty careless performance,[2] and as you rightly judged, too short for the stage—perhaps is only fit to be acted in a private society in the country, like the proverbs now so common in France.[3] On reflection I am very far from thinking it worthy of being exhibited to the public[4]—and of all men living I have the least courage to expose myself in that manner, especially at my age. Conscious of having trespassed too much on the patience of the world and sensible of my own deficiencies, I have long quitted the profession of author; and hope that consciousness of my want of talents will be some excuse for the follies of my younger years; and prove at least that I am not an impenitent offender. You, Sir, cannot want such feeble assistance as mine. The volumes you was so very kind as to bestow on me last winter,[5] and for which I waited on you at Richmond in the summer to thank you, (though I believe you

1. In March 1773 HW had sent anonymously to Colman his one-act 'moral entertainment' *Nature Will Prevail*. Colman was at that time the manager of Covent Garden Theatre. HW declined to reveal his authorship of the piece, but told Colman that he was free to make any alterations he wished if he found it worthy of being performed (*ante* March 1773 and March 1773 *bis*). Colman liked the piece, but thought it was 'too short for the stage' (see below). Nothing further came of it until five years later, when Colman (now the manager of the Little Theatre in the Haymarket) found out the author and wrote to HW expressing his interest and 'approbation.' Colman's letter is missing.

2. 'It was written in two days' (HW to Colman *ante* March 1773)

3. HW had seen *proverbes* acted at Mme du Deffand's in Paris. In her letter to HW 19 Nov. 1777, she mentions 'une musique, des proverbes, tous les plaisirs réunis' (du Deffand iv. 493). The full title of HW's piece when it was performed at the Haymarket later this year was *Nature Will Prevail, A Dramatic Proverb* (*Public Adv.* 10 June 1778).

4. 'In June [1778] was acted "Nature will Prevail," . . . at the little theatre in the Haymarket, with success' (HW's 'Short Notes,' Gray i. 50). For the history of the performances see *ante* March 1773 n. 5.

5. See *ante* 28 Dec. 1776 and n. 2.

did not hear it) confirm my opinion; and the success of the theatre in the Haymarket under your direction,[6] proves the variety of your abilities.

As I am little able to walk and seldom go out in a morning, I should take it as an honour if in your walks you would bestow a quarter of an hour on me at eleven or twelve, when I have rarely any company. I can expect this favour only when you are most at leisure, but shall always be with great regard and gratitude, Sir,

Your obliged and most obedient humble servant

Hor. Walpole

To Charles Bedford,[1] Thursday 23 April 1778

Printed from Cunningham vii. 57, where the letter was first printed. Reprinted, Toynbee x. 226. The history of the MS and its present whereabouts are not known.

Strawberry Hill, April 23, 1778.

Dear Sir,

I SHALL be much obliged to you if you will call tomorrow evening at the Somerset House Coffee-house,[2] and inquire into the truth of the enclosed advertisement;[3] and if you find it a true case, I will beg you to pay what money is wanted, or the whole thirty-nine shillings if no other money has been sent. I will make you no excuse for giving you this trouble, as I am sure you will execute the commission with pleasure.

Yours sincerely,

H. W.

6. Colman was manager of the Haymarket 1777–89.

———

1. (ca 1742–1814), clerk in the office of usher of the Exchequer, 1763; HW's deputy in the Exchequer 1774–97 (ante 27 Feb. 1771, n. 1).
2. No. 166 Strand, at the east corner of the entrance to King's College (Bryant Lillywhite, London Coffee Houses, 1963, pp. 538–40).

3. Not preserved with the letter. The advertisement appeared in the Public Adv. 22 April 1778: 'To the charitably humane, A widow, with two orphan daughters, most humbly addresses her present very unhappy situation, reduced from affluence to a state of the deepest misery. Illness and every ruin has followed her so close, that she is now served with a copy of a Marshalsea Court writ, which admits no bail, for thirty-nine shillings; which, if

To Edward Gibbon, ? May 1778

Printed from a photostat of the MS among the Gibbon papers in the British Museum (Add. MS 34,886, f. 106). First printed in *Miscellaneous Works of Edward Gibbon, Esq.*, ed. Lord Sheffield, [2d edn], 1814, ii. 156–8. Reprinted in *Miscellaneous Works*, ed. Sheffield, 1796–1815, iii. 604–5; Wright vi. 30–1; Cunningham vii. 157–8; Toynbee x. 228–30 (printed with letters of Dec. 1778 in Wright and Cunningham, with letters of May 1778 in Toynbee). For the history of the Gibbon papers in the BM see *ante* ca 12 Feb. 1776. A MS copy of the letter, in the hand of an amanuensis, is bound in Lord Sheffield's interleaved copy of the *Miscellaneous Works*, 2 vols, 1796, now in the Yale University Library (vol. I, pt 2, following p. 500).

Dated conjecturally by the publication of Henry Edward Davis's *Examination . . . of Mr Gibbon's History* 2 May 1778 (see n. 1 below).

Dear Sir,

I HAVE gone through your inquisitor's attack,[1] and am far from being clear that it deserves your giving yourself the trouble of an answer, as neither the detail nor the result affects your argument. So far from it, many of his reproofs are levelled at your having quoted a wrong page, he confessing often that what you have cited is in the author referred to, but not precisely in the individual spot.[2] If St Peter is attended by a corrector of the press, you will certainly never be admitted where he is porter.

I send you my copy,[3] because I scribbled my remarks. I do not send them with the impertinent presumption of suggesting a hint to you, but to prove I did not grudge the trouble of going through such a book, when you desired it; and to show how little struck me as of any weight.

not discharged by the return of the writ on Saturday, precipitates her into a gaol, and her family into complicated distress. 'The smallest donations will be thankfully received, and a direction given (to where all will be fully authenticated) at the Wardour Street Coffee-house, Wardour Street, Soho; and at the Somerset House Coffee-house in the Strand.'

---

1. *An Examination of the Fifteenth and Sixteenth Chapters of Mr Gibbon's History of the Decline and Fall of the Roman Empire. In which his View of the Progress of the Christian Religion Is Shown to be Founded on the Misrepresentation of the Authors He Cites: and Numerous Instances of his Inaccuracy and Plagiarism Are Produced*, 1778, by Henry Edwards Davis (1756–84), B.A., of Balliol College, Oxford. Davis's *Examination* was published 2 May 1778 (*Public Adv.* 2 May).

2. Many of these errors of citation are listed in the section headed 'Proofs of Mr Gibbon's Inaccuracy' (*Examination*, pp. 141–56).

3. Missing. Gibbon doubtless had his own copy of the *Examination*; the copy sent by HW to Gibbon is not recorded in Geoffrey Keynes, *The Library of Edward Gibbon*, 1940, p. 107.

I have set down nothing on your imputed plagiarisms, for if they are so, no argument that has ever been employed, must be used again, even where the passage necessary is applied to a different purpose. An author is not allowed to be master of the property of his own works, but by Davis's new law, the first person that cites him would be so. You probably looked into Middleton,[4] Dodwell[5] etc. had the same reflections on the same circumstances, or conceived them, so as to recollect them, without remembering what suggested them. Is this plagiarism? If it is, Davis and such cavillers might go a short step farther, and insist that an author should peruse every work antecedently written on every subject at all collateral to his own—not to assist him, but to be sure to avoid every material touched by his predecessors.

I will make but one remark on such divine champions. Davis and his prototypes[6] tell you Middleton etc. have used the same objections, and they have been *confuted; answering* in the theologic dictionary signifying *confuting;* no matter whether there is sense, argument, truth, in the answer or not.

Upon the whole, I think ridicule is the only answer such a work is entitled to. The ablest answer you can make (which would be the ablest answer that could be made) would never have any authority with the cabal, yet would allow a sort of dignity to the author. His patrons will always maintain that he vanquished you, unless you make him too ridiculous for them to dare to revive his name. You might divert yourself too with Alma Mater the Church employing a goujat[7] to defend the citadel, while the generals repose in their tents. St Irenæus,[8] St Augustine etc. did not set apprentices and acolytes to combat Celsus[9] and the adversaries of the new religion—but early bishops had not five or six thousand pounds a year.

4. Conyers Middleton (1683–1750), D.D., author and controversialist; HW's correspondent. In the *Examination,* pp. 169–85, 271–2, Davis accused Gibbon of frequent 'instances of plagiarism' of Middleton's *Letter to Dr Waterland,* 1731, and of his *Free Inquiry into the Miraculous Powers,* 1749.

5. Henry Dodwell, the elder (1641–1711), scholar and theologian. Gibbon's 'plagiarism' of Dodwell's *Dissertationes cyprianicæ,* Oxford, 1684, and of other historical treatises by him is discussed in the *Examination,* pp. 229–64.

6. 'The monks that have attacked his

[Gibbon's] two famous chapters' (HW to Lady Ossory 14 Jan. 1779, OssoRY ii. 84). For the names of Gibbon's other attackers see ibid. ii. 84 n. 4.

7. 'An army valet; a soldier's boy' (OED, citing HW's use of the word in this letter).

8. Missionary from Asia Minor who lived in Gaul during the second century; Bp of Lugdunum (Lyons); one of the Fathers of the early Christian church. His Greek work *Against the Heresies,* written ca 180 A.D., was directed against Gnostic errors.

9. Roman philosopher of the second

In short, dear Sir, I wish you not to lose your time; that is, either not reply, or set *your mark* on your answer,[10] that it may always be read with the rest of your works.

To Charles Bedford, Wednesday 22 July 1778

Printed from Cunningham vii. 99, where the letter was first printed. Reprinted, Toynbee x. 287. The history of the MS and its present whereabouts are not known.

Arlington Street, Wednesday, July 22, 1778.

I WILL be obliged to you if you will look into the Abbey,[1] and see if Mr Gray's monument[2] is uncovered yet; as, if it is, I will call and see it.[3]

Yours ever,

H. Walpole

century. His *True Discourse* (known through Origen's refutation of it in the third century) was the first serious criticism of Christianity.

10. In Jan. 1779 Gibbon published *A Vindication of Some Passages in the Fifteenth and Sixteenth Chapters of the History of the Decline and Fall of the Roman Empire.* He sent HW a copy of the pamphlet in Dec. 1778; see *post* 25 Dec. 1778.

––––––

1. Westminster Abbey.
2. The monument was executed by John Bacon (1740–99) at the joint expense of Dr James Brown (*ante* 25 Aug. 1772, n. 1), Richard Stonhewer (*ante* 16 Sept. 1771, n. 1), and William Mason. It was placed immediately below the monument to Milton, and is inscribed with a four-line epitaph by Mason (Cole ii. 101 n. 3; Mason i. 279 n. 8).

3. HW wrote Cole 24 July 1778: 'The tomb for Mr Gray is actually erected . . . but the scaffolds are not yet removed. I was in town yesterday and intended to visit it, but there is digging a vault for the family of Northumberland, which obstructs the removal of the boards' (Cole ii. 103). HW saw the monument a month later. He wrote Mason 28 Aug.: 'The absolutely necessary position is very disadvantageous to it, and prevents any grace in the outline; his nose is a little too aquiline, but both his head and the Muse's are well executed; her body is a little flat, and her legs, from the same want of place, too small and crowded; your epitaph and friendship are the most shining ingredients' (Mason i. 439 and illustration).

From JOHN SIMCO,[1] Monday 17 August 1778

Printed from John Doran, *'Mann' and Manners at the Court of Florence,*
1876, ii. 348–9, where the letter was first printed. The history of the MS and
its present whereabouts are not known.

Dr Doran writes of this letter: 'Mann had often been employed in buying
pictures from Italian collectors, for English amateurs. Walpole, to show what
sort of vendor had turned up in England, sent to Mann the following curious
letter, which caused some mirth in the Minister's house' (ibid. ii. 348). We have
found no reference to the letter in HW's correspondence with Mann.

Aug. 17th 1778.

Honourable Sir,

I HOPE you will excuse the rudeness of a plebeian in being thus
bold to address you, but I was encouraged thereto by the mention
of your goodness Mr Grainger makes of you in his *Biographical History,*[2] as I have in my possession an original painting of Seth Ward,[3]
Bishop of Salisbury, which I should be glad to dispose of, and for which
I ask four guineas; and having read an account of your curious
collections at Strawberry Hill,[4] which I long to see,[5] thought you
might be glad to have it to put with them if you had not got one;
so made bold to acquaint you of it, being encouraged thereto by the
mention the gent[leman] aforesaid makes of your amiable disposition,
and being at present under the frowns of Divine Providence, as
being but in the lowest class as a servant, and being out of place at
present, or else would not have parted with it, as I have been curious
in collecting some curiosities myself, having a taste that way, though
cannot afford to do as I would, but have none worthy of your observation besides; therefore if you please to favour me with a line,

1. (ca 1750–1824), bookseller at No. 11
Great Queen Street; later located at No. 2
Air Street, Piccadilly (*The Universal British Directory of Trade, Commerce, and
Manufacture,* 1791, p. 287; W. B. Todd,
*A Directory of Printers and Others in Al-
lied Trades . . . 1800–1840,* 1972, p. 175).
His obituary in GM describes him as 'a
worthy, honest man, long known and re-
spected for his love of antiquities, and his
curious catalogues of topography and biography (from 1788 to the present time)'
(GM 1824, xciv pt i. 186). He specialized
in the sale of extra-illustrated topographi-

cal books, and was patronized by many
eminent collectors.

2. See *ante* 3 April 1764, n. 2. In the
dedication to HW, Granger refers to 'your
writings, which speak for themselves' and
'your virtues, some of which are as well
known as your literary accomplishments.'

3. (1617–89), D.D. (Oxon.), 1654; Bp of
Exeter 1662–67, of Salisbury 1667–89.

4. Simco had perhaps seen a copy of
HW's *Description of SH,* 1774.

5. Simco visited SH in 1789; see *post*
20 Aug. 1789.

directed for John Simco at Mr Hiron,[6] stone mason, the corner of Portpool Lane in Leather Lane, Holborn, where and when to wait upon you with it,[7] shall take it as a great favour. Hoping your great goodness will forgive my present boldness in thus making free with you,

I remain, honourable Sir,

Your very humble servant to command,

John Simco

To Charles Rogers, Tuesday 8 December 1778

Printed from a photostat of the MS in Thomas Kirgate's hand in the Cottonian Collection, Plymouth Museum and Art Gallery, Devon. First printed, Toynbee *Supp.* iii. 34–5. For the history of the MS see *ante* 27 Jan. 1778.
Address: To Charles Rogers Esq. at the Custom House.

Arlington Street, December 8th 1778.

MR H. Walpole was exceedingly mortified when he heard Mr Rogers had done him the favour of calling on him with his most obliging and acceptable present,[1] when it was quite impossible for Mr Walpole to see anybody, being gone to bed in pain. Mr W. had seen Mr Suckling[2] for a moment in the morning, who can tell Mr Rogers[3] how little fit Mr Walpole was to see anybody, having been confined for six weeks to his bed and room with the gout all over him.[4]

Mr Walpole returns Mr Rogers a thousand thanks for this new proof of his friendship, which he values so much, that it makes him unreasonable enough even to beg another present, which is another impression of Mr Rogers's own portrait,[5] Mr Walpole being very

6. Not further identified.

7. HW apparently declined Simco's offer; no oil painting of Bishop Ward is mentioned in the SH sale catalogue.

1. Probably an engraved portrait for HW's collection of English 'heads' (see *ante* 3 April 1764, n. 3).

2. William Suckling, HW's cousin (*ante* 23 Dec. 1775, n. 6).

3. Suckling and Rogers both held posts in the Custom House.

4. HW had kept to his room since 29 October. The vicissitudes of this illness are described in his letters to Lady Ossory; see Ossory ii. 69–75.

5. A mezzotint engraved in 1778 by William Wynne Ryland (after the painting of 1777 by Sir Joshua Reynolds), included as the frontispiece to Rogers's *Col-*

desirous of having one for his collection of English heads, as well as for the magnificent and beautiful work with which his library has already been honoured and adorned.[6]

From Charles Rogers, Thursday 10 December 1778

Printed from a photostat of Rogers's MS copy in the Cottonian Collection, Plymouth Museum and Art Gallery, Devon. First printed, Toynbee *Supp*. iii. 256–7. For the history of the MS copy see *ante* 27 Jan. 1778. The original letter is missing.

Laurence Pountney Lane, 10 December 1778.

Sir,

WHEN I honoured myself with waiting on you last Monday, I was made extremely uneasy by hearing the cause of being prevented paying my particular respects;[1] yet hope, Sir, you will be soon relieved from your severe fit, for which I have some inducement by your being at leisure to attend to such a trifle as a print which can by no means be thought a striking likeness of the person intended to be represented, being far too juvenile, besides the considerable difference between a perruque and hair;[2] but I believe Sir Joshua Reynolds must be acknowledged to excel in hair-dressing, as well as in material branches of his art.

Such as it is, the admitting it, Sir, into your very valuable collection of portraits can be no otherwise than flattering to,

Sir,

Your most obedient and most obliged humble servant,

C[harles] R[ogers]

Honourable Mr Horace Walpole.

---

lection *of Prints in Imitation of Drawings*, 1778. The painting is now in the Plymouth Museum and Art Gallery; see [Hazel Berriman], *Sir Joshua Reynolds, P.R.A.*, Plymouth, 1973, No. 47.

6. Rogers had given HW a copy of his

Collection *of Prints in Imitation of Drawings* in Jan. 1778; see *ante* 27 Jan. 1778.

---

1. See previous letter.
2. Rogers is shown wearing his own hair in the portrait.

To Charles Rogers, Thursday 10 December 1778

Printed from a photostat of the MS in Thomas Kirgate's hand in the Cottonian Collection, Plymouth Museum and Art Gallery, Devon. First printed, Toynbee *Supp.* iii. 35; extract printed in [Hazel Berriman], *Sir Joshua Reynolds, P.R.A.*, Plymouth, 1973, *sub* No. 47. For the history of the MS see *ante* 27 Jan. 1778.

Address: To Charles Rogers Esq. in Lawrence Pountney Lane.

Arlington Street, December 10, 1778.

MR Walpole has received Mr Rogers's second obliging favour, for which he gives him a thousand thanks, and with which he is much more pleased than Mr Rogers seems to be.[1] The portrait is very like, and if it should be a little the younger there is no harm, for in so fine a work that will be lasting, posterity will not know at what age the likeness was taken.[2]

Mr Walpole flatters himself that in a fortnight or three weeks he shall be able to receive company,[3] when there is nobody he shall see with more pleasure and gratitude than Mr Rogers; as, when able to go abroad, Mr W. shall be happy to wait on Mr Rogers whenever he knows a day and hour that will not be inconvenient.

1. See previous letter.
2. Rogers was sixty-six when the portrait was painted.
3. HW wrote Lady Ossory 14 Jan. 1779

that he had had 'two returns of pain and lameness,' but 'By Monday [18 Jan.] I expect company and events' (Ossory ii. 83).

To Lord Dacre, Tuesday 15 December 1778

Printed for the first time from the MS in Thomas Kirgate's hand, now WSL. The MS descended in the Barrett-Lennard family to Sir Richard Barrett-Lennard, 5th Bt; sold Sotheby's 1 Dec. 1938 (property of Sir Richard Barrett-Lennard), lot 1105, to Maggs for WSL.

Dated by the endorsement and by HW's letter to Lady Ossory 12 Dec. 1778, in which he writes: 'I have been very ill indeed ever since this day sennight . . . but it is quite over; and so is my gout, all but in my right hand. I have not been permitted to see but a few of my own family and one or two friends, and scarce to speak to them. Tomorrow I am to see a few more, under Sacrament of being very prudent' (Ossory ii. 75).

Endorsed by Dacre: Mr Horace Walpole December 1778.

Address: To the Right Honourable Lord Dacre, Bruton Street.

Arlington Street, Tuesday evening.

My dear Lord,

I HAVE had the honour of being allowed to call your Lordship friend so long, that I hoped, as we are both invalids too,[1] that you would not have thought it necessary to send me a formal card.[2] I should have called on you again and again, had I been able, and I preferred informing myself about your Lordship from Mr Cowslade,[3] to troubling you with messages, by a servant, from which one never learns any truth. I hope you are recovering, as I am, and shall be happy to hear so.

I trust I have no occasion to inquire after Lady Dacre, but that she is perfectly well. I must entreat her Ladyship to make my excuses to Lord Camden,[4] for not sending, but not having seen Mr Cowslade for some days, nor above one or two other persons[5] till within these two days, I have but just heard of Miss Pratt's[6] illness.

Your Lordship's most faithful humble servant

H. Walpole

1. See headnote and *ante* 8 Dec. 1778, n. 4.

2. Missing.

3. John Cowslade (*ante* 16 Sept. ?1774, n. 1). Cowslade, like Dacre, had a house in Berkeley Square.

4. Lady Dacre's brother.

5. HW had seen Lord Ossory on 3 Dec.

and his cousin William Suckling 'for a moment' on the 7th (Ossory ii. 74; *ante* 8 Dec. 1778).

6. Probably one of Lord Camden's four daughters, three of whom (Elizabeth, Sarah, and Jane) were unmarried at this time (Collins, *Peerage*, 1812, v. 270).

To Edward Gibbon, Friday 25 December 1778

Printed from a photostat of the MS among the Gibbon papers in the British Museum (Add. MS 34,886, f. 105). First printed in *Miscellaneous Works of Edward Gibbon, Esq.*, ed. Lord Sheffield, [2d edn,] 1814, ii. 158–9 (date omitted). Reprinted in *Miscellaneous Works*, ed. Sheffield, 1796–1815, iii. 605 (date omitted); Wright vi. 41; Cunningham vii. 188–9; Toynbee x. 367–8 (dated '[1779]' and signature omitted in Wright, Cunningham, and Toynbee). For the history of the Gibbon papers in the BM see *ante* ca 12 Feb. 1776. A MS copy of the letter, in the hand of an amanuensis, is bound in Lord Sheffield's interleaved copy of the *Miscellaneous Works*, 2 vols, 1796, now in the Yale University Library (vol. I, pt 2, following p. 500).

Dec. 25, 1778.

THE penetration, solidity, and taste, that made you the first of historians, dear Sir, prevent my being surprised at your being the best writer of controversial pamphlets too. I have read you with more precipitation than such a work deserved, but I could not disobey you and detain it;[1] yet even in that hurry I could discern, besides a thousand beauties and strokes of wit, the inimitable 83d page,[2] and the conscious dignity that you maintain throughout over your monkish antagonists.[3] When you are so superior in argument, it would look like insensibility to the power of your reasoning, to select transient passages for commendation; and yet I must mention one that pleased me particularly from the delicacy of the severity,

1. Gibbon had sent HW a copy of *A Vindication of Some Passages in the Fifteenth and Sixteenth Chapters of the History of the Decline and Fall of the Roman Empire*, 1779, his reply to Henry Edwards Davis's *Examination* (*ante* ?May 1778, n. 1). The *Vindication* was not actually published until 'Jan. 14,' as HW noted in his copy, now WSL (Hazen, *Cat. of HW's Lib.* No. 1609:39:10). It is not clear whether this is the copy sent to HW; the letter seems to suggest that HW returned it to Gibbon, since the pamphlet was not yet published.

2. Gibbon writes on p. 83 of the *Vindication*: 'A Theological Barometer might be formed, of which the Cardinal [Baronius] and our countryman Dr Middleton should constitute the opposite and remote extremities, as the former sunk to the lowest degree of credulity, which was

compatible with learning, and the latter rose to the highest pitch of scepticism, in any wise consistent with religion. The intermediate gradations would be filled by a line of ecclesiastical critics, whose rank has been fixed by the circumstances of their temper and studies, as well as by the spirit of the church or society to which they were attached. It would be amusing enough to calculate the weight of prejudice in the air of Rome, of Oxford, of Paris, and of Holland; and sometimes to observe the irregular tendency of Papists toward freedom, sometimes to remark the unnatural gravitation of Protestants towards slavery.'

3. See OSSORY ii. 84 and n. 4. Davis followed Gibbon's *Vindication* with *A Reply to Mr Gibbon's Vindication*, 1779. HW's copy, now WSL, is Hazen, *op. cit.*, No. 1609:41:1.

and from its novelty too; it is, *bold is not the word.*[4] This is the feathered arrow of Cupid that is more formidable than the club of Hercules. I need not specify thanks, when I prove how much I have been pleased.[5]

Your most obliged

H. Walpole

To Thomas Pennant, Saturday 9 January 1779

Printed for the first time from the MS now wsl. For the history of the MS see *ante* 25 May 1773.

Arlington Street, Jan. 9th 1779.

NOTHING could be more acceptable to me, dear Sir, than the kind proof of your remembrance in the letter[1] I have received from you and the print,[2] which I immediately sent for. The latter however is not near so like as the print in my memory; nor can I say it is so like as a miniature[3] you once showed me of yourself—though I never pretend to decide on resemblances, as I am persuaded the eyes of different persons see objects very differently; and that we should be much astonished if we were for a short time to see with the eyes of others; aye, or to hear or taste with their senses, or smell. Feeling, I believe, is the sense in which there is the most general conformity—and yet accompanied with variations, as pain affects

4. 'He [Davis] is even bold enough (*bold* is not the *proper* word) to conceive some hopes of persuading his readers, that an historian who has employed several years of his life, and several hundred pages, on the decline and fall of the Roman Empire, had never read Orosius, or the Augustan History' (*Vindication*, pp. 90–1).

5. In his letter to Lady Ossory 14 Jan. 1779, HW described the *Vindication* as 'the quintessence of argument, wit, temper, spirit, and consequently of victory' (Ossory ii. 84). He wrote to her on 9 Feb.: 'Pray read all Mr Gibbon's pamphlet, and do not fear not understanding it. It is luminous as day, with clearness one of his brightest talents. I am sure the whole will

delight you. It is Mr Gibbon *that can make the dryest subject interesting and entertaining,* and his reply to Davis is the strongest evidence that can be given' (ibid. ii. 91–2).

———

1. Missing.

2. Possibly the portrait engraving by Walker that was published in the *Westminster Magazine* for December 1777. An engraved portrait of Pennant from SH was sold London 652. Gainsborough's portrait of him, painted in 1776, was engraved by W. Ridley for the frontispiece to *The Literary Life of the late Thomas Pennant, Esq. By Himself,* 1793.

3. Not further identified.

some more than others; and the disagreement about heat and cold
is continual; but probably the sense of feeling depends more on the
constitution of our own bodies than on what impresses them: taste
certainly does too in some degree—but our sight does not vary from
one day to another. The same object does not appear to us blue
today and green tomorrow; and yet I doubt whether either colour
appears exactly the same to two different [persons].[4] I have heard of
a family in the north of England, of whom it was almost ascertained
that they saw everything as black, white and shades of brown.[5] There
are actually two brothers of a great family, who seem to have no
precise idea of specific colours[6]—but I am running into an essay
when I meant only to thank you; yet I am so unreasonable, that I
hope I shall have to thank you this winter with the public for another volume of your travels.[7] I am with great regard, Sir,

> Your most obliged and obed[ient] humble servant

> HOR. WALPOLE

To the REV. THOMAS PERCY, Monday 11 January 1779

Printed from a photostat of the MS kindly supplied by its former owner, the
late E. H. W. Meyerstein. First printed in Meyerstein, *A Life of Thomas Chatterton*, 1930, pp. 276–7. The MS is untraced until it was acquired by Sir Ernest
Clarke; two years after Clarke's death in 1923, his executor, Mr. H. C. Wallace,
gave it to Mr Meyerstein, who died in 1952; not further traced.

> Arlington Street, Jan. 11, 1779.

Dear Sir,

AS I should be very unwilling to take any step in the affair of
Chatterton[1] without your good advice and direction, I take the

4. The MS reads 'colours,' but HW presumably meant to write 'persons.'

5. 'It was verified some years ago, as
much as such a matter could be ascertained, that there were two brothers, I
think in the county of Durham, saw everything in chiaroscuro, that is everything
appeared to them black, brown, or white'
(HW's Anecdotes Written 1784–1796, *sub*
1 Oct. 1784, BERRY ii. 253).

6. ' . . . the present Duke of Marlbro
and his brother Lord Robert Spencer have

very imperfect discrimination of colours,
especially of scarlet and green' (ibid.).

7. The second and last volume of Pennant's *Tour in Wales* was published in
two parts, 1781–3 (*post* 15 Oct. 1782,
n. 5). He published *The Journey from
Chester to London* in 1782 (*post* 13 June
1782 and n. 1).

———

1. For Walpole's involvement in the
Chatterton affair see his correspondence

liberty of submitting to you my narrative[2] of that strange history, and of begging that you will honour me with any remarks, additions or corrections that you shall think necessary, except to facts, which I mention on memory; and which, though they may not be perfectly exact, I had rather give as they occurred to me, as a proof of my veracity, though, should they be wrong, I will add a note to say that I am informed of my mistake, if you observe any such.

My intention is to print only 200 copies,[3] and give them away, not to publish for sale;[4] for as this is only the justification of a private character, I think it is impertinent to suppose that the public in general is concerned about an individual, though he has been so publicly and so very unjustly accused. As every page that is printed about this story adds something to it (the common case of lies) the *Monthly Review* of last November (of which I was told but last week, for I very rarely read reviews) seems to suppose that I saw *all* Chatterton's forgeries, or (which would have been a little severe upon me) that I *ought* to have done so;[5] though the truth is, that I certainly did not receive *from him* half a dozen of them,[6] before he

with Chatterton in CHATTERTON 101–118 and Appendix 1; E. R. Wasserman, 'The Walpole-Chatterton Controversy,' *Modern Language Notes*, 1939, liv. 460–2; E. H. W. Meyerstein, *A Life of Thomas Chatterton*, 1930, pp. 253–84.

2. *A Letter to the Editor of the Miscellanies of Thomas Chatterton*, SH, 1779. The MS that HW submitted to Percy for his criticism was apparently a 'fair copy,' in Thomas Kirgate's hand, of which the first fourteen leaves (up to the 'Extract of a Letter from Mr H. W. to Mr W[illiam] B[ewley]') are now in the Yale University Library. The surviving MS contains corrections in HW's hand and is endorsed: 'After Mr Walpole had printed these pages, which he had previously shown to me, he made me a present of his autograph. Thos. Percy.' HW had written a long letter to Bewley 23 May 1778, defending his conduct in his relations with Chatterton; the 'Extract' from this letter forms pp. 29–44 of the printed *Letter to the Editor* (see CHATTERTON 121–34). The introductory remarks (pp. 1–28) were written in late July 1778 and expanded during the fall of that year (MASON i. 423; 'Short Notes,' GRAY i. 50–1).

3. '1779. In January printed 200 copies

of my pamphlet on Chatterton' (*Journal of the Printing-Office* 19). HW's annotated copy is now WSL; see CHATTERTON 348–50.

4. HW distributed copies to friends and others interested in the Chatterton affair. Cole's copy, now WSL, is inscribed: 'Sent to me by Mr Wapole Febr[uary] 14, 1779. Wm. Cole.' HW wrote Mason 14 March 1782: 'I did not publish my letter on Chatterton, because I am sick of most things, and especially of being the subject of talk' (MASON ii. 198).

5. The *Monthly Review* for Nov. 1778, lix. 395, contained a brief notice of *Miscellanies in Prose and Verse; by Thomas Chatterton*, 1778, edited by John Broughton. The notice remarked that 'Had the whole of his [Chatterton's] manuscripts been thought spurious by the ingenious person [HW] to whom he applied, yet the very fabrication of such things by a boy might have excited his curiosity and attention, and that attention might have saved to the public what Mr Warton calls a prodigy of genius.'

6. HW received two long specimens allegedly written by Thomas Rowley in Chatterton's letters to him of 25 and 30 March 1769 (CHATTERTON 101–5, 107–12).

resented my doubts—It would be excellent indeed, if every man on whom a forgery is attempted, were in duty bound to examine *all* the forgeries of such an impostor—and for what purpose?—not to detect him, but to find out whether he were not a great genius!—are not reviewers admirable and just judges?

I will beg, dear Sir, to have my MS returned as soon as you can conveniently, because I have no other tolerably fair copy, and wish to put it to the press as soon as I can, my illness[7] having delayed it too long already. I must beg your pardon too for imposing this trouble on you, but you have accustomed me to your indulgence; and though gratitude is not very common, it is apt to be a little intruding, especially when it hopes for more obligations.

I am with great regard, Sir

Your most obedient and obliged humble servant

HOR. WALPOLE

To Dr Percy Dean of Carlisle.

Jan. 24.[8]

Dear Sir,

THE foregoing letter I sent to Northumberland House[9] a fortnight ago, as you will see by the date; but as you was not in town, I was forced to begin printing,[10] and therefore can only send you now the MS as far as it is printed off,[11] on which I shall be very glad to be honoured with your remarks.[12]

---

7. See *ante* 8 Dec. 1778 and n. 4.

8. This note is written on the inside recto leaf of HW's letter to Percy.

9. Percy, who had been appointed domestic chaplain and secretary to the Earl of Northumberland in 1765, stayed at Northumberland House when he came to London.

10. In his letter to Cole 15 Jan. 1779, HW says that he is 'actually printing' the *Letter to the Editor* (COLE ii. 138).

11. HW later gave this portion of the MS to Percy; see n. 2 above.

12. No reply from Percy has been found.

From SIR HENRY ECHLIN,[1]
ca Sunday 28 February 1779

Printed from a photostat of the MS in the Bodleian Library (MS Toynbee d. 14, f. 29). First printed in *Lettres de la Marquise du Deffand à Horace Walpole (1766–1780)*, ed. Mrs Paget Toynbee, 1912, iii. 500–1. For the history of the MS see *ante* 20 April 1768.

Echlin dated the letter '29ᵉ feb.ʸ 1779,' doubtless a mistake for 28 February or 1 March, since 1779 was not a leap year. According to Mrs Toynbee, the letter was enclosed in Mme du Deffand's letter of 28 Feb. 1779 to HW (ibid. iii. 500 n. 7); but her letter makes no reference to any enclosure, and the postmark on Echlin's letter suggests that his letter was sent independently.

Address: Honourable Horatio Walpole Esq. Arlington Street, London. [in a different hand:] Angleterre. *Postmark:* MR 5.

L'Abbaie,[2] 29 February 1779.[3]

Sir,

I HAVE but one way that will be agreeable to you to express my gratitude and the feeling of my heart for your unspeakable kindness, that of making use of my liberty which your benevolence procures me,[4] to be useful to society and repair former misconduct. I hope you will never have any occasion to repent your humanity, but on the contrary, rejoice to have restored to the world a man who without your assistance would probably have finished his days in prison. The money you have sent will be employed to procure me my speedy liberty *under the directions of the person*[5] you have

1. (1740–99), 3d Bt; sheriff of Co. Dublin, 1762; surveyor of customs at Rush, Co. Dublin, 1788. He lived for some years at Paris; HW met him there in 1766, and gave him money in 1775 ('Paris Journals,' DU DEFFAND v. 300, 413). In 1779 he was imprisoned for debt in the Abbaye, the instance for the present letter. He lived extravagantly and dissipated a great part of the family estates; the decay of the Echlin baronetcy in the nineteenth century is described in Sir Bernard Burke, *Vicissitudes of Families*, 3d Series, 1863, pp. 8–12. For a contemporary account of Echlin see Pierre Manuel, *La Police de Paris dévoillée*, [?1791], ii. 260–2.

2. The prison connected with the Abbaye de St-Germain-des-Prés, at the Marché de la rue Ste-Marguerite. A view of the building as it appeared at the be-ginning of the eighteenth century is given in Adolphe Berty and L.-M. Tisserand, *Topographie historique du vieux Paris*, 1866–97, iii. between pp. 128 and 129.

3. See headnote.

4. Mme du Deffand wrote HW 7 Feb. 1779: 'Je ne me ressouviens point du tout du Chevalier [Echlin] dont vous me parlez, mais cela ne fait rien. Wiart ira à l'Abbaye, et y exécutera ce que vous lui prescrivez' (DU DEFFAND v. 110). HW apparently took pity on Echlin and sent money to pay his debts and secure his release from prison. The release was actually effected by Mme du Deffand and her secretary, Jean-François Wiart. After being freed, Echlin asked Wiart for more money but was refused. See ibid. v. 114–15, 118–19, 121–2, 127, 131, 135.

5. Mme du Deffand.

addressed it to. In a few weeks I hope to have the honour of thanking you in person and of assuring how much I am for life,
   Sir,

Your most obliged and grateful servant,

HENRY ECHLIN

To THOMAS ASTLE, Tuesday 6 April 1779

Printed from a photostat of the MS in the Massachusetts Historical Society. First printed, Toynbee x. 395. The MS is untraced until it came into the possession of Grenville H. Norcross before 1904; given by him in a collection of autographs to the Massachusetts Historical Society, 1938.
   Endorsed by Astle: Mr H. Walpole. [*on the recto:*] 309.
   Address: To Thomas Astle Esq. at Battersea Rise. *Postmark:* 6 O'CLOCK.
   Memoranda (in an unidentified hand):

£2.5.8

2.6.8

West

Strawberry Hill, April 6th 1779.

ANY company that you like to bring, dear Sir, to see this house, will always be very welcome. I am afraid I shall not be able to be here myself to show it to you on Saturday,[1] but I will leave orders that you may see it at your leisure, and am with great regard, Sir,

Your most obedient humble servant

HOR. WALPOLE

From UNKNOWN, Thursday 3 June 1779

HW wrote in his 'Book of Materials,' 1771 (now wsl), p. 68: 'These lines I received anonymously in a letter June 3, 1779. They are very unjust: Mr Coleman was a writer of more parts than Mr Garrick. They were probably written by some author whose piece Mr Colman as a manager had rejected.' The verses

---

1. The reason for HW's absence is not known; he was in Arlington Street on 12 April (COLE ii. 155), and had possibly gone to town a few days earlier.

are printed on a small sheet which HW pasted in his 'Book of Materials'; the anonymous letter that apparently accompanied the verses is missing.

[Enclosure]

On seeing the Portrait of little COLEMAN[1] by Sir Joshua Reynolds, with other portraits by the same hand, of JOHNSON,[2] ROBERTSON,[3] GARRICK,[4] GOLDSMITH,[5] BURKE,[6] etc.[7]

WHEN COLY's picture I discern'd
Thrust in among the wise and learn'd,
With JOHNSON, ROBERTSON confounded,
By GARRICK, GOLDSMITH, BURKE surrounded,
I know (said I) that sneaking air,
But what the deuce brought COLY there?
REYNOLDS, beneath, to crown the whim
Should write 'see how we apples swim.'
CRITO perceiving my surprise
Stepp'd up, and smiling thus replies,
'I see you wonder, so did I
'At COLY in such company,
'But think, and moderate your rage
'Ours is a strange promiscuous age,
'Observe the senate, BOB the waiter[8]

1. George Colman, the elder. Reynolds's portrait of Colman was exhibited at the Royal Academy in 1770, along with portraits by him of Johnson and Goldsmith (both now at Knole in Kent); the whereabouts of the original painting is not known, but there is a copy of it in the National Portrait Gallery (Ellis Waterhouse, *Reynolds*, 1973, p. 178).

2. Reynolds painted four life portraits of Samuel Johnson before 1779, including the one mentioned in the previous notes; see H. W. Liebert, 'Portraits of the Author: Lifetime Likenesses of Samuel Johnson,' in *English Portraits of the Seventeenth and Eighteenth Centuries*, Los Angeles, William Andrews Clark Memorial Library, 1974, pp. 50–7.

3. William Robertson (1721–93), D.D.; historian; HW's occasional correspondent. Reynolds's portrait of him, exhibited at the Royal Academy in 1772, is now in the Scottish National Portrait Gallery (Waterhouse, loc. cit.).

4. Probably the portrait now at Knole, exhibited at the Royal Academy in 1776 (ibid. 179).

5. See n. 1 above.

6. Probably the portrait now in the National Gallery of Ireland, which may have been exhibited at the Royal Academy in 1774 (Waterhouse, op. cit. 178).

7. Where the author of these verses could have seen the six portraits exhibited together is uncertain. The fact that three of the subjects (Johnson, Goldsmith, and Garrick) were at Knole before 1779 suggests that he may have seen them there and was simply mistaken about the identity of other portraits by Reynolds in the Duke of Dorset's collection (C. J. Phillips, *History of the Sackville Family . . . Together with . . . a Catalogue Raisonné of the Pictures and Drawings at Knole*, [1930], ii. 419–20).

8. Robert Macreth, Member for Castle Rising, had been a waiter at White's (HW's MS note in the margin). Sir Robert

'Sits there like any grave debater,
'And when the question's put goes forth
'For *ay* or *no* like Fox[9] or North.
'Arnold[10] and Putnam[11] now appear
'With names which Howe[12] and Clinton[13] wear,
'Each ranks a general and a warrior
'Tho' this a boatman that a farrier.
'Each wight in Scotland who retails
'Three farthings worth of pins or nails,
'By courtesy of northern fashion
'Is styl'd a *Merchant* thro' the nation.
'Thus piddling Coly who by fate
'Seem'd born but humbly to translate,[14]
'Tho' destitute of all pretence
'To genius, fancy, parts, or sense,
'By fathering scenes which Garrick writ,[15]
'Now takes his place with men of wit:
'And as the bardling first was known
'To fame, by labours not his own,
'Now may the touch of Reynolds save
'The mungrel's likeness from the grave:
'Drawn by a hand of such deserving,
'Even frogs and toads are worth preserving.'

Hay-Market.

Mackreth (?1725–1819), Kt, 1795; M.P. Castle Rising 1774–84, Ashburton 1784–1802. Mackreth began his career as a waiter and billiard-marker at Arthur's coffee-house, where White's Club was established; see Mason i. 173 and n. 6.

9. Charles James Fox.

10. Benedict Arnold (1741–1801), at this time Maj.-Gen. in the American army; after his treason in 1780 he entered the British service.

11. Israel Putnam (1718–90), Maj.-Gen. in the American army.

12. Hon. William Howe (1729–1814), K. B., 1776; 5th Vct Howe, 1799; Lt-Gen., 1777; commander-in-chief in America 1775–8; M.P.

13. Sir Henry Clinton (1730–95), K.B.,

1777; Lt-Gen., 1777; commander-in-chief in America 1778–82; M.P.

14. Colman had published a translation of the comedies of Terence in 1765. He also contributed a translation of *The Merchant* to *Comedies of Plautus, Translated into Familiar Blank Verse,* 1769–74, a project begun by Bonnell Thornton. Colman's translation of Plautus's *Mercator* is possibly alluded to two lines above.

15. Colman's first dramatic piece was an anonymous farce of 1760 entitled *Polly Honeycombe;* it was ascribed to Garrick, who later denied the authorship. Colman collaborated with Garrick on the highly successful comedy *The Clandestine Marriage,* first acted at Drury Lane 20 Feb. 1766.

TO CHARLES ROGERS, Sunday 22 August 1779

Printed from a photostat of the MS in the Cottonian Collection, Plymouth Museum and Art Gallery, Devon. First printed, Toynbee *Supp.* iii. 35–6. For the history of the MS see *ante* 27 Jan. 1778.

The year of the letter is established by the references to Sir Charles Hardy and the 'meditated invasion' by the combined French and Spanish fleet (see n. 3 below).

Address: To Charles Rogers Esq. at Richmond.

Aug. 22d late.

MR Walpole is extremely sensible of Mr Rogers's great kindness,[1] and prays to God that Sir Charles Hardy[2] may be victorious over our enemies,[3] who Mr W. is persuaded have the most fatal designs against this country, of which we are not enough aware; and therefore every man in his sphere ought to exert himself to defend his king and country; and, (if too old and weak, like the writer, to serve them) to animate others in so dear a cause.[4] Unless very triumphant at sea, we must expect most powerful attacks in this land, and be prepared to receive and repel them with coolness and intrepidity. It is deceiving ourselves not to believe in the meditated invasion.[5] Delusion and a sudden panic after confidence are most dangerous: but Mr W. hopes that Englishmen know the value of the blessings they enjoy, and will defend them with the valour of their immortal ancestors. Life would be a burthen without liberty.

1. Rogers, who was clerk of the certificates in the Custom House, had perhaps heard a recent report of the movements of the combined French and Spanish fleet, and passed on the news to HW in a missing letter.

2. (ca 1714–80), Kt, 1755; Adm., 1770; commander-in-chief of the Channel fleet 1779–80; M.P.

3. Having assumed command of the Channel fleet in March 1779, Hardy was ordered in late July to remain at sea to prevent an invasion by the combined fleet of France and Spain (OSSORY ii. 119 n. 5). The *London Chronicle* 19–21 Aug. 1779, xlvi. 174, reported various rumours of an engagement either being fought or about to be fought, but the rumours proved to be false. The threatened invasion never occurred.

4. HW wrote Mann 19 Aug. 1779: 'You know me an unalterable Englishman, who loves his country and devoutly wishes its prosperity. Such I am, ardent for England, and ever shall be—it is all an useless old man can do to pray for its lasting prosperity. The events of war must be accepted with constancy, good or bad. . . . Every man must do the utmost he can in his sphere, when his country is concerned, and private duties must be attended to too' (MANN viii. 507).

5. 'The only conclusion to be drawn at this moment is, that they [the combined enemy fleet] will fight Sir Charles Hardy before their embarkation takes place. By what I see much is to be apprehended from so little being apprehended, and from the unaccountable intentions of a landing' (HW to Mason 23 Aug. 1779, MASON i. 460).

To Lady Craven, November 1779

Printed from the *European Magazine,* 1797, xxxi. 379, an 'Extract of a letter written by the late Lord Orford to a lady of high rank, on her requesting him to give her a character of the comedy of "The Scornful Lady," of Beaumont and Fletcher, previous to its being altered to "The Capricious Lady," in 1783.' The first two paragraphs were reprinted (undated) in William Cooke, *Memoirs of Samuel Foote, Esq.,* 1805, iii. 95–6, where the recipient of the letter is identified as 'Lady C——n'. The history of the MS and its present whereabouts are not known.

Nov. 1779.

I RETURN your Ladyship the play,[1] and will tell you the truth. At first I proposed just to amend the mere faults of language and the incorrectness—but the farther I proceeded, the less I found it worth correcting; and indeed I believe nothing but Mrs Abington's acting can make anything of it.[2] It is like all the rest of Beaumont and Fletcher's pieces; they had good ideas, but never made the most of them, and seem to me to have finished them when they were drunk, so very improbable are the means by which they produce their *dénouements.*

To produce a good play from one of theirs, I believe the only way would be to take their plan; draw the characters from nature; omit all that is improbable, and entirely new write the dialogue; for their language is at once *hard* and *pert, vulgar* and *incorrect,* and has neither the pathos of the preceding age, nor the elegance of this— they are grossly indelicate, and yet have no simplicity.[3] There is a wide difference between unrefined and vicious indecency:—the first would not invent fig leaves—the latter tears holes in them after they are invented.

. . . In regard to gallantry, we are Hottentots, and the scorn of

1. *The Scornful Lady,* a comedy by Beaumont and Fletcher (see headnote).

2. *The Scornful Lady* was altered by William Cooke as *The Capricious Lady* and first performed at Covent Garden 17 Jan. 1783, with Mrs Abington in the title rôle (*London Stage* Pt V, i. 585–6). Cooke wrote in his Preface to the printed play (1783): 'To Mrs Abington I principally owe every degree of applause with which this piece has been honoured, as it was this lady . . . who first suggested to

me the idea of an alteration; and the success has fully justified her opinion.'

3. 'But whilst I yielded to the necessity of lopping off a number of *indelicacies* and *coarse allusions,* which the morals of no age ought to bear, I felt some difficulty in complying with the *rigidity of our modern school of politeness,* as by it I found I must give up some part of the wit and humour of the comedy' (Cooke's Preface to *The Capricious Lady*).

Europe. Our newspapers teem with abuse on the prettiest women in England; and even the theatre, that ought to be their temple, is, as your Ladyship knows, a *bear garden,* and puts me in mind of *Slender* in the *Merry Wives of Windsor,* who entertains his mistress with the exploits of Sacherson.[4]

I am going in a few days to Park Place,[5] and will, at my return, have the honour of paying my duty at your Ladyship's cottage,[6] or be proud of receiving a visit at a castle[7] that is but a shed to that of ————,[8] yet far more loyal to its sovereign lady whilst it belongs to your

Most devoted old humble servant,

Hor. Walpole

4. Sackerson, a famous bear exhibited and used in bear-baiting at Paris Garden on the Bankside in Southwark during Shakespeare's time. See *The Merry Wives of Windsor* I. i. 307–11.

5. The seat of HW's cousin and intimate friend Henry Seymour Conway, in Berkshire. Conway returned to London from Jersey ca 22 Nov. (Ossory ii. 142). HW may have planned to visit him at Park Place, but was prevented by an attack of gout at the end of November (ibid. ii. 143–4).

6. Described by Lady Mary Coke in 1781 as a 'cottage which she [Lady Craven] built two or three years ago upon the banks of the Thames near Putney.' 'She has a fine view of the river but no trees except a few just before the building. She has planted two rows of willows which form a close walk on each side of the boundary of her ground and which go down to the river. Upon the whole I think it pretty as everything upon the Thames must be' (Coke, 'MS Journals' 22, 27 June 1781).

7. SH.

8. Doubtless the house of one of her close friends.

To [?Oliver] Tilson,[1] Sunday 21 November 1779

Printed from the MS now WSL. First printed, Toynbee *Supp.* i. 278–9. The MS is untraced until offered by Maggs, Cat. No. 353 (spring 1917), lot 743; sold by Scribner's Book Shop to WSL, March 1934.

The 'Mr Tilson' to whom this letter was sent was probably one of the six sons of Thomas Tilson, of Dublin. Five of the sons attended Eton and Trinity College, Cambridge, and the most likely candidate is the fifth son, Oliver Tilson, who was HW's exact contemporary and lived in Hill Street, Berkeley Square. The year of the letter is established by the reference to the forthcoming publication of the last volume of *Anecdotes of Painting* (see n. 6 below).

Endorsed in an unidentified hand: Mr Walpole note to Mr Tilson.

21 November.[2]

MR Walpole presents his respects to Mr Tilson; but doubts whether Monsieur Duchesne[3] would not be disappointed in Mr W.'s intended sketch,[4] which will be a slight summary of the rise of modern gardening. It has been written and printed in the last volume of the *Anecdotes of Painting* for some time, but kept back from publication for some particular reasons.[5] Mr W. is very sorry it has been talked of enough to reach Monsieur Duchesne, as it will certainly not answer anybody's expectation. It probably will be published before next Christmas,[6] and whenever it is, Mr Tilson shall command a copy.

1. (ca 1717–88), fifth son of Thomas Tilson, of Dublin; Eton and Trinity College, Cambridge (B.A., 1738/9); fellow of Trinity, 1741; commissioner in the Salt Office 1766–88 (*European Magazine*, 1789, xv. 78; *Eton Coll. Reg.;* Venn, *Alumni Cantab.* Pt I, iv. 243).

2. Not in HW's hand; presumably added by Tilson.

3. Antoine-Nicolas Duchesne (1747–1827), French naturalist; author of *Le Jardinier prévoyant*, 1770–81, *Sur la formation des jardins*, 1775, and other horticul-

tural works (*Dict. de biographie française* xi. 1232–3).

4. The *Essay on Modern Gardening*, written in 1770 (dated 2 Aug. 1770) and printed in 1771, but not published until 1780 as chapter vii in the fourth and final volume of *Anecdotes of Painting* (Hazen, *SH Bibl.* 63–5, 131).

5. See *ante* 21 Jan. 1773 and *post* 4 Oct. 1780.

6. The fourth volume of *Anecdotes* was published 9 Oct. 1780 (*Journal of the Printing-Office* 19).

To Robert Jephson, Tuesday 25 January 1780

Printed from Jephson's MS copy, now WSL. First printed, Wright vi. 69–72. Reprinted, Cunningham vii. 316–18; Toynbee xi. 109–12 (closing and signature omitted in Wright, Cunningham, and Toynbee). For the history of the MS copy see *ante* 15 March 1763. The original letter is missing.

Berkeley Square, January 25th 1780.

IT was but yesterday, Sir, that I received the favour of your letter,[1] and this morning I sent,[2] according to your permission, to Mr Sheridan the elder[3] to desire the manuscript of your tragedy,[4] for as I am but just recovering of a fit of the gout, which I had severely for above two months,[5] I was not able to bear the fatigue of company at home, nor could I have had the pleasure of attending to the piece so much as I wished to do, if I had invited ladies to hear it to whom I must have been doing the honours.

I have read your play once, Sir, rapidly though alone, and therefore cannot yet be very particular on the details—but I can say already with great truth, that you have made a great deal more than I thought possible out of the skeleton of a story; and have arranged it so artfully, that unless I am deceived by being too familiar with it, it will be very intelligible to the audience, even if they have not read the original fable; and you have had the address to make it coherent, without the marvellous, though so much depended on that part. In short you have put my extravagant materials into an alembic, and drawn off only what was rational.

Your diction is very beautiful, often poetic, and yet what I admire, very simple and natural; and when necessary, rapid, concise, and sublime.

If I did not distrust my own self-love, I should say that I think it must be a very interesting piece—and yet I might say so without vanity, so much of the disposition of the scenes is your own. I do not

1. Missing.
2. HW's letter is also missing.
3. Thomas Sheridan (1719–88), actor and theatrical manager. For two seasons, 1778–80, he assisted his son Richard Brinsley Sheridan with the management of Drury Lane Theatre (E. K. Sheldon, *Thomas Sheridan of Smock-Alley*, Princeton, 1967, pp. 284–99).

4. *The Count of Narbonne*, freely adapted from HW's *The Castle of Otranto*.
5. The attack of gout came towards the end of November (Mason i. 482; Ossory ii. 143).

yet know, Sir, what alterations you propose to make, nor do I perceive where the second and fourth acts want amendment. The first
in your manuscript is imperfect.[6] If I wished for any correction, it
would be to shorten the scene in the fourth act between the Countess, Adelaide and Austin, which rather delays the impatience of the
audience for the catastrophe, and does not contribute to it but by
the mother's orders to the daughter at the end of the scene to repair
to the great church.[7] In the last scene I should wish to have Theodore fall into a transport of rage and despair immediately on the
death of Adelaide, and be carried off by Austin's orders,[8] for I doubt
the interval is too long for him to faint after Narbonne's speech. The
fainting fit, I think might be better applied to the Countess; it does
not seem requisite that she should die, but the audience might be
left in suspense about her.[9]

My last observations will be very trifling indeed, Sir; but I think
you use noble*ness*, niceness, etc. too often, which I doubt are not
classic terminations for *nobility, nicety*[10] etc. though I allow that
nobility will not always express nobleness. My *children's timeless
deaths* can scarce be said for *untimely*,[11] nor should I choose to employ *children's* as a plural genitive case, which I think the *s* at the
end cannot imply. *Hearted* preference is very bold for preference
taken to heart.[12] Raymond in the last scene says,

> Show me thy wound—oh Hell! 'tis thro' her heart!

This line is quite unnecessary, and infers an obedience in displaying
her wound which would be shocking—besides, as there is often a
buffoon in an audience at a new tragedy, it might be received

6. See following letter.

7. In the play as printed in 1781, Austin
exits at the end of the long scene (IV. iii)
between the Countess, Adelaide, and himself; in the brief following scene (IV. iv),
the Countess orders Adelaide to 'go . . .
to Alphonso's holy shrine' in the convent
church.

8. In the penultimate scene (V. xiv) of
the printed play, Theodore gazes at Adelaide's dead body, then declares that he
finds life intolerable and rushes out, with
the apparent intention of killing himself.

9. According to Jephson's original stage
directions for the final scene (V. xv), the
Countess, 'after looking some time distractedly,' expresses her despair in a

fourteen-line speech and 'falls on the
body of Adelaide.' A note in the printed
play points out that a 'slight alteration
[was] made in the representation of the
last scene of this tragedy, by the friends
of the author, in his absence.' The altered
stage direction states that the Countess
'swoons in the arms of her attendants.'
See *post* 18 Nov. 1781.

10. A line in the Countess's soliloquy
in the printed play (II. v) reads 'the mere
nicety of maiden fear.'

11. 'My children's timeless deaths' was
retained in the printed play (II. vii).

12. Neither phrase appears in the
printed play.

dangerously. The word Jehovah will certainly not be suffered on the stage.[13]

In casting the parts I conclude Mrs Yates, as women never cease to like acting young parts, would prefer that of Adelaide, though the Countess is more suitable to her age;[14] and it is foolish to see her representing the daughter of women fifteen or twenty years younger—As my bad health seldom allows my going to the theatre I never saw Mr Henderson[15] but once. His person and style should recommend him to the parts of Raymond or Austin.[16] Smith[17] I suppose would expect to be Theodore, but Lewis[18] is younger, handsomer, and I think a better actor—but you are in the right, Sir, in having no favourable idea of our stage at present.

I am sorry, Sir, that neither my talents nor health allow me to offer to supply you with prologue and epilogue. Poetry never was my natural turn, and what little propensity I had to it, is totally extinguished by age and pain. It is honour enough to me to have furnished the canvas of your tragedy; I should disgrace it by attempting to supply adventitious ornaments—The clumsiness of the seams would betray my gouty fingers.

I shall take the liberty of reading your play once more before I return it. It will be extraordinary indeed if it is not accepted—but I cannot doubt but it will be, and very successful; though it will be great pity but you should have some zealous friend to attend to it, and who is able to bustle, and see justice done to it by the managers. I lament that such a superannuated being as myself is not only totally incapable of that office,[19] but that I am utterly unacquainted with the managers, and now too retired to form new connections. I was still more concerned, Sir, to hear of your unhappy accident,[20] though

13. Raymond's 'unnecessary' line (in the penultimate scene, V. xiv) and 'Jehovah' were both omitted in the printed play.

14. Mrs Yates was fifty-one at this time. She had the leading rôle in Jephson's *Braganza* in 1775, but did not act a part in *The Count of Narbonne* when it was produced at Covent Garden in 1781.

15. John Henderson (1747–85), actor, called the 'Bath Roscius.' Henderson assisted HW in getting *The Count of Narbonne* accepted at Covent Garden; see *post* 18 July, 26 Aug., 15 Oct. 1781.

16. Henderson played the part of Austin

in the original production (*London Stage* Pt V, i. 476).

17. See *ante* 24 Feb. 1775, n. 15. Smith did not have a rôle in the original production.

18. See *ante* 13 July 1777, n. 9. Lewis played Theodore in the original production.

19. HW nevertheless helped in various ways with the production of the play, and even attended two rehearsals (Conway iii. 386–7).

20. Not identified.

the bad consequences are past. I have the honour to be with the greatest esteem

Your obedient humble servant

Hor. Walpole

To Robert Jephson, Thursday 27 January 1780

Printed from Jephson's MS copy, now wsl. First printed, Wright vi. 72–3. Reprinted, Cunningham vii. 318–19; Toynbee xi. 112–13 (closing and signature omitted in Wright, Cunningham, and Toynbee). For the history of the MS copy see *ante* 15 March 1763. The original letter is missing.

Endorsed by Jephson: (Copy).

Berkeley Square, January 27th 1780.

I HAVE returned your tragedy, Sir, to Mr Sheridan after having read it again, and without wishing any more alterations than the few I hinted before.[1] There may be some few incorrectnesses, but none of much consequence.

I must again applaud your art and judgment, Sir, in having made so rational a play out of my wild tale: and where you have changed the arrangement of the incidents, you have applied them to great advantage. The characters of the mother and daughter you have rendered more natural, by giving jealousy to the mother, and more passion to the daughter. In short, you have both honoured and improved my outlines: my vanity is content, and truth enjoins me to do justice. Bishop Warburton in his additional notes to Pope's *Works* which I saw in print in his bookseller's[2] hands, though they have not yet been published, observed that the plan of *The Castle of Otranto* was regularly a drama[3] (an intention I am sure I do not

1. See previous letter.

2. Charles Bathurst (ca 1709–86), bookseller in Fleet Street.

3. Warburton's observation is part of a long footnote to line 146 ('And ev'ry flow'ry Courtier writ Romance') of Pope's *First Epistle of the Second Book of Horace Imitated* ('To Augustus'), in *The Works of Alexander Pope, Esq.*, ed. Warburton, 1770, iv. 166–7: 'Yet amidst all this nonsense, when things were at the worst, we have been lately entertained

with what I will venture to call, a masterpiece, in the *fable;* and of a new species likewise. The piece I mean, is, *The Castle of Otranto.* The scene is laid in *Gothic chivalry.* Where a beautiful imagination, supported by strength of judgment, has enabled the author to go beyond his subject, and effect the full purpose of the *ancient tragedy,* that is, *to purge the passions by pity and terror,* in colouring as great and harmonious as in any of the best dramatic writers.' The comment does

pretend to have conceived; nor indeed can I venture to affirm that I had any intention at all but to amuse myself—no, not even a plan, till some pages were written).[4] You, Sir, have realized his idea and yet I believe the Bishop would be surprised to see how well you have succeeded. One cannot be quite ashamed of one's follies, if genius condescends to adopt, and put them to a sensible use. Miss Aickin[5] flattered me even by stooping to tread in my eccentric steps. Her *Fragment,*[6] though but a specimen, showed her talent for imprinting terror. I cannot compliment the author of *The Old English Baron,*[7] professedly written in imitation, but as a corrective of *The Castle of Otranto.*[8] It was totally void of imagination and interest; had scarce any incidents; and though it condemned the marvellous, admitted a ghost—I suppose the author thought a tame ghost might come within the laws of probability. You alone, Sir, have kept within nature, and made superstition supply the place of phenomenon, yet acting as the agent of divine justice—a beautiful use of bigotry.

I was mistaken in thinking the end of the first act deficient. The leaves stuck together, and there intervening two or three blank pages between the first and second acts, I examined no farther, but concluded the former imperfect, which on the second reading I found it was not.

As I imagine, Sir, that the theatres of Dublin cannot have fewer good performers than those of London, may I ask why you prefer ours? Your own directions and instructions would be of great advantage to your play; especially if you suspect antitragic prejudices

not appear in Warburton's 1766 edition of Pope's *Works*. HW, who did not own a copy of the 1770 *Works*, was clearly mistaken about when Warburton made the addition.

4. Writing to William Mason 17 April 1765, less than four months after publishing *The Castle of Otranto,* HW mentioned its being 'begun without any plan at all, for though in the short course of its progress I did conceive some views, it was so far from being sketched out with any design at all, that it was actually commenced one evening, from the very imperfect recollection of a dream with which I had waked in the morning' (MASON i. 6). HW gives a more detailed account of its origin and composition in his letter to Cole 9 March 1765 (COLE i. 88). As a professional playwright, Jephson

would have noted at once that the story is divided into five chapters and observes the dramatic unities.

5. Anna Letitia Aikin (1743–1825), m. (1774) Rev. Rochemont Barbauld; poet, essayist, and editor; author of books for children.

6. 'On the Pleasure Derived from Objects of Terror; with Sir Bertrand, A Fragment,' published in J[ohn] and A. L. Aikin's *Miscellaneous Pieces, in Prose,* 1773, pp. 119–37.

7. *The Old English Baron, A Gothic Story,* 1778, by Clara Reeve (1729–1807). HW's copy (untraced) is Hazen, *Cat. of HW's Lib.,* No. 2461. This was a revised edition of Miss Reeve's novel published at Colchester in 1777 with the title *The Champion of Virtue.*

8. See MASON i. 381–2 and n. 24.

in the manager. You too would be the best judge at the rehearsals of what might be improved.[9] Managers will take liberties, and often curtail necessary speeches, so as to produce nonsense. Methinks it is unkind to send a child, of which you have so much reason to be proud, to a foundling hospital. I am with great regard, Sir,

Your most obedient humble servant

HOR. WALPOLE

To the REV. THOMAS PERCY, Sunday 11 June 1780

Printed for the first time from a photostat of the MS in the possession of the Duke of Northumberland, Alnwick Castle, Northumberland, kindly furnished by Mr D. P. Graham through the good offices of Professor Bertram H. Davis (Alnwick Castle MS 93A/19). The MS passed to Percy's descendants until it was sold Sotheby's 29 April 1884 (Percy Sale), lot 216 (with other papers of the Percy family), to the 6th Duke of Northumberland.

Strawberry Hill, June 11th 1780.

I SHOULD be very vain indeed, good Sir, if I thought myself at all entitled to the honour you have done me in consulting me on the epitaph you have drawn with so much judgment and genuine simplicity (the beauty of such inscriptions) for the late Duchess of Northumberland.[1] You, Sir, on the other hand are far too modest in thinking it wants any correction or improvement. It is solely to show I am not insensible to the compliment you pay me, and to mark respect for the commands of a family that I honour so much, and

9. As well as being produced at Covent Garden in 1781, *The Count of Narbonne* was acted with success at both theatres in Dublin during the 1781–2 season, with John Philip Kemble in the rôle of Raymond. Jephson attended the rehearsals (James Boaden, *Memoirs of the Life of John Philip Kemble, Esq.*, 1825, i. 39–40).

1. The Duchess died in 1776. The Duke of Northumberland erected a monument to her memory in Westminster Abbey, near to the Percy family vault in the chapel of St Nicholas. The monument was executed in white marble by Nicho-

las Read, after a design by Robert Adam. The inscription, after mentioning her ancestry and her marriage, describes her character as follows: 'Having lived long an ornament of courts, an honour to her country, a pattern to the great, a protectress of the poor, ever distinguished for the most tender affection for her family and friends, she died December 5th, 1776, aged sixty; universally beloved, revered, lamented' (J. P. Neale and E. W. Brayley, *The History and Antiquities of the Abbey Church of St Peter, Westminster*, 1818–23, ii. 165).

who are pleased to condescend to ask my opinion, that I venture to propose some very slight alterations, and those not in the thoughts and sense, but in the expression.

I would therefore only offer to your consideration these very trifling changes. I should prefer *an* ornament of courts to *the* ornament.[2] The lapidary style ought to be almost as studied as measured verse, and the hiatus between *e* in *the,* and *o* in ornament is a cacophony. Alliteration too would here be a beauty; for which reason in those three lines I would wish to have *an* ornament, *an* honour (as you have put it) and *a* pattern, and *a* protectress, there being no evident reason for using sometimes *a,* and sometimes *the.* It seems to me too that having called the Duchess in one place *an* honour, it would look too exclusive to call her *the* ornament etc. in the others.

I have rather more objection still to *the* pattern of the great, because, though her Grace was a pattern *to* them, I fear she was not the pattern *of* them which would ⟨imp⟩ly that they did imitate her. I should therefore prefer the more common usage, and say, *a* pattern *to* them. One says, I should like a pattern of such or such a thing, and one means a sample or drawing of it—but when one means to say such a person is a pattern *for* others, *for* is strictly best, but *to* seems to me more elegant.

These are such minute criticisms, Sir, that you must perceive I was forced to hunt for them and refine; and you have certainly no reason to be discontented with your own draught[3] from anything I have said; and I flatter myself that you remember that it was a sort of deference in me to start objections.

I did myself the honour of calling on you to condole, soon after the fire at Northumberland House,[4] but fear you never heard of it. I have been since comforted by hearing you lost nothing of im-

2. HW doubtless recalled the penultimate line of the inscription that he himself had written for the monument to his mother in the Abbey: 'And was an ornament to courts.' Percy was probably familiar with the inscription on Lady Walpole's monument, which stood in the adjacent chapel of Henry VII. See *ante* 26 June 1754 and n. 6.

3. A copy of the epitaph with HW's suggested emendations is preserved with the letter among the Percy family papers at Alnwick Castle (see headnote). The inscription on the monument shows that Percy adopted the changes HW proposed.

4. The fire raged for about three hours in the early morning of 18 March, causing extensive damage to the front of the building facing the street; there was no loss of life. An account of the fire appears in the *Daily Adv.* 20 March 1780.

portance to yourself[5] or the public. I have the honour to be with great regard, Sir,

Your obliged and obedient humble servant

Hor. Walpole

To Mrs Abington, Sunday 11 June 1780

Printed from a photostat of the MS in the British Museum (Add. MS 9828, f. 146). First printed, Wright vi. 86–7 (signature omitted). Reprinted, Cunningham vii. 398; Toynbee xi. 219. For the history of the MS see *ante* 1 Sept. 1771.

Strawberry Hill, June 11, 1780.

Madam,

YOU may certainly always command me and my house. My common custom is to give a ticket for only four persons at a time;[1] but it would be very insolent in me, when all laws are set at nought,[2] to pretend to prescribe rules. At such times there is a shadow of authority in setting the laws aside by the legislature itself—and though I have no army to supply their place, I declare Mrs Abington may march through all my dominions at the head of as large a troop as she pleases—I do not say, as she can muster and command, for then I am sure my house would not hold them. The day too is at her own choice, and the master is

Her very obedient humble servant

Hor. Walpole

---

5. Much of Percy's library at Northumberland House was destroyed by the fire (*Shenstone's Miscellany 1759–1763*, ed. I. A. Gordon, Oxford, 1952, p. xv).

1. The 'ticket' was in the form of a written note to HW's housekeeper; see Hazen, *SH Bibl.* 210.

2. Presumably an allusion to the meeting of the Privy Council on 7 June, at which measures were considered for controlling the anti-Popery riots incited by Lord George Gordon. At the meeting 'it was determined not to shut up the courts nor proclaim martial law, but to empower the military to act at their discretion' (*Last Journals* ii. 311). See Ossory ii. 188 and n. 15.

To Richard Bull,[1] Friday 7 July 1780

Printed for the first time from the MS now wsl. The MS is untraced until offered by Maggs, Cat. No. 433 (Christmas 1922), lot 3811; sold by them to Capt. Frank L. Pleadwell, M.D., USN, before Nov. 1928; acquired by wsl from Capt. Pleadwell by exchange, April 1947.

Strawberry Hill, July 7, 1780.

I SHOULD be most ungrateful indeed, Sir, if I were inclined to refuse you any request in my power. If I could forget all your other favours, Queen Catherine[2] would stare in my face and make me blush. The first time I return to town, which will probably be in [a] few days,[3] I will wait on you with the *Mysterious Mother*,[4] and shall be very happy to see any of your amusements, as I am with the greatest regard, Sir,

Your most obedient and most obliged humble servant

HOR. WALPOLE

1. (1721–1805), of Ongar, Essex, and North Court, Shorwell, Isle of Wight; print collector; M.P. 'Endowed by nature with an exquisite taste, Mr Bull early evinced an enthusiasm for the arts, particularly that of engraving, which with much study he cultivated into a refined knowledge almost exclusively his own at that era; and, with a liberality of sentiment, assisted by Mr Horace Walpole, struck out a plan admirably adapted for the purpose of directing the attention of his country to the illustration of history and biography by portraits of those persons whose lives and actions they record. . . . Through the greatest part of a century, this venerable man continued with unabated ardour his favourite pursuit, and has erected for himself a monument of taste and munificence unequalled in Europe, to which the volumes of Bromley and Granger owe infinite obligation, and bear honourable testimony' (GM 1806, lxxvi pt i. 289). Bull was also the chief contemporary collector of Walpoliana; his

passion for 'grangerizing' led him to compose a lavishly extra-illustrated set of *Anecdotes of Painting* in 14 volumes, imperial folio, and a similarly elaborate copy of the *Description of SH*, 1784 (now wsl; Hazen, *SH Bibl.* 128, copy 13). See COLE i. 287 n. 5; J. M. Pinkerton, 'Richard Bull of Ongar, Essex,' *Book Collector*, 1978, xxvii. 41–59.

2. Catherine (1638–1705) of Braganza, m. (1662) Charles II of England. This was 'the original portrait of Catherine of Braganza, that was sent from Portugal previous to her marriage with Charles II and from which Faithorne scraped his print' ('Des. of SH,' *Works* ii. 496). It was found by Bull at a lodge in the New Forest in 1778; HW hung it in the Great North Bedchamber at SH. See OSSORY ii. 472 and n. 28.

3. HW was in London on 24 July, when he wrote to Mann from Berkeley Square (MANN ix. 73).

4. See following letter.

To RICHARD BULL, mid-July 1780

Printed for the first time from the MS pasted on the front fly-leaf of Bull's copy of *The Mysterious Mother*, SH, 1768, now WSL. This copy (Hazen, *SH Bibl.* 84, copy 3) remained in Bull's library at North Court, Shorwell, Isle of Wight, eventually passing by family descent into the possession of the 5th Lord Burgh (1866–1926); sold Sotheby's 29 June 1926 (Burgh Sale), lot 163, to Spencer; purchased from Walter Hill, Chicago, by James C. Dunn in 1927; acquired from Mrs James C. Dunn, of Washington, D. C., by WSL, Feb. 1961.

Dated approximately by the previous letter.

Memorandum by Bull: Mysterious Mother returned, and afterwards sent back again to me. R. B.

M R Walpole has sent Mr Bull the only copy he has left of the play,[1] but begs to have it returned as soon as he has read it, and that he will not let it go out of his hands.[2]

From the PRINCE de BAUFFREMONT,[1] Saturday 5 August 1780

Printed from the MS now WSL. First printed, Toynbee *Supp.* iii. 257–8 (misdated '5 avril 1780'). Damer-Waller; the MS was sold Sotheby's 5 Dec. 1921 (first Waller Sale), lot 90, to Lytton Strachey; later in the possession of Lytton Strachey's brother, Dr James Strachey, who died in 1967; resold Sotheby's 27 Feb. 1973 ('Other Properties'), lot 445, to Pickering and Chatto for WSL.

Except for the signature, the letter is in the hand of an amanuensis.

De Paris, rue de Vaugirard, le 5 août 1780.

V OUS ressouvenez-vous encore de moi, Monsieur, et puis je me flatte que vous n'ayez point oublié le plaisir que j'ai eu de vivre avec vous chez Madame du Defant,[2] et chez Madame la Duchesse de Choiseul.[3] Cette première m'a assuré que vous aviez eu

1. *The Mysterious Mother*, SH, 1768. Only 50 copies were printed (Hazen, *SH Bibl.* 79).

2. Bull's copy of the play, bound in citron morocco, interleaved, is now WSL; see Bull's memorandum quoted in the headnote.

———

1. Charles-Roger de Bauffremont (1713–95), Chevalier de Listenois; Prince de Bauffremont, 1769.

2. According to HW's 'Paris Journals,' Bauffremont had seen HW at Mme du Deffand's on 16 July 1771 (DU DEFFAND v. 334).

3. HW had supped with Bauffremont (then the Chevalier de Listenois) at Mme de Choiseul's on 14 and 19 Sept. 1767 (ibid. v. 320–1).

la bonté de lui parler de moi plusieurs fois dans vos lettres. Je voudrais qu'elle eût été aussi exacte à vous dire combien j'en ai été reconnaissant, mais je lui crois plus d'agrément que d'exactitude. Quoiqu'il en soit, j'ai la confiance de vous adresser et de vous recommander intimement un de mes amis, c'est M. le Chevalier de St-Sauveur,[4] gentilhomme français, né bon protestant, par conséquent sans espérances dans ce pays-ci. Il vous expliquera lui-même ses affaires. Daignez le conduire et le conseiller.[5] Vous ne pouvez me donner une marque d'amitié à laquelle je sois plus sensible. J'ai l'honneur d'être très parfaitement, Monsieur, votre très humble très obéissant serviteur,

LE PRINCE DE BAUFFREMENT

To Mrs Hogarth,[1] Wednesday 4 October 1780

Printed from a photostat of the MS in the British Museum (Add. MS 27,995, f. 25). First printed in Hist. MSS Comm., 13th Report, App. viii (*Charlemont MSS*), 1894, p. 5, n. 1. Reprinted, Toynbee xi. 290–1. The MS is included in a volume of letters and papers relating to William Hogarth acquired by the BM in 1869. HW's transcript of the letter, in Thomas Kirgate's hand (endorsed 'Copy of my letter, sent with the 4th vol. of my *Anecdotes of Painting*, to Mrs Hogarth, to which she returned no answer. H.W.'), is bound in his copy of John Nichols's *Biographical Anecdotes of William Hogarth*, 1781, now WSL (Hazen, *Cat. of HW's Lib.*, No. 2435).

Berkeley Square, Oct. 4, 1780.

M R Walpole begs Mrs Hogarth's acceptance of the volume[2] that accompanies this letter, and hopes she will be content with his endeavours to do justice to the genius of Mr Hogarth. If there are

4. Probably Hyacinthe-Philémon de Grégoire (d. 1784), Chevalier (later Comte) de Saint-Sauveur (ibid. v. 246 n. 1).

5. HW wrote to Mme du Deffand to inquire about Saint-Sauveur (ibid. v. 246). On 8 Oct., after Saint-Sauveur's arrival in England, HW wrote to his cousin Thomas Walpole at Paris: 'If . . . you should happen to see the Prince of Bauffremont, I should be obliged if you would ask him in what way he wishes a Chevalier de St Sauveur, whom he has recommended to me, should be served. I have told both the Prince and him that I have no kind

of interest or credit, and can only direct the latter where to apply. He is a Protestant, and yet it seems odd for a Frenchman to desire to come into our service at present. I know nothing of his history. . . . I don't know what to do with him, and yet I received so many civilities in France, that I will not neglect him' (FAMILY 180).

---

1. Jane Thornhill (ca 1709–89), only dau. of Sir James Thornhill, m. (1729) William Hogarth.

2. The fourth and final volume of *Anecdotes of Painting*, printed at SH in

some passages less agreeable to her than the rest,[3] Mr Walpole will regard her disapprobation only as marks of the goodness of her heart and proofs of her affection to her husband's memory—but she will, he is sure, be so candid as to allow for the duty an historian owes to the public and himself, which obliges him to say what he thinks;[4] and which, when he obeys, his praise is corroborated by his censure. The first page of the Preface will more fully make his apology;[5] and his just admiration of Mr Hogarth, Mr W. flatters himself, will, notwithstanding his impartiality, still rank him in Mrs Hogarth's mind as one of her husband's most zealous and sincere friends.[6]

1771 but not published until 1780 (the actual date of publication was 9 Oct.). HW held it up to avoid offending Mrs Hogarth by his strictures on her husband. See *ante* 21 Jan. 1773.

3. HW has in mind chiefly his criticisms of Hogarth's 'Sigismunda,' but he also disparages Hogarth's attempts at history painting. See *Anecdotes of Painting*, SH, 1762–71, iv. 76–9.

4. *Fari quæ sentiat* ('Say what you think') was the Walpole family motto.

5. 'The publication . . . was delayed from motives of tenderness. The author, who could not resolve, like most biographers, to dispense universal panegyric, especially on many incompetent artists, was still unwilling to utter even gentle censures, which might wound the affections, or offend the prejudices of those related to the persons whom truth forbade him to commend beyond their merits. He hopes, that as his opinion is no standard, it will pass for mistaken judgment with such as shall be displeased with his criticisms. If his encomiums seem too lavish to others, the public will at least know that they are bestowed sincerely. He would not have hesitated to publish his remarks sooner, if he had not been averse to exaggeration' ('Advertisement,' ibid. iv. [v]).

6. Mrs Hogarth did not acknowledge HW's letter (see headnote). Writing to Cole 16 June 1781, HW says that 'she was not pleased with my account of her husband,' and she apparently encouraged John Nichols to publish his own account of Hogarth (COLE ii. 273). Richard Livesay, the Hogarth copyist, wrote to his patron Lord Charlemont 17 June 1784: 'I have got a copy of the letter Mr H. Walpole sent to Mrs Hogarth at the time he presented to her a copy of his book containing Hogarth's life, and as I think it a literary curiosity, I am happy in communicating it to your Lordship' (MS in the Charlemont papers, Royal Irish Academy, Dublin; Livesay's copy of HW's letter is also preserved in the Charlemont papers).

From Lady Lucan,[1] Thursday 5 October 1780

Printed for the first time from the MS pasted in vol. IV of HW's own copy of *Anecdotes of Painting*, SH, 1762–71, now WSL. For the history of this copy see Hazen, *Cat. of HW's Lib.*, No. 2519.

October 5th 1780.

Dear Mr Walpole,

I AM more obliged to you for your charming book[2] than you can imagine. As to the panegyric of my talent in your elegant preface,[3] some future writer of anecdotes may say that you only praise your own gift, as you have given me that merit which you now reward; it seems to me as if you had made over to me for a time the power I have of painting, as I really do not know how I do it, and think you could dispossess me of it whenever you please, so that Mr Caperpillar[4] might prove that I hold my art by a sort of *copyhold* right under you. Pray then let me keep it as long as possible, that my collection

1. Margaret Smith (d. 1814), m. (1760) Sir Charles Bingham, 7th Bt, 1752, cr. (1776) Bn and (1795) E. of Lucan. 'Margaret Smith wife of Sir Charles Bingham of Castlebar in Ireland, had . . . a genius for copying in watercolours. She had been used to paint in crayons, but having never seen any good pictures, did very ill, till in 1773 I lent her all my finest miniatures and enamels; she copied them and improved with such rapidity that in five months she executed above 40, some of which were at least equal to the originals. Her eye was so exact that she copied equally well Guido, Vandyck, Hollar, Zincke, Isaac and Peter Oliver, and never missed the true colouring. . . . She did a few from the life, pretty like, but not quite well drawn, though she drew so very correctly from the works of other painters. Unluckily she had a desire to have a collection of famous persons, and thence copied a vast number of very bad pictures, and copied them so exactly that she never made them better' (HW's 'Book of Materials,' 1771, pp. 18–19 [now WSL]). Hugh Douglas Hamilton's pastel portrait of Lady Lucan, signed and dated 1774 (when she was still Lady Bingham), hung in the Breakfast Room at SH; it is now WSL. For HW's complimentary verses on her

talents as a painter see 'Des. of SH,' *Works* ii. 425; the MS is pasted on the back of the picture. See illustration.

2. The fourth and final volume of *Anecdotes of Painting*. See previous letter, n. 2.

3. In his Advertisement, p. viii, HW writes of 'the wonderful progress in miniature of Lady Lucan, who has arrived at copying the most exquisite works of Isaac and Peter Oliver, Hoskins and Cooper, with a genius that almost depreciates those masters, when we consider that they spent their lives in attaining perfection; and who, soaring above their modest timidity, has transferred the vigour of Raphael to her copies in watercolours' (*Works* iii. 400).

4. *Mr Capperpillar* alludes to Mr Walpole's fable of the Entail, in which he used to pronounce caterpillar, *capperpillar*, in allusion to one Capper a conveyancer, who had behaved ill to him (HW). Francis Capper (1698–1764) was a lawyer involved in the 'Nicoll affair'; see Appendix 1, Gray ii. 193–233. In HW's verse fable 'The Entail,' written in 1754 and first published in *Fugitive Pieces in Verse and Prose*, SH, 1758, the caterpillar is described as 'a subtle slow conveyancer' (*Works* i. 28–9).

LADY BINGHAM, BY HUGH DOUGLAS HAMILTON, 1774

may increase, to which you have now given intrinsic value, for posterity will always believe *you* more than they will their own eyes, and your mentioning my performances would certainly render them forever valuable, if my colours could last as long as your book is certain of being read.

I must also request that you'll grant my daughter Lavinia[5] the same protection you have afforded me, as *she* has an original genius; and if you will scold and encourage her, make her wish to see you, and at the same time dread it, I am certain that she will become upon some future day (which I hope you and I will see) worthy of being mentioned by you in another volume,[6] as I hope while you live you will never cease to write.

I am, dear Mr Walpole,

Your very obliged and humble servant,

M. LUCAN

From JOHN COWSLADE, ?Friday 13 October ?1780

Printed for the first time from the MS now WSL.

The year is established conjecturally by the reference to the fourth volume of *Anecdotes of Painting*, published 9 Oct. 1780 (Hazen, *SH Bibl.* 63–5).

Address: The Honourable Horace Walpole.

Octo[ber] 13th.

THANK you for your early remembrance of the book[1] you promised me for Mr Chute,[2] which I will take the first oppor-

5. Hon. Lavinia Bingham (1762–1831), m. (1781) George John Spencer, styled Vct Althorp 1765–83, 2d E. Spencer, 1783.

6. In his 'Book of Materials,' 1771, p. 127, HW later wrote of her: 'Lavinia Bingham Countess Spencer, daughter of the celebrated copyist Lady Lucan, drew only in bistre, and was happy in expression, but for some time very incorrect in drawing, but improved much and succeeded particularly in the characters of children. Several prints have been engraved from her designs, which were taken from her own children.' Engravings after her designs are included in HW's Collec-

tion of Prints, Engraved by Various Persons of Quality (Hazen, *Cat. of HW's Lib.*, No. 3588).

1. See *ante* 4 Oct. 1780, n. 2.

2. Probably Thomas Lobb Chute (1721–90), a first cousin once removed of John Chute. On John Chute's death in 1776, his cousin inherited the Vyne, Hants. HW was apparently also acquainted with Thomas Lobb Chute's son, William John Chute (1757–1824), who visited SH in 1786–7 (C. W. Chute, *A History of the Vyne in Hampshire*, Winchester, 1888, p. 120; BERRY ii. 227–8).

tunity of delivering to him, and thank you again for the one you have bestowed on me; it came in the most seasonable moment, just as I stepped out of the Salisbury diligence, and with the accompaniment of a dish of tea, was the greatest refreshment I could have had. The garden chapter,[3] like a good air, pleased better on the repetition; indeed I began with it first, and am now amusing myself with the other parts, which are much relieved by the variety of little anecdotes, that are scattered throughout. I think you told me that the new choir to the cathedral at Salisbury[4] was a poor performance. I found it very much so; it will be an everlasting reproach to the architect,[5] as long as it stands cheek by jowl with the original of your little chapel,[6] from whence any one of taste or feeling would surely have taken his idea at least. I am going in the beginning of the next week to pass a few days with Mrs Titchborne[7] at Inglefield Green;[8] when I return thence shall take the first opportunity of coming to Strawberry.

J. C.

3. The *Essay on Modern Gardening*, chapter vii of *Anecdotes of Painting*, 1762–71, iv. 117–51 (*Works* ii. 519–45).

4. In 1777–8 the cathedral underwent 'a material alteration.' The pews and the pulpit in the nave were taken away, 'the Grecian ornaments of the choir were removed, and a very indifferent style of Gothic substituted; additional seats were made in it' (William Dodsworth, *A Guide to the Cathedral Church of Salisbury*, 2d edn, Salisbury, 1792, pp. 35–6).

5. There appears to have been no architect appointed for the alterations to the choir. The work was supervised by Edmund Lush, the Clerk of the Works, no doubt with the advice of Bishop Hume (information kindly communicated by Mr R. O. C. Spring, Clerk of the Works, Salisbury Cathedral).

6. The Chapel in the garden at SH. The design for its façade was 'taken from the tomb of Edmund Audley Bishop of Salisbury, in that cathedral' ('Des. of SH,' *Works* ii. 507). The Gothic chapel of Bishop Audley (d. 1524) stands on the north side of the choir, in the second bay from the east; it was built by the Bishop in 1520 (Dodsworth, op. cit. 52).

7. Not identified.

8. Englefield Green, Surrey, 1½ miles NW of Egham.

To Charles Bedford, Wednesday 18 October 1780

Printed from Cunningham vii. 453, where the letter was first printed. Re-printed, Toynbee xi. 301–2. The history of the MS and its present whereabouts are not known.

Strawberry Hill, Oct. 18, 1780.

Dear Sir,

I AM most exceedingly concerned at the melancholy account I have received of yourself and your family,[1] and pity you from my heart. I wish anything I could say could give you ease and comfort, or anything I could do could relieve your anxiety—but in such afflictions we must submit to the will of God, who I fervently hope will spare those you so deservedly love. You must act like a man, bear your misfortunes with courage and patience, and take care of yourself for the sake of the rest, if any should be taken from you. I hope your tenderness and fears have made you think the danger greater than it is.

Do not think of ceremony with me, who certainly do not expect it; nor, oppressed as you are, write yourself; but let Mr Harris[2] send me exact accounts. I shall be anxious to hear again, but positively will not have you write yourself. Remember, I enjoin this. I never can doubt of your attention to me, and like best that you should show it now, by complying with what I desire. It will give me sincere joy to receive a better account, as I am

Most cordially yours,

Hor. Walpole

---

1. We do not know the nature of Bedford's 'misfortunes.' It would appear that one or more members of his family had become seriously ill, but his wife and two eldest sons, Grosvenor Charles Bedford (1773–1839) and Horace Walpole Bedford (ca 1776–1807), lived on for many years after this letter was written. His youngest son, Henry, probably was not yet born. See Appendix 2.

2. William Harris, HW's clerk in the Exchequer (*ante* 27 Feb. 1771. n. 2).

To Dr William Hunter, ?November 1780

Printed for the first time from a photostat of the MS inserted in Hunter's presentation copy of *Cornélie Vestale*, SH, 1768, in the Hunterian Collection, University of Glasgow Library. The MS passed on Hunter's death to his nephew and executor, Dr Matthew Baillie, to whom Hunter left his library and other collections in trust for a period of thirty years, after which they were to go to the University of Glasgow; transferred by Baillie to the University in 1807.

The letter was written between 30 Aug. 1778, when HW finished printing *The Sleep-Walker* at the SH Press, and 30 March 1783, the date of Hunter's death. In November 1780 Hunter visited HW to talk to him about Greek medals (Ossory ii. 241). The letter may have been written at this time, before political differences cooled their friendship in 1781.

MR Walpole is so much obliged to Dr Hunter for the trouble he was so good as to take about Mr W's servant's wife,[1] that as a mark of gratitude, and knowing Dr Hunter's taste for curious books, Mr Walpole begs he will do him the favour of accepting two of his editions that are not to be bought. Of the English[2] there were but 75 copies printed, and of the French,[3] 150 were sent to France, and only 50 kept in England.

PS. *Cornélie* was written by the celebrated President Hénault.[4]

1. Not identified. HW had several married servants at this time.

2. *The Sleep-Walker*, a translation by Lady Craven of *Le Somnambule*, a comedy by the Comte de Pont-de-Veyle; printed at the SH Press in 1778 in an edition of 75 copies (Hazen, *SH Bibl.* 114).

3. *Cornélie Vestale*, a tragedy by the Président Hénault; printed at the SH Press in 1768 in an edition of 200 copies, 150 of which were sent to France for dis-

tribution (ibid. 77). The copy of *Cornélie* presented by HW to Hunter, with this letter inserted in it, is now in the Hunterian Collection, University of Glasgow Library (Mungo Ferguson and D. B. Smith, *The Printed Books in the Library of the Hunterian Museum in the University of Glasgow*, Glasgow, 1930, p. 174). Hunter's copy of *The Sleep-Walker* is untraced.

4. See *ante* 6 March 1766, n. 8.

From the PRINCE DE BEAUVAU,
ca Sunday 12 November 1780

Printed from an extract quoted in HW to the Hon. Thomas Walpole 24 Nov. 1780, introduced as follows: 'I have . . . received yours of the 12th with one enclosed from the Prince de Beauvau, with which I am not at all pleased. There are mighty fine compliments, but those are not what I want. He says . . .' (FAMILY 185). HW has translated the parts of the extract enclosed in square brackets. The original letter is missing.

Dated approximately by Thomas Walpole's letter to HW 12 Nov. 1780.

[If there are any portraits or characters] qui paraissent compromettre quelqu'un, et qui pourraient par conséquence blesser la mémoire de notre amie,[1] [I shall] les mettre à part.

From the DUC DE GUINES, Monday 12 February 1781

Printed from the MS now WSL. First printed, Toynbee *Supp.* i. 280 n. 2. Damer-Waller; the MS was sold Sotheby's 5 Dec. 1921 (first Waller Sale), lot 136, to Wells; given by him to Thomas Conolly, of Chicago, from whom WSL acquired it in 1937.

The year of the letter is established by HW's reply *post* 23 March 1781.

Versailles, le 12 fevrier.

J E me suis flatté, Monsieur, que vous me conserveriez encore assez de bontés, pour ne pas désapprouver la liberté que je vais prendre. M. l'Abbé Pizzaná,[1] chargé de faire exécuter une édition

1. Mme du Deffand, who had bequeathed her manuscripts to HW. Notification of the bequest came through HW's cousin, Thomas Walpole, who was then in Paris. The legacy was to be sent to HW by the Prince de Beauvau (without his being held accountable for doing so), and the Prince was allowed to make copies of any manuscripts he wished. The bequest was apparently disputed, however, by Mme du Deffand's executor and heir, the Marquis d'Aulan. A series of disagreements ensued, in which HW tried to obtain all of the manuscripts that he believed himself entitled to, particularly Mme du Deffand's 'portraits' of her circle

of friends and the letters of the Abbé Barthélemy. In the course of the dispute, Beauvau sent HW the present letter, saying that he would withdraw any 'portraits' that might compromise living persons. HW (through Thomas Walpole) objected to this decision and requested all of the 'portraits.' The dispute continued into 1781, but by September of that year HW received most of the papers which were originally intended for him. See DU DEFFAND i. xliii–xlv; FAMILY 181–6, 188–94, 196, 202, 204; OSSORY ii. 292.

1. Giuseppe Pezzana (d. 1802), Parmesan man of letters; translator of Voltaire's

complète des œuvres de Métastase,[2] a désiré d'être recommandé en Angleterre à quelques personnes assez distinguées par leur goût, pour que leur suffrage assura son succès. Je ne pouvais lui rendre un meilleur service que de le mettre à portée de vous rendre ses hommages, et de vous supplier de vouloir bien lui être favorable.

Vous avez perdu dans ce pays-ci une excellente amie;[3] j'avais la satisfaction de l'entendre souvent parler de vous avec le plus grand intérêt; ses derniers moments ont été employés à vous donner des preuves de sa confiance, et elle ne pouvait assurément la mieux placer. Il y a cependant une chose bien fâcheuse: c'est qu'elle ne vous avait légué que les papiers inventoriés, et qu'il en existait un grand nombre qui ne l'étaient pas, et qui peut-être ne composaient pas ce qu'elle avait de moins précieux.[4] Cela est regrettable, en ce que personne ne pouvait mieux que vous en faire un excellent usage.

C'est avec infiniment d'empressement que j'ai saisi cette occasion de me rappeler à votre souvenir,[5] et de vous renouveler l'hommage des sentiments de considération et d'attachement avec lesquels j'ai l'honneur d'être, Monsieur, votre très humble et très obéissant serviteur,

LE DUC DE GUINES

L'Orphelin de la Chine and editor of Ariosto. He severed his connection with the Church and left Parma for political reasons in 1772, serving afterwards as Italian master at the French court (Henri Bédarida, Parme et la France de 1748 à 1789, 1927, pp. 197–8).

2. Pietro Metastasio (1698–1782), Italian poet, dramatist, and opera librettist. Pezzana's edition of Opere del Signor Abate Pietro Metastasio was published at Paris in 12 volumes, 1780–2.

3. Mme du Deffand, who died at Paris 23 Sept. 1780 (DU DEFFAND v. 250).

4. Under the terms of Mme du Deffand's will, HW was to receive her 'brochures, feuilles volantes et manuscrits dont Wiart a fait le catalogue jusqa'à présent, et que je lui ferai continuer à l'avenir' (ibid. vi. 7). But the bequest of manuscripts was apparently disputed by her executor and heir, the Marquis d'Aulan. It was eventually decided that HW could have only those papers which were specifically mentioned in Wiart's catalogue, and from these some letters were withdrawn before HW gained possession (ibid. i. xliv; ante ca 12 Nov. 1780, n. 1).

5. De Guines had not seen HW since he was recalled from his embassy in London in Feb. 1776 (ante 18 Feb. 1776 and n. 3).

To the Duc de Guines, Friday 23 March 1781

Printed from the MS now wsl. First printed, *L'amateur d'autographes*, 1866, v. 354–5; extract quoted in Toynbee *Supp.* i. 280. The MS was sold at Paris 3 Dec. 1866 (Vicomte de Fer Sale), lot 780; resold Sotheby's 17 March 1875 (Autograph Letters and Historical Documents Sale), lot 181 to George Moffatt; resold Sotheby's 27 Oct. 1959 (Moffatt Sale), lot 500, to Maggs for wsl.

À Londres ce 23 mars 1781.

L'HONNEUR de votre souvenir, Monsieur le Duc, m'est infiniment précieux. Je voudrais bien être en état d'en marquer ma reconnaissance par des services rendus à Monsieur l'Abbé Pizzana. Peu de crédit et la vie retirée que mon âge et ma mauvaise santé[1] m'ont préscrite, me laissent peu d'occasions de lui être utile; mais assurément je m'efforcerai de lui procurer des souscriptions,[2] et je l'aiderai de tous les conseils qu'il tient à moi de lui offrir.[3] Je n'aurai rien de plus pressé, Monsieur le Duc, que de vous obéir, et de témoigner combien je suis flatté de l'honneur que vous daignez me faire en me recommandant un de vos protégés.

Oui, M. le Duc, j'ai fait une perte irréparable. L'amitié, dont me comblait Madame du Deffand était autant au-dessus de mon mérite, qu'elle était chère à mon cœur. Il est sûr que je ne la méritais qu'en sachant l'évaluer au delà de toute expression. Je ne sais ce qui m'aviendra de sa succession, n'en ayant encore rien reçu.[4] Je n'y avais nulle prétension quelconque, et j'ai fait mon possible pour qu'elle ne me laissât rien. Je n'ai consenti à recevoir ses manuscrits, qu'à condition qu'elle y bornât tout ce qu'elle me destinait:[5] et dès qu'on m'annonçât ce legs, je n'ai eu ni d'objet ni d'intention qu'à m'en montrer digne, en prouvant que je n'en abuserais point. J'ai fait rendre toutes lettres particulières de personnes vivantes; j'ai consenti qu'on publiât sa correspondance avec Voltaire;[6] et j'ai de-

1. An allusion to his annual attacks of gout.

2. For Pezzana's edition of Metastasio's works.

3. We have found no record of a meeting between HW and Pezzana.

4. See *ante* ca 12 Nov. 1780, n. 1.

5. 'After some contest, and various requests from her to name what I would accept, as her books etc. all which I posi-

tively refused, she said, would I at least take her papers? To satisfy her, and as there would be nothing mercenary in that acceptance, I did consent' (HW to Thomas Walpole 26 Oct. 1780, FAMILY 181). See Ossory ii. 235.

6. The Prince de Beauvau had proposed to allow Mme du Deffand's correspondence with Voltaire to be printed in the forthcoming edition of the *Œuvres com-*

mandé instamment qu'on m'envoyât tout le reste jusqu'au moindre chiffon qui fut de sa propre dictée, à deux raisons, l'une, parce que tout ce qui était d'elle, me sera éternellement précieux: l'autre, parce que je ne voulais pas qu'on accusât ma chère amie d'avoir confié légèrement à un indigne ce qui pourrait intéresser qui que ce fût, et ce qu'assurément je ne permettrais pas de transpirer.[7] Je suis très persuadé que cette demande sera satisfaite, si je suis en droit de l'exiger. Si je ne le suis pas, j'ai nul droit de réclamer ce qui n'est pas à moi.

Je vous demande mille pardons, M. le Duc, d'avoir pris la liberté de vous ennuyer de ce qui me regarde personnellement; mais au vrai l'honneur que vous m'avez fait en m'en parlant, semblait exiger que j'y répondisse avec franchise; et ce n'était que pour répondre à l'honnêteté de votre procédé, que j'ai osé vous faire ce détail.[8] Il est impossible qu'un Anglais soit insensible au moindre petit mot d'intérêt dont l'honore M. le Duc de Guines. C'est se faire valoir que d'avoir à se vanter de ses bontés; et de tous les cœurs qu'il a gagné et conservé dans ce pays-ci, pas un ne lui est plus respectueusement dévoué que celui de

Son très humble et très obéissant serviteur

HORACE WALPOLE

---

plètes de Voltaire, [Kehl], 1784–9, edited by Beaumarchais, Condorcet, and Decroix. HW consented to this request; see CONWAY iii. 385 and n. 11.

7. See FAMILY 182, 185–6.

8. HW wrote Thomas Walpole at Paris 25 March 1781: 'I have received a letter [ante 12 Feb. 1781] from the Duc de Guines . . . in which he tells me . . . that Madame du D. left me only such papers as were specified in an inventory, and that there remain a great many, not inserted there, and perhaps not the least precious, which he laments not coming to me. . . . I have answered very guardedly, told him the heads of my story without complaint, and concluded by saying, that having had no pretensions to anything, I certainly can claim nothing but what was left to me' (ibid. 193).

To JOHN HENDERSON,[1] Monday 16 April 1781

Printed from a copy of the MS in the possession of Mr Martin Heath, Ashton House, Worton, Devizes, Wilts, kindly supplied by the late Roland Heath. First printed, Cunningham viii. 28–9. Reprinted, Toynbee xi. 429–30 (salutation omitted in Cunningham and Toynbee). The MS is one of six letters from HW to Henderson that presumably became the property of Henderson's only child, Harriet, who married James Carrick Moore; the letters passed to their daughter, Miss Julia Moore, from whom they were acquired by her residuary legatee, George Heath; they were in turn inherited by his son, Roland Heath, and his grandson, Martin Heath. A MS copy of the present letter, in Isaac Reed's hand, is in the Pierpont Morgan Library.

Address: To Mr Henderson in Buckingham Street.

Berkeley Square, April 16, 1781.

Sir,

EVER since I had the pleasure of seeing you here,[2] I have been uneasy at what you told me, of having seen an extract of my tragedy[3] in a work going to be published.[4] Though I was so imprudent as to print and give away some copies of it,[5] and consequently exposed myself to the risk of what is happening, yet I heartily wish I could prevent that publication, as it will occasion discourse about the play, which is disgusting from the subject, and absurd from being totally unfit for the stage—a reason, which, could I have succeeded better, ought still to have restrained me from undertaking it.

May I take the liberty of asking you if you think it could be stopped? I should be willing to pay for my folly.[6] Do not answer me

1. John Henderson (1747–85), actor, called 'the Bath Roscius' (*ante* 25 Jan. 1780, n. 15).

2. 'Mr Henderson passes this week with Mr Horace Walpole at Strawberry Hill; to this honour Mr H. is said to have been introduced by the *Count of Narbonne*—which, being descended from the *Castle of Otranto,* is considered by Mr W. as his own *grandchild,* and therefore treated accordingly—that is, *dotingly!*' (*Public Adv.* 10 April). HW pasted this notice in his 'Book of Materials,' 1771, p. 79.

3. *The Mysterious Mother.*

4. A new edition of David Erskine Baker's *Biographia Dramatica* was being

prepared by Isaac Reed (see n. 9 below).

5. Fifty copies were printed at SH in 1768. HW gave away a few copies to friends, but most of them are still unaccounted for (Hazen, *SH Bibl.* 79–81). See n. 7 below.

6. HW soon afterwards decided to have Dodsley reprint and publish the play in order to forestall unauthorized editions. The announcement of the intended publication did prevent a spurious edition that had been advertised, but HW later decided to suppress publication of his own edition even though it had already been printed off. See ibid. 82–3.

by a compliment, nor tell me, as civility may perhaps dictate, that it would be pity to deprive the public of such a *jewel*—pray do not think that I seek for, or should like such an hyperbole. I use the word *jewel* most ironically, and do not imagine that a pebble with a great flaw through the whole can have much lustre. There is no affectation in this request: I have betrayed but too much vanity in printing what I knew had such capital faults—but I am too old now not to fear disgusting the public more than I flatter myself with its approbation—yet the impression of only a small number of copies at first will prove, that, when several years younger, I was conscious of the imperfections of my tragedy, and gave them only to those[7] who I knew were partial to me. There are many defects in the execution as well as in the subject—but when the materials are ill-chosen, what would it avail to retouch the fashion? nor, though I have sometimes written verses, did I ever think that I was born a poet.

In short, Sir, I most sincerely wish to have the publication of any part of the play prevented, and you will oblige me exceedingly if you can assist me. Perhaps it is asking too great a favour, when I beg you to take that trouble—if it is, only let me know the editor,[8] and I will undertake the task myself.[9] I am Sir with great regard

Your obedient humble servant

Hor. Walpole

7. The recipients included Samuel Lysons, Thomas Barrett, Charles Bedford, Michael Lort, Richard Bull and Lady Diana Beauclerk (ibid. 79–81). See *ante* mid-July 1780.

8. Isaac Reed (*ante* 11 Nov. 1774, n. 1).

9. Henderson apparently showed HW's letter to Reed, who at that time made a copy of it (see headnote). The new edition of the *Biographia Dramatica* appeared in January 1782. At the conclu-sion of his article on *The Mysterious Mother*, Reed wrote (ii. 249): 'We intended to have given the reader a specimen of it; but having learnt that the sensibility of the author (to whom every respect is due) would be wounded by such an exhibition, we deem ourselves bound to suppress it, however reluctantly.' In his letter *post* 4 March 1782, HW thanked Henderson 'for saving my scenes from the *Biographia Dramatica.*'

'RICHMOND HILL,' BY HENRY WILLIAM BUNBURY

To Henry William Bunbury,[1] Saturday 28 April 1781

Printed from the MS now WSL. First printed in *The Correspondence of Sir Thomas Hanmer, Bart,* ed. Sir Henry Bunbury, 1838, pp. 397–8. Reprinted, Cunningham viii. 33; Toynbee xi. 434–5; J. C. Riely, 'Horace Walpole and "the Second Hogarth,"' *Eighteenth-Century Studies,* 1975–6, ix. 36 (date, closing, and signature omitted). The MS passed to Bunbury's son, Sir Henry Edward Bunbury, in whose possession it was in 1838; sold Puttick and Simpson 2 Aug. 1851 (A. Donnadieu Sale), lot 980, to Thorpe; resold by B. F. Stevens and Brown ca 1922 to Macgill James, of Baltimore, from whom WSL acquired it in April 1935.

Berkeley Square, April 28, 1781.

I AM just come, Sir, from the Royal Academy,[2] where I had been immediately struck, as I always am by your works, by a most capital drawing of Richmond Hill[3]—but what was my surprise and pleasure—for I fear the latter preceded my modesty—when I found your note[4] and read that so very fine a performance was destined for me! This is a true picture of my emotions, Sir—but I hope you will believe that I am not less sincere when I assure you, that the first moment's reflection told me how infinitely, Sir, you think of overpaying me for the poor, though just, tribute of my praise in a trifling work,[5] whose chief merit is its having avoided flattery. Your genius, Sir, cannot want *that,* and still less, my attestation; but when you condescend to reward *this,* I doubt I shall be a little vain, for when I shall have such a certificate to produce,[6] how will it be possible to remain quite humble? I must beg you, Sir, to accept my warmest and most grateful thanks, which are doubled by your

1. (1750–1811), amateur artist and caricaturist. HW greatly admired his work and collected the prints engraved after Bunbury's designs. His two elephant-folio albums of Bunbury prints are now WSL (Hazen, *Cat. of HW's Lib.,* No. 3563). See J. C. Riely, 'Horace Walpole and "the Second Hogarth,"' *Eighteenth-Century Studies,* 1975–6, ix. 28–44.

2. The annual exhibition at the Royal Academy, Somerset House, Strand.

3. Across the Thames from SH. Bunbury's drawing was No. 536 in the Royal Academy exhibition (Algernon Graves, *The Royal Academy of Arts,* 1905–6, i.

337). It was sold SH xxi. 23 to Whitaker for £2.12.6; acquired in 1967 by WSL. The drawing was engraved and published by William Dickinson 1 March 1782. See illustration.

4. Missing.

5. In the Advertisement, dated 1 Oct. 1780, to the fourth volume of *Anecdotes of Painting,* HW refers to 'the living etchings of Mr H. Bunbury, the second Hogarth, and first imitator who ever fully equalled his original.'

6. The drawing was hung on the staircase at SH ('Des. of SH,' *Works* ii. 420). See *post* 17 March 1791.

ingenious delicacy in delivering me in this very agreeable manner from the pain I felt in fearing that I had taken too much liberty with you. I am Sir with great respect

Your infinitely obliged humble servant

Hor. Walpole

To Lord Bagot,[1] Friday 8 June 1781

Printed from a photostat of the MS owned in 1947 by the 6th Baron Bagot, Blithfield Hall, Rugeley, Staffordshire, kindly furnished by the late R. W. Chapman. First printed in *Memorials of the Bagot Family, Compiled in 1823*, Blithfield, privately printed, 1824, pp. 156–7 (misdated 'Jan. 8th 1781').

Endorsed, probably by William, 2d Bn Bagot: Lord Orford's letter to my father concerning a picture at Blithfield.[2]

Berkeley Square, June 8th 1781.

ON examining your Lordship's picture,[3] though I cannot flatter myself with a chance of discovering the personages, you will forgive me, my Lord, if I differ with your Lordship on the subject, which does not appear to me to represent a marriage, but rather a father and mother presenting their son, perhaps previous to his receiving knighthood, to the Virgin.[4] My reasons for this conjecture, and it is no more, are, that the two elderly persons, not only give an idea of parents, but that the young man alone seems introduced to the Virgin. Each has his patron saint behind; the father, St Andrew; the mother, St Catherine; and that mother being in a kind of nun's

1. Sir William Bagot (1728–98); 6th Bt, 1768; cr. (1780) Bn Bagot; M.P. HW described him in 1777 as 'the Tory, Sir W. Bagot, Lord North's particular friend' (*Last Journals* ii. 22).

2. Lord Bagot's seat, near Rugeley, Staffordshire.

3. A tryptich of the Nativity, attributed to the Master of the St Bartholomew Altarpiece (ca 1450–ca 1510/20), a German painter of the late Gothic period (Thieme and Becker xxxvii. 34–6). The picture is doubtless that described as 'Altarpiece with Virgin and Child' in J. P. Neale, *Views of the Seats of Noblemen and Gentlemen in England, Wales, Scotland,*

and Ireland, 1st Series, 1818–23, iii. sub Blithfield). It was sold by the 6th Bn Bagot at Sotheby's 17 Oct. 1945 to Dr James Hasson, of London, who reproduced it in colour, with commentary, in his book *The Banquet of the Immortals*, Edinburgh, 1948, pp. 106–9.

4. The painting is a small altarpiece commissioned ca 1510 by the Baron Holtzhausen to adorn the private oratory of his mansion at Frankfurt. It was intended to commemorate the confirmation of his only son, Martin Holtzhausen, who is shown kneeling before the Virgin and the Holy Child (ibid.).

or religious dress, excludes the idea of a marriage; but she might be dead at the time the picture was painted or have taken the habit out of devotion. But another reason for my thinking it may be previous to the son's knighthood, is, that he has no spurs, and that his patron saint[5] is in armour, though I do not pretend to guess what saint he is.

The arms behind[6] are evidently foreign, the crests particularly so; and neither shield has the least appearance of a coronet. Were the persons of any princely or very illustrious house, they probably would bear some quarterings. I do not know whether foreign heralds used to be accurate as our own were; but the helmet over the man's arms is in profile, and not in front, which latter with us is one of the marks of a sovereign.

I confess I despair of discovering the arms, as I am very illiterate in foreign blazon: nor do I presume to offer anything I have said to your Lordship but as very superficial conjectures, and which I should not have hazarded but in obedience to your Lordship's commands. The picture, besides being well preserved, has a good deal of merit in itself, and is less stiff than most of that age. I am sorry I am not able to answer better to the opinion your Lordship has been pleased to entertain of my knowledge, but I should be doubly undeserving of those too favourable sentiments, if I attempted to impose on your Lordship, and pretended to discover what I own I cannot decipher. I have the honour to be with great respect, my Lord,

Your Lordship's most obedient humble servant

Hor. Walpole

5. St Martin of Tours (ibid. 109).
6. On the back of the two *flügel*, or folding wings, of the tryptich are painted the coats of arms of the Holtzhausen barony and, presumably, of Baroness Holtzhausen's family (J. B. Rietstap, *Armorial général*, 2d edn, 1884, i. 978).

To Charles Bedford, Tuesday 12 June 1781

Printed from Cunningham viii. 50, where the letter was first printed. Reprinted, Toynbee xii. 10. The history of the MS and its present whereabouts are not known.

Strawberry Hill, June 12, 1781.

I THINK, dear Sir, you are so good as to pay my coach-tax.[1] I must beg the same favour of you for that on servants,[2] which I believe is due very soon, with a heavy penalty if not paid within a limited time.[3] My number is five, a *valet-de-chambre*, two footmen, a coachman and gardener.[4] I have another, but in a capacity which nobody else has, and therefore, I conclude, not included—certainly not specified in the Act; it is my printer.[5]

Yours sincerely,

Hor. Walpole

1. An excise duty of £4, to be paid annually on four-wheel carriages kept for private use, as specified in the act of 20 Geo. II (1747), c. 10. An additional duty of five per cent was imposed twice after 1747, the most recent one becoming effective on 5 April 1781, according to the act of 21 Geo. III (1781), c. 17 (*Statutes at Large,* ed. Owen Ruffhead, 1763–1800, vii. 15–21, xiii. 355–6, xiv. 16).

2. The so-called 'Servants Act' of 17 Geo. III (1777), c. 39, declared 'a duty upon all servants retained or employed in the several capacities therein mentioned.' A master, or his agent, was required to furnish a list of all his male servants, stating their names and employ-

ments. The annual assessment for each male servant was 21s. As stated in the amendment of 21 Geo. III (1781), c. 31, the master was to submit the list of servants within 40 days (20 days every year thereafter) after 21 May, along with payment of the duty. The penalty for failing to deliver a correct list on time was £20, plus double the duty for each servant omitted (ibid. xiii. 103–7, xiv. 38–41).

3. In 1781 payment was due by 30 June (40 days after 21 May).

4. See following letter for their names. The 'Servants Act' did not apply to female servants.

5. Thomas Kirgate.

To Charles Bedford, Monday 18 June 1781

Printed from Cunningham viii. 56, where the letter was first printed. Reprinted, Toynbee xii. 15. The history of the MS and its present whereabouts are not known.

Strawberry Hill, June 18, 1781.

Dear Sir,

THE names and employments of my servants are as follow:[1] Philip Colomb,[2] *valet-de-chambre;* David Monnerat and James Sibley, footmen; John Cowie, gardener; and John Jenkins, coachman. You will be so good as to enter them at the Excise and pay for them now, and every year, and put them into your account.[3]

I will send the account myself to Brentford.[4]

Yours sincerely,

H. Walpole

To Lord Charlemont, Sunday 1 July 1781

Printed from the MS now wsl. First printed in Francis Hardy, *Memoirs of the Political and Private Life of James Caulfield, Earl of Charlemont,* 2d edn, 1812, i. 409–10. Reprinted, Wright vi. 132; Cunningham viii. 58–9; Toynbee xii. 17–18. All printings incomplete (see n. 4 below); the last three lack closing and signature. The MS was in the possession of the 2d Earl of Charlemont in 1812; not further traced until sold Sotheby's 17 Dec. 1928 ('Other Properties'), lot 174, to Sawyer; offered by them, Cat. No. 155 (1940), lot 194; sold by them to wsl, March 1940.

Strawberry Hill, July 1st 1781.

I HAVE been exceedingly flattered, my Lord, by receiving a present[1] from your Lordship, which at once proves that I retain a place

1. See previous letter.
2. (d. 1799).
3. As HW's deputy in the Exchequer, Bedford could act as his agent in paying the servants duty at the Excise Office.
4. Brentford was considered the county town of Middlesex (Daniel Lysons, *The Environs of London,* 1792–6, ii. 40). An official notice appearing in the *St James's Chronicle* 12–14 June 1781 stated that the required list of male servants 'must be de-

livered, and duties paid, either at the chief Office of Excise in London, or at the excise office nearest to the place of residence of the persons liable to the payment of such duties.'

_____

1. A copy of William Preston's *Poems on Several Occasions,* Dublin, 1781. This presentation copy (untraced) is Hazen, *Cat. of HW's Lib.,* No. 2933.

in your Lordship's memory, and that you think me worthy of reading what you like. I could not wait to give your Lordship a thousand
thanks for so kind a mark of your esteem, till I had gone through
the volume, which I may venture to say I shall admire, as I find it
contains some pieces which I had seen and did admire without knowing their author.[2] That approbation was quite impartial—perhaps
my future judgment of the rest will be not a little prejudiced, and
yet on good foundation, for if Mr Preston has retained my suffrage
in his favour by dedicating his poems to your Lordship, it must at
least be allowed that I am biassed by evidence of his taste. He would
not possess the honour of your friendship unless he deserved it; and
as he knows you, he would not have ventured to prefix your name,
my Lord, to poems that did not deserve your patronage.[3] I dare to
say they will meet the approbation of better judges than I can pretend to be—and then, I do not doubt but they will receive the seal
of merit, the disapprobation of Dr Johnson.[4] I have the honour to
be with the greatest respect, esteem and gratitude, my Lord,

Your Lordship's most obedient
and most obliged humble servant

Hor. Walpole

2. William Preston (1753–1807), Irish
poet and dramatist. In 1776 Preston published anonymously at Dublin two verse
satires on Richard Twiss's *Travels through
Portugal and Spain*, 1775. The poems,
entitled *An Heroic Epistle from Donna
Teresa Pinna y Ruiz, of Murcia, to
Richard Twiss, Esq.* and *An Heroic Answer from Richard Twiss. Esq., at Rotter-
dam*, were reprinted in London in 1776
and included in Preston's *Poems on
Several Occasions*. HW's copies of the
separately printed poems, bound in his
'Poems of Geo. III' now at Harvard, are
Hazen, op. cit., No. 3222:15:21.

3. 'Lord Charlemont became his [Pres-
ton's] patron, and his friend. At this time

[1781] he aided his genius as far as he
could, by diffusing a publication of his
works throughout such circles in London,
as might fan the blaze of his poetical
fame. He sent several copies to some of
his literary friends there' (Francis Hardy,
*Memoirs of the Political and Private Life
of James Caulfield, Earl of Charlemont*,
2d edn, 1812, i. 408–9).

4. 'and then . . . Johnson' is omitted
in all previous editions and now printed
for the first time. HW speaks disparag-
ingly of Johnson on several occasions;
in *Last Journals* i. 444 he describes
Johnson as a man 'of the narrowest notions and most illiberal mind.'

To John Nichols,[1] Friday 6 July 1781

Printed from Nichols, *Lit. Anec.* viii. 436, where the letter was first printed. Reprinted, Toynbee xii. 25. The MS is untraced until sold Sotheby's 1 Dec. 1906 (George Smith Sale), lot 178 (with two other letters), to W. V. Daniell; offered by Daniell, Cat. No. 8, new series, lot 1443; offered by Maggs, Cat. Nos 373 (Christmas 1918), lot 2651; 405 (summer 1921), lot 1388; not further traced.

Strawberry Hill, July 6, 1781.

MR H. Walpole desires Mr Nichols to accept his grateful thanks for the obliging present of Hogarth's *Tour*.[2]

1. (1745–1826), printer and author.

2. *An Account of What Seemed Most Remarkable in the Five Days Peregrination of . . . Messieurs Tothall, Scott, Hogarth, Thornhill, and Forrest . . . 1732 . . . Imitated in Hudibrastics*, [1781], by William Gostling (1696–1777). Gostling versified Ebenezer Forrest's 'Account' of the tour made by Hogarth and his friends around the Isle of Sheppey in 1732. Nichols originally intended to include Gostling's poem in the first edition of his *Biographical Anecdotes of William Hogarth*, 1781, but suppressed it, printing twenty copies separately 'as a curiosity' in 1781; he did include it in the second edition of the *Biographical Anecdotes* published in 1782 (*Hogarth's Peregrination*, ed. Charles Mitchell, Oxford, 1952, p. [53]). HW's copy (untraced) of the separately-printed *Account* is Hazen, *Cat. of HW's Lib.*, No. 2385.

To John Henderson, Wednesday 18 July 1781

Printed from a copy of the MS in the possession of Mr Martin Heath, Ashton House, Worton, Devizes, Wilts, kindly supplied by the late Roland Heath. First printed, Cunningham viii. 67. Reprinted, Toynbee xii. 29–30 (salutation omitted in Cunningham and Toynbee). For the history of the MS see *ante* 16 April 1781.

Memorandum (probably in Henderson's hand, on the inside leaf of the letter):
<blockquote>
No critic vanquish'd by superior wit
No disappointed tyrant of the pit
No malice baffled no defeated rage
At the pure pathos of thy spotless page
Fully transcrib'd and faithfully exprest[1]
</blockquote>
Address: To Mr Henderson in Buckingham Street in the Strand, London.

Strawberry Hill, July 18, 1781.

Sir,

I WROTE a week ago to Mr Harris[2] with the offer of Mr Jephson's play,[3] but have received no answer at all. I conclude Mr Harris is in the country,[4] as at least he would have been so civil as to say No. Will you be so good as to tell me by a line hither whether I guess rightly—or if you have heard anything about it. I know Mr Jephson will be impatient; and when I have done a disagreeable thing merely to oblige him, I should be sorry to have him think I had neglected it. I beg your pardon for all the trouble I have given and give you, and am

Sir

Your obliged humble servant

Hor. Walpole

---

1. The author originally wrote 'Fully exprest and faithfully rehearst,' later altering the text as printed above.

2. Thomas Harris (ca 1738–1820), proprietor and stage manager of Covent Garden Theatre. HW's letter to him is missing.

3. Robert Jephson's *The Count of Narbonne*. In Jan. 1780 HW had read the play in manuscript, offering his criticisms and advising Jephson about having the play produced; see *ante* 25 and 27 Jan. 1780.

4. Apparently so; see *post* 26 August 1781.

To Mrs Gostling,[1] ?August 1781

Printed from the MS now WSL. First printed, Toynbee *Supp.* iii. 37. The MS is untraced until offered by Maggs, Cat. Nos 396 (autumn 1920), lot 2670; 439 (summer 1923), lot 1168; 473 (spring 1926), lot 698; 504 (summer 1928), lot 1410; *penes* Colbeck Radford and Co., 1930; acquired from Crompton Johnson, of Farmington, Connecticut, October 1932. Mrs Gostling's draft of her reply appears on the inside leaf of the letter.

Dated conjecturally by HW's reference to being 'out of order.' The letter must have been written after France's entry into the war with America in Feb. 1778, and before the earliest published reference to Mrs Gostling's 'present' in the Appendix (printed soon after June 1781) to the 1774 *Description of Strawberry Hill* (see nn. 2, 3, and 5 below).

Address: To Mrs Gostling at Whitton.

Mr Walpole has been out of order,[2] or he should not have neglected waiting on Mr and Mrs Gostling with his personal thanks. In the meantime he begs leave to take the liberty of entreating Mrs Gostling to accept of two cups and saucers of Sève china, not as a compensation for her valuable present,[3] but as a faint mark of his gratitude, and which still he should not presume to offer her, if the late duty on foreign porcelain,[4] not to mention the war,[5] did not prevent the importation of any more of that of Sève, and consequently makes it a sort of rarity.[6]

1. Anne Green (ca 1724–99), m. George Gostling (ca 1714–82), of Whitton Park, Twickenham parish, a proctor in Doctors' Commons. Whitton Place, formerly the property of Lord Ilay (later 3d Duke of Argyll), was acquired by Gostling, who sold the mansion to Sir William Chambers, the architect, and then built a house for himself, Whitton Park (GM 1782, lii. 600; 1799, lxix pt i. 83; R. S. Cobbett, *Memorials of Twickenham*, 1872, pp. 74, 98, 387–8).

2. Possibly alluded to in HW's letter to Lady Ossory 7 Aug. 1781: 'For these four days I have been confined with a pain and swelling in my face' (OSSORY ii. 285).

3. 'On the hearth [in the Gallery, chimney side, on the left] two fine old blue and white jars of porcelain, round and flattish, very uncommon, a present from Mrs Gostling of Witton' (HW's MS note in his extra-illustrated copy, now WSL, of the *Description of Strawberry Hill*,

1774, p. 66). Soon after June 1781 HW printed an Appendix to the 1774 *Description*, in which the porcelain jars are mentioned (p. 135); see Hazen, *SH Bibl.* 109. See also *Works* ii. 462. The jars were sold SH xxiii. 121 to Zimmerman for £3.13.6.

4. The act of 15 Geo. III (1775), c. 37, imposed a duty of £10 10s. 10d. on every £100 *ad valorem* of imported painted earthenware. See F. J. B. Watson, 'Walpole and the Taste for French Porcelain in Eighteenth-Century England,' in *Horace Walpole: Writer, Politician, and Connoisseur,* ed. W. H. Smith, New Haven, 1967, esp. pp. 186–7.

5. The Franco-American treaty of alliance against Great Britain was signed at Paris in Feb. 1778 (MANN viii. 354–5).

6. By her will, dated 13 July 1794 and proved 28 Feb. 1799 in the Prerogative Court of Canterbury, Mrs Gostling left 'To my dear son George Gostling the two fine cups given to me by Lord Orford.'

Mr Walpole cannot repeat his gratitude without renewing, as he must always do, his shame for the impertin[en]ce he was guilty of, though ignorantly, in asking to purchase the two most beautiful jars, which indeed he did not suspect Mrs Gostling had bought for herself.[7] Her generosity and Mr Gostling's great politeness he can never pretend to equal.

From MRS GOSTLING, ?August 1781

Printed for the first time from Mrs Gostling's MS draft on the inside leaf of HW's letter to her *ante* ?August 1781 (now WSL). The letter sent to HW is missing.

Dated conjecturally by the previous letter.

MRS Gostling cannot without confusion[1] acknowledge the receipt of Mr Walpole's great civility and the trouble she has most involuntarily given him. She hopes he will not deem her guilty of too great vanity in exhibiting the matchless[2] pieces of china he has condescended to enrich her with, but which she had not the most distant presumption[3] to expect, nor will it be in her power to avoid enhancing their value by mentioning, but with the utmost respect, the donor.

7. The sale has not been identified.

———

1. 'blushing' crossed out in the MS draft and 'confusion' substituted.

2. 'elegant' crossed out and 'matchless' substituted.

3. 'by no means presumed' crossed out and 'had not the most distant presumption' substituted.

To Thomas Cadell,[1] Monday 13 August 1781

Printed from a photostat of the MS inserted in a copy of W. S. Lewis, *Horace Walpole*, New York, 1961. First printed, Toynbee *Supp.* iii. 450. The MS was at one time offered for sale by R. Atkinson, of Peckham Rye; sold California Book Auction Company 2 Dec. 1978 (Miscellaneous Sale), lot 497, to Mary Anne Flick, of San Francisco.

Dr Toynbee's source for the letter was R. Atkinson's sale catalogue, which gave the date as '[July?] 13, 1781.' The MS clearly reads 'Aug.'

Strawberry Hill, Aug. 13, 1781.

I DESIRE you will deliver to Mr Raspe[2] twenty copies of his book.[3] I am Sir

Your humble servant

Hor. Walpole

To John Henderson, Sunday 26 August 1781

Printed from a copy of the MS in the possession of Mr Martin Heath, Ashton House, Worton, Devizes, Wilts, kindly supplied by the late Roland Heath. First printed. Cunningham viii. 72. Reprinted, Toynbee xii. 41–2. For the history of the MS see *ante* 16 April 1781.

Address: To Mr Henderson in Buckingham Street, London.

Strawberry Hill, Aug. 26, 1781.

I HAVE received a letter,[1] Sir, from Mr Jephson to Mr Harris, which I flatter myself will promote a reconciliation between them;[2] but I think it will be better if I deliver it myself. Mr Harris

---

1. (1742–1802), bookseller in the Strand.

2. Rudolf Erich Raspe (1737–94), German-English writer and mineralogist; author of *Baron Munchausen's . . . Travels and Campaigns in Russia*, 1785.

3. *A Critical Essay on Oil-Painting . . . Printed for the Author by H. Goldney, and Sold by T. Cadell*, 1781. HW had the book printed at his expense and saw it through the press. 250 copies were printed at London, rather than SH, to save time and because the SH Press was 'out of order'; see Dalrymple 145–6. HW's copy, now wsl, is Hazen, *Cat. of HW's Lib.*, No. 2459. 'Mr Raspe, in his curious trea-

tise published in 1781, has proved that oil painting was known long before its pretended discovery by Van Eyck' (*Anecdotes of Painting, Works* iii. 15n).

---

1. Missing.

2. Edmond Malone, acting on behalf of Jephson, had first offered Jephson's play *The Count of Narbonne* to Harris at Covent Garden. Jephson then decided to apply to Richard Brinsley Sheridan, the manager of Drury Lane Theatre. When Sheridan declined to produce the play, HW 'was desired to recommend it to t'other house [Covent Garden]. . . . When

was so obliging as to promise to let me see him at his return to town,[3] which I conclude must now be near, as the season approaches of opening the theatres.[4] I will be much obliged to you therefore, Sir, if you will be so good as to let me know when Mr Harris arrives; but do not mention the letter, as I had rather have some conversation with him before I produce it. I beg pardon for all the trouble I give you, and am

Your very grateful and obedient humble servant

Hor. Walpole

To James Bindley, Friday 7 September 1781

Printed from a copy in an unidentified hand on paper watermarked 1833, now wsl. First printed, Toynbee *Supp.* i. 281. The copy was owned by Frank T. Sabin in 1918; acquired from Gabriel Wells by wsl, July 1932. The original letter is missing.

Strawberry Hill, September 7, 1781.

IT is very true, Sir, that I am forced to confine the number of spectators of my house to four, and I have given such offence on one hand by exceptions, and have had such liberties taken on the other by some whom I have indulged, that I have often been on the point of declaring that I will on no account make any exception.[1] I am very glad, Sir, not to have done so, as it is still in my power to oblige you, to whom I am so much obliged,[2] and as your request is so

---

I applied to Mr Manager Harris, it came out that the Hibernian trustee [Malone] had originally engaged the play to him, and when Mr Harris complained of the breach of promise, he was not softened by the too zealous friend. There had been twenty other mismanagements, and Mr Harris would not hear the play named' (HW to Lady Ossory 26 Oct. 1781 Ossory ii. 301). See HW to Henderson *post* 15 Oct. 1781.

3. Harris's letter to HW is missing.

4. Drury Lane opened its season on 15 September, Covent Garden on the 17th (*London Stage* Pt V, i. 461).

---

1. Three years later HW printed a page of rules for visiting SH. One of the rules stated: 'As Mr. Walpole has given of-

fence by sometimes enlarging the number of four, and refusing that latitude to others, he flatters himself that for the future nobody will take it ill that he strictly confines the number; as whoever desires him to break his rule, does in effect expect him to disoblige others, which is what nobody has a right to desire of him.' See Berry ii. 219–20; Hazen, *SH Bibl.* 225–9.

2. Doubtless for various antiquarian information, such as a fourteen-line poem headed by HW 'Fragment 1775' that begins 'Love tunes the youthful poet's lyre.' In his 'Book of Materials,' 1771, p. 45, HW noted that 'Mr Bindley has this piece which I never saw before; (he gave it to me).'

very reasonable, I therefore enclose a card as you desired for *five*, but hope it will be used as soon as it can be conveniently; I mean for the sake of your friends, that they may see my house in order, for this month is the time when I take down the small pictures and curiosities, and pack them up against damp weather, and as I am going further into the country, they will be removed this year sooner than ordinary.³ I will own to you, Sir, that I am glad to close the showing of my house at Michaelmas, for I am so near London, and so much nearer Hampton Court,⁴ that the resort of visitors is very inconvenient, and I can get a month's quiet by this regulation, though it is a real pleasure to me when my house can give any satisfaction to my friends, in which number I am proud to reckon you, and am with great regard

Your grateful humble servant

Hor. Walpole

To John Henderson, Monday 15 October 1781

Printed from a copy of the MS in the possession of Mr Martin Heath, Ashton House, Worton, Devizes, Wilts, kindly supplied by the late Roland Heath. First printed, Cunningham viii. 91. Reprinted, Toynbee xii. 65 (salutation omitted in Cunningham and Toynbee). For the history of the MS see *ante* 16 April 1781.
Address: To Mr Henderson in Buckingham Street, London.

Strawberry Hill, Oct. 15, 1781.

Dear Sir,

I AM distressed, and know not whither to apply but to you, who I doubt will repent your facility in getting me out of difficulties. If I am not modest, I am at least too conscientious to press the favour I am going to ask, if you do not care to undertake it, or shall hold it imprudent. Mr Harris seems to have forgotten, or chooses to defer, his promise of calling on me.¹ Mr Jephson, I doubt, will be very impatient, and suspect me of carelessness in not having delivered his letter—and yet I am sure it would have better effect, if I heard

---

3. HW left SH 11 Oct. to visit Henry Conway at Park Place in Berkshire, although he had originally proposed going there on 23 Sept. (Conway iii. 384–5 and n. 6).

4. SH is about 11 miles SW of Hyde Park Corner, and about 4 miles north of Hampton Court.

---

1. See *ante* 26 August 1781.

Mr Harris's complaints before I deliver it. I must be in town on Thursday[2] for a day or two. Would it be possible to let Mr Harris know so, that he might call on me in Berkeley Square on Friday morning? Would it look too much like a plot, if you told him so? I truly wish to serve Mr Jephson, and yet I fear, totally innocent as I am, that blame will fall on me, if the play is not acted this winter.[3] You, who are well acquainted with authors and managers, know what jealous waspish folks both branches of those allied families are. You, who are our cousin,[4] have a cross of good humour, that is singularly unlike the rest of our kin. It will make you forgive

Your affectionate relation

Hor. Walpole

To Thomas Pennant, Monday 15 October 1781

Printed for the first time from the MS now wsl, purchased in Dec. 1948 from Henry Stevens, Son and Stiles; its previous history is not known.
Address: To Thomas Pennant Esq. at Downing, Flintshire. *Postmark:* ISLE-WORTH. 15 OC. 16 OC.

Strawberry Hill, Oct. 15, 1781.

I HAVE been absent for a few days at Park Place,[1] Sir, which prevented my answering the favour of your letter[2] so soon as I ought to have done; but I chose to stay till I could consult my notebook,[3] and thence give you more satisfactory answers.

I do not remember a portrait of the famous Countess of Carlisle[4]

2. HW did 'come to town' on Thursday, 18 Oct. (Mann ix. 193).

3. HW wrote Lady Ossory 26 Oct. 1781 that 'in two days [I] so softened the majesty of Covent Garden [Harris], that he has not only engaged to act the tragedy, but by the beginning of December, when my utmost hopes did not expect to see it before spring' (Ossory ii. 301). Anthony Morris Storer wrote to HW's friend George Selwyn 28 Oct.: 'I met Mr Jephson, who mentioned Mr Walpole's name with great respect—you may tell him so, because as Mr Walpole has undertaken to get Mr Jephson's play upon the stage (a very great favour on Mr W's part to him); it may be some service to Mr Jephson to

let him know, how much Mr Jephson is obliged to him for it—and with how much gratitude and respect he spoke of him '(MS now wsl).

4. By virtue of his being an actor.

———

1. Park Place, near Henley, Berks, the seat of Henry Conway. HW left SH to visit him there 11 Oct. (Mason ii. 161).

2. Missing.

3. His 'Book of Materials,' 1759 (now wsl), in which HW recorded his visits to country seats.

4. Lady Lucy Percy (ca 1600–60), m. (1617), as his second wife, James Hay (ca 1580–1636), cr. (1622) E. of Carlisle.

at Woburn, nor do I find one mentioned in my notes.[5] I have one of her in a double picture with her sister Lady Leicester[6] by Vandyck, from Penshurst;[7] and Lord Dysart[8] has at Ham the one[9] from which there is a print by Lombart.[10]

The Earl of Pembroke[11] who wrote poems on, and dedicated them to, Christiana Countess of Devonshire,[12] was the Lord Chamberlain, of whom Lord Clarendon has so admirably drawn the character,[13] and who was the elder brother of the remarkable Earl Philip,[14] of whom there is the famous family piece at Wilton.[15] The poems are a thin small quarto printed in 1660, with responses by Sir Benjamin Ruddier,[16] and other poems by both, on other subjects. I have that book,[17] which is extremely scarce. There is wit and ease in several, but a great want of correction, and often of harmony: I think the following by Lord Pembroke is one of the least faulty:

That he would not be beloved.[18]

Disdain me still, that I may ever love,
For who his love enjoys can love no more:
The war once past, with peace men cowards prove,
And ships return'd do rot upon the shore.

5. See *ante* 25 May 1773, n. 9.

6. Lady Dorothy Percy (1598–1659), m. (ca 1615) Robert Sidney, 2d E. of Leicester, 1626.

7. Penshurst Place, Kent, the seat of the Sidney family. Van Dyck's double portrait of Lady Carlisle and her sister was purchased by HW at Lady Yonge's sale 10 May 1764; see Montagu ii. 123 and n. 4.

8. Lionel Tollemache (1734–99), styled Lord Huntingtower; 5th E. of Dysart, 1770.

9. In his notes on Ham House, Lord Dysart's seat, which he visited 10 June 1770, HW mentions 'In the gallery, many Vandycks or after him, and Lelys. Countess of Carlisle crowned with a chaplet' (*Country Seats* 67). See Montagu ii. 306.

10. Pierre Lombart (ca 1613–82), French engraver who worked in England. The engraving is described in *BM Cat. of Engraved British Portraits* i. 341; it is one in the series known as 'The Countesses,' after portraits by Van Dyck.

11. William Herbert (1580–1630), 3d E. of Pembroke, 1601; lord chamberlain 1615–26.

12. Christian Bruce (1595–1675), m. (1608) William Cavendish, 2d E. of Devonshire, 1626.

13. Clarendon describes Pembroke as 'the most universally beloved and esteemed of any man of that age'; see *The History of the Rebellion and Civil Wars in England,* Oxford, 1707, i. 44–6. HW's copy (untraced) is Hazen, *Cat. of HW's Lib.,* No. 41. See also HW's *Royal and Noble Authors,* 2d edn, 1759, i. 192–4.

14. Philip Herbert (1584–1650), cr. (1605) E. of Montgomery; 4th E. of Pembroke, 1630.

15. Van Dyck's painting (11 x 17 feet) is fully documented in Sidney, 16th Earl of Pembroke, *A Catalogue of the Paintings and Drawings in the Collection at Wilton House,* 1968, pp. 58–60, No. 158.

16. Sir Benjamin Rudyerd (1572–1658), Kt, 1618; M.P.

17. *Poems . . . Many of which Are Answered by Way of Repartee, by Sir Benjamin Ruddier, Knight,* ed. John Donne the younger, 1660, 8vo. HW's copy, now in the Huntington Library, is Hazen, op. cit., No. 207.

18. Pembroke's *Poems,* p. 5. The title is apparently HW's.

Then tho' thou frown, I'll say thou art most fair,
And still I'll love, tho' still I must despair.
As heat[19] to life, so is desire to love,
For these once quench'd, both life and love are done.
Let not my sighs nor tears thy virtue move;
Like basest metals[20] do not melt too soon.
Laugh at my woes, although I ever mourn;
Love surfeits with rewards;[21] his nurse is scorn.[22]

I think, but am not sure, that Dr Donne has celebrated the same lady.[23]

I remember the name of Mrs Lawson[24] as a beauty in the reign of Charles II, but know not a single anecdote of her.

The large emblematic picture of the Duchess of Bedford[25] consigning her daughter the present Duchess of Marlborough[26] to Minerva and the Graces, or Muses, I forget which, to be educated,[27] was painted by Hamilton,[28] who is, I believe, settled at Rome, and who has published a volume of prints from the works of capital painters.[29]

I am glad, Sir, your volume[30] is so well advanced, and if I can contribute any more such slight notices as these, I beg you will not scruple commanding

Your most obedient and obliged humble servant

HOR. WALPOLE

19. The text in *Poems* reads 'heat's.'
20. 'mettle' in *Poems*.
21. 'reward' in *Poems*.
22. Pennant quotes the poem along with HW's comment 'There is wit . . . least faulty' in *The Journey from Chester to London*, 1782, pp. 374–5. He adds in a footnote (p. 374): 'Communicated to me by Mr Walpole; who is in possession of this very scarce book: a thin small quarto, published in 1660. It consists of the Earl's poems, and responses by Sir Benjamin Ruddier; and other poems, by both, on other subjects.'
23. Not so; HW is perhaps thinking of Donne's verse epistles addressed to Lucy, Countess of Bedford.
24. Possibly Abigail Lawson (fl. 1691–1705), actress, who was first a member of the United Company and later of Thomas Betterton's Company in Lincoln's Inn Fields.
25. Hon. Gertrude Leveson Gower (1715–94), m. (1737), as his second wife,

John Russell, 4th D. of Bedford, 1732.
26. Lady Caroline Russell (1743–1811), m. (1762) George Spencer, 3d D. of Marlborough, 1758.
27. 'A large picture by Hamilton of Gertrude, second wife of Duke John, presenting their daughter Caroline to Minerva, the arts and Graces, to be instructed. The painting very moderate; some of the airs, good' (HW's note in *Country Seats* 18). See *The Journey from Chester to London*, p. 352.
28. Gavin Hamilton (1723–98), Scottish painter and art agent resident in Rome.
29. *Schola Italica picturae*, Rome, 1773, folio, containing 40 engraved plates. HW's copy (untraced) is Hazen, op. cit., No. 3571.
30. *The Journey from Chester to London*, published in 1782. See OSSORY iii. 121–2. HW's copy (untraced), part of a nine-volume collection of Pennant's works, is Hazen, op. cit., No. 547.

[?Enclosure][31]

The Queen of Arragon who Sir Hugh Calveley[32] married was probably Sibylla Fortia,[33] fourth queen of Pedro IV King of Arragon, who died in 1388. John of Gaunt[34] went to Spain in 1386 in pursuit of his claim to the crown of Castile, and returned thence in 1388. Sir Hugh was probably of that expedition,[35] and might remain there after the Duke, liking or being liked by Queen Sibylla just then become a widow. Nor had she been of superior rank to him, for Anderson in his genealogic tables p. 457,[36] says that when she married the King, she was widow of Artol de Fosses. The change in her fortune on the King's death might also reduce her to be glad of accepting Sir Hugh's hand, for Père D'Orleans in his history of Spain[37] vol. 2. p. 386, says, that on Pedro's death she was imprisoned, being accused of having given the old King potions, to make him love her. The historian says that the new monarch[38] left her but barely enough to live on: she was however allowed to bewail in repose the change of her fortune; and it was then probably that she married Sir Hugh

31. The following note in HW's hand appears on one side of a leaf that apparently has been torn from its conjugate leaf. An endorsement in Pennant's hand at the bottom of the leaf reads: 'From Horace Walpole Earl of Orford—'. Although the note is written on paper having the same watermark as that of the letter to Pennant 15 Oct. 1781 and was preserved with that letter when acquired by WSL in 1948, it appears to have been written at a different time, or with a different pen. The present letter makes no reference to any enclosure. It has seemed best to print the note here as a possible enclosure, indicating that its date remains conjectural.

32. Sir Hugh Calveley (d. 1393), soldier and adventurer. Pennant wrote of him in The Journey from Chester to London, p. 17: 'History gives him a royal consort, in reward of his valour, and marries him to the Queen of Arragon. If at this period he took a most antiquated piece of royalty; for I can find no other dowager of that kingdom, unless Leonora, relict of Alonso IV who became a widow in 1335, was then alive.' Citing other evidence, Pennant rejected HW's suggestion that

Calveley was married to Sibilia de Forciá.

33. Sibilia (or Sibilla) de Forciá (d. 1406), m. 1 Artal de Foces; m. 2 (1377) Pedro IV (1319–87), K. of Aragon 1336–87 (Isenburg, Stammtafeln, II, taf. 45; Diccionario de historia de España, 2d edn, Madrid, 1969, iii. 658–9).

34. John (1340–99) of Gaunt, cr. (1362) D. of Lancaster.

35. John of Gaunt set out for Spain on 7 July 1386 and returned to England in Nov. 1389. Calveley's missions to foreign countries occurred earlier. Froissart's Chronicles records that Calveley and Lancaster fought together under Sir John Chandos at the Battle of Navarete in 1367 (DNB iii. 714, x. 855, 862).

36. See James Anderson (?1680–1739), Royal Genealogies: or, The Genealogical Tables of Emperors, Kings, and Princes, 1732, table 457, p. 706. HW's copy (untraced) is Hazen, op. cit., No. 558.

37. Pierre-Joseph Dorléans (1641–98), Histoire des révolutions d'Espagne, 3 vols, 1734. HW's (untraced) copy is Hazen, op. cit., No. 3358.

38. John I (1350–95), K. of Aragon 1387–95 (Isenburg, loc. cit.).

Calveley.[39] King in his *Vale Royal*[40] says that King James I knighted Sir George Calveley[41] in consideration of his nobel descent.[42]

To Elizabeth Younge,[1] Monday 22 October 1781

Printed from the MS now WSL. First printed, *European Magazine*, 1797, xxxi. 236–7. Reprinted, Toynbee *Supp.* i. 282–3. The MS is untraced until sold Puttick and Simpson 15 Dec. 1849 (James Winston Sale), lot 844, to Holloway; offered by Maggs, Cat. Nos 299 (Nov. 1912), lot 4213; 317 (Nov.–Dec. 1913), lot 3696; 333 (spring 1915), lot 434; 360 (autumn 1917), lot 2342; 381 (autumn 1919), lot 2218; 417 (Christmas 1921), lot 3253; 457 (1924), lot 3061; and 488 (spring 1927), lot 632; later purchased by Alvin J. Scheuer, New York, and offered by him, Cat. No. 6 (1931), lot 2709; sold by him to Arthur Pforzheimer, of New York; acquired from Pforzheimer, in a collection of autographs, by Goodspeed, who sold it to WSL, Aug. 1949.

Endorsed in an unidentified hand: Letter from Lord Orford to Miss Young.

Strawberry Hill, Oct. 22, 1781.

IT will, I fear, seem impertinent in an absolute stranger, Madam, to take the liberty of asking a favour of you, nor should I use so much freedom, if I were not persuaded that whoever contributes to calling forth your great powers for the stage, does at once serve your talents and the public. Mr Jephson who has long been my friend, and who has proved himself so by making a rational and interesting tragedy[2] out of my wild *Castle of Otranto*, cannot bring it on the stage to advantage, unless you, Madam, will be pleased to appear in the character of Hortensia, the wife of the Count of Narbonne. Mr Jephson has made her a very sublime character, and improved on my sketch by making her a more natural one in giving her jealousy, and thence forming a fine contrast between her piety and that disordering passion. The other female character[3] is one very com-

39. The marriage, though mentioned in Fuller's *Worthies of England*, seems never to have taken place (DNB iii. 715).

40. Daniel King, *The Vale-Royall of England, or, The County Palatine of Chester Illustrated*, 1656, Book II, p. 53. HW's copy (untraced) is Hazen, op. cit., No. 628.

41. He was knighted at his own house, Leigh Hall, near Alford, 23 Aug. 1617 (W. A. Shaw, *The Knights of England*, 1906, ii. 165).

42. A similar note on Sir Hugh Calveley and Sibilia de Forciá appears in HW's 'Book of Materials,' 1771, p. 47.

1. (ca 1744–97), m. (1785) Alexander Pope (1763–1835), actor and painter; actress.

2. *The Count of Narbonne.*

3. Adelaide, daughter of the Count and Countess of Narbonne.

mon in plays, and that admits of none of the violent transitions, which only such a capital actress as you, Madam, are capable of displaying. The daughter is a simple tender maid, bred up in ignorance and devotion, and demands nothing but plaintive innocent tones. Mrs Crauford[4] declined the mother's part, but I believe from resentment on her husband's[5] account, whom Mr Jephson had undervalued. I will not suspect that she had the weakness of preferring the daughter's part for its youth, because she must know the world too well not to be sensible that nothing makes the middle age[6] so apparent, as appearing in too juvenile a light.

If I am not much mistaken, Madam, when you hear the play read, you will be struck with the opportunities that the Countess's part will give you of exerting the variety of your abilities. Devotion and jealousy contrasted are not all—there is conjugal and maternal tenderness too, very different shades, as you know, Madam; there is sovereign dignity, and the philosophic command of pride in wishing to waive that dignity—but unless I were as great a master of the stage as you are a mistress, Madam, I could not describe half that you will call out from the part; and I will trust to your good sense more than to my own rhetoric for the part's making an impression on you.[7] I am with great respect, Madam,

Your most obedient humble servant

HOR. WALPOLE

4. See ante 13 July 1777, n. 2.

5. Thomas Crawford (1750–94), actor. 'When the Count of Narbonne was first acted at Dublin [in the spring of 1782], it was extremely profitable to Daly; and [John Philip] Kemble greatly distinguished himself in the Count—at the rival theatre, Clinch and Crawford played the Count and Theodore—Mrs Crawford, who should certainly from her age have represented the Countess, to the astonishment of everybody, chose to act Adelaide, solely for the purpose of playing the love scenes with her husband' (John Genest, Some Account of the English Stage, Bath, 1832, vi. 222–3; see also James Boaden, Memoirs of the Life of John Philip Kemble, Esq., 1825, i. 39–40).

6. Mrs Crawford was then forty-seven.

7. 'Miss Young refused the part of the mother, because, as she said, Mrs Crau-

ford had refused it. Mr Harris begged me to write to Miss Young. I did, and to turn aside what I guessed to be the real motive of the refusal, I told her, I would not suspect that Mrs Crauford declined the part from preferring that of the daughter, because Mrs Crauford must know the world too well not to be aware that when a gentlewoman of middle age appears in a very juvenile part, it does but make that middle age more apparent. There was so much sugar strewed over this indirect truth, that even there I have succeeded too, and Miss Young has complied. I am to attend rehearsals, and give advice on scenes, dresses etc., and so must be frequently in town' (HW to Lady Ossory 26 Oct. 1781, OSSORY ii. 302). Miss Younge's reply, mentioned in HW's letter to Jephson post 7 Nov. 1781, is missing.

To John Nichols, Wednesday 31 October 1781

Printed from the MS now wsl. First printed, Nichols, *Lit. Anec.* viii. 436–8. Reprinted, Wright vi. 138–40; Cunningham viii. 99–101 (text incomplete in Wright and Cunningham; see n. 23 below); Toynbee xii. 77–80. The MS was sold Sotheby's 27 Feb. 1882 (Valuable Collection of Autograph Letters Sale), lot 85, to Thibaudeau; *penes* Mrs Alfred Morrison in 1904; resold Sotheby's 9 Dec. 1918 (Morrison Sale, Part III), lot 1908, to Maggs; offered by them, Cat. Nos 376 (spring 1919), lot 822, and 411 (autumn 1921), lot 2413; later owned by George A. Gaskill, of Worcester, Massachusetts, who sold it to wsl, Dec. 1939.

Strawberry Hill, Oct. 31, 1781.

I AM glad to hear,[1] Sir, that your account of Hogarth[2] calls for another edition; and I am very sensible of your great civility in offering to change any passages that criticize my own work.[3] Though I am much obliged by the offer, I should blush to myself if I even wished for that complaisance. Good God! Sir, what am I, that I should be offended at or above criticism or correction? I do not know who ought to be—I am sure, no author. I am a private man, of no consequence, and at best an author of very moderate abilities. In a work that comprehends so much biography as my *Anecdotes of Painting,* it would have been impossible, even with much more diligence than I employed, not to make numberless mistakes. It is kind to me to point out those errors; to the world it is justice. Nor have I reason to be displeased even with the manner. I do remember that in many passages you have been very civil to me.[4] I do not recollect any harsh phrases.

1. Nichols's letter of 27 Oct. to HW was offered by Thorpe, Catalogue of Autograph Letters, 1843, lot 2766; not further traced.

2. *Biographical Anecdotes of William Hogarth,* published ca 26 June 1781 (*St James's Chronicle* 26–8 June 1781). The critical remarks were provided by George Steevens, the theatrical anecdotes by Isaac Reed. HW's copiously annotated copy, now wsl, is Hazen, *Cat. of HW's Lib.,* No. 2435.

3. HW's chapter on Hogarth in the fourth volume of *Anecdotes of Painting,* pp. 68–89 (printed in 1771, published in 1780).

4. For example, Nichols writes in *Bio-*

graphical Anecdotes, p. 39: 'On this occasion, though I may be found to differ from Mr Walpole, I am ready to confess how much regard is due to the opinions of a gentleman whose mind has been long exercised on a subject which is almost new to me; especially when I recollect that my present researches would have had no guide, but for the lights held out in the last volume of the *Anecdotes of Painting in England.*' HW wrote Cole 16 June 1781 that Nichols had been 'much civiller to living me than to dead Hogarth. . . . Nay, in general I have gentler treatment than I expected, and I think the world and I part good friends' (Cole ii. 273).

As my work is partly critical as well as biographic, there too I had no reason or right to expect deference to my opinions. Criticism, I doubt, has no very certain rule to go by; in matters of taste it is a still more vague and arbitrary science.

As I am very sincere, Sir, in what I say, I will with the same ingenuity own that in one or two places of your book I think the criticisms on me are not well founded. For instance, in p. 37. I am told that Hogarth did not deserve the compliment I pay him[5] of not descending to the indelicacy of the Flemish and Dutch painters.[6] It is very true that you have produced some instances to which I had not adverted, where he has been guilty of the same fault, though I think not in all you allege, nor to the degree alleged; in some I think the humour compensates for the indelicacy, which is never the case with the Dutch; and in one particularly I think it is a merit, I mean in the burlesque *Paul before Felix*,[7] for there, Sir, you should recollect that Hogarth himself meant to satirize not to imitate the painters of Holland and Flanders.[8]

You have also instanced, Sir, in many more portraits in his satiric prints than come within my defence of him as not being a personal satirist—but in those too with submission I think you have gone too far as, though you have cited *portraits*, are they all satiric? Sir John Gonson[9] is the image of an active magistrate identified, but is not ridiculous, unless to be an active magistrate is being ridiculous. Mr Pine,[10] I think, you allow, desired to sit for the fat friar in the *Gates of Calais*[11]—certainly not with a view to being turned into derision.

---

5. *Anecdotes of Painting* iv. 69 and n.

6. 'Mr Walpole . . . is willing to expose the indelicacy of the Flemish painters, by comparing it with the purity of Hogarth. . . . Shall we proceed to examine whether the scenes painted by our countryman are wholly free from the same indelicacies?' (*Biographical Anecdotes*, p. 36).

7. 'In the burlesque *Paul before Felix*, when the High Priest applies his fingers to his nose, we have reason to imagine that his manœuvre was in consequence of some offensive escape during the terrors of the proconsul of Judæa, who, as he is here represented, conveys no imperfect image of our late Lord Mayor, at the time of the riots in London. Can any man be

said to have discountenanced an idea which he keeps alive by imitation?' (ibid. 37). HW wrote in the margin of his copy: 'This is an unlucky criticism, for the print is a ridicule of Dutch painters.'

8. See *Anecdotes of Painting, Works* iii. 454n.

9. (d. 1765), Kt, 1722; J.P. and chairman of the Westminster Quarter Sessions. Gonson was known for his zealous apprehension of prostitutes, and he is so depicted in plate 3 of *A Harlot's Progress*.

10. John Pine (1690–1756), engraver, called 'Friar Pine' after Hogarth had introduced a portrait of him as a French friar in *The Gate of Calais, or the Roast Beef of Old England*.

11. 'Mr Pine the engraver sat for the

With regard to *the bloody fingers* of Sigismonda,[12] you say, Sir, that my memory must have failed me, as you affirm that they *are* unstained with blood.[13] Forgive me if I say that I am positive that they were so originally. I saw them so, and have often mentioned that fact.[14] Recollect, Sir, that you yourself allow p. 46. in the note, that that picture was continually *altered upon the criticism of one connoisseur or another*.[15] May not my memory be more faithful about so striking a circumstance than the memory of another who would engage to recollect all the changes that remarkable picture underwent?

I should be very happy, Sir, if I could contribute any additional lights to your new publication. Indeed what additional lights I have gained are from your work, which has furnished me with many. I am going to publish a new edition of all the five volumes of my *Anecdotes of Painting*,[16] in which I shall certainly insert what I have gathered from you. This edition will be in five thin octavos, without cuts, to make the purchase easy to artists, and such as cannot afford the quartos, which are grown so extravagantly dear that I am ashamed of it.[17] Being published too at different periods,[18] and being many of them cut to pieces for the heads, since the rage for portraits has been

portrait of the Friar' (*Biographical Anecdotes*, p. 110). In his revision of *Anecdotes of Painting*, 1782, HW noted that 'some of the instances adduced [by Nichols] were by no means caricaturas. Sir John Gonson and Dr Misaubin in *The Harlot's Progress* were rather examples identified than satires. Others, as Mr Pine's, were mere portraits, introduced by their own desire; or with their consent' (*Works* iii. 455n). See DALRYMPLE 142 and n. 3.

12. Painted in 1759, first exhibited in 1761; now in the Tate Gallery. In the picture Sigismunda is shown weeping over the heart of her lover Guiscardo. For HW's opinion of it in 1761 see MONTAGU i. 365.

13. 'On the authority of repeated inspection, I venture to affirm, that the fingers of Sigismunda are unstained with blood, and that neither of her hands is employed in rending ornaments from her head, or any other part of her person. In this instance Mr Walpole's memory must have failed him, as I am confident that his misrepresentation [in *Anecdotes* iv. 78] was undesigned' (*Biographical Anecdotes*, p. 43n). HW wrote in the margin of his

copy: 'It was so represented at first. Hogarth might correct or alter it, on its being so much censured, as it was before his death, as appears from this very note. In p. 46 he owns it was altered.'

14. See, for example, the letter cited in n. 12 above.

15. Nichols quotes 'an old and intimate friend of Mr Hogarth, who has been applied to for information.'

16. 'The third edition, with additions' (vol. iv, 'Second edition') was published in 5 vols, 8vo, in 1782 (Hazen, *SH Bibl.* 65).

17. 'I am ashamed at the price of my books, though not my fault—but I have too often been guilty myself of giving ridiculous prices for rarities, though of no intrinsic value, that I must not condemn the same folly in others' (HW to Cole 7 Aug. 1781, COLE ii. 284).

18. The first two volumes of *Anecdotes of Painting* were published in Feb. 1762, vol. iii and the *Catalogue of Engravers* in Feb. 1764; vol. iv, though printed in 1771, was not published until 1780 (Hazen, *SH Bibl.* 55, 63).

carried so far, it is very rare to meet with a complete set. My corrected copy is now in the printer's hands, except the last volume in which are my additions to Hogarth from your list, and perhaps one or two more, but that volume also I have left in town; though not at the printer's,[19] as to complete it I must wait for his new works which Mrs Hogarth is to publish.[20] When I am settled in town, Sir, which probably will be[21] by the end of next month, I shall be very ready, if you please to call on me in Berkeley Square,[22] to communicate any additions I have made to my account of Hogarth.[23] One or two trifles I have inserted in the margin of your account, which I will now mention, though scarcely worth your adopting.

P. 84. of yours.[24] It is impossible Henry VIII and Anna Boleyn could be meant for portraits of the late Prince[25] and Miss Vane.[26] The stature and faces of both are totally unlike.[27] You ask, Sir, where the picture is or was. It was at Vauxhall in the portico of the old great room on the right hand as you enter the garden. I remember it there.[28]

P. 147. last line.[29] There never was a *Duke* of Kendal, but an infant son of James II.[30] The arms engraved were certainly those of the *Duchess* of Kendal,[31] and the same with those I have in a lozenge. It must have been a mistake, if written Duke, or in a male shield.

19. The title-page of the third edition reads, 'Printed for J. Dodsley, Pallmall. 1782.'

20. HW apparently decided not to wait: the third edition of the *Anecdotes* was published in May 1782, while the new edition of Hogarth's prints was not announced for sale until 27 Jan. 1783 (COLE ii. 319 n. 2; Ronald Paulson, *Hogarth's Graphic Works*, rev. edn, New Haven, 1970, i. 70–1).

21. The MS reads 'me.'

22. There is no record of a meeting.

23. The rest of the letter is omitted in Wright and Cunningham.

24. 'King Henry the Eighth, and Anna Bullen. . . . This plate is supposed to contain the portraits of Frederick Prince of Wales and Miss Vane; . . . Query, for what purpose was the picture painted, and where is it?' (*Biographical Anecdotes*, pp. 84–5). Opposite 'Frederick . . . Miss Vane' HW wrote in his copy 'Certainly not.' Opposite 'where is it?' he wrote 'at Vauxhall.'

25. Frederick Louis (1707–51), P. of Wales.

26. Hon. Anne Vane (1705–36), eldest dau. of the 2nd Bn Barnard; mistress of Frederick, P. of Wales.

27. Nichols was probably confusing Hogarth's engraving with a satiric print of 1736, adapted from Hogarth's composition, in which the Prince and Anne Vane are represented (Paulson, op. cit. i. 139).

28. What HW saw at Vauxhall may have been a copy (ibid. i. 137).

29. 'Arms of a Duke of Kendal' (*Biographical Anecdotes*, p. 147). HW noted in his copy, 'There never was a Duke of Kendal, but an infant son of James II, when Duke of York.'

30. Charles Stuart (1666–7), D. of Kendal.

31. Ermengarde Melusina (1667–1743), Bns von der Schulenburg, cr. (1719) Ds of Kendal; George I's mistress. See Paulson, op. cit. i. 98–9.

P. 148.[32] The print of Monticelli,[33] Cuzzoni[34] and Heydeggre,[35] if etched by him, was not designed by him, but by the last Countess of Burlington;[36] nor is it Monticelli, but Farinelli.[37] Monticelli was not in England till many years after the Cuzzoni.[38]

I do not at present recollect anything more that can be of use to you,[39] and am

Sir

Your obliged and obedient humble servant

HOR. WALPOLE

32. 'Monticelli, Cuzzoni, and Heydegger; the same which has been mentioned under a title a little different in p. 75' (Biographical Anecdotes, p. 148). 'A scene in an opera, with Farinelli, Cuzzoni, and Senesino, singing. The plate of it is preserved. . . . Mr [Charles] Rogers has an etching of Farinelli and Cuzzoni singing a duet. Heidegger sits behind. Farinelli is in the character of a prisoner, being chained by his little finger' (ibid. 75-6). HW noted in his copy: 'This is certainly from a drawing by Lady Burlington, and not by Hogarth.'

33. Angelo Maria Monticelli (ca 1710-64), Italian castrato opera singer (MANN i. 141 n. 7).

34. Francesca Cuzzoni (1700-70), m. (ca 1723) ——— Sandoni; Italian soprano singer (ibid. i. 359 n. 48).

35. John James Heidegger (ca 1659-1749), opera impresario and manager of the Haymarket Theatre (ibid. vii. 271 n. 11).

36. Lady Dorothy Savile (1699-1758), m. (1721) Richard Boyle, 3d E. of Burlington. She was an amateur artist, and a drawing by her was pasted by HW in his Collection of Prints, Engraved by Various Persons of Quality, now WSL (Hazen, Cat. of HW's Lib., No. 3588).

37. Carlo Broschi (1705-82), called Farinelli; Italian castrato singer (MANN i. 190 n. 4). He appears in plate 2 of A Rake's Progress.

38. Cuzzoni arrived in England for the first time ca 1723, Farinelli in 1734 (Grove's Dictionary of Music and Musicians, 5th edn, ed. Eric Blom, 1954, ii. 568, iii. 24). Monticelli arrived in Sept. 1741 on the same boat with HW, who was returning from the Grand Tour (MANN i. 141). The print in question was possibly a reissue of the third state of Berenstadt, Cuzzoni, and Senesino, with the altered inscription Farinelli, Cuzzoni, Senesino. In the second edition of the Biographical Anecdotes, 1782, p. 346, Nichols states that the print was etched by Joseph Goupy. It was probably not the work of Hogarth, but rather John Vanderbank (Paulson, op. cit. i. 294-5).

39. Nichols incorporated all of HW's specific criticisms in the second edition of the Biographical Anecdotes, pp. 29, 54, 62, 146-7, 235-6, 330, 346. See also Albert Smith, 'Nichols' Anecdotes of Hogarth,' N&Q 1957, ccii. 352-3.

To Robert Jephson, Wednesday 7 November 1781

Printed from the MS now WSL. First printed, Wright vi. 140–2. Reprinted, Cunningham viii. 104–6; Toynbee xii. 84–7 (closing and signature omitted in Wright, Cunningham, and Toynbee). For the history of the MS see *ante* 15 March 1763.

Berkeley Square, Nov. 7, 1781.

YESTERDAY, Sir, I received the favour of your letter with the enclosed prologue,[1] and am extremely pleased with it, not only as it omits mention of me, for which I give you my warmest thanks, but as a composition. The thoughts are just and happily expressed, and the conclusion is so lively and well conceived, that Mr Harris, to whom I carried it this morning, thinks it will have great effect. We are very sorry you have not sent us an epilogue too—but before I touch on that, I will be more regular in my details.

Miss Yonge has accepted the part[2] very gracefully, and by a letter[3] I have received from her in answer to mine,[4] will I flatter myself take care to do justice to it. Nay, she is so zealous, that Mr Harris tells me she has taken great pains with the young person[5] who is to play the daughter,[6] but whose name I cannot at this moment recollect.

I must now confess that I have been again alarmed. I had a message[7] from Mr Harris on Saturday last to tell me that the performers had been so alert and were so ready with their parts, and the many disappointments that had happened this season had been so prejudicial to him,[8] that it would be easy and necessary to bring out your play next Saturday the 10th and desired to have the prologue and epilogue. This precipitation made me apprehend that justice would not be done to your tragedy. Still I did not dare to remonstrate; nor would venture to damp an ardour which I could not expect to excite again. Instead of objecting to his haste, I only

1. Both missing. Jephson's prologue to *The Count of Narbonne* was printed with the play in 1781 and also in GM 1782, lii. 36.

2. Of Hortensia, Countess of Narbonne.

3. Missing.

4. *Ante* 22 Oct. 1781.

5. Elizabeth Satchell (1763–1841), m. (1783) Stephen Kemble; actress.

6. Adelaide.

7. Missing.

8. It is not known what Harris's 'disappointments' consisted of. During the 1780–1 season, the receipts at Covent Garden, under his management, were on almost every night greater than those at Drury Lane (*London Stage* Pt V, i. 361).

said I had not received your prologue and epilogue, but had written for them and expected them every minute, though as it depended on winds, one could never be sure. I trusted to accidents for delay;[9] at least I thought I could contrive some, without seeming to combat what he thought for his interest.

I have not been mistaken. On receiving your prologue yesterday, I came to town today and carried it to him, to show him I lost no time. He told me Mr Henderson was not enough recovered, but he hoped would be well enough to bring out the play on Saturday se'nnight.[10] That he had had a rough rehearsal yesterday morning with which he had been charmed, and was persuaded, and that the performers think so too, that your play will have great effect. All this made me very easy. There is to be a regular rehearsal on Saturday, for which I shall stay in town on purpose;[11] and if I find the performers perfect, I think there will [be] no objection to its appearance on Saturday se'nnight. I shall rather prefer that day to a later, as the Parliament not being met,[12] it will have a week's run before politics interfere.

Now, Sir, for the epilogue. I have taken the liberty of desiring Mr Harris to have one prepared,[13] in case yours should not arrive in time.[14] It is a compliment to him (I do not mean that he will write it himself) will interest him still more in the cause; and though he may not procure a very good one, a manager may know better than we do what will suit the taste of the times. The success of a play being previous cannot be hurt by an epilogue, though some plays have been saved; and if it [be] not a good one, it will not affect you. If you send us a good one, though too late, it may be printed with the play.[15]

I must act about the impression just the reverse of what I did about the performance, and must beg you would commission some

9. 'I trusted to accidents and bore that haste. I had no sooner done so, than one of your Milesians [Edmond Malone] took fire and wrote an angry letter to Mr Harris in resentment of the precipitation' (HW to Lady Ossory 15 Nov. 1781, Ossory ii. 308).

10. The play did have its first performance on Saturday, 17 Nov. (London Stage Pt V, i. 476).

11. See following letter.

12. The second session of Parliament opened 27 Nov. 1781 (Journals of the House of Commons xxxviii. 567).

13. By Richard Jocelyn Goodenough (d. 22 Dec. 1781), author (Ossory ii. 308 n. 4). His epilogue was spoken only at the first two performances, being thereafter replaced by one written by Edmond Malone. See ibid. ii. 308 nn. 4, 5.

14. It arrived late and was not spoken. See post 21 Nov. 1781.

15. Only Malone's and Goodenough's epilogues were printed.

friend to transact that affair,[16] for I know nothing of the terms, and should probably disserve you if I undertook the treaty with the booksellers;[17] nor should I have time to supervise the correction of the press. In truth it is so disagreeable a business, that I doubt I have given proofs at my own press of being too negligent—and as I am actually at present reprinting my *Anecdotes of Painting*,[18] I have but too much business of that sort on my hands. You will forgive my saying this, especially when you consider that my hands are very lame,[19] and that this morning in Mr Harris's room, the right one shook so, that I was forced to desire him to write a memorandum for me.

I think I have omitted nothing material. Mr Wroughton[20] is to play the Count. I do not know who will speak the prologue;[21] probably not Mr Henderson, as he has been so very ill; nor should I be very earnest for it, for the Friar's is so capital and so laborious a part, that I should not wish to abate his powers by any previous exertion. Perhaps I refine too much, but I own I think the non-appearance of a principal actor till his part opens is an advantage.

I will only add that I must beg you will not talk of obligations to me.[22] You have at least overpaid me *d'avance* by the honour you have done me in adopting the *Castle of Otranto*.[23]

I am Sir

Your obedient humble servant

Hor. Walpole

16. Malone undertook this business (*post* 10 Nov. 1781).

17. Thomas Cadell. An Irish edition was published at Dublin in 1781, and another at Cork in 1782.

18. See previous letter, nn. 16, 20.

19. From the gout (*post* 10 Nov. 1781).

20. Richard Wroughton (1748–1822), actor.

21. It was spoken by Wroughton.

22. In the epilogue to be written by Jephson. A prologue written by Jephson's friend Luke Gardiner arrived too late to be used; it contained· four lines praising HW (*post* 22 Dec. 1781). This prologue was printed in the Dublin edition of the play, along with an advertisement which states that 'The story of the tragedy is taken from the *Castle of Otranto,* an admirable romance written by the Honourable Horace Walpole.'

23. The *Public Advertiser* 1 Nov. 1781 reported: 'The management of *The Count of Narbonne* is . . . under very good care: Mr Horace Walpole, with a fondness nothing less than fatherly, directs that part of the affair which respects the scenes and dresses, while Mr Henderson takes charge of the rehearsals and the casting the inferior parts. The Priest, who, in the play, is more important than in the romance, is Henderson's own part; and he is to wear a dress which is lent him from among the antiquities at Strawberry Hill.'

To Robert Jephson, Saturday 10 November 1781

Printed from the MS now WSL. First printed, Wright vi. 143–4. Reprinted, Cunningham viii. 106–7; Toynbee xii. 87–8 (closing and signature omitted in Wright, Cunningham, and Toynbee). For the history of the MS see *ante* 15 March 1763.

Address: To Robert Jephson Esq. at the Castle, Dublin. *Postmark:* 12 NO. NO 19. FREE D.

Strawberry Hill, Nov. 10, 1781.

AS I have been at the rehearsal of your tragedy[1] today, Sir, I must give you a short account of it, though I am little able to write, having a good deal of gout in my right hand, which would have kept me away from anything else, and made me hurry back hither the moment it was over, lest I should be confined in town. Mr Malone perhaps, who was at the playhouse too, may have anticipated me, for I could not save the post tonight, nor will this go till tomorrow.

Mr Henderson is still too ill to attend, but hopes to be abroad by Tuesday: Mr Hull[2] read his part very well. Miss Young is perfectly mistress of her part, is pleased with it, and I think will do it justice. I never saw her play so ably. Miss Satchell, who is to play Adelaide, is exactly what she should be: very young, pretty enough, natural and simple. She has already acted Juliet[3] with success. Her voice is not only pleasing, but very audible; and which is much more rare, very articulate: she does not gabble, as most young women do, even off the stage. Mr Wroughton much exceeded my expectation. He enters warmly into his part and with thorough zeal. Mr Lewis[4] was so very imperfect in his part, that I cannot judge quite what he will do, for he could not repeat two lines by heart; but he looked haughtily; and as he pleased me in Percy,[5] which is the same kind of character, I promise myself he will succeed in this.

Very, very few lines will be omitted; and there will be one or two verbal alterations to accommodate the disposition, but which will not appear in the printed copies, of which Mr Malone says he will take the management. As Mr Harris and the players all seemed

---

1. *The Count of Narbonne.*

2. Thomas Hull (1728–1808), actor and dramatist.

3. Her début in this Shakespearean rôle took place at Covent Garden 24 Sept. 1781 (*London Stage* Pt V, i. 463).

4. See *ante* 25 Jan. 1780, n. 18.

5. Lewis played the title rôle in Hannah More's tragedy, first performed at Covent Garden 10 Dec. 1777 (*London Stage* Pt V, i. 133). For HW's opinion of the play see OSSORY i. 404–5.

zealous and in good humour, I would not contest some trifles; and indeed they were not at all unreasonable. I am to see the scenes on Friday,[6] if I am able; and if Mr Henderson is well enough, the play will be performed on the 17th, or immediately after. Some slight delays, which one cannot foresee, may always happen. In truth I little expected so much readiness and compliance both in manager and actors; nor from all I have heard of the stage, could conceive such facilities—From the moment Mr Harris consented to perform your play, there has not been one instance of obstinacy or wrong-headedness anywhere. If the audience is as reasonable and just, you may, Sir, promise yourself complete success.[7] I am

With great regard Sir,
Your obedient humble servant

HOR. WALPOLE

To Robert Jephson, Tuesday 13 November 1781

Printed from the MS now WSL. First printed, Wright vi. 144–5. Reprinted, Cunningham viii. 107–8; Toynbee xii. 90–1 (closing and signature omitted in Wright, Cunningham, and Toynbee). For the history of the MS see *ante* 15 March 1763.

Address: To Robert Jephson Esq. at the Castle, Dublin. *Postmark:* 13 NO. ISLEWORTH. 19 NO. FREE.

Strawberry Hill, Nov. 13, 1781.

I HAVE this minute, Sir, received the corrected copy of your tragedy, which is almost all I am able to say, for I have so much gout in this hand, and it shakes so much, that I am scarce able to manage my pen. I will go to town if I can and consult Mr Henderson on the alterations, though I confess I think it dangerous to propose them so late before representation, which the papers say again is to be on Saturday if Mr H[enderson] is well enough.[1] Mr Malone shall have the corrected copy for impression.

I own I cannot suspect that Mr Sheridan will employ any un-

---

6. 'I have been at the theatre and . . . have been tumbling into trap doors, see-ing dresses tried on in the green room, and directing armour in the painting room' (HW to Lady Ossory 15 Nov. 1781, *sub* Friday [16 Nov.], ibid. ii. 310).

7. See *post* 18 Nov. 1781.

1. The *Public Advertiser* 12 Nov. re-ported that 'Mr Jephson's new tragedy . . . will certainly appear on Saturday next, if Mr Henderson should be suf-

generous arts against your play.[2] I have never heard anything to give me suspicions of his behaving unhandsomely: and as you indulge my zeal and age a liberty of speaking like a friend, I would beg you to suppress your sense of the too great prerogatives of theatric monarchs. I hope you will again and again have occasion to court the power of their crowns, and therefore, if not for your own, for the sake of the public, do not declare war with them. It has not been my practice to preach slavery; but while one deals with and depends on mimic sovereigns, I would *act* policy, especially when by temporary passive obedience one can really lay a lasting obligation on one's country, which your plays really are.

I am glad you approve what I had previously undertaken, Mr Harris's procuring an epilogue. He told me on Saturday that he should have one.[3]

You are very happy in friends, Sir, which is another proof of your merit; Mr Malone is not less zealous than Mr Tighe,[4] to whom I beg my compliments, and am, Sir,

Your most obedient humble servant

HOR. WALPOLE

ficiently recovered from his late severe indisposition, with a new prologue, epilogue, scenery and dresses.' A similar notice appeared in the *Public Advertiser* on 10 Nov.

2. See *ante* 26 Aug. 1781, n. 2. Jephson apparently feared that Sheridan, the manager of the rival theatre, might employ people to ridicule the play during the performance. See following letter.

3. See *ante* 7 Nov. 1781 and n. 13.

4. See *ante* 24 Feb. 1775, n. 9. 'The management of the *Count of Narbonne* is not with Mr Jephson's old dramatic friend Mr Tyghe, who, like all other ministerialists, is obliged to be at the roll call in the Irish House of Commons' (*Public Adv.* 1 Nov.).

To Robert Jephson, Sunday 18 November 1781

Printed from the MS now WSL. First printed, Wright vi. 145–6. Reprinted, Cunningham viii. 110–11; Toynbee xii. 95–6 (closing and signature omitted in Wright, Cunningham, and Toynbee). For the history of the MS see *ante* 15 March 1763.

Address: To Robert Jephson Esq. at the Castle, Dublin. *Postmark:* 19 NO. FREE. NO 25.

Berkeley Square, Nov. 18, 1781.

AS Mr Malone undertook to give you an account, Sir, by last night's post of the great success of your tragedy,[1] I did not hasten home to write, but stayed at the theatre, to talk to Mr Harris and the actors, and learn what was said, besides the general applause.[2] Indeed I never saw a more unprejudiced audience, nor more attention. There was not the slightest symptom of disapprobation to any part, and the plaudit was great and long when given out again for Monday. I mention these circumstances in justification of Mr Sheridan, to whom I never spoke in my life, but who certainly had not sent a single person to hurt you. The prologue[3] was exceedingly liked, and for effect no play ever produced more tears. In the green room I found that Hortensia's sudden death was the only incident disapproved, as we heard by intelligence from the pit;[4] and it is to be deliberated tomorrow whether it may not be preferable to carry her off as if only in a swoon.[5] When there is only so slight an objection, you cannot doubt of your full success. It is impossible to say how much justice Miss Young did to your writing. She has shown herself a great mistress of her profession, mistress of dignity, passion, and of all the sentiments you had put into her hands. The applause

1. Malone's letter to Jephson is missing.

2. 'The Count of Narbonne was played last night with great applause, and without a single murmur of disapprobation' (HW to Conway 18 Nov. 1781, CONWAY iii. 387). See ibid. n. 5 for excerpts from newspaper accounts of the reception. George Selwyn wrote Lord Carlisle 17 Nov.: 'Mr Walpole, more *défait*, more *perclus de ses membres*, than I ever yet saw any poor wretch, is gone tonight to the playhouse, to see the tragedy of Narbonne. The gout may put what shackles it pleases

on some people; *on les rompt, et la vanité l'emporte.* He seems as able to act a part in the drama as to assist at the performance of it' (Hist. MSS Comm., 15th Report, App. vi [*Carlisle MSS*], 1897, p. 532).

3. Written by Jephson, spoken by Richard Wroughton (*ante* 7 Nov. 1781).

4. See *post* 23 Nov. 1781.

5. This change was adopted in subsequent performances; see *ante* 25 Jan. 1780, n. 9.

given to her description of Raymond's death[6] lasted some minutes, and recommenced; and her scene in the fourth act after the Count's ill-usage[7] was played in the highest perfection. Mr Henderson was far better than I expected from his weakness, and from his rehearsal yesterday,[8] with which he was much discontent himself. Mr Wroughton was very animated and played the part of the Count much better than any man now on the stage would have done. I wish I could say Mr Lewis satisfied me; and that poor child Miss Satchell was very inferior to what she had appeared at the rehearsals,[9] where the total silence and our nearness deceived us. Her voice has no strength, nor is she yet at all mistress of the stage. I have begged Miss Young to try what she can do with her by Monday—however there is no danger to your play: it is fully established.[10] I confess I am not only pleased on your account, Sir, but on Mr Harris's, as he has been so very obliging to me. I am not likely to have any more intercourse with the stage, but I shall be happy if I leave my interlude there by settling an amity between you and Mr Harris, whence I hope he will draw profit and you more renown. I am Sir

With great regard
Your obedient humble servant

Hor. Walpole

To Robert Jephson, Wednesday 21 November 1781

Printed from the MS now wsl. First printed, Wright vi. 147–8. Reprinted, Cunningham viii. 112–13; Toynbee xii. 97–8 (signature omitted in Wright, Cunningham, and Toynbee). For the history of the MS see *ante* 15 March 1763.

Address: To Robert Jephson Esq. at the Castle, Dublin. *Postmark:* 21 NO. ISLEWORTH. NO 25. FREE.

Strawberry Hill, Nov. 21, 1781.

I HAVE just received your two letters,[1] Sir, and the epilogue, which I am sorry came so late, as there are very pretty things in

---

6. Act V, Scene xv.

7. Act IV, Scene iii.

8. HW doubtless means Friday, 16 Nov., two days before.

9. See *ante* 10 Nov. 1781.

10. It had a run of nine successive nights, followed by twelve other performances during the 1781–2 season (*London Stage* Pt V, i. 451).

———

1. Both missing. HW wrote Mason 26 Nov. 1781 that although *The Count of*

it; but I believe it would be very improper to produce it now, as the two others have been spoken.[2]

I am sorry you are discontent with there being no standing figure of Alphonso, and that I acquiesced in its being cumbent.[3] I did certainly yield, and think my reasons will justify me. In the first place you seemed to have made a distinction between the statue and the tomb,[4] and had both been represented, they would have made a confusion. But a more urgent reason for my compliance was the shortness of the time, which did not allow the preparation of an entire new scene, as I proposed last year, and this; nay, and mentioned it to Mr Harris. When I came to the house[5] to see the scene prepared, it was utterly impossible to adjust an erect figure to it; nor indeed, Sir, do I conceive were the scene disposed as you recommend, how Adelaide could be stabbed behind the scenes. As I never disguise the truth, I must own too that I did think myself so much obliged to Mr Harris, that I was unwilling to heap difficulties on him, when I did not think they would hurt your piece. I fortunately was not mistaken; the entrance of Adelaide wounded had the utmost effect, and I believe much greater than would have resulted from her being stabbed on the stage.[6] In short, the success has been so complete, and both your poetry and the conduct of the tragedy are so much and so justly admired, that I flatter myself you will not blame me for what has not produced the smallest inconvenience. Both the manager and the actors were tractable, I believe, beyond example; and it is my nature to bear some contradiction, when it will carry material points. The very morning, the only morning I had, to settle the disposition, I had another difficulty to reconcile, the competition of the two epilogues, which I was so lucky as to compro-

Narbonne 'has succeeded perfectly, the author is dissatisfied. I had four sides last week, and tonight another letter of eight pages [also missing] to scold me for letting the statue on the tomb be cumbent instead of erect' (MASON ii. 167).

2. See ante 7 Nov. 1781 and n. 13.

3. 'After all my pains Mr Jephson is not quite satisfied. . . . [Malone] wrote to Mr Jephson that I had given up a material point of the decoration of the last scene, and had consented that the statue of Alphonso should be cumbent, though Mr Jephson had called it standing—which by the way was wrong. The truth was, we

had not time to remedy that contradiction, unless by altering the word, which Mr Friend [Malone] would not allow, nor could we have placed an erect statue in the scene prepared. . . . In short, Mr Jephson has written me a pressing letter to amend that disposition, when it is too late' (HW to Lady Ossory 22 Nov. 1781, OSSORY ii. 311–12).

4. See ibid. ii. 312 n. 8.

5. Covent Garden Theatre.

6. HW's letter to Jephson post 3 Dec. 1781 indicates that the scenery was later changed according to Jephson's wish, with 'no better effect.'

mise too.[7] I will say nothing of my being three hours each time on two several days in a cold theatre with the gout on me, and perhaps it was too natural to give up a few points in order to get home, for which I ask your pardon. Yet the event shows that I have not injured you—and if I was in one instance impatient, I flatter myself that my solicitations to Mr Harris and Miss Young, and the zeal I have shown to serve you, will atone for my having in one moment thought of myself, and then only when the reasons that weighed with me were so plausible, that without a totally new scene, which the time would not allow, I do not see how they could have been obviated. Your tragedy, Sir, has taken such a rank on the stage, that one may reasonably hope it will hereafter be represented with all the decorations to your mind; and I admire it so truly, that I shall be glad to have it conducted by an abler machinist than

Your obedient humble servant

Hor. Walpole

7. See Ossory ii. 310. The *London Courant* 22 Nov. reported that Goodenough's epilogue 'was written to oblige Mr Harris, but Mr Malone having, without that gentleman's knowledge, composed an epilogue at the express desire of Capt. Jephson, the author of the tragedy, Mr Goodenough very politely consented, that his own should be withdrawn. Accordingly that written by Mr Malone, will, from henceforth, be repeated after the tragedy.'

To Edmond Malone,[1] Friday 23 November 1781

Printed from a photostat of the MS formerly in the Elisha L. Palmer Collection, Connecticut College Library, New London, Connecticut. First printed in Sir James Prior, *Life of Edmond Malone*, 1860, pp. 83–5. Reprinted, Toynbee xii. 100–2; extracts quoted in J. M. Osborn, 'Horace Walpole and Edmond Malone,' in *Horace Walpole: Writer, Politician, and Connoisseur*, ed. W. H. Smith, New Haven, 1967, pp. 304–5. The MS is untraced until sold C. F. Libbie and Co. 21 March 1891 (E. H. Leffingwell Sale), lot 6358; acquired before 1912 by Elisha L. Palmer, who bequeathed it with his collection to Connecticut College; stolen from the Connecticut College Library in the early 1950s and not further traced.

Strawberry Hill, Nov. 23, 1781.

Sir,

I HAVE just received the honour of your letter,[2] and do not lose a minute to answer it, though my hand is so nervous and shakes so much that I have difficulty to write.

If you remember, Sir, Mr Harris sent for me out of the box on the first night;[3] I found Dr Franklin[4] in the green room and some of the players. The former was just come out of the pit, and said the audience there disliked the death of Hortensia, and thought it most unnatural that she should die so suddenly of grief;[5] the actors too agreed with him, and it was proposed that she should be carried off, to leave it at least doubtful whether she was dead or not. I am sure, I have never taken the liberty of making any alterations in Mr Jephson's excellent tragedy: it is as true that I have not set up my own judgment against those who have and must have more knowledge of stage effect; and whenever I have acquiesced with them,[6] it has been with the sole view of serving and contributing to the success of the play, or with a view of contenting Mr Harris in little points, who had so readily consented to bring out the play. I flatter myself too that it has not suffered by those little compliances of mine.

It is likewise true, Sir, and I have no objection to Mr Jephson's knowing, that I approve the alterations you have made, and which you do me the honour of proposing to me to be inserted in the

1. (1741–1812), scholar and editor of Shakespeare.

2. Missing.

3. The first performance of *The Count of Narbonne* at Covent Garden on 17 Nov.

4. Thomas Francklin (ca 1721–84), D.D., scholar, translator, and dramatist.

5. See *ante* 18 Nov. 1781 and n. 5.

6. At this point in the MS several words have been crossed out, probably by HW.

printed copy, but I fear I am not at liberty to agree to that idea, as since I saw you, I have received another letter from Mr Jephson,[7] in which he desires me to deliver the last copy to you, Sir, which I had done, and adds these words, 'that he (Mr Malone) may be requested not to suffer any alteration of the text, except as to pointing, which he understands much better than I do.' I confess I think Mr Jephson too tenacious. He has produced such a treasure of beauties, that he could spare one or two. My frankness and sincerity, Sir, speaks this from the heart, and not in secret; I would not for the world say one thing to you and another to Mr Jephson, and therefore have no objection to your communicating my letter to him. You have shown yourself so zealous a friend to him, and I hope have found me so too, that I am sure you will understand what I say as it is meant, and not as flattery to either, or as double dealing, of which I trust I am incapable.

I read with pleasure in the papers, Sir, that your epilogue succeeded as it deserved[8]—but I am much surprised at what you tell me that the audiences have been less numerous than there was every reason to expect.[9] If any burlesque of what is ridiculous can erase taste for genuine poetry, the age should go a little farther and admire only what is ridiculous.

I am much obliged to you, Sir, for the notices[10] you are pleased to send me, which I shall certainly insert in my own trifling works.

Voltaire's letter[11] to me was printed in one of his latter miscellaneous volumes,[12] I do not recollect in which. I do not doubt but it

7. Missing; presumably the letter of 'four sides' mentioned in HW's letter to Mason 26 Nov. (ante 21 Nov. 1781, n. 1).

8. The St James's Chronicle 20–2 November printed Malone's epilogue, noting that 'This epilogue was spoken on the third night of the representation of the Count of Narbonne, and now continues to be spoken after that tragedy; Mr Goodenough's, though a good composition, being supposed rather deficient in stage effect.'

9. Malone's observation is contradicted by newspaper accounts. The London Courant 22 Nov. remarked on the 'very crowded and brilliant audience' the previous evening, and the Public Advertiser 23 Nov. reported 'a numerous and splendid audience' on the 22d. Advertisements for the play refer to the 'great demand' or 'increased demand' for places. The Courant 23 Nov. announced that the scheduled performance of a new opera, The Banditti, had been postponed in order to meet the demand.

10. Possibly some additions or corrections to Anecdotes of Painting, which HW was then revising for a third edition (published in May 1782). In a letter to Lord Charlemont 8 Jan. 1782, Malone mentioned that HW was 'now employed in reprinting his Anecdotes of Painting, in 8vo, without plates, the book having become very scarce and extravagantly dear' (Hist. MSS Comm., 12th Report, App. x [Charlemont MSS], 1891, i. 395). See following letter.

11. Ante 15 July 1768.

12. See ante 30 Jan. 1777, n. 5.

will be reproduced in the general edition preparing[13]—hereafter perhaps another letter of his may appear, in which that envious depreciator of Shakespeare and Corneille may be proved to have been as mean and dirty, as he was envious.

I have the honour to be, Sir, with great respect

Your most obedient humble servant

HOR. WALPOLE

To Edmond Malone, ca December 1781

Printed for the first time from a photostat of the MS pasted by Malone in his copy of HW's *A Letter to the Editor of the Miscellanies of Thomas Chatterton* in the Boston Public Library. This copy was formerly in the collections of Richard Heber, Edward D. Ingraham, and Thomas Pennant Barton; acquired with the Barton collection by the Boston Public Library in 1873.

Dated approximately by the reference to HW's 'little tract' (the *Letter to the Editor of . . . Chatterton*), which Malone doubtless asked to see when he was at work on his refutation of Chatterton's Rowleian poems; Malone's essay, which first appeared in the *Gentleman's Magazine* for Dec. 1781, li. 555–9, 609–15 (published in Jan. 1782), mentions (p. 557) HW's 'unpublished pamphlet on this subject, printed at Strawberry Hill.'

Endorsed by Malone: Horace Earl of Orford, the writer of the above note, died on Thursday March 2, 1797, aged about 82. E.M.

Dated by Malone: (1782).

MR Walpole had a person[1] with him on business, and could not at that moment return his particular thanks to Mr Malone for his very obliging communications, to which he is fortunate in being able to pay proper respect immediately, as the second volume of the *Anecdotes*[2] is within a few leaves of coming to the article of Vandyck, in which Mr Malone's valuable notes shall be inserted.[3]

Mr Walpole has the honour of sending Mr Malone the little tract[4] he desired, which he will see Mr W. was forced to draw up to clear

13. *Œuvres complètes de Voltaire*, ed. Beaumarchais, Condorcet, and Decroix, [Kehl], 1784–9. The letter is printed ibid. lx. 505–12.

1. Not identified.
2. See previous letter and n. 10.
3. 'Since the former edition of this work I have been favoured by Edm. Malone, Esq. with the following notes of some of

Vandyck's prices from an office-book that belonged to the lord chamberlain Philip Earl of Pembroke.' HW quotes two dated entries from the office-book; see *Anecdotes of Painting, Works* iii. 223–4.

4. *A Letter to the Editor of the Miscellanies of Thomas Chatterton*, SH, 1779. Malone's presentation copy is in the Boston Public Library (see headnote).

himself from as unjust aspersions as ever were conceived,[5] and not to take part in a controversy to which he is very indifferent.[6]

To Robert Jephson, Monday 3 December 1781

Printed from the MS now WSL. First printed, Wright vi. 153. Reprinted, Cunningham viii. 124–5; Toynbee xii. 115 (signature omitted in Wright, Cunningham, and Toynbee). The MS is untraced until sold Sotheby's 1 March 1851 (Interesting Autograph Letters Sale), lot 57 (with three other letters), to Bullock; resold Sotheby's 5 Feb. 1876 (Bullock Sale), lot 324, to Naylor; resold Sotheby's 31 July 1885 (Naylor Sale), lot 969 (with two other letters), to Suyster; later *penes* Matthew Chaloner Durfee Borden, of New York, and inserted by him in an extra-illustrated copy of L. B. Seeley's *Horace Walpole and his World,* 1884; sold American Art Association 19 Feb. 1913 (Borden Sale), lot 812; acquired by William D. Breaker, who sold it at Rains Galleries, New York, 27 Nov. 1935, lot 688, bought in; purchased from Breaker by WSL, Sept. 1939. The letter has since been removed from the volume.

Address: To Robert Jephson Esq. at the Castle, Dublin. *Postmark:* 3 DE. FREE.

Berkeley Square, Dec. 3, 1781.

I HAVE not only a trembling hand, but scarce time to save the post, yet I write a few lines to beg you will be perfectly easy on my account, who never differ seriously with my friends, when I know they do not mean ill to me. I was sorry you took so much to heart an alteration in the scenery of your play, which did not seem to me very material, and which having since been adjusted to your wish, had no better effect. I told you[1] that it was my fault, not Mr Malone's, who is warmly your friend, and I am sure you will be sorry if you do him injustice. I regret no pains I have taken, since they have been crowned with your success; and it would be idle in either of us to recall any little cross circumstances that may have happened, (as always do in bringing a play on the stage) when they have not prevented its appearance or good fortune. Be assured, Sir, if that is

5. HW wrote in 'Short Notes' *sub* 1779: 'In the preceding autumn had written a defence of myself ag[ainst] the unjust aspersions in the preface to the *Miscellanies* of T. Chatterton' (GRAY i. 51). See *ante* 11 Jan. 1779.

6. In his letter to Lady Ossory 25 Dec.

1781, HW abjures 'such an idle controversy as whether Rowley or Chatterton was Rowley; which is as indifferent to me, as who is churchwarden of St Martin's parish' (OSSORY ii. 319).

1. *Ante* 21 Nov. 1781.

worth knowing, that I have taken no offence, and have all the same good wishes for you that I ever had since I was acquainted with your merit and abilities. I can easily allow for the anxiety of a parent of your genius for his favourite offspring, and though I have not your parts, I have had warmth, though age and illness have chilled it; but thank God they have not deprived me of my good humour, and I am most good humouredly and sincerely

Your obedient humble servant

HOR. WALPOLE

To RICHARD BULL, Thursday 20 December 1781

Printed for the first time from the MS now WSL. The MS, formerly laid in Bull's extra-illustrated presentation copy of *Mémoires du Comte de Grammont*, SH, 1772, has been removed from the volume; this copy (Hazen, *SH Bibl.* 98, copy 2) was purchased by Elkin Mathews from one of Bull's descendants in Ireland, 1928; sold by them to WSL, 1931.

Address: To Richard Bull Esq. in Stratton Street.

Dec. 20, 1781.

MY reason, dear Sir, for begging to see you, was to show you an uncommon book[1] that I have lately met with, mentioned by me in my *Anecdotes of Painting;* and if you have it not, to offer it to you; but you are so very obliging that I am quite afraid of attempting to show you any attention, lest it should put you to the expense of new kindness. You have now sent me a fresh cargo of curiosities.[2] I shall take the liberty of picking out a few, but several I have, and shall therefore return.

For the *Grammont*,[3] you have conferred too much value on it, especially as I fear I have not one to give you in return.[4] Besides my own copy, bound uniformly with the set of my editions,[5] I had but

1. Not identified.
2. Doubtless books or prints of antiquarian interest.
3. *Mémoires du Comte de Grammont*, SH, 1772.
4. HW presented Bull with a copy, which Bull 'grangerized' with prints; see headnote. Bull wrote on the fly-leaf of

his copy: 'This book was given to me by Mr Walpole; very few copies were printed, and none were sold.'
5. HW had a master set of Strawberry Hill Press publications, bound in calf with the Walpole arms on the sides; they were kept in the Glass Closet in the Library at SH (W. S. Lewis, *Horace Wal-*

a single one left, and that, I fear, I gave away above a year ago. I am not sure, and will look when I go to Strawberry, but I do not remember to have one; and if I have not, I must presume to say that I *will not* take yours.

I beg you will not come out tomorrow if your cold is not quite well. I am in no hurry, and am always at home till one o'clock, and very often the whole morning.

I am much concerned to hear so indifferent an account of poor Mr Morrice,[6] and shall rejoice to hear better news of him. I am dear Sir, with the utmost gratitude for all your goodness and partiality

Your most obliged and obedient humble servant

Hor. Walpole

To Edmond Malone, Saturday 22 December 1781

Printed from the MS now wsl. First printed in Sir James Prior, *Life of Edmond Malone*, 1860, p. 85. Reprinted, Toynbee xii. 128. The MS is untraced until sold Sotheby's 24 July 1918 (Lady Beryl Gilbert Sale), lot 644, to Dobell; resold Stan V. Henkels and Son, Philadelphia, 28 Jan. 1925, lot 322; acquired by Barnet J. Beyer, New York, who sold it to wsl, Oct. 1935.

Dec. 22d 1781.

I AM very sure, Sir, that the four lines with which Mr Gardiner[1] has honoured me,[2] are much too great a compliment, and will be

pole's *Library*, Cambridge, 1958, p. 16). HW's own copy of the *Mémoires . . . de Grammont* is Hazen, *Cat. of HW's Lib.*, No. 2511.

6. Humphry Morice (?1723–85), politician; M.P. Morice was one of the referees named (along with HW) to arbitrate Lord Orford's dispute with Cavaliere Mozzi in the settlement of the Countess of Orford's estate. He had gone to Bath following a severe attack of gout. HW wrote Mann 21 Dec. 1781: 'Mr Morrice is still at Bath, and though not in danger, so weakened by over-bathing, that I hear nothing of his coming to town' (Mann ix. 220).

———

1. Luke Gardiner (1745–98), cr. (1789) Bn and (1795) Vct Mountjoy; M.P. (Ireland); privy councillor, 1780. He had a

taste for the drama and fitted up a theatre at his lodge in Phoenix Park, Dublin (gm 1783, liii pt ii. 1064).

2. Gardiner had written a prologue to *The Count of Narbonne*. The four lines in compliment to HW are as follows:

Yet ere the fable was to verse
   consign'd,
'Twas by a master's skillful
   hand design'd;
Who now, retired, neglects the
   wreaths of fame,
And more than poet, shuns a
   poet's name.

'This prologue, not arriving in London time enough for the first exhibition of the *Count of Narbonne*, was not spoken' (gm 1782, lii. 36–7).

thought so by all who have not some friendly partiality for me. I am not a poet, and though I have written verses at times, more of them have been bad than good. However, as next to vanity, I should dislike to be thought guilty of affected modesty; and as I have no right to expect that in compliment to either, Mr Gardiner's beautiful lines should be suppressed, though he was so obliging as to sacrifice them at the representation, which I confess I could not have stood; I will take no more liberties, nor object to the publication.[3] Yet should I be taxed with consenting, I must comfort myself that I did not acquiesce till I had no right to refuse.

I very seldom go out in a morning, Sir, but will certainly have the honour of waiting on you soon,[4] and am Sir with great respect

Your most obedient humble servant

Hor. Walpole

To Richard Bull, late December 1781

Printed for the first time from a copy, now WSL, supplied by Elkin Mathews to Dr Toynbee for use in his uncompleted *Supp.* iv. The MS at that time was laid in Bull's extra-illustrated copy of *Mémoires du Comte de Grammont* (ante 20 Dec. 1781, headnote), but it was not in the volume when WSL acquired it from Elkin Mathews in 1931, and it has not been found since.

Dated approximately by HW's letter to Bull *ante* 20 Dec. 1781.

Memorandum (by Bull): Mem. Mr Walpole was mistaken in both his conjectures, and perhaps so in this other.

FORGIVE me for telling you, that I believe you have made one, if not two mistakes. I cannot think that the General Hamilton employed in Ireland was either George or Antony. George[1] had married la Belle Jennings,[2] and after his death she married the Duke of Tirconnel, and therefore I conclude George was dead some years before the Revolution.[3]

3. Gardiner's prologue was printed in the Dublin edition of the play (dated 1781 on the title-page). HW's copy, now WSL, was presumably sent to him by Jephson (Hazen, *Cat. of HW's Lib.*, No. 2402).

4. The Rev. William Jephson, a friend of Malone, wrote to him in March 1782: 'We hear that you spend much time with Mr Walpole. I hope it is the case. Such company is exactly to your taste' (Sir James Prior, *Life of Edmond Malone*, 1860, p. 80).

1. George Hamilton (d. 1676), styled 'Sir George' and, in France, 'Comte' Hamilton.

2. See *ante* ? March 1773 *bis*, n. 5.

3. The Glorious Revolution of 1688.

Antony,[4] the writer of the *Memoirs,* died very old and deaf at St Germains,[5] where Lady Jernegan[6] knew him, and I think I should have heard if he had ever commanded in Ireland.[7]

I imagine too that the Beau Sidney[8] was not afterwards the Earl of Romney,[9] but a younger brother of him and Algernon,[10] but I am not positive on any of these points.

Yours etc.

H.W.

4. Anthony Hamilton (ca 1645–1719), younger brother of Sir George Hamilton and brother-in-law of Philibert, Comte de Grammont; author of *Mémoires du Comte de Grammont.*

5. He died at St Germain-en-Laye 21 April 1719 (Wilhelm Kissenberth, *Antoine d'Hamilton, Sein Leben und seine Werke,* Berlin, 1907, p. 43).

6. Mary Plowden (ca 1703–85), m. (1733) Sir George Jerningham (1680–1774), 5th Bt, of Cossey, Norfolk. Her father, Francis Plowden, was comptroller of the Household to James II, and her mother was one of the ladies in waiting to Queen Mary Beatrice. They followed the exiled King and Queen to France and remained attached to the court at St Germain-en-Laye. The future Lady Jerningham was born and brought up at the court, where Anthony Hamilton spent much of his later life (B[arbara] M[ary] P[lowden], *Records of the Plowden Family,* privately printed, 1887, pp. 60–3; GEC, *Baronetage,* i. 172).

7. With the rank of major-general, he commanded a regiment of dragoons, under Lord Mountcashell, at the siege of Enniskillen, was wounded in the Battle of Newtown Butler 31 July 1689, and also fought at the Battle of the Boyne 1 July 1690 (DNB).

8. 'Robert, troisième fils de Robert Comte de Leicester, et frère du fameux Algernon Sidney, qui fut décapité' (HW's footnote identifying 'Le beau Sidney' in the *Mémoires,* SH, 1772, p. 75). See following note.

9. Hon. Henry Sidney (1641–1704), 4th and youngest son of the 2d E. of Leicester, cr. (1689) Vct Sidney and (1694) E. of Romney. Contrary to HW's belief, he was doubtless the 'beau Sidney' of the *Mémoires.* Sir John Reresby in his *Memoirs* (1734) calls him 'the handsomest youth of his time' (*Memoirs of Sir John Reresby,* ed. A. Browning, Glasgow, 1936, p. 55).

10. Hon. Algernon Sidney (1622–83), 2d son of the 2d E. of Leicester; executed for complicity in the Rye House Plot, 1683.